# CONSUMER ECONOMICS
## Issues and Behaviors

### Second Edition

**Elizabeth B. Goldsmith**
*Florida State University*

**PEARSON**
Prentice
Hall

Upper Saddle River, New Jersey
Columbus, Ohio

**Library of Congress Cataloging-in-Publication Data**

Goldsmith, Elizabeth B.
   Consumer economics : issues and behaviors / Elizabeth B. Goldsmith.—2nd ed.
      p. cm.
   Includes bibliographical references and index.
   ISBN-13: 978-0-13-159049-6
   ISBN-10: 0-13-159049-9
   1. Consumer education.   2. Consumption (Economics)   I. Title.
   TX335.G585 2009
   640.73—dc22

                                                             2008014055


**Editor in Chief:** Vernon Anthony
**Acquisitions Editor:** Jill Jones-Renger
**Editorial Assistant:** Doug Greive
**Development Editor:** David Plaskonka
**Production Coordination:** Janet Bolton
**Project Manager:** Alicia Ritchey
**Operations Specialist:** Deidra Schwartz
**Art Director:** Diane Ernsberger
**Image Coordinator:** Janet Portisch
**Cover Designer:** Kellyn Donnelly
**Cover Art/Image/Photo(s):** Superstock
**Director of Marketing:** David Gesell
**Marketing Manager:** Leigh Ann Sims
**Marketing Assistant:** Les Roberts

This book was set in Garamond by Aptara, Inc., and was printed and bound by Edwards Brothers. The
cover was printed by Phoenix Color Corp.

Pearson Education Ltd., London                 Pearson Education Australia Pty, Limited
Pearson Education Singapore, Pte. Ltd.         Pearson Education North Asia, Ltd., Hong Kong
Pearson Education Canada, Inc.                 Pearson Educación de Mexico, S.A. de C.V.
Pearson Education—Japan                        Pearson Education Malaysia, Pte. Ltd.

10 9 8 7 6 5 4 3 2 1
ISBN-13: 978-0-13-159049-6
ISBN-10:    0-13-159049-9

# Contents

## PART 2   CONSUMER PROTECTION        99

### Chapter 4   Consumer Responsibilities, Redress, and Law     101

## PART 3   CONSUMERS IN THE MARKETPLACE                    161

## Chapter 9    Health and Wellness Issues                                    253

## Chapter 10   Ownership, Safety, and Repairs                          287

# Preface

*Human ignorance as well as greed knows no bounds.*
—Gerald Moy

So much has happened since the first edition of *Consumer Economics: Issues and Behavior*. We've had toys recalled because of lead in the paint, outbreaks of E. coli from contaminated spinach, a salmonella outbreak from peanut butter, and pets dying from imported wheat gluten tainted with melamine. If ever there was a time when consumers and their safety were in the forefront, this is it. A total reorganization of food safety inspection and regulation is being called for by consumers. On top of all this, national and world economies are going through ups and downs and populations continue to grow. The U.S. population is over 300 million, and the world population has swelled to over 6.6 billion.

The beginning quote comes from the manager of the World Health Organization's office that monitors chemicals in the global food supply. The worst food problems used to be kept at the local level, but as we have seen in the news, dangerous additives are showing up in the United States and all other countries as the worldwide market expands. We need more international standards and regular inspections of food production, manufacture, packaging, and shipping. Reducing trans fats and fighting childhood obesity are other issues covered in this edition. The goal of a unique Somerville, Massachusetts, study conducted by Tufts Friedman School of Nutrition was to change children's environments with small and inexpensive steps. In classrooms, children sampled and voted on the foods they wanted to eat. This is an example of the consumer-in-control movement, which is introduced in this edition. Consumers want more say about products, advertising, packaging, and promotion.

Two well-publicized safety issues involve credit card theft and identity theft. The sophisticated methods of stealing someone else's identity and gaining access to financial records continues to grow. I am especially pleased that Chapter 11, "The Internet and Issues of Identity Theft and Fraud," was reviewed by law enforcement specialists and contains state-of-the-art information. One young couple dubbed "the modern Bonnie and Clyde" lived the high life and toured the world on other people's money for years until they were caught. In an unsolved case involving a Marshalls clothing store in Minnesota, hackers pointed a telescope-shaped antenna toward the store and used a laptop computer to decode data leading to a central database. The hackers downloaded over 45 million credit and debit cards that could be used for identity theft. To reflect this growing problem and to respond to this edition's reviewers' request, a separate chapter has been added on identity theft and ways to prevent it. This new chapter also covers methods to protect children online and discusses ways that consumers are using the Internet more often for purchases, including participating in online auctions.

To highlight the drama of consumer issues and to engage readers, each chapter starts with a vignette. None of these are made-up stories; each comes straight from the press or an online news source. The purpose of this new edition is to provide updated information on issues and to put the spotlight on the intricacies of consumption, health, law, government regulation, and the economy.

As in the first edition, the emphasis is not only on U.S. consumption but on patterns of worldwide consumption and changes in population. I was pleased to hear from students and professors who used the first edition in Japan, Switzerland, Canada, Germany, Finland, the United Kingdom, and other countries. As we continue on a path of increased urbanization and high-rise living, how can we ignore the impact of pollutants and other environmental problems? Concern about global warming has skyrocketed since the last edition, and former Vice President Al Gore won the Nobel Prize for his writing and films on environmental issues.

The growth of the Internet has been incredible since the first edition. People increasingly use search engines to find things they want to know, music they want to hear, and products they want to buy. All these forces come together in a new section on the environmental impact of the Internet.

These are exciting times for consumer economists and for those who want to explore the crossovers between consumers and producers and their impact. Do we need to be protected as consumers? Yes, we certainly do. When we open a jar of peanut butter, we do not expect to get sick or die from eating the contents. We look to our leaders, legislators, judges, growers, and progressive companies for forward-looking pro-consumer decisions.

Consumer economics addresses who buys what, where, how, why, and when. It looks at the forces that impact consumer choice in an ever-changing and often-turbulent world. Responding to terrorism has led to changes in consumer laws and protections, including the USA PATRIOT Act of 2001 (covered in this edition).

More has been added on basic personal finance so that students can see how their financial decisions interplay with greater consumer issues. Quality of life and well-being are seen as end states that consumers pursue in their decision making. Too often consumer books have focused on problems and complaints; although these are addressed, solutions are also presented in this text. Upbeat examples of consumerism such as good service are also given—not everything is doom and gloom. These are exciting times for consumers because the choices are boundless.

Today's complex marketplace is beyond anything Adam Smith, the founder of modern economics, could have envisioned. He argued that consumers—not kings or parliaments—should rule nations. There is no doubt that the consumer is still sovereign, but controlling and protecting resources is becoming increasingly difficult. "New" consumers are about so much more than saving money and fighting the urge to buy on impulse.

## HIGHLIGHTS OF THIS EDITION

The following highlights how this text's coverage seeks to explain the behaviors and issues surrounding these new consumers:

- The text presents 15 chapters, designed to be manageable in a semester-long course, that detail unique ideas and solutions leading to more successful consumer experiences.
- Students like to read about situations that relate to their own lives, so every effort has been made to use student-based examples, such as dealing with landlord–tenant disputes, sorting through credit card and cell phone offers, purchasing cars and getting vehicle repairs, and choosing travel and various other "deals" wisely. For example, a friend of one of my students lost thousands of dollars over the Internet putting money down on a London apartment sight unseen because it turned out that neither the apartment building nor the "landlord" existed.
- The Internet plays a very big role in this text. Besides the chapter on the Internet and identity theft, there is reference to both throughout the book. Television viewing and newspaper reading are both declining while the use of the Internet as a source of information and entertainment soars. MySpace and Second Life are just two examples of Internet-based innovations.
- Most universities incorporate consumer behavior in their consumer courses, and this combination is reflected in the title and content of this text. Updates on theory include expanded coverage on prospect theory and the theory of mental accounting, which are connected with message framing. The inclusion of theory sets this book apart from others. New sections were added on style preferences and impulse buying. Economic concepts such as utility and diminishing marginal utility are given more coverage.
- A new feature is the renaming of the Circular Flow Model as the Consumer Power Model in order to more directly define what it is and how it works. The consumer is seen as an integral part of an economic model with many players. Interactivity in the market is what consumer economics is all about.
- This edition contains a full and updated chapter on consumption shifts and the consumer movement. It is amazing to see the types of products that consumers once used, often to their detriment (such as their hair falling out), and how the government stepped in to make the marketplace safer. Personalities are included to add "faces" to the policy changes. New photos throughout add a way for readers to visualize the products, services, and people involved.
- What to eat and drink is a daily consumption decision. Chapter 8 on food and beverages proves to be popular with students, and the coverage of organic foods has been expanded. The slow food movement has grown from its origins in Italy to small towns and urban areas everywhere. Nearly everyone can relate to the choice of buying locally and the value of supporting small-town farmers and businesses. The USDA Food Pyramid has been replaced with MyPyramid, which provides a more individualized way to tailor food, suggested weight, and exercise.
- Chapter 9, now called "Health and Wellness Issues," provides an emphasis on wellness. The chapter begins with some historical background, such as the

failed attempt to make alcohol illegal through Prohibition. Skyrocketing health care costs, recalls of medical devices, cosmetics and treatments like Botox, and alcohol and tobacco consumption patterns are explored.

- Chapter 10, "Ownership, Safety, and Repairs," is followed by Chapter 11, on the "Internet and Issues of Identity Theft and Fraud," the number one consumer complaint area. New coverage on biometrics, the use of people's physical traits to verify identity, is included.

- Practical matters such as how to budget; how to purchase homes, cars, and insurance; and how to invest come next. Warranties and guarantees as well as product safety and awareness of get-rich-quick schemes are addressed. The dark side of the marketplace is revealed in money laundering, scams and fraud, and terrorist financing.

- The last chapter focuses on the global perspective, consumer education and financial literacy, and the future. The four drives impacting consumer behavior are used to frame the discussion of globalization and pro-environment consumers. The ENERGY STAR program for energy-efficient solutions is explained, along with specifics such as compact fluorescent light bulbs (CFLs)— the proliferation of CFLs in U.S. homes and businesses has been phenomenal since the last edition. The book ends with a section titled "Consumer Economics Retrospective." We are all consumers regardless of our status, location, or income.

- Key terms are highlighted in the text and appear again in the updated Glossary to aid in study.

- Careers in consumer economics are mentioned throughout the text and again in Appendix A to guide students who want to apply their learning to the workplace.

- Supplements include: Instructor's Manual, Computerized Test Bank of Questions, PowerPoints, and CourseSmart.

## INSTRUCTOR RESOURCES

To access supplementary materials online, instructors need to request an instructor access code. Go to **www.pearsonhighered.com/irc**, where you can register for an instructor access code. Within 48 hours of registering, you will receive a confirming e-mail, including an instructor access code. Once you have received your code, go to the site and log on for full instructions on downloading the materials you wish to use.

# Acknowledgments

Since the first edition, I have gained a daughter-in-law, new editors Jill Jones-Renger and David Ploskonka, and new reviewers. When I wrote this edition, I wanted to retain the basics of the first one and add current information. My students at Florida State University continue to serve as inspiration. I also thank the students at the University of the West Indies in Trinidad and Tobago, where I taught as a Fulbright Scholar in spring 2006. Students provide realistic views on both handling landlord tenant relations and being consumers in today's world.

A textbook such as this serves as a guide for theory and history as well as providing the most current research and information on particular topics. I am indebted to all the researchers whose work is cited in this edition.

The reviewers of this edition provided many useful suggestions about the organization and content of the book. Special thanks are extended to:

| | |
|---|---|
| Joyce Armstrong | Texas Women's University |
| Ruben Berrios | Clarion University |
| Barbara Briscoe | Morgan State University |
| Joyce Cantrell | Kansas State University |
| Thomas Dahlstrom | Eastern University |
| Pat McCallister | Eastern Illinois University |
| V. Ann Paulins | School of Human and Consumer Sciences, Ohio University |
| Patricia Pierson | Northwestern State University of Louisiana |

Also thanked are the reviewers and pioneers of the first edition:

| | |
|---|---|
| John R. Burton | University of Utah |
| Jane Kolodinsky | University of Vermont |
| Julia Marlowe | University of Georgia |
| Patricia Scheeserd | Indiana University of Pennsylvania |
| Anita Subramaniam | Montclair State University (she is now residing and working in India) |
| Jing Jian Xiao | University of Rhode Island |

In addition, I'd like to thank Diana Sindicich, assistant professor at Kansas State University, CyberSecurity Analysts with Secure Florida, and Mark Lino of the U.S.

Department of Agriculture for providing valuable comments to this edition. Thanks also to the government and technical advisory boards such as the Healthy Home Institute that I serve on because I believe in consumer advocacy and try to live it. I also serve on the editorial boards of the *Journal of Family and Economic Issues* and the *International Journal of Consumer Studies*. In addition, I was privileged to serve as a guest reviewer or editor for a number of academic conferences, including the Association of Marketing Theory and Practice as well as Financial Planning and Counseling, and academic journals, including the *Journal of Consumer Affairs* and Kappa Omicron Nu's *Forum*. Much of my writing has been influenced by serving as a U.S. delegate to the International Federation of Home Economics Council Meeting in South Africa and as a consultant/ advisor in a number of capacities, including advising the White House on women's and girls' economic education. I also thank the Financial Industry Regulation Authority Investor Education Foundation for its research support.

Most of all I'd like to thank my family—my husband, Ronald E. Goldsmith, who is Richard M. Baker Professor of Marketing at Florida State University; my two sons, David and Andrew; and my daughter-in-law, Jessica. They add balance and joy to my life.

# Consumer Alerts

Practical tips and information to help students make smart choices.

**Chapter 1**

Covers cancellation rights

**Chapter 5**

Warns people of misleading advertisements and lists Web site

States devices not authorized by FDA to remove skin wrinkles

Warns of product claims to bolster immune system and combat severe diseases

States investing money not guaranteed and not a sport

Discusses broker who siphoned millions from clients over 15 years, covering tracks and forging statements

Discusses William Thompson who separated New Yorkers from their assets

**Chapter 8**

Warns about avoiding "fad" diets and magic pills

Covers quackery and communication (buyer beware what you buy on Internet)

**Chapter 9**

Discusses need for people to be more active advocates in their own health care

Warns of health care frauds regarding cures for cancer

Warns of health care frauds involving HIV and AIDS

Covers buying drugs online from Canada or another country

Notes not all health-related Web sites are safe and reliable

**Chapter 10**

Covers Consumer Product Safety Commission and American Academy of Pediatrics on safe bedding practices for infants

Warns college students not to be susceptible to travel fraud

Warns of phone call, letter, unsolicited fax, e-mail, or postcard saying you won a free or incredibly inexpensive trip

**Chapter 11**

Warns of shill testimonials that are put there by seller or by friends of seller

Warns of damaged goods (note words such as refurbished, flood sale, close-out)

Notes that most victimized age group for identity theft is 18–29.

Notes that elderly living in nursing homes and assisted living centers are at risk of identity theft

Warns to be on the lookout for fraudelent middlemen representing real charities.

Warns of consumer charity fraud on the Internet originating from Nigeria

### Chapter 12

Lists what you need to be aware of before signing a lease

Covers common problem of bait and switch regarding quality of the apartment rented

Warns of scams in real estate

Covers banks aggressively marketing home equity lines (not for everyone)

Discusses how Equal Credit Opportunity Act prevents discrimination

Covers leases from luxury car businesses pushing low payments with severe penalties that occur when car goes over 15,000 miles a year

Helps consumers know good and bad deals when leasing a car

Covers fraud in moving water-damaged vehicles to another state to sell to unsuspecting consumers

Covers financial fraud in car sales (includes case of a state attorney general suing dealership under the state's Unfair Trade Practices Act)

### Chapter 13

States that selling information is legal (but illegal to have banks make withdrawals without consumer permission)

Covers Electronic Fund Transfer Act (for mistake or unauthorized withdrawal from bank account, consumer needs to notify institution)

Discusses careful selection of personal identification number for use at ATMs and other forms of cash management

Covers how ATM thieves target customers in a variety of ways

Lists safety factors involved in online banking

Helps in selecting financial planner (obtain written estimate of what services are to be expected)

Warns to use caution when signing either for a loan or as a cosigner

Covers being turned down for credit card because there is no balance on another card

Notes that each credit bureau keeps separate file on each person with information supplied by creditors

Discusses personal liability for lost or stolen credit cards

Discusses why women have often had trouble establishing good credit history

Notes that people who file bankruptcy still have debts that are not dischargeable

### Chapter 14

Covers how to protect yourself when buying insurance online by researching

Notes that when applying for auto insurance policies, individual needs to disclose past tickets

Notes that housing unit vacant for 30 days in a row can be considered abandoned and insurance may halt coverage

Warns that consumers with insurance from employers may think they are fully covered when they are not

Covers churning, illegal practice of encouraging insured person to switch policies (often in order to generate commissions)

Covers LTC, fairly new form of insurance whose regulation between states varies widely

Notes that investments have advantages and disadvantages

Notes that millions of dollars worth of consumer lawsuits are filed every year but consumers not aware money is owed to them

Discusses how to handle being pressured when investing and lists warning signs of investment con artist

Warns about buying time-shares or vacation homes

Notes that REITs fluctuate with ups and downs on the market and with quality of the investment

Discusses gemstone scandals using heat treatments and additives to turn lesser sapphires and rubies into copies of better gems

Warns of sales pitches and products sold on infomercials that are a half hour or longer

# PART 1

# Consumer Perspectives

### CHAPTER 1
## Consumers in a Changing World

### CHAPTER 2
## The Consumer Movement

### CHAPTER 3
## Consumer Theories and Development of a Model

# Consumers in a Changing World

*The world is so full of things, I'm sure we should all be happy as kings.*

—Steverson

## Learning Objectives

1. Define consumer economics.
2. Explain the market economy.
3. Describe Adam Smith's contribution to consumer economics.
4. Explain the five steps in the consumption process.
5. Explain the three questions economies have to address.
6. Describe the three parts of the business cycle.

---

### Lead Paint in Toys from China: Recalls

Keeping consumers safe, especially children, is fundamental to the study of consumer economics. In recent years, recalls of Chinese-manufactured toys with excessive levels of lead paint have made the headlines. The Consumer Product Safety Commission (CPSC) in cooperation with Mattel announced a recall of nearly a million toys including Barbie accessories and Fisher-Price brand toys between 2006 and 2007.

Mattel issued a statement apologizing to consumers and said it spent more than 50,000 hours investigating its vendors and testing toys. "We've promised consumers that we'd tell them efficiently and openly if we found any additional affected toys, and that is what we are doing today," said Mattel.[1]

"If I were a betting person I'd bet on more lead paint recalls," CPSC Director of Information Julie Vallese told CNN. "It's clear that lead paint on toys is not isolated just to Mattel." She also said, "It is fair to say that we haven't seen the last of product recalls that may be tied to a violation of the lead paint standard. This is a non-negotiable point. China needs to put plans and procedures in place so that products exported to the U.S. are lead-free."[2]

The CPSC is holding meetings with the U.S. Department of Commerce and with Chinese officials. International cooperation is sought and more rigorously enforced standards for exported toys. In the meantime, consumers are asked to stop using affected toys immediately. Also on the inspection block are fireworks, electrical goods, and lighters imported from China.

---

[1]CNNMoney.com, September 5, 2007.
[2]Ibid.

## INTRODUCTION

Written during the rise of the age of consumerism, Steverson's couplet highlights the importance of things and illustrates a childlike wonder about the possibilities set before us. If happiness is consumption, we should strive to acquire more and, if all goes well, in the end live as kings. Unfortunately, it is not as simple as that; even with endless consumption happiness is not so easily attained. What is the connection between happiness and consumption? What do consumers want? What motivates consumers to consume? How do they make choices? Daniel Gilbert, author of *Stumbling on Happiness,* says that money itself doesn't make you happy—what makes a person happy is what is done with the money. Research suggests experiences such as travel may bring more satisfaction than durable goods.

This chapter introduces the fundamentals of consumerism and the changing world in which we live. Since we are all consumers, consumer economics is not esoteric; it is applicable every day. **Consumer economics** is the study of how people deal with scarcity, fulfill needs, and select among alternative goods, services, and actions. It provides an understanding of how the marketplace works, what our role is in it, and how our choices affect our lifestyles. Studying consumer economics:

- Enriches our lives by helping us get the things we want
- Increases our understanding of the factors influencing our choices and the choices of others
- Improves our understanding of how the marketplace works
- Increases our awareness of what is fair
- Encourages us to think carefully about how we spend and invest our money

An end result of studying consumer economics is improved decision making. Each person should be able to look back on decisions made and, for the most part, feel confident they were the right ones.

## WHY STUDY CONSUMER ECONOMICS?

The purpose of this text is to provide the reader with a usable understanding of consumer economics. By following the principles in this book, you will:

- Increase self-awareness
- Understand others' consumption patterns and perspectives
- Approach daily living with enthusiasm and a can-do spirit
- Overcome limitations and weaknesses by knowing your rights and responsibilities
- Improve your consumer behavior
- Participate in actions that bring fairness to the marketplace
- Take control of your happiness (at least as far as consumption is concerned)
- Find ways to make a profit and make your money stretch further
- Discover career options

Most students in consumer economics classes aspire to careers working with people in education, law, business, community development, management, health, merchandising, design, government, communications, human resources, or marketing. Specific examples of careers involving consumer economics will be given throughout the book and in Appendix A.

The challenge that we, as educated citizens, face today is to overcome passivity and hesitation and to take the steps to join in; enter the marketplace; expect, receive, and provide fair treatment; and bring about improved lives. The main objective is to develop the ability to apply consumer economics knowledge to regulatory and social issues, as well as to personal buying decisions.

There is a certain passion, a sense of hope that one brings to consumerism; it is not all reason and dry theory. Caring about the rights of others is central to the field. The consumer advocates and reformers such as Erin Brockovich and Ralph Nader, whom you'll read about, were passionate about making people's lives better and safer. They gave stirring speeches and wrote popular books that changed the way cars and other goods were made in this country, and they crusaded for a cleaner environment. Brockovich exposed pollution in California and became famous in a 1990s movie directed by Steven Soderbergh for which Julia Roberts, playing the role of Brockovich, won an Academy Award. Brockovich and Nader symbolize how one person can make a difference, which is another key concept in consumer economics. There are groups, individual leaders, and politicians who have led or fostered the consumer movement by exposing fraud and corruption. We have all benefited from their efforts. To summarize the role of passion in economic behavior, Alexander Pope wrote in *Moral Essays*, I:

> On life's vast ocean diversely we sail,
> Reason the card, but Passion is the gale.

---

## CONSUMER ALERTS

### Economic Jitters

With the downturn in the U.S. housing market, issues of supply, demand, price, scarcity and abundance came to the forefront. Foreclosures reached all-time highs since the Depression in states such as Florida and California as subprime loans (loans given to people who normally would not qualify for loans) came due. Adjustable mortgage rates rose and homeowners could not pay the higher costs. One woman's monthly payment rose $200, and she said she did not have the extra money. She was trying to refinance her loan or move out. People were simply over their heads, and when the speculation period ended, they could not easily sell. Bankruptcies and foreclosures went up nationwide, and there was talk of a recession.

The downturn affected not only low- and middle-income homeowners but also upper income consumers. "The housing turmoil, the lackluster stock market, and the impact of the subprime debacle on Wall Street business have sent a chill through the upper-income brackets. A Washington Post/ABC News consumer comfort index for respondents with incomes higher than $100,000 fell to a 12-month low."[1] Have you or anyone you know experienced economic jitters? Do you think the housing market will return stronger than ever? If so, when? Do you think banks and mortgage lenders too freely handed out subprime loans? How ethical should lenders be?

Do you think too many consumers speculated? Ben Bernanke, chairman of the Federal Reserve, says that it is not the role of the Federal Reserve to bail out consumers who make poor investment decisions. He says the role is to stabilize the economy.

---

[1]Scott Patterson, "Glum Consumer Adds to Concern over Fate of '08." *The Wall Street Journal*, January 3, 2008, p. C1. Federal Reserve comments from January 17, 2008, congressional hearings.

## WHO CONSUMES AND WHY?

We need to consume to exist. **Consumers** are individuals or groups such as families who obtain, use, maintain, and dispose of products and services to increase life satisfaction and fulfill needs. Consumers are not always efficient in this process. For example, in one shopping study researchers found that many grocery products (usually ones bought for specific recipes or occasions) were never used (Wansink, Brasel & Amjad, 2000). The usual reason given by respondents was that products were not used immediately after purchase and were slowly pushed to the back of the cabinet and forgotten. They called these products "cabinet castaways." It is estimated that about 12 percent of purchased products are never used and eventually are thrown out (Wansink & Deshpande, 1994) and 80 percent of new products fail. Part of the reason for this is that preferences change as people learn and change and some products are ill-conceived. One of the subtopics in consumer economics is how to increase the awareness of purchase and usage habits in order to save money and reduce waste. For example, information search is a good idea, but it can be costly.

> About 12 percent of purchased products are never used and eventually are thrown out.

Consumerism has many definitions. Sometimes the word is used to refer to the positive efforts of the consumer movement (essentially the consumer interest) while other times it refers to runaway materialism. For an excellent description of the word and all its permutations, see Roger Swagler's "Evolution and Applications of the Term Consumerism: Theme and Variations" listed in the reference section at the end of this chapter. For the purposes of this book, **consumerism** refers to the belief that goods give meaning to individuals and their roles in society. This combination of consumption, social roles, and politics was first voiced by Adam Smith (1723–1790), the founder of modern economics. He argued in his book *An Inquiry into the Nature and Causes of the Wealth of Nations* (1776), found in Heilbroner's *Essential Adam Smith* (1986), that the essential task of coordinating national economies should fall to consumers. He wrote:

> Consumption is the sole end and purpose of all production; and the interest of the producer ought to be attended to only so far as it may be necessary for promoting that of the consumer. This maxim is so perfectly self-evident that it would be absurd to attempt to prove it. But in the mercantile system, the interest of the consumer is almost constantly sacrificed to that of the producer. (Heilbroner, 1986, p. 284)

As a professor of moral philosophy at the University of Glasgow in Scotland, who taught classes several days a week (some as large as 90, with students ages 14 to 16), Smith knew consumers well. He did not sit isolated in a country mansion, and although he never married, he traveled and had many friends. He said his 3,000 books (a very sizable collection in that time) were his companions in life. Smith knew that consumers could make mistakes, but he thought for the most part that they could be counted on to be conscientious and careful spenders since this was in their best interest. He proposed that consumers be given freedom and authority in running their own economic affairs, and in the long run he felt this would benefit the nation as well. His doctrine, considered revolutionary in its time, was resisted by the English king and the businesspeople of the day who dominated national deci-

Adam Smith (1723–1790) published *An Inquiry into the Nature and Causes of the Wealth of Nations* in 1776, laying the foundation of economics. He argued that the wealth of nations came from the goods and services produced and consumed. (Courtesy of the Library of Congress.)

sion making about trade. Across the ocean, his book was well received by many of the founders of the United States who were looking for more democratic ways to do things. They liked the idea of the consumer as king; it fit well into building a new country, welcoming new settlers, and encouraging expansion. In Smith's philosophy the wealth of nations was not based on gold and silver but rather on the goods and services produced and consumed by people. His philosophy of the "invisible hand" was directed as much against monopoly as government. He extolled the virtues of the acquisitive process and competitive markets. To put his philosophy into one phrase, Smith's understanding of human nature was that "to be human is to exchange freely."

In more modern times, consumerism expresses the cardinal political ideals of liberty and democracy because being able to choose among a vast array of commodities gives people a sense of freedom (Heilbroner, 1986). Daniel Harris, author of *Cute, Quaint, Hungry and Romantic: The Aesthetics of Consumerism,* writes:

What, after all, would a world without consumerism be like?

Surely not one that I myself would choose to live in. There would be no cities because cities are dependent on trade, nor money because there would be nothing to buy. There would be no insurance companies because there would be no possessions, no realtors because there would be no houses, no lawyers because hunters and gatherers rarely have to untangle the red tape of copyright infringement or haggle over joint stock agreements or fax each other angry letters to cease and desist. To imagine a world without consumerism is to erase oneself. (2000, p. 265)

## GOODS AND SERVICES

Buying or using goods and services is an act of faith—one assumes when purchasing something that the goods (e.g., a sandwich) or services (e.g., dry cleaning) will provide satisfaction or fulfill a need. Goods are tangible objects: things you can see and feel, such as a car. Services are intangible actions: work done to satisfy or provide for others, such as a catering service. Because the general economic meaning of consumer goods encompasses consumer services, in this book when the word *goods* is used, it implies both goods and services. In recent years the growth in the number of new consumer goods has been astounding—distance learning classes, technology-based cellular phones and Internet access, specialty coffee shops and Internet cafés, e-mails, and so forth. As an explanation, one author wrote:

> Consumer goods became a language, defining, redefining, and easing relationships between friends, family members, lovers, and strangers. Cars and clothes gave identity to young and old, female and male, ethnic majority and minority, telling others who they were and how they expected to be treated. Cosmetics and candy expressed both rebellion and authority, thus providing people with an understanding of themselves in an otherwise indifferent and sometimes unfriendly world. Moreover, goods redefined concepts of the past and future and gave a cadence to the rhythms of daily life when people purchased antiques and novelties and when Christmas became a shopping "season." (Harris, 2000, p. 265)

Not all our memories of consumption are such good ones. Consumerism is not always nostalgic. Have you ever purchased something that disappointed? What was it that did not bring you the degree of satisfaction that you hoped? Was it a ticket to a lousy movie or a printer that was always breaking? Perhaps most frustrating of all is a car that is constantly in the repair shop.

Not only does consumption not guarantee happiness, but it can also bring misery, as the car in the repair shop example shows. The dark side of the marketplace exists. For example, according to government estimates, there are over 14,000 fraudulent telemarketing firms in the United States, bilking consumers (usually the elderly) out of $40 billion a year. This illustrates that consumerism is a multifaceted experience: It is attractive and pleasurable, but at the same time it can be fraught with deception. **Injurious consumption** happens when individuals or families make consumption decisions that will have negative consequences, affecting their quality of life in the long run.

> Every year over 10 million American consumers suffer financial losses from their addiction to gambling. . . . There are currently 10 million alcoholics and 80 million cigarette smokers in the United States. . . . Every year 25,000 people die as a result of alcohol-related traffic accidents. . . . All of these disturbing and disturbed behaviors result from consumption gone wrong. (Hirschman, 1991, p. 4)

Shopping is an economic and social interaction experience. In this photo, three generations are shopping together. (Ken Chernus, Getty Images, Inc.—Taxi.)

**Caveat emptor**, translated as "May the buyer beware," is an integral part of the study of consumer economics, and you will see sections of chapters devoted to problems in the marketplace. Even knowing the pitfalls, consumers forge ahead, looking for new and better products and enjoying the discovery of the latest fashions and electronics. A case in point is the refrigerator from LG, a Korean company, that has multifunctions such as a television screen and a keypad built in with Internet capabilities. Why should a refrigerator, an appliance using energy 24 hours a day, have only the purpose of keeping food cold? Constant striving for improvement is part of consumer behavior.

## Human Needs

Less than 35 percent of U.S. families consist of a husband, wife, and children under age 18.

According to psychologist Abraham Maslow, humans have basic needs that have to be met before moving to higher-order needs (see Figure 1.1). In his hierarchy of needs, physiological needs such as hunger and thirst have to be at least partially met before safety, love and belongingness, esteem, and self-actualization can be fulfilled (Maslow, 1954). Multiply these levels of needs across the population and you begin to realize the enormity of human demands and needs.

According to Mark Oleson (2004), there is a relationship between money attitudes and Maslow's hierarchy of needs. In fact, each level of needs (as shown in Figure 1.1) has a specific money attitude related to it; for example, having money affects our

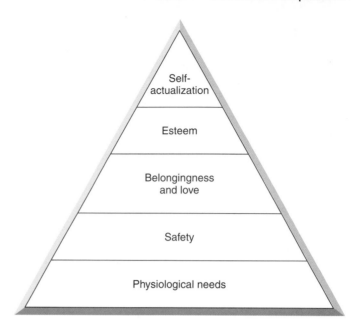

**Figure 1.1** Maslow's Hierarchy of Needs. In this hierarchy of needs, basic physiological needs such as hunger and thirst have to be met before higher-order needs.

needs for esteem and safety. But Oleson (2004) points out that "not all individuals will have the same needs, or combination of needs, at the same time" (p. 91). In his research he found that men's money attitudes were more related to safety needs, whereas women's money attitudes were more linked to esteem. He makes the practical observation that a financial planner or counselor could mix needs with money, for example, by providing lunch or dinner and a comfortable setting during a personal finance workshop with those struggling with lower-order needs such as physiological and safety/security needs.

The last census revealed there are over 301 million people in the United States and over 80 million households. Less than half of all households have a married couple, so unmarried is more common than married or the household has another configuration such as a single mom and child. By U.S. Census Bureau definition, a **household** includes the related family members and all the unrelated persons who share a housing unit. According to the census, "traditional" households, consisting of a husband, wife, and children under age 18, make up less than 35 percent of all U.S. families. Regardless of household type, consumerism is an integral part of every household.

Although consumerism received a boost in the twentieth century, it is not a time-bound concept since, as previously mentioned, humans need to consume to exist. Advertisements etched in stone in ancient Rome, Greece, and Egypt indicate that consumers have desired comfort and style for centuries. What has happened is that the rapid increase in worldwide populations and the market's response to meeting their needs have spurred the current surge in the growth of consumerism. Technological developments have played an important role as well, but it would be limiting to say that consumerism is merely a result of increased populations and subsequent responses from merchandisers and advertisers. Consumerism is a way to define self, family, and community through the ownership, the use, and, ultimately, the disposal of goods. Owning a Lexus sends a far different message than owning a Kia.

## Demography and Demographics

Trying to calculate changes in human needs is an ongoing problem for marketers, educators, advertisers, public policy makers, and manufacturers. In the United States, the idea of a melting pot was popular in the twentieth century. During the twenty-first century, the concept still exists but embraces a more holistic frame of mind, encompassing radically and ethnically diverse groups, both native and foreign born (Frey, 2006). Patterns of groups and their movements have important implications for consumer and voter behavior, economic development, and race relations in metropolitan areas both large and small (Frey, 2006). In the United States, historic ports of entry for Hispanics and Asians have been Miami, New York, Tampa, Los Angeles, San Francisco, and Chicago. Friends, relatives, and universities, in addition to location, affect network patterns, employment, and the settling of minorities in certain areas. The fastest-growing cities in overall population are Las Vegas, Phoenix, and Orlando.

**Demography** is the study of human populations, including characteristics such as size, growth, density, distribution, movement, and other vital statistics. The world population is over 6.6 billion, and the 10 most populous countries in 2002 and projected for 2050 are listed in Table 1.1. Table 1.1 also lists the top 10 populous metropolitan cities. Note that in 2050 it is proposed that India will have a higher population than China and that the United States will stay in the third position.

The term **demographics** refers to data used to describe populations or subgroups. To show how populations change in even a five-year period, here are the shifts in the U.S. population from 2000 to 2005:

- Population grew 4 percent overall.
- African American population grew 5 percent.
- Asian American population grew 15 percent.
- Hispanic/Latino population grew 10 percent.

**Table 1.1**  Most Populous Countries and Megacities

| Countries | | Megacities |
|---|---|---|
| **2002** | **2050 (estimated)** | **2007** |
| China | India | Tokyo, Japan |
| India | China | Mumbai (Bombay), India |
| United States | United States | Mexico City, Mexico |
| Indonesia | Indonesia | New York, USA |
| Brazil | Nigeria | São Paulo, Brazil |
| Pakistan | Bangladesh | Delhi, India |
| Russia | Pakistan | Shanghai, China |
| Bangladesh | Brazil | Kolkata (Calcutta), India |
| Nigeria | Congo (Kinshasa) | Dhaka, Bangladesh |
| Japan | Mexico | Buenos Aires, Argentina |

Demographics are often applied to the study of consumers who are grouped by age, race, gender, income, educational level, marital status, zip code, rented versus owned housing, and number of children in the household. Marketers find these useful ways to segment consumers so they can reach them better than a scattershot approach would provide, but they do not limit their advertising and distribution to demographic characteristics alone. Personality, taste, and lifestyle (in essence, individuality) play a role in consumer behavior as well as in statistical groupings. Consumption of products gives people a way of identifying themselves in groups—displays, advertising, packaging all have ways of attracting certain groups based on the identity that they have or seek. For example, a travel agency specializing in tours for those over age 55 may place ads in publications of the American Association of Retired Persons (AARP) or may find that direct mailings to repeat customers work best. Another example is that short skirts sell better to younger women than to older women; if the demographics change so that there is a shortage of young women, then it would be prudent to consider this in clothing design in order to reach the masses or to sway fashion in general. Failure to realize changes in demographics has been the downfall of many businesses.

## CONSUMPTION PROCESS

Consumer economics, since it has everyday uses for the individual, the family, and the household, is considered an applied social science. Something is going to happen rather than an idea that is merely discussed; in other words, consumer economics is not purely philosophical but is a reality-based, action-oriented discipline. We are all consumers, we all have experiences, and we all want to get better at this practical life skill. Because there are so many aspects to consumption, it can be thought of as a process. In terms of the individual making purchase decisions, the consumption process can be broken down into five parts (see Figure 1.2):

1. Awareness
2. Thinking
3. Planning
4. Implementing/acting
5. Evaluating

The consumption process begins with an awareness that something is needed or desired. Perhaps the stimulus is that something has broken and needs to be replaced, or an occasion or event is coming up that requires new things or actions, or a new product has come on the market that could solve a problem or fulfill a need, want, or goal. Problems are questions or dilemmas and provide a stimulus to act. **Needs** are things that are deemed necessary, such as food, and **wants** are things wished for or desired, such as an expensive car. When consumers become aware, they begin to wonder about the benefits of a purchase and if certain ser-

**Figure 1.2**   Consumption Process.

vices are better than others. For example, cars are not chosen simply to provide transportation; they provide status, identity, or prestige for their owners. Needs are few in number and very general (such as needing something to eat or a car to drive), but wants are limitless and often specific (such as a certain kind of food or car). Economic theory says that human wants are limitless, although this concept can be challenged by individuals who say that the simpler life is better and that there is a level of contentment that can be reached with that approach. In other words, more is not always better. For instance, have you ever had too many clothes and needed to clean out your closet? Needs and wants are usually more immediate than goals. **Goals** are end results, things you are striving for, and are based on values. The value of a good or service is subjective, meaning that preferences differ dramatically among individuals.

After awareness of the need, want, or goal is complete, the process follows these next four steps:

1. *Thinking*. Thinking is a mental exploration of the possibilities: weighing pros and cons and gathering information. Product image or features may be important at this stage.
2. *Planning*. Deciding on an ordered set of steps or activities involves planning. Whom do I need to call? Where do I need to go?
3. *Implementing/acting*. To implement means to put plans into action, to do something, or to go somewhere. This may include sampling a product, visiting Web sites, getting an estimate, or actually buying.
4. *Evaluating*. The final step is to evaluate, a time for reflecting on outcomes. Individuals may ask, "Am I happy with what happened?" To be specific, "Do I like this brand of whole wheat bread or another brand better?" If someone likes another brand better, that person will act differently the next time he or she goes to the grocery store. From the business point of view, evaluation can lead to repurchase behavior. Profitability increases with repeat business, such as multiple haircuts over the course of several months versus a single visit, so a customer may notice extra special treatment during the first visit because the wise barber or stylist tries to establish a relationship or rapport with the customer so that he or she will both return and recommend the place to friends. This relationship can reduce choice for the consumer and makes purchasing decisions easier. By going to the same barber or stylist, a customer simplifies "the cognitive work and mental effort required for buying. . . . The benefits of choice reduction are especially prevalent when the product category is complex, where there is some risk associated with purchase, or if it is time-consuming or difficult for the consumer to specify his or her preferences" (Hofacker, 2002, p. 46).

To discuss the consumption process further, the steps of thinking and planning may seem like the same thing, but they are not. Thinking is a random set of thoughts involving the accepting and rejecting of inputs and ideas, whereas planning is a more advanced stage of decision making when a specific course of action is chosen. It is possible for someone to get stalled in the thinking stage and not move on to the others. Also, the process may be stopped at the awareness level if individuals are too busy to take the time to think or plan about a consumption decision and decide to wait before taking further steps.

## Place of Consumption

The first thought about consumption is that it takes place in a store between buyer and seller, but actually consumption takes place in a variety of settings, including at home, at school, at work, in the community, on trips, and over the Internet. During the course of the day, you may consume water in several places: before leaving home, while walking or driving in the car, when having lunch or dinner, and while working or being in school. Think how bottled water has revolutionized the places water can be consumed—even to the point that an etiquette columnist was asked if it was all right for a guest to swig water from a bottle during a wedding. What do you think was the answer the columnist gave?

Businesses and governments consume, as do individuals and households. There are all sorts of levels of consumption, from the humble to the grand. It explains why in the marketplace there are bath towels that sell for $5 each and others that sell for $75: different markets, different consumers, different needs, different incomes.

## Influences on Consumer Style

Consumers have a characteristic way of prebuying, buying, and postbuying that could be called their **consumer style**—patterns of behaving or ways of making financial decisions and acting on them. Seven factors that influence **consumer style** follow:

1. *Economics.* The condition of national and worldwide economies during times of decision making affects consumer style. The economy is said to follow a business cycle (described in the next section).
2. *History.* The background of a person influences the way his or her decisions are made and acted on. This includes the present as well as family history and the history of the area or region or society in which the individual resides. Why is history an influence? The answer is that we can learn a great deal about consumer behavior from our past and from our general cultural past. In the *Life of Reason,* Santayan wrote, "Those who cannot remember the past are condemned to repeat it."
3. *Culture.* Groups and their behaviors or traditions that surround the individual or family also impact consumer style. This group may be the overall culture and subcultures, including a consumer culture. Do you know what the manufacturer Lea & Perrins makes? You probably know it is Worcestershire sauce, a condiment. Can you even picture what the bottle looks like? It is a glass bottle wrapped in brown paper. This is part of a shared consumer culture.
4. *Personality.* The sum total of an individual's enduring traits, ways of relating, and characteristics, including reaction to risk and opportunity, likes and dislikes, determine consumer choices. Are you between the ages of 25 and 50 and interested in "natural" or environmentally friendly products? If so, the Origins line of the Estée Lauder brand was created for you (Koehn, 2001).
5. *Biology or environment.* The physiology of individuals (such as thirst or hunger) and the environment in which they live influence consumer style. You can see that the Origins line speaks not only to personality but also to

environment. Successful products fulfill several areas of consumer needs or spheres of influence.

6. *Technology.* Technology, a broad term that encompasses machines, techniques, material objects, and processes, is used by individuals to get what they want. Certain individuals are more fascinated by technology than others; entrepreneurs and inventors tend to lead in this area. Henry Ford led in automobiles and Michael Dell led in personal computers; both were fascinated by new technology, constantly taking machines apart and reassembling them (Koehn, 2001).

7. *Politics.* Voters, politicians, organizations, and bureaucrats affect the decisions that alter public policy.

To apply these influences to a specific purchase area, consider clothing. The style, color, and quality selected are affected by what is affordable and available (economics), what has fit or has proven serviceable in the past (history), what others think or what friends wear (culture), what attracts (personality), what keeps a person warm or comfortable (biology or environment), what the cut or weave is (technology), and what sales tax is placed on the garment (politics).

Although, as stated earlier, consumers have a characteristic way of consuming, in recent times more variance in style has been observed by postmodernists. Whereas consumers in the past may have been fairly consistent in purchasing behavior (partly because they had fewer choices), in the twenty-first century there has been a more eclectic mix of goods that may sometimes seem inconsistent to outside observers.

> People do not always remain true to type. Depending on shifts of mood or shifts of situation, the same individual will behave like an upscale achiever one moment, like a downscale bargain hunter the next. The same consumer will buy part of her wardrobe at Bloomingdales and part at K-Mart. (Oglivy, 1990)

## ECONOMICS AND THE BUSINESS CYCLE

So far the chapter has focused on introducing consumerism and some beginning concepts about consumer behavior. Now the chapter moves into the more economic side of consumption.

**Economics** is the study of or science of production, distribution, and consumption. It concerns itself with how wealth is created and managed in households, businesses, regions, and countries. Consumers participate in and react to movements in the economy, and their spending habits affect growth. One of the changes has been a decreased preference for shopping at malls: At least 300 older malls, each with one or two anchor stores, shut down between 1995 and 2001 (Greene, 2001). Another 300 to 500 such malls will follow suit. Why are so many older malls closing? Besides the economic problems the country is going through, another reason may be the glut in retail space. In 2000, the United States had 15 square feet of retail space in shopping centers for every man, woman, and child, up from 11 square feet in 1980, according to National Research Bureau data (Greene, 2001).

In 2000, there were 15 square feet of retail space for every man, woman, and child, up from 11 square feet in 1980.

Periodically, fluctuations occur in the **real gross domestic product (real GDP)**, which is a measure of the value of all the goods and services newly

**Figure 1.3**  Business Cycle. The economy goes through stages that tend to be cyclical. The stages reflect changes in employment, production, and consumption.

produced in a country during some period of time, usually a year or a quarter, adjusted for inflation. **Inflation** is a steady increase in prices. **Deflation** indicates falling prices.

As a way to illustrate the usual expansions and contractions in the economy, there is a **business cycle** (see Figure 1.3). This cycle is made up of three stages:

1. **Expansion** (the preferred stage in the business cycle) is a period of prosperity, growth, higher output, low unemployment, and increased retail sales and housing starts. In general, economic activity, including investing, is growing, and interest rates are low or falling. With low interest rates, consumers find it easier to buy cars, homes, and other expensive goods on credit. For most of the 1990s, the United States was in a time of expansion.

2. **Recession** is a temporary moderate decline or downturn in the economy. It is classically defined by the Bureau of Economic Research as a recurring period of decline in total output, income, employment, and trade, usually lasting from six months to a year, and is marked by widespread contractions in many economic areas. From 2001 to 2003, the United States experienced an economic slowdown. Consumer confidence declined, and there were many layoffs; unemployment rose to 6.1 percent in June 2003. A very deep or prolonged recession is called a depression, and these are rare. The most notable one was the Great Depression of the 1930s, which reached its greatest depth in 1933. Another economic slowdown occurred in 2008.

3. **Recovery**, the period in the business cycle when economic activity picks up, leads to expansion. Economic indicators show that when things are getting better, production and spending rise, consumer confidence improves, and employment picks up. Sometimes this stage includes a rise in interest rates. Signs of recovery are in evidence, with unemployment dipping to 4.5 percent in 2006.

As illustrated, these three stages run in a cycle, but no one knows for sure how long each stage will last or how high or low the swings will go. Changes in the GDP are the main indicators, but unemployment, interest rates, business growth, and other factors play a role.

## Scarcity

Unlimited wants combined with limited supplies create **scarcity**, a condition in which there is an insufficient amount or supply, a shortage. Scarcity lies at the heart of production and consumption. A product may be in short supply, and the manufacturer cannot make enough of the product to meet consumer demand. For example, after the September 11, 2001, destruction of the World Trade Center in New York City and a section of the Pentagon in Washington, D.C., there was a shortage of American flags in the United States. Demand far exceeded supply; it took several weeks for manufacturers and suppliers to catch up.

Scarcity exists on the consumer side as well. A consumer may not have enough money to buy what he or she wants. Scarcity often exists because we have unlimited wants but limited resources to pursue those wants. Scarcity is not the same as poverty. It can exist in a time of abundance and prosperity and is relative to the individual. As we all know, some people are content living on very little, whereas others feel deprived if they cannot immediately get everything they want.

In economic theory, as long as a human need is not satisfied, there is scarcity. In summary, scarcity is a normal part of life, unavoidable and individually defined, and it cycles and flows.

## Supply, Demand, and Equilibrium Price

The American flag shortage mentioned earlier is an example of supply and demand. A worldwide shortage example is that of broadband Internet access: The demand far exceeds the supply, and suppliers are hurrying up to catch up. According to Nielsen rating systems, in the United States, Great Britain, and Canada, over 50 percent of the population has Internet access; worldwide, about one-sixth of the world's population is online (www.nua.ie).

*Over 50 percent of the U.S., Great Britain, and Canadian populations are online.*

In economics, there are a number of theories that partially explain consumer reaction to prices. Some of these theories are elaborated upon in upcoming chapters, but for this introductory chapter, the most basic theory is that of **equilibrium price**, which is reached when supply and demand are equal (see Figure 1.4). Scarcity affects supply. According to the **law of supply**, as the supply of a good or service goes up, the price comes down. In the **law of demand**, as the price of a good or service rises, the quantity demanded of that good or service falls. The price paid for goods and services reacts to these laws. For example, when a color

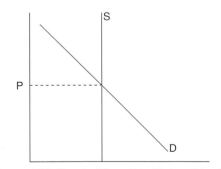

**Figure 1.4**  Links among Supply, Demand, and Price. A change in one affects the others.

Demand (D), Supply (S), and Equilibrium Price (P)

Supply represents the firms' side of transactions.

Quantity Supplied

Demand represents the customers' side of transactions.

Quantity Demanded

Supply shifts are due to:
- Number of competitors
- New inventions, "new and improved" driving out old
- Price of goods needed for production
- Future price expectations
- Government taxes, subsidies, legislation

Demand shifts are due to:
- Preferences
- Access: Ease of purchase
- Prices
- Number of competing buyers
- Consumers' ability to pay
- Expectations of shortages or rising prices
- Price of related goods that could be substituted (example, lamb chops cost more so person buys pork chops instead)

**Figure 1.5**  Supply-and-Demand Shifts.

goes out of style in furniture upholstery, goods in that color are less desired and the price decreases (the goods go on sale). Figure 1.5 gives more details about supply and demand, in particular what causes shifts in each. Supply represents the firms' side of transactions; demand represents the consumers' side of transactions.

Prices based on supply and demand may be on actualities or only on perceptions. For example, in a natural disaster there may be plenty of gasoline available, but people may assume that is not the case and rush to the pumps to fill up. Word of mouth and news media can have a tremendous effect on people's perceptions: An announcement of crop failures in peanuts will motivate consumers to buy whatever they perceive will be in short supply, such as peanut butter. Figure 1.6 shows a diagram of how consumer demand affects supply and eventual resource use.

## SUPPLY, DEMAND, AND DEMOGRAPHICS

Population changes affect consumption patterns. Demand can be explained as the relationship between the price and the quantity demanded by consumers. If the number of consumers increases, then it follows that demand will increase; where populations choose to cluster makes a difference as well. Figure 1.7 shows an example of the spillover effect.

What distinguishes echo boomers from previous generations is their ease with computers.

A successful supplier not only responds to changes but also anticipates buyers' changing preferences and, in the case of population shifts, responds to changes in movement patterns. Regarding U.S. population trends, during the first years of the

**Figure 1.6**  Impact of Consumer Demand on Supply and Eventual Resource Use.

| Consumers move ⟶ | Housing demand ⟶ | Realtors, stores, |
| to a | rises and need | builders, utility |
| certain area | for services | companies respond to |
| | increases | and anticipate demand |

**Figure 1.7**    Spillover Effect: Ways That Moving Affects Others.

twenty-first century there was a surge in the number of undergraduate students going to college, which affected demand for classes, dorm rooms, apartments, and types of goods that people in their late teens and twenties buy.

Most readers of this book belong to Generation Y (the echo boomer generation), the 72 million people born between 1977 and 1994 (see Figure 1.8). (Unless otherwise noted, the population figures given in this section are from the United States.) This group peaked in 1988 when 3.9 million babies were born (the highest number since 1964). They are bringing another wave of high consumption through the nation as they go through their teen years and into early adulthood. What most distinguishes this group from previous groups is their computer fluency. Unfortunately, this group was coming of age when the country was going through tough economic times and more young American adults over age 18 were returning to the family nest. These young adults, called "boomerangers," were most likely to return home because they were experiencing financial pressures (student loans, credit card bills, unemployment) or because they were marrying later. Nearly 4 million or 10.5 percent of the 25- to 34-year-old age group (and 12 percent of those ages 25 to 29) were living in the family home (Greider, 2001). This follows an historic trend: The number of boomerang kids rises when the economy sours. A November 2001 survey by Monstertrak.com found that 60 percent of college students planned to move back home after graduation and more than 20 percent will stay a year or more (Greider, 2001).

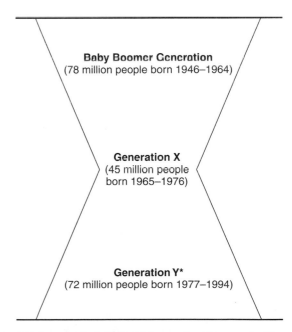

**Baby Boomer Generation**
(78 million people born 1946–1964)

**Generation X**
(45 million people
born 1965–1976)

**Generation Y***
(72 million people born 1977–1994)

**Figure 1.8**    U.S. Age Distribution.

*Also known as the baby boomlet generation. This group is still forming their preferences and behaviors.

The group called Generation X is composed of the 45 million people born between 1965 and 1976. As you can see from Figure 1.8, Generation X is a smaller group representing a shorter span of time than the groups before and after. This group cares about the environment; they like lower prices and a more functional look.

A marked upswing or downswing in the economy can change patterns overnight. If people in any age group feel vulnerable, they will change their spending and saving behaviors immediately.

## Risk and Opportunity Costs

Two other economic concepts that greatly affect consumer purchasing behavior are risk and opportunity. Consumers weigh the risks and opportunities associated with decisions. An individual may be risk averse, risk attracted, or risk neutral.

**Risk** is the possibility or perception of harm, suffering, danger, or loss. In financial risk, this may include the fear of losing money in the stock market or of buying an inferior product. Most people are risk averse, especially when it comes to their money, which is why discussions about how Social Security money should be invested or whether consumers should be allowed to have more say in how their Social Security money should be invested turn into heated debates. Retirement is a time when people want to be secure and comfortable—they don't want surprises.

The psychologist Abraham Maslow said that at any one time people are torn between growth and safety and that safety has the stronger pull, so when given a choice, individuals are more drawn to the familiar and predictable. This is, of course, an overgeneralization, and it is difficult to completely typecast a person as risk averse, risk attracted, or risk neutral because much risk-taking behavior is situational. Someone may be experimental when it comes to trying new food but be predictable when it comes to music or clothing. Usually, a risk-averse person would be attracted to a financial arrangement such as one that has a fixed-rate mortgage of 7 percent on a house versus an adjustable-rate mortgage that varies from 5 to 9 percent because he or she may be more worried about losing money than excited about the prospect of gaining money. A fear of loss is called **loss aversion**. Risk-attracted individuals may be more drawn to the adjustable-rate mortgage, figuring the economy will go in their favor and the mortgage will stay at the lower end of the range and therefore be less costly than the fixed-rate mortgage. A risk-neutral individual could go either way: He or she is indifferent toward risk and uncertainty and would be drawn to expected rates of return.

Research indicates that women avoid risk more than men when it comes to investments. Women are more likely to say they are "careful with money" (31 percent of women versus 24 percent of men), which is probably why they pick safer investments and let banks handle their accounts rather than keeping them with brokerages or mutual fund managers (Whelan, 2001). In the same nationwide study of 31,576 Americans, it was found that female college grads are more likely to put their money in investment products than those who graduated from high school.

In addition, there is true risk and there is perceived risk. What may be pleasurable to one person, such as a thrill ride at an amusement park, may be perceived as a dangerous risk to be avoided by another. In order to reduce perceived risk, individuals diminish their fears by finding out all they can about a product before purchasing it. For example, a person unsure about a thrill ride may watch it go around a few times and talk to others about it before standing in line to get on the ride; another example is that people read about new car model ratings in *Consumer Reports* or *Motor Trend* and talk with friends before purchasing a car. An additional commonly used search mechanism to reduce risk is to gather information on the Internet.

There are other types of risks:

- *Time risk*. Consumers do not want to waste time in finding and purchasing products.
- *Security risk*. Consumers may fear being a victim of crime, perhaps involving their credit card number or Social Security cards.
- *Privacy risk*. Consumers may fear that their buying behavior or personal information is being reported and sold to companies.

**Opportunity** refers to a favorable outlook, a chance for progress, advancement, and action. Economics assumes that people will try to increase their satisfaction by taking advantage of opportunities. However, it is not always easy to tell when something is a risk or an opportunity, such as a job offer in Idaho when you have lived all your life in Alabama. Is this the opportunity of a lifetime, or is it a risky venture that will be regretted? Every choice made means that something else is given up. This is referred to in economics as **opportunity cost**. One alternative is selected over another, and there is a cost attached to this choice. For example, Tiger Woods decided to drop out of Stanford University because he did not have the time to pursue his studies full-time and play golf full-time. He joined the Pro Tour in 1996. He stunned the golfing world with huge victories in 1997; by 1999 he was the top prizewinner on the Pro Tour. In Tiger's case, his scarce resource was time, and taking a risk paid off.

Opportunity cost is related to the concept of **trade-offs**. To get something that is desired, it is necessary to sacrifice something else because of scarcity (of time, of money, of energy). Choosing to study one subject over another is an example of a trade-off, with the maintenance of or improvement of a grade in the selected subject being the hoped-for outcome. Scarcity forces us to make these kinds of choices all the time. An economic principle is that if we worked harder and gave up leisure, we would produce more. Giving up one good or practice for another is the essence of trade-offs.

## Three Questions

Many of the previously mentioned examples are of an individual or personal nature, but large-scale economies tackle similar issues. There are three problems or questions that economies must find a way to solve:

1. What is to be produced? Examples are trucks, television shows, computers, ice cream, and health care. A **product** is anything a consumer acquires or perceives to need. Over 15,000 new or improved products are introduced each year in grocery stores, but not many will succeed.
2. How are these goods produced? Examples include what companies, what types of factories, and how much equipment, material, and labor are needed. International agreements such as the North American Free Trade

Jubilant professional golfer Tiger Woods celebrates after hitting a hole in one on the fourteenth hole at the Greater Milwaukee Open. His decision to drop out of Stanford University to become a pro golfer is an example of opportunity costs, selecting one alternative over another. ( AP Wide World Photos.)

Agreement (NAFTA) have changed the level of competition and reduced international trade barriers. The Internet has also opened up exchange across borders. The general trend is toward freer exchange and less trade restraints, which is usually a good thing for consumers. One of the few negatives is the problem of quality control since many countries in the world do not have strong consumer protection laws (e.g., copyrights, trademarks). Gucci purses, Louis Vuitton luggage, or CDs purchased abroad may be fakes.

3. For whom are the goods produced? Examples can range from the young to the old, from domestic markets to international ones.

## Market Economy and Competition

Most economically developed countries, including the United States, Canada, Australia, Japan, and Western European countries, are referred to as consumption societies, where consumers have a great deal of freedom to buy and sell products as they choose. In fact, people in consumption societies spend more time in consumption than nearly any other activity, including working and sleeping (both of which involve consuming). This is part of being a **market economy**. In a market economy, exchanges are controlled by marketplace forces of demand and supply rather than by outside forces such as government control. This goes back to Adam Smith's philosophy that the market is a self-

Robots prevent people from doing heavy or dangerous work. In the auto industry, robots can weld reliably and safely. (© George Steinmetz, Corbis.)

correcting mechanism—if left alone, it will function well. These exchanges do not exist in a vacuum, however, because untold numbers of dollars are spent on activities that encourage consumption, such as attractive store environments, catalogs, and Web sites.

A market economy is characterized by the free exchange of goods and services in markets and by freely determined prices. This is contrasted with the **command or centrally planned economy** wherein most decisions about what, how, and for whom to produce are made by those who control the government. An example would be the Soviet sphere for much of the twentieth century.

Connected to the market economy is the concept of **property rights**—the legal rights over the use, sale, and proceeds from a good or resource. Property rights are important because they allow people to buy and sell goods. If there were no property rights, anyone could take what you own and sell it. Imagine someone coming into your home, removing everything, and conducting a yard sale on your front lawn. Private property rights include the right to use, the right to protect, and the right to transfer use or ownership. These rights, however, are within the context of the greater society. For example, a homeowner cannot park a giant boat in his front yard if the homeowners' association of the street he lives on prohibits it, but if he lives in a rural area where there are no such rules, he can do what he wants.

In a total or absolute market economy, there would be no restraints placed on the economy by outside forces, which would result in perfect competition and market sovereignty. Perfect competition means that many businesses could offer the same product at the same price. No company could be so large nor its brands so popular that the company could ask a higher price.

## CONSUMER SOVEREIGNTY

**Consumer sovereignty** refers to the premise that consumers decide which goods will survive and that producers cannot dictate consumer tastes. Products do fall in and out of favor. Take the example of ketchup made from tomatoes. Today, we are used to that kind of ketchup, but in the mid-nineteenth century walnut ketchup and mushroom ketchup (as well as tomato ketchup) were established seasonings in the United States (Koehn, 2001). Why did walnut ketchup and mushroom ketchup fall out of favor? Will they come back in style? As another example, people change their minds about what type of leisure activities they want to pursue. It is important to forecast trends in leisure because it generates $535 billion a year and affects fitness clubs, theme parks, marine and cruise industries, and motorcycle and motor sports businesses (Paul, 2001). Research indicates that leisure activities on the rise include swimming, hiking, running, weight training, fishing, golfing, hiking, and using aerobic machines; declining activities include skateboarding, archery, surfing, and racquetball. When people are at home, the biggest leisure activities are reading, spending time with friends and family, and talking on the phone. When they go out, the vast majority of Americans say that eating out is their favorite leisure activity and that they plan to do more of it (Paul, 2001).

The concept of consumer sovereignty is based on Adam Smith's philosophy that consumers should guide the economy—the consumer is king. In many cases the consumer is king, but in looking at the total marketplace environment, consumer sovereignty does not always exist because of outside intervention such as government support for schools and postal services or government controls on imports and exports. For example, recent newspaper reports showed that the United States imports and sells far more Mexican beer than it exports because of consumer preferences and policies making it difficult for U.S. beer to be delivered to and sold easily in Mexico. Each country sets up its own trade agreements and policies regarding imports and exports, which greatly affects what the consumer can purchase. We do not live in a world where the only interaction is between the consumer and the market.

Sometimes, the government steps in to aid industry. For example, in 2001 the federal government gave billions of dollars to airlines to help bail them out when there was a decline in air traffic. In regional or national disasters, the normal balance of supply and demand is disrupted, and the government steps in to restore order and provide funds for rebuilding. This intervention is regarded as necessary for the good of the overall economy as well as for the good of the industry, employees, residents, or region.

## MONOPOLIES

Government also becomes involved in the market economy by discouraging the growth of monopolies. The word *monopoly* comes from two Greek words meaning "single seller." A **monopoly** exists when there is only one producer and there is no substitute, such as there being only one airline or cruise ship line. There are two reasons monopolies are discouraged: Without competition, consumers may have no choice but to pay higher prices, and a monopoly may discourage new inventions or the growth of new companies (new businesses are discouraged when there are high barriers to entry). Rather than being absolute, a monopoly can be thought of as incremental since it is rare for a monopoly to totally control a product or market. An example of a monopoly may be an electricity service in a particular area, but it may not be practical to have competitors in this situation.

**Price** is the amount of money a person pays to buy or use a product. Setting the right price is essential in the consumer–market exchange. If a price is too low, it may indicate low quality; if it is too high, there will be few buyers. Price is affected by demand. For example, there is a higher demand for eggs at Easter than at other times of the year. Sellers can decide whether to raise prices or to use increased holiday consumption as a ploy of attracting customers by reducing the price on eggs in the hopes they will buy other products in the store.

In consumer economics, there is a widely held principle: Competition in the marketplace is good for consumers. Sometimes it may not seem like much of a problem if a monopoly exists; a consumer may think I simply won't buy any more of that type of product (such as a food or drink item), but there are situations in which consumers have no choice, such as a particular medicine that their doctor prescribes. If there are other brands or generic products, it would give the consumer a better range of choices and prices. In recent years, probably the most publicized monopoly case in the United States involved Microsoft.

A successful business has to have a thorough understanding of competitors' goods, capabilities, and strategies. Part of a business's strategy may be to provide superior service so that other businesses will have to upgrade their customer service to compete.

## ECONOMIC SYSTEMS

To summarize the key point of the previous sections, it can be said that for the most part the United States has a market economy. In many ways, we are free as consumers to choose the products and services we want. If we want to go to the store or go online to trade on eBay, we do; if we choose not to purchase new clothes because we don't like the season's fashions, that is also our choice. A market economy is also referred to as **capitalism**, an economic system characterized by open competition in a free market. The ownership and control of resources and businesses are largely held by private individuals, and the forces of supply and demand are relied on to control the production of goods and services. Adam Smith called this perfect liberty, which later became known as laissez-faire capitalism (loosely translated, laissez-faire means "hands off").

**Socialism** is an economic system in which the government (also referred to as the state) centrally plans, owns, and controls most of the capital and makes decisions about prices and quantities. Capital refers to factories, stores, farms, and equipment. The degree of socialism varies by country; for example, Scandinavian countries are generally regarded as more socialistic than the United States. Also, a country could have socialized medicine (such as is found in Canada or the United Kingdom) but have a capitalistic structure in general. **Communism** is a social or economic system in which nearly all capital is collectively owned, and examples (as of the writing of this book) are North Korea and Cuba.

Since most of the world functions as a market economy, this economic system will form the backbone of this book. Today, most people and most nations prefer a high degree of consumer sovereignty.

## INTERNET AND E-COMMERCE

Economic systems cannot remain as isolated as they once were due to the high degree of internationalization of business and the proliferation of the Internet. There is no question that the Internet has revolutionized the worldwide marketplace in terms of communication, entertainment, and exchange and provides an interactive medium as opposed to the conventional modes of mass media such as TV, magazines, billboards, and radio. Mass media are unidirectional (or one-to-many) communication processes (Hofacker, 2000), whereas the Internet provides a wide array of communication patterns between consumers and between consumers and firms.

The new buzz phrase in consumer marketing research is **consumer-mediated environment (CME)**, which refers to buying and selling over the Internet. **E-commerce** is a general term referring to exchange transactions that take place on the Internet, such as buying and selling goods, services, and information. This is in contrast to more conventional modes of exchange transactions, such as in person, over the telephone, or by surface mail. Characteristics of e-commerce include pervasiveness of technology, speed, and globalization.

Many goods and services are sold on the basis of convenience and speed, and buying over the Internet fulfills these needs. For example, at most universities you can buy your textbooks from the campus bookstore and have them delivered to your door or have them available for pickup rather than having to wait in long lines to find the books and purchase them. Campus bookstores had to do this in response to competition from Amazon and other online booksellers that were delivering books straight to dorm rooms and apartments.

E-commerce is such a huge concept that it is useful to break it into two parts:

1. *E-merchandise.* Selling goods and services electronically and moving items through distribution channels, such as Internet shopping for groceries, cars, tickets, music, clothes, hardware, travel, books, flowers, or gifts, are examples of e-merchandise.
2. *E-finance.* Banking, debit cards, smart cards, banking machines, telephone and Internet banking, insurance, loans, financial services and mortgages are all done online and represent e-finance (Goldsmith & McGregor, 2000).

Chapter 11 on the Internet and identity theft will discuss how much things have changed. The top category in terms of percent of traffic (visits) on the Internet is health and medical, followed by education.

Many stores have buildings and Internet sites. An example would be Britain's famous Harrods department store, which has a large building in London and an Internet site (www.harrods.com). Internet retailers are referred to as e-tailers.

Although e-commerce has opened up new ways of trading, it is not without its risks, drawbacks, and critics. Some of the concerns center on the collection and dissemination of consumer information by marketers who participate in online retailing. Specific issues pertain to the privacy and security of consumer data and consumers' perception of such risks: 37 percent of online consumers say they would buy more online if they were not so concerned about privacy issues (Forrester Research, 2001). A more startling statistic was revealed in a survey by the UCLA Internet Project that found that 94.5 percent of consumers express some concern about credit card security online, a number that actually rose from 91.2 percent the previous year (Weber, 2001). An innovation is the growing use of passwords and codes:

> When shoppers buy at a participating site, they will be prompted for the password. But the site won't ever see the secret code. Instead, it will be beamed to the credit card bank, which will then give the retailer an all-clear on the transaction. If it catches on, the approach could cut down on online fraud. (Weber, 2001, p. B1)

*Issue: Should the government regulate online privacy?*

A related concern is how much the government should be involved in regulating online privacy. A nationwide survey revealed that 54 percent of respondents say government should regulate online privacy; this represented a decrease from the previous year of 61 percent (Forrester Research, 2001).

As may be expected, research studies indicate that higher levels of Internet experience lead to lower risk perceptions regarding online shopping (Miyazaki & Fernandez, 2001). In other words, those regularly using the Internet often perceive fewer risks than less frequent users or nonusers. Frequent users have found that their transactions have been protected and that the goods they ordered were delivered as expected. Much Internet shopping takes place during office hours, and this phenomenon is being tracked internationally.

In the third chapter of this book is more coverage on different types of media; later in the book there is more information on legislation and regulations regarding privacy and security when buying and selling over the Internet. For this introductory chapter, the main points are that the use of the Internet is growing and that consumerism as we once knew it is rapidly changing. Economic growth increasingly depends on innovation and the spread of technology.

## SUMMARY

The study of consumer economics covers how people deal with scarcity and choose between alternative goods, services, and actions. Our task is to decide how to allocate limited resources to different competitive uses. Consumption has a purpose: It fulfills a need or want or is used to fulfill or reach a goal. Consumerism is the belief that goods and services give meaning to individuals and their roles in society. According to Adam Smith, founder of modern economics, consumers guide the marketplace, and the goods and services they produce and consume have more to do with the wealth of nations than silver and gold. This consumer power can be referred to as consumer sovereignty.

The chapter addressed the following questions:

Why consume?

Who consumes?

What affects consumption?

Consumption was explained as a process. The ever-changing nature of the marketplace and consumer demands has made consumer economics an increasingly necessary and important field to study. Given the demographic, economic, social, and technological changes in the world, the need for skilled consumption practices (more efficiency, less waste, risk minimization, increased Internet access) at all levels has never been greater. The goal of this chapter is to help the reader understand that part of the economy, to learn to think like a consumer economist (e.g., to understand why competition is good for consumers), and to get an intuitive feel for how scarcity, choices, and economic systems interact.

## KEY POINTS

1. We are all consumers.
2. Consumption is a multistep process.
3. Everyone experiences scarcity (usually of time or money).
4. Scarcity leads to choice; a choice requires consideration of opportunity costs or trade-offs.
5. Three questions that economies face are what, how, and for whom production takes place.
6. The business cycle has three parts: expansion, recession, and recovery.
7. The United States (and most of the world) has a market economy (also referred to as capitalism). A market economy involves freely determined prices, individual property rights, and the freedom to trade, produce, and consume, and it also includes a role for government.

## KEY TERMS

| | | |
|---|---|---|
| business cycle | demography | opportunity |
| capitalism | e-commerce | opportunity cost |
| caveat emptor | economics | price |
| command or centrally controlled economy | equilibrium price | product |
| | expansion | property rights |
| communism | goals | real gross domestic product (real GDP) |
| consumer economics | household | |
| consumerism | inflation | recession |
| consumer-mediated environment (CME) | injurious consumption | recovery |
| | law of demand | risk |
| consumers | law of supply | scarcity |
| consumer sovereignty | loss aversion | socialism |
| consumer style | market economy | trade-offs |
| deflation | monopoly | wants |
| demographics | needs | |

## DISCUSSION QUESTIONS

1. Consider the Duchess of Windsor who said, "I've been rich and I've been poor; rich is better." What do you think about that sentiment? In your opinion, what is the connection between happiness and consumption?
2. Tiger Woods' choice was to continue at Stanford or to potentially make millions of dollars by joining the Pro Tour as a golfer. What would you have done?
3. Give an example of an opportunity cost in your own life. Why did you make the choice that you did?
4. A former head of Revlon said, "In the factory we make cosmetics; in the store we sell hope." What does this quote tell you about consumer needs?
5. Author Daniel Gilbert says that experiences may bring more happiness than durable goods. Do you agree or disagree? Describe two experiences that made you happy.

## E-RESOURCES

**CNET**   *www.cnet.com*
News about e-business, computing, and the Internet

**Electronic Commerce Policy**   *www.ecommerce.gov*
Government source and link to "Business America" about international trade and e-commerce

**NUA Internet Surveys**   *www.nua.ie*
Research statistics on use of the Internet

**U.S. Census Report**   *www.census.gov*
Government source for demographic, social, and economic data

## REFERENCES

Clements, J. (August 16, 2006). Money and happiness. Here's why you won't laugh all the way to the bank. *Wall Street Journal*, p. D1.

Forrester Research. *Privacy issues inhibit online spending* (October 3, 2001), www.nua.ie.

Frey, W. (2006). Diversity spreads out: Metropolitan shifts in Hispanics, Asian, and Black populations since 2000. The Brookings Institute, Washington, DC, 1–17.

Gilbert, D. (2006). *Stumbling on happiness.* New York: Alfred A. Knopf.

Goldsmith, E., and S. McGregor. (2000). E-commerce: Consumer protection issues and implications for research and education. *Journal of Consumer Studies and Home Economics, 24* (2), 124–27.

Greene, K. (December 12, 2001). What a bleak Christmas may mean for older malls. *Wall Street Journal*, pp. B1, B8.

Greider, L. (December 2001). Hard times drive adult kids "home." *AARP Bulletin, 42* (11), Washington, DC.

Harris, D. (2000). *Cute, quaint, hungry and romantic: The aesthetics of consumerism.* New York: Basic Books.

Heilbroner, Robert (Ed.) (1986). *The essential Adam Smith.* New York: Norton. A translation of Adam Smith's (1776). *An inquiry into the nature and causes of the wealth of nations.*

Hirschman, E. (1991). Secular mortality and the dark side of consumer behavior. In *Advances in Consumer Research XVIII,* ed. R. Holman and M. Solomon. Provo, UT: Association for Consumer Research, pp. 1–4.

Hofacker, C. (2000). *Internet marketing.* Dripping Springs, TX: Digital Springs, Inc.

Hofacker, C. (2002). *Internet marketing,* 3rd ed. New York: John Wiley.

Koehn, N. F. (2001). *Brand new: How entrepreneurs earned consumers' trust from Wedgwood to Dell.* Boston: Harvard Business School Press. Also quoted in Michael Dell with Catherine Fredman, *Direct from Dell: Strategies that revolutionized an industry.* New York: HarperCollins, 1999.

Maslow, A. (1954). *Motivation and personality.* New York: Harper & Row.

Miyazaki, A. D., and A. Fernandez. (2001). Consumer perceptions of privacy and security. *Journal of Consumer Affairs, 35* (1), 27–44.

Nicholson, T. (December 2001). You're out! More lose jobs, insurance. *AARP Bulletin, 42* (11), Washington, DC.

Oglivy, J. (February 1990). This postmodern business. *Marketing and Research Today,* 4–21. See also E. C. Hirschman and M. Holbrook (1992), Hedonic consumption: Emerging concepts, methods, and propositions. *Journal of Marketing, 46,* 92–101.

Oleson, M. (2004). Exploring the relationship between money attitudes and Maslow's hierarchy of needs. *International Journal of Consumer Studies, 28* (1), 83–92.

Paul, Pamela. (November 2001). Leisurely occupations. *American Demographics,* 14–15.

Smith, A. *An inquiry into the nature and causes of the wealth of nations,* 1776, as edited by Robert Heilbroner (1986) in *The essential Adam Smith.* New York: Norton.

Swagler, R. (1994). Evolution and applications of the term consumerism: Theme and variations. *Journal of Consumer Affairs, 28* (2), 347–60.

Wansink, B., and R. Deshpande. (1994). Out of sight, out of mind: Pantry stockpiling and brandage frequency. *Marketing Letters, 5* (1), 91–100.

Wansink, B., A. Brasel, and S. Amjad. (2000). The mystery of the cabinet castaway: Why we buy products we never use. *Journal of Family and Consumer Sciences, 92* (1), 233.

Weber, T. (December 10, 2001). What do you risk using a credit card to shop on the net? *Wall Street Journal,* p. B1.

Whelan, David. (November 2001). Investing with care. *American Demographics,* 12–13.

# The Consumer Movement

> In the 19th century novels we first see the caricature of capitalism: the individual who lives for no other purpose than maximizing his profits. How far this all is from Adam Smith.
> —William McGurn

## Learning Objectives

1. Trace the beginnings of the consumer movement.
2. Identify key presidents, writers, and scientists and their contributions to consumer protection legislation and reform.
3. Describe how the consumer movement changed from 1880 to the present.

---

### The Greenest Generation

Some people have called today's college-age students the greenest generation. Do you agree or disagree? Green can mean riding a bicycle to campus instead of driving a car. Other commute alternatives are public transit, carpooling, and walking. According to the last census, 78% of all trips to and from work are drive-alone.

Campuses are holding green transportation rallies with free bike tune-ups, bike races, and entertainment. Companies and campuses are participating in the ENERGY STAR Change a Light, installing compact fluorescent light bulbs (CFLs) that use up to 75% less energy, produce 75% less heat, and last up to 10 times longer than incandescent bulbs. On Earth Day, Home Depot gave away 1 million CFL bulbs. This alone equals the removal of 70,000 cars from the road and resulted in a total greenhouse gas reduction of 196 million pounds.

Do you have a digital camera? They require fewer chemicals and less paper than film and you can delete unwanted shots before printing or share photos through the Internet.

This chapter traces the confluence between the consumer movement and the environmental movement. As we move through the twenty-first century, this confluence continues with emphasis on green travel, sustainable forestry, energy efficiency, healthy homes and workplaces, clean air, and water conservation.

---

*Source:* Adapted from www.energystar.gov and www.eere.energy.gov (the U.S. Department of Energy's Energy Efficiency and Renewable Energy Network for sources of energy savings for homes).

# INTRODUCTION

Adam Smith lived in the eighteenth century; by the nineteenth century, his writings about rational self-interest, freedom, and the marketplace were being challenged by a less noble approach to consumerism: Buy more to get ahead. "The expanding America of the post-Civil War era was the paradise of freebooting capitalists, untrammeled and untaxed. They demanded always a freehand in the marketplace, promising that in enriching themselves they would 'build up the country' for the benefit of all people. . . . Theirs is the story of a well-nigh irresistible drive toward monopoly" (Josephson, 1962, p. v).

In the United States we had a newly launched society, and Mary Elizabeth Sherwood wrote in 1897 that "the tendency to vulgarity is the great danger of a newly launched society." Another author stated, "Waves of immigrants brought their own manners to America, and on the frontier a spoon and fingers were sufficient for a tasty repast" (Crossen, 2001). In short, money and taste did not always go hand in hand, "as was demonstrated during the Gilded Age when wealthy American men collected diamond-encrusted daggers, and women carried 2,000 violet bouquets" (Crossen, 2001). In 1895 the largest home in the United States (and still the largest today) was open to the guests of George W. Vanderbilt in Asheville, North Carolina. With 250 rooms and Renoir paintings, the Biltmore, a visible example of splendorous nineteenth-century consumption, is owned by descendants of Vanderbilt and open to the public.

Smith promoted **rational self-interest**, meaning that people make choices that will give them the greatest amount of satisfaction at a particular time based on information they have at their disposal. As mentioned in the previous chapter, not all consumption is based on reason; other factors such as status come into play. At the end of the nineteenth century, Thorstein Veblen offered his withering assessment of **conspicuous consumption** (Barber, 2007). Conspicuous consumption occurs when someone pays an extremely high price for a product for its prestige value, leading to a much higher demand than a simple price-demand relation would indicate. Material plenty overrides sense. A modern-day example is when a consumer pays $300 for a designer microfiber purse rather than $49 for a store-brand microfiber purse.

One of the difficulties in understanding rational self-interest is that there is a difference between it and selfishness. People acting in their own rational self-interest are not necessarily selfish, nor is conspicuous consumption necessarily a bad thing (depending on your point of view). Is it a form of expression and individual freedom, or is it to be reviled? Some would say that the more stuff one has, the less important it becomes because it is easily replaced. At a certain point individuals begin to search for more meaningful uses for their money, such as helping others through philanthropy and public service, and seek satisfaction from intangibles, such as memorable experiences and self-realization, rather than tangibles. Of course, this usually takes place after people have met their own basic needs for food, clothes, and shelter and their spending becomes more discretionary.

In the nineteenth century, there was an explosion of consumer choice, so a more pragmatic view was evident. Many espoused that the main purpose was, as the opening quote shows, to maximize profits. These times were exciting but at the same time harsh. People relied less on families for support as they moved across the ocean and across the country in their quest to establish new lives. The gap between the poor and the rich was growing, and as a means of distinguishing rich from poor, conspicuous consumption gained in importance, especially in clothes and homes. In cities, things were more crowded; people felt more competitive. Of course, in the nineteenth century you could find individuals who would not fit these generalizations, but an examination of novels and diaries in the nineteenth century reveals a decided switch in attitude from earlier times.

The reason it is important to begin this chapter on the consumer movement with a discussion of the nineteenth century is to provide a bridge between what Adam Smith and his contemporaries thought in the eighteenth century and what came about in the twentieth century. What we shall see is that the twentieth century brought both another attitude change and historical events that necessitated increased government intervention in the form of subsidies and consumer protection. These previous developments and events led to the consumer climate in the twenty-first century, which like all preceding centuries is filled with risks and opportunities.

## DEMOGRAPHIC AND CONSUMPTION SHIFTS

In 1776 the population of the 13 colonies was about 2.5 million (compare this with over 300 million today in the United States), and people were highly self-sustaining and individualistic. In the eighteenth century, most lived in rural areas, but by 1890 nearly 40 percent lived in cities. In 1776, pioneers wanted freedom and independence and were mostly self-sufficient, but by the 1890s citizens had less personal control over the production of goods and relied more on big companies for basics like food and soap. While this transition was taking place, there was a period when dangerous untested products were being sold to unsuspecting consumers, which led to the consumer protection legislation discussed in this chapter.

The trend toward reliance on outside companies and businesses for our basic needs continues. Buyers today are more removed from the production of goods than ever before and are confused by the array of products that are available and most specifically an understanding of how they work. Consider this perspective given by Daniel Harris, author of *Cute, Quaint, Hungry and Romantic: The Aesthetics of Consumerism:*

> My life is suspended above an abyss of ignorance. Virtually nothing I own makes sense to me. What happens when I flick on my light switch? Why does my refrigerator keep my food cold? How does my answering machine record the voices of my friends? When I delete a paragraph on my word processor, what makes it disappear and where in the world does it go? In the interest of saving time, as well as out of pure laziness, I, like most people, have deliberately chosen to leave these questions unanswered. . . . I live quite happily hemmed in on all sides by an impenetrable wall of technological riddles. (2000, p. ix)

During wartime, concerns about consumerism tend to take a backseat as the focus shifts from domestic policy to foreign policy. But during quieter, more prosperous times, a crisis such as widespread illnesses or deaths caused by infected hamburgers or tampered-with medicine bottles rallies the cause for consumer protection. A well-publicized safety problem or court case garners public support for reform.

## CONSUMERISM AND THE CONSUMER MOVEMENT DEFINED

As explained in Chapter 1, consumerism is defined as the understanding of self in society through goods. The **consumer movement** refers to policies aimed at regulating products, services, methods and standards of manufacturing, selling, and advertising in the interests of the buyer. Regulations can be voluntary, by industry initiative, or mandatory, due to written laws or statutes. The movement involves not only policies but also issues and leaders who brought to the public the need for regulations. The objective of the consumer movement is to ensure that consumers pay a fair price for safe, effective, environmentally sound, satisfying goods and services. "A narrow definition of the consumer interest might deal solely with safe, reasonably priced and accurately labeled products. To its credit the consumer movement has never defined the consumer interest so narrowly" (Aaker & Day, 1982, p. 32).

## CONSUMER MOVEMENT WORLDWIDE

For simplicity's sake, most of the coverage in this chapter is on the consumer movement in the United States, which is a recognized leader in consumer legislation, product testing, and advocacy. However, most other countries also have a consumer movement history (meaning a progression of legislation designed to protect consumers and promote fair dealing in the marketplace) so that to be most accurate the consumer movement should be described as a worldwide movement.

One of the linkages between countries is that the substances most likely to be regulated in any country are food and drugs. Another common thread is legislation regarding labeling; for example, the Swedish system of labeling requires labels to describe the main characteristics of the product in easily understood language in under 200 words. Another link between countries is that legislation adopted in one country often leads to the adoption of similar legislation in another. As an example of this, in 1893 England passed a general law entitled the Sale of Goods Act stating that whenever a buyer expressly or by implication makes known to the seller the particular purpose for which the goods are required, there is an implied expectation that the goods sold will be reasonably fit for their intended purpose. England also passed the Adulteration of Food and Drugs Act in 1872, many years before a similar act was passed in the United States. The United Kingdom continues to be a leader in safe food regulation and consumer protection in general.

Another connection between countries is that news of a consumer fraud or health risk spreads from one country to another—information is borderless. Also, consumer courses are commonly taught in many schools and universities around the world.

**GLOBAL CONSUMER**

**Cheers**

Consumer regulation puts more power in consumers' hands. Producers ruled in the nineteenth century and into the twentieth century but gradually consumer rights emerged making it easier to get money back and have avenues for redress. With the Internet, consumer choice has increased and markets and producers have become more accessible worldwide. Our knowledge of companies and countries has increased. A case (yes, there is a joke there) is the production of champagne.

Where would you assume most champagne in the world is produced? You are right if you guessed France. Three in four bottles of champagne sold in the U.S. are bottled by industry leader LVMH (Louis Vitton Moet Hennessey).[1] LVMH dominates the $5.4 billion global market with 18.6% of the global market for champagne by volume according to Impact Databank.[2] The LVMH conglomerate is controlled by Bernard Arnault, the richest man in France. His empire also owns Fendi (handbags, leather goods) and Guerlain (perfume). The global demand for champagne is increasing especially in China and Russia.

Who regulates champagne? The European Union (EU) is the governing body regarding price and opening up competition. Ninety percent of the vineyards in France are owned by independent farmers, and LVMH is the biggest buyer of their grapes.

[1]Christina Passareillo, "To Rule Champagne Market, LVMH Courts Grape Growers," *Wall Street Journal,* January 2, 2008, p. A1.
[2]Ibid.

A further linkage is that countries that share borders (such as the United States with Canada and with Mexico) usually set up cooperative agreements because so many goods transverse borders and workers cross borders for employment. In Europe there are many examples of cooperation between countries, especially those that share borders (which may include rivers or coastlines), regarding water quality/pollution, fishing rights, and transportation issues.

As the global market grows and more goods transverse borders and are manufactured in several countries, more international cooperation and agreement will be sought on quality, labeling, trademark, copyright, finance, and safety issues. An example of international cooperation is the adoption of euro coins and notes replacing the mark, franc, and other currencies as legal tender in European countries.

International consumer conferences and world trade conferences are held regularly to discuss issues, research, and policies. The *International Journal of Consumer Studies* based in the United Kingdom is a leading academic journal with authors and subscribers throughout the world. Names of other consumer journals are listed in Appendix B.

## DECADES OF CONSUMERISM

In the following sections, information is given about the lifestyles of the times and the consumer legislation that was enacted. The growth of the consumer movement is evidenced, as are leaders and issues.

## 1880–1900

In the United States, the early nineteenth century was a time of great promise called "the gilded age." Railroads, appliances, and indoor plumbing became more common. Immigrants came in droves—the flow of immigrants after 1880 came from the Orient and Mexico as well as from Eastern and Southern Europe and Russia, adding diversity to all aspects of American life, including religion and diet. An American style of manners, home design, and cuisine distinct from Western Europe developed. Life became easier for most, but not for all. To name just a few of the problems: Coal miners worked under appalling conditions, gold rushes and land rushes often left people broke and stranded, and the Native American nations were systematically moved against their will farther west to reservations.

> From 1880–1900, the middle class grew. It was not unusual for middle class households to have servants or at least a hired girl in to do the laundry once a week. Domestics who lived in received a room usually in the attic or near the kitchen, board, a small wage, and sometimes used clothes. (Schlereth, 1991)

There was no income tax, so a few very wealthy families emerged unfettered. As described earlier in the chapter, they built palatial mansions such as the Biltmore, owned by the Vanderbilts. The Vanderbilt fortune was built on steamships, railroads, coal mines, and securities. Other famous rich and powerful men included J. P. Morgan (railroads, finance, and banking), Andrew Carnegie (steel), and John Rockefeller (oil). Their influence on the rise of industry and capitalism in this country cannot be overestimated. These captains of industry were also active in politics, educational and humanitarian causes, and the arts, funding museums, libraries, foundations, and universities such as Carnegie-Mellon University in Pittsburgh.

There were a lot of food fads and **hucksterism** (extreme promotion) from 1880 to 1900. Food fads, including diet fads such as fasting, miracle foods, and Fletcherism

The expansion of the United States: Conestoga wagons pulled by horses in a land rush circa 1910s. (Getty Images, Inc.—Image Bank.)

(ritual overchewing of food), abounded. Fletcherism is named after Horace Fletcher, who believed that chewing food 30 times or more would help people digest their food more easily and use it more effectively. Many patent medicines contained alcohol, which is why they gave patients "a lift." Through school and community classes, home economists and dietitians stepped in to give a sensible voice to nutrition. With the growth of railroads, American consumers had far more access to a variety of fresh fruits and vegetables, so in time the American diet became broader, relying less on meat. John Harvey Kellogg and C. W. Post launched their breakfast cereal empires in Battle Creek, Michigan: Kellogg recommended large doses of bran, granola, and graham crackers, and Post developed Grape-Nuts (1898) and Post Toasties; Kellogg challenged Post Toasties with his own version, named Kellogg's Toasted Corn Flakes.

## Early 1900

The start of the twentieth century was exciting. The fashions and attitudes of the previous century were questioned, with materialism and consumerism becoming more complex as inventors and businesses brought many new goods to the market. There was less domestic help, and women's roles began to change. Suburban and small town living began replacing rural living for the masses. As the twentieth century progressed, the former manners and ways of living of the nineteenth century faded: "calling cards, debutante balls, morning coats and finger bowls gave way to backyard barbecues, cocktail buffets and BYOB parties" (Crossen, 2001). Perhaps a sense of elegance was also lost.

In the consumer realm, early consumer protection legislation centered on the control of trade and monopoly and on products closely related to the home (namely, food and drugs). It is difficult to put consumer protection legislation into categories by decade because often the groundwork is laid in one decade and the legislation comes about in the next or even a later decade.

A case in point is the fight for better food quality led by Harvey Wiley—because of his pioneering efforts, Wiley is often called the founder of the modern consumer movement. To give you some idea of his background, he began his career as a chemistry professor at Purdue University and then resigned that post to go to work for the Indiana Department of Agriculture. While there, he tested the ingredients in bags of chemicals purchased by farmers to improve soil. From this experience he went a step further and thought that consumers should also have food products tested and took this quest to the U.S. Department of Agriculture. His role was to determine the safety of the U.S. food supply. In the 1880s he circulated his findings among other professionals; in the 1890s he went public with his research, urging consumers to join in a campaign aimed at getting Congress to initiate laws on food quality.

**Historical Perspective.**   To set Harvey Wiley and his work in historical perspective, in the early twentieth century things were developing so fast that there were very few regulations to manage production and distribution in a consistent way. Food was the largest expense for the factory laborer and for many middle-class families, which is different from today when housing is usually the most expensive item. So the cost and purity of food were especially critical to the well-being of individuals and families. Inventions that we now take for granted had their start during these times: the airplane, the automobile, motion pictures, electric lights and

Harvey Wiley, the founder of the consumer movement, was a pure food reformer. He encouraged the packaging of food to keep it clean. (Courtesy of the FDA History Office.)

appliances, radio, canned soups, detergents, and bottled soft drinks. Let us take, for example, the evolution of Coca-Cola:

> On May 8, 1886, the soft drink was invented by the Atlanta druggist John Pemberton primarily as a headache cure. He and a partner named it Coca-Cola because its ingredients included extracts derived from Peruvian coca leaves and African cola nuts (Schlereth, 1991).
>
> By 1891, it was one of the most popular soft drinks in the United States, and Asa Candler bought controlling shares.
>
> Between 1891 and 1929, Coke gained national distribution, selling for a nickel a bottle.
>
> By 1929, Coke was sold in 66 countries.
>
> In the late 1930s, Pepsi-Cola became a serious challenger. The main way Pepsi challenged Coke was by selling at a lower price.

Coke and its competitors raised the question: Are brand names and advertising important? Yes, they are. "Coca-Cola stands today as the second most widely understood term in the world, after okay" (Tedlow, 1990, p. 24). The basic goal of the advertising campaign was to make consumers think of Coke when they were thirsty and to assure them that Coke was the best choice to quench that thirst (Tedlow, 1990).

When Coca-Cola came of age, the timing could not have been better: Prosperity, affluence, and expansion ruled. Americans had more purchasing power than ever before and a growing array of goods to choose from, and they also had more free time. The six-day workweek was common in 1900. Between 1900 and 1930 Americans extended their time in school by going beyond the eighth grade, finishing high school became more the norm, and more students went on to college. Additional time in school meant more time for leisure, increased exposure to peer pressure, and a better educated citizenry. Home economists taught food and consumer classes in schools and in communities and prepared pamphlets for the poor, based on the theory that educated consumers could combat high prices; they publicized food purity concerns in their classes (Strasser, 1989).

Another invention, the automobile, liberated middle-class youth as well as families. In short, in the early twentieth century to consume took on whole new meanings and luxury was part of it (Cross, 2000). One author states, "Materialism became Americanism" (Schlereth, 1991, p. 302).

However, before we go any further, it should be pointed out that laboratory testing methods in the late nineteenth and early twentieth centuries were primitive compared with those of today. In 1902, in order to test food additives, Wiley set up a group called the "Poison Squad." The squad was made up of healthy young adults, mostly college students, who ate unadulterated food and also ate the same diet with food additives over a five-year period. He compared their weight and physical condition and found that preservatives readministered continuously in small doses negatively affected their digestion, appetite, and general health.

> The men, of course, knew they were eating potential poisons. They didn't know, however, which foods contained the substances. At first borax was added to butter, to which the men developed a sudden distaste. Wiley then tried it in milk, meat, and coffee. Borax is a hydrated sodium borate (borate is a salt of boric acid used as a preservative). Evidently, as the men determined which food contained the substances, they began eating less of it and eventually avoided that food altogether. (White, 2002, p. 14)

Wiley, observing this, eventually started putting preservatives inside gelatin capsules. The Poison Squad became a sensation with the press and the public (reporters were interviewing the chef through a basement window). Wiley decided he better cooperate, so he ended up sharing the details of the experiments with reporters. The experiments stopped when the men couldn't function or work. Wiley's efforts led to the regulation of food additives. What happened to the Poison Squad? There are no scientific reports, but anecdotal reports indicate that none were harmed. William O. Robinson of Falls Church, VA, a member of the Squad, lived to be 94 years old.

Wiley became the symbol of food and drug reform. Reformers were interested in two main issues: fraud and poison. The kinds of frauds included the extension of flour, mustard, and ground coffee with cheap fillers, including sawdust and chalk (Strasser, 1989). Besides the alcohol already mentioned, patent medicines were found to contain cocaine and opium.

Wiley's results caught the attention of the American Medical Association (AMA), which began analyzing drugs and medicines. Not everyone rallied behind Wiley and the AMA; many business groups said the research was antibusiness and even anti-American. Business was a tremendous force during this era, and improvements were made in transportation, advertising, packaging, machinery, and corporate growth and coordination (Cross, 2000). It was the golden age of national name brands such as Ralston Purina and Quaker Oats. As an example, cereals were no longer just breakfast foods but were promoted as having all kinds of health benefits,

Not everyone backed Harvey Wiley's quest for better food safety. Some business groups said his work was antibusiness—even anti-American.

The Pure Food and Drug Act of 1906 was the first federal law in U.S. history specifically enacted to protect consumers.

The poison squad. (Courtesy of the FDA History Office.)

including inspiring confidence and providing a good start to one's day. So Wiley was up against a formidable enemy, but he persevered and his work paved the way for the Pure Food and Drug Act of 1906, which was considered the first federal law in U.S. history specifically enacted to protect consumers. This act dealt with the production, transportation, and sale of food and drugs in the United States.

**Upton Sinclair and President Theodore Roosevelt.**   Another piece of legislation came to the forefront whose source was not the laboratory but a stirring novel written by a journalist. In 1906, public uproar over the exposé of the Chicago meatpacking industry depicted in the novel *The Jungle* by Upton Sinclair led to the passage of the Meat Inspections Act. Sinclair graduated from the College of the City of New York in 1897 and went to graduate school at Columbia University. He supported himself by journalistic writing, and *The Jungle* was his sixth novel. His purpose was to write about immigrant families and their struggle, but his story of the squalor and impurities in processed meats aroused widespread public indignation. He said, "I aimed at the public's heart and by accident I hit in the stomach." Here is a passage from the book:

> There was never the least attention paid to what was cut up for sausage; there would come all the way back from Europe old sausage that had been rejected, and that was mouldy and white—it would be dosed with borax and glycerine, and dumped into the hoppers, and made over again for home consumption. There would be meat that had tumbled out on the floor, in the dirt and sawdust, where the workers had tramped and spit uncounted billions of consumption germs . . . rats were nuisances and the packers would put poisoned bread out for them, they would die, and then rats, bread, and meat would go into the hoppers together. (Sinclair, 1905, p. 136)

Sinclair became known as a **muckraker**, a term for writers, politicians, journalists, and public speakers who search out and expose political or commercial corruption. *The Jungle*, which is still in print today, was first published at Sinclair's own

American author Upton Sinclair writing by the light of his desk at home in California. His most famous book was *The Jungle*, which exposed wrong-doing in the meatpacking industry. (Murray Garrett, Getty Images, Inc.—Hulton Archive Photos.)

expense and became a best-seller. He wrote more books, including *Oil!* (1927), based on the Teapot Dome Scandal, and *Boston* (1928), based on the Sacco-Vanzetti case, but none had the enduring impact of *The Jungle*. His works were popular abroad, including in Russia before and after the Revolution of 1917. In later years he ran as Democratic candidate for governor of California and lost. He was known throughout his life as a fighter for social causes. Sinclair was not alone in his crusade and was joined by many others, who formed the first Consumer's League in 1891; in 1899, this was followed by the National Consumers League, which fought for justice in the marketplace. What was happening was the development of a consumer consciousness. There is no question that consumer consciousness—through organizations, books, the press, and word of mouth—was raised during this era.

President Theodore Roosevelt, writer, rancher, explorer, and soldier whose years in office were 1901 to 1909, was outraged by *The Jungle* and called for an investigation, just as he had earlier by assigning eminent chemists to review Wiley's work (Strasser, 1989). Food reformers had a friend in Roosevelt, who had testified before a Senate investigating committee that he would just as soon have eaten his old hat as the canned food that, under a government contract, had been shipped to the sol-

Theodore Roosevelt, the twenty-sixth president of the United States, sitting at his desk working. He was a champion of consumer rights and an antimonopolist. (Getty Images, Inc.—Hulton Archive Photos.)

diers in Cuba during the Spanish-American War (Downs, 1963). The investigation of the Chicago meatpacking industry revealed that the book did not exaggerate; in fact, conditions were worse than Sinclair had reported. Based on this, Roosevelt joined Congress in calling for federal legislation to correct the matter. On June 30, 1906, he signed both the Pure Food and Drugs Act and the Meat Inspection Act.

Theodore Roosevelt, a Republican, is known as a president who expanded the powers of the federal government on the side of public interest in conflicts between big business and big labor. In 1902 he established a Bureau of Corporations with powers to inspect the books of all businesses engaged in interstate commerce. He was also a trust-buster, bringing suit against 44 major corporations during his presidency.

Roosevelt's most successful suit was against the Northern Securities Company using the Sherman Anti-Trust Act, which was passed in 1890 but was largely ignored until Roosevelt invoked its power. **Antitrust laws** prevent business monopolies and are aimed at establishing and maintaining competition so that consumers get fair prices as well as goods in adequate quantities. The rights of buyers and competitors fall under the general category of **common law**, which is based on custom and is the unwritten system of law that is the foundation of both the English and U.S. legal systems (excluding Louisiana whose laws are based on the Napoleonic Code). The Sherman Anti-Trust Act made monopoly and price-fixing illegal so that firms were prevented from unfairly harming their competitors. Roosevelt was first and foremost a crusader, a person who overcame physical weakness in his youth to become a lifelong competitor and adventurer, but he is also considered a leader in the modern concept of consumer protection.

In 1908 the first court case using the Pure Food and Drugs Act was tried. The product under investigation was deemed worthless: It did not cure headaches as it was supposed to do, nor did its usage make consumers more intelligent. The manufacturer was ordered to change the label and was charged a $700 fine. As was common, this fine was a mere slap on the wrist because the manufacturer had already made millions of dollars. This is an ongoing problem in consumer protection today—the fines are often minuscule compared with the profits. By the time advertisements are pulled or companies are sent to court, they have already made all the money they set out to make. Another problem is that corporate lawyers are usually better paid and have more staff support than government lawyers, which makes for uneven battles.

## 1910s

More consumer legislation followed. In 1914 the Federal Trade Commission (FTC) Act was passed to enforce antitrust laws and to spell out unfair methods of competition, including deceptive advertising. The FTC, for example, can issue a **cease-and-desist order**, an administrative or judicial order forcing a business to cease "unfair or deceptive acts or practices." For a listing of key consumer laws passed between 1880 and 1929, see Box 2.1. Also in 1914, Christine Frederick published *The New Housekeeping: Efficiency Studies in Home Management*, which extolled the virtues of an orderly labor-saving home and the need for more packaged goods and for fairer deals in the marketplace. She testified before Congress on behalf of consumers.

**BOX 2.1   Key Consumer Legislation 1880–1929**

During this time period, over 50 consumer laws were passed in the United States. Here is a sample:

| | |
|---|---|
| 1887 Interstate Commerce Act | Power to regulate commerce was reserved to the states. |
| 1890 Sherman Anti-Trust Act | It prohibits monopolies and price-fixing and encourages competition. |
| 1906 Pure Food and Drug Act | It prohibits adulteration of food and drugs and mislabeling of such sold in interstate commerce, requires disclosure of narcotics and alcohol contents on patent medicine labels, and prohibits manufacturers from claiming ingredients that are not present. |
| 1906 Meat Inspection Act | It provides for meat inspection. There had been an earlier act in 1891 that set up the Federal Meat Inspection Service. |
| 1914 Federal Trade Commission Act | It prohibits deceptive advertising and unfair and deceptive trade practices. The FTC Act was used in the battle against trusts. Examples of early trusts (combinations of firms that got together to reduce competition and control supplies and/or prices in an industry or region) included sugar, whiskey, matches, and fuel. |

The Federal Bureau of Standards established a national system of weights and measures; as its name implies, it standardized how goods were weighed and sold. To raise consumer awareness, at food expositions and state and county fairs consumers were shown measuring devices with false bottoms and nonregulation-size milk bottles and bushel baskets (Strasser, 1989).

The Sixteenth Amendment was added to the U.S. Constitution in 1913 allowing for the collection of income tax.

Other developments include the establishment of Better Business Bureaus (BBBs) in 1912 that discouraged dishonest business practices. In 1913 the Sixteenth Amendment to the U.S. Constitution was passed giving Congress the right to collect income taxes. The amendment stated, "The Congress shall have the power to lay and collect taxes on income." The first tax was only 1 percent of income. By 1915, to be middle class meant to have electricity, and the expression "chain store" came into being. Chain stores that bought in bulk passed savings on to consumers. It was more common for people to eat cereal out of a box for breakfast instead of the previously home-cooked breakfast of beefsteak, bacon and eggs, fried potatoes, wheatcakes and sausage, porridge, donuts, and fruits (Schlereth, 1991).

In 1917, the United States became involved in World War I, so concern switched from domestic to international affairs. The war led to a quiet period in the consumer movement.

## 1920s

The 1920s began with relief that the war was over. Parties, extravagant lifestyles, gambling, bobbed hair, and flapper dresses marked the first years, and consumer incomes rose steadily while prices remained stable. However, by 1928 discontent was expressed in *Your Money's Worth* by Stuart Chase and F. J. Schlink, who exposed false advertising and high-pressure sales techniques. They called for more testing of products and improved standards. As a result in 1929 Consumers' Research, Inc. (of which Schlink became technical director), was formed to perform testing work. Although there was a dearth of consumer protection legislation during this decade, the government was actively involved in testing the effectiveness of "germ-killing" products and enforcing the 1906 Pure Food and Drug Act, seizing defective food and drugs before they were shipped. In October 1929 the stock market crashed in the United States, and a depression began not only in this country but also worldwide. A **depression** is characterized as a drastic and long-lasting decline in the economy, with high unemployment, falling prices, and decreasing business activity.

## 1930s

The lowest point of the Great Depression was in 1933. Although there was a panic and a run on the banks in late 1929, no one really knew what was happening until well into the 1930s; more importantly, at first no one really knew what to do about it. There was no question that people lost faith in American industry and in American banks.

> The Depression hit America like a typhoon. One half the value of all production simply disappeared. One quarter of the working force lost its jobs. Over a million urban families found their mortgages foreclosed, their houses lost to the bank. Nine million savings accounts went down the drain when banks closed, many for good.

Against this terrible reality of joblessness and loss of income, the economics profession, like the business world or government advisers, had nothing to offer. Fundamentally, economists were as perplexed at the behavior of the economy as were the American people themselves. (Heilbroner & Thurow, 1998, p. 30)

**Economist John Maynard Keynes.**   During these troubled times, English economist John Maynard Keynes (pronounced "canes") published *The General Theory of Employment, Interest, and Money* (1936), a more complicated and technical book than Adam Smith's *Wealth of Nations*. It had a central message that was easy to grasp: Economic activity in a capitalist system is determined by the willingness of its entrepreneurs to make capital investments (Heilbroner & Thurow, 1998). Sometimes this willingness is blocked, and the import of Keynes' theory was that if there is no self-correcting property in the market system, such as prolific business investment to keep capitalism growing, other solutions have to be found. The solution in this case was increased government spending on public works. Since his book was published during the Great Depression, it influenced President Franklin D. Roosevelt, his economic/political advisors, and their policies. He founded a school of thought called Keynesian economics that emphasizes the role government plays in stabilizing the economy, and his influence extends to today.

FDR signed into law the 44-hour workweek in 1938 and reduced it to 40 hours in 1941.

**President Franklin D. Roosevelt.**   Franklin Delano Roosevelt (FDR), a Democrat who became president in 1933, rose to the challenge that the Depression presented. As evidence of his popularity and effectiveness, he is the only president to be reelected three times; his years in office were from 1933 to 1945 (a complete list of U.S. presidents and their terms in office are given in Appendix C). He used the federal government's powers to bring about a national economic recovery, which was called the New Deal, and he was president during World War II. Therefore, during his administration his policies were not the hands-off kind of government recommended by Adam Smith because Roosevelt thought that the crisis demanded a more hands-on approach, and Keynes' book provided the theoretical background for much of the approach that was taken. Examples of Roosevelt's policies include signing the Fair Labor Standards Act in 1938, which established the 44-hour workweek; in 1941 this was reduced to the standard 40-hour workweek that we use today.

By way of background, Roosevelt went to Harvard and studied law at Columbia University. In 1905, he married Eleanor Roosevelt, an outspoken consumer advocate and the niece of Theodore Roosevelt. In 1910 he was elected to the New York Senate and later became governor of New York. He rose up through the ranks, and as president he promoted sweeping economic programs that provided relief, loans, and jobs through federal agencies.

During his years in office many consumer laws were passed, including the Food, Drug, and Cosmetics Act of 1938. This act amended the 1906 act by adding cosmetics and allowing inspectors to remove dangerous products from store shelves while tests were being completed. Congressional leaders and Roosevelt were horrified by the disfigurements and the nearly 100 deaths caused by the new sulfa wonder drug named Elixir Sulfanilamide.

There were other problem products as well. The respectability in the use of cosmetics and beauty salons grew tremendously in the 1930s, but with it came abuse in the form of face creams that burned and dyes that caused hair to fall out: "A once

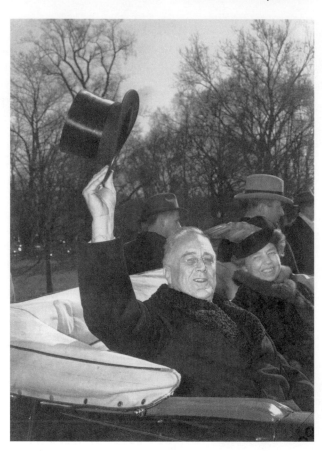

President Franklin D. Roosevelt raises his hat while riding in a convertible with his wife, Eleanor Roosevelt. They were both consumer activists who fought for better working conditions and product safety. (Corbis/Bettmann.)

pretty matron was blinded by Lashlure, an eyelash dye" (Aaker & Day, 1982, p. 27). Adding fuel to the fire was the 1933 *100,000,000 Guinea Pigs* by Arthur Kallet and F. J. Schlink when they introduced the public to a number of cosmetic, food, and drug problems, including the use of a well-known rat poison as the active ingredient in the depilatory cream Koremlu. The book gave the following case, first documented in the *Journal of the American Medical Association,* about a woman, age 24:

> [She] came to the Cleveland Clinic complaining of severe pains over the soles of both feet and ankles, weakness of both feet and legs, and intense burning of both feet. . . . Four and one-half months prior to entering the clinic, the patient had first noticed intermittent epigastric [abdominal] pains which gradually increased in severity to sharp, cramp-like pains throughout the entire abdomen. . . . The patient had become very nervous, cried easily, had lost about ten pounds, and felt continually tired. . . .
>
> It was discovered that she had been using a depilatory cream, "Koremlu," nightly for the preceding five months, beginning its use two weeks before the appearance of the first symptoms. A quantity sufficient only to cover the upper lip and the chin had been used on each occasion. (Kallet & Schlink, 1933, p. 82)

Kallett and Schlink (1933) went on to make the following point:

> Purchasers of ordinary foods and drugs have little enough assurance of safety, despite the control (as some term it) provided by the Federal Food and Drugs Act and by various state agencies. The purchaser of cosmetics has no protection whatever. No

Federal agency has jurisdiction over cold creams, depilatories, skin lotions, hair dyes, or any other substance intended for external use and not for the treatment of disease. (p. 78)

Although it was still the Depression and news of fraudulent products abounded, consumers bought what they could. Inexpensive treats such as nickel movies and gum sold well. The Snickers candy bar was introduced in 1930.

> There were signs of downscaling. Sales of men's suits dropped sharply. . . . Thin wallets led to record sales of glass jars for home canning. The "live at home movement" meant foregoing the night on the town and instead listening to the radio. . . . As common as cutting back, however, was a very different response—a refusal to retrench. Many Depression-era Americans were unwilling to abandon the "luxuries" of the 1920s. Cigarette smokers could not give up the habit. . . . Americans held on to their old Model Ts. (Cross, 2000, p. 69)

**Economist John Kenneth Galbraith.**    John Kenneth Galbraith (1908–2006) was a Canadian who lived most of his life in the United States. A prolific writer, one of his most famous books was *The Affluent Society,* published in 1958. In this book he called for less emphasis on production and more emphasis on public service. He was a key advisor to John F. Kennedy and served as ambassador to India (1961–1963) before returning to Harvard.

Earlier during the FDR years, Galbraith also served in several government posts. FDR rode out the storm very well and was highly regarded by contemporaries and the general populace. John Kenneth Galbraith, the Paul Warburg Professor of Economics Emeritus at Harvard University, at age 93 had this to say: "Franklin D. Roosevelt was good on great issues or small. A great war. A great depression. He presided over both. No question about it—he's the person who most impressed me. In my life, he had no close competitor" (Fussman, 2002, p. 60).

## 1940s

World War II turned everyone's attention to the war front, and interest in consumer legislation faded. Food and gasoline were rationed here and abroad, so people were more interested in getting goods than worrying about their quality. "Here is a partial list of what you could not get for Christmas in 1943: beer mugs, bird cages, cocktail shakers, radios, doll carriages, rubber boots, bicycles or tricycles, typewriters, griddles, toasters, hair curlers, phonographs, alarm clocks or balls that bounced. America's armed forces, fighting overseas, needed all the metal, rubber, chemicals and food they could get" (Crossen, 2002, p. B1). Because household income had grown substantially from the depression years, for many men and women working at jobs in the United States this was the first time they could not buy something they were able to afford. According to recorded oral histories and exhibits at the D-Day Museum in New Orleans, this was the first time many women went to work outside the home, becoming welders and shipbuilders, thus earning their own wages. The economic freedom this provided was unprecedented and set the groundwork for the future expansion of women's employment.

Because of the wartime shortage of gasoline, travel was curtailed. The lack of basics such as eggs, milk, and butter led to the development of recipes for cakes such as fruitcakes that used none of these ingredients. With shortages came a growing black market. To lessen hoarding and to provide commodities fairly, the federal government instituted rationing and price limits.

> Every man, woman and child received a monthly ration book, giving them a certain number of red points (for meat, cheese, and oil) and blue points (for canned goods). A person might get 64 red points a month, but a pound of butter could require as many as 24. . . . So strict were the rules, that government employees would scan newspaper death notices and send letters to families asking them to return ration books. (Crossen, 2002, p. B1)

Another response to the shortages was provided by the advertising industry. Instead of promoting consumption, they came up with slogans such as "Use it up, wear it out, make do or do without" (Crossen, 2002, p. B1).

Homeowners were encouraged to grow victory gardens for personal consumption so that foods canned in factories could be shipped overseas. Nylon was used in the war effort, so it could not be used for stockings, and women drew pencil lines up the back of their legs to simulate stocking seams. "In 1943, the season's most coveted gifts were a carton of cigarettes or a pair of nylon stockings" (Crossen, 2002, p. B1).

American homes were growing more technologically complex: Flush toilets were considered standard, telephones were owned by 36 percent of families, and refrigerators were in 91 percent of households (Cross, 2000). Even though there were shortages, the average household improved substantially during the war years and immediately afterward. The teen market was also growing and paving the way for resurgence of bobby sox power in the 1950s. *Seventeen* magazine was introduced earlier in 1944.

Box 2.2 shows that no major federal consumer legislation was passed in the 1940s and only a few laws were passed during the 1950s. On the marketplace side of things, during the 1940s and 1950s advertising surged and demand for consumer goods was never higher. Production was more important than protection, with cigarette smoking glamorized.

Advertisers gained respect when they produced effective propaganda for the war effort.

> More important, they shaped popular opinion by addressing the critical question: "What are we fighting for?" Their answer was well summarized by one ad: "For years we have fought for a higher standard of living, and now we are fighting to protect it against those who are jealous of our national accomplishments." A Nash-Kelvinator ad showed a paratrooper affirming, "We have so many things, here in America, that belong only to a free people . . . warm, comfortable homes, automobiles and radios by the million." (Cross, 2000, p. 84)

## 1950s

When the war ended in 1945, everyone wanted new houses, cars, furniture, washing machines, and every other kind of consumer good imaginable. The emphasis was on increasing production to meet these needs, and modern American and European business was born. In the United Kingdom, rationing continued longer than in the United States, but when it was over, it was replaced by an up-

**BOX 2.2    Key Consumer Legislation 1930–1979**

| | |
|---|---|
| 1938 Federal Food, Drug, and Cosmetics Act | Extended coverage of the earlier act, added cosmetics, and gave federal agencies the power to remove untested products from stores. |
| 1938 Federal Trade Commission Act | It updated the 1914 act and prohibits deceptive and unfair trading practices. |
| 1939 Wool Products Labeling Act | It requires accurate labeling of wool products. |
| 1951 Fur Products Labeling Act | It requires proper labeling of fur products. |
| 1953 Flammable Fabrics Act | It prohibits selling highly flammable clothes. |
| 1957 Poultry Products Inspection Act | It requires inspection of poultry. |
| 1958 Textile Fiber Products Identification Act | It covers advertising and labeling of all textile products not covered in the Wool and Fur Products Labeling Acts. |
| 1960 Hazardous Substances Labeling Act | It requires warning labels on dangerous household products. |
| 1964 Civil Rights Act" | It guarantees consumer choice, the "full and equal enjoyment of the goods, services, facilities, privileges, advantages, and accommodations of any place of public accommodation." |
| 1965 Cigarette Labeling Advertising Act | Warning labels are required of possible health hazards (this act grew out of growing evidence that tobacco caused cancer). |
| 1965 Immigration and Nationality Act | It opened up the United States to large numbers of immigrants from Latin America and Asia. |
| 1966 Child Protection and Toy Safety Act | It bans dangerous toys and requires childproof devices and special labeling. |
| 1966 Fair Packaging and Labeling Act (more commonly known as Truth in Packaging Act) | It requires that weight and content information be given on product labels (thus enabling consumers to comparison-shop). |
| 1966 Child Protection and Toy Safety Act | Childproof devices and labeling are required. |
| 1966 National Traffic and Motor Vehicle Safety Act | New car dealers must be informed by manufacturers of any safety defects found after the manufacture and sale of autos. |
| 1967 Wholesale Meat Act | It updates 1906 legislation and provides for higher standards in slaughterhouses of red-meat animals. |
| 1968 Interstate Land Sales Full Disclosure Act | It requires accuracy of information on interstate land sales. |
| 1968 Consumer Credit Protection Act (Truth in Lending Act) | It protects and regulates credit transactions, demands that lenders inform debtors of annual interest rates, and limits the practice of garnishing wages. |

**BOX 2.2    Key Consumer Legislation 1930–1979** (*continued*)

| | |
|---|---|
| 1970 Public Health Cigarette Smoking Act | It prohibits cigarette advertising on television and radio. |
| 1970 Fair Credit Reporting Act | It protects consumers' credit reports. |
| 1970 Clean Air Act | It authorizes the Environmental Protection Agency to establish national air-quality standards and requires states to develop plans for reducing pollution emissions by 90 percent in five years. |
| 1970 Bank Secrecy Act | It establishes record-keeping and reporting requirements for national U.S. banks and federal branches and agencies of foreign banks. |
| 1972 Consumer Product Safety Act | It establishes the Consumer Product Safety Commission; regulates hazardous items, especially those related to the home such as toy, baby, and play equipment and household products; and provides for a continuous review of products. |
| 1972 Odometer Act | It protects consumers by stating that used-car odometers cannot be rolled back or disconnected. |
| 1972 Water Pollution Control Act | It endeavors to make major waterways clean enough for fishing and swimming by 1983. |
| 1973 FTC** Door-to-Door Sales Rule | The FTC regulates door-to-door sales contracts. |
| 1973 FTC Rules of Negative Options | It spells out FTC rules regarding book and record clubs. |
| 1974 Real Estate Settlement Procedures Act | It requires the disclosure of home buying costs. |
| 1974 Equal Credit Opportunity Act | It prohibits discrimination regarding credit. |
| 1974 Fair Credit Billing Act | It protects against billing errors and establishes procedures for resolving mistakes on credit card bills. |
| 1975 Magnuson-Moss Warranty Act | It governs content of warranties, including full and limited warranties. Warranty information must be given to the consumer before he or she makes a purchase. |
| 1977 Fair Debt Collection Practices Act | It limits debt collectors and their methods and prohibits abuses such as harassment. |

_____

*This is far more than a consumer protection law. It was directed at ending racial discrimination, the humiliation of segregated facilities, and the denial of access by minorities to consumer choices.
**Federal Trade Commission.

surge in choice and availability (Lyon, Colquhoun & Kinney, 2004). Both in the United States and abroad, modern grocery stores and shopping plazas replaced corner mom-and-pop stores; checkout lines and counter service became the wave of the future. Everyone wanted to buy what was new and to put the war behind them.

For homeowners who already had washing machines, they upgraded from wringer washers to automatic washers and from clotheslines to electric dryers. Television grew tremendously during this decade, and *The Mickey Mouse Club* premiered in 1955. College towns and campuses grew substantially during the late 1940s and the 1950s as the GI Bill allowed returning soldiers to go to college, swelling enrollments in universities. There was renewed interest in science and invention that would benefit homes and industry.

By 1954, Frigidaire was selling 10 kinds of appliances; demand was high and consumers wanted choices (Tedlow, 1990). Some of the innovations—especially the early dishwashers—were less than successful. To make them appear more useful, they were sold as multifunction appliances: For example, it was suggested that meat could be defrosted and cocktails (in shakers) could be mixed in the dishwashers while washing dishes.

The 1950s was a decade of private consumption, capitalism gone full tilt. To consume was to be free (Cross, 2000). In the mid to late 1950s, loud was in—loud colors, loud television westerns, loud fashion, and loud music with rock 'n' roll and Elvis Presley. Food preferences changed too, with chips and dip replacing sand-

A Barbie doll from 1959 in a striped swimsuit. Barbie revolutionized the toy market and still is a top-seller worldwide, although she now comes in countless variations. (AP Wide World Photos and Peter Arnold, Inc.)

wiches for when guests dropped by (Cross, 2000). The split-level house was introduced as a change from the rectangular ranch; inside, unlikely combinations of the old and the new, such as knotty-pine cabin-like paneling and kitchen cabinets mixed with plastic formica tables and counters, occurred. The decade ended with the introduction of Mattel's Barbie in 1959.

Businesses became more sophisticated in their understanding and use of market research. By the end of the decade, a new muckraker emerged: Vance Packard. His 1957 book *The Hidden Persuaders* exposed the manipulative methods that businesses use to stimulate sales. The book stated that "supermarket operators are pretty well agreed that men are easy marks for all sorts of impulse items and cite cases they've seen of husbands who are sent to the store for a loaf of bread and depart with both their arms loaded with their favorite snack items" (Packard, 1957, p. 95). Packard (1957) also related the following:

> An Indiana supermarket operator nationally recognized for his advanced psychological techniques told me he once sold a half ton of cheese in a few hours, just by getting an enormous half-ton wheel of cheese and inviting customers to nibble slivers and cut off their own chunks for purchase. They could have their chunk free if they could guess its weight within an ounce. The mere massiveness of the cheese, he believes, was a powerful influence in making the sales. "People like to see a lot of merchandise," he explained. "When there are only three or four cans of an item on a shelf, they just won't move." (p. 94)

In 1959, the Food and Drug Administration (FDA) seized boxes of Pillsbury blueberry pancake mix for misbranding. The ingredients list and the picture on the box included blueberries, but there were none in the product. Also, in 1959 a cranberry crop scare shook the nation. Cranberries were being sprayed with chemicals that caused cancer, so the FDA called for the end of distributing cranberries until this problem was solved. By the end of the 1950s, with books like Packard's and the cranberry exposé, there was a return to interest in consumer protection and the groundwork was being laid for advances in the consumer movement in the 1960s.

## 1960s

In 1962, American biologist Rachel Carson, founder of the modern environmental movement, exposed other environmental pollution problems in her book *Silent Spring*. **Pollution** refers to any undesirable change in biological, chemical, or physical characteristics of air, land, or water that harms activities, health, or survival of living organisms. Carson advocated the use of natural pests or deterrents rather than chemicals and questioned the soundness of runaway consumption.

Since the 1960s, **environmentalism** (defined as concern for the environment) has become a very important part of the modern consumer movement. Extensive media coverage of both environmental ills and disappearing species and a growing appreciation of the natural world spurred interest in environmentalism. There may be another reason as well: "Most consumers lack the scientific background to understand many environmental issues and few have relevant previous experience to guide them in assessing the relative environmental merits of market-place alternatives. Thus, the potential for consumer fraud and deception is great" (Cude, 1993, p. 207). President John F. Kennedy, a Democrat, read Carson's *Silent Spring* and decided to take action. His interest in her work led to his Consumer Message to

Rachel Carson (1907–1964) is considered the founder of the modern environmental movement. She was an American biologist who wrote *Silent Spring,* an exposé on pollution. (Erich Hartmann, Magnum Photos, Inc.)

Congress in March 1962; in the preamble, Kennedy gave the famous Consumer Bill of Rights:

1. The right to safety (to be protected from hazards to health and life)
2. The right to be heard (to be protected from fraud, deceit, or grossly misleading information including advertising and labeling)
3. The right to choose (to have access to a variety of products and services at competitive prices)
4. The right to information (to be assured of fair and expeditious treatment from government and in policy formation)

He particularly cited the need for revision of laws pertaining to food and drugs. Later presidents added the following three rights:

1. The right to a decent environment (influenced by several presidents)
2. The right to consumer education (added by President Gerald Ford)
3. The right to reasonable redress for physical damages suffered from using a product (added by President Richard Nixon)

In January 1964, President Lyndon B. Johnson, a Democrat, created the new White House post of special assistant for consumer affairs and appointed outspoken consumer advocate Esther Peterson to fill it. He also promised he would support new consumer legislation. The 1965 Immigration and Nationality Act and landmark

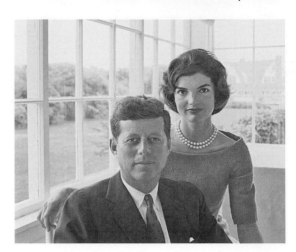

President Kennedy, shown here with his wife Jacqueline, was a pro-consumer leader. (Photo Researchers, Inc.)

civil rights laws opened up the United States in many ways, including new job and educational opportunities and an influx of newcomers from Latin America and Asia.

The 1960s was the age of dominance of large national general merchandise and department stores over small local mom-and-pop stores as well as the spread of fast-food brands. In 1965, the leader in sales and profits was Sears, Roebuck & Company, followed by J.C. Penney and Montgomery Ward (Tedlow, 1990). Ray Kroc bought out the McDonalds brothers in 1960 and franchised McDonald's restaurants. In the 1960s the FDA also seized bogus bust developers such as Lady Ample.

Any discussion of consumer protection in the 1960s would be incomplete without recognizing the enormous contribution that muckraker Ralph Nader made in his 1965 book *Unsafe at Any Speed,* which highlighted the need for more auto safety, including cushioning and seat belts. "The automobile had been around for seventy years before Ralph Nader got general recognition of the fact that autos included unsafe design features and sometimes were ill-engineered," according to authors David Aaker and George Day (1982, p. 31). A series of horrendous accidents caused by poorly manufactured cars led to a call for reform. Nader spoke out against industrial pollution and the abuse of corporate power not only in the car industry but also in the home repair industry, the food industry, and securities, to name a few. He testified extensively before Congress and still advocates on behalf of consumers, particularly regarding environmental concerns, and he founded consumer groups that are still active.

In 1968, Paul Erlich's *The Population Bomb* made the case that there are too many people, too many cars, too much of everything and that if the trend continued unchecked, then famines and other catastrophes would occur. His book influenced the debate on the use of birth control methods and a reconsidering of optimal family size.

Another important book in 1968 was *The Dark Side of the Marketplace* by Senator Warren G. Magnuson and Jean Carper, who explained how the consumer movement had vastly expanded its scope "from sales deceptions and safety standards to concern over the environment—air and water pollution—and the ominous trend toward economic concentration which threatens consumers' welfare" (1968, p. 2). In the first chapter, the authors discussed how elderly couples were being bilked out of thousands of dollars by con men selling aluminum siding door-to-door. This influenced the passage of the 1973 FTC Door-to-Door Sales Rule. Magnuson and Carper asserted that deceptive selling by the unscrupulous few cheated Americans out of more money than is lost to "robbery, burglary, larceny, auto theft, embezzlement, and forgery combined" (1968, p. 13). Their disturbing conclusion was that the public is not being adequately protected, including not knowing enough about the hazards of smoking. Their book influenced the passage of the 1970 Public Health Cigarette Smoking Act (see Box 2.2); also notice the 1975 act that bears Magnuson's name.

## 1970s

As Box 2.2 shows, there was a great deal of consumer protection legislation in the 1970s led by Presidents Richard Nixon (Republican), Gerald Ford (Republican), and Jimmy Carter (Democrat). Nixon, a lawyer by training, signed numerous pieces of consumer legislation into law and led the way to the development of small claims courts throughout the United States, while Gerald Ford promoted consumer education. Carter called for conservation and reduction of energy consumption. He was personally interested in solar power and other environmental technologies and appointed numerous strong consumer advocates to government posts, including Esther Peterson as special assistant for consumer affairs. Because of this and the legislation he supported, Carter is considered a strong pro-consumer president.

Other developments during this decade included the end of the Vietnam War and changes in consumer buying patterns. Discount stores and malls grew, and with them the growth in credit cards, and more stores were open on Sundays.

Faux exercise devices, including different models of the Relaxacizor, were seized by the FDA several times during the 1970s. The FDA has a museum with collections of these types of devices, as well as cosmetics that came under regulation, biological

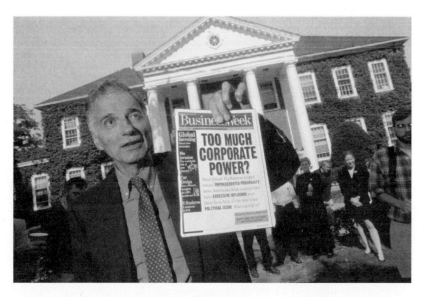

Consumer advocate and presidential candidate Ralph Nader shows off a magazine cover that supports his platform outside the Franklin Pierce Law Center. Nader is a lifelong consumer activist. His famous book, *Unsafe at Any Speed,* revolutionized car safety. (© Dan Habib, *Concord Monitor,* Corbis. All rights reserved.)

agents, foods, medical devices, and quack products of every sort. The museum is part of the FDA History Office, whose mission is to increase knowledge of the history, mission, and activities of the FDA and its predecessor, the Bureau of Chemistry of the U.S. Department of Agriculture. Besides this Washington-based museum, objects are on loan to the St. Louis Science Center, the Science Museum of Minnesota, and also Washington's Smithsonian Institution.

Many of the 1970s acts, because they are landmark legislation, are still influential today (for example, the Equal Credit Opportunity Act and the act establishing the Consumer Product Safety Commission). Especially significant was the previously mentioned 1973 FTC Door-to-Door Sales Rule, which came about because high-pressure salespersons were rushing consumers into buying things they did not want, such as encyclopedias, magazine subscriptions, vacuum cleaners, and home improvements. Because consumers were approached at their homes, many people, particularly women and the elderly, felt threatened if they didn't sign for the product or felt vulnerable in some other way. With the legislation, a consumer could cancel within a three-day cooling-off period. The problem, as the Consumer Alert box shows, is that not all types of contracts were covered. This is often the case with consumer legislation: It stops some of the blatant abuses, but while it is well intentioned, it only covers certain problem areas; additionally, over time it becomes dated as new situations and products arise that were not anticipated and covered in the original legislation.

## 1980s

With President Ronald Reagan, a Republican, at the helm from 1981 to 1989, there was a renewed look at consumer protection in this country. Agencies were reorganized, and some would say they became less powerful. As an advocate of supply-side economics, Reagan mostly took the view that the market should regulate itself. He thought his predecessors may have been overzealous regarding reform, and there was evidence that citizens in the 1980s were tired of restrictions and conserving. The general attitude was that consuming, after all, is fun for most people, most of the time. Movies about greed and Wall Street abounded, college students flocked to business schools, video games came into style for children, the term *yuppie* was used to describe trend-setting dual-earner childless couples, and name brands such as BMW and Ralph Lauren promised prestige.

Consumers were encouraged to use the laws already on the books. Nevertheless quite a bit of consumer protection legislation was passed during the Reagan terms, as shown in Box 2.3. According to public opinion polls, Reagan was a popular president. He was followed by George Bush (1989–1993), also a Republican, who took a similar consumer protection stance.

During the 1980s, there was a corporate thrust behind consumer education because for-profit companies preferred consumer education to more legislation. Increased consumer education is worthwhile if it hits the right audience at the right time, but there is only so much it can do as the following quote makes clear: "Even genuine consumer education cannot, of course, solve consumer problems by itself. If all meat prices go up it's little help to tell consumers to buy the lower-price cuts. These usually go up the most. Nor can consumer education help much in restraining high mortgage interest rates or high medical and hospital fees" (Margolius, 1982, p. 56).

**BOX 2.3    Key Consumer Legislation 1980–Present**

| | |
|---|---|
| 1981 FTC* Used-Car Rule | It requires used-car dealers to disclose to consumers specified types of information. |
| 1984 FTC Funeral Home Rule | It requires disclosure of prices and services. |
| 1984 Counterfeit Access Device and Computer Fraud and Abuse Act | It prohibits counterfeit credit cards and other unauthorized access to credit. |
| 1984 Automobile Restraints | It requires all new cars sold after September 1, 1990, to have restraints (seat belts). |
| 1984 Toy Safety Act | By this act, CPSC** can more quickly recall hazardous toys and equipment for children. |
| 1984 Generic Drug Act | It allows the FDA† to speed up acceptance of generic drugs on which patents have expired on original drugs. |
| 1986 Smokeless Tobacco Act | It requires labeling of hazards on smokeless tobacco products and prohibits advertising of these products on television and radio. |
| 1988 Home Equity Loan Consumer Protection Act | It requires fuller disclosure of loans and prohibits lenders from changing contracts after signage. |
| 1990 Clean Air Act | It updates the 1970 act and establishes new pollution limits and standards for automobile, power plant, and cancer-causing substance emissions. |
| 1990 Children's Advertising Act | It directs the FCC‡ to limit TV advertising directed at children. |
| 1990 Food Labeling Act | It establishes new labeling standards. |
| 1993 Truth in Savings Act | It requires that financial institutions report APY (annual percentage yield) in the same way. |
| 1994 Dietary Supplement Health and Education Act | It requires manufacturers to provide product safety information to the FDA. |
| 1994 Fair Credit Reporting Act (Amended) | It increases access to credit. |
| 1994 NAFTA (North American Free Trade Agreement) | It gradually eliminates tariffs among Mexico, Canada, and the United States on most products. Agreement is in full force in 2008. Included is a dispute-resolution program. |
| 1998 The Digital Millennium Copyright Act | It adapted U.S. legislation to the WIPO treaties. The World Intellectual Property Organization (WIPO) had two treaties, laid down in Geneva, that adapted copyright rules for e-commerce. Copyright laws cover physical copies, broadcasting, books, songs, and films distributed online. The treaties, ratified by 41 countries, went into effect in 2002. |
| 2001 USA PATRIOT Act | It requires every bank to adopt a customer identification program. |

---

*Federal Trade Commission.
**Consumer Product Safety Commission.
†Food and Drug Administration.
‡Federal Communications Commission.

**CONSUMER ALERT**

There is no universal three-day cooling-off period. Do not be misled into thinking that you have an automatic three-day or other cancellation period for all purchases. Only a few types of contracts give you a right to cancel. Federal law, for example, gives you the right to cancel certain door-to-door contracts within three days, and some states provide cancellation periods for such things as health and dating club contracts. Check with your state and local consumer office for more information about cancellation rights.

*Source:* Federal Consumer Information Center.

## 1990s

President Bush, the forty-first president, was followed by Bill Clinton, a Democrat, who held office from 1993 to 2001. Although it is not considered consumer protection legislation per se, Clinton signed the North American Free Trade Agreement (NAFTA), which greatly impacted trade, employment in certain industries, and prices. His vice president, Al Gore, was known for his interest in environmental and family issues and wrote the book *Earth in the Balance,* which is about environmental problems. In 2007, Al Gore was awarded the Nobel Peace Prize for his environmental efforts. A modern-day muckraker, Erin Brockovich, was in the news, and there was an award-winning movie about her investigative work on exposing health-endangering pollution in a small town in California.

This was a decade of affluence, expansion, and low unemployment. The stock market rose steadily, hitting century highs near the end of the decade. The Dow Jones Industrial Average of 30 major American companies hit a twentieth-century high when it closed at 10,000 in 1999. At the same time there were a number of books, magazines, television shows, and writers advocating a simpler, less materialistic life. A book entitled *Affluenza* and public television documentaries *Affluenza* and *Escape from Affluenza* recommended that people go hiking, spend time with their families, or volunteer rather than go to the mall. Although not everyone chose to scale down their consumption, some did, and there was a nationwide switch to more recycling. Schoolchildren were encouraged to participate. It became the American way in this decade and into the twenty-first century.

Holders of wealth changed greatly in the 1990s. By the time Sam Walton, founder of Wal-Mart, died in 1990, he was the richest man in the United States, but within a few years the richest man in the world (not just in the United States) was Bill Gates, founder of Microsoft. The consumption story of the 1990s cannot be told without a nod to computers and the Internet, the growth of e-mail and online buying, and the trend toward working and shopping at home. Few consumer goods have become obsolete so fast: The "286" processor was replaced by the "386," then the "486," and then the Pentium in 1993, advancing to the Pentium IV and an operating system introduced by Microsoft called Windows XP—the list goes on. To meet demand, office-supply, computer, and electronic stores grew. As an alternative, consumers could buy computers online, customizing the system they wanted and getting home delivery.

To stay competitive, by the late 1990s most leading store chains, including department stores and gift shops, offered both **bricks and clicks**, meaning a physical store and an online store. The Mall of America opened in suburban Minneapolis in 1993, showing that entertainment, tourism, leisure, and shopping could all happen underneath one roof; it sports two indoor lakes and an amusement park. Across the country, old malls were closing, there was a partial return to free-standing stores, grocery stores had their own delis and bakeries, and there were more superstores open 24 hours a day. Large mass-market and department stores regrouped; others (such as Kmart) filed for bankruptcy and closed many of their stores. This trend continued into early 2000.

## 2000–Present

A recession ran from 2001 to 2003 and was followed by a period of recovery and another recession in 2008. Unemployment reached 6.1 percent in June 2003 and dropped to around 4.5 percent in 2007. The recession affected the types of jobs that college grads could readily get, so many added greatly to their student loans as college tuition increased significantly. A study released by Collegiate Funding Services found that more than 30 percent of college graduates said they had to take a job other than the one they really wanted in order to pay off their loans, whereas a year earlier the percentage was 20 percent (Kim, 2003). The average debt ranged from $10,000 to $40,000, with some students reporting being over $120,000 in debt in 2007, particularly students attending private colleges and those going on to graduate school, medical school, or law school.

In 2000, the 66-year-old consumer activist Ralph Nader ran as the presidential candidate of the Green Party, garnering about 3 percent of the vote. To learn more about his views on politics, read his book *Crashing the Party: How to Tell the Truth and Still Run for President* (2002). A theme running throughout is that both major political parties "routinely savage the interests of the American people by ignoring such fundamental concerns as corporate control, environmental pollution and the widening gap between rich and poor" (Nader, 2002, p. A12). He ran again in 2004.

As of the writing of this chapter, it was too soon to give a full report on the legacy of consumer protection legislation under George W. Bush, the forty-third president. During his presidency, much of his attention was drawn to the war on terrorism, the war in Iraq, and related security issues. The 2001 USA PATRIOT Act required every bank to adopt a customer identification program as part of its compliance with the Bank Secrecy Act. His early years as president were marked by business scandals about financial mismanagement and improper reporting of funds. Corporate responsibility to employees and stockholders was questioned, as well as the adequacy of outside auditing procedures, and in response, the Securities and Exchange Commission strengthened rules about reporting procedures and increased investigations.

During the Bush administration, there were waves of mergers and turnovers in economic advisors. His Council of Economic Advisors noted that merger activity was well above average levels and had been growing for several decades. Mergers escalated for several reasons:

- Antitrust legislation was less enforced.
- Deregulation spread.

- Large companies benefited from mergers.
- A weakened economy made smaller companies more vulnerable and willing to sell.

Here are some examples of mergers taken from a February 25, 2002, article titled "Why the Sudden Rise in the Urge to Merge and Form Oligopolies?":

> Twenty years ago, cable television was dominated by a patchwork of thousands of tiny, family-operated companies. Today, a pending deal would leave three companies in control of nearly two-thirds of the market. In 1990, three big publishers of college textbooks accounted for 35% of industry sales. Today they have 62%. . . . In 1996, when Congress deregulated telecommunications, there were eight Baby Bells, today there are four, and dozens of small rivals are dead. (*Wall Street Journal*, p. A1)

Regarding consumer organizations and issues during this decade, in 2002 the Consumers Union launched Consumer WebWatch (www.consumerwebwatch.org), a project to help make Web sites more accountable for the accuracy of their information. The site provided news alerts for Web-savvy consumers and research results. The growth of the Internet as an information and selling source is a hallmark of the first decade of the twenty-first century. Evidence of this was apparent in the passage of international legislation and the signing of treaties between countries regarding legalities and the Internet. The globalization of the economy continued with the spread of factories and sales.

## CONCLUSION OF THE DECADES OF CONSUMERISM

The more recent legislation and issues discussed in this chapter may ring a bell. Perhaps you heard about them on television or learned about them in school. Most of you probably do not remember a time when seat belts were not required or when food labels were not as extensive as they are today, nor do you remember presidents much before Presidents Clinton and George W. Bush. To avoid fatiguing the reader, the chapter ends at this point with the intention of exploring the most current legislation and related issues further in upcoming chapters. It should also be noted that for brevity's sake not all persons and organizations that contributed to consumer protection in the United States are mentioned. The consumer movement, much as the Internet, is borderless, free-ranging, and growing. Food crises continue, with outbreaks of illness from contaminated spinach, peanut butter, and pet food, to the point where people ask, "What next?" One of the values of studying the history of the consumer movement is to increase awareness of past crises and to learn how regulation helps prevent future outbreaks. When food crises occur, food regulation and inspection come to the forefront.

Crises such as threats to our health draw attention to faulty products, inspections, health systems, or services that need correcting. The range of problems includes everything from faulty tires to improper food processing. The FDA has been enormously important in testing foods and seizing misbranded food (such as blueberry pancake mixes with no blueberries in them), with many of these seizures being well publicized. We become aware of crises or misrepresentations through the news and the Internet. In the past, newspaper articles and books written by muckrakers rallied support for product or financial reform. Sometimes, reform has arisen out of invention or a natural evolution of things—new scientific discoveries disclose new ills or inventions such as computers or credit cards require new rules for handling their potential abuse.

This chapter focused on consumer rights and legislation, but this is only one side of the coin. Chapter 4 explores consumer responsibilities. The government cannot be everywhere, so how do consumers look out for themselves? What is their responsibility in the marketplace?

## SUMMARY

Unquestionably, the twentieth and twenty-first centuries can be seen as times of increasing affluence. But with affluence come abuses in the marketplace that necessitate more consumer protection. The twenty-first century began with a rocky start as the national and the worldwide economy experienced a slowdown, and a series of corporate scandals led to a loss of faith in the dependability of business standards and practices. Through it all, the consumer movement has been active. In the United States, the modern consumer movement can be traced from the 1880s. The earliest concerns were about food quality, but over time many more product areas came under scrutiny, including drugs, cosmetics, toys, and broader social, technological, and financial concerns. The consumer movement embraced the environmental movement, and they are so coupled today that it is difficult to separate them. The late 1960s and early 1970s were the heyday of environmental concerns spurred by well-publicized oil spills that wrecked coastlines and killed wildlife. In more recent decades, concerns shifted back to food quality and purity as well as other health-related issues.

Certain decades produced more consumer protection legislation than others; particularly active decades were the 1930s and the 1960s through the 1980s. Presidents from both the Republican and Democratic parties have provided leadership in consumer protection. Senators, scientists, writers, corporate employees, and organizations have stirred the public interest by bringing to light shoddy and questionable practices and products. Ralph Nader and other consumer activists provided leadership and put the spotlight on food, environmental, and car problems. Some may question whether the phrase "consumer movement" is the best term since it is no longer an ideological movement because consumerism is a regular part of our everyday experience. If a product breaks or causes injury, we expect remedy or justice—consumer protection is a given in our daily lives. We rely on regulations to facilitate our reasoned choice and, in particular, to protect the young, elderly, and defenseless from unscrupulous practices.

Consumer protection needs arise in response to:

- New technological developments
- Changing conceptions of the social responsibilities of consumers, businesses, and nations
- Exposés of the dishonest, greedy, and selfish fringe that break the rules and take advantage

In conclusion, as long as there are consumers, there will be a need for consumer protection.

## KEY POINTS

1. From 1776—the year of the publication of Adam Smith's book—to the present, there has been a growing trend of consumer reliance on business to provide goods. With the decrease in self-production of goods comes the necessity to rely on business or government to ensure quality and safety.
2. Abuses in the marketplace lead to the need for consumer protection legislation.
3. The consumer movement refers to policies aimed at providing regulations and standards.
4. Harvey Wiley, chemist, is the founder of the consumer movement, and some would say the founder of the FDA. He is famous for his Poison Squad experiments on the effects of food additives.
5. Food reformers were most concerned about fraud and poison.
6. World War II brought shortages and rationing. Consumer legislation took a backseat to concerns about obtaining goods. Immediately after the war, increased production for houses, household goods, and cars became paramount.
7. Rachel Carson, biologist and author of *Silent Spring*, is the founder of the modern environmental movement.
8. Muckrakers such as Upton Sinclair, author of *The Jungle,* led to reforms in meat processing, and others such as Ralph Nader, author of *Unsafe at Any Speed,* led to reforms in car safety.
9. Two economists—John Maynard Keynes and John Kenneth Galbraith—and their contributions were introduced in this chapter. Keynes, whose book *The General Theory of Employment, Interest, and Money* was important during the Depression, made the case for more government intervention. Galbraith, author of many books including *The Affluent Society,* served in various government roles during World War II; later, as an advisor to John F. Kennedy and ambassador to India, he influenced public policy and promoted public service.
10. Several presidents were key figures in influencing consumer legislation. Particularly noteworthy is John F. Kennedy who, in his Consumer Message to Congress, outlined the four basic principles of consumer protection—the rights to be safe, to be heard, to choose, and to have information.
11. Consumer legislation is necessary and well intentioned. However, loopholes nearly always exist, and the acts or rules do not cover everything. For example, the 1973 FTC Door-to-Door Sales Rule only allows a consumer to cancel a few types of contracts within three days. In all cases, caveat emptor (meaning "May the buyer beware") holds true.

## KEY TERMS

| | | |
|---|---|---|
| antitrust laws | conspicuous consumption | hucksterism |
| bricks and clicks | consumer movement | muckraker |
| cease-and-desist order | depression | pollution |
| common law | environmentalism | rational self-interest |

## DISCUSSION QUESTIONS

1. If President John F. Kennedy was alive today, would he be pleased with the state of consumer protection in this country? List his four consumer rights, and give a current example of each from your own life or from a friend's or relative's experience.
2. After reading the excerpt from *The Jungle*, do you think reforms were necessary in the meat-processing industry in 1906? Explain your answer. What was President Theodore Roosevelt's role in meat-processing reforms?
3. It isn't easy being a reformer. Who did not support the work of food safety reformer Harvey Wiley?
4. Select one of the e-resource Web sites listed next. What did you find on the site?

## E-RESOURCES

**Center for Science in the Public Interest** *www.cspinet.org*
A nonprofit membership organization that conducts research, education, and advocacy on food safety, nutrition, health, and related issues.

**Consumers Union** *www.ConsumerReports.org*
Consumers Union, the publisher of *Consumer Reports*, is a nonprofit organization chartered in 1936 that provides information on consumer goods such as toothpaste, toys, toasters, and cars and conducts tests.

**Consumer WebWatch** *www.consumerwebwatch.org*
A Consumers Union site, it helps make Web sites more accountable for accuracy and provides research results and news alerts for consumers.

**FDA History Office** *www.fda.gov*
The office provides information about its evolution, function, the oral history program, the museum collection, and the staff.

**Federal Trade Commission** *www.ftc.gov* and *www.consumer.gov*
This government commission offers consumer information on many subjects, including labeling, advertisements, and monopolies.

**North American Free Trade Agreement (NAFTA)** *www.mac.doc.gov/nafta/*
Issues and information are given on CBP.gov site, which is of use to exporters, public policy experts, and economists.

## REFERENCES

Aaker, D., and G. Day. (1982). *Consumerism: Search for the consumer interest,* 4th ed. New York: Free Press.

Barber, B. R. (2007). *Consumed.* New York: Norton.

Carson, R. (1962). *Silent spring.* Boston: Houghton Mifflin.

Chase, S., and F. Schlink. (1928). *Your money's worth.* New York: Macmillan.

Cross, G. (2000). *An all-consuming century: Why commercialism won in modern America.* New York: Columbia University Press.

Crossen, C. (December 28, 2001). Etiquette for Americans today. *Wall Street Journal,* p. W13.

Crossen, C. (December 18, 2002). In wartime holidays of the past, patriots curbed their spending. *Wall Street Journal,* p. B1.

Cude, B. (1993). Consumer perceptions of environmental marketing claims: An exploratory study. *Journal of Consumer Studies and Home Economics, 12,* 207–25.

Downs, R. B. (1963). Afterword to *The Jungle,* 4th ed., by Upton Sinclair. New York: New American Library, pp. 343–50.

Erlich, P. (1968). *The population bomb.* New York: Ballantine Books.

Frederick, C. (1914). *The new housekeeping: Efficiency studies in home management.* New York: Doubleday.

Fussman, Cal. (January 2002). Interview with John Kenneth Galbraith. *Esquire,* p. 60.

Galbraith, J. (1958). *The affluent society.* Boston: Houghton Mifflin.

Gore, A. (1992). *Earth in the balance.* New York: Penguin Books.

Harris, D. (2000). *Cute, quaint, hungry and romantic: The aesthetics of consumerism.* New York: Basic Books.

Heilbroner, Robert (Ed.) (1986). *The essential Adam Smith.* New York: Norton. A translation of Adam Smith's (1776). *An inquiry into the nature and causes of the wealth of nations.*

Heilbroner, R., and L. Thurow. (1998). *Economics explained.* New York: Simon and Schuster.

Josephson, M. (1962). *The robber barons.* New York: Harcourt, Brace & World.

Kallet, A., and F. Schlink. (1933). *100,000,000 guinea pigs.* New York: Grosset & Dunlap.

Keynes, J. (1936). *The general theory of employment, interest, and money.* London: Macmillan.

Kim, J. (September 2, 2003). More college graduates postpone their "dream jobs" to pay loans. *Wall Street Journal,* p. C1.

Lyon, P., A. Colquhoun, and D. Kinney. (2004). UK food shopping in the 1950s: The social context of customer loyalty. *International Journal of Consumer Studies, 28* (1), 28–39.

Magnuson, W., and J. Carper. (1968). *The dark side of the marketplace.* New York: Prentice Hall.

Margolius, S. (1982). The consumer's real needs. In *Consumerism: Search for the Consumer Interest,* 4th ed., David A. Aaker and George S. Day. New York: Free Press, pp. 48–56.

Nader, R. (1966). *Unsafe at any speed.* New York: Pocket Books.

Nader, R. (2002). *Crashing the party: How to tell the truth and still run for president.* New York: Thomas Dunne Books.

Packard, V. (1957). *The hidden persuaders.* New York: Pocket Books.

Schlereth, T. (1991). *Victorian America: Transformations in everyday life 1876–1915.* New York: HarperCollins.

Sinclair, U. (1905). *The Jungle.* New York: New American Library of World Literature.

Smith, A. (1776). *An inquiry into the nature and causes of the wealth of nations,* as edited by Robert Heilbroner (1986) in *The Essential Adam Smith.* New York: Norton.

Strasser, S. (1989). *Satisfaction guaranteed.* New York: Random House.

Tedlow, R. (1990). *New and improved: The Story of mass marketing in America.* New York: Basic Books.

White, S. (November–December 2002). The "poison squad" and the advent of food and drug regulation. *FDA Consumer.*

Why the sudden rise in the urge to merge and form oligopolies? (February 25, 2002). *Wall Street Journal,* p. A1.

# Consumer Theories and Development of a Model

*If we do discover a complete theory, it should in time be understandable in broad principle by everyone, not just a few scientists.*
—Stephen Hawking

## Learning Objectives

1. Explain different theories and their relevance to the study of consumer economics.
2. Describe the components of the Consumer Power Model.
3. Explain factors that affect the model.
4. Explain how consumer well-being, including consumer confidence, is defined and measured.
5. Describe the basic functions of business and the nature of entrepreneurship.

---

### Environment and You: Part of the Consumer Power Model

Consumer organizations including college activist groups specializing in protecting the environment are exploring the varied dimensions of consumerism. Eco-reps are students encouraging eco-friendly lifestyles among their peers. About 40 colleges including Harvard University have eco-reps and more colleges are participating.

"One unseasonably warm morning in late October, the University of Vermont paid a group of students to do something kind of rowdy on the Burlington campus: spread 680 pounds of trash on the ground in front of the David Student Center for all to see and smell. The effort worked."[1] Passersby demanded an explanation and they got it along with a discussion of how two tons of food waste goes from the center to the land-fill every week. When it comes to consumer issues, drama often works.

The goal of the eco-reps is to show students how to lessen their environmental footprint. Administrators like it because it saves them money and shows social awareness. Harvard University saved $170,000 yearly in electricity costs because of a 5-year campus energy saving program. Sustainability is the name of the game. Can you give examples on your campus of energy saving or recycling programs? This is all about behavior change and sometimes it happens in small steps. Peers tend to be more effective in bringing about change than higher-ups, hence the success of the eco-reps. "Students can't change out a boiler or negotiate an electricity contract or erect a large wind turbine," says Sarah Hammond Creighton of the Tuft's Office of Sustainability, "but they can turn their lights off."[2]

---

[1] G. Jeffrey MacDonald, "Students Teach Students to Waste Less on Campus," *USA Today*, November 5, 2007, p. 4D.
[2] Ibid.

# INTRODUCTION

*The rationality of consumers to the exclusion of other factors is being questioned by economists.*

We learned in the first chapter that the founder of modern economics, Adam Smith, believed that "to be human is to exchange freely." That idea—of humans wanting the freedom to exchange unrestricted by outside forces—is a theory that Adam Smith espoused. He believed in an orderly, progressive, and harmonious commercial society.

In today's world, many economists follow the teachings of Smith (summarized as faith in the market), while others believe, as did John Maynard Keynes, that the more complicated world we live in necessitates more government intervention. Economists generally agree that consumers have **rationality** (the ability to reason) and **acquisitiveness** (a strong desire for things, ideas, and information).

Recent developments in economic theory and research have questioned the nature of rationality. For example, the 2002 Nobel Prize in economics went to Daniel Kahneman and Amos Tversky, who published an article highlighting the irrational nature of people when it comes to consumption. They represent a growing area of economics called **behavioral economics** or **behavioral finance** or **neuroeconomics**, which is "pushing the frontiers of research by introducing psychologically realistic models of economic agents into economic theory" (Robinson-Brown, 2002, p. 1). Their particular contributions about judgment, attitudes, and decision making are discussed in this chapter. Economics is about studying choices and decisions. Neuroeconomics is a subset focusing on personal choices (versus those of firms and institutions) and the mental changes that affect choice selection, and it confirms that emotions are important factors in selection (Glimcher, 2003). It extends the beginning theories on choice by adding observations of the nervous system so that, for example, full brain scans or other such measures may be performed to understand economic decision making (usually some recording mechanism is involved).

Regarding the acquisitive nature of human behavior, Harvard University Professor Juliet Schor (1998) wrote that what we acquire is tightly bound to our identity. Theories such as these form the bulk of this chapter, which explores the nature of theories and their roles in consumption. The chapter ends with discussions of consumer well-being, including measures of consumer confidence.

# THEORY, EXCHANGE PROCESS, AND UTILITY

*Theories are useful for guiding research and explaining consumer behavior.*

A **theory** is an organized system of ideas or beliefs that can be measured. Theories are essentially systems of principles or assumptions, and because of the measurement aspect, theories are useful in guiding research and explaining behavior. A research project may start with questions or hypotheses that are predictions of

A fundamental consumer theory backed by research is that past purchasing behavior is a strong predictor of future purchasing behavior.

future occurrences; for example, a researcher might predict that if a consumer has bought Tide detergent for the last 10 years, he or she will likely continue to do so. In consumer research it has been proven many times over that past behavior is a strong predictor of future behavior. Knowing this, many companies work hard at building brand loyalty in young people. As an example, consider the number of credit cards that have been offered to you during your college years. Even though you may not have much money now, the credit card companies know that you will soon and that you are unlikely to change credit cards once you graduate.

In the following pages, we explore various theories about how people plan, decide, buy, and exchange goods given scarce resources. Several theories exist because many factors or groups impact different kinds of consumers, and as time goes on, new theories are formulated to describe behavior. Consumers come in all shapes, sizes, ages, nationalities, income levels, and so forth, although discernible patterns and statistics are useful in determining these groupings. For example, in the United States, women account for about 80 percent of consumer spending (Allon, 2001). That makes gender a factor in consumption behavior. A specific example of this is that in the United States most women use body wash, but only 45 percent of men use body wash and "most are using women's products and half are using them secretly. Their partners typically do not know that they're using it" (Neff, 2002, p. 8). Hoping to change this behavior and directly market to men, Procter & Gamble Co. launched Old Spice High Endurance body wash in January 2003 and marketed it to men. This is called a **brand extension** because Old Spice already comes in aftershave, antiperspirant, and deodorant. Note also the words "high endurance," which sounds masculine rather than feminine.

In the United States, women account for about 80 percent of consumer spending.

Since consumer economics can be described most simply as the study of exchange activities, it is important to define what this encompasses. The **exchange process** occurs when people (as individuals, family members, employees, members of religious groups, etc.) negotiate with a goal of reaching an agreement, such as an agreed-on price or date of delivery. When the exchange is fulfilled, it is called a **transaction**.

Another useful consideration in consumer economics is the concept of **utility**, which generally refers to the usefulness of a product, service, or idea. In economics, **diminishing marginal utility** means that in a given time period, a consumer will receive less satisfaction from each successive unit (such as a food item) consumed; for example, a second piece of chocolate cake is less satisfying than the first.

In summary, consumer economics and behavior are affected by many variables. To make the study of these variables more organized, this chapter will incorporate theories and models, and they serve as guides to explaining consumers' choices and the influences on their behavior.

## THEORY OF REASONED ACTION

Although consumers are generally considered to be rational (as explained in the Introduction), the newer thought is that they do not always behave rationally. And if one looks back, there is much evidence of irrationality in the past. Consider this example:

In the late 19th century, teacher-turned-snake-oil-seller Lydia E. Pinkham used her image and signature to help sell her eponymous vegetable compound as a cure-all for faintness, flatulence, depression and other "female" complaints. While her product may have been suspect—a main ingredient was alcohol—her marketing strategy was sound. Ads that appeared in newspapers and on barns were so persuasive that women wrote her detailing their aches and pains. They always received a letter back signed by Lydia—even long after the lady died, thanks to those who kept the company going. (Well, 2001, p. 124)

Was it rational for women to think of Lydia Pinkham, a person they never met, as a friend? Do women think of modern-day media moguls Oprah Winfrey and Martha Stewart as friends? Do their companies promote these relationships much as Lydia Pinkham's did? This connection between attitudes, social relationships, and consumer behavior has been explored by several theorists. Probably the most commonly cited theory of this kind is the **theory of reasoned action** developed by Martin Fishbein and Icek Ajzen (Ajzen & Fishbein, 1980). Their theory states that behavioral intentions are based on a combination of the attitude toward a specific behavior, the social or normative beliefs about the appropriateness of the behavior, and the motivation to comply with the normative beliefs (Sheppard, Hartwick & Warshaw, 1988). In the theory of reasoned action, what is important is the consumer's attitude toward behaving a certain way and the consumer's subjective norm, which is his or her belief about others' evaluations of his or her actions.

Regarding this second point, what the consumer believes to be a rational or reasonable purchase or course of action may or may not be shared by his or her family, coworkers, or friends. For example, if a 55-year-old bald man buys a red sports car, he may or may not wonder what others think. If he senses disapproval (for example, he is perceived as having a midlife crisis), he may select another color or a pickup truck instead. This middle-aged man is not alone. "Many of us are continually comparing our own lifestyle and possessions to those of a select group of people we respect and want to be like, people whose sense of what's important in life seems close to our own" (Schor, 1998, p. 3). The theory of reasoned action shows that consumption is based on beliefs and attitudes, that it has consequences, and that it takes place within a social context.

## PROSPECT THEORY AND THEORY OF MENTAL ACCOUNTING

As mentioned in the Introduction, economists for the most part follow a central tenet that people are logical with their money and that the market operates sensibly. The problem is that when the stock market reverses and companies go bankrupt, economists and others wonder how sensible the market really is. It appears to be capable of irrational behavior, and the corollary to this is that consumers also act in illogical ways. When people do not have all the answers or ways of systematically approaching decisions, it does not stop them; they proceed and do what they can. In other words, they do not let uncertainty get in the way of making decisions.

In 1979, an American psychologist named Daniel Kahneman (noted for his pioneering work in behavioral finance) and Amos Tversky (who died in 1996) published "Prospect Theory: An Analysis of Decision Under Risk" in *Econometrica,* a journal of economics. In this article, "[they] argued that people's degree of pleasure (their 'utility' in social science-ese) is more dependent on the change in their condition than on the absolute level. In other words, a rich man who loses $10 is

Lydia Pinkham's Vegetable Compound. Marketed to women, the compound had alcohol as its main ingredient. (Drug Enforcement Administration.)

apt to feel bad, whereas a poor man who wins $100 is apt to feel rich. This concept broke ground with classical economics, which held that rich always feels better than poor" (Lowenstein, 2003, p. 42). This was called **prospect theory**. It is an economic theory that explains choice under uncertainty and led to the idea of loss aversion. This idea holds that people feel more pain from loss than pleasure from profit. This explains why people hold on to stocks that are performing poorly (they are doing so to avoid pain even if they can afford the loss), although it would probably be more rational to sell the stocks and put the money into a better-performing investment. Prospect theory describes decision-making processes and includes the steps of editing and evaluating: We are exposed to countless advertising pitches a day that we have to edit and evaluate, we subjectively frame messages, and we determine the utility we expect to receive from our decisions.

An outgrowth of prospect theory is the impact of **message framing**. For example, an advertising or marketing campaign may indicate you will be happy if you buy this product or sad if you do not. Think of all the advertisements that use these approaches. Consider the saying "At these prices, run in before everything is gone." This is an example of a *negatively framed message* since it says you will be sorry if you pass up this deal. *Positively framed messages* let consumers know the benefits to be gained from the purchase: "You will smell better and have more friends if you use this deodorant." Both types of messages are about purchasing behavior, and the messages connect risk or negative consequences if consumers do not act. Initially it appears that negative framing of a choice has more impact than positive framing, but a warning or negative message can act as a boomerang by making the risky behavior more attractive. This is referred to as **reactance**. A warning sign posted outside a roller-coaster ride might stimulate more desire to experience it than if there was no sign at all. Likewise a group of golfers might be stimulated to hit their balls harder if they see a sign posted at a swampy area on the course that says "Beware of snakes and alligators"; in other words, they need to hit their balls over this swampy area or they will lose them. Playing this risky hole may be more challenging to them than hitting in an open fairway or chipping up to a pretty azalea-lined green.

In regard to Kahneman's contribution, his department chairman, Gene Grossman, said, "He's challenged the basic model of how individuals behave economically. The standard model is that everybody is rational, self-interested, calculating; he's suggested that more psychological motives determine people's behavior and that these motives are important for economic phenomena . . . I think there is now a broader range of thinking about certain issues, especially savings behavior and participation in the stock market" (Robinson-Brown, 2002, p. 2).

Kahneman and Tversky were collaborators with Richard Thaler. Thaler, who teaches at the University of Chicago, studied with Kahneman (a Princeton professor who teaches Psychology 101 and has never taken or taught a course in economics) and came up with the **endowment effect**. In experiments Thaler found that "[s]ubjects who have been given a present—they used a coffee mug—will demand a higher price to sell it than people who don't have the mug would be willing to pay for one" (Lowenstein, 2003, p. 42). This finding contradicts the widely held classical economist view that in a free market, one price fits all. Again, human behavior (in this case, a sense of ownership) affects what people set as an appropriate price. Thaler took this a step further and developed the **theory of mental accounting** in which people frame or put into context their buying and selling: "People who obsess over saving $5 on groceries will happily blow $1,000 on a vacation because they account for it differently" (Lowenstein, 2003, p. 42). They are, therefore, uneven in their response to money. Thaler, other economists, and family and consumer economists around the country are exploring other dimensions of saving and spending behavior through surveys and experiments.

## INNOVATION THEORY

Innovators or early adopters of new products and services are of interest to consumer economists and marketers. Research surrounds certain questions:

- Who are these first people to buy?
- Why do they do it?
- Does the trend toward buying first affect all product categories, or is it product specific?

**Innovators** are the earliest buyers of new brands, services, products, and store or other market offerings, and they like new ideas and technologies as well. They are attracted to grand openings of stores, advertisements of new products, door prizes, and excitement. Does this describe you or someone you know? The theoretical background for this phenomenon was provided by E. M. Rogers, author of *Diffusion of Innovations:*

> He defined a process through which an individual . . . passes (1) from first knowledge of an innovation, (2) to forming an attitude toward the innovation, (3) to a decision to adopt or reject, (4) to implementation of the new idea, and (5) to confirmation of this decision. (1995, p. 161)

An innovative consumer is highly involved and wants to know what is happening. He or she may be an avid reader or follower of the news or may talk with friends about new products and services. Online consumer communities are central to creating and spreading the buzz. As mentioned in the Introduction, economists believe that people are acquisitive—they need to know what is going on in the marketplace and to acquire (or at least to think about or look at) new things such as cars, houses, or electronic items (digital cameras, flat-screen televisions). Rogers posited that there is a theme in consumer behavior of adoption and diffusion of innovations.

What is curious about innovation adoption is that a person can be an innovator in one category, such as wearing the latest fashions, but a laggard in another category, such as going to see the latest movies. This makes sense because it would be very expensive, time-consuming, and exhausting to be an innovator in all areas of consumption, so people make choices about where to put their time, effort, and money. Many choose to ignore the latest ideas or products altogether and prefer the tried-and-true. One thinks of the expression, "If it ain't broke, don't fix it." One example involves a nutrition professor who has a 1980s Amana microwave oven in her home kitchen; the oven is huge, and family and friends kid her about it, but it still works, she is used to it, and she sees no reason to change.

A consumer innovator is more likely to take risks and be more venturesome than later buyers. If marketers can find the innovators in a particular product class, promotion and distribution should be directed to them first. Marketing researchers would want to know what magazines and newsletters innovators read, what clubs they belong to, what sporting events or arts events they attend, and so on. Generally, innovators are more upwardly mobile and less price sensitive than later adopters. One product class that attracts innovators is computers and computing services. Another public relations approach could involve advertising and direct marketing, such as holding a launch party for magazine editors or hosting exhibit booths at conventions to display new wares. More subtle approaches include such things as sponsoring community or cultural events or sports teams, contributing to high school yearbooks, and buying tickets to charity events. The parties or events may involve gift bags with the new product or at least a discount coupon on its purchase.

An innovation may be new to one social or cultural group or country, whereas it may not be perceived as new by another. It can be said that the innovation diffuses, or moves through, a social system over time—some pick it up early, some pick it up late, and the vast majority fall somewhere in between. People in the middle are interested in what is new but are wary of things that are brand-new. They may think that if they wait, the kinks will be worked out of the new product (such as a car model) or that the price will come down. Rogers developed a bell-shaped curve to illustrate the rate at which new products, services, or ideas are typically adopted. At the beginning is 2.5 percent of the population, designated as the innovators. They are followed by 13.5 percent, who are the early adopters; 34 percent, who are the early majority; 34 percent, who are called the late majority; and ending with the last group to adopt, who are called the laggards and are estimated as 16 percent of the population. The nutrition professor with the old microwave oven would be a laggard.

## SCIENTIFIC METHOD

At this juncture, it would be useful to describe the scientific method that consumer researchers follow (as do biologists and chemists). Following are the five steps in the scientific method:

1. Describe what is happening (recognize the problem or opportunity).
2. Explain why it is happening (make assumptions).
3. Develop a model.
4. Predict what will happen in the future.
5. Control, check, or test what is happening.

The problem may be "I need shoes." The opportunity may be "I need new shoes even though I already own 30 pairs." Assumptions are commonly held beliefs or statements that are accepted as true without proof. Someone may assume that the new pair of shoes will give more wear, satisfaction, and status than the shoes already owned. He or she may predict or imagine what will happen when wearing the shoes, what compliments will be received, what outfits the shoes will go with, and so on.

In step five of the scientific method, the word *control* refers to the things people do to check their course of action or to test what they have purchased. Checking, tests, or trials are used to determine whether a theory is consistent with the facts or the outcomes. For example, if someone theorized that saving money was better than spending it, he or she could set up an automatic deduction of $50 from his or her paycheck that goes directly into a savings account. The control aspect would be checking on how the savings account is building. Did it bring the desired effect? Did the person feel too limited by having the $50 deducted from each paycheck? When individuals make purchase or financial decisions, they are trying to predict what will happen (how much pleasure or pain they will derive from the decision); on the basis of that analysis, they change or alter their behavior accordingly.

Some of us are more visual learners than others and enjoy things being drawn or demonstrated. An example in a work setting would be seeing a flow chart of the officers' or administrators' names and titles. With drawings, plans, and charts, one can instantly visualize relationships. **Models** are representations or schematics or illustrations of relationships. They take abstractions from the real world and allow us to visualize the connections between ideas or between people or institutions. A common model is a blueprint, which is a flat drawing of a house. Another way to visualize the building of a new house or the remodeling of an existing home is to use computer simulations of floor plans and elevations. In the next section of the chapter, frameworks (which are outlines or connections of ideas) are discussed first, followed by more theories and models. In the course of this discussion, a new consumer model is proposed and illustrated.

## BASIC FRAMEWORK FOR MODEL DEVELOPMENT

### Exchanges

Consumer economics involves processes of exchange between two or more parties. The process occurs when parties negotiate (this can be verbal or nonverbal)

**Figure 3.1**   Exchange Process
between Consumers and Markets.   *Includes reactions and inactions.

and reach an agreement. The fulfillment of the exchange process is called a transaction (as mentioned earlier) and is illustrated in Figure 3.1.

An everyday example of this is when a person goes to the grocery store to
buy a gallon of milk and then pays for it—the exchange is completed. This is
what happens on the surface, but the exchange process is not really that simple. Behind the scenes, there are many forces and parties. The cows produce
milk, and the farmers and suppliers get the milk to market; then come the regulators, grocers, marketers, and promoters. Public policy may also be involved in
the form of taxes, farm subsidies, exports, or regulations so that prices or supplies are affected. A government agency may reinforce the rules that regulate
product dating, and the stores will have to stamp the appropriate pull date on
the milk. Government inspectors make sure this is done correctly and consistently.

Other relationships are also formed in exchanges, such as market-to-market
transactions (businesses selling to each other) and consumer-to-consumer transactions (such as people buying and selling at yard sales or college students selling
used textbooks to each other). Consumer-to-consumer relationships are often com-
municated by word of mouth or referral networks such as local newspapers or
signs. Because this book is about consumer economics, the focus is on where and
how the majority of consumer transactions take place, which is between consumers and markets.

While most consumer–market exchanges are satisfactory, meaning that both
sides are satisfied, sometimes things go wrong, creating a **consumer–market conflict**. Getting an agreement or reconciling differences may be difficult. Here is
where public policy steps in: It anticipates potential areas of conflict and deals with
them before, during, and after they have happened, and as such it plays a very
important role in the consumer–market exchange and deserves a place in our model
(see Figure 3.2).

**Figure 3.2**   Consumer
Exchange. This model shows the
interaction between three
fundamental components in the
consumer exchange: consumer,
public policy, and markets.

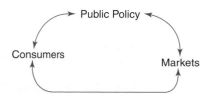

## Public Policy

Figure 3.2 shows a traditional view of the consumer–market exchange wherein public policy serves as a moderator or mediator. The role of public policy is to make sure the exchange is fair in terms of competition, labeling, access, advertising, and pricing. The arrows in Figure 3.3 Consumer Power Model show more complex relationships. As an example, the market (through for-profit and non-profit organizations) may hire lobbyists to sway public policy in its favor, and this lobbying effort may lead to fewer restrictions on the organization, reduced taxes, or advertisements in new mediums.

The Consumer Power Model shows how all the pieces fit together.

Consumers want useful, safe, environmentally sound products at fair prices, and they also want selection. **Public policy** is a plan or decision by government to act in a certain way or go in a particular direction, such as to keep products safe, open up competition, eliminate poverty, allocate more money to medical research or the space program, or clean up the environment. This is in contrast to private matters or concerns, such as how an individual or family acts. Public policy makers exist at all levels, from the smallest town to the federal government, and they work in the executive, legislative, and judicial branches. Individuals and families get involved in public policy through an aspect of their consumer well-being referred to as political well-being, which is a reflection of each individual's internal sense of power and autonomy and of what is right and wrong. Freely making decisions, voting, and choosing products in the marketplace are part of political well-being.

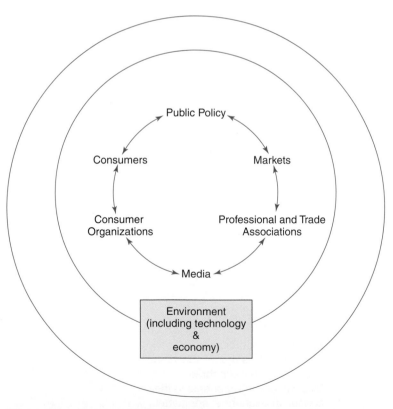

**Figure 3.3**   Consumer Power Model.

Public policy responds to issues, problems, causes, and influences such as those of voters, activist citizens, consumer organizations, and lobbyists. At any given time, one set of constituents' goals may be in conflict with those of another set of constituents, or they may not agree or support proposed policies or actions. When conflicts occur, difficult decisions have to be made, usually in the interests of the greater good. Most public policy is designed to promote the general public interest but is influenced by politics and the support of certain individuals, groups, and organizations.

A common role of government is regulation. Through regulation, society allows a bureaucracy to promote certain public or community interests, causes, or goals. An ongoing debate is how much regulatory power government should have versus allowing the market to exist unhampered. In the final analysis, it comes down to a series of trade-offs involving decisions about both how much regulation is in the best interest of consumers and whether the costs involved in regulation are worth the money spent.

## Consumer Organizations

Consumer organizations assist, protect, and advocate for consumers.

Besides consumers, regulators, and markets, other groups of consumer organizations come into play and include the Consumers Union, the National Consumers League, and the American Association of Retired Persons (AARP) (see Box 3.1 for a sample list of organizations). As their names imply, consumer organizations may cover a wide range of interests or may specialize in one area such as senior citizens' concerns. They may push for the passage of legislation in the public interest, they may send staff members to testify before Congress, or they may hire lobbyists or support people to run for political office in order to sway public policy their way.

The main mission they have in common is to assist and protect consumers and provide consumer advocacy. Most try to improve the health and safety of consumers and better their lives, including improving their financial health and promoting their fair treatment in the marketplace. In the model, they could be placed under consumers as a subgroup, but not all consumers support or appreciate the work of consumer advocacy groups. In many ways, they are a force in and of themselves, so they deserve their own spot in the model. An updated and revised model includes other influences and groups such as trade and professional associations, which are discussed next.

## Trade and Professional Associations

Companies that manufacture similar products or offer similar services often belong to trade and professional associations that serve to resolve problems between consumers and member companies and that also provide consumer information and education through Web sites and publications. One example is the American Bankers Association (www.aba.com), which provides consumer education materials; another is the Food Marketing Institute (www.fmi.org), which conducts programs in research, education, industry relations, and public affairs on behalf of its members (grocery retailers and wholesalers). Both of these associations are located in Washington, D.C., as are many others. They offer career opportunities for those trained both in consumer economics and in public policy. Since trade and professional associations are most associated with markets, they are placed under markets in the model being developed in this chapter.

BOX 3.1    Examples of National Consumer Organizations*

Alliance against Fraud in Telemarketing and Electronic Commerce (AAFTEC)

American Association of Retired Persons (AARP) (Consumer Issues Section)

American Council on Consumer Interests (ACCI)

American Council on Science and Health

Center for Science in the Public Interest

Center for the Study of Services

Coalition against Insurance Fraud

Community Nutrition Institute

Consumer Action

Consumer Alert

Consumer Federation of America

Consumers for World Trade

Families USA Foundation

HALT: An Organization for Americans for Legal Reform

Health Research Group

Jump$tart Coalition for Personal Financial Literacy

National Association of Consumer Agency Administration

National Coalition for Consumer Education

National Community Reinvestment Coalition

National Consumer Law Center

National Consumers League

National Fraud Information Center/Internet Fraud Watch

National Institute for Consumer Education

Public Citizen, Inc.

Self Help for Hard of Hearing People (SHHH)

Society of Consumer Affairs Professionals in Business (SOCAP)

United Seniors Health Cooperative

U.S. Public Interest Group (U.S. PIRG)

─────

*This is not a comprehensive list. More national organizations exist, and some come and go. Local, state, and international organizations also exist.

Besides these organizations, more has been added to the model (shown in Figure 3.3), such as the influence or impact of the environment and technology on the economy. Both of these are discussed in the following sections.

## Environment

When we use the word *environment* in consumer economics, it refers to the space in which all its transactions or potential transactions occur. Probably the best way to think of an environment is its all-encompassing external conditions. To give a specific example, a shopping mall is a consumer environment. An individual or family may window-shop or may actually buy a specific good, with prebuying, buying, and postbuying all being part of the consumption process. Environments affect what is being offered and how well it is received, so attractive displays and pleasant music are important. Consumption, therefore, takes place in an environmental context. Think of sitting in a dentist's chair or shopping in a grocery store and the music you hear—probably a preprogrammed tape with soothing instrumental music from old movies such as *The Sound of Music* or *Sleepless in Seattle*.

**Regional subcultures** exist in the United States due to differences in the natural environment and resources, characteristics of immigrant groups, and other social forces, including history and traditions. Beer consumption, advertisements, and formulas vary widely, resulting in the rise of microbreweries. To compete, large firms such as Anheuser-Busch have regional formulas and **targeted advertising**. For example, Anheuser-Busch divided Texas into regions and developed unique advertising for Budweiser in each: In the northern part of the state, it used a cowboy image, while in the southern part a Hispanic identity was stressed (Hawkins, Best & Coney, 2001). As other examples of environmental effects, hot donuts and coffee sell better in cold climates than in warm climates, and iced tea is on the menu year-round in the South but may be a summer-only item in New England and Canada (around the world, partly because of the huge populations in Asia, tea is the most consumed beverage).

If consumers do not like or need a product, they will not buy it or will try it once and reject it. It is estimated that 90 percent of new products fail. When this book went to press, it was yet to be seen if Old Spice High Endurance body wash would succeed or fail even though it had a better chance than average since it is a product extension and the product launch was backed by an estimated $15 million to $20 million in marketing support (Neff, 2002).

Failed products are an enormous expense to companies, so every effort is made for them to succeed, but even very successful companies make mistakes. Examples of failed products by established businesses include Harley-Davidson wine coolers, Levi Strauss tailored suits for men, Life Savers gum, and Country Time apple cider (Hawkins, Best & Coney, 2001). Each of these major product launches was an expensive loss. A new movie, for example, could cost millions of dollars to distribute, advertise, and merchandise. Why products fail is a subject of consumer research. One finding is that products are not pretested to the degree they should be; another is that manufacturers do not take into account regional differences or shifts in consumer preferences. Whatever the reason, a company has to be well capitalized to withstand the wins and the losses. In 1968 when Estée Lauder launched Clinique, a new line of skin care products and makeup, it lost money for several years before it became one of the market leaders that it is today (Koehn, 2001).

Sometimes companies reinvent themselves. The restaurant chain Boston Chicken changed its name to Boston Market and became a wholly owned subsidiary of McDonald's Corporation, operating more than 650 company-owned restaurants in 28 states. It also sells a line of frozen entrees and jarred gravies and broths, manufactured by H. J. Heinz Co. The newer restaurants or remodeled restaurants have booths and softer colors and lighting. Alyson Kim, communications manager for the Golden, Colorado–based chain, said, "Customers said they loved our home style food, but the dining experience didn't match it. . . . They wanted a warm, homey atmosphere" (Sams, 2001).

Tea is the most consumed beverage in the world.

About 90 percent of new products fail.

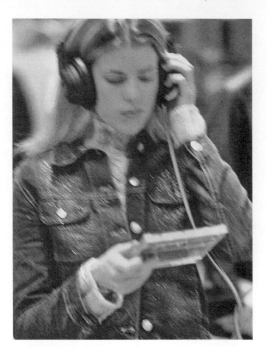

Technology has allowed for a
proliferation of ways to listen to music.
(Martin Riedl, Photo Researchers, Inc.)

To conclude, the term *environment* is used in the model in its broadest sense, referring to the environment in which consumer–market interactions take place. Environment encompasses the natural environment and human-made environment and includes the following: cultural, educational, technological, physical, social, political, economic, situational, chemical, and biological influences. It is a view of the world in which we live and everything contained in it, including measures of time and place and all other external conditions affecting our lives.

Since environment is such a large concept, some theorists have divided it into two parts—microenvironment (meaning close to the home and the individual) and macroenvironment (everything that surrounds the microenvironment). It used to be that the microenvironment was the context in which most production and consumption took place, but with the proliferation of world trade, radio, television, and the Internet, consumption even at the individual level is very much influenced by both parts of the environment. For example, you may buy a Hostess cupcake at the local convenience store, but the ingredients (wheat, sugar, and flavoring) and the packaging may have come from anywhere in the world (ingredients are listed on the package label, but not sources).

## Technology

**Technology** is the application of scientific knowledge to useful purposes. In the model, technology is considered part of the environment. One example of consumer technology is the introduction of machine-read bar codes on products that are used in grocery and discount stores; another is the introduction of automatic teller machines (ATMs) used in financial transactions.

A paradox exists in technology—a specific technology may save time but may also require time or take time away from using other technologies or being involved in other behaviors. Paradoxes increase conflict in decision making; in other words, they make life more complicated. Here is an example of a technology-based decision situation: Should you use a dishwasher to wash six dinner plates, glasses, and forks, or should you wash them by hand? What is the best use of your time? The trade-off between using a computer and cell phone versus other means of communication or information search is another example. Research shows that time spent on the Internet and e-mailing (in the evening especially) is taking away from time spent watching television. As another example, American cell phone users ages 25 to 34 are more than four times as likely to use their mobile phones as their primary phones than are those over age 35 (Gardyn, 2001a).

If a product becomes outdated soon after purchase or before it is worn out, a consumer experiences **technological obsolescence**. Products such as computers and video cameras lose value because they so rapidly become technologically out-of-date. No one can anticipate every new product or upgrade, so the best someone can do is to keep abreast of changes and/or buy equipment or devices that can be upgraded with add-ons. As seen in the previous case of the nutrition professor, another option is to hold on to old technologies and let the new technologies pass you by—new is not always better or necessary.

## Media

**Media** is a term for a means of mass communication, such as newspapers, magazines, television, or the Internet, that revolutionizes human life in developed and developing countries. To get an idea of the impact of different media, it is useful to look at earlier technologies such as radio and television.

In 1947 there were 200,000 TV sets in the United States; by 1949 there were 2 million.

Radio exposed listeners to mass advertising, and television let them see it as well as hear it. The heyday of radio was from the 1920s through the 1940s, but by the late 1940s it had a competitor in the form of television. By 1947, 200,000 U.S. homes had black-and-white television sets; in 1948, there were enough viewers to make a national audience for the *Ed Sullivan Show* and *Milton Berle Show;* and by 1949, there were 2 million television sets in the United States, showing a very rapid adoption of this form of technology (Goldsmith, 2002). Although available in the 1950s, color television did not become common until the 1960s. In the late 1970s a device for projecting television onto a large screen became widely available, and this technological advance was followed by videocassette recorders (VCRs). Presently, over 95 percent of U.S. homes have televisions.

The first radio shows often had only one sponsor, and the show was often named after that sponsor. Several early television shows also were named after their sponsor (such as the 1940s and 1950s *The Texaco Star Theater*), but eventually television shows were so expensive to produce that they had multiple sponsors, which is the format we are familiar with today. If we watch a televised football game, we expect to see many different advertisements (razor blades, cars, snack foods) rather than advertisements from a single company. The reason this is important to point out is that with only one sponsor the advertiser had quite a bit of control over program content as well as the show's stars and guests, but

Computers have opened up the world to commerce and communication. (Photo Researchers, Inc.)

multiple sponsors provide more freedom of expression and a greater differentiation between the ads and the show.

Today, radio and television can provide background noise, and the listener or viewer may only really notice it when a special song or an interesting show or announcement comes on. In this way, radio and television are different from print forms such as books and magazines that require more focus and usually require the reader to sit down. An exception to this is audiobooks, which people listen to while driving.

With the advent of the remote control, people gained even more options because television and radio advertising could be muted and channels could be changed more quickly without getting up. Similarly, Internet users can mute certain messages and ignore others or create musical tapes of only the songs they want to hear. The Internet is different from radio and television in that it is still undergoing vast experimentation. Advertisements can be changed every few seconds, whereas a television advertisement may take months to create and may be repeated for months. Can you think of any advertisements that you are tired of or that you find irritating?

**Growth of the Internet.**    The development of the Internet is just part of the development and proliferation of computers. The Internet can be seen as part of media. No one planned the Internet, and it still has few controls. Since no one company or government controls it, it is difficult to set policies or to screen what information is put on the World Wide Web, the information retrieval system.

**Internet Interactivity.**    The Internet is useful in providing services and information, a communication exchange between customers and providers. It is interactive to a greater degree than most other forms of media. Billboards, magazines, radio, and television are mostly one-way exchanges from the publication, station, or program to the reader, listener, or viewer. An exception to this is that magazines have added the interactive feature of providing aftershave, perfume, or grapefruit samples (to increase grapefruit juice sales) that can be smelled; the addition of smell (usually in scratch and sniff samples) was a true innovation in print medium. Children's books have had similar interactive experiences for years (think of *Pat the Bunny*) before the magazines found a way to inexpensively mass-market an interactive experience. Other examples of more interactivity are radio or television call-in or fax-in shows or shows with e-mail messages being sent and responded to on the air.

An interesting mix of Internet and television can be experienced in shows such as *Oprah* that continue after the show goes off the air via oprah.com, where viewers can go online and follow the discussion that takes place after the show is over. But most typical television shows are one-way exchanges, and you usually can't call in during the program and talk with the actors and suggest plot changes, although some shows broadcast live and some stage plays have experimented with this format. In these plays, the characters are presented to the audience at the beginning of the show, and the audience votes as to who shall play what roles. Internet games allow for these types of interactivity, so the general trend is for most forms of media to move to more interactivity. Higher involvement usually leads to more sales, so sponsors and advertisers want to encourage as much interactivity as possible. This is why they hand out perfume samples in department stores—if you try it, you are more likely to buy it.

Besides being a source for information and communication, the Internet is a useful tool for buying and selling financial services, software, tickets, collectibles, and computers. According to Connie Johnson, an analyst at Forrester Research (Forrester Research Online, forresterresearch.com), the following are the top online retail stores:

eBay: 10 percent of all retail sales

Amazon: 5 percent of all retail sales

Wal-Mart, Target, J.C. Penney, and most other major retailers: 1 percent each of all retail sales

**Internet Buying Trend: Upward.**   For example, Internet sales go up each holiday season. Consumers report that the main reason they shop online is that it is easier. In 2006, 6 percent of November/December holiday purchases were made online; this jumped to 10 percent in 2007. The number of Americans shopping online was about 65 million in 2001 compared with 49 million in 2000, according to Jupiter Media Matrix Inc., a market research firm. The total number of dollars was over $34 billion in 2001 compared with $24 billion the previous year (Landau, 2001). Since the numbers are constantly changing, memorizing the numbers is less important than witnessing the phenomenon—the upward trend in buying online.

**Media and the Model.**   The purpose of media is to inform consumers about goods, services, news, and events and to provide purchase opportunities. Figure 3.4 illustrates the information transaction process. Negotiations may include price, conditions, model, quantity, and delivery. The transaction is completed when both sides are satisfied and a purchase is made with an order, money, or a contract.

---

The process can be diagrammed as:

information sent ⟶ information received ⟶ transaction negotiated ⟶ transaction completed

---

**Figure 3.4**   Information Transaction Process.

There are two major media categories:

1. *Print.* Print media include magazines, direct mail, newspapers, mass transit (that is, signs in subways, buses), billboards, and dealer promotions such as free calendars.
2. *Broadcast.* Broadcast media encompass the Internet, cable, television, and radio.

The newspaper is the most basic of print media. Many national and international newspapers and magazines have regional editions so that advertising and stories can be targeted to certain markets. Newspapers or magazines may have special teen editions, such as *Teen People* or *The Wall Street Journal Classroom Edition.* In economically developed nations, the most pervasive forms of media are radio and television. In some countries, radio and television are state run and accept no advertising but may run government-sponsored spots announcing programs or events.

## CONSUMER POWER MODEL

So far, the chapter has built a model of consumer economics that focuses on the transactions that take place between consumers and markets, given other conditions and players. Consumer economics can be described as a collection of activities, situations, or exchanges among several parties that take place within an environment. It assumes that individuals seek to maximize their satisfaction from the decisions they make and that they seek fair trade and justice in the marketplace. It also assumes that, for the most part, consumers will gather information (a type of resource) before making decisions. The **Consumer Power Model** shows how all the pieces fit together. A circle is used instead of a square because the process involves a fluid motion, a feeling of constant motion rather than an angular or linear beginning-and-end exchange. Relationships are indicated by the arrows that serve as channels or mediums for exchange.

Theory, research, and common sense suggest that consumers select what messages to receive and process.

The model incorporates theories from many areas. For example, consumers are bombarded daily with hundreds of messages. They cannot evaluate every message, so they selectively choose the ones to listen to or read about. Much of this selection is automatic as new perceptions are made to fit comfortably with existing knowledge or cognition (Foxall, Goldsmith & Brown, 1998).

## CONSUMERS

Although the model shows consumers as only one player in a series of players, they are the most important part. The consumer drives the system, or to use the wording from Chapter 1, the consumer is king. This is true, for the most part, but even kings don't always get their way. For example, a consumer may go to a store to buy a certain product and then learn that the store no longer carries that product nor does anyone else in town; in this situation, the consumer feels more like a pawn than a king. Given that it is an imperfect and complicated world and that the

## CONSUMER POWER MODEL

**Power of Social and Consumer Networks**

The Consumer Power Model illustrates in a diagram all the main players in the consumer domain. A growing field of study explores the impact of social and consumer networks. The focus in consumer economics is on how information influences the decision process, examples of which are online social or consumer networks such as eBay, MySpace, and Facebook. These have opened up consumers to more opportunities to be influenced and to influence than ever before through discussion boards and reviewer comments as well as private conversations. Do you have online friends (ones you have never met in person)? Have you asked them about a product or service? If so, give an example. Do you think this widening of information is a good or a bad thing? What are the implications for the marketplace and for the way people search for information and ultimately purchase? What types of advertising have you noticed on network sites? Should there be limits on advertising? As a final note of clarification, social and consumer networks always involve person-to-person interactions—it is not about one-way interaction, such as a person noticing an advertisement in a magazine or on a billboard. Data indicate that these networks are increasing in size and power, with the most recent figures showing that the average person in the United States spends two and a half hours a day online.

demands of the mass market have to be considered in the mix of goods that are offered, the individual consumer is shown as a player in an interactive environment rather than being placed at the center of the process.

In the model, consumers are placed directly across from markets because as the first illustration in this chapter shows, the primary relationship or exchange is between consumers and markets. Consumers participate when they spend, save, barter, trade, and invest; they are involved in public policy when they vote or act to influence public policy in some other way; and consumers use and dispose of goods, gather information and opinions, and react to media and other forms of communication. By behaviors such as voting and gathering information, consumers hope to improve their **quality of life**, which is their perception of and satisfaction with their lives. During lean economic times, Americans focus more energy and money on keeping their homes and families secure (Gardyn, 2001b).

**Consumption** refers to the using up of goods. Consumers have a **level of living**, which is the way they are actually living, but they aspire to a **standard of living**, which is a certain quality of life. The difference is between how one actually lives and how one would like to live—actual versus ideal. This is connected to one's self-concept, and self-concept is important in all cultures. There is the private self (how someone sees himself or herself) and the public or social self (how others see that person). A strong disconnect between the private and public self can cause confusion. Public figures, such as actors and politicians and their families, are confronted with this all the time, but the majority of people experience it to a lesser degree. **Lifestyle** is how one lives and includes patterns of time use and living space; it also involves what one thinks is important and how one spends money. Have you ever heard the expressions "contented housewife," "business tycoons," or "social climber"? These are phrases that describe lifestyles. "Researchers have speculated that our happiness is influenced not by what our absolute level of wealth and income is but rather by how our financial situation compares with that of friends and colleagues" (Clements, 2006).

Much of consumption behavior is directed toward improving one's lifestyle, which is linked to self-concept. For example, someone may say, "Next year I'm moving into a better apartment" or "Someday when I'm working full-time, I'm going to buy Ralph Lauren clothes." When millions of consumers make similar choices, this is called **mass consumption**, which has a tremendous impact on the general economy.

## Consumer Decisions and Experiences

The relationships within the Consumer Power Model are based on the fact that consumers hope to increase their well-being through consumption (something they have to do to exist) and that there are various indicators of well-being. One of these is environmental well-being. In consumer economics, we are concerned about the quality of the natural environment and the sustaining of it for future generations. Environmental well-being refers to a concern for society's role in the earth's diminishing resources, which affect the overall well-being of individuals, families, and communities.

Our consumer life is also influenced by our experiences. Think of all the experiences you have had visiting restaurants, hotels, theme parks, bakeries, national parks, grocery stores, schools, and friends' homes. As a specific example, what have you observed about birthday cakes? At birthday parties, were the cakes store-bought or homemade? Which do you think is better? What is the tradition in your family? Do you blow out candles on the cake? Do you sing "Happy Birthday to You"? Or do you completely ignore birthdays? Many of our traditions and consumer experiences have their roots in our early life.

Based on our childhood experiences, we make assumptions about how other people live. College is often a real awakening to the differences in how people live—what they eat, what they consider cleanliness, what their sleeping habits are, and so forth. For instance, one male student reported that his roommate bought a sack of potatoes and existed almost exclusively on baked potatoes. He said, "It freaked me out." Another male student reported that he ate cereal and bananas 90 percent of the time because it was an easy meal to fix. An 18-year-old boy coming home from two college friends' apartment told his mother that all they had in the refrigerator was water and milk. He said, "Doesn't everyone at least have orange juice?" His assumption was based on his home refrigerator, which was well stocked.

Another area to look at is the type of experiences that businesses provide (for example, Carnival describes itself as "The Fun Ship" or "The Most Popular Cruise Line in the World"). Many companies are not only selling products or services but also selling experiences or entertainment. Consider theme restaurants such as Rainforest Cafe, Hard Rock Cafe, and McDonald's. Note the use of the word *café*. What images does that word conjure up? Compare those with images for the words *tearoom, roadhouse,* and *diner.* When stores decorate for the holidays, they are also providing a fun shopping experience and are getting customers in a shopping mood. Spas try to get their guests to relax through massages, creams, lotions, aromatherapy, and soft lighting and music.

How do experiences relate to public policy and consumer organizations (the remaining parts of the model)? Nearly everyone has experiences with rules and regulations, with government, with elections and politics. Out of these experiences come policy opinions about who should be U.S. president, what is the right and wrong way to do things, and what would be best for the greater good. Consumer organizations provide consumer education and advocate for change on behalf of consumers. In terms of public policy, most legislation is based on previous laws and regulations, but as the economy and consumers change, legislation and the causes that consumer organizations take up need to be updated.

## Consumer Well-Being

**Definition.**    As mentioned earlier, a key aspect of consumers' lives is their well-being. Well-being is made up of a variety of factors, including material, social, and spiritual dimensions (Chambers, 1999). In the Introduction we said that consumers are acquisitive, which means they want more things, ideas, and information, and they have to replace things that are worn out or used up. People consume or spend money to take care of basic needs such as food, clothing, and shelter and to take care of future needs through investing in retirement plans, by making estate plans or setting up trusts, and by buying insurance. Through such activities, they are providing for their own well-being and that of their family members.

Consumer well-being is an umbrella term encompassing the following five areas:

1. *Economics or financial well-being.* The degree to which individuals and families have economic adequacy and security reflects their financial well-being. It is the desire for or extent of protection against the economic risks people face in their daily lives (such as loss of employment, illness, bankruptcy, bank failures, poverty, destitution in old age). Economic well-being also includes an overriding sense of economic equity or economic justice and involves the concept of fairness, not only within one's own community and nation but also internationally. The setting of a minimum wage is an example of economic equity or justice; another is child labor laws.

2. *Physical well-being.* Personal safety and goods and services that provide one's physical needs impact physical well-being. Threats to physical well-being include, but are not limited to, unsafe or irresponsible personal conduct as well as unsafe or irresponsible actions of others; illness, disease, and malnutrition; lack of or inappropriate exercise; dangerous and hazardous products; adulterated foods; incompetent and irresponsible service delivery; and environmental degradation (McGregor & Goldsmith, 1998).

3. *Social well-being.* The social space of the family or the group provides for a sense of emotional well-being, caring, and working together. "The crux of social well-being is interpersonal relationships and the dynamics of familial interaction to fulfill six basic functions: procreation, socialization, economic consumption and production, social control, physical care and maintenance, and love and emotional support" (McGregor & Goldsmith, 1998, p. 123). **Socialization** refers to the process of learning to interact with others, forming cooperative relationships, participating in society, and learning the ways of daily life. Parents and family are very important in the socialization of children. As social beings, we have a need to

belong, which leads us to join groups, form families and circles of friends, buy certain brands, or wear certain types of clothes or adornments.

4. *Psychological or emotional well-being.* The mental state of an individual within the family or other groups reflects the degree of that person's psychological or emotional well-being. The emphasis in social well-being is on the group, whereas the emphasis in psychological or emotional well-being is on the individual. Emotions are strong feelings that affect one's behavior and attitudes, general temperament, and demeanor. Consumer socialization is part of emotional well-being as well as part of social well-being. Consumer and family life specialists are interested in how well people are socialized to be consumers—how they process information and make decisions, how they react to advertising, and how they seek remedy or recourse when a consumer difficulty arises. When something goes wrong, do they fly into a rage, or do they follow the steps necessary to get a refund? Psychological or emotional well-being is associated with thought and reflection, a sense of self, and self-preservation.

5. *Environmental well-being, political well-being, and spiritual well-being.* The first two realms (environmental and political) were introduced in previous sections; spiritual well-being "captures a layer of well-being, a sense of insight, and ethereal, intangible evolution not readily imparted by either social or psychological well-being as conventionally defined" (McGregor & Goldsmith, 1998, p. 124). A very broad definition of spiritual well-being encompasses the joy and sense of completeness associated with a connectedness with the world as well as peace, hope, and faith gained from insights and moments of growth and enlightenment. It is not simply about organized religion, although many people experience spiritual well-being in this way. Nearly 90 percent of Americans claim a religious affiliation (Kosmin & Lachman, 1993).

If we consider the concepts of trade-offs and opportunity costs introduced in Chapter 1, we can see that individuals may choose to spend their time in different ways, such as in church or as a choir member, in a mall, at a movie, or in the woods communing with nature; they may give to charities or choose a more consumption-oriented activity such as buying another $10 T-shirt. This is not to imply that spiritual well-being and consumption activities are always opposites. Someone may find looking at a beautiful Christmas display at a store to be a joyful, spirit-lifting experience, while another may get a lift from singing the school song or the national anthem at a football game. Spiritual well-being may include beauty or aesthetics, music, patriotism, appreciation of nature, and all sorts of other qualities or reactions, individually defined and appreciated.

**Measurement.**    Discussing well-being or the qualities that make up human welfare is one thing, but measuring it is another since so much depends on people's attitudes and responses. The United Nations Development Programme's **Human Development Index (HDI)** puts a number on (quantifies) well-being by combining several measures of human well-being. The HDI is broader than consumer well-being per se but touches on it. The HDI compares the progress of nations by using the same measures of quality of life across the globe, and it uses an adjusted measure of real per capita gross domestic product (GDP) as one component of an index that includes school enrollment ratios, adult literacy, and life expectancy.

## Consumer Price Index and Consumer Expenditure Survey

The Consumer Price Index (CPI) provides a statistical measure of the nation's economic well-being.

Consumer durables last three or more years.

Connected to the discussion of well-being are other factors that consumer psychologists and economists look at as indicators of the strength of the economy. Consumers need confidence to buy high-ticket items such as consumer durables and homes, and because of the lasting nature of these products, consumers look for quality. **Consumer durables** are products bought by consumers that are expected to last three years or more and include automobiles, appliances, and furniture. Companies such as Maytag and Electrolux that make these types of products are considered consumer durables manufacturers. In contrast, consumer nondurables manufacturers make more immediately consumable items such as food or medicines.

The **Consumer Price Index (CPI)** measures prices each month of a fixed list ("market basket") of 400 goods and services (durables and nondurables) bought by a typical consumer. The market basket on which the CPI is based includes shelter, transportation, tires, utilities, entertainment, health care, clothing, and services. The CPI is published by the Bureau of Labor Statistics (BLS) in the Department of Labor and is based on a score of 100 in 1982. The following information is taken from the BLS Web site (www.bls.gov):

> The process by which the Bureau measures price changes to consumers each month requires the efforts of hundreds of BLS employees and the patient cooperation of thousands of individuals in households and retail outlets throughout the country. The cycle begins during the first week of the month when BLS data collectors (called economic assistants) gather price information from selected department stores, supermarkets, service stations, doctors' offices, rental units, etc. For the entire month, about 80,000 prices are recorded in 87 urban areas. During these monthly visits, the economic assistant collects price data on a specific good or service. If available, the economic assistant records the price. If not available or if there are changes in the quality of an item, the assistant selects a new item or records the quality change. This sampling technique is used because it would be impossible to gather the price of every good or service bought each month in the United States. The entire process takes about 20 days for the reviewing, analyzing, and publishing of the data.

The CPI is widely held as a cost-of-living benchmark that affects adjustments in Social Security payments and other pay schedules and tax brackets. The thinking is that if it costs more to live, then the government should respond by increasing payments, for example, to the elderly. The president, Congress, and the Federal Reserve Board note trends in the CPI and use them for formulating policy. The CPI is used to adjust wages and payments, such as to keep pensions, rents, royalties, alimony, and child support payments in line with changing prices. At the headquarters in Washington, D.C., and in regional offices, specialists check the incoming data for accuracy and consistency, and computer programs calculate the weighted changes in prices. By the time the CPI is reported on the television news, the process has started all over again, and the next month's data are being gathered.

The CPI is actually a series of interrelated samples. These include the **Consumer Expenditure Survey** collected from a national sample of over 30,000 families that provides detailed information on spending habits. According to the BLS Web site (www.bls.gov), "This enables BLS to construct the CPI market basket of goods and services to assign each item in the market basket a weight or importance based on total family expenditures. Another national sample of about 16,800 families serves as the basis for a Point-of-Purchase survey that identifies the places where households purchase various types of goods and services." The BLS uses census data to determine which urban areas are selected for price checks. BLS job openings, including positions for economic assistants, economists, and administrators as well as internships and summer employment, are listed on its Web site, www.bls.gov.

## Consumer Confidence

Another measure of consumer well-being is consumer confidence. **Consumer confidence** is measured and nationally reported by two organizations:

1. Conference Board (a New York–based organization)
2. Survey Research Center (at the University of Michigan in Ann Arbor)

The Conference Board specializes in consumers' plans to buy cars, houses, and appliances and to participate in activities such as traveling. The Board does this by sampling the attitudes of 5,000 consumers with multiple-choice questions and analyzing the results. According to the Conference Board, consumer confidence was declining in October 2001, dropping to 85.5 from 114 in August—the steepest fall since October 1990. According to the survey, fewer than 1 in 5 consumers rated business conditions as favorable, down from more than 1 in 4 the previous month (Paul, 2001).

During the same time period, the Survey Research Center found a similar drop in consumer confidence. The Survey Research Center measures a sample of 500 consumers' expectations about the economy and their own personal finances and tries to determine attitudes about consumption and changes and trends therein. Both these organizations seek to determine how consumers view the health and direction of the economy and how they are responding to it, so the measures are very much about perception; for example, optimism about the economy makes the consumer feel more confident about spending and more willing to acquire debt (credit cards and loans). Consumer confidence levels are reported in the news and used by government and business so they can make better policies and plans of action.

To provide more updated figures, the Conference Board reported a high of 110.2 in March 2002 compared with the previous six months (Eisinger, 2002). Likewise, the U.S. Commerce Department reported that in March 2002, personal income, savings, and spending rose. The general thinking is that if consumer confidence appears to wobble, consumer spending will fall; if confidence is up, then spending goes up. Investors watching these figures react in terms of what companies they will invest in and what stocks they may sell. A large reported gain or dive will impact investor reaction more strongly than a slight rise or dip.

When consumer confidence is down, how might consumers and businesses respond? This is the type of question investors would ask themselves. During times of uncertainty, familiar brands such as Procter & Gamble's Ivory Soap provide reassurance. An article published after the economic downturn caused by the September 11, 2001, tragedies put it this way:

> Marketing messages should be straightforward, honest and down-to-earth. This is
> not the time for messages about luxury or indulgence, which can come across as

*During uncertain times, consumers are drawn to familiar brands.*

insensitive and irrelevant. Neither is it the moment for cheap solutions and quick fixes. People want to feel confident that what they're getting is the "right" product, something they can count on, something that will deliver on its promise. (Paul, 2001, p. 23)

In contrast, how should businesses respond when consumer confidence is up? In 2002, consumers were marching to a different drummer than they were in 2001. Luxury became attractive again, and consumers were buying upscale appliances, cars, electronics, travel, and homes. "Millions of Americans who once made up the vast middle of the nation's $7 trillion consumer market migrated upscale toward premium and luxury goods" (White & Leung, 2002, p. A1). Helmut Panke, an executive at German automaker BMW, stated that "today's auto market is increasingly shaped like an hourglass," meaning there are many high-end and low-end purchases and not many in the middle. When interviewed, many consumers say for a few thousand more they would rather have a premium car than an ordinary car (White & Leung, 2002). For another example of this trend toward high-end consumption, consider the following:

> Who would pay $2,200 for a washer-dryer set with stainless-steel drums, 12 different wash cycles, rounded styling, baby-blue trim and room for 22 bath towels? Whirlpool Corp. thought it knew the answer when it introduced its Duet line last year: a niche of affluent laundry-doers willing to pay about three times the price of the company's midrange machines. Whirlpool expected the Duet would make up only 5% of its North American washer and dryer sales. Instead, in its first six months on the market, the Duet line is on track to double Whirlpool's projections. (White & Leung, 2002, p. A1)

As an example of a typical family who bought a Duet, the Boyd family with four children, who live in suburban Chicago (the mother is a substitute teacher, and the father is a field manager in a construction company), said they bought the Duet because "we find in the long run it's more cost-effective to have high-quality products," because they perform better and last longer (White & Leung, 2002, p. A8). As this book went to press, consumer confidence was shaken and gasoline and food prices were rising rapidly.

## BUSINESSES AND MARKETS

*The goal of business is to maximize profits.*

As the preceding quotes illustrate, today's businesses need to be sensitive to consumers' perceptions and actions at any given point in time. The goal of businesses is to maximize profits, and they pursue this goal while cooperating with government, listening to consumers, and watching sales figures closely.

Businesses cannot get so stuck on current conditions and issues that they lose the bigger picture—planning for the future. For example, Albertson's, a food and drug retailer based in Boise, Idaho, updates its grocery stores' appearance every 10 years. When the retailer plans its redesigns, it has to imagine what future grocery stores will look like: Will there be the usual 21-aisle store with freezer cases? Will people still push carts up and down the aisles, or will groceries be ready for customers at the door of the store or delivered directly to their homes? Experiments with both are taking place, but it is not yet clear what the future holds except that history shows that we can expect changes, not just in store design and layout but also in products. The typical 1950s North American grocery shopper would not have known what zucchini squash or sushi or pesto was.

In ancient times, markets were actual places where consumers and producers came together to trade.

Going back several steps into our past, in ancient times most markets were physical locations where consumers and producers came together to make trades, and they set prices by arguing over what would be the right price. In many countries today, including the United States, Northern Ireland, France, Finland, Costa Rica, Trinidad and Tobago, and Mexico, farmer's markets coexist with modern grocery stores. Some markets allow or encourage bargaining, but most have set prices. Other examples are the New York Stock Exchange and tobacco and cattle markets where buyers and sellers come together to buy and trade. The Internet and other modern telecommunications services and devices have made being in the same location less important than it was in the past.

## Typical Company Functions

In the old markets, selection was limited by season and availability. With modern transportation and growing methods, seasons are less important in terms of what is offered. A concern for the future is deciding how much choice consumers can handle. For example, most large grocery stores and Home Depot–like supply stores offer 40,000–50,000 products, and some of the superstores go as high as 100,000. How much more selection do consumers need? Is there an optimum number of products or size of store?

Average-size grocery stores have 40,000–50,000 products.

To handle these sorts of questions, a typical company that markets to consumers has various divisions, including top management, marketing, finance, human relations, research and development (R&D), purchasing, manufacturing, and accounting as well as product design and in-house public/media or consumer relations and investor relations. Here are their functions:

- Top management sets the goals, missions, objectives, and strategies and often answers to a board of directors.
- Marketing promotes, sells, conducts survey research (or conducts focus groups to gather consumer opinions), and distributes goods. (The next section provides additional information on marketing and consumer psychology.)
- Finance balances current funds and procures more funds. A chief financial officer (CFO) may visit banks to get loans for factory expansion or may give presentations to mutual fund managers in hopes that they will buy substantial numbers of shares in the company.
- Human relations departments take care of employee needs such as hiring and benefits.
- R&D focuses on developing new and exciting, yet safe and effective, products. An example is Post-it notes used in offices that were developed in the R&D department of 3M (Minnesota Mining and Manufacturing).
- Purchasing gets supplies and materials, such as raw materials, at a good price.
- Manufacturing oversees the production of a quality product and handles decisions on quantity.

- Accounting watches the books and checks costs and expenditures. Sometimes a head tax accountant moves into the finance department, and there may be other movements within companies among different groups noted in this section.
- Product design may be part of marketing or R&D or may be free-standing.
- For major public relations campaigns, including advertising, large companies usually hire outside firms, but they may have an in-house division to handle day-to-day media inquiries such as a newspaper columnist asking for a media kit with press releases and photos or slides.
- Consumer relations departments in large companies that sell consumer goods or services have to handle consumer inquiries and complaints and report consumer trends to higher management. Thousands of companies, from airlines to toy and food manufacturers, have such departments. Choose nearly any packaged food product off a shelf at the grocery store or at home, and on the label there will be the toll-free number and address of the consumer relations department. For example, on the back of a Progresso French Onion soup can it says: "Questions or Comments? Call 1-800-200-9377 weekdays 8–6 CT. Information from label on end of can will be helpful. Consumer Relations, P.O. Box 555, Vineland, NJ 98360."
- An investor relations department is usually found if the company has stock that is publicly traded (in other words, the stock is available in a stock exchange). An investor owning stock or thinking of buying stock can contact the investor relations department to find out more about how the company is doing and in particular inquire about the influences on stock. Figure 3.5 shows all these components.

**Figure 3.5** Components of typical consumer product companies. Note that in a smaller company, many of these functions may be performed by one employee or outsourced to another company. For example, accounting, public relations, or marketing may be done by an outside firm, and manufacturing may take place in another country. In a large multinational company, top management and many other functions may be spread throughout the world.

## Marketing and Consumer Psychology

Throughout the book we're talking about consumer psychology, but let's pause for a few minutes here to revisit the topic, given changes in the global economy and technology. Reaching consumers is easier in some ways than before with the Internet, but in some ways it is harder because there is less personal interaction. People report spending more time at home than in the last few decades, so reaching them has to be done differently. The likelihood they will come into a physical store is diminishing; consequently, retailers are shifting gears. Let's take the example of cereal maker Kellogg Company:

> To help sell Frosted Flakes, Kellogg offers a Web site where kids can send emails or make trading cards featuring Tony the Tiger. On another site, the company offers behind-the-scenes clips of "American Idol" stars on tour. Beyond the Internet, Kellogg has tried word-of-mouth campaigns, where the company taps loyal customers to tell others about new products, and in-store marketing. (Steinberg, 2006, p. R1)

Note the use of the practice of making original cards and the words "word-of-mouth campaign." In the quote, Kellogg has made loyal customers part of a campaign. This is part of the **consumer-in-control movement**, meaning consumers want more say about products and services. They want to design ads, products, and packaging; send e-mails; and let others know about their input, their insider's knowledge of what is available or what is to come. **Customization**, specifically designed products such as shirts with logos or custom-made drapes and coordinating pillows in another fabric, is a result. Companies can encourage this (as seen in the Frosted Flakes example). Children especially enjoy creating original designs. We can also envision the consumer-in-control movement as part of the Consumer Power Model as more and more consumers have control of the marketplace.

Related to this is the concept known as **market mavens**, opinion-leading consumers who are very involved in the marketplace. They are enthusiastic, energetic buyers and shoppers who talk about what is for sale. They may not be wealthy, but they are more involved than usual consumers. For example, they may enjoy knowing that a new grocery store or Starbucks is opening in their community, and they will visit early and tell others about their experience. Was the food good or bad? How was the service? What was the atmosphere like? Consumer researchers are intensely interested in the way these people disseminate information through frequent interactions with other consumers. Market mavens have a willingness to try new things. They are unique and willing to seek social status through consumption (Goldsmith, Clark & Goldsmith, 2006). Are you a market maven? If so, in what category are you most interested and knowledgeable? Examples would be fashion, cars, shoes, travel, movies, sporting events, hunting, fishing, technology, organic food or gardening, store openings, and restaurants. Do you know any market mavens? "As consumers increasingly use the marketplace to express their self-concepts and to show their status, they come more and more to *seek out unique products*. This behavior can be studied via uniqueness theory, which proposes that individuals vary in the extent to which they wish to be different" (Goldsmith, Clark & Goldsmith, 2007). Uniqueness theory will be further discussed in Chapter 7.

## Entrepreneurship

Businesses don't exist without leadership. Unique industry-changing leaders are called **entrepreneurs**. Entrepreneurs pursue new business opportunities relentlessly without becoming deterred by the limited resources they initially controlled (Stevenson, 1985). Few are called and even fewer succeed. Entrepreneurs such as Bill Gates and Michael Dell are rare, and timing is everything. When they started their computer businesses, only a small number of people owned a personal computer, let alone one that was made to order or designed for individual purposes. Many students enrolled in consumer economics classes are interested in some day forming their own business, selling a product, or offering a service. The opportunities are limitless.

The concept of entrepreneurship is not new. In 1759 in the midst of the Industrial Revolution, Josiah Wedgwood founded his own pottery workshop with the idea of making affordable but well-designed dinnerware for the masses. He noticed that with the improved economy, more people wanted consumer goods, including china, linens, clocks, tea, tobacco, chocolate, window curtains, books, and cutlery (Koehn, 2001). China was fast replacing the wood and pewter dishes that Britons had used for centuries. Within a few years the Wedgwood brand was well established and continues to be a leading brand of quality china, housewares, and giftware today. Besides developing new methods of production, Wedgwood was a master at organizing, and he established good public relations by making special sets for royalty that were displayed at special events and exhibitions.

How did Josiah Wedgwood become a successful entrepreneur? What qualities or characteristics does one need to succeed in today's competitive business environment? In her study of six entrepreneurs documented in *Brand New: How Entrepreneurs Earned Consumers' Trust from Wedgwood to Dell* (2001), Nancy Koehn writes that each entrepreneur "intended to make the most of the moment to construct a name, brand and organization that would endure, and each succeeded brilliantly, in substantial measure" (p. 320). She lists the following five reasons (Koehn, 2001, p. 320):

- They had deep knowledge and personal experience of their product or service.
- They learned quickly from their mistakes and made rapid adjustments.
- They created meaningful brands that distinguished their offerings and responded to consumers' changing priorities.
- They initiated a process of reciprocal learning with their customers that resulted from ongoing two-way communication with them.
- They created a range of organizational capabilities that delivered on the promises of their respective brands.

Their efforts have important consequences for businesses and for consumers. Without their energy, foresight, and sheer drive, products may have remained unchanged and needs gone unfulfilled for many years.

## Women as Entrepreneurs

In the United States, most of the entrepreneurs have been men, but that trend is changing. As recently as 1973, women owned just 4.6 percent of the U.S.

businesses, but by 2000, that percentage rose to nearly 50 percent. Between 1987 and 2000, the number of women-owned businesses doubled from 4.5 million to 9.1 million in the United States (Allon, 2001). These businesses employ more people than the Fortune 500 companies; in other words, businesses run by women are flourishing, and part of the reason may be that women understand the needs of female consumers better. This is important because (as mentioned in the Introduction) women account for 80 percent of consumer spending in this country. Go to the grocery store and who do you see? Go to the mall and who is shopping? Go to a Gap Kids store and who is there? One might assume most shoppers in Home Depot or Lowe's are male, but recent surveys show that about one-half the shoppers in Home Depot and Lowe's are women.

## SUMMARY

Adam Smith, founder of modern economics, said that "to be human is to exchange freely." This chapter explored theories that explain or provide insight into consumer behavior and presented a multifaceted Consumer Power Model. It was also stated that consumer researchers follow the scientific method, a five-step method of analyzing issues: They recognize problems, make assumptions, develop models, make predictions, and check, control, or test facts or outcomes. Researchers are concerned about scarcity and how consumers make transactions in a complex market involving public policy and other input. Theory and the exchange process were also defined, and examples of various theories that explain consumer behavior and the variances thereof were given.

Consumer decisions take place in an overall environment, including technology, and are based on experiences. When someone makes a new purchase, it is influenced by past purchase experiences as well as media and other factors. Public policy serves as a mediator or rule maker, and consumer organizations seek to protect, educate, and advocate for consumers. Consumer well-being was introduced as an umbrella term referring to many aspects of life, including economic, psychological or emotional, environmental, political, and spiritual well-being. Measures of consumer well-being include the Human Development Index (HDI), the Consumer Price Index (CPI), and consumer confidence. In business, unique leaders called entrepreneurs emerge who substantially change industries; examples include Michael Dell, Bill Gates, and Josiah Wedgwood.

*Consumer economists are curious about why people behave as they do.*

The Summary section in Chapter 2 challenged you to think like a consumer economist. Here is another facet this chapter has added: Consumer economists are curious—they want to know why people spend money and behave as they do. This is what consumer economics is all about. Given scarce resources, why do people buy what they do? Who are market mavens? What is the impact of the consumer-in-control movement? How much are consumers influenced by family and friends? How can they become better consumers? How can consumer well-being be improved as part of the greater picture of improving human welfare? Theories help us predict future behavior, and models help us visualize the interplay among various groups and influences, including individuals' real and perceived self-concepts.

## KEY POINTS

1. The objective of consumer economics is to understand the real world and how it operates, how exchanges or transactions take place, and what factors (such as environment and experiences) influence them.

2. Theories and models are abstractions of the real world; they are used to organize and visualize thoughts and connections or relationships.

3. The theory of reasoned action is a consumer behavior theory that states that one's own attitudes and those of others matter when it comes to a purchase decision.

4. Prospect theory argues that people make consumption decisions even when they are uncertain. They are not always rational, self-interested, and calculating. Kahneman and Tversky, authors of prospect theory, won the Nobel Prize in recognition for their work integrating psychology with economics and in so doing laying the groundwork for behavioral economics and behavioral finance.

5. Innovation theory is a consumer behavior theory that indicates that innovations diffuse through social systems and that some people are innovators (early buyers or adopters), whereas others are late adopters or laggards. Research indicates that the differences vary by product category.

6. The Consumer Power Model was introduced. In this model the key players are consumers, business, public policy, media, and consumer organizations interacting within an environmental and experiential context. The growing field of study of social and consumer networks is a result of more people going online to discuss everything (including goods and services).

7. Consumer economics is an applied social science. Perceived wants are unlimited and resources to satisfy them are limited, so consumers make decisions about how to allocate scarce resources.

8. Level of living (actual) is different from standard of living (ideal). Much of consumption behavior is directed at raising one's level of living. The Consumer Price Index (CPI), calculated monthly by the Bureau of Labor Statistics (BLS), is a leading measure of inflation and buying power.

9. Consumer confidence is tracked each month by two main organizations: the Conference Board of New York and the University of Michigan's Survey Research Center. Consumer confidence fluctuates, and to be successful, markets have to be responsive to changes in how consumers feel and act.

10. There are several components of consumer well-being. The United Nations has attempted to compare human welfare conditions (including PPP$, which refers to purchasing power of goods in relation to income) across many nations using the Human Development Index (HDI).

11. In ancient times, markets were physical locations where buyers and producers haggled over prices. Some markets of this type (such as farmer's markets) still exist, but for the most part, consumers and producers do not physically meet—there are many middlemen in between. Modern businesses have numerous divisions that have specialized functions.

## KEY TERMS

| | | |
|---|---|---|
| acquisitiveness | diminishing marginal | public policy |
| behavioral economics | utility | quality of life |
| behavioral finance | endowment effect | rationality |
| brand extension | entrepreneurs | reactance |
| consumer confidence | exchange process | regional subcultures |
| consumer durables | Human Development | socialization |
| Consumer Expenditure | Index (HDI) | standard of living |
| Survey | innovators | targeted advertising |
| consumer-in-control | level of living | technological |
| movement | lifestyle | obsolescence |
| consumer–market | market mavens | technology |
| conflict | mass consumption | theory |
| Consumer Power Model | media | theory of mental |
| Consumer Price Index | message framing | accounting |
| (CPI) | models | theory of reasoned action |
| consumption | neuroeconomics | transaction |
| customization | prospect theory | utility |

## DISCUSSION QUESTIONS

1. What do you think of prospect theory? Give an example of when you were uncertain but went ahead and made a consumption decision anyway. Describe the outcome (positive or negative) of the decision.
2. Give an example of a product that you were an innovator in (an early buyer) and an example of a product that you have been a laggard or in the late majority in buying. Describe why you were an early buyer in one case but a late buyer (or nonbuyer) in another.
3. According to Pamela Paul, "Americans want good quality and good value from good companies doing good things." Do you agree or disagree? Explain your answer. How does a recession affect consumers' behavior, especially their need for value?
4. Give an example of how companies can go along with and even encourage the consumer-in-control movement.

## E-RESOURCES

**Better Business Bureau**    *www.bbb.org*
Business-supported organization concerned with advertising and product- and service-quality issues

**Center for Neuroeconomic Research at the University of South Carolina**
*www.neuroeconomicresearch.org/*
University source of research on choice and decision making.

**Center for Media Education**   *www.cme.org/cme*
Organization concerned with children and advertising

**Federal Trade Commission**   *www.ftc.gov*
Government source for advertising and labeling

## REFERENCES

Ajzen, I., and M. Fishbein. (1980). *Understanding attitudes and predicting social behavior.* Englewood Cliffs, NJ: Prentice Hall.

Allon, J. (2001). *Turn your passion into profits.* New York: Hearst Books.

Chambers, R. (1999). *Whose reality counts?* London: Intermediate Technology Place.

Clements, J. (August 16, 2006). Money and happiness: Here's why you won't laugh all the way to the bank. *Wall Street Journal,* p. D1.

Eisinger, J. (April 30, 2002). Ahead of the tape: Today's market forecast. *Wall Street Journal,* p. C1.

Foxall, G., R. Goldsmith, and S. Brown. (1998). *Consumer psychology for marketing,* 2nd ed. London: Thomson Business Press.

Gardyn, R. (December 2001a). Phone home. *American Demographics,* 18–19.

Gardyn, R. (December 2001b). The home front. *American Demographics,* 34–36.

Glimcher, P. (2003). *Decisions, uncertainty, and the brain: The science of neuroeconomics.* Cambridge, MA: MIT Press.

Goldsmith, E. (2002). Colgate Palmolive. In *Encyclopedia of advertising,* ed. John McDonough and Karen Egolf. New York: Fitzroy Dearborn.

Goldsmith, R., R. Clark, and E. Goldsmith. (2006). Extending the psychological profile of market mavenism. *Journal of Consumer Behaviour,* 5, 411–19.

Goldsmith, R., R. Clark, and E. Goldsmith. (2007). The desire for unique consumer products and innovativeness. Proceedings of the Academy of Marketing Science Annual Meeting, Coral Gables, FL.

Hawkins, D., R. Best, and K. Coney. (2001). *Consumer behavior,* 8th ed. Boston: Irwin McGraw-Hill.

Kahneman, D., and A. Tversky. (1979). Prospect theory: An analysis of decision under risk. *Econometrica, 47,* 263–92.

Koehn, N. F. (2001). *Brand new: How entrepreneurs earned consumers' trust from Wedgwood to Dell.* Boston: Harvard Business School Press.

Kosmin, B., and S. Lachman. (1993). *One nation under God.* New York: Harmony Books.

Landau, M. D. (October 22, 2001). Holiday hints. *Wall Street Journal,* p. R4.

Lowenstein, R. (January 2003). A salute to the irrational. *SmartMoney,* 42–43.

McGregor, S., and E. Goldsmith. (Summer 1998). Expanding our understanding of quality of life, standard of living, and well-being. *Journal of Family and Consumer Sciences,* 122.

Neff, J. (December 30, 2002). P&G shores up Old Spice with body-wash extension. *Advertising Age,* 8.

Paul, P. (December 2001). Pulse: A critical look at American views. *American Demographics,* 22–23.

Robinson-Brown, L. (December 19, 2002). Daniel Kahneman wins Nobel Prize. *News from Princeton University,* Office of Communication.

Rogers, E. M. (1995). *Diffusion of innovation,* 4th ed. New York: Free Press.

Sams, R. (December 13, 2001). Third Boston Market on the way. *Tallahassee Democrat,* p. E1.

Schor, J. B. (1998). *The overspent American*. New York: Harper Perennial.

Sheppard, B., J. Hartwick, and P. Warshaw. (December 1988). The theory of reasoned action. *Journal of Consumer Research,* 324–43.

Steinberg, B. (July 10, 2006). The marketing maze. *Wall Street Journal,* p. R1.

Stevenson, H. (1985). A perspective on entrepreneurship. In *New Business Ventures and the Entrepreneur*, ed. H. H. Stevenson, Michael J. Roberts, and H. Irving Grousbeck. Homewood, IL: Richard D. Irwin, pp. 2–15. See also William A. Sahlman, Howard H. Stevenson, Michael J. Roberts, and Amar Bhide, eds. (1995). *The entrepreneurial venture*. Boston: Harvard Business School Press.

Well, M. (December 10, 2001). Less than perfect pitch. *Forbes,* 122–24.

White, G., and S. Leung. (March 29, 2002). Middle market shrinks as Americans migrate toward the high end. *Wall Street Journal,* pp. A1, A8.

# PART 2

# Consumer Protection

## CHAPTER 4
### Consumer Responsibilities, Redress, and Law

## CHAPTER 5
### Government Protection, Nongovernmental Pro-Consumer Groups, and the Media

# Consumer Responsibilities, Redress, and Law

*Why should there not be patient confidence in the ultimate justice of the people? Is there any better or equal hope in the world?*
—Abraham Lincoln

## Learning Objectives

1. Define fraud, and explain why identity theft is the number one fraud.
2. Explain consumer responsibilities.
3. Discuss consumer service problems.
4. Explain the steps to follow before buying.
5. List the steps to follow to complain effectively.
6. Discuss how small claims courts work.

---

### Youthquake

They're called the Millennials, ages 18 to 29, and they are fed up with the economy and politics as usual. They want change and they are not afraid to complain about issues or under-performing products. According to the Census, nearly 43 million people fall in this age category or about 20% of registered voters. "I think about the costs of having a family, and it's going to be so difficult," says Edward Summers, 25, assistant to the president of Marist College in Poughkeepsie, N.Y.[1]

This generation has watched corporate scandals and their parents lose jobs. They are keenly aware of how difficult it is to stay secure. "They saw their parents get burned," says Claudia Tattanelli, CEO of Universum Communications, a research firm that specializes in Millennial workplace issues. "They watched 401(k)s that never got paid, parents losing health plans."[2]

"As the government and employers shift more responsibility for benefits like health care and retirement onto the shoulders of individuals, many Millennials see themselves as unwitting victims. Although that trend has been building for decades, this may be the first generation to fully feel the great shift of risk in their bones." 'This is a group of people who understand what it means to have no safety net,'" says Elizabeth Warren, a Harvard University School of Law professor.[3]  Wielding their power for change is the hallmark of this generation.

---

[1]Michelle Conlin, "Youthquake," *Businessweek*, January 21, 2008, pp. 32–36.
[2]Ibid.
[3]Ibid.

# INTRODUCTION

If it sounds too good to be true, it probably isn't.

Chapter 2 documented the growth of the consumer movement, and the emphasis was on consumer protection legislation that was passed to remedy or curtail abuses in the marketplace. This chapter discusses the other side of the coin: the responsibilities that consumers have in the marketplace. For example, it is their responsibility to spend and invest wisely and to consider the environmental implications of their consumption not only for themselves but also for future generations. They also have a responsibility to carefully examine products and avoid falling victim to fraudulent schemes. This is easier said than done because consumers are exposed daily to get-rich-quick schemes, miracle diets, and mechanical belts that shake off fat. Who buys these things, such as pharmaceutical-grade, industrial-strength olive oil pills to build muscles, especially when they know that they don't work? Nearly all of us are vulnerable to sales pitches, some more sophisticated than others, that promise improved appearance or increased bank accounts. If we can take a pill rather than exercise to build muscles, that is pretty attractive, and maybe it is true that people in the Mediterranean have the secrets to a long life and now their secret (olive oil) can be ours! Hope often triumphs over experience or common sense. This is not to say that hope is bad—a certain amount is important, as the opening quote by Abraham Lincoln illustrates—but hope has to be tempered with a degree of skepticism. One of the sayings in consumerism is that if it sounds too good to be true, it probably isn't. What complicates the process of sorting the legitimate from the fraudulent is that often fraudulent products are sold by legitimate stores such as drugstores or pharmacies and that the fraudulent products may have some basis in fact, although greatly exaggerated. In this chapter, the steps to follow if a person becomes a victim of any kind of fraud or buys a faulty product will be covered as well as ways to reduce the chances of it happening. This chapter also discusses the more general topic of customer service and the steps to follow in the complaint process regardless of the nature of the complaint. When all else fails, the last resource is the court system.

# TOP CONSUMER FRAUD COMPLAINTS

Poor-quality products need to be differentiated from fraud. **Fraud** is an intentional deception perpetrated to deprive another person of his or her assets. Consumers deal with many frauds, but the fraud area rising the fastest is identity theft, which is the leading consumer fraud complaint, far exceeding gripes about Internet auctions and services. Of the 380,000 complaints compiled by the Federal Trade Commission (FTC), 43 percent were about identity theft, up from 42 percent the previous year (Ho, 2002). The hijacking of a person's identity information, such as Social Security numbers or credit card numbers, to steal money or commit fraud is one of the fastest-growing crimes in the United States. The number of people victimized is estimated at 700,000 a year and increasing. Most victims do not know how or when their identity was stolen. It costs the average victim more than $1,000 in expenses to cope with the damage to accounts and reputation. "This is a crime that is almost solely on the shoulders of the victim to resolve," said Beth Givens, director of the Privacy Rights Clearinghouse. "They're beleaguered, they're tired, they're angry, and it takes them a good deal of time to recover." In some cases, recovery of one's financial identity, getting bank accounts and financial records straightened out, can take as many as five years. The most likely use of another person's identity is for credit card fraud, but other major categories include fraudulent bank and cell phone accounts. The top consumer fraud complaints compiled by the FTC (percent of complaints) are as follows:

Identity theft (43 percent)

Internet auctions (13 percent)

Internet services and computers (6 percent)

Advance fee loans and credit protection (5 percent)

Shop-at-home and catalog sales (5 percent)

Foreign money offers (4 percent)

Prizes, sweepstakes, and lotteries (4 percent)

Business opportunities and work-at-home plans (3 percent)

Telephone services (2 percent)

Health care (2 percent)

Magazines and buyers clubs (2 percent)

*Identity theft tops the list of frauds.*

With shopping over the Internet making up the second- and third-highest categories of complaints, not only are there real risks but also perceived risks of privacy and security involved in online shopping. Until these real and perceived risks are resolved, Internet shopping will be used hesitantly by some consumers. Obviously, new methods of protecting one's identity are also needed, and credit card and bank companies are devising better methods of protecting their clients' identities.

---

 **CONSUMER POWER MODEL**

**Protecting ATM Cards**

Have you ever complained about a product or a service? Have you ever been ripped off? Has your identity been stolen? Have you lost credit cards or had them stolen? Identity theft tops the list of the most common fraud or complaint according to the FTC. If you follow the news, most likely you have seen reports of someone stealing someone's ATM (automated teller machine) card and going to the machine to remove cash. The problem from the criminal's point of view is the need for the password code or number to get into the account. Have you noticed how banks are trying to track and limit this sort of crime? Cameras on the machines taking photos of those using cards is one way, and more sophisticated means of identifying cardholders are in development.

## CONSUMER RESPONSIBILITIES

Consuming takes time, but complaining takes even more time.

As discussed in Chapter 2, President John F. Kennedy gave a list of consumer rights to Congress. Unfortunately, a formal list of consumer responsibilities does not exist, but over the years it has become evident that consumers can look out for themselves in several ways:

1. *Be honest with merchants and manufacturers.* For example, consumers should be honest when filling out job applications, mortgage applications, warranty information, sales of used cars, returns of purchased clothing, and so forth.

2. *Be realistic in possible outcomes and expectations.* Cologne or toothpaste will not dramatically change one's life regardless of what advertisements say.

3. *Avoid nuisance or frivolous lawsuits.* File complaints or lawsuits only when necessary. Complaining takes time, and Americans have less time today than they had 30 years ago (DeGraff, Wann & Naylor, 2001; Schor, 1992). What is frivolous is in the eye of the beholder (or more specifically, in the mind and body of the sufferer and the lawyers who represent them). A widely publicized case dealt with overweight people suing fast-food restaurants, charging that their weight gain was a result of eating the fattening food served. See the case box about a particular lawsuit that was thrown out. Many people reading or hearing about this case thought it was frivolous since the decision to eat in these restaurants and what to choose to eat were a personal responsibility rather than a corporate responsibility. In another case it was the restaurant chain's responsibility when it said it fried potatoes in vegetable oil when it turned out there was beef lard in the frying oil, which was not in keeping with the diet requirements of vegetarians. The restaurant had to own up to the practice and change its oil immediately to vegetable oil only. A very controversial legal area is asbestos (used in fireproofing, electrical insulation, and building materials) and its harmful effects. In 2002, 90,000 new asbestos claims were filed—triple the number filed in the two previous years. Asbestos lawsuits (usually about lung abnormalities) now run more than $200 billion, and the amounts awarded are increasing. The claimants (some of whom are sick, while others are neither sick nor impaired) and the tort lawyers are pitted against an ever-widening group of defendants (corporations, builders, and owners of buildings, including schools and businesses). When it is not a legitimate claim (no illness or injury), it can be considered a fraud in and of itself. In response, some law professors are calling for Congress to limit fraudulent claims, putting a cap on how much can be awarded (Brickman, 2003). Others would say this is not a good idea and would like to continue the present system wherein the courts decide on the amount of awards.

4. *Keep within the law when protesting or boycotting products or companies.* Safety is paramount, and there are many ways to effect change. Consumers have the right to be heard and informed but not to injure themselves or others in the process as they exercise the First Amendment right to free speech.

5. *Report faulty goods.* Producers want to know when a product doesn't work because they want satisfied customers. And there is a larger aspect to this; for example, if cars or tires are faulty, reporting problems may save lives.

6. *Report crime and wrongdoing.* It is important to report crime and wrongdoing to the proper authorities or government agencies as a way to protect oneself and others.

In 2003, a federal judge dismissed a class action lawsuit filed on behalf of New York children that claimed McDonald's food caused them to suffer health problems, including diabetes, high blood pressure, and obesity. "One necessary element of any potentially viable claim must be that McDonald's products involve a danger that is not within the common knowledge of consumers. Plaintiffs have failed to allege with any specificity that such a danger exists," stated U.S. District Court Judge Robert Sweet in a 65-page ruling.

*Source:* McDonald's, January 23, 2003, p. E1.

7. *Take responsibility for ill-conceived actions.* If the garment label says to dry-clean only and the consumer washes a sweater in hot water in a machine, the maker cannot be held responsible. Likewise, if signs at a national park tell tourists not to go into certain areas because of lava or geysers, tourists should obey or possibly suffer negative consequences.

8. *Recognize that consumption has an effect on the environment and future generations.* According to Juliet Schor (1998), "A necessary first step toward becoming an educated consumer is to learn about the impact your consumption has on the environment. Only then can you make responsible and informed choices" (p. 156).

9. *Get referrals before signing a contract.* Check out a contractor's recommendations with local consumer protection agencies and the Better Business Bureau (BBB). The more substantial the investment or cost is, the more time should be spent checking out the business.

10. *Get estimates from at least two companies.* In such areas as making home improvements, removing trees, or moving furniture, a consumer should get more than one estimate and should have a firm understanding of all charges, licenses, and potential liabilities.

11. *Lessen the chances of identity theft.* By not leaving credit card receipts where they can be found and not writing Social Security numbers or home phone numbers on checks, consumers can lessen their chance of becoming victims of identity theft. Also be careful about what gets put in a mailbox that anyone can get into (for example, checks can be stolen out of letters).

12. *Deal with reputable, socially responsible companies.* More and more consumers expect companies to take **social responsibility**, a broad-based term referring to caring about the community and the environment (Mohr, Webb & Harris, 2001).

What do all these consumer responsibilities add up to? They are really about using common sense; being aware of surroundings, business dealings, and potential victimization; and thinking about others as well as oneself.

## CUSTOMER SERVICE

The consumer experience includes not only what someone actually buys but also what happens during the entire shopping experience. Potential areas of complaint include problems with delivery and in-store customer service.

Clueless clerks roaming the aisles at Home Depot. Flight attendants in need of "anger management" counseling. Telemarketers calling promptly at dinner time to sell long-

**Table 4.1**   Corporate Reputation Rankings—Top 10 Companies, 2006

1. Microsoft
2. Johnson & Johnson
3. 3M Company
4. Google
5. The Coca-Cola Corporation
6. General Mills
7. United Parcel Service (UPS)
8. Sony Corporation
9. Toyota Motor Corporation
10. The Procter & Gamble Corporation

*Source*: Adapted from Harris Interactive, 2006 Reputation Quotient Survey.

distance service. These are just some of the consumer gripes that proved costly to companies in the third annual corporate reputation survey conducted by Harris Interactive Inc., an online market-research firm. (Alsop, 2002, p. B1)

Consumer gripes are costly to companies because dissatisfied shoppers can take their business elsewhere. "When a company provides great service, its reputation benefits from a stronger emotional connection with its customers, as well as from increased confidence that it will stand behind its products," said Joy Sever, a senior vice president at Harris. The survey of 21,630 revealed that emotional appeal is the primary driving force behind corporate reputation. Johnson & Johnson has held the number one spot in the Harris polls for several years, cultivating a powerful image as "the caring company" and being associated with products for cuddly babies. Quality products and services play into how people responded in the survey. One of the respondents, a 42-year-old grocery clerk, said he got a burgerless Big Mac from the drive-through window at his local McDonald's.

Besides Johnson & Johnson, companies that score high in exemplary service are United Parcel Service, Microsoft, and Toyota. Since this survey is taken every year, the names on this list change, but the point is that customer service is part of the consumer experience and that an individual's buying experience as well as the company's reputation plays into customer satisfaction and expectations. The customer with the burgerless Big Mac says now he double-checks his bag before driving off.

Smart companies react to these types of polls. When Home Depot dropped to nineteenth place in 2001 from fourth in 2000, it made some changes, such as having salespeople unpack merchandise at night so they could help customers during prime shopping hours and putting more employees on the floor on weekends. Table 4.1 lists the top companies and their reputation rankings.

## STEPS TO FOLLOW BEFORE BUYING

In subsequent chapters, there will be information on specific products and services such as buying houses or leasing cars. But here are some general buying guidelines that consumers can follow to avoid potential problems:

1. Decide in advance what is needed and affordable.
2. Research the product or service by using resources (including the Internet) to comparison-shop or to find out rules and regulations governing goods or businesses. Also find out if a company has a complaint record through the BBB or local consumer affairs offices.
3. Ask friends, family, and coworkers for recommendations about companies and products.
4. Shop around in person, comparing quality and prices.
5. Read and understand contracts and warranties, labels and tags; check licenses. For example, if you are hiring a contractor to repair your roof, you would make sure first that he or she is properly licensed to do roof repairs.
6. Find out about refund and return policies.
7. Get things such as receipts in writing, and keep credit card receipts.
8. Be wary of buying from door-to-door salespeople, at the side of the road, out of a motel room, or from any other type of business without a permanent address. Be wary about buying over the Internet from unknown companies or private individuals. For example, a woman felt bad for two men who stopped at her front door in early December selling steaks door to door from the back of their truck. One of the guys kept saying, "Help me out; I need to make this sale for my bonus." . . . "It was before Christmas," the woman said. "I did feel sorry for him" (Rosica, 2003, p. 1B). She wrote a check for $329.50, and the men filled her freezer with steaks. She paid for 120 steaks and got 117, but the main problem was the quality: Some of the cuts could not be identified, and much of the meat was hamburger patties and thin steaks rather than the steaks the men had shown her initially. When she complained, she could not get her money back. Their out-of-town company would not return phone calls. The men did not have a license to sell in her county, and she discovered from the BBB in the company's city that it had an "unsatisfactory record . . . of no response to customer complaints brought to [the Bureau's] attention," according to the bureau's Web site. As of the writing of this book, she was continuing her efforts, but it was not promising because she waited a month before filing a complaint and the state has a three-day cooling-off rule in which contracts can be cancelled from day of purchase. "The best thing to tell people is 'caveat emptor'—Latin for 'let the buyer beware,'" said Dr. James Varley, a food safety specialist with the state's Department of Agriculture and Consumer Services. When it comes to buying meat, he said, "You'd do better at a name-brand grocery store" (Rosica, 2003, p. B1). In those stores, they pay attention to cleanliness and keep the meat properly frozen. The woman said she learned a valuable lesson. "Shut the door," she said. "There's no point in trying to be polite to these people. And they are very aggressive" (Rosica, 2003, p. B1).
9. Do not sign contracts until all blanks or changes are properly initialed or filled in.
10. Know which areas are complaint prone. Besides the identity theft already discussed, there are a number of other prominent fraud areas. Every year the Consumer Federation of America and the National Association of Consumer Agency Administrators survey government consumer protection offices to find out what transactions generate the most complaints. Following are those most commonly on the list:

| | |
|---|---|
| Sales of new and used cars | Credit and lending |
| Auto repairs | Mail-order and online orders |
| Home improvements | Auto leasing |
| Retail sales | |

## STEPS TO FOLLOW AFTER BUYING

### Consumer Redress

Before using any new product, read the instructions or labels, send in the warranty card, and keep all contracts, sales receipts, cancelled checks, owner's manuals, and warranty documents. If even after acting in this responsible manner, there are problems with a product or service, consumers have the **right to redress**, which is the right to seek and obtain satisfaction for damages incurred through the use of a product or service. Consumer redress means that consumers could not foresee or protect themselves against faulty goods or services and after the fact can seek satisfaction for damages incurred. **Consumer satisfaction** is a construct or idea that performance perceptions and service expectations are met or, better yet, exceeded. For example, the brakes on a car should work because if they don't, the driver will not be safe.

Consumer redress is complicated because it is not always easy to determine fault and to decide who to approach for redress. Accidents may be the fault of many parties or manufacturers as well as the consumer himself or herself. The *Statistical Abstract of the United States* (2000, p. 146) lists the number of home accidents per year connected to consumer products:

1. Stairs, ramps, landings, and floors        1,971,685 accidents
2. Bicycles                                                         566,085 accidents
3. Knives                                                           444,604 accidents
4. Beds                                                              400,648 accidents[*]
5. Doors                                                            318,185 accidents

Routine activities such as those listed below also cause injuries:

| Activity | Injuries per Year |
|---|---|
| Barbecuing | 15,952 |
| Bicycling | 534,883 |
| Bowling | 17,916 |
| Driving | 2,788,000 |

### Ways to Complain Effectively

Before hiring an attorney or running off to court, there are less time-consuming and less expensive remedies to try first. Figure 4.1 gives the order of steps to follow when seeking redress. The following sections provide descriptions of each step.

---

[*]You may wonder how one get hurts by a bed; a common accident is a child getting hurt from falling off or jumping off of a top bunk bed.

**Figure 4.1**   Steps to Follow When Bringing a Complaint.

**Local Business.**   The first step is to go back to the local business where you bought the product, such as returning rotten strawberries immediately to the store where you bought them and getting a refund. Before taking this step, make sure you have the paperwork. In the case of the strawberries, you may need the grocery receipt with the item circled as well as the strawberries. Go to the customer service desk at the grocery store, and get a cash refund. Many stores won't even require the receipt because the bar code on the plastic container has the needed price information. A more expensive product, such as a car, is going to require more documentation, but still the first step is to contact the business that sold you the item or performed the service. Most consumer complaints can be resolved at this level.

**Business Headquarters.**   If the local business does not provide satisfaction, you may want to go directly to the headquarters of the company. For example, if the local department store does not provide satisfaction, you would contact its headquarters by letter, e-mail, or phone. To find a company's headquarters and customer service office, go to www.companyname.com, click on customer service or a similar name, and report the problem. Calmly and concisely, describe the problem and what action you would like, such as a refund, repair, or replacement. If you file a complaint by e-mail, there will be a form to fill out or a place to type in your complaint, which is easier than composing a formal letter and mailing it. The advantages of e-mail are that it is free and it is 24/7, whereas many complaint toll-free phone lines are only open during normal business hours Monday through Friday. Increasingly, more people are using e-mail for complaint filing with companies or with government agencies. Companies and the government prefer e-mail to phone calls because they can manage the round-the-clock e-mails better than they can a surge of phone calls flooding the phone lines at certain times of the day.

**Manufacturer.**   Another option is to go to the manufacturer or maker of the product. Let's say an electric ceiling fan does not work right and the local home supply store where it was purchased will not give a refund. Besides going to the supply store's headquarters, an option would be to contact the manufacturer directly. There may be a regional office (rather than a central office) that will help you. Most products have a consumer complaint toll-free phone line or mailing or e-mail address on the box or product label. Telephone companies and libraries can also be of assistance, or check www.standardandpoors.com for a registry of manufacturers. At a manufacturer's main offices (just as at retail stores' headquarters), there is a chain of command going from the entry-level person you first contact all the way up to the president or chief executive officer (CEO) of the company. A last resort would be to send a letter and copy of receipts and/or correspondence to the president or CEO.

Over 1,500 companies have consumer affairs departments in the United States and Canada.

Consumer affairs or consumer relations departments are set up within companies because they want to hear from consumers. Many of the companies are members of the **Society of Consumer Affairs Professionals (SOCAP)**. Founded in 1973, this international professional organization offers training, conferences, and publications to encourage and maintain the integrity of businesses in their transactions with consumers and in communications with government regulatory groups and agencies. Their goal is to improve the marketplace for consumers through addressing their concerns with corporate structures. Examples of companies belonging to SOCAP are AAMCO Transmissions Inc., American Express Company, Ball Park Brands, and Campbell Soup Company.

As consumers go through these levels of complaint steps, they should keep a record of efforts to resolve the problem. When you e-mail or write to the company, describe the problem, what you have done so far to resolve it, and what solution you want. See Figure 4.2 for a sample complaint letter. When you call, keep notes of whom you spoke with and what they said and include dates.

An additional piece of advice is to allow time for the person you contacted to resolve your problem. Save copies of all letters to and from the company. Don't give up if you are not satisfied—there are self-regulatory organizations (discussed next), trade associations, media programs, national consumer organizations, and legal assistance programs listed throughout this book that may be able to assist you.

**Self-Regulatory Organizations.**    There are also self-regulatory groups, which may be known as **third-party complaint-handling sources** or dispute resolution groups. The reason they are called "third party" is because consumers are involving someone besides themselves and the source of the complaint. A third party is necessary when the local business, company headquarters, or manufacturer refuses to do anything to resolve the complaint. Nonprofit third-party organizations exist to resolve disputes between buyers and sellers, and probably the best known of these is the Better Business Bureau (BBB), which has offices in about 150 larger communities in the United States; there are also 16 BBBs in Canada. BBBs are nonprofit organizations supported mostly by local business members. In other words, citizens are not paying taxes to run these organizations; rather, legitimate businesses in the community pay to run them because they know it is good business to support an ethical marketplace and to provide an alternative place for dispute resolution. To find the office in your area, go to www.bbb.org. Generally, BBBs offer the following:

- Consumer education materials that encourage honest advertising and selling practices and expose scams
- Answers to consumer questions
- Information about a business including whether there are unanswered or unsettled complaints or other marketplace problems
- Help in resolving buyer/seller complaints against a business, including mediation and arbitration services
- Information about charities and other organizations that seek public donations

BBBs are nonprofit organizations supported by the business community that offer many services to consumers, including dispute resolution.

What won't BBBs do? They do not judge or rate individual products or brands, handle employer–employee wage disputes, or give legal advice. Local BBBs are listed in the telephone directory, and some offer 900 telephone numbers that charge a certain rate for the first four minutes, with a lesser charge per minute afterward up to a maximum charge. Some numbers require a major credit card.

## Sample Complaint Letter

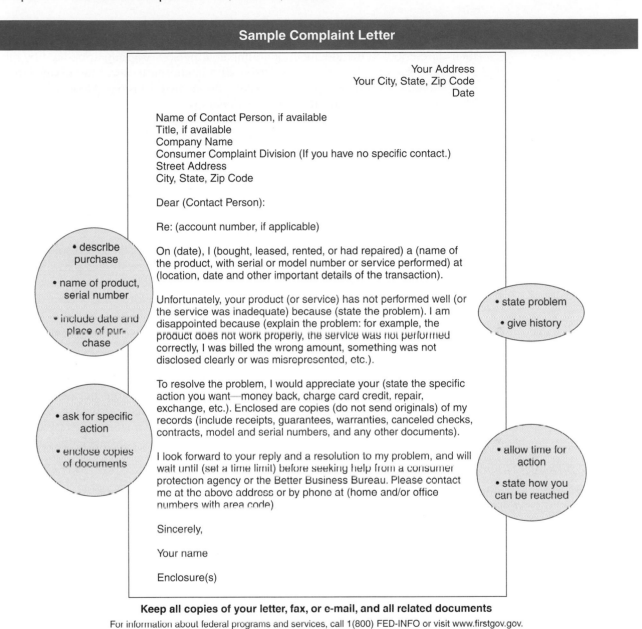

Your Address
Your City, State, Zip Code
Date

Name of Contact Person, if available
Title, if available
Company Name
Consumer Complaint Division (If you have no specific contact.)
Street Address
City, State, Zip Code

Dear (Contact Person):

Re: (account number, if applicable)

On (date), I (bought, leased, rented, or had repaired) a (name of the product, with serial or model number or service performed) at (location, date and other important details of the transaction).

Unfortunately, your product (or service) has not performed well (or the service was inadequate) because (state the problem). I am disappointed because (explain the problem: for example, the product does not work properly, the service was not performed correctly, I was billed the wrong amount, something was not disclosed clearly or was misrepresented, etc.).

To resolve the problem, I would appreciate your (state the specific action you want—money back, charge card credit, repair, exchange, etc.). Enclosed are copies (do not send originals) of my records (include receipts, guarantees, warranties, canceled checks, contracts, model and serial numbers, and any other documents).

I look forward to your reply and a resolution to my problem, and will wait until (set a time limit) before seeking help from a consumer protection agency or the Better Business Bureau. Please contact me at the above address or by phone at (home and/or office numbers with area code)

Sincerely,

Your name

Enclosure(s)

- describe purchase
- name of product, serial number
- include date and place of purchase

- state problem
- give history

- ask for specific action
- enclose copies of documents

- allow time for action
- state how you can be reached

**Keep all copies of your letter, fax, or e-mail, and all related documents**

For information about federal programs and services, call 1(800) FED-INFO or visit www.firstgov.gov.

**Figure 4.2**  Sample Complaint Letter.

How do BBBs work exactly? The consumer calls or contacts the BBB; the BBB takes the consumer's records and takes up the complaint with the company involved. The company gets to tell its side of the transaction and what went wrong. A company could choose not to respond, but this is unusual because the company does not want to have a bad record at the BBB and does not want to have its membership dropped in the BBB. If the call or letter from the BBB does not settle things, then the BBB may offer mediation or arbitration. **Mediation** is the process of negotiating to resolve differences, an attempt to bring about a peaceful settlement or compromise between the consumer and the business through the intervention of a third party. **Arbitration** is the process by which the parties in the dispute submit their differences to the judgment of an impartial person or group appointed by mutual consent. The arbitrator is the person who is chosen to settle the disagreement and who has the ability or power to make authoritative decisions. Mediation and arbitration are less expensive than legal proceedings.

So far the emphasis in this section has been on BBBs, but there are other organizations that offer mediation and arbitration. Another option is the consumer action panels (CAPs) that many industries have set up to handle industry-wide complaints. Below are examples of CAPs dealing with automobile disputes:

- Automotive Consumer Action Program (AUTOCAP) at www.nada.org
- Center for Auto Safety (CAS) at www.autosafety.org
- BBB Auto Line at www.bbb.org

Besides mediation and arbitration, there is a third type of dispute resolution program: conciliation. **Conciliation** means to reconcile, to make things pleasant again. A consumer offered a choice of these programs should select the one most appropriate by asking for a copy of the rules of the program before filing a case. The ruling may be binding for both the business and the consumer, or it may apply only to the business. If the program turns down your request, then the next step may be contacting consumer protection agencies or going to court.

**Government Consumer Protection Agencies.**    Some people may go to agencies before they go to third-party dispute resolution organizations because they feel it is more appropriate or there is no BBB in their community, as well as for a variety of other reasons. Which level of government is appropriate varies by location and type of complaint. State, county, and city government consumer protection offices do the following:

- Mediate complaints
- Conduct investigations
- Prosecute offenders of consumer laws
- License and regulate a variety of professions and professionals (this varies by state but may include banking, insurance, securities, utilities, doctors, lawyers, home improvement contractors, auto repair companies, debt collection agencies, and child day care businesses)
- Promote strong consumer protection legislation
- Provide educational materials
- Advocate in the consumer interest

County and city offices may have a better idea of local problems and businesses, so that would be the place to start; however, if a consumer does not have access to these, the next step is to contact the state consumer office or agency. Often these offices are part of the attorney general's office (this is the case in Arizona, Arkansas, Michigan, and Minnesota, to name a few) or the governor's office, but other times they are either separate entities or part of another unit. See Box 4.1 for a list of the primary state offices dealing with consumer complaints. For example, Florida has a Division of Consumer Services within the Department of Agriculture and Consumer Services, and they handle over 25,000 consumer complaints a month, so that gives you an idea of volume. Florida also has other

**BOX 4.1     State Consumer Protection Offices**

Please note: Although states may have many consumer protection offices, the primary one for each state and the District of Columbia is listed here as a beginning contact. Also be aware that phone numbers and e-mail addresses change; the ones listed were accurate when this book went to press. In addition, most of the toll-free numbers only work within the state, so persons outside the state may have to pay for a phone call.

**Alabama**

Consumer Affairs Division

Office of the Attorney General

800-393-5658

www.ago.state.al.us/consumer.cfm

**Alaska**

Consumer Protection

Office of the Attorney General

907-269-5100

www.law.state.ak.us/department/civil/
consumer/cpindex.html

**Arizona**

Public Advocacy Division

Office of the Attorney General

800-352-8431

www.azag.gov/consumer

**Arkansas**

Consumer Protection Division

Office of the Attorney General

800-482-8982

www.ag.state.ar.us/consumers_protection
.html

**California**

Department of Consumer Affairs

800-952-5210

www.dca.ca.gov

**Colorado**

Consumer Protection Division

Attorney General's Office

800-222-444 or 303-886-5189

www.ago.state.co.us/consumer_protection.cf
m?MenuPage=True

**Connecticut**

Department of Consumer Protection

800-842-2649 or 860-808-5400

www.ct.gov/AG/site/default.asp

**Delaware**

Fraud and Consumer Protection Division

Office of the Attorney General

800-220-5424

http://attorneygeneral.delaware.gov/
consumers/protection/safeguarding.html

**District of Columbia**

Office of the Attorney General

202-727–3400

http://occ.de.gov/occ/site/default.asp?

**Florida**

Consumer Services

Department of Agriculture and Consumer
Services

800-435-7352

www.800helpfla.com

**Georgia**

Governor's Office of Consumer Affairs

800-869-1123 or 404-651-8600

www.consumer.georgia.com

**Hawaii**

Office of Consumer Protection

Department of Commerce and Consumer
Affairs

808-586-2630

http://hawaii.gov/dcca/areas/ocp

**Idaho**

Consumer Protection Division

Office of the Attorney General

800-432-3545

www2.state.id.us/ag/consumer

**Illinois**

Office of the Attorney General

800-243-0607 (Carbondale)

800-243-0618 (Springfield)

800-386-5438 (Chicago)

http://www.illinoisattorneygeneral.gov/

**BOX 4.1    State Consumer Protection Offices (*continued*)**

**Indiana**

Consumer Protection Division

Office of the Attorney General

800-382-5516

www.indianaconsumer.com

**Iowa**

Consumer Protection Division

Office of the Attorney General

888-777-4590 or 515-281-5926

www./iowa.gov/government/ag/
protecting-consumers/
index.html

**Kansas**

Consumer Protection Division

Office of the Attorney General

800-432-2310 or 785-296-3751

cprotect@ksag.org

www.ksag.org/content/page/id/39

**Kentucky**

Office of Consumer Protection

Office of the Attorney General

888-432-9257

http://ag.ky.gov/consumer

**Louisiana**

Public Protection Division, Consumer
Protection/Environmental Section

Office of the Attorney General

800-351-4889

www.ag.state.la.us

**Maine**

Attorney General's Office

Consumer Protection Division

207-626-8800

www.maine.gov/ag/consumer/
index.html

**Maryland**

Consumer Protection Division

Office of the Attorney General

410-528-8662

www.oag.state.md.us/consumer/
index.html

**Massachusetts**

Consumer Protection and Antitrust Division

Office of the Attorney General

617-727-8400

www.mass.gov

**Michigan**

Consumer Protection Division

Office of the Attorney General

877-765-8388 or 517-373-1140

www.michigan.gov/ag

**Minnesota**

Consumer Services Division

Minnesota Attorney General's Office

800-657-3787

www.ag.state.mn.us

**Mississippi**

Consumer Protection Division of the Office
of the Attorney General

800-281-4418

www.ago.state.ms.us/index.php/sections/
consumer

**Missouri**

Attorney General's Office

Consumer Protection Division

800-392-8222

http://ago.mo.gov/divisions/
consumerprotection.htm

**Montana**

Department of Justice

Consumer Protection

800-481-8696

www.doj.mt.gov/consumer

**Nebraska**

Attorney General's Office

Consumer Protection Division

800-727-6432

www.ago.ne.gov/consumer

**Nevada**

Bureau of Consumer Protection

800-326-5202

http://ag.state.nv.us/org/bcp/bcp.htm

**New Hampshire**

Office of the Attorney General

Consumer Protection and Antitrust Bureau

603-271-3641

http://doj.nh.gov/consumer

**New Jersey**

New Jersey Division of Consumer Affairs

Office of Consumer Protection

973-504-6200

www.state.nj.us/lps/ca/ocp.htm

**New Mexico**

Consumer Protection Division

Office of the Attorney General

800-678-1508

www.nmag.gov/office/consumerInfo/
default.htm

**New York**

New York State Consumer Protection Board

800-697-1220

donna.ned@consumer.state.ny.us

www.consumer.state.ny.us

**North Carolina**

Consumer Protection Section

Office of the Attorney General

877-566-7226 or 919-716-6400

www.ncdoj.com/consumerprotection/
cp_about.jsp

**North Dakota**

Office of the Attorney General

Consumer Protection and Antitrust Division

800-472-2600 or 701-328-3404

www.ag.state.nd.us/CPAT/CPAT.htm

**Ohio**

Ohio State Attorney General's Office

Consumer Protection Section

877-244-6446

www.ag.state.oh.us/citizen/consumer

**Oklahoma**

Oklahoma Attorney General

405-521-3921 or 918-581-2885

www.oag.ok.gov

**Oregon**

Financial Fraud/Consumer Protection Section

Department of Justice

877-877-9392

www.doj.state.or.us/finfraud

**Pennsylvania**

Office of the Consumer Advocate

800-684-6560

www.oca.state.pa.us

**Puerto Rico**

Departmiento de Asuntos del Consumidor

787-722-7555

www.gobierno.pr/DACO/Inicio

**Rhode Island**

Consumer Protection Unit

Department of Attorney General

877-982-4357 (ID Theft) or 401-274-4400

www.riag.state.ri.us/civilcriminal/
consumerprotection.php

**South Carolina**

S.C. Department of Consumer Affairs

800-922-1594 or 803-734-4200

www.scconsumer.gov

**South Dakota**

Office of the Attorney General

Consumer Protection Unit

800-300-1986

www.state.sd.us/attorney/office/divisions/
consumer

**Tennessee**

Division of Consumer Affairs

800-342-8385 or 615-741-4737

www.state.tn.us/consumer

**Texas**

Attorney General of Texas

800-621-0508

www.oag.state.tx.us/consumer

**Utah**

Division of Consumer Protection

800-649-2424 or 801-530-6601

www.dcp.utah.gov

**BOX 4.1    State Consumer Protection Offices (continued)**

| | |
|---|---|
| **Vermont** | **West Virginia** |
| Consumer Assistance Program | Consumer Protection and Anti-Trust Division |
| for Consumer Complaints & Questions | Office of the Attorney General |
| 800-649-2424 or 802-656-3183 | 800-368-8808 |
| www..atg.state.vt.us | www.wvago.gov/consumers.cfm |
| **Virginia** | **Wisconsin** |
| Office of the Attorney General | Department of Agriculture, Trade, and |
| Consumer Assistance | Consumer Protection |
| 800-552-9963 | 800-422-7128 |
| www.oag.state.va.us/CONSUMER/index.html | www.datcp.state.wi.us |
| **Washington** | **Wyoming** |
| Office of the Attorney General | Attorney General's Consumer Protection Unit |
| 800-551-4636 | 800-438-5799 or 307-777-7874 |
| www.atg.wa.gov/safeguardingConsumers/default.aspx | http://attorneygeneral.state.wy.us/consumer.htm |

areas of state government that handle complaints, including the Department of Insurance and the Attorney General's Office. To keep the list in the box manageable, only one main source is given for each state; for example, for California, the Department of Consumer Affairs is listed because it is the leading consumer department in a large and complex state with many consumer relations areas.

When contacting a state department or office about a consumer complaint, the first contact should be a phone call on their toll-free line or by e-mail. The consumer hotline person or responder to e-mail will know how to direct your call or tell you what steps to take in filing a complaint. Investigators may be put onto cases involving several complaints such as travel fraud, auto repair, or health club fraud. They are interested in helping the consumer who has filed a complaint and also in preventing similar problems from happening.

How often do people file complaints? Although toll-free lines or e-mails gather tens of thousands of complaints a month in populous states, this is only the tip of the iceberg. An American Association of Retired Persons (AARP) study found that less than 2 percent of consumers who believe they've experienced a major fraud complain to their state's attorney general's office (Sichelman, 2002). Why? The two most likely reasons are they don't want to bother or don't know where to turn for help.

Less than 2 percent of consumers who have experienced a fraud complain to their state's attorney general.

State consumer protection agencies may license and regulate a variety of professions and professionals. They may oversee boards that issue rules and regulations; prepare and give examinations; issue, deny, or revoke licenses; bring disciplinary actions; handle consumer complaints; and provide referral services. The agency may contact a professional on your behalf, may conduct an investigation, and may take disciplinary action, which may include probation, license suspension, or license revocation for that business.

Regarding identity theft, state governments and the FTC's consumer protection agency are actively investigating consumer complaints in this area, trying to lessen their occurrence and changing laws and procedures in the process. For example, in Florida, a statewide grand jury that is searching for ways to stop identity theft recommended tighter restrictions on the distribution of personal data, more frequent in-person driver license renewals, and a swifter response from law officials. Although identity theft is a growing national problem, certain areas are reporting more complaints than others: The District of Columbia had the highest rate of identity theft in 2001, with 77 victims for every 100,000 people; California and Nevada followed, with 45 and 41 victims, respectively (Ho, 2002).

As mentioned previously, besides the general consumer protection office in the state, certain divisions may have their own toll-free lines or Web sites to handle complaints in specific areas, such as auto repairs or insurance. For example, if a consumer was having problems with a repair shop or an insurance agency or policy, after trying to remedy the problem with the local company, its headquarters, and the BBB, the consumer could call the Auto Repair Division or the Department of Insurance in his or her state and find out what to do next. If there is a specialized agency, the consumer should contact it first rather than the general consumer complaint agency.

The federal government may handle individual complaints in certain areas, such as investment fraud on a national scale, but more likely the consumer should start at the city, county, or state level. For information and complaints regarding investments, a consumer could call the Securities and Exchange Commission (SEC) Office of Investor Education and Assistance toll free at 1-800-SEC-0330 or send an e-mail to www.sec.gov.

Besides government agencies, on occasion private consumer organizations will try to help a member with a complaint, but generally consumer groups do not assist individual consumers with their complaints and encourage members to go through the steps previously outlined. For example, a group such as AARP has a consumer issues section that is mainly charged to examine those consumer problems and issues that impact the financial security of people 50 years of age or older and to help its members protect themselves from marketplace fraud and deception. AARP employs a variety of strategies to keep members informed of wrongdoings but does not pursue individual complaints on a regular basis.

To avoid unnecessary duplication of effort, state consumer protection offices meet regularly to inform each other about scams that are drifting through the United States. It is common for states to form coalitions leveling charges of fraud or deception against a repeat-offender company. For example, the attorney generals of several states may charge a company with false and misleading claims. An out-of-court settlement may be reached wherein the company stops making such claims and pays each state an amount of money to cover the costs of their investigations and legal efforts. In so doing, the company is stopped, and the states bring issues to federal attention. It also takes the load off the courts.

Another way states have taken the load off the courts is by instituting systems of ombudspersons. The office of the **ombudsperson** mediates disputes, offers counseling and mediation services, and uses other out-of-court means to resolve conflict. Ombudspersons work with the court system to accelerate the bureaucratic process.

States also work together through the **Uniform Commercial Code (UCC)**, whose main purpose is to set a standard by which merchants operating in more than one state can more easily comply with that state's laws. This statute has been

This a real story about a student and what happened to her in small claims court. The student was a middle-age female who was an American citizen born in Mexico. Her husband worked for the U.S. Post Office, and she was very proud of her family and American citizenship. One Christmas she was shopping for gifts at a store and left the gifts to be wrapped at the gift wrap department. On her return, the gifts were missing, and the store insisted that she had made it all up and that she had not purchased anything. As the argument escalated, the store managers used racial epithets. On the basis of her consumer economics class, she decided to go to small claims court. While waiting outside for her case to be called, the store managers said they wanted to settle out of court and would give her the money. She said, "No, I want my day in court" and went in. Not only was she awarded the money, but it turns out she exposed a ring that was working in the gift wrap department. They had an accomplice outside the backdoor whom they would give the merchandise to when a shopper's back was turned. The judge awarded her the money she had lost. The student said that had it not been for the class, she would not have known what to do nor had the courage to do it. When she reported what had happened to her classmates (she did not tell anyone at the time, including her family, because she did not know what would happen), they applauded and congratulated her. As a prevention technique, classmates also mentioned that shoppers should get proof that their gifts are being wrapped if they leave them (often stores have a ticket for this purpose) or should keep their purchase receipt or stay and wait for the gifts to be wrapped. (In the case of this student, the wrappers not only took the gifts but also took her receipt, so she had no proof of purchase.)

adopted at least partially by all states and regulates most sales of goods. It makes it easier for sellers to conduct business in several states.

**Small Claims Courts or Civil Courts.**   When all the previous steps have failed, a consumer can go to **small claims court** (in some places it is called conciliation court or magistrates court). This is a form of civil court that allows **litigants** to claim damages or resolve disputes that involve modest amounts of money. Each state sets the maximum allowed; in some states the maximum is $5,000. In small claims courts, consumers speak for themselves, the business also gives its side of the story, and a judge listens and decides the outcome. It is rare, but some states have juries instead of judges. Usually the consumer wins. Often businesses do not show up or try to settle out of court because they can't spare the court time (usually there is some waiting time involved). A business owner's time may be worth more than the amount of money in dispute. Typical cases involve ruined clothes at dry cleaners, landlord—tenant disputes, and faulty home repairs. The judge, for example, may have the dry cleaner give a newlywed $1,000 for a ruined wedding dress. Cases involving more than the maximum allowed amounts or more complications would go to another civil court. The process that is usually followed in a small claims court is given in Box 4.2.

## CIVIL VS. CRIMINAL CASES

Civil court involves the hiring of attorneys, more formality, and more money than small claims court. If the litigant loses, there are routes of appeal within the court system that go all the way up to state supreme courts. This is a costly and time-

Arguing a case before a judge in small claims court.
(Alan King, Getty Images, Inc.—Artville LLC.)

consuming process. If a person cannot afford a lawyer, he or she may qualify for free legal help from the office of a legal aid agency or a Legal Services Corporation (LSC) office or may receive help on a contingency basis. Telephone directories list the addresses and telephone numbers of legal aid offices, or consumers can go to www.nlada.org. The LSC was created in 1974 by Congress to provide financial support for legal assistance in noncriminal proceedings for low-income consumers; it has offices in all 50 states, as well as Guam, Puerto Rico, Micronesia, and the Virgin Islands, and the Web site is www.lsc.gov.

Sometimes if the litigant wins and is awarded the money, the defendant refuses to pay, which may necessitate going back to court. **Civil cases** involve the settling of private conflicts between people or between businesses. Common cases involve landlord–tenant disputes, contract disputes, and ruined products; usually the wrongdoer is asked to pay or remedy the situation in some way, so compensation is involved. A **tort** is a civil wrong that causes either emotional or physical injury (or both). Torts can be intentional or negligent.

Crimes are acts that society forbids or punishes through legislative bodies or courts. **Criminal cases** involve prevention, punishment, and rehabilitation. In criminal cases, a violation is deemed to have taken place or an injustice committed against the government, which brings charges against the person or persons who committed the crime. A person committing a crime is prosecuted, and if found guilty, he or she is punished by the government according to its statutory laws.

## CONSUMER LAW

The law provides safeguards to buyers. Laws pertaining to consumers can be broken down into statutory law, regulatory law, common law, and constitutional

**Box 4.2   Typical Small Claims Court Process**

- First, the "wronged" consumer initiates the process by speaking with the clerk of the court (usually the consumer must live, work, or do business in the locale in question).
- If the clerk advises the consumer to proceed, he or she files a claim and becomes known as the **plaintiff** (the initiator of the lawsuit). Everything on the forms must be accurate. There may be a small fee for filing a claim, and businesses as well as consumers can file suits.
- Once the plaintiff files suit, the court issues a **summons**, which is a notice to appear in court as a juror, defendant, or witness, or a **subpoena**, which is a legal writ requiring an appearance in court to give testimony. The **defendant** is the person required to answer the lawsuit. Upon receiving the summons, about one-quarter of the cases will be settled out of court; in such an occurrence, the consumer should get the agreement in writing and file it with the court.
- If the case goes on and the defendant does not show up at court, then the court will often grant the claim by default. Usually there are no lawyers unless there is a substantial amount of money involved. Some states prohibit lawyers from presenting at these cases because generally the setting is informal, and plaintiffs should be able to represent themselves. In preparation for a case, college students can often get free legal advice at their university (call student services to find out if your college offers legal services to students). A common student problem is landlord–tenant disputes.
- If both sides show up at the court case, then they both give their sides of the story and present evidence in the form of photos, receipts, letters, contracts, cancelled checks, and so on. A calm, simple explanation is advised. Visitors, friends, and families can watch cases in progress.
- The judge usually decides the outcome right then; occasionally the judge may wait a few weeks and send the verdict by letter.

law. There are hundreds of federal statutory and regulatory laws related to consumers. **Statutory laws** are enacted by the legislative branch of government, which at the federal level means the U.S. Congress. **Regulatory laws** are laws, rules, or regulations enacted to protect consumers through agencies of the federal or state government. At the federal level, the FTC is often the agency that protects consumers, but there are over 100 federal government regulatory laws, and these involve many agencies, from food safety to airline safety. Examples of

### Advice on Finding an Attorney

To find a lawyer, ask family and friends for references, and check with the lawyer referral services in your area. The bar association is listed in the telephone directory; also see the E-Resources section near the end of this chapter. As mentioned earlier, as a college student you may have access to free legal help on your campus; contact student services.

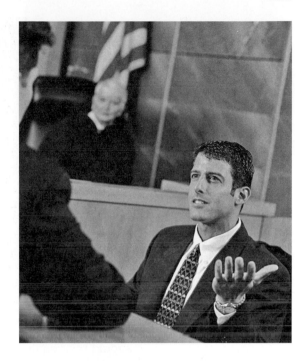

A businessman gestures while testifying in courtroom. (Corbis RF.)

other agencies are the Department of Agriculture and the Food and Drug Administration. At the state level, the most likely agencies or offices are the state attorney general's office or consumer affairs departments or divisions (listed in Box 4-1).

Common law is based on judicial decisions and embodied in reports of decided cases that have been administered by the common-law courts of England since the Middle Ages. These laws evolved into the type of legal system we now have in the United States and Canada, for the most part. The trend is away from common law to statutory law. **Constitutional law**, as the name implies, is based on the U.S. Constitution, which is the fundamental law of the U.S. federal system of government. An example of a right discussed in the Constitution that affects consumers is the right to a fair trial.

## LICENSING BOARDS

Much of the state consumer protection activity takes place through state licensing boards before something reaches the complaint level. The boards issue licenses to professionals such as barbers, physicians, attorneys, and funeral directors. When you have had your hair cut, you have probably seen the license of the barber or cosmetologist prominently displayed. The boards have the power to issue and revoke licenses and charge fees, and in so doing, they protect the consumer from deceptive, harmful, or ineffective services. Critics of boards feel that some are not as consumer-oriented as they ought to be (depending on the makeup of the board members and the kinds of information they are given, this may or may not be true) and that they are inclined to be more in favor of the professional. Most boards try to do the right thing, and they perform important preventive services. Aren't you glad that someone has checked out your barber or cosmetologist before he or she takes scissors or a razor to your head or uses chemical dyes?

## WARRANTIES AND GUARANTEES

Many products offer warranties or guarantees. The terms *warranty* and *guarantee* can be used interchangeably according to the Magnuson-Moss Warranty Act, which became law in 1975. This act requires that consumers be given warranty information, if it exists for a particular product or part of a product, before making a purchase. The act does not require that manufacturers give warranties, but if a warranty is given, it must be clearly stated as either a full or a limited warranty. See Box 4.3 for a list of what a full warranty promises and what a limited warranty means according to the act. A product such as a washing machine can have a full warranty on some parts and a limited warranty on others. Violations of the act should be reported to the FTC (www.ftc.gov).

Besides full and limited warranties, there are also implied and express (or written) warranties. Automobile manufacturers issue **written warranties**, which are written promises that the character and quality of the product are as the manufacturer represents them. Usually the guarantee specifies what is covered for a specific number of miles or years (when leases are involved) or months. **Implied warranties** are not written but are inherently understood in the transaction. The **implied warranty of fitness** for a particular purpose means that the warranty holds for the correct use of the product; for example, the seller guarantees that a shampoo will clean hair, but he or she does not guarantee that it will clean car seat covers. The **implied warranty of merchantability** is more open than the implied warranty of purpose and simply means that the product should work, that it is salable and fit for the market; as an example, a blender that doesn't blend would be unmerchantable. Products delivered to your home should be as merchantable as they were in the store. The seller is obligated to deliver the product in a reasonable amount of time (reasonable means what an average responsible adult would expect given the circumstances). A **reasonable person** is rational, attentive, knowledgeable, and capable of making judgments in his or her best interest.

## CONTRACTS

Agreements or promises that are legally enforceable are called **contracts**. Most significant contracts in consumer law are written, but they may also be oral or implied. Obviously, written contracts are more easily defended in court and in the complaint process. A contract is an understanding reached between parties having

**BOX 4.3    Magnuson-Moss Warranty Act**

The Magnuson-Moss Warranty Act is the federal law passed by Congress in 1975 that governs consumer product warranties. It requires manufacturers and sellers of consumer products to provide consumers with detailed information about warranty coverage. In passing this act, Congress specified a number of requirements that warrantors must meet. The act affects the rights of consumers and the obligations of warrantors under written warranties. The following is a description of parts of the act and its objectives (for further information, go to www.ftc.gov).

Below is a list explaining the act's contents:

- It enables consumers to comparison-shop for warranties.
- It encourages warranty competition.
- It promotes timely and complete performance of warranty obligations.
- It does not compel the consumer to be given a written warranty. (The act does not apply to oral warranties; only written warranties are covered.)
- It does not apply to warranties on services.
- It says that a product is "merchantable," meaning it is supposed to do what it claims. For example, one assumes that an oven will bake food at a controlled temperature selected by the buyer, so if it does not heat or heats improperly, an implied warranty of merchantability would be breached.
- It implies warranty of fitness for a particular purpose, which means that customers rely on sellers to make a product for a specific use. An example given on the FTC Web site is that if an appliance manufacturer says that a washing machine will handle a 15-pound load, it should be able to handle 15-pound loads.
- It implies a standard or level of performance at time of purchase. Implied warranties do not cover problems caused by abuse, misuse, ordinary wear, failure to follow directions, or improper maintenance. However, the normal durability of an appliance, for example, would be considered. Used merchandise may have implied warranties when the seller is a merchant who deals in such goods, not when a sale is made by a private individual.
- It discusses the concept of selling "as is." You cannot sell "as is" in some states; in others, merchandise has to be clearly marked as defective or damaged. Sellers have to be careful when selling a product "as is" because they may be liable if it is dangerous or causes personal injury to someone.
- It distinguishes between a full warranty (and the promises thereof) and a limited warranty. In short, a limited warranty lets consumers know that the warranty offers less than a full warranty. Caution is advised because limited may mean that only certain parts will be replaced for free or that the buyer may have to pay for labor costs.

the legal capacity to agree and something of value is exchanged between them, and a contract is formed when the parties involved may be held liable or responsible. Contracts are made for the present and the future—not the past. The pros and cons of service contracts or extended warranties are covered in Chapter 10; the present chapter's coverage serves as an introduction and emphasizes the legal ramifications of contracts.

A legally binding contract requires the following:

- There must be a mutual agreement.
- Competent participants are involved. For example, the people must be of age (usually 18 years or older). A person who is intoxicated or in some other way incapacitated is usually not legally held to a contract signed under those conditions.
- The subject matter is legal.
- There must be consideration (an exchange of goods, money, or services, that is, something involved beyond just words).
- A legal form is required. The form varies by state; in some states, contracts have to be written.

## CONSUMER LEGAL TERMS

The chapter has already introduced some legal terminology and provided some basic information about courts. Naturally, there is much more, and Box 4.4 lists other basic definitions of legal terms. The intent of this chapter is not to turn you into an attorney but to expose you to "legalese" relevant to the study of consumer economics. Many students who have found this part of the course interesting have gone on to law school or to graduate school in public administration or public policy; others work in businesses or nonprofit settings where they interact with lawyers, so it is useful to have a beginning understanding of legal terminology.

## MEDIA SOURCES FOR REDRESS

At any point in the complaint process, a consumer may seek help from a media source. In most cities, there is a hotline or action-line column in the newspaper or a consumer reporter or a consumer segment on the radio or the television news programs. Many of the columnists or reporters will go to bat for wronged consumers and try to get answers. To find these services, contact the local newspaper (usually the business section editor will know whom to contact) or call radio or television stations. Media are most likely to take up your cause if they feel that it affects other viewers or readers and that it would be a public service. Newspapers and television news shows also perform a valuable public service by providing information about current fraud schemes, telling what is happening and how to avoid being victimized. A well-known, long-standing national television program is *60 Minutes,* which for years has broadcast investigations into wrongdoing, much of which is consumer-linked, such as health fraud investigations or telemarketing and investment schemes.

Another media resource is Call for Action, Inc. (www.callforaction.org). Several decades old, it is an international nonprofit network of consumer hotlines operating in conjunction with broadcast partners. Its purpose is to educate and assist consumers and small businesses with consumer problems. Box 4.5 gives a list of its hotlines in major markets that are staffed with trained volunteers who offer advice and mediate complaints at no cost.

**BOX 4.4  Consumer Legal Terms**

Here are some legal terms relevant to the study of consumer economics that have not already been defined in this chapter. These will not be listed in the Key Terms section at the end of the chapter because they are given mainly as a reference.

*action:* a judicial proceeding; a lawsuit contested in court.

*adversary proceeding:* a legal procedure involving opposing parties, such as a plaintiff and a defendant.

*adversary system:* a system with a trial where the truth will emerge (the system we are used to in the United States).

*answer:* the defendant's written response to the plaintiff.

*breach of contract:* the failure (without legal excuse) to fulfill any promise that is part of a contract.

*class action:* an action brought by a group or class of plaintiffs or defendants who share the same interests in the litigation.

*complainant:* the group or person who files a complaint.

*complaint:* the initial pleading that begins a lawsuit and includes allegations and remedies sought.

*default:* the failure to do something (such as pay a loan or show up in court), the failure to comply.

*deposition:* a statement or testimony made under oath.

*discovery:* the methods used to obtain information held by the other party that can be used in civil or criminal actions.

*dismissal:* the termination of an action or claim; the end of a lawsuit.

*enjoin:* to impose, constrain, attach; to stop a person from a specific act.

*fiduciary:* a person acting on behalf of another (such as managing money or property); a person acting in good faith (such as being an executor of a will or a guardian of a minor).

*garnishment:* a device used by creditors to get back money owed to them (a third party, such as an employer, can garnish wages of an employee and send that money through the court to creditors).

*injunction:* a remedy by a court order compelling a party to do or refrain from doing a specified act (such as the court ordering a person to leave a celebrity alone).

*joint and several liability:* a joint liability imposed on all the parties involved, and if one party does not pay, the other parties must (liability may vary by jurisdiction and considerations of fault).

*joint tenancy:* two or more parties being held equally responsible; a form of legal co-ownership.

*liability:* the position of being answerable according to law, of being held responsible (such as being an accomplice in a crime).

*negligence:* the failure to exercise the right amount of care in protecting others.

*rebuttal:* the giving of evidence or argument that rebuts or refutes previous testimony or evidence given by an adversary.

*settlement:* an agreement reached that terminates the lawsuit.

*verdict:* the decision of the jury for the plaintiff or the defendant; in criminal actions, the finding of guilty or not guilty.

**BOX 4.5   Call for Action, Inc., Hotlines in Major Markets (TV and Radio)**

- Altoona, PA: WTAJ-TV, www.wearecentralpa.com, 814-944-9336
- Atlanta, GA: WAGA-TV, www.fox5atlanta.com, 404-879-4500
- Boston, MA: WBZ, www.wbz.com, 617-787-7070
- Buffalo, NY: WIVB-TV, www.wivb.com, 716-879-4900
- Cleveland, OH: WJW-TV, www.fox8cleveland.com, 216-578-0700
- Colorado Springs, CO: KKTV-TV, www.kktv.com, 719-457-8211
- Detroit, MI: WXYZ-TV, www.detnow.com, 248-827-3362
- Fort Myers, FL: WINK-TV, www.winktv.com, 239-334-4357
- Greensboro, NC: WFMY-TV, www.wfmy2.com, 336-680-1000
- Kansas City, MO: KSHB-TV, www.kshb.com, 816-932-4321
- Milwaukee, WI: WTMJ-TV, www.touchtmj4.com, 414-967-5495
- New York, NY: WABC Radio, www.wabcradio.com, 212-268-5626
- Philadelphia, PA: WPVI-TV, www.abclocal.go.com/wpvi, 866-978-4232
- Phoenix/Flagstaff, AZ: KPNX-TV and KNAZ-TV, www.12news.com, 602-260-1212
- Pittsburgh, PA: WTAE-TV, www.thepittsburghchannel.com, 412-244-4698
- Providence, RI: WPRI-TV, www.wpri.com, 401-228-1850
- St. Louis, MO: KTVI-TV, www.fox2ktvi.com, 636-282-2222
- Tampa, FL: WFTS-TV, www.abcactionnews.com, 866-428-6397
- Toledo, OH: WTOL-TV, www.wtol.com, 419-255-2255
- Washington, DC: WTOP AM & FM, www.wtopnews.com, 301-652-4357

For phone number updates and additional stations, go to www.callforaction.org.

*Source:* Adapted from Call For Action Web site, www.callforaction.org.

## SUMMARY

The study of consumer economics includes learning how to effectively complain and how to avoid fraud. Identity theft tops the list of consumer fraud complaints according to the Federal Trade Commission.

Legitimate businesses want satisfied customers (because they are more likely to return and provide good word of mouth to friends and family), so for the most part they will seek to remedy problems. This chapter gave a list of consumer responsibilities and steps to follow when seeking redress. The chapter addressed the following questions:

What do I do first if I have a faulty product or get poor service?

When is it appropriate to contact a third-party complaint-handling organization-such as a Better Business Bureau or a government consumer agency?

When is it appropriate to go to small claims court or civil court?

The goal of this chapter is to help the reader feel in charge, to know what to do when a purchase goes wrong, how to complain effectively, and who to turn to for help.

Most consumers do not complain. An AARP study found that only 2 percent of consumers who experience a major fraud complain to their state attorney general's office.

Knowing legal terminology and understanding basic consumer rights and responsibilities are useful consumer skills. Reading newspaper articles and watching television programs that expose fraud help keep consumers abreast of current scams; these are examples of knowledge being power. A lot of consumer complaints can be avoided by being wary (for example, not buying from door-to-door salespeople or from people at the side of the road) and by making wise purchases and seeking redress when necessary (for example, by immediately returning faulty products or cancelling a contract within three working days if necessary).

## KEY POINTS

1. Consumers have responsibilities (for example, to be honest in their dealings).
2. There are steps to follow in the complaint process. The recommended first step is to talk to the people at the place the faulty product or service was purchased.
3. More people are using the Internet as a way to contact manufacturers and resolve complaints.
4. Most companies want good customer relations and will try to resolve complaints.
5. In most small claims court cases, lawyers are not necessary, and there is usually a judge who decides the case instead of a jury.
6. Warranties, of which there are several kinds, protect consumers.
7. State government consumer protection departments and related units and media sources are ready to help consumers in their quest for complaint resolution.

## KEY TERMS

arbitration
civil cases
conciliation
constitutional law
consumer satisfaction
contracts
criminal cases
defendant
fraud
implied warranties
implied warranty of
    fitness

implied warranty of
    merchantability
litigants
mediation
ombudsperson
plaintiff
reasonable person
regulatory laws
right to redress
small claims court
social responsibility
Society of Consumer

Affairs Professionals
    (SOCAP)
statutory laws
subpoena
summons
third-party complaint-
    handling sources
tort
Uniform Commercial
    Code (UCC)
written warranties

## DISCUSSION QUESTIONS

1. Regarding the list of consumer responsibilities in the chapter, does it make any difference to you if a company that you buy from is socially responsible? For

example, would you more likely shop in a department store that regularly gives to charities and sponsors charity events than one that does not? If the prices were the same in competitive stores for the same pair of shoes that you are buying, would a store that is more community or environmentally responsible get your business? Explain your answers.

2. What has been your experience with customer service? Name one company that provided good service and one that did not. What happened in each case?

3. Do you know anyone who went to small claims court? If so, what was the case about, and what was the outcome?

4. Go to www.bbb.org and find the Better Business Bureau nearest your campus. Also find out about a charity; select one and see what it says. Go to www.bbbonline.org and ask about an online business (e.g., eBay); report on what you find out.

5. Go to refdesk.com, select a newspaper, and find an article on consumer fraud. Print the article and write a half-page summary of what the problem is and your solution (what you think should happen).

6. Go to lawyers.com and either click on "Ask a lawyer" to try a question out or click on legal resources and find out more information beyond what the chapter covered.

## E-RESOURCES

**American Bar Association**   *www.aba.org*
Nonprofit organization source for legal help and information on dispute resolution

**BBBOnLine**   *www.bbb.org*
Nonprofit organization source
Site that verifies the legitimacy and privacy practices of online businesses

**Better Business Bureau**   *www.bbb.org*
Nonprofit organization source for business and charity reports
Source to check out a company on the BBB Web site

**Lawyers.com**   Web site that offers definitions of legal terms and legal resources

**refdesk.com**   Web site that provides access to over 50 leading newspapers, including consumer articles and fraud coverage

## REFERENCES

Alsop, R. (January 16, 2002). Reputations rest on good service. *Wall Street Journal,* p. B1.

Brickman, L. (January 6, 2003). The great asbestos swindle. *Wall Street Journal,* p. A18.

DeGraff, J., D. Wann, and T. Naylor. (2001). *Affluenza: The all-consuming epidemic.* San Francisco, CA: Berrett-Koehler Publishers.

Ho, D. (January 24, 2002). Identity theft tops list of frauds. *Tallahassee Democrat,* p. 1E.

McDonald's. (January 23, 2003). *Tallahassee Democrat,* p. E1.

Mohr, L., D. Webb, and K. Harris. (2001). Do consumers expect companies to be socially responsible? The impact of corporate social responsibility on buying behavior. *Journal of Consumer Affairs, 35* (1), 45–72.

Rosica, J. (January 7, 2003). Freezer full of unwanted steaks has woman steamed. *Tallahassee Democrat,* p. B1.

Schor, J. (1992). *The overworked American: The unexpected decline of leisure.* New York: Basic Books.

Schor, J. (1998). *The overspent American: Why we want what we don't need.* New York: Harper Perennial.

Sichelman, L. (January–February 2002). Protect your move. *Century 21 House & Home* (a publication of Hachette Filipacchi Media U.S., New York).

# Government Protection, Nongovernmental Pro-Consumer Groups, and the Media

Nothing is easier than spending the public money. It does not appear to belong to anybody. The temptation is overwhelming to bestow it on somebody.
—Calvin Coolidge

## Learning Objectives

1. Explain how to contact an elected official.
2. List the functions of government agencies most involved with protecting the consumer interest.
3. Discuss the reasons for regulation and deregulation.
4. Describe the three primary interests of nongovernmental pro-consumer groups.
5. Explain the mission of consumer media.

---

### Food Recalls: Humans and Pets Falling Ill

Food recalls are continually in the news. The food can be imported or domestically grown or raised for humans or for pets. An example is when the agribusiness company Cargill Inc. recalled more than 1 million pounds of ground beef that may have been contaminated by E. coli bacteria. They learned that the meat may have been contaminated after the Department of Agriculture found a problem with a sample.

The Cargill recall was voluntary. They worked to track down and recall the potentially contaminated meat. It was found that most of the ground-beef patties were distributed at Sam's Club stores and recalled after four Minnesota children and four Wisconsin adults who ate the food developed E. coli illness. News releases provided a toll-free number for consumers to call Cargill for more details.

In other cases, Canadian meat and poultry were found to have bacteria-contaminated meat that sickened 40 people in eight states. "The Canadian firm, Rancher's Beef Ltd., of Balzac, Alberta, was linked in October to a multistate outbreak of E. coli infections involving Topps Meat Co. A massive recall, the second-largest beef recall in U.S. history, forced New Jersey-based Topps out of business. Rancher's Beef also ceased operations."[1]

The U.S. Department of Agriculture is calling for tightened restrictions on imported meat and poultry, and consumers are asking for more inspections.

---

[1]"Cargill Voluntarily Recalls Ground Beef in 10 States," *Wall Street Journal,* November 5, 2007.

## INTRODUCTION

Government spending goes up every year. "When consumer and corporate spending declines in difficult times, government spending acts as a buffer for the economy. And currently, the federal government has a major budget surplus, helping to ensure government spending can continue, even when tax receipts decline" (Lynch, 2001, p. A8). Perhaps you have an opinion on an issue such as government spending that you would like to share with an elected official. This chapter begins with a description of how to reach elected officials, including the president and vice president.

Although President Coolidge criticized those who loosely spend government money, we all need the services government provides, and that includes consumer protection. In an American customer satisfaction survey conducted by the University of Michigan, consumers were just as satisfied with services they received from federal government agencies as they were with services from private companies (Jones, 2002). A striking example was that respondents were more satisfied with the service from the Internal Revenue Service (IRS) than from McDonald's.

This chapter builds on topics introduced earlier in the book: government, proconsumer groups, and media—all parts of the consumer power model of consumerism (see Figure 5.1). Some of the topics to be covered include product recalls, regulation and deregulation, and Web sites for information. This latter point

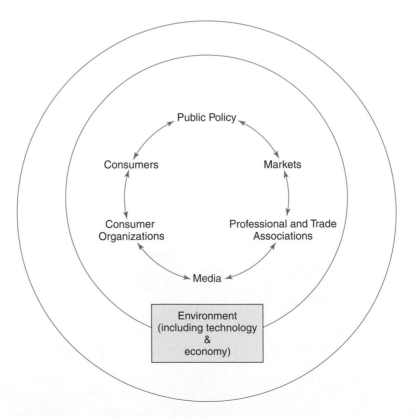

**Figure 5.1**    Consumer Power Model of Consumer Economics.

We are living in an information economy.

is important because we are living in an **information economy**—those who produce, have access to, and influence the spread of information have power in the global society.

## WAYS TO CONTACT ELECTED OFFICIALS

It takes only a few minutes to write to an elected official, but it can make a difference if there is an issue you care about. When elected officials receive enough letters from constituents or even a single stirring letter, it will sway their vote or stance on an issue. Often elected officials will read parts of the letters when they give testimony or make other types of public pronouncements. For greatest impact, follow these six guidelines:

1. Use your own paper and your own words; write clearly and concisely.
2. Focus on one subject per letter or e-mail.
3. Refer to specific legislation by name and/or number.
4. Request a specific action, such as voting in a particular way, or suggest public hearings.
5. If you work or live in the elected official's district, say so.
6. Insulting words or lack of courtesy will not work; polite wording will get more of the kind of attention and action you want.

To find addresses of state and local representatives, check your phone book. U.S. senators and representatives can be reached at the following addresses:

| | |
|---|---|
| The Honorable _____ | The Honorable _____ |
| [name] | [name] |
| U.S. Senate | U.S. House of Representatives |
| Washington, DC 20510 | Washington, DC 20515 |

"The Honorable" in front of a person's name is a title of respect in the United States and is reserved for those who hold or have held high office at the federal, state, and city levels. Members of Congress also have local addresses in their districts as well as e-mail addresses and Web sites. For a directory, go to http://lcweb. loc.gov/global/legislative/email.html. The salutation on the letter should be Dear Senator _____ or Dear Mr. _____ or Ms. _____ for a U.S. representative (putting the person's last name in the blank).

You can e-mail the president at *president@whitehouse.gov* and the vice president at *vice.president@whitehouse.gov*. E-mails or letters should have the following salutation: Dear Mr. President or Dear Mr. Vice President. In the event of a female president or vice president, it would be Dear Ms. President or Dear Ms. Vice President unless she announces another choice.

The correct salutation for a governor is Dear Governor or Dear Governor _____ (add the last name). An e-mail or letter to a state governor would be addressed:

The Honorable

_____ [name]

Governor of _____ [state]

Address

For the closing of a business letter, "Sincerely" is always appropriate; for the president or another high official, it is appropriate to use "Respectfully yours." In a letter, skip three spaces down and then type in your name. In the space above, handwrite your signature.

## AGENCIES AND COMMISSIONS

### Federal Consumer Protection

The federal government is empowered to act on behalf of consumers through a series of acts, rules, regulations, and legislation. Several federal government agencies provide recall information, perform product tests, conduct research studies, and enforce product safety regulations. The agencies most involved with consumer protection are the Federal Trade Commission (FTC), the Consumer Product Safety Commission (CPSC), the Food and Drug Administration (FDA), the U.S. Department of Agriculture (USDA), the Department of Justice (DOJ), the Securities and Exchange Commission (SEC), and the National Highway Traffic Safety Administration (NHTSA). Also included in this section is the Federal Consumer Information Center (FCIC), which announces recalls and distributes the *Consumer Action Handbook* as well as booklets and pamphlets on specific consumer topics (see E-Resources for its Web site).

**Federal Trade Commission (FTC).**   At the federal level, the FTC is the government's most aggressive agency in rooting out fraud, violations of consumers' privacy, and deceptive marketing practices in the emerging point-and-click marketplace (Simons, 1999). The FTC was established in 1914 by the Federal Trade Commission Act, and since then its powers have broadened. In 1938, the Wheeler Lea Amendments clarified the FTC's role in regard to including "unfair or deceptive acts or practices," and by these amendments, deceptive advertising came under the FTC's jurisdiction. Warranties and other trade regulations were added under the 1975 Magnuson-Moss Warranty Act, which also extended FTC's ability to enforce its rules (previously it had to go through the Department of Justice). In the 1980s, the FTC established an Office of Consumer and Competition Advocacy to identify and respond to issues regarding government intervention in the market. The FTC is continually balancing the need to protect legitimate business while going after fraudulent businesses (as shown in the Consumer Alert box).

   This agency pursues Internet-related enforcement actions, including garden-variety fraud cases such as get-rich-quick pyramid schemes and miracle weight-loss drugs. The FTC is responsible for the laundering instructions sewn into every piece of clothing sold in the United States and also wrestles with regulating television advertising and curbing telemarketing fraud. The agency has enforcement powers based on its statutes; for example, it can insist that advertisers run **corrective advertising**. This type of advertisement disclaims previous false advertising claims and is run by a firm to cause consumers to "unlearn" inaccurate information from prior advertisements. Here are two examples of corrective advertising messages (Hawkins, Best & Coney, 2001, p. 728):

- "Do you recall some of our past messages saying that Domino sugar gives you strength, energy, and stamina? Actually, Domino is not a special or

**CONSUMER ALERT**

"Retirees! Moms! Earn extra cash while working at home!" We have all seen these classified ads that promote work-at-home scams in newspapers. The person answers the ad by sending money or charging a toll call to a credit card to get details. And what does he or she get in return? He or she receives instructions for running more ads or setting up a business, a box of trinkets for assembling, or envelopes for stuffing, after which the person mails the items back at his or her own expense and supposedly earns a fee. Often the person's work is then said to be shoddy, so the company offers more expensive kits—or more likely the company then disappears. Common sense should tell people that they will not be paid huge sums of money to sit at home and do simple work. This is where the FTC steps in: It warns people about misleading advertisements. To learn more about scams and how to spot them, log on to FTC's Web site (www.ftc.gov), click on Consumer Protection, and then go to Franchise & Business Opportunities.

unique source of strength, energy, and stamina. No sugar is, because what you need is a balanced diet and plenty of rest and exercise."

- "If you've wondered what some of our earlier advertising meant when we said Ocean Spray cranberry juice cocktail has more food energy than orange juice or tomato juice, let us make it clear: we didn't mean vitamins and minerals. Food energy means calories. Nothing more."

The Federal Trade Commission enforces consumer protection laws against any illegal acts that are considered unfair methods of competition or unfair or deceptive practices. It was considerably strengthened in terms of enforcement power by the Magnuson-Moss Warranty Act.

Although the effectiveness of corrective advertising has been questioned, the FTC continues in this effort as a means to bring accurate information to the public. In order for the FTC to insist on corrective advertising, the false impression that is made has to be very strong. Indirect effects or flattering words are difficult to define, so puffery and fluff in advertising are legitimate and pervasive.

One of FTC's biggest challenges is enforcing labeling and trade violations from overseas. With the advent of the Internet, more and more problems are coming from other countries where consumer laws are usually weaker. For example, Web sites abroad are offering prescription drugs without doctors or licensed pharmacies being involved.

One of its newer realms of coverage is dealing with telemarketers. The FTC steps in regarding violations of no-call requests (Box 5.1 gives information about how to reduce unwanted calls). Florida established the first state no-call list in 1991. To give you an idea of how such legislation comes about, this particular law was supported by Carl Carpenter, a state legislator whose elderly disabled mother could hardly get to the phone, and when she did get to it, the call would be from some firm selling aluminum siding or bulk beef. She told him there should be a law to protect people from unsolicited sales calls, so Carpenter fought for it and won.

Since FTC's jurisdiction is so vast, it has divided its functions into several divisions with different responsibilities:

- Advertising
- Marketing
- Credit
- Enforcement
- Service industries

**BOX 5.1   Getting Relief from Telemarketers' Calls**

The National Do Not Call Registry is open for business, putting consumers in charge of the telemarketing calls they get at home. The federal government created the national registry to make it easier and more efficient for you to stop getting telemarketing calls you don't want. You can register online at www.donotcall.gov or call, toll-free, 1-888-382-1222 (TTY 1-866-290-4236), from the number you wish to register. Registration is free.

The Federal Trade Commission, the Federal Communications Commission, and the states are enforcing the National Do Not Call Registry. Placing your number on the registry will stop most, but not all, telemarketing calls.

The FTC does not act on individual complaints but rather looks for a pattern of complaints and then decides which ones to investigate. Complaints can come from a variety of sources, including consumers or consumer organizations, whistleblowers, congressional leaders, and scholars and institutes. If after an investigation the FTC believes that a business has violated the law, it will ask the business to stop a specific action and/or issue a complaint. If the business will not stop and no settlement is reached, the case may go forward. Formal hearings may take place; then an administrative law judge may issue a decision. Decisions can go all the way to the Supreme Court. Along the way, an FTC rule may be challenged in a U.S. Court of Appeals. The rules or trade regulations are FTC's most effective means of protecting consumers and legitimate businesses.

Another area of jurisdiction of the FTC is that of monitoring mail-in rebate offers. For example, the FTC has taken action against electronics makers, such as manufacturers of scanners, that routinely paid out rebates months later or not at all (Spencer, 2002). More valuable rebates are the ones that most often come into question. Some offer as much as $400 off computer purchases, for example, while a charcoal rebate offer on a $4.99 bag of charcoal may be for only a $1 (when you take off the cost of the stamp, that isn't much of a rebate). For the low-end offers, the percentage of consumers mailing in rebate coupons, known as **claim rates**, may be only 5 percent, but for the high-end electronics offers, the percentage may go as high as 40 percent (Spencer, 2002). The rebates attract customers and move merchandise, but they can trip up a company that does not plan wisely. One dot.com filed for bankruptcy court protection because it owed customers $90 million in rebates; one particularly enthusiastic shopper was owed $90,000 (Spencer, 2002).

The FTC also issues sets of guidelines such as voluntary guidelines for green claims (the word *green* meaning environmentally sound), and Box 5.2 offers examples of these guidelines.

**Consumer Product Safety Commission (CPSC).**   The CPSC, headquartered in Bethesda, Maryland (outside Washington, D.C.), was created in 1972 by Congress under the Consumer Product Safety Act; it began operating in 1973. It has three regional offices: New York City, Chicago, and Oakland, California. There are about 100 CPSC investigators, compliance officers, and consumer information specialists throughout the country, and in total the CPSC has approximately 500 employees and monitors the safety of over 15,000 kinds of consumer products. It

*Consumers vary in their response rate to rebate offers, which ranges from 5 percent to 40 percent, depending on the deal.*

*Trade regulations or rules are developed by federal and state agencies that define and prohibit various industry activities.*

**BOX 5.2    Examples of Environmental Guidelines Issued by the Federal Trade Commission**

- An ad calling a trash bag "recyclable" without qualification would be deemed misleading because bags aren't ordinarily separated from other trash at incinerators and landfills.
- A shampoo advertised as "biodegradable" without qualifications wouldn't be deceptive if there is reliable scientific support showing it will decompose in a short time.
- A "recycled" label on a bottle made from recycled material wouldn't be considered misleading even if the cap isn't made from recycled material.

is an independent agency, meaning it doesn't report to nor is it part of any other federal department or agency. Its basic function is to protect consumers against injuries and deaths associated with consumer products; the kinds of products most often involved are toys, baby and sports equipment, and household products such as coffeemakers and lawn mowers. The CPSC does not have jurisdiction over some categories of products such as automobiles, tires, boats, drugs, food, cosmetics, pesticides, and medical devices. The CPSC Web site lists its activities:

- To develop voluntary standards with industry
- To issue and enforce mandatory standards for consumer products (or ban them if no feasible standard would adequately protect the public)
- To obtain the recall of products or arrange for their repair
- To conduct research on potential product hazards
- To inform and educate consumers through the media, state and local governments, private organizations, and responses to consumer inquiries

One of the problems involved in monitoring the safety of babies and young children is that because they live with adults and older brothers and sisters, they are exposed to products that are not made for them. The worst-case scenarios result when babies suffocate in water beds, swallow parts from their older siblings' toys, and get strangled in window blind cords. Toy and household product manufacturers that are aware of such risks do what they can to reduce the risks; for example, one leading window manufacturer places the blinds between two panes of glass and in so doing removes the blind cords as a safety measure for children. Parents and other caregivers have a responsibility to watch over children and to remove potential hazards. Seemingly safe products such as a bucket with wash water for floors can turn deadly if a toddler puts his or her head in it, can't get out, and drowns. Childproofing a house, yard, and pool area, coupled with active supervision, is essential. The CPSC offers suggestions on how to prevent accidental injuries in its publications and on its Web site.

The CPSC does not recommend brands or test products. It provides information to consumers on what safety features to look for in products and announces recalls.

A product is recalled if it presents a significant risk to consumers because the product either is defective or violates a mandatory standard issued by the CPSC. If a product is recalled, you should stop using it and find out from the CPSC what to do next by sending an e-mail to info@cpsc.gov or calling 1-800-638-2772. If a toy, for example, is found to be unsafe, the recall may only apply to products manufactured and dated at a specific time. When you check into a recall order, sometimes you get your money back, and sometimes you don't. The CPSC regularly updates recall information on its Web site.

Typical product recalls by manufacturers in cooperation with the CPSC have included those for strollers, activity gyms, baby clothes, electric ranges, glue guns, dishwashers, and pull toys. Regarding these particular problems and their remedies, the strollers, for example, often collapsed and injured children who fell. To remedy this, the manufacturer sent a free repair kit so that the parent could make the stroller safer. In the case of activity gyms that had detachable rattles that posed a choking hazard, refunds were offered from the stores where the activity gyms were purchased. The baby clothes had a zipper pull that posed a choking hazard, so a refund was offered. When sparks or flames from the electric range were possible, a free in-home repair was offered. For glue guns that overheated, causing burn risks, a refund was offered. With the dishwashers in question that could ignite, free rewiring or rebates were offered from the company. For the pull toys that had plastic connectors on a string that could detach and put children at risk of choking, the manufacturer offered replacement.

If someone is hurt by a consumer product, the CPSC wants to know. Unsafe products and injuries from products can be reported online, at hazard@cpsc.gov; by phone, 1-900-638-2772, extension 650; or by letter. A letter to the consumer will then be sent from CPSC's National Injury Information Clearinghouse because the CPSC will want to know more details and to confirm the accuracy of information already given. The complaint will be sent to the manufacturer.

It should be noted that not all complaints are investigated. The CPSC receives reports of over 10,000 product-related injuries and deaths a year, and due to its small staff size, it can only investigate some of these. Even if the product is not investigated, the information sent is a valuable resource because it is put into CPSC's database and is used to warn others, to set up safety guidelines, and to possibly influence rule making.

**Food and Drug Administration (FDA).**   The FDA, located within the Department of Health and Human Services, is an influential federal agency designed to protect consumers. Its mission is to promote and protect the public health by helping safe and effective products reach the market in a timely way and by monitoring

The FDA looks out for the safety of the
U.S. food supply. (© Dorling Kindersley.)

products for continued safety after they are in use (see the example shown in the Consumer Alert).

The FDA considers its work as a blending of law and science aimed at protecting consumers. FDA-regulated products account for about 25 cents of every consumer dollar spent in the United States.

According to the FDA Web site, from the beginnings of civilization people have been concerned about the quality and safety of foods and medicines. In 1202, King John of England proclaimed the first English food law, the Assize of Bread, which prohibited adulteration of bread with such ingredients as ground beans or peas. In the United States, regulation of goods dates from early colonial days (Chapter 2 of this text highlights legislation passed in the twentieth century). Remember the discussion of Dr. Harvey Wiley, the father of the Pure Food and Drugs Act of 1906? He unified a variety of groups, including the media and the public, behind this federal law to prohibit the adulteration and misbranding of food and drugs.

Federal controls over the drug supply began with inspection of imported drugs in 1848. For example, in 1998 the Federal Food and Drug Administration Act, which offered gravely ill patients easier access to experimental drugs and cut the waiting period for approval time, was passed. More on the history of food, drug, and cosmetic controls, with a focus on health, is found in Chapter 8. The emphasis in this chapter is on the present and the ways these agencies function and affect our daily lives.

As the Consumer Alert shows, the FDA has jurisdiction over human drugs, but as its name ("Food and Drug") implies, it also oversees most food products (other than meat, poultry, and egg products). In addition, the FDA is in charge of animal drugs; therapeutic agents of biological origin; medical devices; radiation-emitting products for consumers and for medical and occupational uses; cosmetics; and animal feed. The staff size is approximately 9,100 employees (about one-third work in the Washington, D.C., area), and it has a budget of over $1 billion. Agency scientists evaluate applications for new human drugs and biologics, medical devices, food and color additives, infant formulas, and animal drugs (Swann, 2002).

To give a broader picture, listed below are the types of products that the FDA regulates and the issues it is involved in:

*Food:* foodborne illnesses, nutrition, and dietary supplements

*Drugs:* prescription, over-the-counter, and generic

*Medical devices:* pacemakers, contact lenses, and hearing aids

> Every day, every American comes in contact with products that the FDA regulates.

---

 **CONSUMER ALERT**

Shock your wrinkles away? Yes, this was a product promoted by actresses as the secret for younger-looking skin. Put this battery-operated device on your face every day, and the companies making the device suggest that the appearance of wrinkles will be reduced. The device sold for between $99 and $250, depending on the company. Testers who tried it said they felt pain and tingling. The FDA said the devices weren't authorized for removing wrinkles and sent warnings to the companies. The bottom line was that muscle stimulation may produce temporary swelling, but according to dermatologists, it cannot permanently remove wrinkles.

*Source:* GH Institute, 2001.

## CONSUMER ALERT

"They claimed their products could bolster the immune system and treat several serious diseases, including AIDS and cancer. But Allen J. Hoffman of Finksburg, Maryland, and a Virginia physician are now serving prison terms for fraudulently peddling an intravenous mixture containing aloe vera to treat autoimmune and other conditions." They billed up to $18,000 for a two-week treatment of intravenous aloe vera. Patients traveled from the United States to the Bahamas and Mexico for treatments. The investigator's report stated that "it is clear that some people were misled and defrauded into trying dangerous, unapproved and ineffective alternative treatments."

*Source:* Michelle Meadows, "Maryland Man, Virginia Physician Sentenced for Illegally Marketing Aloe Vera 'Teatments.'" *FDA Consumer,* May–June 2002, p. 34.

*Biologics:* vaccines and blood products

*Animal feed and drugs:* livestock and pets

*Cosmetics:* safety and labeling

*Radiation-emitting products:* cell phones, lasers, and microwaves

> Poisoning, much of it from food sources, is the nation's third most common form of unintentional death.

To give a specific example, the FDA announced a nationwide recall of Susie Brand imported cantaloupe due to salmonella (rod-shaped bacteria that can cause illness). It should be noted that poisoning, much of it from food sources, is the nation's third most common form of unintentional death; other sources are household cleaning products and medicines (usually swallowed by children). On the same day as the cantaloupe alert, there were other recalls and alerts as well as recent approvals of new products.

**Department of Agriculture (USDA).** The USDA, headquartered in Washington, D.C., has offices and testing centers throughout the United States (examples of some centers or divisions are given in Box 5.3). The USDA began in 1862 under President Abraham Lincoln when 48 percent of the people were farmers who needed good seeds and information to grow their crops. With less than 2 percent of the American population now living on farms, the mission and outreach of the USDA have broadened to include all segments of the population. Its range of activities has grown to include food and water safety, research, education, and conservation, and well as oversight of a number of programs such as food stamps and school breakfasts and lunches.

Regarding food, the USDA is responsible for the safety of meat, poultry, and egg products, which falls under Food Safety, a division that administers the federal meat and poultry inspection system and educates industry and consumers about food safety. Inspection of meat products is required by federal law. In 1996 the Meat and Poultry Rules were passed that allowed inspectors to use microscopes to detect E. coli and salmonella bacteria, making it much easier to determine if products carry these potentially deadly organisms. Another area of the USDA, the Food, Nutrition, & Consumer Service, runs the federal food assistance programs and coordinates nutrition research and policy.

The Cooperative State Research, Education, and Extension Service of the USDA has been a source of information and assistance to consumers for over a century.

BOX 5.3    Centers and Divisions within the USDA Most Related to Consumer Issues

- Animal and Plant Health Inspection Service, Riverdale, MD; www.aphis.usda.gov
- Center for Nutrition Policy and Promotion, Washington, DC; www.usda.gov.cnpp
- Cooperative State Research, Education, and Extension Service, Washington, DC; www. reeusda.gov (you may also consult county government listings in local telephone directories for the number of local Cooperative Extension Service offices)
- Meat and Poultry Hotline, Washington, DC; www.fsis.usda.gov

The mailing address for the USDA and all its agencies is U.S. Department of Agriculture, Washington, DC 20250.

Educators are located in nearly every county to bring research-based knowledge directly to families and communities with programs that include personal finance issues, such as budgeting and retirement, as well as programs on food and nutrition and safe housing. College students who have completed coursework in consumer economics and related areas can consider the Cooperative Extension Service, as well as the other agencies and commissions covered in this chapter, as a place for internships and employment.

**Department of Justice (DOJ).**    The mission of the DOJ, according to its Web site, is to enforce the law and defend the interests of the United States based on the law, to provide federal leadership in preventing and controlling crime, to seek just punishment for those guilty of unlawful behavior, to administer and enforce the nation's immigration laws fairly and effectively, and to ensure fair and impartial administration of justice for all Americans. The part of the DOJ most connected to consumer economics is the Antitrust Division, which promotes and protects the competitive process through the enforcement of antitrust laws. A more common way to refer to the antitrust function is "trust busting." The following are practices that restrain trade:

- Price-fixing conspiracies
- Corporate mergers likely to reduce the competitive vigor of particular markets
- Predatory acts designed to achieve or maintain monopoly power

Monopolies occur when there is only one producer (a single firm) that controls or dominates an industry and for which there is no substitute. Because we live in a market economy, we want to be free, as consumers, to choose the products and services we want—we like selection. On the other hand, Adam Smith, founder of economics, recognized the desire of businessmen to monopolize trade by joining forces, and "although he was not able to specify what the monopoly price would be, he recognized that monopolists would extract a higher price by restricting output" (Landreth & Colander, 2002, p. 83). In other words, monopolies would ultimately result in higher costs to consumers, so he encouraged competition. "He saw competition as fundamentally requiring a large number of sellers; a group of resource owners who were knowledgeable about profits, wages, and rents in the economy; and freedom of movement for resources among industries" (Landreth & Colander, 2002, pp. 82–83).

A **merger** occurs when two or more companies combine into a single unit and can be classified by its economic function: horizontal, vertical, market, product, or conglomerate. A **horizontal merger** combines direct competitors in the same product lines and markets, with an example of a horizontal merger being two department stores in the same town merging. A **vertical merger** combines supplier and company or customer and company, an example of which is when a producer of a raw material also manufactures and wholesales the material. A **market extension merger** combines firms selling the same products in different markets; for example, one grocery store distribution company buys another, increasing the area to which it distributes. A **product extension merger** combines firms selling different but related products in the same market, as when a soft drink company acquires a snack food company thus extending or expanding the product line. The catch-all merger category is the **conglomerate merger**, which combines companies with none of the previously mentioned relationships or similarities; an example of a conglomerate merger would be a beer manufacturer joining with a furniture company. Sometimes the federal government blocks or slows the growth of mergers, but other times it lets them go by or only focuses on certain types. Many mergers involve small companies that do not have much consumer impact, and because cases are usually costly in terms of personnel and money, the emphasis is on larger companies or precedent-setting cases. There are a number of other factors as well, such as the general economic climate and the presidential administration. Now and then, Congress steps in (usually in response to a company scandal or consumer uproar) and insists on the need to strengthen antitrust laws.

Historically, the goal of antitrust laws is to protect economic freedom and opportunity through promoting competition. What are the benefits of competition?

- Competition provides businesses with the opportunity to compete on price and quality, on a level playing field, in an open market, unhampered.
- It tests and strengthens American companies at home, making them better able to succeed abroad.
- Competition within the United States or globally leads ultimately to lower prices, better quality, and greater choice for consumers.

The Antitrust Division prosecutes serious and willful violations of antitrust laws by filing criminal suits. Possible outcomes include fines and jail sentences. Civil action, which would forbid future violations of the law, is also possible. These statutes are enforced by the Antitrust Division:

- *Sherman Anti-trust Act.* This 1890 act deals with restraint of trade and monopolies. The main purpose of this act is to maintain a competitive economy. It was named after Senator John Sherman, who was quoted on the Senate floor as saying, "If we will not endure a King as a political power, we should not endure a King over production, transportation, and sale of the necessaries of life." The first case tried under this act decided by the Supreme Court was *United States* v. *E. C. Knight Company* (1895). The American Sugar Refining Company controlled 98 percent of the U.S. sugar-refining industry. Cases since then have included monopolies in aluminum, oil, tobacco, steel, telephone, and computer industries.
- *Clayton Act.* This act, passed in 1914, includes statements about discrimination in price, services, or facilities. It discusses corporate mergers, exclusive contracts, and other processes that lessen competition.

- *Wilson Tariff Act.* This act encompasses imports and fairness of trade. There are also codes and statements regarding falsifying, concealing, or covering up, by any trick, scheme, or device, a material fact or in any other way using misrepresentation, including frauds and swindles by mail, wire, radio, or television. Defrauding through the mail became a federal crime under the Mail Fraud Act of 1872.

**Securities and Exchange Commission (SEC).** The SEC, headquartered in Washington, D.C., is the investor's advocate. Its primary mission is to protect investors and maintain the integrity of the securities (a word referring to stocks and bonds) markets. This agency was created by the Securities Exchange Act of 1934 to administer that act and the Securities Act of 1933, formerly under the jurisdiction of the FTC. The SEC is composed of five commissioners who are appointed by the president on a rotating basis for five-year terms; the chairman of the SEC is designated by the president, and no more than three members of the commission may be of the same political party. The SEC supports full public disclosure and protects the investing public from malpractice in the securities market.

As the quote from the SEC Web page in the Consumer Alert indicates, millions of Americans and foreign investors have money invested in the stock market, either directly through individual stocks or mutual funds or through retirement accounts, so the work of the SEC is crucial to people's financial future. The SEC watches for fraud and deception in the securities market and provides investor education. It may also investigate allegations of wrongdoing on its own or join with other groups; for example, in 2002 the SEC, the New York Stock Exchange, and the regulatory arm of the National Association of Securities Dealers launched a joint examination of Wall Street compliance that was spurred by a broker in Cleveland who took an estimated $125 million from clients (see the Consumer Alert), and since other brokers were found to have committed similar fraud, the joint examination included a plan to canvass nearly 6,000 registered brokers to see if there were other gaps in monitoring the actions of brokers.

The laws and rules that govern the securities industry in the United States require public companies to disclose meaningful financial and other information to the public. The SEC promotes a steady flow of timely, comprehensive, accurate information so that investors can make sound decisions. The SEC oversees stock exchanges, broker-dealers, investment advisors, mutual funds, and public holding companies.

---

 **CONSUMER ALERT**

"As more and more first-time investors turn to the markets to secure their futures, pay for homes, and send children to college, these goals are more compelling than ever. The world of investing is fascinating, complex, and can be very fruitful. But unlike the banking world, where deposits are guaranteed by the federal government, stocks, bonds and other securities can lose value. There are no guarantees. That's why investing should not be a spectator sport; indeed, the principal way for investors to protect the money they put into the securities markets is to do research and ask questions."

*Source:* "What We Do." www.sec.gov. Accessed May 23, 2002.

**CONSUMER ALERT**

"Frank Gruttadauria, a star Lehman Brothers broker in Cleveland, siphoned an estimated $125 million from clients over 15 years, covering his tracks with forged account statements, federal regulators say. Where was the local Lehman official who was supposed to monitor his conduct? He reported to Mr. Gruttadauria. In Miami, R. Christopher Hanna used strikingly similar methods over 10 years to steal $15 million from his clients at Credit Suisse First Boston (CSFB), regulators say. The former CSFB branch manager who was supposed to be overseeing Mr. Hanna may not have noticed because he was busy as a broker in his own right, handling accounts for wealthy customers."

*Source:* Gasparino & Craig, May 23, 2002, p. A1.

**National Highway Traffic Safety Administration (NHTSA).**  The NHTSA, in the Department of Transportation (DOT) headquartered in Washington, D.C., works to reduce injuries and develops minimum performance standards by enforcing safety standards on motor vehicles, including bicycles, motorcycles, automobiles, trucks, buses, mopeds, and recreational vehicles, as well as all accessories for these vehicles (for example, safety belts come under their jurisdiction). NHTSA's goal is to reduce highway deaths, injuries, and property losses. Defects may require recalls so that corrections can be made. Visit its Web site for information on air bags, auto safety, child seat inspections, crash statistics, and crash tests.

**Federal Consumer Information Center (FCIC).**  The FCIC, located in Pueblo, Colorado, is part of the U.S. General Services Administration. This center was established to help federal agencies and departments develop, promote, and distribute useful consumer information to the public. The center can also tell consumers whom to contact for help with problems. The FCIC enables consumers to send complaints directly to companies and agencies through its Web site (see E-Resources), but it does not handle consumer complaints. One of the ways it disseminates information is by publishing a new *Consumer Information Catalog* four times a year. Its catalog lists more than 200 free or low-cost booklets on topics such as these:

   Cars (what to look for when buying new and used cars)

   Computers (how to avoid Internet investment scams)

   Education (how to financially plan for college)

   Employment (how to create resumes and cover letters)

   Family (how to find resources for aging parents)

   Federal government (how to find out about public land for sale and disability rights laws)

   Food (how to locate diabetes recipes and reports on food allergies)

   Health (how to find out about drug interactions)

   Housing (how to buy a new home and find information on indoor air hazards)

   Money (how to save for a rainy day)

   Records (how to obtain vital records on births, deaths, marriage, and divorces)

Small business (where to get loans)

Travel (how to get national park system information and maps and how to get a passport)

For a free catalog, go to www.pueblo.gsa.gov. At the Web site, search for topics of interest or the latest consumer news, and use the links to other federal agencies and consumer offices.

This concludes the federal government section of this chapter, but it should be noted that there are many other federal departments and commissions that affect consumers. For brevity's sake, not all of them can be covered here, but many are covered in other areas of the book. For example, the Federal Reserve System (the "Fed") will be covered in Chapter 13 on banking.

## State Consumer Protection

As mentioned in previous chapters, state governments provide consumer protection through agencies, commissions, boards, attorney generals' offices, departments of insurance, and offices of consumer affairs as well as other units. They serve an important role in handling consumer complaints in their states; some states have better protection measures than those of federal government agencies, and in some cases, states handle the same sorts of complaints and cases as the federal government. In an earlier section, it was noted that the FTC can go after companies that are consistently late in paying rebates; likewise, state government attorney generals can go after companies slow to pay up. Examples are Texas, which settled with CompuServe, and Florida, which filed a complaint against the same company for failing to pay $400 rebates to dozens of customers who had signed up for three years of Internet service (Spencer, 2002). Box 5.4 gives a list of places to turn to if your rebate does not arrive in a reasonable time.

Certain fraudulent and deceptive practices tend to occur in specific areas of the country more often than in others, so in many cases localized solutions make more sense than federal intervention, and there is also a history in the United States of states' rights. Regarding targeted fraud, in Florida, California, and other states in the

**BOX 5.4    Where to Turn When Your Rebate Fails to Come**

---

To move merchandise, companies are offering record numbers of rebates for everything from computers to charcoal. If your rebate is late beyond a reasonable amount of time, here are places to turn:

- You can contact your state attorney general's office. To find the address and phone number, go to www.naag.org, which is the Web site of the National Association of Attorneys General.
- You can file a complaint either by going online to www.FTC.com or by calling 1-877-FTC-HELP.
- You can gripe or hear other people's horror stories at www.RipOffReport.com or www.Planetfeedback.com.
- You can track rebate offers on electronics and computers by going to www.RebatePlace.com.

Sunbelt, state governments are well aware that their high concentration of elderly makes them attractive to fraudsters, so additional protections are needed. Con artists may come in the form of telemarketers, nursing homes salespersons, financial planners, sellers of gold coins and foreign lottery tickets, roof repairers, and fortune-tellers. It is difficult to track financial crimes against the elderly because those crimes are less obvious than product purchases, and the elderly are less likely to report fraud than the general population. Sometimes the elderly simply don't know what happened to them; other times they are too embarrassed to speak out. Other types of fraud common in the Sunbelt, desert areas, Hawaii, and mountain resort areas are phony land deals and tourist scams.

Besides the obvious consumer units, states have public health commissions that provide information on health care and look out for the health of citizens. They have other divisions that test foods (such as citrus fruit) grown within the state for diseases. States also have human rights commissions, boards of review, departments of transportation, and other departments similar to those at the federal level that handle consumer concerns. State and local courts also handle consumer cases, especially those involving contracts.

## Local Consumer Protection

Counties, cities, small towns, and military bases have their own consumer affairs, financial, or police departments that investigate consumer complaints, hear tenant–landlord disputes, conduct investigations, prosecute offenders of consumer laws, and advocate in the consumers' interest. If there are criminal acts involving finances, threats, and scams, the police become involved. Crimes of this type investigated by police may come under the category or division called bunco or, more commonly, **bunko**, referring to swindles in which an unsuspecting person or group of people is cheated. Police departments in recent years have had to spend more time on these types of crimes, a trend that has been shaped by economic, legal, technological, and social forces along with the perennial problem of runaway greed. There are always people who want to get rich quick or to get rich without working for it.

As readers of this book know by now, fraud is not new. "Old scams never die—they just change hands, passed along from one grifter to the next" (Adams, 2002, p. 240). A **grifter** is someone who uses his or her position to derive profit or advantages by unscrupulous means. **Extortion** is the illegal use of position, power, or knowledge to obtain money, goods, funds, or favors. In nineteenth- and twentieth-century novels, the main type of extortion was blackmail. The plot would revolve around the blackmailer holding a scandalous letter or photograph of a person, and the blackmailer would then threaten to show the letter or photograph to interested parties unless he or she was paid money or given a position. With advancements in copy machines, this type of blackmail no longer makes sense since there can easily be more than one copy in circulation so that the victim would never know if his or her secret was safe by burning the original letter or photograph. More recently, tape recordings and e-mails have been used by blackmailers.

The terms **confidence man** and **con man** refer to a person who carries out a particular type of swindle in which victims are defrauded after their confidence has been won. The confidence or con game may take minutes, weeks, or years to pull off, based on the amount of money involved and the complexity of the fraud. Movies such as *Oceans 11* (with George Clooney) and *The Sting* (with Paul Newman and

**CONSUMER POWER MODEL**

**Consumer Rights on the Ski Slopes**

Consumer rights and regulations include all sorts of issues including the rights of snowboarders vs. skiers. In the United States, Taos Ski Valley in New Mexico was one of the last places of snowboard-free skiing and that changed in 2008. Snowboarders are now allowed on the slopes. "Relations between skiers and riders (as snowboarders are known) have never been chillier. An age gap helps put the group at odds. The majority of skiers who skied more than a day at a U.S. resort this past year were older than 25, according to the National Ski Areas Association; the majority of snowboarders weren't old enough to rent a car."[1]

Skiers say boarders are reckless and boarders say skiers are old and stuffy. What do you think? Can these two groups coexist and use the same areas? Besides the managers of the slopes, real estate developers and restaurants/hotels are involved. Many think real estate will take a downturn if riders are allowed. "They bring their lunch to the mountains instead of buying it," says Liz Jamison, a real estate agent and ski instructor at Taos for 22 years.[2] Can you think of another consumer rights issue where there is an age divide?

------

[1] Hannah Karp, "Snowboarders Invade Another Ski Shrine," *Wall Street Journal*, December 22–23, 2007, p. W1.
[2] Ibid.

Robert Redford) have glamorized con games, but in reality con games are not glamorous and can result in years in prison. Although the term *con man* is masculine, there are con women as well (*con artist* is a generic term). A common crime occurs when female housekeepers or caregivers steal either from the households they are hired to clean or from the people they are hired to care for, especially the elderly. Besides stealing jewels and money, these people may get hold of the elderly person's checkbook or credit card and scam undetected for a long time. Banks are on the lookout for any unusual movement of large amounts of money and may report suspicious activity to the account holder. Before leaving the subject of con games, it should be pointed out that they occur in business as well as in personal life; accountants or bookkeepers can siphon off company funds for a long time before they are caught. On a national scale, rigged television game shows and fake company sweepstakes have been exposed in the past. As a result, con games can be petty or involve

 **CONSUMER ALERT**

"In 1848 William Thompson came up with a disarmingly simple trick for separating New Yorkers from their assets. Well-dressed and polite, he approached a genteel-looking stranger on the street. After a bit of conversation, he asked, 'Have you confidence in me to trust me with your watch until tomorrow?' When a sucker did, Thompson walked off richer by a watch. This dodge gave birth to a new term: 'Confidence man' or con man for short."

*Source:* Adams, 2002, p. 240.

millions of dollars. Regarding fraud directed at individuals, it is becoming more common for con artists today to be less personal than the example in the Consumer Alert, with contact with the victim more likely coming through advertisements in newspapers, on television, over the telephone, or on the Internet.

In summary, as the marketplace becomes more complex, so does the need for protection. It behooves all of us to pay more attention to what is occurring right in front of us, right now. We need to be curious about what is going on, what we are buying, and what we are eating and drinking. Being present in the moment will help us avoid injuries and fraud by being more careful of the environment that surrounds us, which leads us to the next subject to be discussed—injurious consumption.

## INJURIOUS CONSUMPTION

The government agencies described in this chapter actively work to reduce injuries caused by consumer products and their use. Injurious consumption occurs when individuals or groups make consumption decisions that have negative consequences or misuse products in such a way as to cause injury to themselves or others. For example, every year 25,000 people die as a result of alcohol-related traffic accidents; some of these people were drunk or alcohol impaired, and others were innocent victims. There are about 10 million alcoholics and 80 million cigarette smokers in the United States (Faber, 1985; Hirschman, 1991). Companies promoting such products are often the culprit, but the government is not immune if one considers the number of state-sponsored gambling activities, including lotteries, and companies that make potentially harmful products that are given subsidies or tax breaks.

In summary, consumers often engage in harmful activities, and businesses (and even the government) can be the source of injurious consumption. "Economics is about events in the real world" (Landreth & Colander, 2002). So even though it is difficult to point out that people consume for reasons that are not always healthy or in their best interest, it has to be done. The Landreth and Colander quote points out that economics (and especially consumer economics) is about the real world, and the outcomes of consumption are not always attractive.

## REGULATION AND DEREGULATION ISSUES

So far, this chapter has talked about rules, legislation, and agencies to protect consumers as well as some types of fraud and injuries that may befall consumers. Government, through its policies on taxes (such as placing high taxes on cigarettes) and spending, affects consumer behavior. It decides how schools will be funded, what roads will be built, and whether Social Security recipients will receive a raise each year and how much. Once an agency is created, it has the authority to develop rules and regulations. It is usually easier to have rules and regulations set up than to have legislation pass through state legislatures and Congress. Besides developing rules, agencies have to see that they are enforced. In terms of consumerism, a **rule** or **regulation** is an attempt by government to control the workings of the marketplace. Rules and regulations are necessary because policy makers believe that it is in the best interest of consumers and the overall economy as well as the development of certain industries if monopolies are held in check because they reduce competition in the marketplace. This reduction could lead to price-fixing, poor service, and scarcer choices. This stance, of course, is opposed to the general philosophy of Adam Smith, who argued that government interference, for the most part, is undesirable because it infringes on the natural rights and liberties of individuals. However, his greatest concern was about the regulation of international trade rather than domestic trade (Landreth & Colander, 2002).

Rules and regulations relevant to consumer economics do the following:

- Educate consumers
- Protect consumers
- Regulate sellers
- Discourage unfair, deceptive, or dangerous business practices
- Change the relationship between buyers and sellers, making certain practices or products illegal

Many rules protect children in terms of the advertising content and images targeted at them. For example, in 1996 the Federal Communications Commission (FCC) issued new rules under the Children's Television Act that required stations to air three hours of educational programming per week targeting children 16 years old and under and tightened the definition of what constitutes educational programming. Most people would agree that children need protection in the marketplace.

Regulations placed on products aimed strictly at adults are more controversial. Some economists and many corporations (especially those that are under investigation and those who represent them) feel that government intervention has gone too far and would argue for more public choice. They believe that government regulation is ineffective or too restrictive of trade and agree with Adam Smith's philosophy of laissez-faire (let the marketplace run itself). Given the countless numbers of products and services available, it is safe to say that for the most part the marketplace is not regulated. For example, "supplements are largely unregulated by the federal government and are not monitored for potency, purity or correct dosage; older adults on other medications may be particularly susceptible to overdoses or adverse reactions" (Pope, 2002). Many in the population applaud government intervention and would like more of it, especially as new problems crop up. When it comes to the unknown and the untested, the public looks to government to serve as a protector. To summarize and extend the arguments already presented, as the marketplace becomes more impersonal, as small local stores disappear and consumers deal with sellers in an impersonal environment, fraud is more easily promulgated. Product complexity has also grown, requiring more knowledge of companies, products, and services, and advertising is more intrusive. All these factors make a case for the necessity for regulation.

Below is a list of several areas of regulation:

- *Pricing.* A maximum price may be set for a product or service.
- *Licensing.* A license may be required to be an interior designer, a nail technician, or a barber.
- *Standard setting.* Safety standards can be set in factories, as can standards regarding how much beef should be in a can of beef noodle soup.

- *Subsidies.* Government can become involved in regulating supplies of imports, such as oil, and provide incentives or subsidies for growing specific crops or developing certain businesses.
- *Privacy.* Standards regarding privacy in financial transactions can be determined.

In the 1970s, proponents of reform and some lawmakers began to question the wisdom of too much government regulation of industry. They argued that too much regulation was restricting trade and that in the long run consumers may gain from deregulation. **Deregulation** removes or reduces government intervention and allows the free market to operate. Below are examples of deregulated industries:

- *Airlines.* Deregulation of airlines in 1978 covered fares, schedules, and routes. Under discussion is a passenger bill of rights as well as better airfare disclosures.
- *Banking.* Deregulated in the 1980s, banking practices affect savings rates, fees, and lending standards. When some banks failed in the 1980s, they were bailed out by the government; mergers ensued. The opening up of interstate banking came in 1994. In the United States, the top 25 banks controlled 51 percent of deposits in 1998, compared with 29 percent in 1980 ("Deregulated," 2002). Under discussion is more protection from unreasonable rate hikes, especially in the area of ATM charges.
- *Cable television.* The cable television industry was regulated and deregulated throughout the 1980s and 1990s, which affected rates and services. This industry often ranks low in consumer satisfaction surveys.
- *Electricity.* Deregulation of electricity providers in certain areas in the 1990s was controversial. Problems with blackouts in California, for example, caused that state to suspend deregulation in 2001.
- *Telephone.* In 1984 telephone equipment was deregulated; long-distance service was partly deregulated in 1984, and domestic service began to be deregulated in the 1990s and is continuing. There are problems with customer confusion over rates and services.

*Consumers need government protection through regulations and legislation, but they also can benefit from deregulation because of more competitive pricing.*

Box 5.5 provides a list of criteria to use in judging how well deregulation has worked.

If it works as intended, deregulation should lead to more competitive pricing, product and service innovations, and more options for consumers. In deregulation, sometimes smaller companies rise to the top; for example, Southwest Airlines, once a small regional airline which is now nationally known, has consistently high consumer satisfaction ratings on service and prices. When deregulation does not work out well, there are problems, such as the blackouts in California noted in Box 5.5. In deregulation, services may suffer, prices may not decrease, and the number of choices can lead to customer confusion. An example of this is the confusion of many consumers over which telephone company or computer server to choose and arguments over improper or misleading charges. Because of the variance in industries and in consumer needs, each deregulated industry has to be judged individually. Traditionally it was assumed that for the most part, the positive aspects (in particular, better prices) far outweighed the negative aspects, but there have been articles that question how much consumers really benefit from deregulation ("Deregulated," 2002). If an industry is deregulated, it does not mean that the government is no longer involved because government is watching for abuses in the

**BOX 5.5    Deregulation Criteria**

There are arguments for and against deregulation. The reason a clear-cut pro and con list cannot be given is that deregulation in certain industries may be better for urban dwellers living in concentrated high-profit centers because they experience increased service and more competitive prices, whereas people in rural areas may experience less service and higher rates. In the list below, the usual criteria listed are used to decide if deregulation is working from a consumer point of view.

*Choice.* Are consumers given more choices?

*Consumer rights.* Are consumers given more rights, or are the rights they already have upheld?

*Innovation.* Are better products offered? Are new ways of manufacturing and production encouraged?

*Safety.* Have security and safety increased?

*Savings.* Are consumers saving money? Are prices lower?

*Service.* Are consumers being served better? Are services dependable?

*Source:* Adapted from "Deregulation," 2002.

system, such as runaway rate hikes or discrimination, and is prepared to step in when things get out of hand or existing laws are violated.

Another type of deregulation is when government turns to **privatization**, which means turning over some of the functions of government to business. The trend in many states is toward more privatization or outsourcing of formerly government-based work. This may involve government workers losing their jobs, being offered early retirement, or shifting from government to business occupations. There is debate on both sides (government and business) as to whether privatization leads to better service and (in the long run) to more efficiency and cost savings for citizens.

## SPECIAL INTERESTS

Businesses, organizations, and government do not operate in a vacuum—they influence and are influenced by many groups. **Special-interest groups** are units of two or more persons who have a common interest and seek to influence government policy and enforcement. They may do this by lobbying. **Lobbyists** represent special-interest groups. A study by the Center for Public Integrity found that lobbyists vastly outnumber and overwhelm elected state officials and are also a significant presence in Washington, D.C. The top lobbying interests in the nation are given in Table 5.1. The number of lobbyists is highest for the insurance industry, followed by those representing health services. There are different opinions about the worth and the functioning of lobbyists, with some calling them swarming locusts and others calling them useful resources. They definitely serve a function—to influence legislation on behalf of their client, which may be an organization, industry, or employer—and are another voice in the legislative process. According to a study titled *The Fourth Branch* by the Center for Public Integrity in 2002, lobbyists spend more than $570 million per year influencing legislation in states across the country. States have laws

**Table 5.1**   Top-Ranked Lobbying Interests in the United States

| | |
|---|---|
| 1. Insurance | 6. Business services |
| 2. Health services | 7. Electric utilities |
| 3. Education | 8. Pharmaceuticals |
| 4. Local government | 9. Oil and gas industries |
| 5. Health professionals | 10. Lawyers/law firms |

*Source:* Center for Public Integrity, *The Fourth Branch*, 2002 report.

regulating how much legislators can accept from lobbyists; for example, in Florida, the limit is $100 per occurrence that a lobbyist can spend on a lawmaker, and this money can go for dinners, hunting trips, and sporting events tickets.

A study by Public Citizen and the Center for Responsive Politics in 2001 reported that the following two industries did the most political spending from 1999 to 2000: pharmaceuticals ($177 million in lobbying and $20 million in campaign contributions) and insurance ($128 million in lobbying and $41 million in campaign contributions). So there are a number of public-action groups and centers monitoring political spending, tracking advertisements, and documenting promotions. According to University of Pennsylvania's Annenberg Public Policy Center, which tracks issue ads, "When it comes to issue advocacy money is indeed speech, with the largest bankroll having the loudest voice and the voice of those with limited means effectively drowned out" (Drugmakers, May 2002, p. 14).

## ENLIGHTENED COMPANIES AND CONSUMER PROTECTION

The activities of lobbyists as well as new laws and regulations will continue to grow, but enlightened companies encourage their managers to look beyond what the rules say and simply to "do the right thing." In other words, well-run companies will self-regulate. Socially responsible firms actively seek ways to protect the long-run interests of their consumers and the environment (Kotler & Armstrong, 2002). They do not rip off consumers by selling products that stop or reverse the aging process, for example. Since it is not currently possible, anyone who does this is lying, even if he or she is a doctor, according to S. Jay Olshansky, a demographer at the University of Chicago (Pope, 2002).

How businesses run themselves as well as the products they produce has come under public scrutiny. For example, recent well-publicized corporate scandals have drawn the public's attention to the pitfalls of poor business practices, including shoddy accounting. Businesses more than ever before are being expected to use common sense and to be above reproach. Many industries and professional associations have adopted a code of ethics or a set of guidelines for standards of behavior and accountability. The development of e-commerce and the Internet has pushed this agenda even further, and privacy issues have moved center stage. Legislators and company managers are asking: What are the rules in cyberspace? Written laws from the government have often not kept pace with this fast-moving technology, and existing laws are often difficult to apply or enforce in cyberspace.

If companies don't self-regulate, the government can and does step in. An example is the 1998 case of America Online (AOL), which paid a $2.6 million penalty and agreed to update its business practices to settle a deceptive-marketing complaint brought forward by 44 state attorney generals. AOL failed to notify consumers clearly that the "50 free hours" in its online service's much-touted trial memberships must be used within a one-month period and that users would incur subscription fees after the first month (Kotler & Armstrong, 2002). Unethical marketing tactics are part of an area called social marketing. In **social marketing**, marketing strategies and tactics are applied to alter or create behaviors that have a positive effect or that try to reverse negative outcomes for individuals, society, and the environment. For example, social marketing could be used to encourage recycling or to reduce smoking (in the case of smoking, this could be done through dramatic advertisements showing close-ups of the ruined teeth, wrinkled skin, or blackened lungs of lifelong smokers).

Leading corporations support social marketing by considering their own business practices and by advertising to try and help the communities in which they are located. They want consumers to have the information they need to make sound choices. Successful businesses know that good products, information, and word of mouth are essential to their continuing success in the marketplace, and smart consumers look for reliable companies they can trust. Legitimate businesses know it is in their best interest to have good relations with consumers, and that is why they get involved in issues of consumer protection. They provide full disclosure through warranties and labels, especially for health care products both because they want to have happy customers and repeat business and because they want to drive out illegitimate or quasi-legitimate businesses that give business in general a bad name. They may join Better Business Bureaus (BBBs) or associations whose primary goal is to help legitimate businesses maintain good reputations in communities by accepting consumer complaints.

As mentioned in the previous chapter, over 2,600 members representing more than 1,500 companies (such as Dial Corporation and Delta Air Lines) belong to the Society of Consumer Affairs Professionals (SOCAP), which provides training, conferences, and publications. SOCAP exists to encourage and maintain the integrity of business in transactions with consumers; to encourage and promote effective communication and understanding among businesses, government, and consumers; and to define and advance the consumer affairs profession. Contact information is given in the E-Resources section.

## NONGOVERNMENTAL PRO-CONSUMER GROUPS

There are literally thousands of nongovernmental pro-consumer groups, ranging from Centers for Economic Justice to Legal Aid Societies. Some have the word "consumer" in their titles and others don't, which makes some of them difficult to identify or classify without closely examining the issues or the people they represent. For example, the American Cancer Society would not be thought of primarily as a consumer organization, but it is a research and consumer advocacy group on the specific subject of cancer prevention and the search for cures. To summarize the main emphases, consumer groups are concerned with three things:

1. Do consumers have full knowledge of what they are buying?
2. Are products safe?
3. Are products environmentally sound?

Chapter 3 provided information about leading national organizations that look out for consumers' interests. One of the oldest, largest, and most visible is the Consumers Union (CU), which publishes *Consumer Reports,* a monthly magazine, as well as other publications and media. The CU researches and tests consumer goods and services and publishes the results. CU is an independent nonprofit organization.

The Consumer Federation of America (CFA), founded in 1968, is a large nationally recognized advocacy organization working to advance pro-consumer initiatives. CFA focuses much of its advocacy on several areas:

- Financial services
- Utilities
- Product safety
- Transportation
- Health care
- Food safety

Located in Washington, D.C., it mainly serves as a lobbying federation. Staff members testify before Congress, the White House, federal and state regulatory agencies, and the courts on consumer issues, and their testimony is based on facts gathered and issues analyzed. CFA also is an educational organization and coordinates the efforts of over 285 organizations, including trade unions, credit unions, and rural electric cooperatives, and in so doing serves as a clearinghouse of information. Because of this, CFA represents a wide constituency and range of interests versus some groups that are more focused. CFA is especially concerned about the needs of the less affluent and less educated consumers who have little discretionary income and are especially vulnerable to deceptive or fraudulent sales. A partial list of some of the thousands of nongovernmental pro-consumer groups and their primary functions are listed in Table 5.2. There are other organizations that

**Table 5.2**   Nongovernmental Pro-Consumer Groups and Their Primary Functions

| Group | Function |
| --- | --- |
| American Association of Retired Persons (AARP) | Information (especially for those 50 years and older), lobbying, research, publications |
| American Council on Consumer Interests (ACCI) | Academic-based organization, information, journal |
| American Standards Association (ASA) | Research on products, standard setting |
| Better Business Bureaus (BBBs) | Business supported organizations, consumer protection |
| Center for Auto Safety | Car complaints, testing, lobbying |
| Center for Science in the Public Interest | Legal-based organization, lobbying, nutrition |
| Center for Study of Responsive Law | Legal-based organization, lobbying |
| Consumer Federation of America (CFA) | Coordinating, lobbying |
| Consumers Union (CU) | Testing, publications |
| Public Citizen | Legal defense, lobbying, information |
| Public Interest Research Groups (PIRGs) | Lobbying, research, presence on some college campuses |
| Tax Reform Research Group | Has subgroups such as Congress Watch |

are primarily academic in nature such as the American Council on Consumer Interests (ACCI), which publishes the *Journal of Consumer Affairs,* and the Association for Financial Counseling and Planning Education, which publishes *Financial Counseling and Planning.*

# CONSUMER PUBLICATIONS

## Mission

**Media mix** refers to the combination of media vehicles, nontraditional media, and marketing communication tools whose mission is to reach a targeted audience (Wells, Burnett & Moriarty, 2000). In consumer economics, the target is the consumer, and the messages could include how to stimulate shopping or search behavior or how to be more cautious and selective in purchasing behavior. A successful media campaign will deliver on its objectives:

- Increase sales
- Increase awareness
- Change attitudes

Consumers can be divided into two groups: those who buy the product or service and those who use the product or service. For example, parents buy baby food, but the baby eats the food. In terms of consumer protection, a parent may be interested in putting screens or limits on Internet access to certain sites for their teenager; the user would be the teenager, but the purchaser of the product or service would be the parent. In both cases, the parent is the targeted consumer.

A major source of consumer information is the many newspapers and magazines published about health; about personal finance, such as *Money* or *Better Investing,* or about the results of product tests, recalls, travel bargains, or other consumer news, such as car testing results in *Motor Trend* magazine. These publications, combined with radio, the Internet, and television throughout the world, reach millions of consumers and perform a great public service.

## Consumer Reports

As mentioned previously, there are generalized consumer groups and sources of information, and there are also specific publications with "consumer" in the title. The most famous of these is *Consumer Reports* (and Consumer Reports Online and Consumer Reports on TV in the United States and Canada) published by Consumers Union (CU), an independent nonprofit testing and information organization. The magazine's subscribers number between 4 and 5 million. CU's mission since its inception in 1936 has been to test products, inform the public, and protect consumers. CU has a president, a board of directors, and a staff of more than 450. Its Consumer Policy Institute and testing and research center is in Yonkers, New York, and is the largest nonprofit education and consumer product testing center in the world. All the products are tested off the shelf, meaning the staff buy them just as a consumer would. The staff send back free products sent by manufacturers. What do they test? In more than 50 labs, the staff test appliances, autos, chemicals, electronics, food, home environment products, public service, and recreation and home improvement products. Cars and trucks are tested at the auto-test facility in East Haddam, Connecticut. The staff also survey readers to find out about repair reliability and to rate services. The Consumer Policy Institute conducts research and education projects on such issues as air pollution, food safety, biotechnology, and right-to-know laws. It calls itself "America's #1 Consumer Product Test Center." *Consumer Reports* does not take advertising but does engage in sales of its own services, products, and publications, such as the *Consumer Reports Travel Letter*, and uses inserts for new subscriptions or subscription renewals. Further, inside the magazines there are statements and advertisements that encourage subscribers to remember CU in their wills. The following was found on paper wrapped around an issue mailed to a subscriber:

> Your next issue will be your last issue! It's alarming, but true . . . unless you renew now! You're about to lose the money-saving, safety preserving, rip-off preventing independent research results and recommendations compiled in every issue of *Consumer Reports*. So, quick! Check the term you prefer on the postage-free card and mail it today. (*Consumer Reports,* October 2002)

So it could be said that *Consumer Reports* meets the three media objectives listed earlier: increased sales, increased awareness, and changed attitudes.

CU has three advocacy offices in Washington, D.C., San Francisco, and Austin, Texas. Advocacy staff testify before federal and state legislative and regulatory bodies on issues such as health care, financial policies, and food and product safety, and they also petition government agencies and file lawsuits on behalf of consumers. This brings us back full circle to the beginning of the chapter, which stressed that we are living in an information society. As consumers, we need to know what is going on, what the results of product tests are, and how we can make the best choices.

## SUMMARY

The media are an important element in our information economy. The mission of media is to inform. *Consumer Reports,* published by CU, is an example of a nongovernmental, consumer-oriented publication. Government is one of the main gatherers, sorters, producers, and monitors of information and produces many useful publications, including the more than 200 publications about everything from buying cars to making wills found in the *Consumer Information Catalog* by the FCIC. The federal government is empowered to act on behalf of consumers in a number of ways, such as rules and regulations.

The chapter began with a description of how to contact elected state and federal officials about issues and concerns and moved on to explain the workings of the main federal government agencies related to consumerism. Because their jurisdictions differ, it is not always easy to differentiate one from the other. For example, the USDA handles meat, poultry, and egg product testing, whereas the FDA handles other food sources. Some agencies test products and others don't, and some have more investigation and enforcement powers than others. The different agencies also cooperate with each other and may each have a say in a particular part of a case or investigation. All are involved in providing consumer information to the public through their Web sites. State and local governments are also active in consumer protection, as are some corporations, associations (such as SOCAP), and nongovernmental pro-consumer groups (such as the CFA).

As the marketplace becomes more complex, the need for more consumer protection increases, but it was also pointed out that consumers often engage in injurious or risky behaviors. It is impossible to remove all consumer risks, but reducing risks and providing better consumer information are goals of government agencies and consumer organizations.

## KEY POINTS

1. The Federal Trade Commission (FTC), established in 1914, is responsible for handling complaints of false advertising, fraud, and product safety and administering antitrust and consumer protection legislation. The FTC looks for patterns of noncompliance, fosters free and fair business competition, and prevents monopolies and activities that restrain trade.

2. As the name implies, the Consumer Product Safety Commission (CPSC) handles consumer product safety, mainly in the areas of toys, baby and sports equipment, and household items.

3. The Food and Drug Administration (FDA) has as its mission to promote and protect public health by helping safe and effective products reach the market in a timely way and by monitoring products for continued safety after they are in use.

4. The U.S. Department of Agriculture (USDA) helps farmers and ranchers and leads in the food stamp, school lunch, and school breakfast programs. It researches human nutrition; encourages stewardship of the land, conservation, and community development; and monitors the safety of meat, poultry, and egg products.

5. The Department of Justice (DOJ) enforces antitrust laws and promotes competition.

6. The Securities and Exchange Commission (SEC) advocates for the investor and provides investor education. It looks for fraud and deception in the securities markets.

7. The Department of Transportation (DOT) oversees highway safety and monitors seat belts and other safety devices.

8. State and local governmental units, including police, get involved in consumer protection.

9. There are pros and cons to deregulation. In theory, the pros may include lower prices, expanded choices, and enhanced services, but in practice this has not always been the case when industries are deregulated.

10. Thousands of nongovernmental pro-consumer groups look out for the consumer interest.

11. The media, including *Consumer Reports* published by the Consumers Union, inform consumers about product quality, possible fraudulent schemes, and recalls. Magazines and newspapers (and their Web sites) may also provide information, including up-to-date ratings, on auto trends, cell phones, running shoes, digital cameras, and other products in the marketplace.

## KEY TERMS

bunko
claim rates
confidence man
conglomerate merger
con man
corrective advertising
deregulation
extortion
grifter

horizontal merger
information economy
lobbyists
market extension
    merger
media mix
merger
privatization

product extension
    merger
regulation
rule
social marketing
special-interest groups
vertical merger

## DISCUSSION QUESTIONS

1. Why does the Department of Justice get involved in the violation of antitrust laws?
2. How do the police get involved in consumer protection? What sort of cases might they investigate? What is extortion, and why would the police become involved in investigating extortion?
3. What is an example of injurious consumption? Why do consumers engage in activities that put themselves and others at risk?
4. Consumer advocacy comes in many forms. Go to the Consumer Federation of America Web site at www.consumerfed.org, and list the current issues that they are working on (click on What's New).

## E-RESOURCES

The U.S. government Web site that leads to all the others is www.firstgov.gov.

**Center for Public Integrity (CPI)**    *www.publicintegrity.org*
Nonprofit center, reports on lobbyists

**Consumer Federation of America (CFA)**    *www.consumerfed.org*
Washington-based advocacy organization, education

**Consumer Product Safety Commission (CPSC)**    *www.cpsc.gov*
Federal government agency, news updates, employment information

**Consumer Reports**    *ConsumerReports.org*
Current consumer news, alerts, online shopping site e-ratings, interactive product selectors

**Department of Justice (DOJ)**    *www.usdoj.gov*
Federal government agency

**Department of Transportation (DOT)**    *www.dot.gov*
Federal government agency

**Federal Consumer Information Center (FCIC)**   *www.pueblo.gsa.gov*
Federal government center, recalls posted, other consumer news, pamphlets

**Federal Trade Commission (FTC)**   *www.ftc.gov*
Federal government agency, consumer protection, Consumer Sentinel (program to fight consumer fraud and scams)

**FirstGov for Consumers**   *www.consumer.gov*
Consumer information from over two dozen federal agencies

**Food and Drug Administration (FDA)**   *www.fda.gov*
Federal government agency

**National Fraud Information Center**   *www.fraud.org*
Nonprofit center, exposure of fraud, Internet Fraud Watch (click on Internet Tips)

**National Highway Traffic Safety Administration (NHTSA)**   *www.nhtsa.dot.gov*

**Securities and Exchange Commission (SEC)**   *www.sec.gov*
Federal government commission, information on stocks and investing

**Society of Consumer Affairs Professionals (SOCAP)**   *www.socap.org*
Nonprofit association, consumer concerns within the corporate structure

**U.S. Department of Agriculture (USDA)**   *www.usda.gov*
Federal government agency

## REFERENCES

Adams, S. (June 10, 2002). May I hold your watch? *Forbes,* p. 240.

Center for Public Integrity. (2002). *The Fourth Branch.* Washington, DC.

Deregulated. (July 2002). *Consumer Reports,* pp. 30–35.

Drugmakers. (May 2002). *AARP Bulletin.* Washington, DC, pp. 13–14

Faber, R. (December 1985). Two forms of compulsive consumption. *Journal of Consumer Research,* pp. 296–304.

Gasparino, C., and S. Craig. (May 23, 2002). Broker watchdogs face scrutiny as investor complaints mount. *Wall Street Journal,* p. A1.

GH Institute Report. (August 2001). Shock away your wrinkles? *Good Housekeeping,* p. 16.

Hawkins, D., R. Best, and K. Coney. (2001). *Consumer behavior: Building marketing strategy.* Boston: Irwin McGraw-Hill. Examples cited from I. Teinowitz, FTC faces test of ad power. *Advertising Age,* March 30, 1998, p. 26.

Hirschman, E. C. (1991). Secular mortality and the dark side of consumer behavior. In *Advances in Consumer Research XVIII,* ed. R. Holman and M. R. Solomon. Provo, UT: Association for Consumer Research, pp. 1–4.

Jones, D. (December 17, 2002). More consumers give government services thumbs-up. *USA Today,* p. A1.

Kotler, P., and G. Armstrong. (2002). *Principles of marketing activebook.* Prentice Hall. www.prenhall.com/myactivebook.

Landreth, H., and D. Colander. (2002). *History of economic thought,* 4th ed. Boston: Houghton Mifflin Company.

Lynch, P. (October 15, 2001). What's next? *Wall Street Journal,* p. A5.

Pope, E. (June 2002). 51 top scientists blast anti-aging idea. *AARP Bulletin,* pp. 3–5.

Simons, J. (July 30, 1999). FTC has a committed foe of Internet fraud. *Wall Street Journal,* p. A20.

Spencer, J. (June 11, 2002). Rejected! Rebates get harder to collect. *Wall Street Journal,* pp. D1–2.

Swann, J. P. (May 14, 2002). History of the FDA. From www.fda.gov. Adapted from George Kurian, ed. (1998). *A Historical Guide to the U.S. Government.* New York: Oxford University Press.

Wells, W., J. Burnett, and S. Moriarty. (2000). *Advertising: Principles & practice,* 5th ed. Upper Saddle River, NJ: Prentice Hall.

# Buying Process, Brands, and Product Development

*In commerce, bygones are forever bygones; and we are always starting clear at each moment, judging the values of things with a view to future utility.*
—William Stanley Jevons

## Learning Objectives

1. List the six steps in the buyer decision process.
2. Explain the motivations of companies, including the handling of consumer complaints and reactions to competition.
3. Discuss the four stages in product development.
4. Explain population trends, including changes in families and households.
5. Identify the four stages in the household life cycle.

---

### Brands: Who Owns What?

Brands are distinctive names and packaging identifying a product or manufacturer. But, even the most famous brands and product divisions can be bought and sold, merged, or acquired.

Kraft Foods, Inc., recently put their Post cereals business up for sale. PepsiCo, Inc., General Mills, Kellogg, and Del Monte Foods, Co. (the San Francisco-based maker of canned fruits and vegetables), considered pursuing Post, but it appears that Ralcorp Holdings, Inc., is the frontrunner. You've probably heard of all of these except Ralcorp so who are they? And, why is Kraft selling off their Post cereals?

Ralcorp is a St. Louis private label maker of cereals and other foods like frozen waffles. They are interested because they can extend their product line and gain more shelf space in grocery stores. It also gives Ralcorp more purchasing power of wheat and other raw materials needed in their products.

About Kraft, "a sale would be part of Kraft's push to get rid of slow-growth assets under Chief Executive Irene Rosenfeld. The Post cereals business, which includes Raisin Bran, Grape-Nuts, and a variety of Pebbles children's cereals, is the No. 3 U.S. cereal maker by sales after Kellogg Company, and General Mills, Inc., but its sales have been stagnant. Sales of Post cereal at food retails, excluding Wal-Mart Stores, Inc., fell 2% to $699 million in the first months of the year, according to market research company Information Resources Inc."[1]

Deals such as these not only affect established brands and who owns what but affect the rise and fall of the stocks of the companies involved in sales and acquisitions. Investors are wise to follow such large brand moves and the companies who make them.

___
[1]Matthew Karnitschnig and Julie Jargon, "Kraft Is Near Sale of Post Cereals," *Wall Street Journal*, November 5, 2007, p. A 3.

## INTRODUCTION

As was typical of early writers, Adam Smith (1723–1790) saw numerous connections between many areas of society—things that today are studied by economists, political scientists, philosophers, sociologists, marketers, and family and consumer scientists—particularly in consumer behavior. **Consumer behavior** refers to the buying behavior of consumers—the individuals, families, and households that buy goods and services for personal consumption. Our task in this chapter is to build on Smith's contribution by continuing to explore the interconnectedness of the economy, with a particular emphasis on the connections among consumers, business, and the media. "One of the fundamental premises of the modern field of consumer behavior is that people often buy products not for what they do, but for what they mean. This principle does not imply that a product's basic function is unimportant, but rather that the roles products play in our lives go well beyond the tasks they perform. And the deeper meanings of a product may help it stand out from other, similar goods and services" (Solomon & Rabolt, 2004, p. 27). The chapter begins with the steps consumers go through in the buying decision.

## STEPS IN THE BUYER DECISION PROCESS

Consumers go through six steps in the buying process (shown in Box 6.1) that are part of prepurchase, purchase, and postpurchase behavior.

**BOX 6.1    Steps in the Consumer Buying Process**

**Prepurchase**

1. Assessing need
2. Searching for information
3. Evaluating alternatives
4. Selecting a product or service

**Purchase**

5. Buying

**Postpurchase**

6. Evaluating after purchase through use and comparisons

## Prepurchase

Purchase intentions are one of the most studied areas in consumer behavior. Of particular interest is **prepurchasing**, which focuses on what consumers are thinking about and how they are behaving that lead up to an actual purchase. One of the factors of note is perceived quality, which has a direct effect on purchase intentions and involvement (Tsiotsou, 2006). If someone believes a product or service is best, he or she is more inclined to buy it. If the individual is truly involved, he or she may talk about it with others, sharing knowledge and information. This person would be a market maven (a type of consumer discussed in Chapter 3). Marketers want to know consumer purchase intentions so that they can make a **forecast** of sales of existing products or demand for those in development. According to Box 6.1, prepurchasing involves four steps: assessing needs, searching for information, evaluating alternatives, and selecting a product or service, and each of these will be discussed.

**Assessing Needs.**   In prepurchasing, the consumer tries to determine how much pleasure or pain will be derived from a product or service. What is the anticipated performance? How much enjoyment can be expected? The first step, assessing need, results when problems or decision situations are recognized because people sense a discrepancy between their current state and a desired state. Need recognition can emerge internally ("I am thirsty") or externally ("There is no milk in the refrigerator"). The difference between needs and wants was presented in earlier chapters, which included the discussion of Maslow's hierarchy of needs that begins with the importance of fulfilling our most basic physiological needs (hunger, thirst, shelter) before moving on to more advanced needs. Table 6.1 shows examples of needs and wants.

In terms of employment, most people need work skills, people skills, benefits, transportation, a gathering place and/or communication system, and, of course, pay. Wants can include nearly anything—the sky is the limit. Examples would be corner offices, special phones, designer clothing, boats, private jets, sports cars, state-of-the-art computers and sound systems, swimming pools, vacations, and fitness equipment.

Needs and wants can be complex. In marketing, the term **need set** is used to reflect the fact that most products satisfy more than one need. For example, a house offers more than shelter: At a minimum, it offers storage for possessions and a place to sleep and eat, besides serving as a shelter from the wind and weather; it also offers status and services, which can be seen as an extension of the self. For instance, a homeowner told an interior designer who was suggesting a brown sofa

**Table 6.1**   Differences between Needs and Wants

| Needs | Wants |
| --- | --- |
| Basic clothes for school, leisure, and work | Stylish clothes for special events |
| Transportation for school and work | Brand-new high-end car |
| Apartment or room | House with a pool, a tennis court, and a view |
| Healthy, affordable food | Maine lobster (5 lb.), steak (16 oz.), loaded baked potato, and cheesecake |

and beige walls, "I need color. I cannot live without color." For the homeowner, color is a need—not simply a want—she cannot live in a brown world. Someone else may not care about color if a sofa is needed right away and the price is right. Another way to look at needs is to consider the types of relationships that individuals form with products, according to Susan Fournier (1998). Following are four relationships:

1. *Self-concept attachment*. Products help establish the user's self-concept and identity (for example, a professor carrying a briefcase or a student carrying a backpack).
2. *Nostalgic attachment*. When the product serves as a link with one's past, such as a favorite childhood brand of cereal, there is a nostalgic attachment. Kellogg's Frosted Flakes commercials show a middle-age woman ashamed to admit that the bowl of Frosted Flakes is for her, not for her children.
3. *Interdependence*. A product that is part of someone's daily routine, such as a specific soap and shampoo or a certain brand of orange juice, creates interdependency. Most people also have a favorite seat in the living room or family room, so they and the chair or sofa are interdependent.
4. *Love*. The product may elicit love, warmth, passion, or another strong emotion from the consumer. Examples would be stuffed toys or red roses at Valentine's Day. Expressions of love can be conventional, like red roses or a heart-shaped box of candy, or unique. One husband gave his wife a jar of honey every Valentine's Day.

Marketers take an individual's basic needs a step further by grouping consumers with similar need sets because they do not want to offer products that appeal only to one customer but to many. Once this group or segment is determined through research and/or demographics, then marketers focus their attention on the **target market**—the largest, most likely group to purchase. Once this market is determined, then **marketing strategy** is formulated that addresses the question "How can we give excellent customer value to this target market?" The question is answered by providing the proper **marketing mix**, which includes communications or information (to be discussed next) as well as product, price, distribution, and service.

**Searching for Information.**   The second step in the consumer buying process is searching for information. In this step, information is accessed either internally or externally. Nonrisky behavior, such as choosing what flavor of Snapple to buy, requires less search behavior than a riskier purchase, such as which car to buy. The information search involves sorting behavior. Consumers search for information before they buy: They may conduct an **internal search**, going over in their minds what they know about a product based on past searches or personal experiences, or they may conduct an **external search**, looking at advertisements, reading articles, going on the Internet, or asking others what they think about a product. An internal search is easier and more common than an external search because an external search requires activity such as talking with individuals or groups, reading marketing information, or experiencing the product itself (for example, test-driving cars or sampling foods at the grocery store).

Convenience plays a large part in consumer decision making.

Advertisers and businesses want to reach today's consumers who are actively conducting internal searches, and they also want to influence consumers' external searches. This is a challenging task because consumers don't always have the time, energy, or money to conduct extensive searches, either internal or external. Have you ever heard someone say, "I just don't have time to think about that right now"? This means that an internal search would take more time than he or she currently has. Regarding external searches, if a carload of people are running out of gasoline, they will drive into the nearest gas station regardless of cost or brand. But if they come to an intersection with two gas stations, then they may choose the one they prefer because of cost or brand preference or may select the one on the "right" side of the street. Convenience plays a large part in consumer decision making, which explains how two Starbucks (coffee shops) or convenience stores located only a block from each other can succeed.

The following are part of external searches:

- *Opinions, attitudes, and behaviors of others.* Friends, family members, neighbors, club members, television personalities, and even strangers, such as those contacted over the Internet, can influence searches.
- *Direct experiences.* Consumers' searches are also based on their own product inspections, trials, or observations. For example, an attorney could observe that in her law firm the attorneys drive BMWs and the secretaries drive Toyotas or Saturns.
- *Reading materials.* Articles and professional publications provide consumers with external search information.
- *Marketing communications.* External searches are impacted by advertising, public relations, coupons, labels, packaging, billboards, in-store displays, and other signals and messages that a company provides about itself and its products, which are termed **marketing communications**. One of the newer forms of market communications is product placement in movies and television shows where the viewer sees a box of cereal or a can of soda prominently displayed or used by a likable character. To reach the target market, the products and the communication mode should match—you wouldn't expect to see the giant purple Barney swigging down liquor or Spiderman eating prunes.

When consumers conduct a search, sometimes it is deliberate and sometimes it is not. For example, if someone needs an airplane ticket immediately, he or she will go on the Internet and search for airplane routes, availability, and prices. If there is more time, then the search may be less deliberate and the person may think, I wonder what flights there are between New York and London and what they are going for; then he or she may search the Internet out of curiosity or skim a full-page newspaper advertisement for discount fares. Another way to look at search behavior is to consider an **ongoing search**, which is conducted to acquire information for possible later use. One person, for example, may enjoy paging through fashion magazines with an intention of future clothing purchases, while another individual may like going to open houses or looking at housing or building magazines for ideas. Camping equipment, cars, computers, boats, recreational vehicles, and trips may all be part of ongoing searches. Go to any bookstore and you will see consumers thumbing through books and magazines mostly for recreational purposes.

Searching for information takes time and energy. The **information search rule** states that a consumer will search as long as the cost of the search is less than or equal to the expected savings from the search. Businesses help reduce search costs

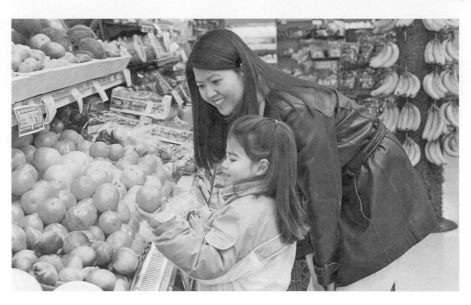

Food is an "experience" good. (Pearson Learning Photo Studio.)

by locating near each other (for example, auto dealerships and malls). The cost of the information search should be mentally added to the total cost of the product.

**Experience goods** refer to those about which the consumer gets relevant information after purchasing them, such as food and entertainment. Until consumers eat the food or see the movie, how can they tell if it was a pleasurable experience or not? Often with these types of goods, free samples or taste tests of food are given, and previews provide partial experiences of movies. **Credence goods** are those for which consumers can never get all the needed and relevant information and/or cannot evaluate the goods themselves, so these goods are often under government regulation and protection. An example of credence goods would be drugs.

Because so much consumer information exists and information overload is a distinct possibility, consumers make decisions about what types of information to access. They may use the following criteria:

- *Attractiveness*. Are they drawn to the information? For example, does the cover of a magazine attract? Does a movie preview look interesting?
- *Appropriateness*. Does the information fit their lifestyle? If they never travel, it is unlikely they will read travel books.
- *Existence of various alternatives*. Does one form of information fit better than another?
- *Performance characteristics*. What features (including cost) are provided? Is the information free or readily available? If a magazine costs $4.95, is it worth buying for the information and entertainment value that it contains?
- *Usefulness or caring*. Do they care what the information is about? If an article is about foot care for diabetics, it is unlikely that a ten-year-old would be interested.

Information may be passively or actively acquired. **Passive information** is encountered when one is doing something else. For example, most people have the radio on when they are jogging, working at a desk, driving a car, reading a magazine, or doing housework but do not just sit and listen to the radio. Because of this, radio ads have to break through consumers' inattention, but radio does have the advantages of sound effects, the human voice (for example, the announcer) and songs to reach listeners. Passive information is provided by a billboard at the side of the road; another source of passively acquired information is a **banner ad** that comes up at the top of a Web site, and there is currently debate in the marketing literature about how successful (or how irritating) banner ads are. **Actively acquired information** is sought after for its own sake (for example, test-driving a car or going to a fashion show). If you are planning a Disneyland or Disney World vacation, you could go on the Disney.com Web site, call the Disney phone number for information, read about Disney in books or travel magazines, or use a travel agent or travel Web site—all are methods of actively seeking information about the trip using a variety of sources. Marketers are very interested in how an active external search goes and may use surveys ("How did you hear about us?"). Other sought-after information includes how many stores or Web sites the person visited, the number of alternatives considered, the number of personal sources used, and the overall combination of measures and factors that influenced the final choice. Another way that marketers can target consumers is by asking for their zip code at the time of purchase because the zip code information will show them where to send circulars and catalogs.

**Evaluating Alternatives.**   In the third step, the person evaluates the alternatives based on the information search. Likes and dislikes, beliefs about the product or brand, on-site visits to several stores or Web sites, pricing, and availability help the consumer narrow the choices. In the case of which flavor of Snapple to buy, a consumer could eliminate all flavors with lemon in them if he or she doesn't like lemon, which narrows the field. Another evaluation involves sorting behavior—picture someone looking at the products on the shelf or reading labels or warnings.

Price, the amount of money one pays to obtain the right to use a product, is very important in alternative evaluation. An individual paying a price can own a product outright or may pay to rent or lease a product or service. One may assume that a lower price would sell more products, but price is also an indicator of quality. Would you feel comfortable paying $150 a month for a one-bedroom apartment, or would you feel suspicious, thinking something must be wrong with an apartment that could be rented at such a low price? The same could be said for the pricing of any other object or service. For example, retailers have witnessed the phenomenon of a bin of the same sale-priced sweaters selling better at $39.99 than they did at $25.00. Setting a price requires a thorough knowledge of not only the product but also the potential market for that product.

Potential buyers will also consider the **consumer cost**, which is the total cost involved in owning or using the product; this is also called the nonprice cost. For example, if someone buys a car, the consumer costs include the cost of gasoline, repairs, parking fees, depreciation, tire replacement, and so forth. A car that gets good mileage with regular gasoline will cost less to run than a car that uses premium gasoline. Sellers of products often will promote the cost savings.

Availability has an effect in the alternative evaluation. If the product is not readily available, a substitute product may be offered in its place or the purchaser may decide to wait until more selection is available. This relates to the marketing concept of **distribution**, that is, products being available in places near target customers. A truckload of snow tires in Florida will just sit there, but in January they may be a "hot" item in Minnesota. This is an obvious example, but less obvious examples are differences in food preferences throughout the United States, which successful grocers have to be aware of or they are stuck with slow-moving merchandise.

Consumers will also evaluate **service**, any activity performed to enhance and sustain the primary product or service. For example, when consumers buy from a local distributor of appliances, they may inquire whether the seller will also service an appliance when it breaks down. If they buy appliances over the Internet, they may wonder who will install and service the appliances. Other service considerations may be free pickup and delivery. Will the company take away the old appliances and install the new appliances, all at no cost? With people's busy lives, convenience becomes more and more important.

Information is a key input into the alternative evaluation, but there are other factors such as resources and product characteristics. Resources include time, energy, and money, as well as anything else that is useful to the decision and subsequent planning and action. Resources can be current or anticipated.

Since it would be impossible to taste every food in the grocery store, consumers evaluate the alternatives based on the amount of their shopping time and on a product's characteristics (such as sweet or sour, highly caloric or low-fat, bitter or smooth). Does chunky peanut butter taste better than regular? What is your preference? Consumers evaluate product characteristics based on the following:

Cost

Accessibility or availability

Features

Style

Perceived risk

All day long we make consumer decisions—we have to if we are to eat and drink and keep ourselves alive. We also consume to fulfill social functions since we are social beings. For example, a mother may be baking a birthday cake from a mix at home that requires three eggs, but when she opens the refrigerator, she finds there are only two eggs. Should she bake the cake using two eggs (taking a risk), should she go to the store for more eggs, or should she forget baking and go to the bakery? Her final decision will rest on energy, time, money, availability of the store and bakery, transportation, desired features or style of the cake, and so on. A connected decision is the candles, which are another resource, as are the matches to light the candles. One consumer decision builds on another, forming a chain of decisions.

**Selecting a Product or Service.**   To return to the prepurchase process, the fourth step is selection. The consumer takes the product off the shelf and puts it in his or her shopping basket; if it is a large purchase, he or she may tell the salesperson when and where to deliver it. If shopping online, the consumer clicks the desired selection and puts it in his or her virtual shopping basket. What if consumers see something they like better on the way to the checkout? They may change their minds, put the object back, and proceed to the next step.

## Purchase

The next phase is the actual purchase—the consumer buys the product. At the point of purchase, consumers think they have made the best choice by weighing all the factors, and the item or service is purchased, with money being spent or a trade being made. Things usually go smoothly, and the consumer can relax—unless his or her credit card isn't accepted, there isn't enough money to cover the purchase, or a computer is down.

## Postpurchase

After the purchase, buyers evaluate their purchase and seek reinforcement. Was the best decision really made? This third phase, called postpurchase behavior, encompasses the consumer deciding if it was a good or bad purchase by comparing the expected performance internally and externally. For example, internally a postpurchase consumer may decide that a food tastes good or bad. External reactions may include what others say or how they react to the consumer's new product; at a gas station, for example, he or she may notice the make of other cars and talk to owners who own the same car to see if they like the way their car is performing.

The tendency is to accentuate the benefits (in other words, look for reinforcing information that the consumer made a good purchase) and downplay the deficits, which is called **cognitive dissonance**. Consumers look for reinforcement and seek acknowledgment of the characteristics that are important to them. Being reassured brings pleasure to the decision-making process because a right decision removes doubt and uncertainty. It is generally more profitable for companies to retain customers than to replace them with new customers, so it behooves them to be concerned with factors such as cognitive dissonance as part of overall **customer satisfaction**, which is a function of the prepurchasing, purchasing, and postpurchasing experience (including that derived from the value of the product while it is in use).

Companies knowing all this seek to build loyalty in their customers. Ways to do this include frequent-flyer programs, discounts on future purchases, gifts, discount coupons, and loyalty points, such as those offered by Nordstrom. As an example, a woman may be given a bottle of free shampoo at the salon she frequents or a 10 percent discount on her next beauty treatment. Another way to do this is to give the purchaser a consumer satisfaction survey (at the time of purchase, at the end of a service such as a cruise or hotel stay, or immediately upon his or her return home by a survey sent in the mail). Accompanying the survey may be a newsletter with discounts or other encouragement to buy again.

If things go wrong, the final evaluation of a product or service is an important step that many consumers choose to ignore because they want to avoid pain or negative thoughts. They don't want to revisit bad clothing decisions, so they will put ugly clothes at the back of their closet or get rid of them. The problem with an unworthy product may be its style or other characteristics, the brand, unrealistic expectations, or the place where the purchase was made. In order to avoid wasting money again, the postpurchase step is a necessary part of the consumer process. The consumer may decide that the store or Web site should be avoided in the future and that alternative sources of products should be explored.

## MOTIVATIONS OF MARKETERS

In previous chapters we've discussed how businesses interact with consumers and government, but how do they operate internally? What are their motivations and concerns? Specifically in terms of marketing, what are their goals? We know that consumers want the best products at the best prices. Businesses want to participate in this process by bringing these sought-after goods to market and in so doing maximize profits. Marketing is key to this outcome.

*Effective consumer complaint handling is a way to keep customers and maintain good word of mouth.*

Listed below are four things marketers want to maximize:

1. *Consumer awareness.* They want you to notice their goods and services, their promotions and advertisements.
2. *Consumption.* They want you to try their products and buy more the next time. From a business perspective, greater levels of consumption are seen as a way to better things for both the consumer and the seller. As covered in previous chapters, not everyone agrees with this perspective (the scornful indictment of consumerism expressed in *The Overspent American* by Juliet B. Schor), but this section of the chapter is about how firms view consumption and their place in it.
3. *Loyalty.* As mentioned in the last section, marketers want to see you again. For example, you could be invited to join a loyalty club, such as the Crown & Anchor Club for repeat Royal Caribbean International cruisers (you are a gold member after completion of one cruise and a platinum member after five cruises; the incentives go up with each category, and there are separate cruises just for repeat customers). Fund-raisers for universities, sororities, fraternities, and charities often distinguish levels of givers, and the names or titles provide prestige. Metals and gems may denote different levels (it is better to be gold than silver and platinum than gold), and often at the top are diamonds or diamond categories (such as 5-diamond).
4. *Consumer satisfaction.* Although marketers want repeat customers, they want not only volume but also quality. They want to know that consumers like what they buy and that their product or service satisfies a need in a style or way that is pleasurable or comfortable. This is less easily measured than the number of products sold, but it is important to the long-running success of a business. Handling consumer complaints promptly and efficiently falls under this category (as well as the previous one of loyalty).

## COMPANIES AND COMPETITION

In order to meet customer needs, companies have to efficiently manage their finances, production, research and development, delivery, human resources, facilities, technology, and image and reputation. Managing the company image and reputation goes beyond producing effective advertising because image and reputation include other areas such as displays in stores or at conventions and news stories about managers and the health of the company, including present and future worth, growth, community leadership, treatment of employees, and environmental friendliness. If a scandal (such as a tampered-with consumer product) breaks out,

The following happened to the author of this book. I found a dead ladybug in a bag of prepackaged salad mix bought at the grocery store. The bug was found after half the salad mix had been eaten, to which my family replied, "Oh, gross!" I called the manufacturer's toll-free number and got the Consumer Care line. After explaining what happened and reporting that no one had gotten sick, I was offered a check for $15 or coupons worth about that much for future purchases. The Consumer Care person said that the salad mix is chlorinated in California and then shipped, so the bug was chlorinated as well and posed no health threat to anyone. However, she said that she would report the bug to quality control and thanked me for providing the code on the label information so she could track the place of origin. She also said I could take the complaint further and possibly get more money, but she said that rarely works. She advised me to take the $15, which I did. The check arrived, along with an apology letter, a few days after the call. The letter writer's title was "Consumer Response Specialist." In the second paragraph she wrote, "We are concerned when a product does not meet our high quality standards. Ready-to-use items, such as our pre-cut salads, are triple washed. The process should remove field debris or insect material. We informed our Quality Assurance staff of your report. The information will be helpful to prevent this in the future."

how does the company handle it? Does it act like nothing happened, or does it quickly try to remedy the problem? Often positive news is sent out to counteract bad news: When one drug fails in a pharmaceutical company, management puts out news about a promising drug that is undergoing research and development; in a movie production company, a failed movie is pushed aside, and the promotion effort switches to the next upcoming film. Where to put time and how much energy and resources to expend are continual issues for companies, but making those decisions is what managers are paid to do.

Competition is a continual threat and a stimulator. If companies are to succeed, they need to keep up with or surpass as well as anticipate competition. They can respond to competition in several ways:

- Reduce prices
- Increase advertising or change ad placement
- Introduce a new product
- Buy out the competition through mergers
- Develop a new strategic plan
- Improve customer service, giving better value such as offering free gift wrap or delivery
- Improve product quality

Across the United States and in many other places in the world, a common phenomenon is when a large company such as Wal-Mart or Home Depot comes into a small community and disrupts the existing mix. Since they deal in such large volumes, they often offer lower prices than smaller dealers can, so in order to stay alive, the smaller stores have to make themselves distinctive by offering easier parking, more services, or unique products. In the long run, competition allows companies to grow to be more efficient and profitable and serve customers better. Government policy plays a part in this competition through changes in zoning and in treaties or trade agreements such as the North American Free Trade Agreement (NAFTA), which greatly reduced trade barriers and increased the level of competition.

## GLOBAL CONSUMER

### Perking Up Coffee

Keeping established brands fresh and competitive is an ongoing concern of businesses. "Howard Schultz, whose vision 25 years ago took Starbucks from a handful of stores to an international behemoth with 15,000 locations worldwide, has returned as its CEO with this promise: Starbucks is returning to its roots. 'I am dissatisfied more than anyone else where we sit today,' he said in a hastily called conference call with industry analysts. 'We have a lot to do.' Starbucks' competitive map has changed drastically. The CEO change came the same day that McDonald's began to detail aggressive plans to invade Starbucks' turf by selling—at lower prices—such Starbucks favorites as cappuccino and lattes."

For Starbucks, the plan is to return to the basics, [removing] some of the non-coffee products and adding new "better for you" products. Boosting international growth is also on tap.

*Source:* Bruce Horowitz, "Starbucks Orders an Extra Shot." *USA Today,* January 8, 2008, p. B1.

## Customers and Brand Loyalty

Companies use **product positioning** to give brands a specific and unique image or position in the minds of consumers within a target segment (Foxall, Goldsmith & Brown, 1998). Their goal is to make their brand the most popular with the group they are trying to reach. It involves "creating the appropriate image of a product in the minds of consumers in the targeted markets" (Echtner & Ritchie, 1993). Generally, the greater the match is between a consumer's

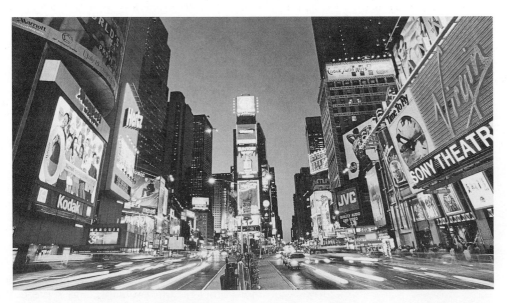

Times Square in New York City is full of advertising. Can you think of other places in the world with highly visible advertising? (Creative Eye/MIRA.com.)

image of a product and the self-concept of the individual, the greater the likelihood the individual will have a favorable attitude toward the product and the more likely that he or she will purchase it (Sirgy & Su, 2000). To do this, a company such as Unilever makes many kinds of toothpaste (including Aim and Pepsodent) that are positioned for different markets. As another example, tourist destinations can be marketed by product or image positioning (Sirgy & Su, 2000). Marketing managers determine the best product positioning through research, testing, and experience.

From a customer's point of view, familiar brands make it easier to shop—a sure thing is easier than experimentation each and every time one shops. For example, if a family is on vacation looking for a place to stop for lunch, they know the menu, quality, and prices they can expect from a Cracker Barrel restaurant versus an unfamiliar local "home-cooking" restaurant. Another aspect of branding is that given economies of scale, widespread distribution of certain brands should save money for producers and sellers, and the savings should be passed on to the consumers. A **brand** is a distinctive name identifying a product or a manufacturer; an example of a popular brand for a product would be Ivory, and a popular company would be Coca-Cola or Gillette. Sometimes the product or object is so popular that it becomes synonymous with a brand name—someone may be more likely to say "Hand me a Kleenex" than "Hand me a tissue." Examples of famous brands (besides those already named) are Campbell, Crayola, Hilton, Nabisco, Marriott, Chevrolet, Ford, Maytag, and Sears. As you can see from this list, brands can originate with manufacturers (such as Nabisco) or with dealers (such as Sears). Sometimes manufacturers and dealers are one and the same or have a close relationship through a franchise. You can also see on this list competitive brands such as Hilton and Marriott or Ford and Chevrolet.

When the same brand name is given to several products, it is termed a **family brand**, examples of which are Tom's Snack Foods and Frito-Lay. A family brand makes the most sense when the brands are of the same category, such as a food or a household cleaning product line. Unique packaging promotes and protects products. As mentioned in earlier chapters, the Federal Fair Packaging and Labeling Act of 1966 requires that consumer goods be clearly labeled in easily understood terms. There are ethical issues regarding packaging: The picture on the label on the front of a can or package should be similar in appearance to the product within, labels of competitive brands should be different enough so that consumers are not confused about which product they are buying, and the size of the package should be similar to the amount of contents found inside. The latter is particularly a problem with potato chips and cereals that settle, but manufacturers remedy this by stating ounces and giving a warning on the label that contents may settle in transit.

**Store brands** may be packaged in simply designed cans and boxes (examples include toilet paper and green beans). Because of the simplicity of these products and no markup for brand names and advertising, they are usually less expensive than similar products on the same shelf. Store brands are common in chain grocery stores and discount grocery chains, as well as in less developed countries, the latter being true because there is less exposure to advertising in those countries, so branding may not be part of the consumer culture, and people are actively seeking low prices.

## Product Development

Products go through four stages in their development:

1. *Introduction.* In the introductory stage, the product is developed and introduced to the market.
2. *Growth.* In the growth stage, easily recognized brands are aggressively marketed, such as using product placement in movies or increasing advertising, to keep sales growing, and gimmicks, including coupons, games, add-ons, and giveaways, may be used. An example of an add-on is when a popular shampoo is bundled with a conditioner; a giveaway takes place when a bank gives $500 to every five hundredth new customer.
3. *Maturity.* In the mature stage, the product is well known and accepted (for example, Crest toothpaste), but it may be reenergized with new formulas or packaging.
4. *Dormancy/decline (and possibly revitalization).* A product in the last stage may no longer be manufactured (for instance, a book may be out of print and available only on the used-book market). But let's say a movie comes along that popularizes the book (an example would be *Forrest Gump*); then the book is in demand again and is reprinted. Likewise, cartoon characters, toys, and jewelry can become popular again and be remarketed.

To explain further, let's look at how new products in stage one are introduced:

- A product could be new. An example of a totally new product would be chocolate-flavored french fries (although it could be said this is an off-shoot of chocolate-flavored or -dipped potato chips or pretzels that already exist). It is difficult to come up with a totally new product.
- A product could be a line extension, such as Coke Vanilla. (If it sells, will they try Coke Cinnamon?) A new flavor of potato chip could be developed by an existing potato chip company.
- A product could be a brand extension, such as Mello Yellow Candy.

Since new product development is costly, it is critical that extensive consumer research take place before the product is introduced to the market. Research shows that certain individuals are more likely than others to quickly try something new—these people are called innovators. An **innovation** is something that is perceived as new or different. Those attracted to innovations are important from a company perspective because they are heavy users of new products, often paying full price or a premium for newness. They may drive hours to see a car show or buy a new product, or they may book an exotic trip to go somewhere none of their friends have gone. Usually people choose their innovative categories, such as computer equipment, software, cameras, music, clothes, or restaurants. Innovators give valuable feedback to companies through their buying habits and their reactions to specifics about product features; in the marketplace, they encourage future sales through positive word of mouth (the consumer innovation curve was described in Chapter 3).

Although so far the discussion has been about products, there can be innovators in other areas:

- Ideas
- Sources

- Brands
- Practices
- Strategies, plans, or actions

Following innovators are the early adopters; then come the early majority, the late majority, and the laggards, who are the last people to adopt an innovation. They may want to wait until all the information is in before they make a decision or may be waiting for the price to fall before purchasing. Since people pick the category or categories they are innovators in—an individual can be a laggard in clothes but an innovator in electronics.

Innovativeness is linked to personality. A broad personality trait may be an affinity for trying something new versus having a more cautious outlook. Innovators are more likely to be risk takers than later adopters. Innovativeness is also linked to socioeconomic class since it takes discretionary income (extra money) to buy new products. Innovators are usually exposed to more media than laggards.

Everett M. Rogers, a leader in innovation theory, defined the innovation decision process as "the process through which an individual . . . passes (1) from first knowledge of an innovation, (2) to forming an attitude toward the innovation, (3) to a decision to adopt or reject, (4) to implementation of the new idea, and (5) to confirmation of this decision" (1995, p. 161).

To put this into a list, think of these as stages in the process (Foxall, Goldsmith & Brown, 1998):

- Knowledge
- Persuasion
- Decision
- Implementation
- Confirmation

To demonstrate how this works, take a magazine about shopping, such as *Lucky,* or a lifestyle magazine, such as *Real Simple.* Your introduction to it may be through a friend or family member or through a store display. You would form an opinion of whether it is right for you or not and then decide to thumb through it or not. If you like it, you may buy a copy or a subscription, and after a while you could decide if the purchase was a good decision or not. If you do not like the magazine, you might just give it back or put it back on the display.

## BRANDS, COUNTERFEITING, AND PIRATING

Brand names can be trademarked, which means they can be protected by law. A **trademark** is a legal term that includes words, symbols, or marks that are legally registered for use by a company. An example of a trademark is Big Mac for McDonald's; no other competing fast-food restaurant uses the term *Big Mac.*

Counterfeiting refers to making a look-alike copy, and counterfeiters sell knockoffs, products that look like the real thing but aren't (for example, counterfeit copies of CDs, Gucci handbags, Levi's jeans, or Rolex watches). Most consumers know that if the item is being sold on the street or at an extremely low price, then the item is probably a copy. If someone buys the product with this understanding, that is one thing, but if it is bought without this knowledge, then a deception has taken place, as has a rip-off of the legitimate manufacturer, artist, singer, or designer.

Counterfeiting is especially common in countries that do not honor international trademark or copyright laws or that have a culture in which counterfeiting is not considered unethical. In recent history in China and South Korea, there were many counterfeit products and few protections for internationally known brands in such areas as clothing, music, and books (including the popular Harry Potter books).

However, it is important to point out that low-income nations steal from other low-income nations, so it is not a question of the products of richer nations being pirated by poorer ones. A case in point is the Ghana textile industry (the average annual income in Ghana is $400) that continually combats cheap knockoffs by China, Pakistan, Nigeria, India, and the Ivory Coast. These other countries make cheap copies of the most popular Ghana textiles, smuggle them back into Ghana, and snatch sales from potential customers of the original high-quality fabrics (Phillips, 2002). "The fakes aren't hard to spot. They tend to be made of flimsier, less regular fabric, often synthetic such as rayon, instead of cotton. The colors don't always line up with the shapes" (Phillips, 2002, p. B1).

**Pirating** means stealing an original idea or product and selling it. Currently, "entertainment companies have a variety of techniques at their disposal to make it harder for people to share music, movies and software over the Internet" (Wingfield, 2002, p. D3). Following are some examples of these techniques:

- *File spoofing*. In file spoofing, a song or movie is labeled as something else. The user often experiences bursts of static or hears only part of a song's chorus.
- *Redirection*. Redirection happens when instructions are inserted into a bogus file; a possible outcome is the sending of the user to a commercial music site.
- *Interdiction*. Interdiction overloads a computer, jamming the computer with traffic.

Obviously these techniques are controversial and could be considered extreme or anticonsumerism. Pirating is not a new concept—ever since the advent of tape recorders, music could be taped and copies shared, and with VCR and DVD equipment and cameras, movies can now be copied. Because only a few people used to be involved in swapping activity, it was hard to prosecute or to work up much energy over the practice, but the Internet has made it much easier and more pervasive through file-swapping Web sites. Traditional industries are fighting back. "We think copyright owners ought to be able to do whatever they can that's lawful to protect their rights and their artists' careers," says Cary Sherman, president of the Recording Industry Association of America (Wingfield, 2002, p. D1).

## BRAND PERCEPTION AND IMAGE

**Brand perception** refers to how consumers view or rate a brand: How do they classify the brand? Do they think the brand is reliable or untrustworthy, innovative or old-fashioned? "An image of a product, person, brand, or place is formed when people develop beliefs, ideas, perceptions, or impressions about a product, person or place" (Deslandes, Goldsmith & Bonn, 2002). An individual can have an **image**

(an impression or attitude) about a vacation destination, for example, without having ever been to that place, and this image can come from the general media, educational sources, family, friends, travel agents, or brochures. It is widely assumed that an appropriate image can make or break a vacation destination; for example, news of terrorism or civil unrest can wreak havoc with a country's tourist industry, but visions of swaying palm trees, beautiful beaches, and cool drinks attract tourists.

**Brand image** refers to the set of perceptions that consumers have formed about a brand, such as a brand being perceived as targeting the young. Mello Yello soft drink is marketed to young people, with its advertisements showing shirtless teenage boys swinging on ropes out from cliffs, letting go, and dropping into a lake or pond. One would assume that a brand extension, such as Mello Yello candy, would appeal to a similar group. Since consumers tend to resist change and keep buying the same brands or brand extensions, firms especially like to attract young people because once young people like a brand, they have a lifetime of buying ahead of them. It often takes a crisis such as nonproduction of a good or a true innovation to move someone away from his or her established brand preferences.

Early brand perception is part of the socialization process in families. Think about any brands that your family routinely buys (a particular detergent, soap, toothpaste, or cleaning product). Assume your family buys Lysol. What is your perception of Lysol? Will it get things clean? Will it be strong? Usually one of the earliest consumer experiences outside the home is the child accompanying parents to the grocery store—think of all the toddlers you have seen in their carriers in grocery carts. This, among other reasons, is why it is important to turn our attention next to families and households in terms of population trends.

## POPULATION TRENDS

The U.S. population is growing more in states such as Arizona and Nevada than in others, and this affects market demand and the stress on natural resources such as water. Likewise, worldwide growth is uneven and impacts market demand and the use of resources. Population trends are important to study in consumer economics because one has to know where the humans are now and where they are likely to be in the future. By 2050 the U.S. population could be more than 500 million. Rather than being overwhelmed by this number, it is important to remember that this country has been growing steadily since colonial times and that solutions will be found to accommodate everyone. There are vast spaces in this country that are wilderness areas; other areas are actually losing or barely maintaining their population.

Here are some population trends:

- The greatest growth is expected in the West in states such as Alaska, Arizona, Colorado, Idaho, Nevada, New Mexico, Utah, and Wyoming.
- Rapid growth is also expected in Florida, Georgia, North Carolina, Oregon, Tennessee, Texas, and Washington.
- Slower-growing states include those in the Midwest and the states of Connecticut, New York, and Pennsylvania—although the largest metropolitan area in the United States is New York City with over 19 million inhabitants.
- Much future growth will come from immigration.

- The average age of the U.S. population is about 36 years and is rising.
- There are more empty nesters (those between 50 and 64 years old whose children have grown) as well as senior citizens (those over age 65) and elders, affecting health care, cars, food services, finances, housing, and tourism. Life expectancy in the United States is 74.8 years for men, 80.1 years for women.
- There are more teens now. In 2010, 30 million U.S. teens are anticipated, and they will influence sales of clothing, recreation, cars, and music.
- Since World War II, the most popular move has been to the suburbs, affecting transportation (cars are a necessity), jobs, stores, and homes. In the twenty-first century, there is a countermove back to cities, where people are renovating homes and rejecting long commutes. Although there is a return to urbanism and planned developments, with access to green spaces, there is also a segment of the population favoring "the new ruralism," a return to small-acreage farms or homes with two acres or more of land.
- Mobile populations are higher consumers than people who stay in one place because each move necessitates consumption of products and services. In the retired population, the main choices are to stay put, move permanently to a new location (usually in a warm climate), or be nomads, changing homes every three to five years while looking for the best location near family, friends, and services such as health care, shopping, airports, restaurants, and entertainment.
- More people have middle- and upper-class incomes.
- There is increased diversity. About 1 in 10 U.S. homes is non-English-speaking (or combined English- and non-English-speaking), and the percentages are much higher in certain areas than others, which affects education and all sorts of consumer preferences from food to entertainment.
- Baby boomers' kids are having babies. In 2006, 4.3 million babies were born in the United States—the largest number in a single year since 1961. This increase is affecting toy sales, future educational needs, and media.

## Changing Families and Households

A household may be made up of one or more persons; a family is made up of two or more persons. Since 1980 the percentage of households that are families has declined.

The household is the most basic consumer unit. Households drive the consumer market in their selection of housing, food, transportation, entertainment, financial services, and clothing. The U.S. Census Bureau defines a household as comprised of all persons who occupy a "housing unit," that is, a house, an apartment or other group of rooms, or a single room that constitutes "separate living quarters." A household can contain related family members as well as unrelated persons such as foster children, lodgers, wards, or employees who share the same housing unit. A household may be made up of one person or many, but the trend is for the household size to be smaller.

By U.S. Census Bureau definition, a **family** consists of two or more persons related by birth, marriage, or adoption and residing together in a household. It should be noted that some groups and family specialists do not like this definition of family because it does not include gay couples or other groups such as young heterosexual couples or nonmarried elderly couples who live together. The American Red Cross has a much broader definition of family, which they used when they determined who was eligible for aid after the September 11, 2001, tragedy. As another example of a broader definition, an advertisement intoned that family is whoever is around the dinner table, and for many this is a better definition than the Census Bureau's. Numbers show that **nonfamily households**, made up of householders who live either alone or with others to whom they are not related, are a growing group, accounting for almost 30 percent of all households in 2000. Another phenomenon is extended families, which may include a core family and aunts, uncles, grandparents, in-laws, or other family members. Extended families living together are more common in China, India, and South Korea than they are in the United States.

Since 1980, the percentage of households that are families has declined and the percentage of people living alone has risen. There are more households than ever before, but household composition is changing. Less than half of all households have two parents and children under the age of 18 years living at home. Americans are also marrying later. Some cities such as Boston, New York, San Francisco, and Washington, D.C., have large populations of singles.

What does all this mean for consumerism? For one thing, advertising has to reflect changes in households and families. If the marketer is trying to attract extended families, then a grandmother should be in the television advertisement and should have lines to say along with the two parents and children (a Holiday Inn advertisement about a family traveling to Las Vegas had just such an assortment). Appealing to families can be tricky because members of the same family have differing tastes and desires. For a family vacation destination or cruise line, the advertisement should show fun activities for children and adults. For example, the Disney and Carnival cruise lines use advertisements that show a variety of activities for the whole family. The family emphasis may have to be toned down to attract the more than 30 million unmarried men and women living alone in the United States. What sort of vacations would single, working 35-year-olds like? Are they likely to travel alone, or are they more apt to travel with friends or family or with a tour group?

Size and structure of the household affect products and advertising. In terms of housing, several questions arise: How many bedrooms and bathrooms should the featured home have? How large should the garage or the master bedroom suite be? Are supersize stainless-steel refrigerators or smaller ones with more compartments and features desired?

The household life cycle can be segmented into four stages, and each poses problems and opportunities:

- *Stage 1.* The first group consists of unmarried and married individuals under age 35. This can be further subdivided into those under age 25 and those between 25 and 35 years. In the younger group, the persons may have recently graduated from high school or college and may be starting work and setting up households. Movement is common in this age group. For those age 25 to 35 years, more stability sets in regarding employment, friends, and family. Marriage and divorce may occur in this stage; children may be born or adopted. In the United States, the average age at first marriage is 24.4 years for women and 26.5 years for men, and higher-educated individuals tend to marry later than national averages. Whether married or not, younger people spend more money than other groups proportionally on movies, take-out food, alcoholic beverages, and clothes.

- *Stage 2.* The second group encompasses married or single parents with young children. Whether by adoption, birth, or remarriage, adding children

Young children add to household expenses and change leisure and travel choices.

brings with it changes in lifestyle and consumption. Housing needs increase; baby clothes, furniture, and equipment are bought; televisions are tuned to kid shows; and restaurant and food choices change. Cereal consumption goes up (remember the slogan "Kix is for kids"?). Hamburgers, pizza, macaroni and cheese, and spaghetti take the place of quiet romantic dinners, and noisy restaurants or restaurants with play spaces or overhead televisions are preferred. This is one of the most expensive stages in terms of what needs to be bought. If one parent does not work, reduced income is another outcome, but if they both work, child care costs go up. This can be a time of high debt and other financial problems, so advertisements on television about consolidating debt services are directed at this age group, which spills over into stage 3. Since people are having children later in life than earlier generations, it is difficult to separate stages 2 and 3, so no age range is given for stage 2.

- *Stage 3.* Middle-aged single or married individuals, with or without children, make up stage 3. These people are between 36 and 64 years of age and comprise the middle years of life, although some prefer to start the clock of middle age ticking at age 45 or 50. Putting a number on an age or stage is not an exact science because age is not only a chronological issue but also a frame of mind or attitude. Since the midyears represent such a wide time span and remarriages or blended families are common from age 35 to age 64, there may be young children or children in the middle, teen, or college years or the family may be experiencing the empty-nest syndrome. Households with teens and children in their early twenties experience high costs associated with car insurance and college tuition.

  Middle-aged singles without children generally live alone and have higher incomes and less expenditures than those with families, yet they still need dishwashers, cars, and so forth. Single-person households tend to have the same equipment as multifamily households, but singles' preferences may include condominiums or homes with small yards, expensive restaurants and wine, luxury automobiles, jewelry, and travel. They tend to be heavy gifters; they also contribute to charitable groups and organizations.

  People in middle age may also be part of the **sandwich generation**, meaning they are supporting or taking care of children as well as aging parents; consequently the time and energy and strain may be enormous. Vacations, maid services, yard services, pet care, and other types of services may target them.

  Middle-aged marrieds with no children travel extensively, prefer dining out, and buy time-saving services (such as housecleaning, yard care, laundry, and shopping) and luxury items (such as expensive haircuts or spa treatments, jewelry, sports bikes, or fitness club memberships). They may take up tennis, yoga, or golf and may be interested in long-term care insurance because there are no children to take care of them in their old age. In addition, middle-aged marrieds become more focused on funding for retirement.

- *Stage 4.* Older married persons and singles in the 65 years and older group are in stage 4. Most are now on their own, with the exception of grandparents who are taking care of grandchildren full-time and those elders who are living with adult children. Most are not working full-time (although 1 in 5 men and 1 in 10 women work full-time after the age of 65), so they have extra time for travel and recreation. They may be interested in part-time work, volunteer positions, or seasonal jobs. As long as their health holds out, they may favor retirement communities or new multiage developments (with walking paths or other recreational facilities), vacations, and recreational vehicles. Many elders are active Internet users. The consumption patterns of young retirees (those ages 65 to 75 years) are quite distinct from those of older retirees: Often the younger ones are heavier travelers and users of recreation than the older ones; elders tend to follow the news and the weather more than younger groups. Since people are living longer and staying healthier than ever before, the age range of active retirement keeps getting pushed upward, so what may be considered a young retiree could expand upward to age 80 and beyond. In the later years, estate planning, insurance issues, health care, and assisted living and retirement homes become important.

## Groups and Market Segmentation

In the last section, the discussion was mainly about households and families, but people belong to other groups as well. One of these is **reference groups**, which are collections of people that influence your decisions and behavior. The family stands out as the most important reference group because of its longevity, emotional attachments, shared genetics, and intensity. Other than family members, reference groups can include teachers, neighbors, religious groups, political parties, racial or ethnic organizations, clubs, colleagues, and students. If there is frequent contact, then the reference group is considered primary; if contact is infrequent or in the past, it is considered secondary. In consumerism, reference groups exchange information, offer advice and guidance, provide identity, and serve as a measuring stick or as a means of comparing. Belonging to certain groups may require uniforms or other forms of appearance. For example, college students usually dress casually, so if a student shows up for class in a suit, the other students will assume that student is giving a presentation or going to a job interview.

Thus, group members engage in usual ways of behaving and may share other characteristics such as age, gender, education, social class, lifestyle, occupation, income, religion, and race and ethnicity. In terms of social class, it is estimated that about 14 percent of Americans are upper class, 70 percent are middle class, and 16 percent are lower class (Hawkins, Best & Coney, 2001). The most widely used determinant of this is the **socioeconomic index (SEI)**, an index based on education level and occupation. For example, in the SEI, bartenders and stevedores are rated lower than engineers and dentists (Stevens & Cho, 1985). Studies have shown that income does not cause direct consumption nearly to the extent that education and occupation do (Hawkins, Best & Coney, 2001). Americans are becoming more educated and taking more white-collar positions.

The average American visits malls 3.2 times per month and spends 75 minutes each time.

Working women are the most important sales generators in malls, with 42 percent of mall sales (Fetto, 2002). On average, Americans visit the mall 3.2 times per month and spend an estimated 75 minutes each time (Fetto, 2002).

Companies as well as families have a social and cultural context. According to Charles Holliday, CEO of DuPont, "It's part of our culture to think about doing the right things and we're not going off on any short-term whims" (Hymowitz, 2002). He says he feels responsible to four distinct stakeholders: employees, investors, customers, and the public. He adds, "We're not changing our core values, including concern about the safety of our products and our people" (Hymowitz, 2002).

Shopping with others offer social
benefits. (Corbis Digital Stock.)

Businesses and the media study what groups exist and who belongs to which
**market segment** (a specific group of consumers). "A market segment is a portion
of a larger market whose needs differ somewhat from the larger market. Since a
market segment has unique needs, a firm that develops a total product focused
solely on the needs of that segment will be able to meet the segment's desires better than a firm whose product or service attempts to meet the needs of multiple
segments" (Hawkins, Best & Coney, 2001). The segment has to be sizable enough
to generate enough sales, whether the product be radio time or toothpaste.

To determine a market segment, consumers are first grouped by similar needs;
for example, young families may be interested in backyard swing sets. In order to
establish this need, a company may conduct focus groups, interviews, or surveys,
with questions being asked about features, such as how many swings are needed,
whether a slide is desired, and which building materials and colors would be preferred. Once this need set is delineated, then attention turns to the most likely consumers. What is their lifestyle? Where do they live? What media do they use?

Everyone belongs to a dominant culture as well as subcultures. People identify
with their core culture and their subcultures, each of which has values, norms, and
customs. Holiday celebrations and foods are often connected with cultures and
subcultures. Ethnic subcultures include members with shared behaviors and beliefs
based on a common language, background, or race.

In a directive from the federal Office of Management and Budget, all federal agencies are to report statistics according to the following recommended race and ethnicity categories: American Indian or Alaskan Native, Asian, Black or African American, Native Hawaiian or Other Pacific Islander, White, and Hispanic or Latino. The different groups have different consumption patterns and store preferences. According to Simmons Market Research, whites shop at home improvement stores more than African Americans, Asians, or Hispanics (Frequent Shoppers, 2003). But for the most part, profession or income may be more of an indicator of consumption than race or other criteria. For example, "African American, Hispanic and Asian American cable households are significantly more likely than their non-cable counterparts to be luxury car owners, homeowners, and college graduates with annual incomes exceeding $75,000, according to MRI research. . . . Consumers in these groups are also more likely to have professional/managerial jobs" (Karrfait, 2003, p. S4).

In the 2000 census, about 10 million Americans refused to pick a race or ethnicity category. Some people object to being classified in categories; others find making a selection difficult, especially if they are of mixed heritage. The three largest ethnic/racial categories are the Hispanic or Latino population, the African American population, and the Asian American population. Census data show that Hispanics, African Americans, and Asians are more likely to live in large metropolitan areas than the population as a whole, but they are increasingly likely to live in the suburbs and in rapidly growing job centers in the South and West.

**Hispanics/Latinos.**    The term *Hispanic* is used to describe an ethnic group with Spanish-speaking heritage. Hispanics constitute 13 percent of the U.S. population (about 35 million people), outnumbering African Americans (at 12 percent) for the title of the largest minority group in the nation. In the 2000 census, respondents were asked if they were Spanish/Hispanic/Latino. After responding yes, they could select a nationality group of Mexican/Mexican American/Chicano, Puerto Rican,

Hispanics and Latinos are the largest minority group in the United States. (Pearson Learning Photo Studio.)

Cuban, or Other. Hispanics are the largest ethnic group in areas of Arizona, Florida, New Mexico, and Texas and one of the fastest-growing groups nationwide due to a high birthrate as well as immigration, making them an attractive consumer segment. Their households are larger (3.5 people) than those of the general population (2.7 people). By the year 2050, the U.S. Census predicts Hispanics will comprise 23 percent of the nation's population.

Hispanic populations are spreading out from traditional metropolitan centers. In 2004, 23 percent of the nation's Hispanic population lived in the Los Angeles and New York metropolitan areas; in 1990 it was 30 percent.

Hispanic advertising is a hot area. Given the results of the census, advertising firms, many of which are owned and staffed by Hispanics, are catching up. According to Hispanic Business, the total ad budget for Hispanics is currently about $2.2 billion a year, compared with $234 billion for the mainstream market (Raymond, 2002). The number of radio stations for Hispanics is lower than the number for African Americans. One of the best-known brands directed at the Hispanic market is the food powerhouse Goya, whose products include Mexican chilies, Caribbean fruit juices, and Spanish olive oil. It is the fourth-largest Hispanic-owned company in the United States (Bianchi & Sama, 2002). Competitors include Unilevers' Iberia Foods and La Cena Fine Foods Ltd. as well as smaller companies. According to Marino Roa, vice president of sales at Le Fe Foods Inc., "Latinos are very loyal to their brands" (Bianchi & Sama, 2002). Latinos visit grocery stores an average of 4.7 times a week, compared with 2.2 times for the average American, and also outspend other Americans $117 to $87 per week (Bianchi & Sama, 2002).

Hispanics and Latinos are a highly diverse group.

Since Hispanics are a growing market and high food spenders, grocery stores such as Albertsons Inc. are considering all-Hispanic stores; Kmart and Wal-Mart are considering similar initiatives. Meanwhile, retailers are expanding the number of products that they offer in their current stores that are attractive to Hispanics. This group is often called a sleeping giant because although retailers have been slow in the past to market to this group, that is rapidly changing.

Hispanics eat out less often than most Americans, averaging only 1.2 times per week. At home, meals are prepared mainly from scratch. Convenience foods are less important than foods made with care. In urban markets, there are television channels and magazines devoted to Hispanics, and with cable television nearly everyone gets at least one Hispanic channel. Hispanics' incomes and education levels are rising dramatically. The Hispanic market is not homogeneous, meaning that being Hispanic may be less important than country of origin, so care must be taken in how they are approached in terms of products (such as food) and music and media messages. Hispanics also pay more for phone services, furniture, and apparel and spend a higher proportion of their income on housing and transportation than the general population (Karrfait, 2003).

M. Isabel Valdes, in her book *Marketing to American Latinos: A Guide to the In-Culture Approach, Part 2,* emphasizes the "in-culture" approach, which is a philosophy that encourages marketers to thoroughly understand consumers' culture and origin before attempting to court them. She says there are vast differences in spending power and consumer viability among Hispanics based on age, geographic distribution, and country of origin.

**African Americans.**　When it comes to grocery shopping, African Americans spend slightly more per week than the total U.S. market but less than Hispanics. They constitute about 12 percent of the U.S. population, with a concentration in the South and in urban areas. The U.S. Census estimates they will make up 14 per-cent of the population in 2050. Currently, they are somewhat younger than the general U.S. population; their household incomes range from low to high, but overall their incomes place them in the middle between Caucasians and Hispanics. Many of their consumer preferences are linked more to SEI than to race. Generally they spend less on housing and more on clothing, personal care items and ser-vices, and shopping trips to upscale malls and retailers (Fisher, 1996). On average, the African American woman spends three times as much as a Caucasian woman on hair-care products (Solomon & Rabolt, 2004), and companies such as Clairol, L'Oreal, and Alberto-Culver have extensive ethnic lines.

Magazines such as *Essence, Jet, Black Enterprise*, and *Ebony* are directed at the African American market. For example, *Jet* claims to reach 90 percent of the black male market (Solomon & Rabolt, 2004). Advertisements in these magazines include product categories such as skin and hair care, cosmetics, and food and beverages. Another marketing approach is to offer promotions or sponsor events targeted to African Americans, such as sporting events or concert tours. African Americans tend to view shopping as more recreational than other groups and appreciate a pleasant and fun shopping environment, and they have more buying power than any other ethnic group. They watch 40 percent more TV than the general market; what they watch differs from programming for general audiences (Karrfait, 2003). "Because many more African American men love sports than any other group, they have pur-chased more large screen TV sets, with price tags of $500 or more," according to Willis Smith, principal researcher of the *Urban Market Report* (Karrfait, 2003, p. S4).

The largest percentage of Asian Americans are Chinese.

**Asian Americans.**   As with all groups, sensitivity is needed when appealing to Asian Americans. A mistake was made when an American company used a Chinese model in an advertisement for a Korean product, which demonstrates that even though this section is discussing different racial and ethnic groups, within these groups there are vast differences. There is not a single Asian American market, just as there is not one for Hispanics. Asian American children and adults are often seen with groups of people in ads especially for fashion, toys, electronics, food, and bars.

Asian Americans are more highly educated and have higher household incomes than the general population. At 4 percent of the population, they are smaller in num-ber than Hispanics or African Americans, but they are slated to grow to 10 percent by the year 2050. The largest numbers are Chinese and Filipinos, followed by Koreans, Vietnamese, and others. They are mostly concentrated in urban areas, especially Chicago and New York, as well as California and Hawaii. One of the challenges to reaching this group is the diversity of languages: Chinese (25 percent), Filipino (18 percent), Indian (17 percent), Vietnamese (11 percent), Korean (11 percent), and Japanese (8 percent). About 70 percent of the 12 million Asian Americans in the United States are foreign born, compared with 44 percent of Latinos (Karrfait, 2003).

Grocery stores devote sections to foods used exclusively by Asian Americans and to those of the general population who like Oriental cuisine. Some Asian Americans (estimated at about 49 percent) strongly identify with their original culture, and about half of them know their native language (Hawkins, Coney & Best, 2001). Younger groups and those brought up in the United States have less traditional as-sociations. Asian Americans are stronger savers than the general population, are quality oriented regarding the goods they seek, and are heavy users of computers and the Internet. Name brands and status appeal to a sizable number of Asian Americans, who prefer BMW, Mercedes Benz, and other premium car brands, as well as designer handbags and clothes. They are generally affluent and the best educated of the major ethnic groups. Asian Americans and Hispanics spend more than other groups or the general population during visits to the mall (Fetto, 2002). Although their current numbers are small, this is a fast-growing segment of the U.S. population. According to Simmons Market Research, they are more likely to shop in home electronics stores and home furnishing stores than whites, African Americans, or Hispanics (Frequent Shoppers, 2003).

Young Asian Americans are also displaying a new ethnic pride in their heritage, helped by role models such as the seven foot, six inch Yao Ming of the Houston Rockets, who beat out Shaquille O'Neal in fan votes to start in this year's NBA All Star game (Ming appears in commercials for Visa and Apple Computers and just signed a five-year deal to represent Gatorade.) "It's never been so hip to be Asian, as kids across all demographics are learning" (Karrfait, 2003, p. S5).

**Gays and Lesbians.**   Because many people are offended by or uncomfortable with images of gay lifestyles if they are portrayed in general audience publications, many companies, including American Express, Sony, and Subaru of America, make specific advertisements designed for the gay media. Many of the ads are for prosaic products and services such as financial planning. One reason this is a special concern for gays and lesbians is that employers may not provide benefits or coverage for partners to the extent that they do for heterosexual married couples. The ads may show same-sex couples embracing, holding hands, or looking off into the future.

Research shows that homosexuals tend to be more highly educated than the general public; are dedicated to their careers; have more discretionary income; enjoy change, humor, and trends; and are more informed politically and socially. "A Simmons study of readers of gay publications found that compared to heterosexuals, these consumers are almost twelve times more likely to hold professional jobs, twice as likely to own a vacation home, and eight times more likely to own a computer notebook" (Solomon & Rabolt, 2004, p. 157). They are heavy users of the Internet. They also use other media:

> They prefer to read newspapers targeted at them and more upscale sections of the newspaper; the same is true for magazines. They prefer more intellectual and upscale TV and radio programs [and] use catalogs, 800 numbers, and online forms of direct marketing. (Wells, Burnett & Moriarty, 2000, p. 99)

High-profile gay figures in advertising include actors, comedians, and singers. Gays and lesbians are more likely to be urban dwellers than rural dwellers. Advertisements even for general audience publications often show homosexual relationships, so watch for changes in how and where this group is depicted. The exact proportion of the population that is gay or lesbian is difficult to say; the numbers vary based on source and location.

## SUMMARY

This chapter explored the meaning of consumption. For example, it was shown that individuals have relationships with products that go beyond mere function. How functional are a dozen red roses? Consumer behavior refers to the buying behavior of individuals, families, and households that buy goods and services for personal consumption. Consumers go through six steps in the buying process: assessing needs, searching for information, evaluating alternatives, and selecting a product or service (prepurchase); buying (purchase); and evaluating the product or service afterward (postpurchase). In this last step, companies or organizations want to build loyalty and relationships and to enjoy positive word of mouth.

Companies compete with each other for consumer dollars and use product positioning to give brands specific and unique images. Products go through four stages of development—introduction, growth, maturity, and dormancy/decline.

Some consumers are more innovative than others. Innovativeness is linked to personality.

Brand names can be trademarked. Counterfeit means look-alike copies, and pirating refers to stealing an original idea or product and selling it.

The household is the most basic consumer unit. The household life cycle can be broken down into four stages, beginning with young adults and ending with older singles and married persons.

## KEY POINTS

1. Consumers go through six steps in the buying process.
2. Businesses want to maximize profits by offering sought-after goods.
3. A brand, such as Nike or Reebok, is a distinctive name identifying a product or manufacturer.
4. About 14 percent of Americans are upper class, 70 percent are middle class, and 16 percent are lower class. The most widely used determinant is the socioeconomic index (SEI).
5. Studies show that income does not cause or direct consumption nearly as much as education and occupation do.
6. Media and businesses study market segments, which are groupings of people.
7. The three largest ethnic/racial groups in the United States are Hispanics/Latinos, African Americans, and Asian Americans. Each group has individual characteristics and consumption needs that differentiate them from the general population. More and more marketers are aware of ethnic groups' consumption needs and market to them. New networks are springing up to serve a growing demand for multicultural fare.
8. A baby boom is going on in the United States. In 2006, 4.3 million babies were born—the largest number in a single year since 1961.

## KEY TERMS

| | | |
|---|---|---|
| actively acquired information | consumer behavior | family |
| | consumer cost | family brand |
| banner ad | credence goods | forecast |
| brand | customer satisfaction | image |
| brand image | distribution | information search rule |
| brand perception | experience goods | innovation |
| cognitive dissonance | external search | internal search |

marketing communications
marketing mix
marketing strategy
market segment
need set
nonfamily households

ongoing search
passive information
pirating
prepurchasing
product positioning
reference groups
sandwich generation

service
socioeconomic index (SEI)
store brands
target market
trademark

## DISCUSSION QUESTIONS

1. What are the steps in the prepurchase process? Why is so much time taken before purchase?
2. What are the stages in product development? Give an example other than those in the chapter for each stage.
3. Go to the Procter & Gamble Web site (www.pg.com) and click on P & G Products. Find out the brand names of different laundry detergents or shampoos. Why would the same company offer different products that essentially perform the same function?

## E-RESOURCES

Thousands of company, government, and organization Web sites could be mentioned here, but for brevity's sake, a few have been chosen for each category.

**Market Leaders in Consumer Goods**

**Procter & Gamble**   *www.pg.com*
Is a leading maker of soaps, shampoos, detergents, diapers, and other household and personal care products

**Wal-Mart Stores, Inc.**   *www.wal-mart.com email letters@wal-mart.com*
Is a leading grocer in the United States and spreading internationally

**Government Agencies**

**Federal Trade Commission (FTC)**   *www.ftc.gov*
Promotes fair trade, protects the public

**Food and Drug Administration (FDA)**   *www.fda.gov*
Sets labeling and packaging requirements

**Organization Data Sources**

**CAB Multicultural Marketing Resource Center**   *www.cabletvadbureau.com/mmrc*
Provides information and resources about ethnicity and consumption

**International Data Corporation**   *www.idc.com*
Provides market data

**Simmons Market Research**   *www.simmonsmarketresearch.com*
Supplies information on adults, teens, children, and Hispanics

# REFERENCES

Bianchi, A., and F. Sama. (July 9, 2002). Goya Foods leads an ethnic sales trend. *Wall Street Journal,* p. B4.

Deslandes, D., R. Goldsmith, R., and M. Bonn. (2002). Measuring destination image: Do the existing scales work? A working paper, Florida State University, Tallahassee, FL.

Echtner, C. M., and J. E. B. Ritchie. (1993). The measurement of destination image: An empirical assessment. *Journal of Travel Research, 31* (4), 3–13.

Fetto, J. (March 2002). Mall rats. *American Demographics,* 10.

Fisher, C. (September 1996). Black, hip, and primed to shop. *American Demographics,* 52–59.

Fournier, S. (March 1998). Consumers and their brands: Developing relationship theory in consumer research. *Journal of Consumer Research, 24,* 343–73.

Foxall, G. R., R. E. Goldsmith, and S. Brown. (1998). *Consumer psychology for marketing,* 2nd ed. London: Thomson Business Press.

Frequent shoppers. (May 2003). *American Demographics,* 8.

Hawkins, D., R. Best, and K. Coney. (2001). *Consumer behavior: Building a marketing strategy,* 8th ed. Boston: Irwin McGraw-Hill.

Hymowitz, C. (July 9, 2002). CEOs must work hard to maintain faith in the corner office. *Wall Street Journal,* p. B1.

Karrfait, W. (May 2003). A multicultural mecca. *American Demographics,* S4–S6.

Phillips, M. (July 12, 2002). Pilfered patterns. *Wall Street Journal,* p. B1.

Raymond, J. (March 2002). ¿Tienen numeros? *American Demographics,* 22–25.

Rogers, Everett M. (1995). *Diffusion of innovations,* 4th ed. New York: Free Press.

Schor, Juliet B. (1998). *The overspent American.* New York: HarperCollins.

Sirgy, J., and C. Su. (2000). Destination image, self-congruity, and travel behavior: Towards an integrative model. *Journal of Travel Research, 38,* 340–52.

Solomon, M., and N. Rabolt. (2004). *Consumer behavior in fashion.* Upper Saddle River, NJ: Prentice Hall.

Stevens, G., and J. Cho. (1985). Socioeconomic indices. *Social Science Research, 14,* 142–68.

Tsiotsou, R. (2006). The role of perceived product quality and overall satisfaction on purchase intentions. *International Journal of Consumer Studies, 30* (2), 207–12.

Valdes, M. I. (2002). *Marketing to American Latinos: A guide to the in-culture approach, Part 2.* New York: Paramount Market Publishing.

Wells, W., J. Burnett, and S. Moriarty. (2000). *Advertising principles & practice,* 5th ed. Saddle River, NJ: Prentice Hall.

Wingfield, N. (July 11, 2002). Behind the fake music. *Wall Street Journal,* p. D1.

# Decision Making and the Influence of Advertising

*In very few instances do people really know what they want, even when they say they do.*
—Advertising Age

## Learning Objectives

1. Understand the role of decision making in consumer buying decisions.
2. Explain uniqueness theory.
3. Understand the role of advertising in relation to buying decisions.
4. Know the pros and cons of advertising in relation to consumers.
5. Explain the government agencies that affect advertising.
6. Understand the value of public service announcements.

---

### DVRs vs. Live Audiences: Effects on Television Advertising

Higher ad rates are charged for highly rated shows. This makes sense and reflects supply and demand. Broadcast networks used to pit popular shows against each other so that consumers had to pick a show and watch it along with the commercials. This traditional practice is being challenged by DVRs (digital video recorders). More viewers are opting to record rather than watch live. Television programmers are forced to rethink their strategy since DVRs allow viewers to skip through commercials.

"The latest Nielsen figures have been eagerly anticipated: They represent the first look at how many people actually watch the commercials during the fall primetime season, when advertisers spend the most on ads. Previous Nielson data looked only at viewership of the shows. Six of the top 10 most-recorded shows during the first three weeks of the fall season air on Thursday night, according to Michael Mellon, senior vice president of research for Walt Disney's ABC. One example is ABC's hit *Grey's Anatomy*."[1]

Grey's Anatomy according to the data was recorded by 20% of its viewers; the overall audience is growing but the live audience is dropping. Similar viewer behavior is evident for CBS's Survivor show. Analysts say that the move away from live viewership and toward playback has not affected ad rates for specific shows yet, but it is simply a matter of time.

Complicating the matter further is that owners of DVRs are more upscale. They are an attractive market to advertisers.

---

"One of the things you've seen this year is there are really no breakouts of new programs, in part because people capture the shows they already know they like on DVR,
and they're leaving live shows to watch DVR shows,"[2] says Michael Nathanson, a senior analyst at Sanford Bernstein. Mr. Nathanson calls this a "logjam" effect.

[1]Rebecca Dana, "Latest Ad Challenge: Must-Record TV." *Wall Street Journal*, October 31, 2007, p.
B4.

[2]Ibid.

## INTRODUCTION

This chapter builds on the last one on buying process, brands, and product
development. It delves further into how consumers make decisions and how
advertising influences those decisions. We discuss why people buy what they
do, why they want to be unique, and how they react to advertising. We also explore how advertising works and in particular why those irritating jingles stay
in our minds. The secret is called "locking power." The chapter also discusses
the influence of cultural or societal groups and lifestyles in relation to consumerism.

## DECISION MAKING AND TIME

In the last chapter, we discussed the steps that consumers go through in the
buying process, including prepurchase, purchase, and postpurchase behavior.
Another way to say this is that consumers are involved in preselection, selection,
and postselection. Consumers try to make good decisions, but this is becoming
more difficult because (1) time is limited, (2) the number and complexity of
products have increased, and (3) consumers have become further and further
removed from the origin or basis of products. For example, rather than buying
fruits and vegetables from a neighbor or nearby farmer, fruits and vegetables
are bought in an impersonal grocery store, and the origins of the produce may
be anywhere in the world. Even local farmer's markets today sell produce from
nearly anywhere (mixed in with local produce), and the labels on the boxes
near their stand reveal the distances that the produce may have traveled.

Regarding time as a scarce resource, we all have to make decisions about the best
way to manage time. In consumption there are countless examples of time and
consumption trade-offs, such as cooking a meal from scratch that would take several hours versus popping a preprepared frozen dinner in the microwave that will
take minutes to heat. Another time-saver is using the telephone or the Internet to
search for products. For example, a recent search for a certain brand of popcorn
popper revealed that none of the local stores had one and that the only way to get
the popper was by ordering online direct from the company. The good part was
that ordering online saved time and could be done at 11 o'clock at night when
stores were closed, and it also saved gasoline; the negative was the shipping
charge (versus buying in person).

**Parkinson's law** states that a job expands to fill the time available to accomplish the task, such as finding and purchasing a product. A person who has all day to shop will view the shopping task differently than a person who has to buy something quickly on his or her lunch hour. Thus, Parkinson's law shows the elasticity of time and consumption behavior. It was named after an English historian, C. Northcote Parkinson, who studied the Royal Navy in 1977 and found that the more people hired, the more work was created without increasing output. So in consumption, the analogy would be that more time spent in shopping does not necessarily mean there will be increased return for that effort. There is a point at which comparison shopping (and the time and energy that it involves) is wasteful, and going to several stores a day could become a full-time occupation.

Another law or principle relevant to consumption is the **Pareto principle**, also known as the 80-20 rule, which states that 20 percent of the time expended produces 80 percent of the results and that 80 percent of the time expended results in only 20 percent of the outcomes. Essentially this means that people waste a lot of time on nonproductive activities, so again the message would be to use time wisely, to seek information and shop efficiently. This principle was named after Vilfredo Pareto, a nineteenth-century Italian economist and sociologist who found that in any series of elements to be controlled, a select small fraction of the elements accounted for a large fraction of effectiveness.

## TECHNOLOGICAL OBSOLESCENCE

As discussed in Chapter 3, technological obsolescence means that a product loses value even though it is not worn out yet because it can be replaced with a more technologically advanced product. Good examples are appliances, televisions, printers, cell phones, video cameras, calculators, and computers. The more rapid the advances, the more quickly the product will undergo **depreciation**. Not only do you not want the product anymore, but it is not worth very much to anyone else. New cars depreciate around $2,000 right after they are driven off the lot by the owner; however, over time, the rate of depreciation slows or else the car could be worthless in a month. So what should you do? First, accept technological obsolescence and depreciation as facts of life. Second, think before you purchase—ask yourself if it would be better to wait. Third, realize that sometimes you cannot wait before making a purchase (such as a drug for a life-threatening disease or a business suit for an interview).

Computer companies are particularly aware of how rapidly computers are changing and have been very forthcoming with information about new releases to prospective buyers. For example, a college student ordered an Apple laptop and was called by the company to tell him that if he waited two weeks, he could have a newer model at a similar price. Now that is customer service. Because he was a long-time Apple user, the company wanted to keep him happy, so it gave him the choice of going with the model he ordered or getting the newer model with more bells and whistles. What would you do?

**CONSUMER POWER MODEL**

**Who Owns Music?**

The battles over who owns music and how much consumers should pay continue. Sony BMG Music Entertainment says it is selling digital albums, similar to gift cards, without copyright protection. The estimated price is $12.99 at retailers. This allows consumers to download MP3 files onto their home computers, making it easier to play music and transfer songs to various equipment. Other companies are changing the way they offer music as well, such as Warner Music Group who has a deal with Amazon.com's download store and Universal Music Group. The EMI Group was the first major company to remove the protection in a deal with iTunes.

Have you tried any of these digital albums? What do you think of this trend?

*Reference*: Bloomberg News, January 8, 2008, "Sony BMG Will Sell Music without Copyright Protection," *New York Times*, p. C13.

## THEORY AND STYLE PREFERENCE

One way consumers reduce the amount of options is to use **rules of thumb**, principles that guide purchases (such as only buying certain brands, only shopping in certain stores, or only buying certain styles). **Style** refers to the distinctive qualities of a product that set it apart from others of its kind. Consider the following in regard to consumers and style:

*Buying style. Consumers* can be rational, slow, comparative, or impulsive, and they have certain preferences, maybe choosing bargains rather than new merchandise at full price and shopping at small stores instead of large ones.

*Preference for certain styles and colors.* A person may like or dislike red, stripes, polka dots, or plaids.

*Desire for either conformity or uniqueness.* People vary in whether they want to stand out from the crowd or fit in. The appeal of owning something that is one of a kind is often the driving force behind auction bidding. Scarcity or uniqueness explains why someone would pay $145,000 at an auction for John Travolta's leisure suit from the movie *Saturday Night Fever.* When the auctioneer was asked later if the price seemed excessive, he remarked graciously, "Well, it certainly was a record for polyester" (Cialdini, 2001, p. 227). Another example of a high payment for memorabilia was $807,000 paid for the black dress worn by actress Audrey Hepburn as Holly Golightly in the 1961 film *Breakfast at Tiffany's.* A charity had received the dress from the designer, and the proceeds of the auction went to the City of Joy Aid, which helps India's poor.

**Uniqueness theory** proposes that individuals vary in the extent to which they wish to be different. This can be measured by the Desire for Unique Consumer Products (DUCP) scale by Michael Lynn and Judy Harris (1997). For example, the DUCP scale can be used to measure general innovativeness, innovativeness for fashionable clothing, and conformity (Goldsmith, Clark & Goldsmith, 2007). In the expanding global marketplace, consumers are exposed to an ever growing array of products and brands. What they select is connected with their self-realization, identity manifestation, and self-expression (Solomon, 2003). Utility or usefulness for some may be less of a draw than **authenticity**, the quality of being genuine and trustworthy. Consumers want authenticity and have "a desire for original, innovative, and distinctive products and services" (Lewis & Bridges, 2000, p. 4). A monogram, for example, is a way to make a product unique to the owner; other examples are the purchasing of memorabilia (such as the Travolta suit or the Hepburn dress), each a famous one-of-a-kind item. In summary, uniqueness stimulates people to embrace new things, defy convention, and pursue rare and unusual objects.

To go back to the second point on the above list, having a preference in either a buying style or the color of a product or design is common to all of us. We like certain types of shopping experiences and colors and fabrics. Preferences save a lot of time and anxiety. A person who hates crowds would be well advised to avoid malls on Black Friday, the Friday after Thanksgiving in the United States which is the kick-off of the holiday buying season. Likewise, an individual who hates used or damaged goods would be well advised to stay away from antique stores or flea markets, used-book stores, or consignment shops. If conformity is appealing, in department stores a male consumer can pick from a display of dozens of the same blue shirts. When it comes to apparel, style is "a particular combination of attributes that distinguishes it from others in its category" (Solomon & Rabolt, 2004, p. 6). Examples would be styles of shirts, pants, dresses, and skirts (dress or skirt length used to be a determinant of the latest style, a way of being fashionable).

## IMPULSE BUYING

**Impulse buying** means to walk in a store or to look at a catalog or Web page, see something attractive, and purchase it without taking the time to think about the ramifications, such as cost, benefits, values, or needs. Sellers exploit impulse buying by putting displays at the front of the store or the checkout counter. Online or by catalog phone order, they may offer an add-on at the end; for example, if you spend $10 more, you will receive a bonus or a slight discount. Impulse items are often inexpensive or fun, like a candy bar, magazine, or tabloid newspaper. Buying a refrigerator is rarely an impulse item, but a digital camera or a set of golf clubs may be. Style is often more important than substance in product categories such as clothing, restaurants, furniture, and architecture, and it certainly is in packaging. This is why a hamburger ranges in price from $0.59 to $20 depending on the restaurant, although there are size and quality differences, too.

Packaging attracts the impulse buyer and adds to image and branding. If you are going to throw out a package or display item anyway (such as a cardboard box for cosmetics or those tiny hangers used to display socks in stores), why would the style of the package or display matter? Packaging does matter because it attracts your attention, helps you differentiate the brand from those of competitors (for example, the light green boxes of Clinique cosmetics versus other brands), and is useful for other aspects of display. In many cases, part of image is aesthetic appeal and status, but beyond that it is personal expression. For example, no one really

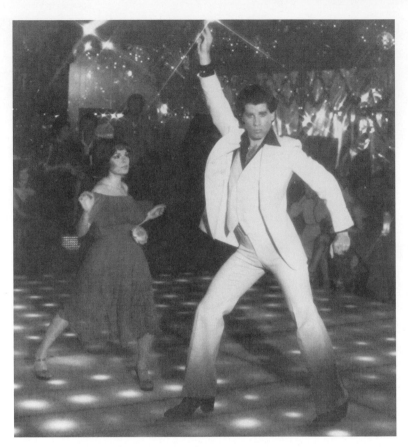

Would you pay $145,000 for John Travolta's suit? Someone did.
(Corbis/Bettmann.)

needs a $1,000 glass bathroom sink embedded with copper, but it may be more pleasing to look at and certainly more unique than a typical $40 white porcelain sink. Both of the sinks function the same; the difference is in the style. Other examples are $600 antique door knobs and $7,000 custom-made copper range hoods when ordinary ones would cost much, much less. Can an expensive item be an impulse item? Most definitely! Many time-shares, high-end jewelry, art, and boat purchases are impulse items.

If a product makes consumers feel good and they can afford it, it can be thought of as a **consumer payoff**, a positive result from searching and making the best choice. The optimum behavior is to seek the highest quality at the lowest price (the essence of consumer economics), but as we have discussed, this is not always the case. Sometimes to get the highest quality, one has to pay the highest price because there is no alternative, such as when purchasing a piece of art, an antique, or a collectible. To connect this with the section on decision making and time at the beginning of the chapter, a consumer would seek the largest expected payoff from the least time and energy expenditure, especially given the price of the item. For example, one would assume a consumer would spend less time selecting a mouthwash than a computer. A truly busy person with a high income may send out a personal assistant to search for information. For example, an owner of a horse farm/estate sent her personal assistant to look at fabric for drapes; the assistant reported back what she had found, and then the owner went to the store. Most of us do not have personal assistants, but we may have little time and find other ways to cut corners such as using shopping bots (sites on the Internet that gather shopping information and provide choices, outlets, and prices).

Consumers reach a point where the cost of searching further is greater than any possible benefit that can be derived from this practice. Comparison shopping over a distance for a single can of soda does not make financial sense.

**Price variation** refers to a situation when a single seller may charge the same consumer different prices at different times for the same item. In the case of a large, heavy antique armoire, an antiques seller will probably be willing to sell it at a lesser price the last hour of a three-day antiques show than at the beginning—the reason being the problem and expense of packing it up and taking it to the next show. More common examples of **price discrimination** (different prices for the same product or service based on purchaser and/or date) include the different prices charged by hotels, airlines, and cruise lines, depending on when the trip is booked, by whom it is booked (meaning a travel agent versus a private individual), and the days on which the travel will take place. Price discrimination can be illegal if it is proven that an individual or a group is discriminated against in an unfair manner. For example, if a hotel charged a different price for the same room on the same day to people of different races or ethnicity, that could be grounds for claiming discrimination.

Another rule of thumb is that people use seals of approval or trademarks as guides. Sometimes a new competitor will use only a slightly different brand name than a successful, established product, but if it is too close, the established brand may sue over name rights. Quasi-fraud charities are notorious for using names that are very close to those of legitimate charities. An additional rule of thumb involves price. For example, if broccoli is being sold for $1.99 a bunch, the consumer will buy, but if it is $4 a bunch, then he or she will pass and substitute another vegetable while waiting for the price on broccoli to go down. However, price is not the only guide (as noted in earlier chapters).

Price often serves as a rule of thumb guiding selection and purchase.

Consumers may ignore a rule of thumb if they are in a hurry and really need a product, such as disposable diapers. This explains why they will pay twice the normal price for milk at a convenience store than at a full-service grocery store or twice what they would normally pay for a hotel room if they are exhausted, are in the middle of a snowstorm, and want to get off the road. Because of **budget constraints** (the relationship between what someone can spend and what someone will spend), most people can afford to pay double the price on a gallon of milk whereas they could not afford to pay twice as much for a desired house. This is impacted by the **ability to trade**, meaning trading one good for another. Let's say it is a new development of houses, all very similar, and the houses are lined up in a row. House A is right next to House B and is essentially identical; the prices differ by $5,000, so the preference will be for the less expensive house. Things get a little more complicated when the trade is between slightly dissimilar items, such as lamb chops for pork chops or watermelon for cantaloupe, and get much more complicated when choosing between vastly dissimilar items, such as ham and lobster or rutabaga and lettuce. In the case of dissimilar items, the consumer will have to decide how to maximize satisfaction given the conditions (price, quality, selection) that exist and then trade or purchase accordingly. Information will be part of the transaction—consumers will not buy a rutabaga if they do not know what to do with it or are unsure of the taste, whereas a choice between iceberg lettuce and romaine lettuce may be easier to make.

Besides the purchase price of the item, there are additional expenses such as cost of use, maintenance, or end-result preparation. Examples of after-purchase expenses are house taxes or gasoline and repairs for cars. There are even added-on costs for simple things like food. Take, for example, the choice of buying a pound of hamburger: This could be a low-budget item or a mid- to high-priced meal, depending on where it is consumed and what goes with it.

## READING CUSTOMERS' MINDS: CAN IT BE DONE?

Consumers use rules of thumb (price, time, style, etc.) to guide decisions, but new research and testing are under way that may totally change how we think about and certainly how we measure consumers' decision-making process. Gerald Zaltman, the author of *How Customers Think* and a marketing professor at Harvard Business School, "uses brain scans, psychotherapy-like interviews and his patented Zaltman Metaphor Elicitation Technique (ZMET) to help the likes of Procter & Gamble, Pfizer, General Motors, and Coca-Cola get inside the consumer's head" (Useem, 2003, p. 48).

Zaltman says that at least 95 percent of the thinking that drives our behavior occurs unconsciously. Much of what we think were the steps we went through are actually after-purchase constructions—in short, people are buying products for reasons they are not fully conscious of. The brain scans involve monitoring blood flow in the brain and seeing cortices light up. A new product can be shown to a subject, and the person experiences it negatively or positively; the brain scan picks up his or her reaction. To bring this out of the laboratory into a larger setting, new technologies are being developed, such as caps that people can wear. So far Zaltman and his colleagues have studied positive responses (joy and happiness) rather than negative reactions (disgust and turnoff). In the long run, you have to know what repels consumers as well as what attracts them. Zaltman sees many applications of the new technology and testing, particularly in certain industries such as cosmetics and personal appearance.

Another testing method that Zaltman uses involves asking people to bring in eight-by-ten pictures that represent their thoughts and feelings about something such as snack foods. One person brought in a picture of someone covered with bees. The trained interviewer asked what the bee picture meant, and the woman responded that she had a lot of confidence that she wouldn't get stung—"that she could safely indulge in snack foods without running the risks of harm that everyone else talks about. So there was a bit of defiance to it" (Useem, 2003, p. 48). You can see from this example that this method is in the experimental stages (and some would question the interviewer's interpretation), but it is presented as a wave of the future, a consumer research area that will draw attention and will grow. What Zaltman would say is that simply asking people why they buy what they do falls far short of what really happens.

## CONSUMERSPACE

Michael Solomon, director of a consulting firm called Mind/Share, an Auburn University professor, and the author of *Conquering Consumerspace,* differentiates marketspace (a commercial system in which companies sell to us) from consumerspace (a commercial system in which they sell *with* us). His concept is that business no longer calls the shots—consumers do. He describes a trend called **identity marketing** that fuels the fire of consumerspace. In identity marketing, consumers wear or display in their homes product logos (for example, T-shirts and shoes with Nike on them or lamp shades with a university name on them). In Great Britain, an ad agency paid students to wear temporary tattoos of product logos on their foreheads. Would you do this? And if so, at what price and for how long?

According to Solomon, branding provides security and clarity in a complicated world where nationalities are less important. To summarize, the bedrock of our identities is formed by allegiance to common value systems, often expressed concretely through affiliation with common product sets. In the preface he writes: "Welcome to consumerspace. Where reality is branded. Where we avidly search for the products and services that define who we are and who we want to be. Where we are what we buy—literally" (2003, p. xiii). Not everyone in consumer economics will be comfortable with this notion, feeling it is going too far and believing that people are much more (their identities are much more) than what they purchase and use. But he is expressing a point of view that business listens to, and anything that might become a trend naturally is interesting to watch. He wonders what consumerspace will look like and what firms will help build it and even control it, and he posits that people will move seamlessly between offline and online worlds, something which in many ways is already happening. Have you ever searched for a product online and then bought it at a store? Or have you found something in a store that you liked but that was not available in the right color or size or model so you went online to purchase it or to find a lower price?

According to Solomon, "People hunger for unique products that help them express their individuality in an impersonal world. We have what psychologists call a need for uniqueness" (2003, p. 128). We can add that to the list of needs that Abraham Maslow posited in his hierarchy of needs. Solomon says that everyone needs to feel special, and perfumes are often marketed as smelling differently on each person. This leads us to our next section on advertising where mass-marketed products boldly carry the messages "as individual as you are" or "making you feel your best."

## ADVERTISING

We discussed earlier the importance of the information search in the consumer buying process. The chapter now turns its spotlight on **advertising**, defined as any paid form of nonpersonal communication about an organization, product, service, or idea by an identified sponsor (Alexander, 1965). The word *nonpersonal* means that mass media forms, such as newspapers, radio, and television, are used that can transmit to or reach large groups. The message is sent to an anonymous audience who does not respond back to the source of the message. Advertising is part of the promotional mix that sellers use to reach customers. It can be produced in-house, a separate advertising agency may be hired, or the promotional mix could involve a combination of both.

Advertising as a form of mass communication can be classified in several ways:

- *National advertising.* National advertising is the biggest category; some of the largest consumer brand advertising budgets belong to Procter & Gamble and General Motors.
- *Retail and local advertising.* Examples of retail and local advertising would be fitness clubs and local restaurants.
- *Political and cause-based advertising.* Political slogans and public service announcements would come under political and cause-based advertising.
- *Direct-response advertising.* In direct-response advertising, the customer reads the information and can choose to buy direct from the company through the mail, by telephone, or on the Internet.
- *Industrial advertising.* Business and health care publications would be grouped under industrial advertising.
- *Professional advertising.* Professional advertising targets groups such as doctors, teachers, and lawyers.

Advertising is based on the goals of the advertisers. What do they want to achieve? Most likely one or more of these would be on the list:

- Increased sales
- Attitude or perception change
- Increased product and brand awareness
- Provision of reminders and reinforcements

To achieve these types of goals, the advertisements have to be attractive, creative, well executed, and placed in the right form of media. Familiar advertisements for familiar products reinforce past purchases and remind people to buy again. The message can be simple, such as "Got Milk" from the American Dairy Association, or complex and multileveled. Notice that simple messages have mental staying power. The message can be broken down into five parts: perception, awareness, understanding, persuasion, and retention/memorability (Wells, Burnett & Morarity, 2000). In this way the message can be seen as a multilevel process, and it is only part of developing the total end-result advertisement.

An effective advertisement encompasses the following:

- Memory (the consumer remembers it)
- Exposure (the right consumer sees and/or hears it)
- Attention-grabbing power (the consumer notices it)
- Interpretation or understanding (the consumer gets the message)

Advertisers can determine these factors in a number of ways, including recall reports, recognition tests, diary reports, and sales figures (after an ad has been shown). More intrusive measures would be wiring people and putting them in a special research room as they watch ads to measure eye pupil dilation or using brain wave analysis or brain scans (as in the Gerald Zaltman studies mentioned earlier).

Usually there is a link between the cost of the advertisement space and the potential size of the market. Thus, one ad during the Super Bowl game (usually airing the last

Sunday in January) costs over a million dollars but has the potential of reaching more than 500 million people because the game attracts not only the U.S. audience but international viewers as well. Originality counts, so many advertising firms and companies try to show off with their best talent, to the point that many viewers remark that the ads are better than the game. About 48 percent of the viewers are women, so it is not strictly a male market. Some start-up companies only advertise on the Super Bowl, putting their entire advertising budget on that one opportunity; they would be focusing on building awareness, making a first impression. Most companies, such as giant, established beverage manufacturers and carmakers, would use the Super Bowl as only one venue among many, and their goal would be to keep the public interest alive in their brands and maybe to push a new flavor, model, or version.

Timing is also important. The most expensive ads on the Super Bowl come at the beginning of the game when viewership is highest. Depending on how the game goes, viewership may remain constant or drop off, a factor on which advertisers take a risk. Besides the large audience, another reason that the Super Bowl is so popular as a showcase is because of **association**—advertisers like to link their products with a fun experience. Football has a pleasant association because it is a game, a contest that is all-American. Likewise, political candidates like to surround themselves with actors and other celebrities, such as successful football coaches, as a way of building their popularity. Olympics sponsors also use association, a candy bar or a brand of sportswear may be the "official" product for the Olympics in a particular year, boosting sales.

Advertisers use association to build or maintain images.

With the opening up of global markets, advertisers have to address global markets as well as local markets. Naming products is difficult because an acceptable name in the United States may not be acceptable elsewhere. Similarly, settings or environments and types of models used have to be appropriate to the market. Advertising has to be adaptive and accountable and accurate to succeed.

Advertising push is uneven. Some products, such as food and beverages (that is, goods that are used often and used up), are heavily advertised, but other products are rarely advertised and then only in small targeted markets. Candy may be advertised only at Halloween and Easter. Because of economies of scale, large advertisers have an advantage—they are already known and accepted by markets. It is difficult for a new smaller firm to break into established, heavily branded markets such as cereals, which are dominated by three major brands.

It is also necessary to point out that some ads don't work even if they are advertising a good product. The ad may be inappropriate or offensive. Have you ever watched an ad and wondered what it was about? Obviously, the sales point was not made. Probably the least effective advertising is direct mail that goes to mass markets: It is estimated that 98 percent of junk mail is thrown out. Examples of this are high-rise apartment dwellers receiving circulars for tires, middle-age women without children receiving catalogs for children's clothes, and rural Midwesteners receiving reviews of the latest restaurants in Manhattan.

## Is Advertising Necessary?

A home freezer may not be about keeping food cold or saving money; it may be about security, warmth, and safety.

Do you recall the discussion in Chapter 2 of muckracker Vance Packard, author of *The Hidden Persuaders*? At the beginning of his book, he wrote:

This book is an attempt to explore a strange and rather exotic new area of American life. It is about the large-scale efforts being made, often with impressive success, to channel our unthinking habits, our purchasing decisions and our thought processes by the use of insights gleaned from psychiatry and the social sciences. Typically these efforts take place beneath our level of awareness, so that the appeals that move us are often, in a sense, "hidden." (Packard, 1957, p. 1)

There is no doubt that, as Packard suggests, advertising can be manipulative and that it uses psychology for profit and advantage. He says some of the manipulating is amusing because it is so obvious (for example, beautiful models draped on cars or rock stars drinking colas). But he says some of it is disquieting, intense, and potent. For example, the Weiss and Geller Advertising Agency became suspicious of the reasons people gave for buying home freezers because economically it didn't make much sense considering the initial cost, the added utility costs, and the amount of frozen leftovers thrown out. Researchers, whom Packard called "probers," found that families filled freezers because they were trying to fill their inner anxieties brought on by the uncertainties in their lives. The probers concluded that a full freezer is reassuring because it means there will always be food in the house, which means security, warmth, and safety. Economics had very little to do with the real reason for a home freezer purchase, so the advertising and sales pitches were adjusted accordingly (Packard, 1957).

Packard goes on to say:

> Probers have found out why we are afraid of banks; why we love those big fat cars; why we really buy homes; why men smoke cigars; why the kind of car we drive reveals the brand of gasoline we will buy; why housewives typically fall into a hypnoidal trance when they get into a supermarket; why men are drawn into auto showrooms by convertibles but end up buying sedans; why junior loves cereal that pops, snaps, and crackles. (1957, p. 2)

Of course, consumer behavior and advertising research have come a long way since the 1950s, but the basic premise he puts forth has merit.

The industry would counter by saying that advertising is important for consumer information—it lets the consumer know what is out there and by doing this stimulates choices and competition. Advertising also communicates availability by saving consumers the time of comparison shopping and needlessly shopping at stores that do not carry certain brands or products. For example, a television ad for a new movie says that it opens on March 3. This is useful information, saving the filmgoer the trouble of going to the theater in February.

Advertisers would also say they are primarily recommenders, for example, offering samples as a way to try something out. They would say they do not create needs but rather help to fulfill them. In the transaction process, advertisers and marketers cannot create demand, so they try to fill the demand that is already there. So is advertising necessary? Yes, it probably is because it fulfills a function in the marketplace.

The power of samples can be explained by the rule of reciprocation. In a classic psychology study, a university professor sent Christmas cards to perfect strangers. He was amazed at the number of people who sent holiday cards back addressed to him, and most did not inquire into his identity (Kunz & Woolcott, 1976). They appeared to have some sort of automatic drive—get a card, and send a card. The **rule of reciprocation** means that we try to repay what someone has given us. A free sample will often encourage people to buy the full-size product, and individuals receiving samples may feel obligated to the salesperson or the company. Samples or free gifts are often for food or shampoo but also may be higher-priced items such as certificates for free T-shirts or scarves, accompanied with a letter from the company president appreciating their business, given to frequent buyers at a national clothing chain. The rule of reciprocity has been tested and found to be true in many societies around the world. Sociologists and anthropologists theorize that our ancestors developed networks of sharing and learning, so this feeling of indebtedness is deeply ingrained in us.

The dark side to the rule of reciprocation is explained by Robert Cialdini in his book *Influence: Science and Practice*. What he says is that some people take this too far and may make a person feel uncomfortably indebted by expecting a favor in return. This could be a tactic of door-to-door salespeople or charities; for example, a common tactic is to receive unsolicited gifts such as address labels or notecards from charities or nonprofit organizations. A person may also try to get someone to comply with a request. There are two approaches to dealing with unwanted samples, gifts, or favors: reject them outright, or see the offers for what they are and not for what they are represented to be. Cialdini states, "We should accept initial favors or concessions in good faith, but be ready to redefine them as tricks should they later be proved as such. Once they are redefined in this way, we will no longer feel a need to respond with a favor or concession of our own" (2001, p. 50). It all boils down to a need for self-regulation when it comes to advertising—the informed consumer knows when to respond and when not to respond

## Color in Advertising

Are you attracted to black-and-white photos of pizza? No, the advertisement or circular that comes in the mail or in your newspaper needs red for the tomato sauce and yellow for the cheese to be effective. Color has the power to create brand imagery, convey moods, and stimulate taste buds. Red is a common color in political advertising because it attracts attention, and red, white, and blue are a popular combination for a patriotic appeal. The attractions of certain colors vary by intended message, targeted age group, and other classifications. Parkay margarine in electric blue and shocking pink targeted to children was a surprise to many doubting adults who asked, "Who would use that stuff?"

Blue is the most favored color overall, but the second most popular color varies by ethnicity and race. Whites like green, Hispanics and African Americans lean toward purple, and Asian Americans prefer pink. Older people like sky blue much more than younger people. Blue-and-silver cars sell well. It used to be there was more impact based on gender, but increasingly men and women are agreeing on house paint colors and car colors (Paul, 2002). Reasons given for this trend are that gender roles have loosened up and that men are being exposed (through the world of sports) to masculine men wearing uniforms of purple and teal. There are limits; for example, you can't put GI Joe in pink according to Richard Brandt of Landor Associates (Paul, 2002).

Another trend is toward brighter and more complex colors. Crayola crayons come in 120 different hues, so children are exposed early to a wide range of colors. When marketing to Hispanic children, the emphasis is on warmer tones of yellow and red, according to Margaret Walch of the Color Association of the United States (Paul, 2002). But any generalization can vary around the country since a consumer's palette is dependent on light, temperature, and location as well as on how he or she spends time. Mexicans favor reds, blues, and blacks, whereas

Florida Hispanics like pastels, pinks, and salmons for fashions and interiors (Paul, 2002). African Americans experiment with colors from chartreuse to brown; they are also attracted to yellows and reds. To be effective, advertising needs to keep up with trends in ethnic and racial preferences. Although this section is on color, it should be pointed out that typeface, font, size, and legibility also affect how ads are perceived; for example, elderly people cannot and will not read small print. On television, advertising can use motion, so Gap, Old Navy, and Target ads often feature people dancing while wearing those companies' products.

## Value of Repetition

A successful advertisement can stay in our heads for decades. Baby boomers can sing the Mickey Mouse Club song from their younger days, and the elderly remember jingles and slogans from their youth for products that no longer exist. Memorability or **locking power** is a goal that advertisers strive for. Advertising plays on two forms of memory—recognition (sight) and recall (more complex associations). For example, shoppers who see hot dog buns realize they do not need the buns, but seeing them is a cue that they need hot dogs or mustard or ketchup. Likewise, a Krispy Kreme ad triggers a memory that causes a consumer to say, "Oh yes, I need to remember to stop by and get donuts on the way to work tomorrow."

Repetition can be used as a memory-jogging device over many years or over a short time span. For example, during the 2003 Super Bowl an advertisement for Anheuser-Busch (the world's largest brewery), featuring singer Tim McGraw promoting responsible drinking, was shown in all four quarters of the game. Is it worth the expense to be repetitive? Usually, the answer to this is yes. Many people will ignore a first or second ad, but it is difficult to ignore the fourth ad shown during a single event or evening. And when it comes to the major TV broadcasting advertising event of the year—the Super Bowl—the timing becomes even more complicated. "These days, PepsiCo releases its commercials about a week in advance of the game 'to capitalize' on the buzz surrounding Super Bowl, says Dave DeCecco, senior manager of public relations for Pepsi-Cola North America. The beverage and bottling concern got an estimated $10 million in free publicity for a 90-second Britney Spears performance it used to promote Pepsi soda last year" (Vranica & O'Connell, January 21, 2003, p. B1).

Memory devices include **jingles** (music), **slogans** (short phrases), and **taglines** (end messages). Repetition thrives on rhyme, catchy melodies, and repeating sounds. An example of a repeating sound is the sound of an Alka-Seltzer tablet dissolving in a glass of water accompanied by the jingle "Plop, plop, fizz, fizz, Oh what a relief it is." Can you sing the Oscar Mayer Weiner song? Characters such as cartoon characters or animals can also assist with repetition and locking power; for example, the Aflac duck promotes insurance, a product that is difficult to visualize or make attractive.

## Economics and Advertising Pros and Cons

Advertising is part of the free market system. It encourages competition and fosters economic growth, which is good for consumers. New products are developed and offered, stimulating the economy. Volume sales can lead to lower production costs, and those savings should be passed on to consumers in the form of lower prices.

These are all pros. The main negative is that advertising adds to the cost of marketing goods, and this cost is also passed down to consumers. The debate about the economic value versus the possible negative effects of advertising may never be resolved. Some economists take a negative view of advertising, others feel that "it depends on your point of view," and still others are very positive. Consumer economists are not critical of advertising per se but may be critical of techniques or type of appeal. All agree that advertising is a powerful institution integral to the workings of the market.

From an economic standpoint, advertising provides information about alternatives and provides consumers with recall cues that help them make substitutes at the time of purchase. The more alternatives that consumers can think of, the greater is the price elasticity. They may say that they can't afford this product but can afford another that will easily substitute. Advertising succeeds best in environments where choices exist and there is disposable income. The basic economic role of advertising is to let people know what is available, and that helps them make consumption decisions.

## Deceptive Advertising

Among other things, advertising should be accountable, it should be accurate, and it should give a fair portrayal of the product or service. But advertising can be deceptive or misleading. How much so is difficult to pinpoint; it is also difficult to know where to draw the line between persuasiveness and manipulation. In political advertisements, mudslinging occurs and misleading statistics are presented, both of which alter people's perception of the truth. There have been studies that show decisively both that purchases are consumer driven based on needs and that advertising is simply an information source. Other studies show that consumers become aware of a new product and then the need or want follows. Critics say vulnerable groups, such as young children, teens, and the elderly, too easily succumb to marketing messages and that businesses take advantage of their vulnerability. Evidence to prove this is shaky, except in the area of very young children who cannot distinguish between an advertisement and a cartoon show.

Puffery is legal.

Accuracy or accountability refers to whether the advertising message, either direct or subtle, is accurate. Most watchers of television know that a new face cream will not improve their social life, but where do you draw the line? **Puffery** refers to advertising that exaggerates the characteristics of a product. If an advertiser said its face cream would remove all wrinkles, that would be puffery, but it is okay for the company to say a moisturizer used as directed will reduce the "appearance of wrinkles." Puffery is legal. A common phrase of puffery is "the world's best pizza." The Uniform Commercial Code (UCC) is a set of laws about sales and other commercial matters that in essence says it is okay for ads to make general statements praising a product or service. Therefore it is all right for Silversmith's to advertise that it is the area's leading jeweler, but it is not okay for the store to advertise that "all our gold jewelry is 18 karat gold" when it also sells gold of lesser quality.

The Federal Trade Commission (FTC) says an advertisement is unfair if it causes or is likely to cause substantial consumer injury which is not reasonably avoidable by consumers themselves and is not outweighed by countervailing benefits to consumers or to competition. The FTC says an ad is deceptive if it contains misrepresentation or omission. It also uses the average man rule, which is based on whether an average person would be deceived by the advertisement; if that is true, then the ad is ruled misleading. As has been discussed in other chapters, there are other groups besides the FTC that monitor advertising messages and images.

Here are more examples of deceptive advertising:

- A hamburger is made to look large by putting it on a very small plate or in the hands of a small child.
- A toy race track set appears to have cars that go fast by using camera tricks and angles when in reality the cars putter around a dull oval-shaped track.
- Vegetables and beef are added to a bowl of vegetable beef soup for a TV ad so that it looks like there are more vegetables and beef than would be found in an actual can. (An old trick was to put weights in the bottom of the bowl so that the vegetables and beef floated to the surface.)
- Cars are driven off-road by professionals, a practice that would actually wreck the cars if they were driven by ordinary people. In an effort to be more truthful, some television ads have small print on the bottom of the screen that says "driven by professional drivers."
- People appearing to be doctors give testimonials or are supporters of diet products when in fact they are not medical doctors or are doctors whose specializations have nothing to do with diets.
- Someone says a product is low in calories when it is actually high in calories.

Examples of ethical concerns (morals, principles, or values) include the sharing of buyer lists and personal information about consumers by companies, the promotion of harmful substances such as tobacco and alcohol to teens, and questionable or rigged sweepstakes and contests. When it comes to court action against companies, it often boils down to figuring out if the advertisers were deliberately untruthful or misleading. This can be proved by e-mails, letters, and employees' testimony. Legitimate companies and advertisers want to eliminate flagrantly deceptive advertising because shady advertising of any kind reflects poorly on the advertising industry as a whole.

Does advertising encourage materialism (a preoccupation with material things)? It is hard to argue that this is not the case. After all, it encourages consumption and also affects our sense of what constitutes status, success, and achievement. For example, a wine campaign could equate wine with elitism and elegance. Drinking wine could say, "I've arrived."

Does it create dissatisfaction? Many consumer economists would give a resounding yes in response to this question. They would say that advertising encourages the throwing out the old in favor of buying something new. In the world of advertising, "new" is almost always better, the exception being eBay and similar Web sites. Advertisers say that they did not create materialism—they are simply providing information, supplying a service. They think advertising has become a scapegoat for all of society's ills, as a maker of values rather than as a reflector of values. They will also say that no amount of advertising can sell a lousy product. Since products fail all the time, there is some merit to this argument—people will not buy what they don't like or can't use.

Does advertising portray an unreal world, a world of perfection? Yes, it often does. The models have perfect teeth and hair; everyone in the ad is happy and secure. Viewers or readers accept this because they want a better life and like attractive people and settings.

Advertising also preys on people's insecurities: fear of being a victim of theft (to sell home security systems), fear of dying penniless (to sell funeral burial policies and financial products), and fear of smelling bad (to sell deodorants, soaps, shampoos, body washes). Baldness remedies are sold to men on the basis of fear—of losing their youth and of what other people are saying about them. The basic message is that if you buy this product, you will look or feel better. Current events play into the type of advertising that is run and the products that sell. Following the September 11, 2001, tragedies in the United States, life insurance sales skyrocketed. War news curtails foreign travel and has the effect of increasing domestic travel, especially destinations within easy driving distance of home.

Does advertising pay for television and radio shows? The answer is yes. The commercials are most obvious on commercial television and radio and are more subtle but nevertheless present on PBS when company names splash across the screen. PBS television and radio also rely on viewer and listener contributions and federal government support. According to the PBS Annual Report, leading corporate underwriters of shows that target kids, such as *Sesame Street,* include over $1 million from Playskool, W. K. Kellogg Foundation, General Mills, Lego Co., and LookSmart Ltd. In the next category of corporate underwriters, at the $500,000 to $1 million level, is KB Kids.com Inc., Libby's Juicy Juice, and Chuck E. Cheese. There are ethical issues involved in this level of corporate support, with some feeling it has gone too far. "It used to be 'the following program is brought to you with support from Mobil,'" says Robert Thompson, director of the Center for the Study of Popular TV at Syracuse University in Syracuse, New York. "Now it is a moving video and some of it is pretty substantial—it's longer, it's a full-fledged commercial. It's no longer a mention. It's a commercial pure and simple and sometimes not so pure and not so simple" (Beatty, 2002, p. B1).

For television viewing in general, experiments have been conducted where people paid for television shows without commercials, but these experiments failed. We have become accustomed to "free" television and radio. With the advent of mute and fast-forward buttons on remotes, we are paying less of a price.

Not all advertisements are difficult to watch. Some are entertaining, using the latest music, or amusing as well as informative, especially on the first exposure; repeated exposure lessens the pleasurable effect. Curiously, though, some of the dullest commercials sell the most products.

Bait and switch as a fraudulent sales practice was discussed earlier in the book, but it needs to be added here because it is a common advertising fraud. A person reads an ad for a digital camera selling for $125, and since that is a very low price, he or she goes to the store wanting to buy it. The store says the camera is sold out and tries to switch the customer to a $500 digital camera. State attorney generals' offices or other consumer affairs areas can look into bait-and-switch fraud, and consumers can file individual or class-action suits demanding compensation.

## Subliminal Advertising

Subliminal advertising has embedded images for a product that aren't noticed on a conscious level.

We assume that advertising is seen and/or heard. **Subliminal advertising** operates below the level of consciousness. It refers to messages "transmitted in such a way that the receiver is not consciously aware of receiving it" (Wells, Burnett & Moriarty, 2000, p. 41). The symbols or words may be too faint or too fast for the conscious mind to pick up. Many would say this is foul play, whereas others would say this is like the creature Big Foot—it does not exist. Comedian Steven Wright has a joke that goes something like this: "I saw a subliminal advertising executive the other day, but only for a second."

Subliminal advertising is a favorite topic of psychology and consumer classes. The question is: Is it possible to manipulate the mind of consumers with faint or hidden messages? In experiments when psychologists or communications experts have tested subliminal advertisements that they designed, it appears that they do not work. Consumers will not buy products they do not need regardless of either overt or subliminal advertising messages. The advertising industry does not like the insinuation that its members use subliminal advertising and says that accusations of its use are damaging and false. Common accusations target movie theaters, which are said to use subliminal messages in premovie advertisements to increase popcorn or soda sales.

Author Wilson Keys suggested that most embedded ads appeal to sexuality (Weir, 1984). An example is that of an attractive woman's body embedded in ice cubes in a print advertisement for an alcoholic beverage. Research indicates that an advertisement such as this may trigger a like or dislike for the product, but it appears unlikely that a subliminal advertisement will cause someone to drink whiskey if they do not normally drink whiskey. Although subliminal advertising may not exist, it has been shown to be largely ineffective in experiments. It may be possible in the future for more sophisticated forms to be developed that may be capable of manipulating consumers. This is the reason that this subject is worth mentioning in a book on consumer economics, and given the previous section on the Zaltman research studies, perhaps there is more merit to studying unconscious thought regarding consumption than was previously thought.

## Distasteful Advertising

Taste is about not only what is artistically pleasing but also what seems appropriate. Table 7.1 gives a list of ethical and/or taste issues facing advertisers. In Europe, an advertising firm painted advertisements on the sides of cows standing in fields (with the permission of and payment to the owners), and animal rights activists objected, saying it was in bad taste because it took advantage of the cows. Do you agree or disagree? Also in Europe, a baby carriage manufacturer had a contest, and the winners received expensive baby carriages with company advertising on the side of the carriages. People said this was in bad taste, too. Do you agree or disagree?

Taste, as a value-laden word, is in the eye of the beholder, and this includes where the viewer or consumer lives. Taste can refer literally to what tastes good. For example, cheese flavor is not appealing to most Chinese, so to sell Frito-Lay's Cheetos in China the company tried out over 600 different flavors in taste tests. Although the end product is still called Cheetos, the flavor we are used to in the United States cannot be found in most of China. What flavors is the company selling? American Savory and Japanese Steak are two of the favorites. In regard to advertising, what passes for bad taste in one country or area of the world may be considered appropriate in others. In Australia and Western Europe, women's breasts are shown in television commercials, whereas in the United States this is considered poor taste and not allowed. In the United States, the time of day and the type of show that beer ads can appear on are regulated. Beer ads are not allowed on Saturday cartoon shows, but it is okay to have them on Saturday

**Table 7.1** Ethical and/or Taste Issues Facing Advertisers

| Issue | Types or Examples |
|---|---|
| Controversial products and ads | Should alcohol, tobacco, lotteries, and gambling be advertised? |
| Intimate products | How should ads sell feminine hygiene products, impotency cures, lingerie, and underwear? |
| Advertising to children | Should there be guidelines for ads targeting children in terms of type of ad, placement of ad, and time of day? |
| Bias or stereotyping | What should be done about offensive depictions in ads of racial/ethnic groups, the elderly, the disabled, or other groups? |
| Puffery | What is legal exaggeration in an ad, and does it include the use of the word "best"? |
| Social responsibility | Do ads hurt or help causes? Do some ads go beyond legal lobbying rules? |
| Use of models and spokespersons | Does the model or spokesperson really use the product? Is proof of use necessary? |
| Use of former public figures | Should former presidents, governors, legislators, or generals endorse products? Which products are off-limits? |

afternoon football games. Since children may be watching the games or playing in the room while their parents are watching the games, they are exposed to beer commercials. So although there are some guidelines to protect children, this example shows that they are exposed to adult product advertising on a regular basis. Children also see roadside billboards for adult entertainment clubs and other adult fare.

U.S. consumers complain that much advertising, regardless of whom it is directed to, is in poor taste. They say it is irritating, repetitive, insulting to their intelligence, and humorless, as well as degrading to certain individuals and groups. Beer ads and advertising for bars are often degrading to women, Asian Americans, African Americans, Hispanics, and the elderly have also been the target of stereotyping. The kinds of ads said to be obnoxious often have to do with personal care, such as deodorants, dandruff shampoos, and denture creams. Irritating ads can have close-ups of dogs crunching dog food or a doorbell or telephone ringing that gets someone up off a couch to answer the door or phone. Nauseating ads may have close-ups of people chewing with their mouths open, little children smearing food all over their faces (some find this cute), or women spooning cat food from a can. Music or jingles can be especially irritating.

**Infomercials** are program-long advertisements that can run an hour or more for cooking products, cosmetics, tools, and diet programs/supplements. Traditionally, these were shown late at night when airtime was inexpensive, but increasingly infomercials are airing at noon during the week and on Saturdays. Some people find these irritating, while others enjoy the advice, demonstrations, and comfortable conversational style. Infomercials go in and out of style, some dropping off the air and being replaced with others.

## Marketing to Children

Monopoly and other games like Electronic Mall Madness by Milton Bradley en-courage children to be acquisitive, aggressive, and shrewd in their spending deci-sions. The objects of the games are to make the most money or to have the money spread as far as it will go. In the case of Electronic Mall Madness, the ob-ject is to get the most stuff and get back to the parking lot first. It is quite an in-troduction to the world of credit cards, consumption, and competitiveness. Some would say this is too much for ten-year-olds; others would say it is good life training since grown-ups are exposed to a continuous barrage of sales ads, credit card offers, and car salesmen screaming at them from the television set about new, low prices.

Games involving money or gambling aimed at children are nothing new, nor are advertisements aimed at children. In 1912, Cracker Jack was offering a toy inside so that children would ask for it. Before television, children were saving box tops for prizes; the practice of putting toys in cereal boxes to attract children has been going on for decades, although lately coupons for products or discounts are be-coming more common. McDonald's has had Happy Meals for years, as have com-petitors (using slightly different names for their meals), with prizes marketed to children.

Children are exposed to about 200 television commercials a day, and the commer-cials have changed considerably from the ads that their parents viewed (DeGraaf, Wann & Naylor, 2001). In earlier ads, parents were shown as authority figures,

Today, children play computer games at a younger age than in the past. (Photo Researchers, Inc.)

people who would help the children out by explaining how products worked or who could be relied on to put products together. Newer ads often leave out parents and are more likely to show peers or cartoon-type characters showing children how products work—in other words, a mom and dad are no longer shown as the wise figures (value setters) that they used to be.

## Government and Advertising

Government agencies, such as the Federal Communications Commission (FCC) and the FTC, and legislation affect both the advertising industry and its practices (see Table 7.2).

**Role of FCC in Advertising.**   One of the agencies that has not been discussed extensively before is the FCC, formed in 1934 to protect the public in regard to broadcast communications. The FCC has limited control over broadcast advertising through its ability to issue and revoke licenses to stations. The FCC's concerns with radio and television stations and networks include advertising that is perceived to be in bad taste or that is deceptive, and as such, the FCC works closely with the FTC (discussed in the next section).

As this chapter and previous ones have shown, the government and the advertising industry are often at odds, but sometimes they cooperate and work together.

**Table 7.2**   Government Agencies Affecting Advertising

| Agency | Effect |
|---|---|
| Bureau of Alcohol, Tobacco, and Firearms (AFT) (a division of the U.S. Treasury Department) | Regulates advertising of alcohol; can revoke permits for distillers, wine merchants, and brewers |
| Federal Communications Commission (FCC) | Issues and revokes licenses for radio and television stations; can eliminate deceptive or poor-taste ads |
| Federal Trade Commission (FTC) | Regulates advertising, labeling, and packaging; issues warnings; requires advertisers to validate claims |
| Food and Drug Administration (FDA) | Regulates labeling, packaging, and manufacture of food and drug products as well as safety and purity of cosmetics |
| Library of Congress | Watches over copyright protection issues such as coined phrases and well-known slogans in ads |
| U.S. Patent Office | Watches over trademark registration |
| U.S. Postal Service | Controls advertising through the mail; handles complaints of unsolicited ads and products that come in the mail (such as obscenity, contests, fraud)* |
| State agencies | Regulate unfair and deceptive trade practices within states (often including advertising) |

*Consumers who receive sexually offensive material in the mail can request that no more mail be delivered from that sender. The postmaster general has the power to stop offensive mail or questionable offers sent through the mail such as get-rich-quick schemes.

For example, on October 6, 2000, President Clinton signed an executive order at the White House that included language to establish the first multicultural advertising guidelines for federal government departments and agencies. The main point was to encourage inclusiveness and fairness throughout the marketing and advertising processes, from employment and career advancement to competition and compensation for creative services. The American Advertising Federation (AAF) and the AAF Foundation formed a committee that drafted the *Principles and Recommended Practices for Effective Advertising in the American Multicultural Marketplace*. Companies such as DaimlerChrysler, Kraft General Foods, and other agencies have committed to adopting the principles laid out in the report. For a complete report, go to www.aaf.org.

**Role of FTC in Advertising.**   In an earlier chapter, there was a lengthy description of the oversight and powers of the FTC, but here is a brief review with a focus on advertising. The FTC receives complaints and inquiries each month about advertising; it investigates problems and may take action, depending on the case. A first step is a **consent decree** in which the FTC notifies the advertiser that its ads are deceptive and asks the advertiser to sign a consent decree saying it will stop the deceptive practice. Most do sign it and thus avoid a possible fine of $10,000 per day and the bad publicity for refusing to do so.

**Role of Legislation in Advertising.**   For consumer redress, one of the strongest pieces of legislation is the **Magnuson-Moss Warranty–FTC Improvement Act of 1975**. It empowers the FTC to obtain consumer redress when a person or firm engages in deceptive practices such as false or misleading advertising. This includes the ad agency as well as the manufacturer of the product. For example, one case of misleading advertising of a shaving product ended with both the company and the agency paying $1 million each to the government, and they had to halt the advertising campaign. On behalf of consumers, the FTC can order any of the following:

- Cancellation or reformation of contracts
- Refund of money
- Return of property
- Payment of damages
- Public notification

One of the strongest actions that the FTC can take is cease-and-desist orders. A hearing, similar to a trial, takes place in which the company presents its defense. An administrative law judge presides, and FTC staff attorneys represent the commission. If the FTC succeeds in proving that an ad is unfair or misleading, then it issues a cease-and-desist order requiring the ad to stop; if the company does not do so, it is given a stiff fine. The advertiser can appeal.

**Counteradvertising**, also called corrective advertising, is new advertising that is undertaken pursuant to an FTC order for the purpose of correcting false claims about the product. The new ad can be on radio, in print, or on television and gives information to correct former misinformation. The purpose is not to punish the advertiser but rather to act in the best interest of consumers. A classic case was Warner-Lambert's Listerine campaign that ran for nearly 50 years. In this ad campaign, the claim was that the product prevented colds or reduced the severity of colds and sore throats. The cost of the corrective advertising was $10 million and ran for 16 months, mostly on television (Wells, Burnett & Moriarty, 2000).

Whether counteradvertising works or not (whether it changes consumer behavior) is questionable. For example, Warner-Lambert found that after the corrective advertising was ended, 42 percent of Listerine users still believed that the mouthwash was being advertised as a remedy for colds and sore throats, and 57 percent of users rated cold and sore throat effectiveness as a key reason for purchasing the brand (Wilke, McNeil & Mazis, 1984).

## ROLE OF PUBLIC SERVICE ANNOUNCEMENTS

It is fitting to end this chapter on a positive note. We have all benefited from **public service announcements (PSAs)**, defined as messages on behalf of some good cause such as stopping drunk driving (Mothers Against Drunk Driving) or preventing forest fires. A leader in creating these announcements is the Ad Council, a private nonprofit organization whose mission is to identify a select number of significant public issues and stimulate action. The Ad Council often teams up with government agencies or nonprofit organizations to get a message out to the public. For example, currently the Ad Council and the U.S. Department of Health and Human Services have a joint campaign to inspire healthier lifestyles. One of the first Ad Council campaigns was during World War II, using the slogan "Loose Lips Sink Ships." Here are some slogans that you were brought up with that were developed by the Ad Council:

- McGruff the Crime Dog's "Take a Bite Out of Crime"
- Smokey Bear's "Only You Can Prevent Forest Fires"
- "Keep America Beautiful"
- "A Mind Is a Terrible Thing to Waste"
- "Friends Don't Let Friends Drive Drunk"

According to the Ad Council's Web site, 68 percent of Americans exposed to the "Friends Don't Let Friends Drive Drunk" advertisements say they have personally stopped someone who had been drinking from driving. The United Negro College Fund's slogan "A Mind Is a Terrible Thing to Waste" has helped raise more than $1.9 billion, used to help 300,000 minority students graduate from college.

## SUMMARY

Time, technological obsolescence, and depreciation all affect buying decisions. Gerald Zaltman of Harvard University has conducted research that indicates that much of consumer decision making may be unconscious. More research is under way to determine the extent to which this is true. In 1957, Vance Packard's *The Hidden Persuaders* exposed the advertising industry and its manipulative ways. Government agencies and the advertising industry are often at odds with each other, but sometimes they cooperate on social advances and initiatives. A positive side of the advertising industry is the public service announcements (PSAs) that they create, often in cooperation with government agencies or nonprofit organizations, to bring about positive social change.

Price often serves as a rule of thumb—a guide for narrowing down choices. A $200 cashmere sweater may be out of the question, but one marked down to $69 may be considered. Scarcity plays a part as well and explains why famous oil paintings go for $75 million and John Travolta's leisure suit from the movie *Saturday Night Fever* sold for $145,000 at auction.

Researcher Michael Solomon, author of *Conquering Consumerspace,* suggests that the traditional way of doing business in which companies call the shots is obsolete; the trend now is for businesses to work with consumers. He describes a world where boundaries between branded commodities and everyday life are blurred and nationalities are less important. More and more people will move seamlessly between the offline and online domains.

Advertising is part of the free enterprise system. It provides exposure to choice and competition, but in the long run it is added on to the price of consumer goods. There are many levels or steps in advertising—getting the message across is an underlying purpose. Advertisers like their goods to be associated with pleasant experiences (like football games) or attractive lifestyles. Because of economies of scale, large advertisers have an advantage over smaller ones or beginners in a market. It is debatable whether subliminal advertisements exist or not, but there is no question that we are exposed to obnoxious and distasteful advertising. The Federal Communications Commission (FCC) has the authority to issue and revoke licenses to broadcasting stations and works closely with the Federal Trade Commission (FTC). The FTC is the government's main watchdog on deceptive advertising. It can issue consent orders and cease-and-desist orders and can request counteradvertising (also known as corrective advertising). Research studies question whether counteradvertising is effective.

## KEY POINTS

1. Consumers vary in their ability to trade, based on the amount of time and the amount of money they have (budget constraints), which affects their decision making in the marketplace. Some seek bargains; others are content with full prices. Style matters to some and not to others, with price usually being a strong guide (but not the only guide) to purchasing.

2. Uniqueness theory proposes that individuals vary in the extent to which they wish to be different.

3. Impulse buying is encouraged by sellers by various means such as check-out displays of candy or magazines or add-ons from catalog or Internet sales. Impulse items can be expensive items.

4. Advertising is part of the free market system. As such, it encourages competition and fosters economic growth, but it also ultimately costs the consumer. Consumers often find advertising irritating, objectionable, and in bad taste, but this varies by consumer, by region, and by country.

5. Puffery, exaggerated claims such as "the world's best pizza," is legal.

6. Children are exposed to about 200 television commercials a day.

7. Public service announcements (PSAs), developed on a volunteer basis by advertising and communications professionals, inform the public about critical social issues such as drunk driving and forest fires.

## KEY TERMS

ability to trade
advertising
association
authenticity
budget constraints
consent decree
consumer payoff
counteradvertising
depreciation
identity marketing
impulse buying

infomercials
jingles
locking power
Magnuson-Moss
    Warranty–FTC
    Improvement Act
    of 1975
Pareto principle
Parkinson's law
price discrimination
price variation

public service
    announcements
    (PSAs)
puffery
rule of reciprocation
rules of thumb
slogans
style
subliminal advertising
taglines
uniqueness theory

## DISCUSSION QUESTIONS

1. What have you bought on impulse? Was it a good or bad purchase? Explain why.
2. What do you own that has depreciated in value? Do you accept this depreciation or not? Explain your answer.
3. Select two print ads and compare their messages. What are they selling? Who is their audience or target market? How effective are the ads in grabbing your attention?
4. Do you think there should be more or less government regulation of advertising? Support your answer with examples.
5. Go to the FTC Web site and see what it says about advertising. What are the current issues they are involved in?

## E-RESOURCES

**Advertising Industry**

**Advertising Age**   *AdAge.com*
Trade publication

**American Advertising Federation (AAF)**   *www.aaf.org*
Trade association representing 50,000 professions in the advertising industry

**Ad Council**   *www.adcouncil.org*
Private nonprofit organization founded in 1947 that marshals volunteer talent from the advertising and communications industries and the media to produce

public service advertising to address critical social issues in American government agencies

**American Association of Advertising Agencies**　　*www.aaaa.org*
National trade association founded in 1917 representing the advertising agency business

**Government Agencies**

**Federal Communications Commission (FCC)**　　*www.fcc.gov*

**Federal Trade Commission (FTC)**　　*www.ftc.gov*

**Food and Drug Administration (FDA)**　　*www.fda.gov*

# REFERENCES

Alexander, R., ed. (1965). *Marketing definitions*. Chicago: American Marketing Association.

Beatty, S. (July 11, 2002). PBS and corporate underwriters: Too close for comfort? *Wall Street Journal,* p. B1.

Cialdini, R. (2001). *Influence: Science and practice*. Boston: Allyn and Bacon.

DeGraaf, J., D. Wann, and T. Naylor. (2001). *Affluenza: The all-consuming epidemic*. San Francisco, CA: Berrett-Koehler Publishers.

Goldsmith, R., R. Clark, and E. Goldsmith. (2007). The desire for unique consumer products and innovativeness. Proceedings of the Academy of Marketing Science Annual Meeting, Coral Gables, FL.

Kunz, P. R., and M. Woolcott. (1976). Season's greetings: From my status to yours. *Social Science Research, 5,* 269–78.

Lewis, D., and D. Bridges. (2000). *The soul of the new consumer*. London: Nicholas Brealey Publishing.

Lynn, M., and J. Harris. (1997). The desire for unique consumer products: A new individual differences scale. *Psychology & Marketing, 14* (6), 601–16.

Packard, V. (1957). *The hidden persuaders*. New York: Pocket Books.

Paul, P. (February 2002). Color by numbers. *American Demographics,* 31–35.

Solomon, M. (2003). *Conquering consumerspace*. New York: American Management Association.

Solomon, M., and N. Rabolt. (2004). *Consumer behavior in fashion*. Upper Saddle River, NJ: Prentice Hall.

Useem, J. (January 20, 2003). This man can read your mind. *Fortune,* p. 48.

Vranica, S., and V. O'Connell. (January 21, 2003). For immediate release! *Wall Street Journal,* p. B1.

Weir, W. (October 15, 1984). Another look at subliminal facts. *Advertising Age,* p. 46.

Wells, W., J. Burnett, and S. Moriarty. (2000). *Advertising principles & practice,* 5th ed. Saddle River, NJ: Prentice Hall.

Wilke, W., D. McNeil, and M. Mazis. (Spring 1984). Marketing's "Scarlet Letter": The theory and practice of corrective advertising. *Journal of Marketing, 26.*

Zaltman, G. (2003). *How customers think*. Cambridge, MA: Harvard Business School Press.

# Food and Beverage Issues

*Eating is an art—the only art everyone can participate in.*
—Alice Waters

## Learning Objectives

1. Discuss food and beverage consumption patterns, retailing, and issues.
2. List the agencies and laws that protect our food and water.
3. Explain what organically grown means.
4. List the different points of view regarding genetically altered foods.
5. Discuss health and legal issues as well as government protection of food and beverages.

---

### UM Study Shows Organic Farming Can Produce

One of the myths surrounding organic farming is that it is nice in small patches or for home growers, but it is not productive enough to sustain large numbers of people. Ivette Perfecto, Professor at the University of Michigan's School of Natural Resources and Environment, says, "My hope is that we can finally put a nail in the coffin of the idea that you can't produce enough food through organic agriculture."[1]

Perfecto along with co-researcher Catherine Badgley found in an exhaustive review of existing data that in developed countries, yields were almost equal for organic and conventionally grown crops. And in developing countries, food production can double and even triple using organic methods, which are less environmentally harmful. They defined organic as "practices referred to as sustainable or ecological; that utilize non-synthetic nutrient cycling processes; that exclude or rarely use synthetic pesticides; and [that] sustain or regenerate the soil quality."[2]

"Perfecto said the idea that people would go hungry if farming went organic is 'ridiculous. . . .'" This is especially good news for developing countries, where it's sometimes impossible to deliver goods from outside, so farmers must supply their own. "Yields in developing countries could switch dramatically by switching to organic farming," Perfecto says.[3] Their findings have implications for consumers, growers, manufacturers, and nations. The goal is to use land and other resources more efficiently.

---

[1]"Organic Farming Can Feed the World, U-M Study Shows." News Service, November 7, 2007; www.ns.umich.edu/htdocs/releases/story.
[2]Ibid.
[3]Ibid.

# INTRODUCTION

This chapter turns its attention to a specific area of consumer behavior: food and drink. As Chapter 2 showed, food is usually the first area of consumption that is government regulated because it is such a fundamental human need and people can get extremely ill or die from contaminated food. Since the first food and drug law was enacted in 1906, the federal government has taken an active role in ensuring the quality of our food supply. Food and drink are such integral parts of our daily lives that they are important areas to single out in terms of discussions about consumerism. We may buy only a few cars in the course of our lives, but we will buy countless amounts of food and drink.

Eating and drinking with friends and family scores high on happiness rating scales. People generally have a positive view of food, farms, and agriculture, including organic foods (Gifford & Bernard, 2006). Not all is well, though, when it comes to food; there are many issues. For example, **trans fats** have been under scrutiny. They are made when manufacturers add hydrogen to vegetable oil in a process known as hydrogenation. The average American consumes about five pounds of trans fats a year, a number that should go down because many fast-food chains, theme parks, school systems, and in some cases entire cities are eliminating trans fats.

Technology has provided the means for great advances in food and beverages. Did you know the Defense Department's combat-feeding program has come up with a barbecued chicken sandwich that has a shelf life of 3 years? Military rations (now called MREs, for Meals Ready to Eat) have come a long way from the tinned foods and Spam of World War II. Speaking of Spam, did you know that the number one state in Spam consumption is Hawaii? Products sold to the general public such as powdered milk, freeze-dried coffee, and processed cheese have their origin in GI rations. Currently, the military says it has found a way to keep lettuce and tomatoes fresh for 50 to 60 days at room temperature. One of the main developers of MREs is the feeding director for combat troops, Gerald Darsch, who has been described as a wry man with a great deal of intestinal fortitude. He is a modern-day example of the poison squad you read about in Chapter 2. "His distinguished combat-food record includes taste-testing 12-year-old canned ham and lima beans. 'It was ugly' is all he'll say about it, apparently trying to forget" (Stipp, 2003, p. 46). Another technological advance is our ability to track tainted food through DNA matching. This advance, which has enormous health and legal implications, is covered later in this chapter.

Although eating is one of life's greatest pleasures, nearly all Americans are on a diet or concerned about their weight, so people enjoy eating but worry about it at the same time. The concern about weight gain is so great that it has been called a national obsession. "The single most important issue in nutrition right now is gaining weight, and that's a matter of calories," says Marion Nestle, chairwoman of the Department of Nutrition and Food Studies at New York University. "It doesn't matter if they're healthy calories or unhealthy calories—calories are calories" (Parker-Pope, 2003, p. D1).

According to the Centers for Disease Control and Prevention (CDC), more than 60 percent of U.S. adults are either overweight or obese, but the question is what to do about it, if anything. Is it a problem that government and business should get involved in, or is it a matter of individual choice? At this point, consumers have to sort through lots of fads, misinformation, and downright fraudulent information coming from innumerable sources. Who should they believe? What should they do? What makes it even more complicated is that seemingly low-calorie, healthy-sounding foods are often not either; for example, a Fresh City Chicken Teriyaki Wrap has 968 calories and 33 fat grams, and Baja Fresh Ensalada Chicken contains 857 calories and 57 fat grams. What drives up the calories and fat grams are the sauces and dressings. A ham sandwich at Fresh City only has 547 calories by comparison, but most consumers would assume this is higher in calories than a Chicken Teriyaki Wrap. Nutritionists would like calorie information available at the counter or on the packaging. "Nobody can tell how many calories are in food they haven't prepared themselves," says Dr. Nestle. "Even a trained nutritionist can't tell, not even a really good one" (Parker-Pope, 2003, p. D1). Restaurant chains such as Wendy's International that owns Baja Fresh say that consumers can always get wraps or salads without the sauces or dressings and that they offer low-cal items like Mahi Mahi tacos, with 216 calories and 11 fat grams. In short, nutritionists, consumer economists, and health advocates want to educate the public about food and health risks, encourage participation in healthy behaviors, and make sure that useful and valid information is available to the public.

Although many of the examples in this chapter are from North America, it should be pointed out that food and beverage quality, availability, and consumption patterns are worldwide concerns. For example, fast-food consumption varies greatly by country. According to *Euromonitor*, the United States leads in per-person spending on fast food, followed by Canada, the United Kingdom, and Australia. In some countries there are great divides between rural and urban consumption and shopping patterns; as may be expected, choices may be more limited in rural areas, but fresher produce may be available. In a study in Scotland, the researchers found that consumers living in rural areas accepted a lack of shops and more expensive products, and they concluded that distance from retail centers strongly influenced shopping behaviors (McEachern & Warnaby, 2006). Have you noticed differences in food availability in the different places you have lived?

Writing about food and beverage issues has its share of pitfalls because it is such a fast-moving area, making it difficult to be absolutely accurate and up-to-date. Every effort has been made to provide balanced and current coverage, but because of the rapid pace of discoveries, the best advice is for readers to keep up with new developments from reliable sources and consult with their own physicians. Government sources were heavily relied on for the information provided in this chapter, and the government Web sites in the E-Resources section near the end of the chapter should supply the latest updates. The chapter begins with a discussion of food and beverage consumption patterns.

## FOOD AND BEVERAGE CONSUMPTION

### Basic Terminology

**Foods** are products from plants or animals that can be taken into the body for energy and nutrients to sustain life and growth. The food and beverages consumed are one's diet. **Nutrition** is the science of foods and nutrients and their actions within the body. The six classes of nutrients are carbohydrates, lipids, minerals, proteins, vitamins, and water. Your body obtains nutrients through the digestive process, in which foods are broken down in the gastrointestinal tract into compounds that the body can absorb. A kilocalorie is a measure of energy content in food.

## Brief History

In early Colonial America, food often consisted of whatever came out of a large pot set above the flames of the fireplace, and food was plain (except for the rich). Alcohol consumption (beer, wine, liquor, and cider) was high, estimated at six gallons per year for Americans over the age of 15. Around the time of the American Revolution, the most common main dish served was ham, except in the South, where it was chicken. Accompanying these were breads and desserts, cheese and other dairy products. Vegetables, seafood, and fruits depended on the season and consumer location, although importing was beginning from the Caribbean. By the 1820s, finer dining and restaurants were in evidence in the cities, and manners, etiquette, and utensils improved; by the 1830s and 1840s, extensive menus were available. Dining out became high fashion from New Orleans to Boston. Railroads and ships brought fine cuisine to the West. A famous dinner at New York's Delmonico's held in 1868 to honor English author Charles Dickens involved nearly 40 sumptuous dishes (Mariani, 1991). By the end of the 1890s, with advances in refrigeration and transportation, nearly any food was available anywhere. Americans went oyster mad, with an average consumption of 660 oysters per year, compared with 120 in the United Kingdom and only 26 in France (Mariani, 1991). This points out how consumption has changed over the years and how it varies by country. Do you normally eat 660 oysters a year?

In 1900 the hamburger patty on a bun was introduced, followed immediately by a hot dog in a bun. In the 1920s the widespread use of refrigerators revolutionized food and beverage storage, and dairy products, including pasteurized milk, became popular. In 1924 Clarence Birdseye sold the first frozen food—fish. Snack foods and candies prospered during the 1930s depression, with the Twinkie being introduced in 1930.

The first TV dinner was sold in 1954 by C. A. Swanson & Sons. The first affordable home microwave oven was introduced in 1965, and it became a common household appliance by the 1980s. In 1990 Oscar Mayer launched Lunchables, packs of meat, cheese, and crackers, leading the way to more individualized servings. In 2000 Smucker's introduced Uncrustables, packages of frozen peanut-butter-and-jelly sandwiches. Throughout the twentieth century, baking from scratch became less and less common. Prepackaged, prewashed salad mixes made their debut in the 1990s. Look in any large grocery store and notice how much space is devoted to salad mixes versus heads of lettuce. Changes in shelf space are good indicators of changes in American shopping habits. Another development in the twentieth century was the increase in snack food space: What once occupied a back corner of the store now has a whole aisle. Other changes include a wider variety of foods from other cultures and a greater variety of fruits and vegetables.

## Today's Practices and Habits

What are Americans eating and drinking today? Figure 8.1 shows the daily beverage consumption of Americans. Water is the highest category, followed by coffee and bottled water, then soft drinks and milk, and on down the list. Probably most

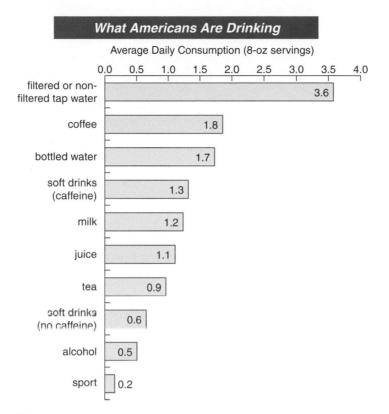

**Figure 8.1**   What Americans Are Drinking. (International Bottled Water Association.)

surprising in recent years is the explosive growth of sales in bottled water. This may seem like a new phenomenon, but water has been bottled and sold far from its source for thousands of years. The Food and Drug Administration (FDA) regulates bottled-water products that are sold interstate under the Federal Food, Drug, and Cosmetic Act. Under this act, manufacturers are responsible for producing safe, wholesome, and truthfully labeled food products, including bottled-water products (Buller, 2002). Box 8.1 gives the FDA classifications of bottled water.

Food and beverage choices and practices constantly change for individuals, families, households, communities, and nations. A good example of this is that carrying individually sized bottled water was a rarity until the 1990s in the United States. People decide what to eat and drink and when and where to do it. Several things determine their choices:

- Personal preferences and tastes
- Habit
- Background, ethnicity, heritage, and history
- Convenience, availability, and location
- Emotions (comfort foods, positive and negative associations)
- Values (religion, vegetarian, fresh versus prepared foods)
- Cost (for example, hamburger versus steak)

**BOX 8.1   FDA Classifications of Bottled Water According to Its Origin**

*Artesian well water.* Artesian well water comes from a well that taps an aquifer (layers of porous rock, sand, and earth that contain water). According to the Environmental Protection Agency (EPA), water from artesian aquifers is often more pure.

*Mineral water.* Water from an underground source that contains at least 250 parts per million of total dissolved solids is called mineral water. Minerals and trace elements must come from the source, not be added later.

*Spring water.* Spring water comes from an underground formation from which water flows naturally to the earth's surface.

*Well water.* Water obtained from boring or drilling a hole into the ground and tapping an aquifer is classified as well water.

In addition:

*Tap water.* Tap water comes from municipal sources and is usually treated.

Sparking water, seltzer water, soda water, tonic water, and club soda are not included as bottled water under the FDA's regulation; historically these have been considered soft drinks.

- Body image
- Nutrition and health benefits
- Innovation and marketing

As an example, coffee consumption fell 50 percent over four decades until Starbucks Corp. made a brand out of a commodity; coffee consumption has inched upward since 1995 (Kilman, 2002). Another example of a food with a consumption history is chocolate. A nineteenth-century gourmet, Jean-Anthelme Brillat-Savarin said that Spanish ladies in the New World were so enamored with hot chocolate that they sometimes had it brought to them in church. Chocolate consumption has been rising steadily in the United States. In 2000 total U.S. chocolate consumption rose to 3.3 billion pounds, up almost 7 percent from 3.1 billion pounds in 1996, which amounts to almost 12 pounds for every man, woman, and child (Constant Cravings, 2002). Other items increasingly consumed are salty snacks like chips, popcorn, and pretzels. According to a report released by Chicago-based Mintel Consumer Intelligence, 17 percent of Americans report they "can't help snacking on salty snacks" (Junk-Food Nation, 2001).

Different colors and taste combinations keep being developed. H. J. Heinz Co. introduced an Ore-Ida line extension called Funky Fries. This kid-oriented product, found in the freezer section of grocery stores, has new colors and flavors, including Cocoa Crispers (chocolate fries). This product comes on the heels of the success of neon-colored ketchup by the same company.

Unusual uses for foods also are on the horizon. Four football players at Sacramento State applied ConAgra Food's Pam nonstick cooking spray to one another during a game with the University of Montana. They lost the game, but the Big Sky Conference launched an investigation into the "slippery actions of the players."

Waiting for fruits and vegetables to be in season is a thing of the past. We get apples, grapes, and lettuce year-round. When it is winter in the United States, it is

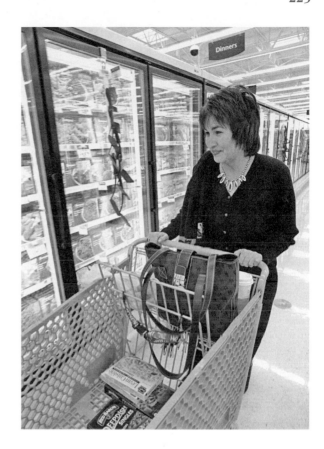

Woman shopping in frozen
dinner section of grocery store.
(PhotoEdit Inc.)

summer in New Zealand and Chile. With transportation and shipping advances, anything can be brought fresh to market.

## U.S. Spending on Food

In the typical family's budget, the most expensive monthly item is housing, followed by transportation and then food. Low-income families spend a higher proportion on food than high-income families, so rising food prices hit low-income families harder than high-income families. According to the U.S. Department of Agriculture (USDA), food expenses consist of food and nonalcoholic beverages purchased at grocery, convenience, and specialty stores, including purchases with food stamps, dining at restaurants, and household expenditures on school meals. Consumer spending on food dropped 10 percent between 1990 and 2000 (Weiss, 2002). The Food Marketing Institute says that is because there are a lot more places to buy food, which means competitive pricing. But it is more complicated than that; for example, items such as health care products are taking a larger share of the family income.

Those under the age of 25 spend more on fresh fruit than other age groups. Across the whole population, in the decade from 1990 to 2000, spending went up for poultry, fish, and seafood and down for beef, eggs, and dairy. Think of the appearance of sushi display counters in grocery stores in the 1990s; they weren't there in the 1980s. Beef consumption has been declining over the last 25 years, but the fresh meat counter is still a major moneymaker for grocery stores, ringing in over $60 billion in sales each year (Kilman, 2002). New attempts are being made to remarket beef as precooked microwaveable roasts. In 2001, 474 new beef products were launched, compared with 70 in 1997 (Kilman, 2002).

Over the next decade, there are several probable trends:

1. More convenience
2. More healthy foods
3. Smaller packages for smaller households
4. More flavor (watch for words such as *zesty* and *spicy*)
5. Increased food safety
6. More ethnic foods and regional distinctions (especially watch for more Hispanic and Asian foods)

## MYPYRAMID PLAN

The MyPyramid plan developed by the USDA is a guide to helping choose the foods and amounts that are right for different age groups and physical activity levels. The information (available online at www.mypyramid.gov) shows how to make smart choices from food groups and how to get the most nutrition out of calories. It describes a healthy vegetarian diet as well as other kinds. For a quick suggested estimate of what and how much to eat, go to this Web site and enter your age, sex, and activity level. See Figure 8.2.

## CROSSOVER BETWEEN FOOD AND DRUGS

We used to know what a food was and what a drug was, but that difference is blurring. Fresh fruits and vegetables are most likely to still be classified as foods, but what about a "healthy" flaked cereal, which is a grain product that has been sprayed with vitamins, or a prepackaged frozen lasagna with over 40 ingredients, many of which have lengthy chemical names on the label? Foods that have additives and supplements are more expensive and may be somewhere between a food and a drug. Manufacturers say that foods have been engineered to promote health, and if the alternative is rapid spoilage or fewer nutrients, they have a point. But consumers are very much on their own to determine, for example, if a candy bar full of sugar and fat is healthy because it also contains herbs.

## LABELS

Labels provide information about nutrient content and compare similar foods, so they are useful up to a point. They do not tell the amounts in products, however; they simply give a list. The first item on the list is the one with the highest amount,

# Anatomy of MyPyramid

## One Size Doesn't Fit All

USDA's new MyPyramid symbolizes a personalized approach to healthy eating and physical activity. The symbol has been designed to be simple. It has been developed to remind consumers to make healthy food choices and to be active every day. The different parts of the symbol are described below.

### Activity
Activity is represented by the steps and the person climbing them, as a reminder of the importance of daily physical activity.

### Moderation
Moderation is represented by the narrowing of each food group from bottom to top. The wider base stands for foods with little or no solid fats or added sugars. These should be selected more often. The narrower top area stands for foods containing more added sugars and solid fats. The more active you are, the more of these foods you can fit into your diet.

### Personalization
Personalization is shown by the person on the steps, the slogan, and the URL. Find the kinds and amounts of food to eat each day at MyPyramid.gov.

### Proportionality
Proportionality is shown by the different widths of the food group bands. The widths suggest how much food a person should choose from each group. The widths are just a general guide, not exact proportions. Check the web site for how much is right for you.

### Variety
Variety is symbolized by the six color bands representing the five food groups of the pyramid and oils. This illustrates that foods from all groups are needed each day for good health.

### Gradual Improvement
Gradual improvement is encouraged by the slogan. It suggests that individuals can benefit from taking small steps to improve their diet and lifestyle each day.

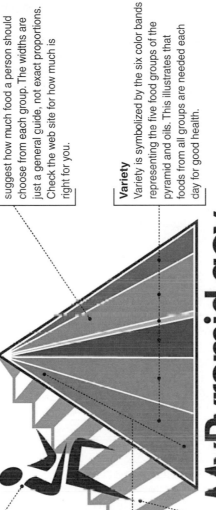

## MyPyramid.gov
### STEPS TO A HEALTHIER YOU

GRAINS · VEGETABLES · FRUITS · OILS · MILK · MEAT & BEANS

**USDA** U.S. Department of Agriculture
Center for Nutrition Policy
and Promotion
April 2005 CNPP-16

*USDA is an equal opportunity provider and employer.*

**Figure 8.2** MyPyramid. (Courtesy of U.S. Department of Agriculture.)

so if the first ingredient listed in a candy bar is sugar, then sugar is the leading ingredient, but the consumer will not know if it makes up 80 percent or 20 percent of the product. In soft drinks, the first ingredient is water. Consumer advocacy groups, weight-loss groups, and those with certain diseases have been asking for years that amounts be put on labels, but manufacturers insist they have the right to have "secret formulas" or recipes and that lengthy labels are impractical and ultimately costly to the consumer.

The labels on food products should show the quantities per serving in the following easy-to-read format:

- Total food energy (kcalories)
- Food energy from fat (kcalories)
- Total fat (grams)
- Saturated fat (grams)
- Cholesterol (milligrams)
- Sodium (milligrams)
- Carbohydrates, including starch, sugar, and fiber (grams)
- Dietary fiber (grams)
- Sugar (grams)
- Protein (grams)

Also, labels must present vitamin A, vitamin C, iron, and calcium information. Sometimes, the manufacturer chooses to add other nutrient information. To encourage consumers to read labels, various campaigns have been launched through alliances with the food industry, government agencies, consumer advocacy groups, and educational and health organizations. Notice that some foods such as fresh fruits and vegetables do not have labels; part of this is practicality—it does not make sense to have a tiny label on every cherry or grape.

Can all labels be believed? The answer is no. When nutrition experts heard about a product called Poi English Muffins that had only 70 calories each, which is about half the amount in other standard-size brands, they did some testing. The muffins had taro root, a Hawaiian delicacy, and weight-loss magazines were raving about the muffins as a speedy low-calorie breakfast. The Good Housekeeping Institute sent two bags to an independent laboratory. The report came back that each muffin actually contained 160 calories and 30 grams of carbohydrates, equivalent to two slices of bread (Low-Cal Muffins: Too Good to Be True? 2001). The Poi English Muffins were definitely not a weight-loss food and should not be marketed as such.

## ACTIVITY, DIET, AND EATING

Dr. William Dietz of the Centers for Disease Control and Prevention (CDC) says that we should opt for smaller portions, turn off the TV, walk rather than drive, and don't make cleaning the plate a requirement for kids and that if a child refuses a healthy meal, it's not up to the parents to prepare something else. The thinking here is that a hungry child learns to eat what is served; if the child is not hungry, he or she should not be forced to eat.

**CONSUMER POWER MODEL**

**Keeping It Simple**

"Every year, millions of people resolve to lose weight. According to a Gallup Poll of 1,006 adults ages 18 and older for *USA TODAY* and *Discovery Health*, 76% of people say they have tried to lose weight at some point. Women (82%) are more likely than men (69%) to have tried."[1] How about you or someone you know?

[1]Nanci Hellmich, "Simplicity Stays the Course." *USA TODAY*, January 8, 2008, p. 6D.

About 27 percent of the American population is obese, and the percentage has more than doubled in the last 40 years. Obesity is the number two cause of preventable death in the United States (after smoking) and accounts for almost 10 percent of the money spent on health care. Some people blame the growing preference for fast food and snacking, but as Dietz mentions, there is more to it than that. The solution cited in source after source is that it is not just about food— inactivity and cultural practices play a part. As the next section points out, some are questioning the wisdom of our practices and preferences.

## FAST FOOD

About 14 percent of Americans consume a diet comprised almost entirely of fast food.

Fast food came into vogue in the twentieth century because of the frantic pace of life, multiple roles, and the need to pick up a quick meal. Today, about 50 percent of Americans visit a fast-food restaurant each month, and 30 percent go 6 to 10 times (Addicted to Grease, 2002). It is estimated that about 14 percent of Americans consume a diet comprised almost entirely of fast food; the ones most likely to say this are between the ages of 18 and 24 (Junk-Food Nation, 2001).

The term *fast food,* popularized in the 1960s in the United States, referred to something quite specific—the preparation and service of hamburgers, french fries, milk shakes, fried chicken, and pizza at a chain restaurant where people order their meals from a cashier who sets the prepackaged order on a tray with a regimented, almost robotic quickness that sends the customer on his or her way without further ado (Mariani, 1991). The McDonald brothers led the way by firing carhops, cutting their 25-item menu to 9 choices, minimizing the number of employees, getting rid of china and metal flatware, and passing their savings on to customers (Mariani, 1991). McDonald's hamburgers sold for 15 cents, french fries for 10 cents, and milk shakes for 20 cents in the late 1940s and early 1950s. The first McDonald's with the trademark arches opened in 1953 in Phoenix, Arizona. In 1961, Ray Kroc bought out the McDonald brothers for $2.7 million and expanded the business, experimenting with drive-through windows that are the staple of many fast-food restaurants today (Mariani, 1991).

There is no question that McDonald's led the charge for fast food and that all other competitors—even those that had been in business before McDonald's—followed that lead. . . . There were fast-rising Mexican restaurants like Taco Bell of Irvine,

California, and Chi'Chi's (Louisville), roast beef and steak restaurants like Arby's (Atlanta), Roy Rogers (Bethesda, Maryland), and Ponderosa (Dayton, Ohio), and pizzerias, which in the 1980s registered astounding growth, led by Pizza Hut (Wichita, Kansas), Little Caesar's (Farmington Hills, Michigan), Godfather's (Omaha), and Domino's (Ann Arbor, Michigan), whose selling point was the delivery of its pizzas to the customer's door. And there were fried chicken restaurants like Bojangles (Charlotte, North Carolina), Popeye's (Jefferson, Washington), Church's (San Antonio), and the granddaddy of them all, Kentucky Fried Chicken. (Mariani, 1991, p. 172)

The cities of origin or headquarters are given to show how the fast-food movement is spread across the United States; there is no one place or one corporation that owns it all. Also it is curious to see how Western-sounding restaurant names like Roy Rogers or Ponderosa are headquartered in the East and Midwest.

Coming back to the cultural changes that led to the popularity of fast food, Roxburgh (2002) found that heavy time pressures are related to the number of roles consumers occupied. In answer to the question "Who are the time pressured?" she found in a study of 734 full-time workers that they were the affluent, parents, caregivers, and those with high-demand, low-control jobs. She concluded that time pressure is experienced by both men and women. Regarding home-related activities, Haas (1999) found that women spend more time than men engaged in activities considered traditionally female such as meal preparation, dishwashing, laundry, housecleaning, and grocery shopping, while men spend their time in traditionally male activities such as minor household repairs, bill paying, gardening, and car repairs.

## SLOW FOOD MOVEMENT

Nearly everyone knows what fast food is, but fewer are aware of the expression "slow food." Slow food is about enjoying local cuisine, slowing down, and buying locally produced products.

Social commentators have argued that life has accelerated because of capitalism and that people are engaged in the relentless pursuit of consumer goods to the point that the true pleasures of life, such as fine dining, have been all but ignored (Schor, 1992). Having overloaded schedules and being busy have become cultural ideals that symbolize economic and social success (Daly, 1996; Hochschild, 1989).

In the twenty-first century, people around the world began to question the value of this increased pace. The slow food movement started in Italy (now it is worldwide) as a way to defend endangered local foods, and as the name implies, it serves as a counterpoint to the trend toward mass-produced fast foods and the range of foods offered in modern supermarkets. Slow food advocates favor local cheeses, wines, and meat products such as sausages and disdain the commercial overprocessing that is commonly done for shipping and storing purposes. Fresh is the emphasis; genetically modified food is reviled. The movement embraces organic methods of agriculture to produce foods more slowly even though it may cost more to do so. Many hail it as a return to taste and regional differences. The slow food movement supports authentic regional cuisine and the turning away from generic international cuisine. Guides for tourists are published indicating local wines, restaurants, and food stores. The headquarters of the slow food movement is in Italy, and its Web site is www.slowfood.com. The United States also has a slow food association.

The slow food movement can be likened to the "buy local" movement. They both inspire consumers to get more of their food from local sources and resist an increasingly globalized agriculture industry. For example, a study by the Leopold Center for Sustainable Agriculture found that grapes make an average trek of 2,143 miles before arriving on Americans' plates. Produce shipped such long distances can lose freshness and flavor along the way, and there are also concerns about the environmental costs (electricity for cooling, gasoline for transportation). Driving the system is consumers' demand for a consistent marketplace where locally or even nationally out-of-season fruit is available year-round, which is possible with worldwide growing and shipping practices. If we are trying to get people to eat healthier, a wide range of foods is usually preferable, but this is in itself an issue. A takeoff on the slow food and buy local movements is the 100-mile diet (or something similar), whose underlying principle is that people should try to eat only foods that are grown within a 100-mile circle drawn around where they live; following this practice, people only eat locally and seasonally available foods. Depending on where someone lives, this is easier to do for some than for others.

In summary, food fads, diets, and trends are in continual motion, and the slow food movement is one approach that is gathering advocates. It combines tourism, community development, environmental awareness, and foods in an interesting way.

## ORGANICALLY GROWN FOODS

**Organically grown foods** are crops grown and processed according to USDA regulations. Many of the foods have gone mainstream and are sold not only at a natural foods store such as Whole Foods Markets but also at the more conventional grocery chains such as Kroger, Albertson's, and Publix. The products may be displayed in a separate section or may be integrated throughout the store (for example, organic canned vegetables on the shelf with the other canned vegetables). Usually the color green is associated with organic products and labels. The most accurate term is *organically grown food,* but often the word *organic* is used for simplicity's sake. An advertisement for Publix promoted its "greenwise market" and a "naturally tasty night" complete with tastings and natural/organic foods gift basket door prizes. Here is some copy from the ad:

> Publix knows you're trying to live healthier. By eating natural and organic foods. Using products that are environmentally sound. And taking a more wholesome approach to raising your family. Now we've made it easy, with our extensive selection of quality health products—in Produce and in Frozen Foods, on our Grocery aisles and in our Dairy case, in our Deli and our Seafood departments. If you know what's good for you—and especially if you don't—join us for our naturally tasty night, Thursday, January 16, 4 until 7 P.M. (*Tallahasee Democrat,* January 12, 2003, insert)

Manufacturers of conventional foods also sell organically grown versions (for example, Heinz sells organic ketchup).

Organic food has grown from a niche market to mainstream in the space of a few years in the United States, Canada, Europe, and Asia. A study of Norwegian consumers showed a positive attitude toward the consumption of organic food (Honkanen, Verplanken & Olsen, 2006). In the United States, organic food has gone well over the $15 billion mark in sales per year. One can see the growth in the number of products lining grocery store shelves and in the marketing of basic foods like cereals in organic forms. The USDA established the USDA National Organic Program in 2002 with specific, detailed national standards. University departments of agriculture are offering organic food classes, and the University of Florida has one of the nation's first organic-agriculture growers associations. Growers, farmers, consumers, and megafirms like Kellogg's are devoting more attention to anything organic—there is organic milk, organic beef, and nearly every other organic food product imaginable.

Why would someone choose organically grown foods?

1. To enjoy improved taste
2. To avoid artificial ingredients (this includes synthetic colors and flavors)
3. To reduce "bad" foods in a diet (artery-clogging partially hydrogenated oils are not allowed in organic food)
4. To limit exposure to pesticides
5. To be more environmentally friendly

Under the USDA rules, organically grown produce cannot be treated with synthetic pesticides, but this does not mean that organically grown foods are pesticide free because chemicals linger in the soil and the air. This can happen if an organic farm is next to a conventional farm that uses pesticides. One study found organically grown foods contain a third of the residues present on conventional produce. Another reason some consumers prefer organically grown foods is to protect the environment; organically grown foods reduce spraying and water contamination, improve soil quality, and enhance wildlife habitats.

Many consumers are willing to pay more for organically grown foods. These foods typically cost 15 to 50 percent more than nonorganic. This potential for additional profit makes them attractive to manufacturers, farmers, and grocery store owners.

Why do consumers pay more for organically grown foods? The main answers have already been suggested, but in the end it comes down to individual choice. Cheryl Rezendes Rulewich became a big believer in organic foods when her five-year-old son's food allergies cleared up when she switched him to an organic diet (de Lisser, 2002). She also believes organic foods are healthier and taste better for the whole family. "Conventional fruit and vegetables, with their bright colors and waxy, unblemished surfaces, look unnatural to her eyes. 'They look like Play-Doh food,' she says" (de Lisser, 2002, p. D4).

Not everyone would agree, so the debate continues as to whether organic foods are truly healthier or even preferred given the greater price. "Nelda Mercer, a registered dietitian and spokeswoman for the American Dietetic Association, says there is no scientific evidence showing that organically produced foods are nutritionally better than their conventional counterparts" (de Lisser, 2002, p. D4). What does this mean for consumers? Most agree that organic and sustainable foods are better for the planet, and because organic foods use fewer pesticides, it follows that people who eat organic will have lower levels of pesticides in their bodies. Partly what weighs in is cost and how we respond to advertising messages and images of what is healthy and what isn't. Consumers have to consider the costs and the benefits

**Figure 8.3**   USDA Organic Seal. The seal tells consumers that a product is at least 95 percent organic. Organic food differs from conventionally produced food in the way it is grown, handled, and processed. (Courtesy of the U.S. Department of Agriculture and the Department of Health and Human Services.)

about organic versus conventional food, just as they do in other consumption areas. Another issue is whether or not to buy meat or milk from cloned animals and how these products should be labeled. Should they be mixed in with the more conventional products, or should they be displayed separately?

USDA regulations define the use of synthetic fertilizers, herbicides, insecticides, fungicides, preservatives, and other chemical ingredients. Organic products cannot have been irradiated, genetically engineered, or grown with fertilizer made from sewer sludge (Whitney & Rolfes, 2002). Dairy and meat products may be called organic if the livestock have been raised according to USDA regulations, which include grazing conditions and the use of organic feed, hormones, and antibiotics.

Foods that have met USDA standards may have a seal on their label. To get this green-and-white USDA seal, a product must be at least 95 percent organic. Examples of products with the seal are fruits and vegetables and cereals that are 100 percent organic, but if a product is at least 70 percent organic, the label can say, for example, "made with organic corn." Another label designation states that the product contains "organic ingredients," which means that less than 70 percent of the product is organic. In this latter case, "organic" cannot be used on the front of the package, but the manufacturer can list organic ingredients on the back.

Implied in the marketing of organically grown foods is that they are healthier than foods grown by conventional methods—this may or may not be the case. There are advantages and disadvantages to both, and consumers have to ask questions about pesticide and fertilizer use and other conditions. These can be difficult questions because the use of fewer chemicals is inherently appealing, but properly used pesticides can yield more crops. If pesticides are used improperly, they can be hazardous to human health; for example, organic fertilizers such as unprocessed animal manure can have ill effects. In the home, consumers can remove or reduce pesticide residues by peeling fruits and vegetables; washing fresh produce in warm water, using a scrub brush; and rinsing thoroughly. Further information can be obtained 24/7 from the EPA's National Pesticide Information Center Hotline at 1-800-858-PEST.

## GENETICALLY ALTERED FOODS

One of the hottest controversies worldwide is the topic of genetically altered foods. Some consumers feel uneasy about the possible risks associated with genetically engineered foods, and others don't see the problem because foods have always been altered genetically either by nature or by man. "One theory of the origins of agriculture holds that domesticated plants first emerged on dump heaps, where the discarded seeds of the wild plants that people gathered and ate—already unconsciously selected for sweetness or size or power—took root, flourished, and eventually hybridized. In time people gave the best of these hybrids a place in the garden, and there, together, the people and the plants embarked on a series of experiments in co-evolution that would change them both forever" (Pollan, 2001, p. 186).

**Genetic engineering** is defined as the use of biotechnology to modify the genetic material of living cells so that they will produce new substances or perform new functions (Whitney & Rolfes, 2002). One of the first foods to be genetically engineered was the tomato, introduced into the market in 1994. Prior to this development, tomatoes did not last long on the shelf, and because they were somewhat fragile, many did not make it to market. More recently, experiments have been carried out on potatoes. "NewLeaf" is the name of a genetically engineered potato by the Monsanto Corporation (Pollan, 2001). This potato produces its own insecticide. What might the future hold? Possibilities include potatoes that are genetically modified to absorb less fat when fried, corn that can withstand drought, lawns that don't ever have to be mowed, "golden rice" rich in vitamin A, and bananas that deliver vaccines (Pollan, 2001). **Biotechnology** is the use of biological systems or organisms to create or modify products. Examples of biotechnology include the use of bacteria to make yogurt, of yeast to make beer, and of cross-breeding to enhance crop production (Whitney & Rolfes, 2002). Plant engineering, a type of biotechnology, is being conducted worldwide. China's bioengineers have worked with more than 50 species of plants, adding genes for traits such as resistance both to viruses and to insects in everything from peanuts to papayas; as a consequence, they are reporting major fiscal and public health gains (The Shape of Biotech to Come, 2002, p. 130).

The reason that the controversy has heated up in recent years is that the twenty-first century has brought very rapid advances in agriculture and food production, and the public is more aware than ever before about these dramatic changes. Through genetic engineering, scientists can introduce a copy of a specific gene that will produce a desired trait, with the goal of improving crops or livestock. So the process has been speeded up, and this worries some people because it does not feel "natural"—it is tampering with nature. Others would argue that ever since crop rotation, selective breeding, and grafting, nature has been tampered with. The beginnings of agriculture and food production can be traced to before 8000 B.C. in Southwest Asia (the Fertile Crescent) and soon spread to Europe and North Africa (Diamond, 1999). But there is no question that genetic engineering is speeding up the changes in how farmers farm and how foods and drugs are processed. On the plus side, genetic engineering improves the nutrient content in foods, lengthens shelf life, usually means less use of pesticides, and makes land more usable. In terms of government control, much of the approval responsibility falls to the FDA, the EPA, and the USDA.

Consumer advocacy groups want genetically altered foods labeled as such so that consumers know what they are buying. The problem with this is what to say and how much to say. In recent years, some foods have been pulled from the market when the public felt misled regarding contents. This dispute is not settled yet. For the most part, the scientific community (and this includes the FDA) contends that biotechnology can deliver a safe and better food supply and needs to continue and that genetically altered food will serve more people and reduce hunger around the world. Today, one person in every five in the world suffers from persistent hunger, and tens of thousands die every day from starvation (Whitney & Rolfes, 2002). For more information on organic methods, go to the USDA Biotechnology Information Center at www.nal.usda.gov/bic. (the pro side) and to Greenpeace at www.greenpeaceusa.org or www.ucsusa.org (the con side). According to Whitney and Rolfes (2002), the con side worries about the following:

Disruption of natural ecosystems

Introduction of diseases and newly created viruses

Creation of biological weapons

Ethical concerns (including furthering the gap between the haves and have-nots)

## IRRADIATED FOODS

Exposing any food to radiation for commercial purposes is called **food irradiation**. To say this another way, "Food irradiation is the treatment of foods with gamma rays, X-rays, or highvoltage electronics to kill potentially harmful pathogens, including bacteria, parasites, insects, and fungi that cause food-borne illness. It also re duces spoilage and extends shelf" (Insel & Roth, 2002, p. 348). For example, irradiated strawberries can last unspoiled in the refrigerator for up to three weeks versus the usual three to five days for untreated berries. Lengthening the shelf life of products has great value for grocers and ultimately consumers because it cuts down on the amount of food thrown out. Irradiated foods are very useful in situations such as camping, space exploration, and military operations when people are away from fresh sources of food for long periods of time. Since 1963, the government has allowed certain foods to be irradiated, starting with wheat and flour and now including fruits, poultry, herbs, vegetables, and meats. Irradiation is also used on contact lenses, medical supplies, teething rings, milk cartons, and plastic wrap. Although irradiation has been endorsed by the CDC, the American Medical Association (AMA), and the World Health Organization (WHO), the general consuming public is skeptical. They have the following concerns (legitimate or not):

- Essential nutrients may be destroyed.
- Eating irradiated foods may cause cancer or other ill effects.

**Figure 8.4** Flowerlike Radura Symbol. This symbol signifies something is irradiated. (Courtesy of USDA Food Safety and Inspection Services.)

- Employees exposed to irradiation or who live near factories that use irradiation could be hurt.
- Foods treated with irradiation may taste different or odd.

The bottom line is that the foods are tampered with, and many consumers feel this is unnatural. Irradiated spices or ingredients embedded in complex products do not have to be labeled as irradiated, but primary goods such as fruits, vegetables, and meats that have been irradiated should carry a flowerlike radura symbol and a brief information label. Studies show that when consumers are given information about irradiation and its benefits, most want to try the foods (Insel & Roth, 2002).

## FOOD ADDITIVES

**Additives** are substances added to food either intentionally or by accident. Examples of "by accident" are bits of conveyer belts and packaging, soil, feathers, rocks, pesticide residues, or insects that can fall into products during processing or while in storage. If, for example, rocks being in food sounds absurd, notice the packaging on dry split peas or beans; often it will say to sort and rinse the peas or beans before use, looking out for rocks and stones. Since rocks and stones can look and weigh the same as beans, no machine can completely sort them out, so the consumer must do this before making split-pea or bean soup or forget the whole thing and buy already prepared or canned soups.

"Today, some 2800 substances are intentionally added to foods for one or more of the following reasons: (1) to maintain or improve nutritional quality, (2) to maintain freshness, (3) to help in processing or preparation, or (4) to alter taste or appearance" (Insel & Roth, 2002, p. 348). These substances make up less than 1 percent of our food, however. Most additives are preservatives that help prevent spoilage; others make food taste or look better.

**Preservatives** are antimicrobial agents, antioxidants, and other additives that retard spoilage or maintain desired qualities, such as softness in baked goods (Whitney & Rolfes, 2002). Regarding appearance, think of the colors in M&M candies—they are the result of color additives that make the candy look better. Color is also added to margarine, cheeses, pastas, soft drinks, and baked goods. Nutrient additives include iodine in salt, vitamins A and D in milk, calcium and vitamin C in fruit juices, and thiamin in bread.

Additives are approved by the FDA, but the manufacturer has to show that the additives are effective (do what they are supposed to do), detectable and measurable in the final product, and safe. Additives have initial and periodic re-reviews. Regarding safety, the risk of cancer is not tolerated. The **Delaney clause** (a clause in the Food Additive Amendment to the Food, Drug, and Cosmetic Act) states that no substance that is known to cause cancer in animals or human beings at any dose level shall be added to foods. Over time, this tough clause has been difficult to administer, a case in point being the popular artificial sweetener saccharin. When animal tests in the 1970s revealed a possible cancer hazard, leading to talk of removing it from the market, there was a public outcry, and it is still on the market. The key problem is the phrase "at any dose level" because it has been shown in animal testing that huge amounts of a single additive may prove harmful, but very few people would consume the necessary amount to cause the problem (for example, people would not normally drink 50 cups of coffee sweetened with saccharin daily). Instead of zero risk, a more likely standard that the FDA uses is "negligible risk" or minimal risk.

The food additives that have long been in use and are believed to be safe are on the **GRAS List**, which stands for "generally recognized as safe." Examples are sugar, salt, and herbs.

## CALORIES, WEIGHT, AND DIETS

**Calories** are units by which energy is measured. Food energy is measured in kilocalories (1,000 calories equal 1 kilocalorie), abbreviated kcalories or simply kcal. You can lose weight by eating fewer calories and increasing physical activity. Just because a product is fat-free does not mean it is calorie-free—it can be loaded with sugar and other sweeteners. There is also a tendency for consumers to eat more of a food that is low-fat or fat-free, thinking this will save them calories, but if the portion size is larger than normal, any potential calorie savings may be lost.

The surgeon general says that only one in five U.S. adults gets the recommended amount of physical activity (30 minutes on most days is recommended for various health reasons). Overweight and inactivity affect the rate of coronary heart disease and increase the risk of developing diabetes, hypertension, and colon cancer. About 30–40 percent of U.S. women and 20–30 percent of men consider themselves overweight, and about 5 percent of U.S. adults are underweight.

### Questionable Claims

The market for weight-loss diets and books is estimated at $33 billion a year in the United States (Whitney & Rolfes, 2002). There is no doubt that some diets will provide short-term weight loss, but improved health and long-term weight loss (or maintenance of a preferred weight) are rarer. Consumers need to watch out for common fad diet claims:

- You can lose weight by eating only at certain times of the day.
- Certain combinations of foods will help you lose weight.
- Some diets energize the brain.
- Certain products can rewire your genetic code.
- There are surefire remedies for weight problems.
- Millions of people have been successful at permanent weight loss using this plan.

Also consumers should beware of programs that insist on large sums of money up front. Regarding the role of genetics, genes may not cause obesity, but genetic factors may influence the food intake and activity patterns that lead to it and the metabolic pathways that maintain it (Heitmann et al., 1997). Studies have shown that adopted children tend to be similar in weight to their biological parents, not to their adoptive parents. In experiments it has been shown that some people gain more weight than others even given the same energy intakes. Clearly, genes play a role in gaining and losing weight, but what can be done about this is still under in-

**CONSUMER ALERT**

**Avoid "Fad" Diets and Magic Pills**

Examples of fad diets are those involving one particular food or type of food. The food may be cabbage or grapefruit or a group of foods, such as high-protein items. Although there is initial weight loss, these are hard diets to maintain for a lifetime, and there are potential negative health effects to concentrating on only one food or type of food for long periods of time.

So-called magic pills are to be avoided, but the FDA has approved prescription drugs that may help obese people who have difficulty losing weight through diet and exercise alone. Before trying any radical diet or medicine for weight reduction, a person should contact his or her doctor to discuss treatment, options, and possible side effects.

vestigation. To conclude this section, given that people are saying obesity is a major health problem in many countries and study after study stresses the importance of not being overweight, there are certainly benefits to maintaining a healthy weight.

## FTC's Fight against "Miracle" Weight-Loss Products

An FTC study analyzed 300 ads for products and services that promised quick fixes for shedding weight and found more than half featured at least one claim that was very likely to be false or that lacked adequate proof. Howard Beales III, director of FTC's Bureau of Consumer Protection, said, "'Lose weight while you sleep' and 'Exercise in a bottle' are claims that editors and publishers ought to be able to recognize as problematic. . . . Most newspapers don't run pornographic ads and it's not by accident. It's because they looked. That same level of looking should identify the kinds of [weight loss] claims that are clearly not true" (December, 2002, p. D7). In a magazine directed to the elderly, weight-loss claims included foods that make you sleep sounder (if you are not awake, you can't eat). As a counterpoint to this argument, publishers and broadcasters would say that it is difficult to verify advertisements, meaning newspapers and TV stations do not have scientific laboratories to conduct experiments on advertised products.

**CONSUMER ALERT**

**Quackery and Communication**

The days when a wagon would wheel into town and the huckster would get up on the top and extol the virtues of his new food, miracle drink, or cooking device to anyone who would listen are long gone. In its place are other forms of misinformation and unproven products: the Internet, glossy magazine advertisements and articles, "health" magazines, television infomercials, in-home sales, and so on. The Internet is a particular problem because in many countries of the world there are few (if any) controls on what is sold and advertised in terms of health-related products. More than ever, remember the words "may the buyer beware."

**BOX 8.2    Questionable Ad Claims for Weight Loss**

Common advertising claims and techniques are used by weight-loss ads. Here is a list of the FTC's examples of questionable ad claims:

"The fastest all-natural diet known for rapid weight loss without a prescription!"

"Amazing fat-fighting diet pill produces an extremely fast weight loss . . . even if you cheat or refuse to diet."

"It can make a delicious, juicy hamburger as low in fat as a lean turkey sandwich."

"Major weight loss breakthrough: New carb-killer lets you cheat and eat like crazy and still get skinny lightning fast!"

"Our amazing 'Herbal Bullet' blasts fat and flushes it out of your body!"

There is also the question of profit incentives. Full-page ads for weight-loss products bring in a lot of revenue to magazines and newspapers, as do infomercials on television. Publishers and broadcasters also hesitate to compromise freedom of speech and think that they have the right to run ads with the idea that the reader or viewer will be smart enough to read between the lines. The FTC is intent on promoting stricter media self-policing of obvious fraudulent claims.

Where are these ads placed? The FTC found fraudulent ads in broadcast and cable television, infomercials, radio, magazines, newspapers, supermarket tabloids, direct mail, commercial e-mail, and Web sites. When the FTC compared current ads with ones from a decade earlier, it found weight-loss ads not only appeared more frequently but also promoted 159 percent more products and carried a dramatically different tone. Box 8.2 shows some of the common advertising claims used by weight-loss ads.

As this book went to press, the FTC was considering holding media liable for disseminating products' false claims, including cable channels, newspapers, and magazines that run diet and health ads making dubious claims. The FTC could sue the media outlets for carrying the ads—from a legal standpoint there is precedent since regulators have used the argument that advertising of certain products (such as liquor, tobacco, and gambling) has harmful effects. The FTC has gone after fraudulent marketers and manufacturers before. Some media outlets have said that it is easier to determine what is wrong in liquor, tobacco, and gambling ads than it is for food and beverage ads (that is, what is misleading and what isn't) and that copyeditors are not trained in nutritional analysis.

## FOOD-BORNE DISEASES

It used to be when people got sick from tainted food, it was difficult to trace the source. Although it is not foolproof, DNA analysis (genetic testing) is an objective way to link each sick person with a particular food or product. For example, the CDC found that a 68-year-old woman's death was caused by a strain of E. coli bacteria with a DNA fingerprint that matched a strain found 1,300 miles away at a meat-processing plant; tainted ground beef was probably the culprit. "For epidemiologists, the genetic match was a powerful illustration of the role DNA fingerprinting can play in food safety and public health. Plaintiffs' lawyers, meanwhile, say the technique has become a formidable legal weapon in product-liability cases against food companies. The number of lawsuits stemming from food-borne illnesses is small, but the implications of using genetic fingerprinting are huge" (Abboud, 2003, p. B1). If an attorney can prove that a person became seriously ill or died from a food and the source is known, the only question is how much the settlement should be. Consumers will benefit because the food industry will be even more aware than usual of the importance of food safety.

A totally risk-free food supply is a goal to shoot for, but the reality is that the most that can be hoped for is increased risk reduction. Canned and packaged goods sold in grocery stores are largely controlled, and sources of problems can be traced through codes. Accidents occur, for example, when contaminated foods make their way to market or when seals or packages are broken, intentionally or unintentionally. Consumers should immediately report any concerns they have to the store where the item was purchased and to the toll-free consumer complaint number on the package or can. Everyone—from producers to suppliers to consumers to parents (especially)—should be involved in maintaining a safe food supply.

In recent years, E. coli outbreaks have been traced to contaminated spinach and lettuce, and a fast-food chain had to close several restaurants for over a month due to consumers getting sick. Responding to public outcry, several U.S. senators introduced legislation that would form a central food agency. Another problem was contaminated imported wheat used in pet food, which caused illness or death of many pets in 2007.

In summary, food-borne diseases can cause illness or even death. The estimates are that annually there are 76 million illnesses, 325,000 hospitalizations, and 5,200 deaths in the United States from food-borne illnesses (Landro, 2002). Especially at risk are infants, small children, and the elderly. The FDA's Food Safety and Applied Nutrition site (www.cfsan.fda.gov) has information on everything from the risk of bacterial infections from eating raw sprouts to how to spot spoiled seafood. The other government Web sites and nutrition information groups listed in the E-Resources provide further information and warnings. According to the Partnership for Food Safety Education, there are many bugs to look out for:

- Botulism caused by botulinum toxin, found in canned goods and luncheon meats
- Campylobacteriosis caused by *Campylobacter jejuni,* found in meat, raw poultry, and unpasteurized milk
- Listeriosis caused by *Listeria monocytogenes,* found in cold cuts, seafood, and unpasteurized milk
- Perfringens food poisoning caused by *Clostridium perfringens,* found in foods not kept properly hot
- Salmonellosis caused by salmonella bacteria, found in raw meats, dairy products, shrimp, and poultry
- Shigellosis (bacillary dysentery) caused by shigella bacteria, found in milk and dairy products, poultry, and potato salad (the food becomes contaminated when hands aren't washed)
- Giardiasis caused by *Giardia lamblia,* found mostly in contaminated water

- Hepatitis A caused by hepatitis A virus, found in oysters, clams, mussels, scallops, and cockles (usually when their beds are polluted by untreated sewage)
- Staphylococcal food poisoning caused by *Staphylococcus aureus* bacteria, found in bacteria that grows on food left at room temperature

## OTHER FOOD CONCERNS

One food issue is research conducted on animals. The degree to which animal testing is necessary is controversial, and some activists call for no further testing on animals. When shopping, their mission is to find foods that have not been tested on animals: They may frequent stores or Web sites that sell products that do not use animal testing, they may boycott companies and products that use animal testing, or they may conduct protests at government or university laboratories that do tests on animals. Others would say that it is better to run tests on animals than on humans, so the lesser of the two evils is to only conduct animal testing when absolutely necessary to protect human health. Some would differentiate between types of animals, feeling more comfortable with experimentation on mice and rats than on larger animals. The general consensus is that animals should be treated in as humane a way as possible and that testing should be done only when absolutely necessary.

A **food allergy**, which is a bodily reaction to a substance that is more severe than food intolerances such as lactose intolerance or reactions to food coloring or MSG, is another issue. "A true food allergy is a reaction of the body's immune system to a food or food ingredient, usually a protein. The immune system perceives the reaction-provoking substance, or allergen, as foreign and acts to destroy it" (Insel & Roth, 2002, p. 349). The reaction (hives, swelled tongue, cramps, asthma, or in severe cases a loss of blood pressure called anaphylaxis) can occur in minutes. Trigger foods such as nuts, milk, eggs, wheat, fish, and shellfish must be avoided, and people at risk should carry medications to treat their reactions. Many infants outgrow food allergies, but it is estimated that about 2 percent of the adult population has food allergies (Insel & Roth, 2002). A good first step in determining whether you have a food allergy or just an intolerance is to keep a diary or log of foods eaten and reactions to determine a pattern, with consultation with a physician being the next step.

A final food concern to discuss is use of a **boycott**, a (usually group) decision to avoid purchasing a product or doing business with a company. Stated another way, a boycott is "an attempt by one or more parties to achieve certain objectives by urging individual consumers to refrain from making selected purchases in the marketplace" (Friedman, 1999, p. 4). No one knows when boycotts began, but there is evidence of them throughout history, from boycotts in England and Ireland long ago to the 1773 Boston Tea Party to the beef boycotts in 1973 (when protestors stood in front of selected grocery stores and asked people not to buy beef). There are commodity boycotts (for example, against beef) or boycotts against a company or a single product (for example, Starkist tuna). Boycotts can last a couple of days to several months. Techniques range from boycotters with signs to sit-ins, call-ins, mail-ins, e-mails, and signed petitions; they may also include more drastic measures such as obstruction—using physical presence or obstacles and not allowing people to shop at stores or to work at their jobs (such as harvesting grapes or unloading boats of fish). Examples of food companies that have been boycotted include Bumble Bee Seafoods and Heinz (the company that makes Starkist tuna, with the issue being dolphin-safe tuna). The media are involved through coverage of events. The subject of consumer boycotts is much more comprehensive than food only; for a complete guide to the subject, read Milton Friedman's *Consumer Boycotts* (1999).

## JUNK FOOD CRITICS AND LAWSUITS

How much should food and beverages be regulated is a central issue in this chapter. Junk food is of particular concern. Many consumer advocates are fighting to keep snack and soft drink beverage vending machines out of elementary, middle, and high schools. The question can be asked: Does this work, or do children bring snacks in their lunches from home or go off school grounds to buy snacks at neighboring convenience stores, thus enhancing their risk of being hit by cars, being late for school, or skipping classes? These are not easy questions. It is all about freedom of choice, as well as what children prefer to eat versus what they should eat. What were the rules in the schools you attended? Were vending machines available on school grounds?

One approach to lessening the availability of snacks and soft drinks is to bring lawsuits against the industry (similar to the way the antitobacco lobby conducted itself). A drawback is that snack food is less easily defined than tobacco products because a wide range of foods can be considered snacks. Most of the lawsuits have been directed at fast-food restaurants rather than at food and beverage manufacturers. The most newsworthy was the July 2002 lawsuit in which a "272-pound New York City man sued four fast-food chains, alleging that their food contributed to his obesity, heart disease and diabetes" (McKay, 2002, p. A1). One of the restaurants in the lawsuit was Kentucky Fried Chicken. The National Restaurant Association came out with a statement dismissing the lawsuit as "senseless, baseless, and ridiculous" (McKay, 2002, p. A10). But ridiculous or not as a defensive maneuver, fast-food chains are responding by using healthier oils.

Trans fats are no longer used in many restaurants and products. For example, a package of baked snack crackers or cheese-flavored crackers with peanut butter filling may have on the label 0g trans fat or zero grams trans fats.

Steven Reinemund, chairman and chief executive officer of PepsiCo, says, "The trend is clear: More consumers are concerned about nutrition, and 'we need to be prepared to deal with it.' Already, low-fat snacks such as baked potato chips and pretzels account for 20% to 25% of Frito-Lay sales" (McKay, 2002, p. A10). In the case of PepsiCo, some of its less caloric products have succeeded, but some (like Wow! Chips with their unpleasant side effects) were less successful. Salt sprinkled on the surface of chips and pretzels helps with "flavor delivery" because salt is one of the first elements to hit the tongue, meaning that many products contain less salt than a lot of people think because salt is just on the surface while the products seem to taste best. Attempts to reduce salt have been less than successful; in some cases low-salt products have sold, but no-salt products have not.

Besides using better oils, what else can fast-food or snack manufacturers do to produce healthier foods? PepsiCo is experimenting with adding broccoli, carrot, and tomato flecks to chips, and more snacks may have oats, soy, and/or dairy products. It is tricky to find the right combinations because as Reinemund says, "The consumer wants a balance of indulgence, as well as 'better for you.' And if we overreact . . . in either direction, we won't get the balanced growth that we want" (McKay, 2002, p. A10).

## NAVIGATING THE GROCERY STORE

Grocery stores seek to develop and maintain long-term ties with their customers because they know loyal customers return again and again. Loyalty is often based on familiarity, availability of desired products, and good customer service. In a study of large-format retailing, Morganosky and Cude (2000a) found that attending to the details of the food retail business (accurate pricing, product availability, continuity of personnel) is a way to improve the consumer experience. But there are problems such as misleading promotions and advertisements as well as scanning errors at the checkout and coupons and rebates that don't always work.

**End-of-aisle displays** may feature products at a higher cost than similar products placed mid-aisle. For example, grape juice may be $3.99 on the end of the aisle and $2.99 on the shelves where there is a less expensive competitive name brand or a store brand. **Tie-ins**—where complementary products are placed side by side, with one price jacked up to compensate for the **loss leader** (a very-low-priced advertised special to bring shoppers in)—are common. For example, hamburger may be on sale, but the price on the buns or ketchup next to it may be jacked up. Food and wine samples also encourage sales, as do the pleasant aromas circulating from the bakery; sometimes, the aromas from the deli or bakery are piped out the front door so that the sensory experience starts before customers enter the store.

Most stores are set up so that a consumer has to go around the perimeter to get the basics such as meat, milk, cheese, bread, and fruits and vegetables, with the frozen-food aisles in the middle of the store. The longer the customers stay in the store, the more they will spend, hence the perimeter layout (which encourages them to go up and down all the aisles), free samples, relaxing music, and tantalizing aromas. The addition of precooked foods, pharmacies, in-store restaurants, floral section, cards, magazines, paperback books, and deli areas also slows consumers.

At the checkout area, there are the last-minute impulse items: candy (at child height), magazines, tabloids, small gadgets, gum, and other sundries. Checking the foods you have at home, reading the advertisements, clipping coupons, and making a list before shopping will save you money in the store, but studies show that fewer and fewer people are doing these things. One way stores are responding to this is by having coupons placed right on the products or in a coupon dispenser attached to the shelf.

**Unit pricing** refers to the presentation of price information on shelves on a common basis such as per ounce, which is valuable information for making price comparisons within brands and between brands. Sometimes unit pricing reveals that the middle-size box of cereal or tube of toothpaste is actually less expensive per ounce than a larger size.

**Open dating** is a system of placing a date on perishable products that indicates when the product should be sold or consumed. Other dates are the **pull date** (the last day the product should be sold), **expiration date** (the last day the consumer should use the product), **quality assurance date** (the last day when the product is at its peak), and **pack date** (when the product was packaged or manufactured). Quality assurance dates or statements may be found on bread wrappers: "The quality of this product is best if purchased by September 1." Sometimes consumers know these dates, such as an open date stamped on a gallon of milk, and sometimes they do not. For example, a loaf of bread may have a green, blue, or red twist tie that tells the person stocking the shelves when to remove the bread, but the color means nothing to the consumer who doesn't know the code. The tendency is for shoppers to pick the freshest product (in other words, the one with the freshest date), so if milk is set out with dates of July 31 and August 1, shoppers will take the August 1 date even if it is July 24 and they intend to use the whole gallon that day.

Not everyone shops at large grocery stores; convenience stores do a lot of business and their prices are generally higher, but like anywhere else there are sales and deals to be had if one reads ads and compares shelf prices. Drug stores increasingly sell food and beverages.

A new technology called **radio frequency identification (RFID)** puts a tiny chip in products that allows for the automatic tracking of products. It was test-marketed in a prototype grocery store in Germany and is spreading to other countries including some in the United States. RFIDs would replace bar codes on products. RFID tags fall into three broad categories: passive, semiactive, and active. Passive tags are the simplest and least expensive; they obtain power from the radio frequency field of the reader and therefore do not require an integrated power source. Semiactive and active tags use an on-board power source to achieve a greater range or the ability to record data from a sensor. There are several reasons why RFIDs are favored by grocery stores: The main one is faster, more detailed inventory, which makes stocking and ordering easier, and others include more accurate pricing and less shoplifting. Consumers worry about a loss of privacy. Will their products be tagged all the way to their homes? Technology exists for consumers to have their goods detagged before leaving the store, but this may involve standing in another line—not an attractive option. Since this is such a new technology, all the pros and cons have not been worked out yet, but it is something to watch unfold.

The largest grocer in the United States is Wal-Mart Stores Inc. This is an amazing story of the growth of a business because Wal-Mart started selling food in 1988 and in 2002 became the nation's largest grocer with more than $53 billion in grocery sales:

> Wal-Mart sells groceries in at least 1,258 supercenters, 180,000 square foot grocer/discount store combinations and in 49 small Neighborhood Markets. Most of the stores are in the South and Southwest. If Wal-Mart's supercenters continue to expand at their current pace, within this decade, more than three-quarters of the nation's Krogers and Albertsons Inc. stores and more than half the Safeway Inc. outlets could be within 10 miles of a Wal-Mart supercenter, according to Trade Dimensions, a market-data provider. (Callahan & Zimmerman, 2003, p. B1)

The largest U.S. grocer is Wal-Mart.

Wal-Mart pushes rivals to match its low costs. It does this by cutting down on excess labor, improving its inventory-tracking systems, doubling or tripling discount coupons, and building customer loyalty with discount-card plans. "Studies show that items at Wal-Mart cost 8% to 27% less than at Kroger, Albertsons or Safeway, including discounts from these competitors' loyalty cards and specials" (Callahan & Zimmerman, 2003, p. B1).

## GROCERY SHOPPING ONLINE

Various grocery stores in the United States, Canada, and Europe have experimented with online grocery sales. Some experiments have worked and some have failed. There are online retailers and online grocery shopping services; some offer weekly home deliveries of groceries as well as other services such as picking up videos, dry cleaning, and UPS packages. Charges can be a percentage, a monthly flat rate, or a minimum charge per delivery, but some services waive the delivery fee if the order is above a specified amount (such as $75). Another way to avoid a charge is for consumers to place their grocery order by computer and pick up the preselected groceries (all bagged) on their way home. This works well for branded prepackaged foods such as crackers, cookies, and canned goods that are always the same but does not work so well for meat, fruit, and vegetables because shoppers might like to see or feel these products before buying them.

Regarding home delivery, the concern is having someone there to receive the groceries or having a unit in the garage or a housing unit where a delivery person can leave frozen or refrigerated food. Naturally, there are also security concerns.

Convenience is the most-cited reason why a consumer uses online shopping (Morganosky & Cude, 2000b). Shopping online is also a boon to customers with physical constraints, such as disabilities or injuries, or lack of transportation. The future success of online grocery sales is not clear, and experiments are still going on; some services are making it while some have gone bankrupt.

## BOTTLED-WATER CONSUMPTION

The difference in the quality (taste, consistency, safety) of tap water versus bottled water is controversial. Tap water may smell or look different from bottled water, but you can't always tell by that because most of the dangerous contaminants are those consumers cannot see, smell, or taste (Buller, 2002). Tap water is constantly tested for harmful substances. One of the controversies is the addition of fluoride to tap water; fluoride is added to drinking water to promote strong teeth and prevent tooth decay. There is a concern that children who drink only bottled water will have more dental problems. Again, this is controversial, and if you are concerned, you should ask your dentist or your children's dentist. To complicate things, some bottled-water products contain fluoride and some contain vitamins. To find out if the bottled water you drink has fluoride in it, you need to contact the individual company directly.

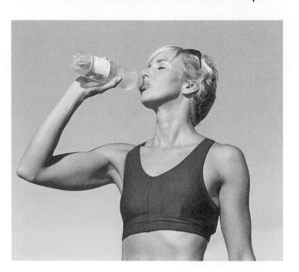

Water is important when exercising and bottled water makes it convenient. (Getty Images—Stockbyte.)

Why do consumers, especially young health-oriented people, buy bottled water? Jeremy Buccellato, age 31, of Ramsey, Minnesota, says he's heard the arguments "that tap water is just as good if not better than bottled water. A glass from his own tap, however, provides water that's discolored, chlorinated, and tastes like 'pool water.' Buccellato says the extra money he spends on bottles of Dasani water is worth it" (Buller, 2002, p. 18). Portability is certainly also a plus.

Does bottled water ever go bad? No, according to the International Bottled Water Association, assuming that it has been treated by the bottler according to guidelines set by the FDA coupled with state and industry standards. Bottled water should contain nothing to attract and grow pathogens that pose a threat to human health. To preserve taste, it is recommended that bottles should be stored in cool, dry places away from odors and toxic substances. Some bottles have two-year expiration dates stamped on them, but this has nothing to do with product safety; it is a number that store owners use to rotate bottles on the shelves.

"Generally, over the years, the FDA has adopted EPA standards for tap water as standards for bottled water," says Dr. Henry Kim, a supervisory chemist at the FDA's Center for Food and Safety and Applied Nutrition, Office of Plant and Dairy Foods and Beverages. "As a result, standards for contaminants in tap water and bottled water are very similar" (Buller, 2002, p. 16). Box 8.1 (earlier in chapter) shows the FDA classifications of bottled water based on origin.

Bottled-water sales are growing at a faster pace than soft drink sales.

In bottled-water consumption, there is the battle of the brands. As this book went to press, the top-selling brand was Aquafina by PepsiCo Inc., followed by Dasani by Coca-Cola Co. These age-old rivals in the soda drink market have found a new battleground in the water wars. It makes sense that they would be major players because they have the water-purifying and bottling plants and distribution systems already. Competitors include regional and imported bottled waters. In recent years bottled water has grown at a faster pace than soft drink sales, with annual supermarket sales of over $13 billion for soft drinks and over $3 billion for bottled water.

## AGENCIES AND LAWS

In an earlier chapter, you learned that the FDA regulates food, including the areas of food-borne illnesses, nutrition, and dietary supplements; drugs, including prescription, over-the-counter, and generic; medical devices and biologics; and cosmetics, including safety and labeling issues. The FDA monitors Web sites for products that may endanger the public health. In 1994, the Dietary Supplement Health and Education Act established specific labeling requirements and authorized the FDA to promulgate good manufacturing practice regulations for dietary supplements. This act defined the terms *dietary supplements* and *dietary ingredients* and classifies them as food; it also established a commission to recommend how to regulate claims.

Box 8.3 lists the government agencies (including the FDA) that monitor the food supply. The USDA has a Food Safety and Inspection Service (FSIS), which inspects meat and poultry and monitors slaughterhouses and processing plants. States also monitor parts of the food supply, particularly the wholesomeness of foods grown in their own state; for example, California and Florida actively test and look out for problems in their citrus industries.

Both the FDA and USDA are active in consumer education, spending millions of dollars each year on education (and in the case of the USDA, on promotion of agricultural products). The USDA has government-sponsored trade associations, including the Egg Board, the National Pork Board, the Cattlemen's Beef Promotion and Research

### BOX 8.3    Government Agencies Monitoring the Food Supply

Each government agency listed below deals with the food supply, is involved in consumer education, alerts the public to health concerns, and conducts research. Following is a very brief description of these agencies and their activities:

- *Centers for Disease Control (CDC)*, www.cdc.gov. About one-fourth of the U.S. population experiences a food-borne illness each year. The CDC monitors food-borne diseases, which are illnesses transmitted to humans through food and water. In homes, food-borne illnesses can be prevented by keeping a clean kitchen, avoiding cross-contamination, keeping hot foods hot, and keeping cold foods cold.
- *Environmental Protection Agency (EPA)*, www.epa.gov. The EPA is responsible for regulating pesticides and establishing water quality standards.
- *Food and Agricultural Organization (FAO)*, www.fao.org. Part of the United Nations, the FAO has responsibilities that include international monitoring of pesticides.
- *Food and Drug Administration (FDA)*, www.fda.gov. The FDA is responsible for ensuring the safety and wholesomeness of foods processed and sold in interstate commerce, except for meat, poultry, and eggs (which the USDA monitors). The FDA also inspects food plants and imported foods. It cannot possibly sample all foods—it is a monitoring agency that sets standards—but it samples foods regularly and acts promptly when problems occur or when there is suspicion of a potential problem.
- *U.S. Department of Agriculture (USDA)*, www.usda.gov. Enforcing standards for the wholesomeness and quality of meat, poultry, and eggs produced in the United States is the domain of the USDA.
- *World Health Organization (WHO)*, www.who.ch. The WHO is an international agency that adopts standards on pesticide use and reports statistics on world food shortages.

Board, and the National Dairy Promotion and Research Board. A consumer issue is whether using taxpayer dollars for promotional efforts is a good idea or not as well as whether it is an example of the crossover between government, industry, and media.

As we learned in previous chapters, the FTC is responsible for food advertising and industry competition. It does not distinguish between various claims and products (for example, whether a substance is a food or a drug), so there is this gray area of confusing policy whereby food labels are more closely watched or restricted than television commercials or magazine advertisements. Here is an example. A magazine advertisement can say that ketchup may reduce the risk of prostate and cervical cancers, but the label on the product will not say this even though ketchup contains cooked tomatoes that have pytochemical lycopene, which is thought to reduce certain types of cancer. This brings us to the topic of **structure–function claims**, claims that are made about products by their producers and that are not regulated by the FDA. Health claims are fairly tightly regulated by the FDA, but structure–function claims can be made without FDA approval; for example, products can be said to "improve memory" or "build stronger bodies" without proof. Advertisers are careful to skirt the issue by not mentioning specific diseases, a fine distinction often lost on consumers. Here is another example. Milk contains calcium, which may reduce the risk of osteoporosis—this health claim and the nutrient content need FDA approval. But an advertisement that goes further and makes the structure–function claim that milk helps to promote bone health does not need FDA approval—the phrase "helps promote" is often the key and is considered an easy way out. Box 8.4 gives more examples of structure–function claims.

The FTC does not have the resources to keep up with every U.S.-based Web site offering products with health claims, and it certainly does not have the resources to keep up with foreign Web sites. Therefore, do not assume that law enforcement agencies can protect everyone from Internet food swindles.

**BOX 8.4   Structure–Function Claims**

These product claims, which may be largely untested or not regulated by government, may be found in advertising:

- Helps maintain body weight
- Builds strong bones and teeth
- Lifts your spirits
- Slows aging
- Improves memory
- Boosts your immune system
- Helps you relax so you can finally get some sleep
- Promotes heart health
- Reduces the risk of colds*
- Promotes relaxation and good karma
- Increases alertness
- Enhances mood

*This one is a borderline claim that has gotten some companies in trouble. A way around it is to mention the cold or flu season while using actors with red noses who are holding tissues and sneezing on each other and then let viewers draw their own conclusions. Actions or settings are less easily regulated than words.

## SUMMARY

Food and beverage consumption patterns in the United States have changed considerably since colonial times. Currently the top U.S. beverage is tap water, followed by coffee and then bottled water. Coffee consumption was dropping considerably until it was reinvigorated in 1995 by Starbucks and its competitors. Many innovations in food (such as freeze-dried coffee) have their origins in military research (for example, the development of MREs, referring to Meals Ready to Eat).

The Food and Drug Administration (FDA) regulates bottled water as well as the safety of most foods, while the U.S. Department of Agriculture (USDA) monitors the wholesomeness of meat, poultry, and eggs. The Federal Trade Commission (FTC) is active in food labeling and monitoring advertising.

Outbreaks in illnesses and deaths from contaminated human and pet foods have made many concerned about the safety of food supplies. Another issue is that many frauds in the food and health industries exist, especially in the area of weight reduction as well as any product or service that promises a more attractive appearance.

The slow food movement (also called the "buy local" movement) is worldwide. It began in Italy as a reaction both to the increased use of fast food and to the toll that the spread of fast food was taking on unique and often more flavorful regional cuisines. Advocates of slow food emphasize local and fresh foods as alternatives to global internationalized foods.

In the typical family budget, food is the third most costly item, behind housing and transportation. Online grocery shopping is being experimented with, convenience being the main positive feature.

Organic foods may or may not be healthier than conventional foods, and they may cost more. The added health benefits of eating organically grown foods are controversial, as is the eating of genetically altered or irradiated foods. Genetically altered foods are controversial because in many people's minds the process seems to go against what nature intended, although advocates of the value of genetically altered foods would point out that man has been altering nature for centuries through a variety of food production and agricultural practices. Irradiated foods are also met with skepticism. Some people think we have gone too far; others think we have not gone far enough. Starvation still exists on this planet, and advocates of genetically altered foods would suggest that higher crop yields and the reduction of hunger far outweigh worries about tampering with nature. Everyone agrees that as the world population grows, better methods of food production and land use are needed—the dispute is over the best way to do this.

## KEY POINTS

1. The USDA MyPyramid offers a way to individualize choices of foods and amounts, and it encourages exercise.
2. Not all foods have labels, and not all labels are truthful.
3. It is difficult for consumers and even trained nutritionists to determine how many calories are in foods that they haven't prepared themselves. Many consumers think they are eating a low-calorie, healthy food in restaurants

based on the name of the item, but many times that is not the case. Calorie information should be available on counters or packaging.

4. Weight and health effects and weight control are highly personal and complicated issues.

5. Bottled-water guidelines are set by the FDA.

6. The FDA regulates what is considered an organically grown food. These foods cost 15 to 50 percent more than conventionally grown foods.

7. The largest grocer in the United States is Wal-Mart.

8. A number of government agencies monitor the U.S. food supply; most important are the FDA and the USDA.

9. DNA matching (genetic testing) can be used to track tainted food, which has enormous health and legal implications.

10. Food allergies are rare, affecting about 2 percent of the adult population. Food intolerance, an adverse but not life-threatening reaction, is more common. Through trial and error, most people learn what foods their bodies will not tolerate.

## KEY TERMS

| | | |
|---|---|---|
| additives | foods | pull date |
| biotechnology | genetic engineering | quality assurance date |
| boycott | GRAS List | radio frequency |
| calories | loss leader | identification (RFID) |
| Delaney clause | nutrition | structure–function claims |
| end-of-aisle displays | open dating | tie-ins |
| expiration date | organically grown foods | trans fats |
| food allergy | pack date | unit pricing |
| food irradiation | preservatives | |

## DISCUSSION QUESTIONS

1. How have food preferences changed in the last 100 years? Give at least three examples.

2. What does the Delaney clause refer to? What does negligible or minimal risk mean?

3. Why do people buy branded bottled water? What government agency regulates bottled water?

4. What is your opinion of organic foods? Why have they grown in popularity? Are they worth the extra money?

5. Select a Web site in the E-Resources section and report on what you find on a specific body-related issue such as food or beverages.

## E-RESOURCES

**American Dietetic Association**   *www.eatright.org*

**American Journal of Clinical Nutrition**   *www.faseb.org/ajcn*

**American Medical Association (AMA)**   *www.amaassn.org*

**Centers for Disease Control and Prevention (CDC)**   *www.cdc.gov*

**Dietitians of Canada**   *www.dietitians.ca*

**Food and Drug Administration (FDA)**   *www.fda.gov* (if you have questions, e-mail webmail@oc.fda.gov)

**Healthfinder**   *www.healthfinder.gov*

**Tufts University Nutrition Navigator**   *www.navigator.tufts.edu*

**USDA Food and Nutrition Information**   *www.nal.usda.gov/fnic*

**U.S. Health and Human Services Office on Women's Health**
*www.4women.gov*

## REFERENCES

Abboud, L. (January 21, 2003). DNA matching helps track tainted meat. *Wall Street Journal,* p. B1.

Addicted to grease. (May 2002). *American Demographics,* 56.

Buller, A. C. (July–August 2002). Bottled water: Better than the tap? *FDA Consumer,* 14  18.

Callahan, P., and A. Zimmerman. (May 27, 2003). Price war in aisle 3. *Wall Street Journal,* p. B1.

Constant cravings. (May 2002). *American Demographics,* 56.

Daly, K. (1996). *Families and time.* Thousand Oaks, CA: Sage.

de Lisser, E. (August 20, 2002). Is that $5 gallon of milk really organic? *Wall Street Journal,* p. D1.

December, R. (September 18, 2002). New miracle weight-loss product? Fat chance! *Wall Street Journal,* p. D7.

Diamond, J. (1999). *Guns, germs, and steel.* New York: Norton.

Friedman, M. (1999). *Consumer boycotts.* New York: Routledge.

Gifford, K., and J. Bernard. (2006). Influencing Consumer Purchase Likelihood. *International Journal of Consumer Studies, 30* (2), 155–63.

Haas, L. (1999). Families and work. In *Handbook of Marriage and the Family,* ed. M. Sussman, S. K. Steinmetz, and G. W. Peterson. New York: Plenum Press.

Heitmann, B. L., et al. (1997). Are genetic determinants of weight gain modified by leisure-time physical activity? A prospective study of Finnish twins. *American Journal of Clinical Nutrition, 66,* 672–78.

Hochschild, A. R. (1989). *The second shift: Working parents and the revolution at home.* New York: Viking.

Honkanen, P., Verplanken, B., and S. Olsen. (2006). Ethical Values and Motives Driving Organic Food Choice. *Journal of Consumer Behavior, 5* (5), 420–30.

Insel, P., and W. Roth. (2002). *Core concepts in health,* 9th ed. Boston: McGraw-Hill.

Junk-food nation. (November 2001). *American Demographics,* p. 25.

Kilman, S. (February 2, 2002). A roast is a roast? Not in the new game of marketing meat. *Wall Street Journal,* p. A1.

Landro, L. (2002). The informed patient: Knowledge is half the battle in avoiding infectious diseases. *Wall Street Journal,* p. C2.

Low-cal muffins: Too good to be true? (October 2001). *Good Housekeeping,* p. 18.

Mariani, J. (1991). *America eats out.* New York: William Morrow.

McEachern, M., and G. Warnaby. (2006). Food shopping behavior in Scotland: The influence of relative rurality. *International Journal of Consumer Studies, 30* (2), 189–201.

McKay, B. (September 23, 2002). Fit to eat? PepsiCo challenges itself to concoct healthier snacks. *Wall Street Journal,* p. A1.

Morganosky, M., and B. Cude. (2000a). Large format retailing in the US: A consumer experience perspective. *Journal of Retailing and Consumer Services, 7,* 215–22.

Morganosky, M., and B. Cude. (2000b). Consumer response to online grocery shopping. *International Journal of Retail & Distribution Management, 28* (1), 17–26.

Parker-Pope, T. (January 14, 2003). That veggie wrap you just chowed down is more fattening than a ham sandwich. *Wall Street Journal,* p. D1.

Partnership for Food Safety Education, www.fightbac.org

Pollan, M. (2001). *The botany of desire.* New York: Random House.

Roxburgh, S. (2002). Racing through life: The distribution of time pressures by roles and role resources among full-time workers. *Journal of Family and Economic Issues,* 121–45.

Schor, J. B. (1992). *The overworked American: The unexpected decline of leisure.* New York: Basic Books.

Shape of biotech to come. (September 2, 2002). *Fortune,* p. 130.

Stipp, D. (January 20, 2003). Son of Spam. *Fortune,* p. 46.

Weiss, M. (April 2002). Inconspicuous consumption. *American Demographics,* 31–39.

Whitney, E., and S. Rolfes. (2002). *Understanding nutrition,* 9th ed. Belmont, CA: Wadsworth.

# Health and Wellness Issues

*Good health and good sense are two of life's greatest blessings.*
—**Publius Syrus (42 B.C.)**

## Learning Objectives

1. Explain what it means to be well, and list the types of wellness.
2. Discuss the reasons why fraudulent health claims are rampant.
3. List ways to reduce health care costs.
4. Discuss the issues and players involved in medical malpractice insurance.
5. Explain the market for cosmetics and the reasons people use them.
6. Discuss addictions, such as to alcohol and tobacco, and the related consumer issues of health, safety, advertising, and cost.

---

### Recall of Toy with "Date Rape" Drug

Australia and the United States pulled over 4.2 million of Chinese-made children's toys after regulators learned a chemical on the toy beads turned into a powerful "date rape" drug when swallowed. The toys were called Aqua Dots in the United States and Bindeez Beads in Australia. The beads could be arranged into designs and came with accessories such as a drying fan, applicator pen, and templates.

"Children who swallow the beads can become comatose, develop respiratory depression or have seizures," a CPSC statement warned.[1] "Anyone with Aqua Dots at home should throw them out," CPSC spokeswoman Julie Vallese said.[2] The toy was named toy of the year in Australia and recently made Wal-Mart Store Inc's list of top 12 Christmas toys. Wal-Mart, on hearing the news, immediately removed the toy from both its shelves and its top toy list.

The arts and crafts kit was aimed at children ages four and older and was made in China and distributed from Canada, but children as young as two got sick. This is an example of how global many products, including toys, have become and the possible health hazards. It also shows that once toys are in the house, all children—regardless of age—may play with them.

Australian officials said that instead of the safe chemical 1,5-pentaneidol, the potentially dangerous chemical 1,4-butanediol was used during manufacturing. When ingested, 1,4-butanediol becomes gamma hydroxybutyrate (GHB). GHB can cause drowsiness, vomiting, loss of consciousness, seizures, coma, and death. Three children in Australia swallowed the beads and were hospitalized. "I was so

---

> frightened because I thought she wasn't going to make it," Heather Lehande told CNN affiliate Network 7 of her 10-year-old daughter, Charlotte, who was among those children.[3]
>
> ———
> [1]CNN.com, November 8, 2007.
> [2]Ibid.
> [3]Ibid.
> *Reference:* Jayne O'Donnell, "Chinese-Made Beads Turn into 'Date Rape' Drug When Ingested." *USA TODAY,* November 8, 2007, p. A1. More information can be found at www.spinmaster.com.

# INTRODUCTION

*What is healthy is very subjective.*

The last chapter focused on food and beverage issues, and this chapter extends the discussion by turning its attention to the general topic of health and wellness. This is a more difficult topic than one would assume because "healthy is a very subjective definition," says Gene Cameron, vice president of marketing for Baja Fresh (Parker-Pope, 2003, p. D1). Health and body issues are important to study from a consumer economics standpoint because so much money is spent on health and body products, so much consumer protection legislation and regulation revolve around these issues, fraud is rampant, and, most important, individual and family health are critical. Subtopics to be covered include vaccines, brand-name versus generic drugs, cosmetics, and tobacco and alcohol use. The emphasis in this chapter is on legal drug use, not illicit drugs such as cocaine and marijuana (the Harrison Act of 1914 prohibited the use of cocaine, morphine, and opiates for nonmedical purposes).

*Prohibition began in 1919 and ended in 1933.*

Throughout the twentieth century and into the present century, there has been an ongoing battle over the definition of what is a socially acceptable desire or habit and what is an addiction. The Eighteenth Amendment of 1919 (more commonly referred to as Prohibition) outlawed most alcohol use, with the purpose of eliminating or drastically reducing alcohol consumption. The amendment challenged the free market; it was protested by distillers, brewers, and importers and was supported by the American Medical Association (AMA), reformers, and religious groups. In the end, the experiment failed, and the act was repealed in 1933 by the Twenty-First Amendment to the Constitution. Most of the enforcement efforts were directed at sellers rather than consumers, so Prohibition introduced a new kind of criminal—the bootlegger—the most famous of whom was Al Capone. It also forced otherwise law-abiding citizens into a position of circumventing the law, which made many people uncomfortable. There was a concern that if citizens were acting illegally in this area, they were more likely to ignore the law in other areas as well. After Prohibition, a few states continued to prohibit or control the sale of alcohol, but by 1966 liquor control became more a local control issue rather than a statewide or nationwide effort.

Life has gotten more complicated since the days of Al Capone and bootleg whiskey. Drugs, legal and illegal, have introduced a new set of health concerns. "Recent ads in newspapers and magazines claim that it's now legal to import drugs into the United States for personal use: In fact, some ads on the Internet and elsewhere claim that people can legally bring up to a 90-day supply of their prescription medications bought outside the United States home with them. Neither of these claims is true," says Ray Formanek Jr., editor of the *FDA Consumer* (October 2002, p. 2). Under the Federal Food, Drug, and Cosmetic Act, unapproved, misbranded, and adulterated drugs are prohibited from importation into the United States. This quote points out the interaction between the consumer, business, media, and government in the marketplace, as shown in the consumer power model of consumerism; it also emphasizes the importance of the Internet in terms of obtaining drugs and information about both drugs and medical treatment. Health information sites on the Internet get an incredible amount of traffic (for example, the Mayo Clinic reports over 2 million visitors a month).

Due to the following, life improved during the twentieth century for most Americans:

- Availability of vaccinations for childhood diseases
- Fluoridation of drinking water
- Safer workplaces, homes, and schools
- Recognition of the severe health problems caused by tobacco use
- Healthier mothers and babies as well as improved obstetric care
- Increase in life expectancy
- Control of infectious diseases
- Improved sanitation

It is assumed that the readers of this chapter have learned about the harmful short- and long-term effects of alcohol and drug abuse in previous classes; for individual health advice, they should consult their physician. The E-Resources section also has Web sites with further information. This chapter begins with a discussion of wellness and well-being.

## WELLNESS AND WELL-BEING

"Everyone knows the feeling of waking up after a long illness and suddenly, miraculously, feeling full of life again! Being anxious to dive back into things that have been neglected, and try new things, too. Not feeling isolated, powerless, or estranged anymore" (De Graaf, Wann & Naylor, 2001, p. 231). **Wellness** is the ability to live life fully with optimal health and vitality, encompassing physical, emotional, intellectual, spiritual, interpersonal, social, and environmental well-being (Insel & Roth, 2002). Thus, wellness is an expanded idea of health, going beyond just the absence of physical disease. It can be said to transcend health— for example, when individuals with serious illnesses or disabilities rise above their physical or mental limitations to live rich, meaningful, and vital lives. **Well-being** is the state of being healthy, happy, or prosperous. Well-being is about being both mentally and physically healthy and having the finances to keep healthy, comfortable, and contented. The term *well-being,* then, is about someone's present health and his or her expectation of a good life, which includes excellent health in the future.

Why do we study health, wellness, and well-being in consumer economics? The answer is that health is an asset; in fact it is generally agreed that it is your greatest asset. "Some aspects of health are determined by your genes, your age, and other factors that may be beyond your control. But true wellness is largely determined by the decisions you make about how to live your life" (Insel & Roth, 2002, p. 2). According to Insel and Roth, wellness is made up of six components or subtypes:

1. *Physical wellness.* Exercising, eating well, avoiding harmful habits, making responsible decisions regarding sex, and getting regular dental and physical care all contribute to keeping physically well.
2. *Emotional wellness.* Emotional wellness includes having the ability to share feelings and being optimistic and trusting.
3. *Intellectual wellness.* Curiosity, a sense of humor, openness to new ideas, a love of learning, and the capacity to question and to think creatively are all components of intellectual wellness.
4. *Spiritual wellness.* Being spiritual well includes both having a set of guiding beliefs, values, or principles that adds meaning to life and thinking beyond oneself.
5. *Interpersonal and social wellness.* Developing satisfying relationships is an important part of interpersonal and social wellness.
6. *Environmental or planetary wellness.* Environmental or planetary wellness includes an appreciation for and care of one's surroundings, both natural and man-made (and increasingly, personal health depends on the health of the planet).

Well-being is promoted by sensible behaviors such as paying attention to safety (wearing safety belts), eating well (good nutrition), and regularly exercising. Economists perceive that maintaining good health and safety is linked to personal behavior. The consumer of health care services is called the **principal**; the provider of health care is an **agent**. Apart from self-help (such as wearing seat belts), the consumer as principal needs to find the right agent—the right doctor or health services provider and health insurance provider.

Preventive health care includes being careful while driving, maintaining friendships and families, taking time to exercise and play, using a buddy system when swimming, and having smoke alarms installed at home. Families are important

According to the AMA, 90 percent of patients don't get good explanations of tests or treatments from their doctors.

**CONSUMER ALERT**

Do you ever return from a doctor's visit and realize all the questions you should have asked? Or have you ever forgotten what the doctor said? There are several solutions, including preparing ahead by going to the E-Resources section and looking up symptoms and treatment options, taking someone with you to take notes, or bringing paper to take your own notes. Patient advocates and medical professionals agree that patients need to become active advocates for their own care. Arming yourself with information and questions before the visit begins is a good start. During the exam, carefully frame the discussion about medical concerns. The American Medical Association (AMA) reports that 90 percent of patients don't get good explanations of tests or treatments from their doctors.

socializing influences for teaching their children the do's and don'ts of safe behavior. Moderation is also important as a means to avoid overexertion and injury. Avoiding risk, another key economic concept, involves avoiding certain consumption behaviors such as heavy smoking and drinking.

**Consumer health** is an umbrella term encompassing the decisions that consumers make about health care, including products and services that they buy or that their insurance covers, and the decisions that they make about their lifestyle that affect health care needs. Because health decisions are often made in a hurry, time is involved as well as money and information. Health information is available through many media, and consumers like buying over the telephone or computer in their own homes because of the privacy it provides. But because of the personal or privacy issues involved, consumers who are gypped are less likely to complain or ask for a refund in this area of consumption than they are in less personal areas. The result is that many **quacks** (unscrupulous individuals specializing in medical or health swindlers) and quasi-legitimate products and programs continue to exist because of the lack of complaints. This is worrisome because not only is there a money and esteem loss, but also there may be a health loss because the consumer did not seek legitimate advice or treatment.

## FRAUDULENT HEALTH CLAIMS VS. SCIENCE

Because health is so fundamental to our sense of well-being and people want to appear as well as feel healthy, people are susceptible to products and services that offer a healthy glow or appearance. From Abraham Maslow's perspective, health and cosmetic products and services meet the full range of needs (see Figure 9.1).

Health frauds are perpetrated against all segments of the population, but some age groups are particularly vulnerable to certain types of frauds: Teenagers are susceptible to acne cream, bust developers, and diet claims; the middle age group is prone to products offering wrinkle reduction and perpetual youth; and the elderly fall victim to fraudulent hearing aid schemes, medical quackery and gadgetry, and arthritis remedies. Usually the fraud victim loses time, money, and dignity. For example, consumers spend an estimated $2 billion a year on unproven arthritis remedies such as honey and vinegar mixtures, magnets, and copper bracelets—none of these remedies have been proven to offer long-term relief. Some products and treatments can cause serious harm and even death; many are expensive because health insurance rarely covers unapproved treatments.

Consumers spend $2 billion a year on unproven arthritis cures.

Fraudulent health claims run the gamut from inflated claims about mouthwash to very serious life-threatening treatments. As noted in Chapter 7, a classic case arose in the 1960s when the Federal Trade Commission (FTC) greatly stepped up efforts to regulate television advertising, attacking the exaggerated health claims of Listerine mouthwash. Fundamental to a study of consumer behavior is the acceptance that there is always a market for products that will beautify or make consumers more socially acceptable.

The question is not why consumers buy health-related or appearance-related products but why they continue to buy obviously questionable products. The simple

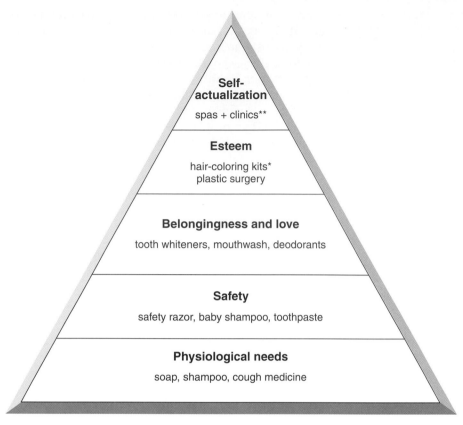

*For example, ads that say "I'm worth it."
**For example, ads that say "You have arrived."

**Figure 9.1**  Maslow's Hierarchy of Needs. This hierarchy includes examples of drugs or cosmetic products.

answer is that successful fraud trades on false hope. But as people become more educated and sophisticated, shouldn't they be more skeptical of especially improbable product claims such as "lose 10 pounds while you sleep"? What can be done? Perhaps the answer lies in encouraging people to be less gullible (easily deceived or duped) by being more scientific in their approach to consumption, such as asking for proof. Robert Park (professor of physics at the University of Maryland, frequent commentator on TV news programs, and author of *Voodoo Science: The Road from Foolishness to Fraud*) states:

> Of the major problems confronting society—problems involving the environment, national security, health, and the economy—there are few that can be sensibly addressed without input from science. As I sought to make the case for science, however, I kept bumping up against scientific ideas and claims that are totally, indisputably, extravagantly, wrong, but which nevertheless attract a large following of passionate, and sometimes powerful, proponents. I came to realize that many people choose scientific beliefs the same way they choose to be Methodists, or Democrats, or Chicago Cub fans. They judge science by how well it agrees with the way they want the world to be. (2000, pp. viii–ix)

He makes a strong case in his book that the media play a major role in promoting false health claims and that even the supposedly investigative shows or evening news shows have promulgated obviously fraudulent products. He says that if scientists can fool themselves and make mistakes, "how much easier is it to craft arguments deliberately intended to befuddle jurists or lawmakers with little or no scientific background? This is junk science." **Junk science** is a term for when there is little or no evidence or proof to support claims.

Health fraud trades on false hope. It promises quick results and easy solutions.

Here are two further questions: Why is it that some people faced with the same set of facts choose to believe and others choose to doubt? Why do some people need more proof than others? Partly this has to do with the ability to discern patterns and accumulate observations, and some people are stronger at this than others. It should also be understood that not everyone desires a world that is predictable and measurable through scientific reasoning and testing; they prefer a little adventure and mystery. It is more fun to believe that a $55 tiny jar of moisturizer will cause wrinkles to vanish than to face up to the fact of being old enough to have wrinkles.

**Science** is systemized knowledge that is the object of study. To put it another way, "Science is the systematic enterprise of gathering knowledge about the world and organizing and condensing that knowledge into testable laws and theories" (Park, 2000, p. 39). When considering a new product or claim, scientists would apply two rules:

1. Expose the idea and/or result to independent testing and replication by other scientists.
2. Abandon or modify accepted facts, theories, or procedures in light of the new evidence.

Many inventors of new products or claims do not allow them to be tested by independent scientists or doctors, so one of the first rules of determining whether a new health or cosmetic discovery is legitimate or not is to find out what sort of testing was done and by whom. Box 9.1 lists the various words in advertising or labeling that might lead one to believe that fakery (or at least puffery) is at hand. A way to lessen the chance of people being taken in by false claims is to encourage **scientific literacy**, the promotion of science education in the schools and in the community. Park adds that what is needed is a broader scientific worldview, by which he means an understanding that we live in an orderly universe governed by natural laws that cannot be circumvented by magic or miracles.

In Box 9.1 it mentions that the consumer should beware of ads that use testimonials, especially full-page ads for such things as weight reduction and miracle cures. Here is an example from *FTC Facts for Consumers:* "My husband has Alzheimer's disease. He began eating a teaspoonful of this product each day. And now in just 22 days he mowed the grass, cleaned out the garage, weeded the flower beds and we take our morning walk again" (2003, p. 9).

To go back to the beginning of this section, the FTC continues to do everything it can to lessen misleading advertising, putting particular emphasis on advertising and products directed to children under the age of eight. For adults, a new concern is the marketing of brand-name prescription drugs on television and in magazines; the ads on evening television and in magazines suggest that consumers ask their doctor for a brand-name drug the next time that they have an appointment. The

**BOX 9.1    Health Fraud Buzzwords and Scams**

Look out for before-and-after photos, testimonials, limited supplies (so hurry!), and the following claims about a product:

- Shrinks tumors
- Improves sex life and cures impotency
- Is an ancient remedy
- Why the medical community is keeping this discovery secret
- Is fast/safe/easy
- Is guaranteed to work for everyone
- Is amazing
- Is a new product breakthrough
- Is a miracle
- Contains a secret formula
- Is exciting
- Is painless
- Can help you sleep well every night and wake refreshed
- What primitive tribes can tell you
- Will improve your popularity
- Can end baldness forever
- Is recommended by three out of four doctors

problem is that these ads are designed for the general public and may not fit an individual's health status or symptoms. There is real potential for self-diagnosis, which most likely will be off the mark. The counterpoint to this is that someone may recognize symptoms in themselves for a disease like depression and know that there is help.

 **CONSUMER ALERT**

Beware of health frauds about cures for cancer. Because a diagnosis brings feelings of fear and hopelessness, people will try just about anything. They are susceptible to exotic cures or remedies. Cancer is a name given to a wide range of diseases, and each requires different forms of treatment that are best determined by a specialist, a health professional trained in that field.

The FTC turns up hundreds of Web sites touting unproven cures or treatments for cancer. One site pushes more than 100 alternative cancer treatments that it claims are safe, effective, and nontoxic. Some of these sites are by medical doctors, so just because a product or treatment is endorsed by medical doctors does not mean it is safe. Types of cures include herbal teas and fish extracts—even electronic zappers. The FTC obtained "a $4.3 million judgment against BioPulse International Inc., for making unsubstantiated claims about two cancer 'treatments' it offered in Tijuana, Mexico. One of them, billed as 'hypoglycemic sleep therapy,' involved placing cancer patients in a series of insulin-induced comas over a seven-week period at a cost of nearly $40,000. Some patients, according to news accounts, died from their cancers soon after receiving the treatment" (Fleck, 2003, p.18). To learn more about quackery in cancer treatments, go to www.quackwatch.org.

**CONSUMER ALERT**

Beware also of health care frauds involving HIV and AIDS. According to the FTC, although legitimate treatments can extend life and improve the quality of life for people with AIDS, there is no cure for the disease so far. People diagnosed with HIV, the virus that causes AIDS, may want to try untested drugs or treatments, but trying unproven products or treatments, such as electrical and magnetic devices and so-called herbal cures, can be dangerous and may cause HIV-positive individuals to delay seeking medical care. The government has information at www.hivatis.org.

## GOVERNMENT AGENCIES AND THEIR HEALTH CARE TASKS

As the Consumer Alert shows, the FTC is one of the active government agencies engaged in guarding the public's health. Table 9.1 gives a partial list of key agencies and their main tasks. Figure 9.2 shows the different groups impacting one particular agency, the Food and Drug Administration (FDA). Two goals of regulatory agencies are to help people attain a high level of health at a reasonable cost and to protect them from being misled or taken in by outright fraud. Many issues surround the competency, credentialing, cost, and access to medical care.

## SKYROCKETING HEALTH CARE COSTS

The United States has the most expensive health care in the world, and the costs are rising. "Medical costs increased 10 to 15 percent in 2001, after averaging 5 to 6 percent

**Table 9.1**   Partial List of Government Agencies and Their Health Care Tasks

| All agencies are involved in some form of education or public outreach; beyond that, some of their main tasks and responsibilities are given below. | |
| --- | --- |
| **Agencies** | **Tasks/Responsibilities** |
| Centers for Disease Control and Prevention (CDC) | Disease control, accident prevention, and the search for cures |
| Environmental Protection Agency (EPA) | Environmental protection, cleanup and disposal of toxic waste, and protection of water supplies |
| Food and Drug Administration (FDA) | Testing and regulation |
| Internal Revenue Service (IRS) | Taxes and tax policy regarding deductions |
| National Institutes of Health (NIH) | Research |
| Occupational Safety and Health Administration (OSHA) | Monitoring of the nation's workplaces for potential health hazards |
| U.S. Department of Health and Human Services, the Surgeon General's Office, and state and county health departments | Help for ill people, policy setting, and oversight of the nation's public health |

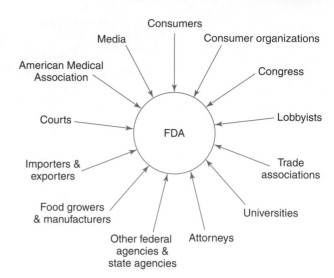

**Figure 9.2** Groups Impacting the Food and Drug Administration.

for a decade. Hospital spending accounted for about 45 percent of increased health care costs in 2000. Unnecessary admissions and labor shortages are among the factors that make hospitals the primary driver of rising costs. Some hospitals have demanded increases of 40 percent to 60 percent for certain services" (Florida Blue State Edition, 2002). Health care premiums rise as medical costs and services rise. Hospitals are for the most part for-profit organizations that have to be enterprising to survive; unprofitable hospitals close totally or close down unprofitable services. As of the writing of this book, the country's largest hospital chain is HCA, Inc., followed by Tenet Healthcare Corporation of Santa Barbara, California. Both of these compete in buying up smaller hospital chains and individual hospitals.

Because it is so expensive, about 40 million Americans do not have health insurance. In 2003, 17,500 employees of General Electric Co. (GE) went on a two-day nationwide walkout to protest higher out-of-pocket health costs. It was the first national walkout at GE since 1969, which shows that employees of GE do not lightly make the decision to go on strike. This also illustrates that even employees with health insurance provided by their employers have to pay for part of the coverage (the GE workers were protesting an average copay increase of $300 to $400 annually). In Chapter 14, there will be more coverage on health insurance availability through employers (HMOs and so on), but here are eight general guidelines to follow to reduce health care costs:

1. Get good health care coverage from your employer. Find out about your health plan/program in terms of copayments, deductibles, and choice of physician. For example, find out if you can visit a nonnetwork physician, and if you can, what the cost differences are between a network and nonnetwork physician.
2. Use generic drugs instead of a brand-name drug. A **generic drug** is a lower-cost copy of a brand-name drug that becomes available after the brand-name product's patent expires, typically after 15 years or more. The usual cost is 30 percent less than the brand-name drug but is sometimes as much as 75 percent less. More information on generic drugs is given in the next section.

3. Try a mail-order program or shop around for the best price when you use a drug regularly.

4. Choose a physician who participates in your health plan/program when you are traveling. If you choose a nonparticipating provider, your deductible and coinsurance amounts may be higher. One of the biggest plans, Blue Cross/Blue Shield, has 400,000 providers in the United States who participate in the plans, and these providers can be reached at www.bcbs.com or by calling 1-800-810-BLUE.

5. Ask how much it is going to cost you. Can the payments be stretched out?

6. Get free samples from the physician.

7. Comparison-shop for the best health care coverage at the best price if your employer (or your spouse's) does not offer health care insurance. One suggestion is to check group policies offered by universities, credit unions, clubs, associations, and other groups that may offer better deals than you could find buying insurance as a nonaffiliated individual.

8. Ask the pharmacist any further questions when getting a prescription filled. Pharmacists are an underused resource.

One of the basic tenets of consumer economics is trying to get the best product at the lowest cost (time and money), but when it comes to your health, perhaps this is not always the wisest course. For example, before agreeing to surgery, you should seek a second opinion; fortunately, most insurance companies will cover the cost of a second opinion. Peace of mind is worth a great deal.

## Medicare Fraud

*Medicare is the nation's largest health insurance program.*

Frauds and scams drive up the cost of health care for all of us. The federal government has been working for years to reduce the money loss through Medicare fraud, and it instituted a volunteer program called the Senior Medicare Patrol sponsored by the U.S. Administration on Aging. **Medicare** is the federal health insurance program for people age 65 or older and for many people with disabilities. It covers over 40 million Americans and is the nation's largest health insurance program; by 2030, this number will double, and there are concerns about how to keep this program solvent. Fraud prevention will help. Medicare is subject to a number of errors and abuses, partly because it is so large. Someone who gets Social Security at age 65 is automatically enrolled in Medicare, which has two parts: hospital insurance and medical insurance that helps pay for doctors' services, outpatient care, tests, home health visits, and other services.

Medicare fraud, abuse, and billing errors, which together cost taxpayers $12 billion a year, are being investigated through the Senior Medicare Patrol by volunteers who are retirees (often retired medical doctors) looking into possible improper Medicare charges, based on tips from beneficiaries, or who serve as educators to other seniors about the potential for problems. As one example, after two days of training, volunteers worked one on one with beneficiaries to track down suspicious charges on the beneficiaries' monthly Medicare summary notices, or billing statements. Even when fraud is found, sometimes beneficiaries do not want to become involved in clearing it up, fearing bureaucracies and the time loss; volunteers can help with this, making it easier for fraud victims to come forward by showing them the ropes and helping with the paperwork. Other volunteers may be trained to do educational programs because in the long run the biggest gains may come from prevention of fraud, abuse, and error rather than fixing things after they occur.

What kinds of frauds exist? Examples of fraud are Medicare payments for people long since dead, reconditioned wheelchairs billed as new, saline solutions sold as painkillers, and bills for home health services never rendered. "Scam artists are really, really smart. There's a new gimmick every day," says Shirley Merner, state coordinator for Operation Restore Trust of Iowa, a Patrol project that has about 1,500 senior volunteers (Engstrom, 2002, p. R6).

## Brand-Name Drugs and Generic Drugs

Drugs are chemicals other than foods intended to affect the structure or function of the body.

The Food, Drug, and Cosmetic Act defines drugs by their intended use: "(A) articles intended for use in the diagnosis, cure, mitigation, treatment, or prevention of disease . . . and (B) articles (other than food) intended to affect the structure or any function of the body of man or other animals" (Food, Drug, and Cosmetic Act, section 201g1). A simpler way to say this is that **drugs** are any chemical other than food intended to affect the structure or function of the body (Insel & Roth, 2002).

**Prescription drugs** are obtained by a written instruction, usually from a physician, for the preparation and use of a drug. It is illegal to write your own prescription or modify an existing prescription from a doctor. Since drugs have side effects, undesirable reactions and interactions, consumers are given warnings on labels and in advertising. Nonetheless it is estimated that nearly 200,000 people die every year from adverse drug reactions, making it one of the leading causes of death. Most of the medications sold are for **over-the-counter (OTC) drugs** (nonprescription drugs) because most people choose to self-medicate or are treating minor illnesses or discomfort such as headaches, stomachaches, or pain relief with an analgesic.

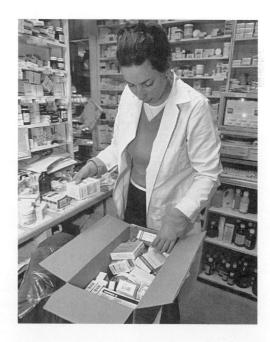

A pharmacist checks through a delivery of packaged drugs. (Photo Researchers, Inc.)

According to the *FDA Consumer,* a bimonthly publication of the FDA, when the pain reliever acetaminophen was developed in the 1950s, it was only available under the brand name Tylenol. Today, acetaminophen can be found in many generic and store-brand versions such as Pamprin, Midol, and Anacin. Similarly, many drug products, both prescription and over-the-counter, have generic versions available. An estimated 44 percent of all prescriptions in the United States are filled with generic drugs. The biggest seller is aspirin, which is acetylsalicyclic acid; it is sold by nearly 500 companies and may be mixed or coated with other substances. Anacin, Excedrin, and Bayer are common brand names. In using OTCs, the potential for misdiagnosis is very high, resulting in side effects, hospitalization, overuse, overdose, lack of efficacy, and failure to get professional care. **Lack of efficacy** means that the pill or treatment fails to produce the desired effect or outcome.

The biggest-selling OTC drug is aspirin.

Drugs are continually being changed from prescription to OTC drugs. An FDA committee decides whether to approve or disapprove the change from one category to another; once approved, the agency is concerned about OTC labeling so that consumers know what they are buying, as well as any warnings. The FDA's purpose is to protect human health while at the same time providing freedom of choice in the marketplace—something that isn't always easy to attain. Public participation is sought, and this is happening more often as consumers take an active role in acquiring health information.

Given the possible savings, why doesn't everyone switch to generics? In an American Association of Retired Persons (AARP) study, 95 percent of respondents were aware of generics, but only 31 percent asked for them from their doctors ("Generics May Be Cheaper, But Consumers Resist," 2002). About 28 percent of the respondents worried that the drugs would be less effective, of inferior quality, or in some other way different from brand-name drugs. As this section shows, this is not the case since generics must pass strict standards to earn FDA approval.

The way the approval process works for brand-name drugs is that companies develop new drugs and patent them, and in so doing, they earn the right to sell the drugs for a certain number of years. When the brand-name drugs near their expiration dates, manufacturers can apply to the FDA to sell generic versions. The Drug Price Competition and Patent Term Restoration Act of 1984 allows for this approval process. To summarize, generic drugs are safe, effective, and FDA approved (see Box 9.2). People can use them with total confidence, according to Gary Buehler, M.D., director of the FDA's Office of Generic Drugs.

## Imported Drugs

**Safety Concerns.**   "With an unapproved drug, you can't be sure that it has been shipped, handled, and stored under conditions that meet U.S. requirements" (Meadows, 2002b, p. 19). Unapproved drugs that come into the United States carry innumerable health risks. The Internet, as well as increased travel (much of it between Mexico and the United States), has made it easier for unapproved drugs to come into this country. "We've found drugs that were stored in time containers and car trunks," says Daniel Hancz, a pharmacist with the Health Authority Law Enforcement Task Force (HALT) in Los Angeles (Meadows, 2002b, p. 18). Some criminals claim to have a medical background, and they not only sell drugs but also give injections illegally. Some of the drugs are very old, others have side effects, some cause death. Through the Food, Drug, and Cosmetic Act, the interstate shipment of

**BOX 9.2   Frequently Asked Questions about Generic Drugs (and FDA's Answers)**

1. Are generic drugs as safe as brand-name drugs?
   Yes. The FDA requires that all drugs be safe and effective.
2. Are generic drugs as strong as brand-name drugs?
   Yes. The FDA requires generic drugs to have the same quality, strength, purity, and stability as brand-name drugs.
3. Do generic drugs take longer to work in the body?
   No. Generic drugs work in the same way and in the same amount of time as brand-name drugs.
4. Why are generic drugs less expensive?
   Generic drugs are less expensive because generic manufacturers don't have the investment costs of the developer of a new drug. New drugs are developed under patent protection, and the patent protects the investment—including research, development, marketing, and promotion—by giving the company the sole right to sell the drug while it is in effect.
5. Does every brand-name drug have a generic counterpart?
   No. Brand-name drugs are generally given patent protection for 20 years from the date of submission of the patent. This provides protection for the innovator.
6. If brand-name drugs and generics have the same active ingredients, why do they look different?
   In the United States, trademark laws do not allow a generic drug to look exactly like the brand-name drug, but a generic drug must duplicate the active ingredient. Colors, flavors, and certain other inactive ingredients may be different.

*Source:* Adapted from *FDA Consumer,* September–October 2002, p. 24. For the sake of brevity, the key point of the answer is given; for additional information, refer to this publication or the FDA Web site at www.fda.gov/cder/ogd.

any prescription drug that lacks required FDA approval is illegal, and interstate shipment includes importation. The FDA works with the U.S. Customs Service. If a bag or package arouses suspicion, the FDA or the Drug Enforcement Agency (DEA) will be contacted. The U.S. Customs Canine Enforcement Team inspects arriving international mail for illegal pharmaceuticals. For information about the U.S. Customs Service, visit the agency's Web site at www.customs.ustreas.gov.

To summarize, there are several potential health risks with imported drugs:

1. Quality assurance concerns
2. Counterfeit potential
3. Presence of untested substances
4. Risks of unsupervised use
5. Labeling and language issues
6. Lack of information

**Crossing of National Borders to Buy Drugs.**   On the evening news shows, there are segments showing elderly Americans going on bus trips to Canada to save money on prescription drugs. It is estimated that tens of thousands of Americans are going across the border on buying trips or are buying drugs online from Canadian pharmacies (Parker-Pope, 2002). There can be real cost savings because drugs such as Celebrex (for arthritis) and Tamoxifen (for breast cancer) sell in

Canada at less than half of American prices in U.S. dollars (Parker-Pope, 2003). Another example is the cholesterol-lowering drug Zocor. In 2002, it cost $327.86 for a three-month supply from U.S.-based drugstore.com, but at hometownmeds.com (based in Manitoba, Canada), the price was $189.55 (Parker-Pope, 2003). Depending on the drug and shipping charges, savings may be more or less than this. When a married couple is using a dozen drugs between them, the savings can be $300 or more a month, so it is worth shopping around. The U.S. and Canadian government regulators are looking into increased online shopping behavior, and Canadian regulators are cracking down on unaccredited Canadian pharmacies that are staffed with unregistered pharmacists.

The FDA says people are taking a risk when they buy outside the United States, but not everyone sees it that way, including many physicians, congressmen, and senators. The concern according to *FDA Consumer* is that some of the drugs may be exact and some may not. Consumers report that one problem is that certain doses carried in the United States aren't always available or are sold in quantities that do not match their prescription quantity. The FDA does not have authority to approve drugs sold in Canada. Canada, which is cooperating with U.S. authorities, is having to deal with some of the same regulatory issues, including their citizens buying from other countries over the Internet. Although this section has been primarily about Americans going to Canada, there are similar issues regarding Americans living in the Southwest going to Mexico to find less expensive drugs, and people in other countries traveling to neighboring countries around the world to save money. Crossing borders, physically or online, to buy drugs is an issue to watch, and more international agreements between countries in this regard are under way.

## Doctors Online

"Almost 30% of doctors have their own Web sites, according to the American Medical Association" (Reagan, 2002, p. D4). Web sites have several functions.

- Provide information such as telephone numbers and office addresses
- Attract new patients
- Increase efficiency (for example, an online feature allows patients to fill out their medical history before a visit, thus saving five minutes in the waiting room)
- Announce availability ("We have flu shots available for $15 from October 1–November 15")

**CONSUMER ALERT**

When buying drugs online from Canada or any other country, the U.S. consumer should deal only with a pharmacy that requires a prescription from a U.S. doctor. Also, the consumer should be able to speak to the pharmacist filling the prescription. To be really sure, the consumer should ask the pharmacy what country the drugs are from, request a copy of the pharmacy's license, and ask if the delivery date is guaranteed and in what manner.

Thorny online issues for physicians include whether they should respond to patients' e-mail requests for information and whether they should post warnings (such as "The flu season has arrived"). Many patients would like more interaction with their doctors, but doctors who are already overworked may have a hard time responding to individual e-mails or keeping up-to-date information posted. Another issue is the privacy of e-mail exchanges because messages sent through unsecured servers can be intercepted. Under the Health Insurance Portability and Accountability Act (HIPAA) of 1996, doctors can be fined for compromising the confidentiality of patients' records (Reagan, 2002). In spite of all this, the overall trend is toward more online consultations.

Medem Inc., of San Francisco, is the leading provider of Web sites for doctors. What it has found is that when major changes in medical news hit the media, such as the June 2002 study results that showed potential risks of hormone replacement therapy (HRT), thousands of women scrambled to Web sites for advice. Doctors pay Medem $2.50 per "online visit" and set their own fees for patients, which averaged about $26 when this book was being written. A competitor, Medfusion, offers a secure message system and other features, so as with any other new business, there will be a back-and-forth network between providers, charges, and consumers.

Almost 30 percent of doctors have Web sites and the trend is upward, including the development of a national system of health record access for patients, parents, and health care professionals.

The bottom line is that what works on e-commerce sites may not necessarily work in health care issues because their highly personal and individualistic nature requires special thought and discretion. Clearly, there are ethical, technological, and cost issues to be worked out, but the trend is toward more doctors going online and toward developing a national system where patients, parents, and doctors can easily access health records, such as vaccination records of children, online. A national system would save lives and reduce pain and suffering because Xrays, tests, and other records could be sent immediately to offices, emergency rooms, and operating rooms—the wait or float time while records are being found and sent would be erased. When doctors close their offices, there will be no more announcements or rushes to get records because they will automatically be in the system—they will never be lost. It would also be a boon to the majority of people in this country who move around a lot or are traveling—their records could be accessed immediately, anywhere. Eventually, there will be a worldwide system, or at least cooperative relationships among a number of countries so that people who travel abroad can be assured of their records being available when needed.

# BIOLOGICS

Following a series of tragic deaths from tainted biological products, Congress enacted the Biologics Control Act in 1902. This law gave the FDA's Center for Biologics Evaluation and Research (CBER) authority to regulate biological products and ensure their quality. **Biologics** include vaccines, blood and blood derivatives, allergenic patch tests and extracts, tests to detect HIV and hepatitis, gene therapy products, cells and tissues for transplantation, and new treatments for cancers and arthritis (100 Years of Biologics Regulation, 2002). Key developments since 1902 include polio vaccine, measles vaccine, pertussis vaccine (for whooping cough), blood and plasma products, and the screening of the blood supply. A hundred years ago, the average American could expect to die by age 47. Whooping cough, flu, pneumonia, and diphtheria could kill whole families; if someone got cancer, he or she did not usually live for long. Today 4 out of 10 patients are alive 5 years after diagnosis, and we are nearing additional permanent cures. Life expectancy has greatly increased.

## HEALTH CHALLENGES

The main challenge is to find ways to reduce the three leading causes of death in the United States:

1. Heart disease (31 percent of total deaths)
2. Cancer (23.2 percent of total deaths)
3. Stroke (6.8 percent of total deaths)

Other challenges include ethical issues surrounding tissue transplants and research on gene therapy and the growing costs of health care and prescription drugs. Another challenge is reducing the cost of health care while expanding services to underserved populations—the young, the elderly, rural dwellers, and the poor.

**Malpractice insurance** (insurance doctors or clinics have in case they are sued by patients) is one of the things driving up the costs of health care and shaping the decisions doctors make about what specializations to go into and where to practice because malpractice insurance rates vary by specialization and by state. Many doctors pay over $100,000 a year for malpractice insurance. "An analysis by the American Medical Association finds that the escalating cost of medical-liability insurance is causing doctors to quit, relocate or abandon high-risk practices, creating a health-care crisis in 12 states," including Washington, Oregon, Nevada, Texas, Ohio, West Virginia, Pennsylvania, Florida, New York, New Jersey, Mississippi, and Georgia (Cummings, 2003, p. A4). Doctors have staged rallies in several of these states. On January 1, 2003, West Virginia surgeons "walked out of four hospitals to protest the rising insurance premiums that are driving some to quit and others to abandon high risk specialties such as obstetrics, some surgeries and trauma treatment" (Cummings, 2003, p. A4). Generally, malpractice insurance premiums are highest for obstetricians and orthopedic surgeons. Physicians are pressuring Congress to cap damage awards as one means of bringing down premiums (their payments to insurance companies).

Several powerful groups, including trial lawyers and patients' rights groups, oppose the doctors. These groups make the following two points:

1. Capping awards may not work (and may hurt consumers, especially families with young children who have had severe medical problems and face life-long care and medical expenses).
2. The medical profession could do a better job of policing their own physicians since only a small percentage account for most of the malpractice suits. They would say here is a good opportunity to root out less-than-adequate doctors. They would also say that government boards could do a better job of reprimanding or taking licenses away from errant physicians.

The end of this is not in sight. Two of the proposals being considered are to limit noneconomic patient damages (such as legal and court fees) to $250,000 and to shorten the statute of limitations for filing complaints (Cummings, 2003). In a move

**CONSUMER POWER MODEL**

### On the Treadmill

Body fitness products abound from treadmills to elliptical trainers. *Consumer Reports* tested dozens of treadmill models ranging in price from $500 to $3700. "For the most part, you get what you pay for, especially with treadmills,' says Robert Tiernan, the magazine's editor. A treadmill should have a solid platform with some give or flexibility to it, he says. The top-rated machines cost about $3,000."[1]

Tiernan says you can save money if you are only going to walk, not run. Before you buy any equipment, test it out to see if it fits your stride and typical workout method. Once home, most people use their equipment less than they thought they would and many a treadmill ends up as a coat rack. Watch out for the January effect too, the New Year's fitness resolution which often fizzles by the end of the month.

---

[1] Nanci Hellmich, "Tilting Toward Buying a Treadmill?" *USA Today,* January 8, 2008, p. 6D.

---

toward political activism, in 2003 the AMA moved all of its leadership meetings to Washington to give doctors plenty of opportunity to lobby and influence representatives. From the consumer point of view, what it really comes down to is doctor availability, and there are very critical health concerns connected with this. Patients in primarily rural states have died because the nearest available specialist was six hours or more away. Why? The specialists moved to states with better malpractice insurance rates. This is a many-sided issue involving states, the federal government, the medical profession, attorneys and courts, patients' rights, and consumers' choices.

Another factor driving up the cost of health care is the nursing shortage. Nurses are now being offered signing bonuses, scholarships, more flexible hours, and significantly higher salaries than in the past.

Another substantial cost is the money poured into research and development (R&D), the search for cures. Pharmaceuticals commit a higher percentage to R&D than any other industry—it costs an average of $500 million to discover and develop a single new medicine. Of the thousands of compounds screened for medical potential each year, only a few will pass enough hurdles to get to the human testing stage and be approved by the FDA. If drug prices were lowered or more controlled, would it reduce R&D? Those representing pharmaceutical companies and researchers in the United States and Europe say yes, but those representing consumer groups are more likely to say no. Some consumer advocacy groups argue that the companies should plow more of their profits into R&D. The industry replies that this is not realistic, that price controls are harmful to innovation and discovery, and that cutting back on R&D would be harmful to patients in the long run.

## VACCINES: CONSUMER SAFETY ISSUES

In the early twentieth century, many people died as a result of common infectious diseases and poor environmental conditions such as unrefrigerated food, poor sanitation, and air and water pollution. **Infectious disease** is defined as a disease that is communicable from person to person; the causes are invading microorganisms such as viruses and bacteria. These are different from **chronic disease**, which is a disease that develops and continues over a long period of time. Chronic disease is usually caused by a variety of factors, including lifestyle; examples of chronic disease are heart disease and cancer.

Bioterriorism threats in the twenty-first century have forced a reexamination of the nation's vaccine supply. Do we have enough vaccines? Vaccine shortages frustrate parents, patients, and doctors alike.

> There are many reasons for the shortages. A major reason is the fact that there are relatively few manufacturers in the vaccine business. It's also difficult to make vaccines; from start to finish, a particular batch of a given vaccine requires roughly a year of production time. Unlike most drugs, vaccines are produced from living cells and organisms. Most require growing the immunizing agent, whether it's bacteria or viruses, in a production facility where growth conditions are complex. (Meadows, 2002a, p. 12)

Of particular concern is smallpox vaccine, a possible tool in the war on bioterror. In its recorded 3,000-year history, smallpox has killed hundreds of millions of people. The problem with the vaccine is that it causes life-threatening reactions in 15 of every million people vaccinated, killing 1 or 2 of them (Chase & Hitt, 2002). At highest risk of reaction are babies, pregnant women, people with the common skin rash eczema, and those with weakened immune systems. So doctors are wary to give the vaccine unless it becomes necessary, and government policy makers are tackling the issue of who should get the vaccine first. One idea favored by federal health officials is to offer smallpox vaccinations to the 500,000 hospital workers viewed as most likely to come in contact with patients with smallpox should there be a widespread bioterrorism attack (Chase & Hitt, 2002).

Several vaccines have been in short supply in the past:

1. *Diphtheria, tetanus toxoids, and acellular pertussis (DTaP).* The DTaP supply has returned to normal and is used the most for children ages 6 weeks to 6 years.
2. *Measles, mumps, and rubella (MMR).* The first dose in the two-dose MMR regimen is given between ages 12 and 15 months and the second between ages 4 and 6 years. Supply is now normal (this vaccine has been stockpiled since 1983).
3. *Chickenpox (varicella).* Normally, the recommendation is one dose of varicella vaccine between 12 months and 18 months or at any age after 18 months if a child has not had chickenpox or the vaccine. Supply is now normal.
4. *Pneumococcal conjugate.* Infants normally receive a series of four shots, with the final shot at age 12–15 months. According to manufacturers, supplies were low until 2003.
5. *Tetanus and diphtheria toxoids for adults (Td).* Tds are given as booster shots to adolescents and adults; supply levels are adequate.

A number of government groups, in particular the FDA and the CDC, are working together to ensure a steady supply of vaccines. Discussions are under way regarding how to speed up production and how to stockpile more vaccines. Check with your health care provider about whether you need any of these vaccines as well as others such as flu (influenza vaccines) and hepatitis B vaccine (HBV), which protects against hepatitis B virus. Hepatitis B is spread through contact with blood and body fluids of an infected person. To access the recommended schedule of adult vaccines, go to www.cdc.gov/nip/recs/adult-schedule.htm.

## HARMFUL EFFECTS OF TANNING

A different subject is a health issue that is, for the most part, under our control—how much or how little to tan. **Tanning** is the body's response to skin exposed to ultraviolet radiation (UV) from the sun. The darker side of tanning includes increased risk of skin cancer, eye damage, skin aging, and allergic reactions. Health problems can occur from using sunlamps and tanning beds, as well as from natural sunlight. If using artificial means to tan, the consumer should use goggles and other protective gear and should watch the timing carefully. Using a sunscreen appropriate to exposure and skin type is recommended. The consumer should also be careful about any possible reactions that may occur from the use of certain medications while being exposed to the sun.

Besides the physical problems associated with excessive tanning, consumers should be careful before signing contracts with tanning salons. Tanning salons often go in and out of business, so contracts may not be fulfilled. Individual questions about tanning salons, skin damage, and tanning from the sun should be directed to physicians.

Why do people spend time and money getting a deep tan given the negative health effects? Obviously, they do it to improve their appearance, but it goes beyond that. Getting a tan before going to the beach for the first time may provide

A woman lying on a tanning bed. Note that she is wearing protective goggles.
(Eric Kroll, Omni-Photo Communications, Inc.)

freedom from ridicule—a strong motivator. Also, in consumer theory, there exists a dimension of the want-satisfying nature of products described as **hedonism**, referring to the fact that many products and behaviors (such as tanning) provide sensory benefits—in short, they taste, feel, look, or smell good to us. It is not difficult to understand why someone would want to escape a long, snowy winter to find the sun in the Caribbean or Hawaii.

# BOTOX

Botox is a drug.

Is botox a cosmetic or a drug treatment? Advertisements to the contrary, botox is a drug by FDA definition. **Botox** is made from a toxin produced by the bacterium *Clostridium botulinum.*

> Botulinum Toxin Type A is a protein complex produced by the bacterium *Clostridium botulinum,* which contains the same toxin that causes food poisoning. When used in a medical setting, small doses of an injectable form of sterile purified botulinum toxin blocks the release of a chemical called acetycholine by nerve cells that signals muscle contraction. By selectively interfering with underlying muscles' ability to contract, existing frown lines are smoothed out and in most cases are nearly invisible in a week. (Lewis, 2002, p. 11)

The FDA approved the use of the drug under certain conditions. Drugs, including those used for cosmetic purposes such as Botox, are subject to the FDA approval process. Part of the confusion is that the FDA regulates the products but not how they are used. Botox treatments have been given by nonmedical personnel, which is against the law. Sometimes, a doctor oversaw a clinic or gave his or her name to be used in advertisements, but the actual injections were given by nonmedical personnel such as cosmetics/spa workers or beauticians. Unauthorized people who are caught giving injections are arrested and charged.

Botox gained public attention because it was marketed to groups of people in a party setting. At the parties, adult men and women gathered, paid a fee, signed a consent form, ate snacks and had drinks; then they were led off one by one to treatment rooms where they were sedated and the numbing treatments given (sometimes the numbing does not wear off easily). Common Botox treatment side effects include headache, nausea, respiratory infection, and flu syndrome. One of the main places for injections is the frown lines or wrinkles above the nose. It is not uncommon for someone to go in for Botox treatments every three months. For more information on Botox, see the E-Resources section at the end of this chapter.

# MEDICAL DEVICES, TREATMENTS, AND PROCEDURES

Since the beginnings of recorded time, people have been experimenting with various devices and procedures to restore health. Even today, there are so many fake devices and procedures that it is difficult to put them into categories; many of them defy categorization because they claim to cure so many different kinds of ills. The

## CONSUMER ALERT

Be careful when using health-related Web sites. There are thousands of them, and not all are safe and surfable sites. Examples of reliable sites are given in the E-Resources section of this chapter. When you are deciding about the worthiness of a site, consider the following:

- Who the source is
- Where the information comes from, who wrote it or what institution stands behind it, and how old the information is
- Why the source exists and what it is selling (avoid sites that sell or have testimonials as a sales gimmick, and avoid sites that offer easy or "natural" cures for serious, complex disorders)
- What the message is (look for names you know and trust, and remember that a fraudulent name can be very close to a legitimate source name)

best advice is that if it seems to be too good to be true, it probably is. Some products are harmful and others are merely ineffective. As an example, do warmed-up fist-size stones placed on your back give long-lasting health results? What do you think? Is the treatment worth the $150 spa charge?

The FDA cannot keep up with every device, treatment, or product sold in the marketplace, especially those from foreign countries advertised on the Internet or those cooked up in someone's kitchen and sold at in-home sales parties. The FDA tries to review products, especially those sold nationally, to see if they are effective and do not present unreasonable risk to patients. In short, not everything is thoroughly tested, and most medical devices are cleared only through the premarket notification process, a less rigorous process. Examples of medical devices are contraceptives, defibrillators, lasers, heart devices, breast-imaging devices, wart removal systems, contact lenses, and weight-loss devices. The FDA Web site lists newly approved devices and procedures.

The FDA regulates prescription, OTC, and generic drugs as well as radiation-emitting products such as cell phones, lasers, microwaves, and mammogram machines. The 1993 Mammography Quality Standards Act was reauthorized in 1998 and is set to be revisited in the twenty-first century. Under this act, facilities are initially certified as meeting certain quality standards and then must continue to pass annual inspections. In 1994 a landmark Dietary Supplement Health and Education Act established specific labeling requirements, provided a regulatory framework, and authorized the FDA to promulgate good manufacturing practice regulations for dietary supplements. In 1999 the Food and Drug Administration Modernization Act mandated the most wide-ranging reforms in agency practices since 1918; its provisions included measures to accelerate review of devices and regulate advertising of unapproved drugs and devices. Examples of medical devices regulated by the FDA include pacemakers, contact lenses, and hearing aids.

The challenge of preventive medicine is to get people to focus on feeling better rather than looking thinner or making whatever other appearance change is desired. Many frauds in the health industries have their root in the promise of a more attractive appearance and an easy way to get it, which leads us into the next section on cosmetics.

## COSMETICS

The FDA is the main regulator of cosmetics in the United States—it has its work cut out for it. The number of products grows every day, and there are 13,500 officially recognized cosmetic ingredients, according to the *International Cosmetic Ingredient Dictionary.*

Different types of cosmetics are marketed to different demographic groups around the world. In some countries, skin care is emphasized; in others, the emphasis is more on products that provide color to the skin and lips or a combination of skin care and color enhancement.

The 77 million baby boomers (Americans born between 1946 and 1964) are prime targets for antiaging products, from facial creams to hand lotions. Over the past few years, sales of antiaging products have been growing incredibly fast worldwide. Expensive cosmetics produced in France, Switzerland, and Japan can run as high as $500 an ounce for creams or serums infused with silk extract or gold particles. In a *Consumer Reports* study, the top performer out of nine antiwrinkle brands was the lowest-priced cream selling for $18.99, which beat out competitive brands running as high as $335. So when it comes to cosmetics, "May the buyer beware."

The Food, Drug, and Cosmetic Act defines **cosmetics** (products made to beautify the body by their external application) by their intended use. According to the act, cosmetics are "articles to be rubbed, poured, sprinkled, or sprayed on, introduced into, or otherwise applied to the human body . . . for cleansing, beautifying, promoting attractiveness, or altering the appearance (FD&C Act, section 20[i]). Among the products included in this definition are skin moisturizers, perfumes, lipsticks, fingernail polish, eye and facial makeup preparations, shampoos, permanent waves, hair colors, toothpastes, and deodorants, as well as any material intended for use as a component of a cosmetic product.

Famous name brands may be **aspirational products**, such as Chanel No. 5, meaning that consumers aspire to own them. A perfume or famous-brand cosmetic may fulfill a consumer's desire for acceptance, affiliation, esteem, achievement, prestige, and status. Another consumer may have no interest in what another individual or group thinks but may aspire to own a certain fragrance or cosmetic to fulfill a personal sense of happiness, beauty, or pleasure.

Companies try to satisfy different needs and may even position a product to fulfill several levels of needs. Thus, advertising for the same product may vary greatly from media outlet to media outlet. Depending on the **cues**—ads, signs, packaging, and other stimuli—the individual will respond positively, neutrally, or negatively. If there is a positive response, it is because the cue worked, that is, it somehow struck a nerve or fulfilled a drive. When no one responds, the marketers or product manufacturers have missed their target. Research studies show that when consumers purchase cosmetics, they pursue convenience, enjoyment, prestige maintenance, utility, and fulfillment and experience a cancellation of a sense of uneasiness (Yoo, Hong & Jung, 2006). If people are unsure about their appearance, cosmetics may be bought for reassurance, and the wise salesperson knows this.

A few years ago, manufacturers and advertisers tried to get most of the American adult population interested in applying a special foot deodorant to their feet on a daily basis, just as they apply deodorant under their arms. Consumers failed to pick up the cues because they didn't perceive foot odor to be an everyday kind of problem deserving their attention. This is a good example of consumers driving the marketplace—they will not buy a product if they do not perceive a need.

When it comes to cosmetics, some consumers are experimental, meaning they like to try new brands and products, whereas others are brand loyal, preferring the tried-and-true. In fact, the latter type gets quite upset when their favorite lipstick or scent is no longer available. Cosmetics companies play into both experimental and stick-to-it types with promotions or samples of new products coupled with a few conventional products. Samples, as a type of cue, create the perception of a want or a need. Once a sample is tried, a certain percentage of customers will buy a full-size product—if not for themselves, then for someone on their gift list.

Can a product be both a drug and a cosmetic? Yes, some products meet both definitions. For example, a shampoo is a cosmetic because it is intended to clean hair, but an antidandruff shampoo also contains a drug to treat dandruff, so it is both a drug and a cosmetic. Other examples of duo products are toothpastes that contain fluoride, deodorants that are also antiperspirants, and moisturizers and makeup that provide sun protection.

The FDA only regulates cosmetics after products are released to the marketplace; ingredients or products are not reviewed or approved by the FDA prior to being sold to the public. If the FDA wishes to remove a cosmetic from the market, it must first prove in a court of law that the product may be injurious to users, is improperly labeled, or otherwise violates the law. The FDA inspects cosmetics manufacturing facilities, collects samples to check, and takes action through the Department of Justice. Foreign products may be refused entry into the United States.

## Labeling

Personal care products can produce unwanted effects such as skin irritations and allergies. About 10 percent of the population has adverse reactions to cosmetics and toiletries ("The Hype in 'Hypoallergenic,'" 2002). Fragrance is the most common irritant, but emulsifiers and preservatives can also be irritating. One of the ways consumers can minimize adverse effects is to know their skin type and read labels. The drawback to suggesting that consumers read labels is that they would have to be chemists to understand many of the ingredients.

> About 10 percent of the population has adverse reactions to cosmetics and toiletries. Fragrance is the most common irritant.

According to the FDA Web site, federal regulations require ingredients to be listed on product labels in descending order by quantity. Consumers can check the ingredient listing to identify ingredients they want to avoid. Based on the amount used, an ingredient such as water is usually found at the beginning of the product's ingredient list while color additives and fragrances (usually present in small amounts) are normally seen at the end of the listing. These rules apply only to products for home use; professionally used products are not required to have ingredient declarations. The FDA regulates the labeling directly on the product, and ads for cosmetics in magazines, in newspapers, or on television are monitored by the FTC.

## Hypoallergenic Products

A common claim is that cosmetics are hypoallergenic. Consumers with sensitive skin are drawn to them, but in reality there are no federal standards or definitions governing the term *hypoallergenic*. What consumers find on a list of ingredients on the product label are ingredients that usually are compatible with sensitive skin, but there are no guarantees. Manufacturers are not required to disclose the components of fragrances, which (as stated earlier) are the most common irritants. To help fill this gap in consumer information, the Consumer Union has an Eco-Labels program and a Web site (www.eco-labels.org) that explains labels such as "hypoallergenic" and "unscented." So if you want to know if a cosmetic is, for example, alcohol-free, then you can go to the Web site and find the information about a specific product. Besides toiletries, this site also discusses cleaning products, food, and wood products.

## Organic Beauty: Natural or Environmentally Friendly Products

Certified organic beauty products must contain at least 70 percent certified organic ingredients that come from natural sources such as nuts, flowers, and fruits.

Just as there are organic foods, there are organic beauty products. Are they better? How much is hype? To be certified organic, a beauty product must contain at least 70 percent certified organic ingredients, which means they come from natural sources such as nuts, flowers, and fruits. They should be cultivated in pesticide-free soil and be free of spraying. Regular and organic cosmetics are formulated to be irritation-free, but an individual may have a reaction. Differences may be found in scents, preservatives, colors, and emollients (oils, essential fatty acids). Organic products may not last as long as regular cosmetics with preservatives, so the rule of thumb is to use the product in a timely fashion and to throw out anything that smells, separates, or looks bad. There have been reports that organic cosmetics are more likely to have purity problems. Choosing organic or environmentally friendly products comes down to personal preference; they may be more compatible with both your skin and your politics than conventional products. Connected to this are concerns about the use of animals in product testing. Many consumers prefer cosmetics that do not use animal testing in research and development, so some companies put this on their label or manufacture whole lines of products in North America and in Europe that do not use animal testing.

## Tooth Whiteners: Road to Glamour

It used to be that entertainers had to frequent a Hollywood dentist to get really white teeth, with the treatments being done over several weeks' or months' worth of appointments in the dentist's chair. But with new technologies and inventions, there are now more effective in-office dental treatments and home-based do-it-yourself kits. Is there a market? Yes—a whopping 93 percent of Americans worry about their teeth being yellow or stained according to a survey by Trident. The dental-bleaching business has gone from nearly nothing to billions of dollars in annual sales for oral-care kits within the last few years. Sales for "tooth polishes" more than doubled in 2002, and Procter & Gamble alone had $1 billion in oral-care sales (De Lisser, 2003). Teeth darken with age, so treatments work best on those over 30 years of age and those with a history of coffee drinking and smoking.

Whiteners come in a variety of ways, including bottles, swabs, little brushes, strips, and tooth trays to collect the drool. Prices range from $15 to nearly a $1,000. Do they work? The answer is that it depends on the product and the person's teeth, as well as on how well the person follows the directions. Journalists and *Consumer Reports* have been testing the dental-bleaching products, and since these products are being perfected, it is best to continue watching for the best-performing products. To establish a baseline (what your teeth are like before treatment), a dentist can use a shade guide; then he or she can check your teeth to see how much they have whitened after the treatment is completed. While at the dentist's office, ask what treatment may be right for you. When looking at whitening toothpastes, look for the American Dental Association (ADA) seal of approval. For more information, visit the ADA Web site at www.ada.org.

One of the most expensive treatments is the Zoom! Chairside Whitening System (about $825, depending on the dentist). In this treatment, gel is applied to teeth and activated by a special light. The actual whitening takes close to 90 minutes. During this time, the patient sits in a chair, he or she wears protective goggles, and his or her mouth is stretched open with a dental expander. Some people get panicky or experience claustrophobia while they wait, but the outcome of whiter teeth has been documented (De Lisser, 2003). For much less expense, Colgate Simply White is a gel applied to individual teeth with a tiny brush, twice a day for 14 days, at home. One of the most advertised products is Crest Professional Whitestrips, which are plastic strips worn on the top and bottom teeth for at least 30 minutes twice a day. It should be noted that most of the treatments involve some form of tooth pain afterward that tapers off.

The point of this section is that consumers are always interested in new health or cosmetic products, especially ones that have the promise of enhancing their appearance. Different generations tend to focus on different parts of the body, such as shiny hair or whiter teeth. Fads come and go, but the fact that consumers want to improve their appearance is a permanent human condition.

## ALCOHOL AND TOBACCO CONSUMPTION

Now the chapter turns its attention to the more serious topic of potentially addictive behavior—alcohol and tobacco consumption. **Addictions** are habits that have gotten out of control, resulting in a negative impact on one's health that often spills over into other aspects of life such as personal relationships or the ability to do work.

### Alcohol Consumption

**Alcohol**, a colorless, pungent liquid, is the intoxicating ingredient found in fermented liquors (Insel & Roth, 2002). The common use of the word *alcohol* refers to the intoxicating ingredients found in beer, wine, and distilled spirits (hard liquor); chemists would use the term *ethyl alcohol* or *ethanol*. A drink is an alcoholic beverage that delivers one-half ounce of pure ethanol. Examples are 5 ounces of wine, 12 ounces of beer, and one-half ounce of distilled liquor (80-proof scotch, rum, vodka, or whiskey). People have different tolerance levels, so it is difficult to determine what would be a moderate amount. The generally accepted definition of moderation is not more than one drink per average-size woman and two drinks per average-size man per day (Whitney & Rolfes, 2002). Alcohol consumption has both short- and long-term effects. The most horrifying long-term effects are those of babies born to mothers who abused alcohol, which is called **fetal alcohol syndrome**.

Why is alcohol abuse a consumer issue? Society pays a very high price for alcohol abuse, including the harm caused by drunk-driving accidents, homicides, suicides, and unintentional injuries, not to mention the health effects, insurance costs, lost workdays, and lower productivity. The average American spends 61¢ a day on alcohol, compared with 59¢ a day on prescription drugs. A 5-ounce glass of wine has about 100 calories, a 12-ounce regular beer about 150 calories, and 1.5 ounces of 80-proof distilled spirits about 100 calories.

The liquor industry has voluntary advertising guidelines, including self-imposed bans, but according to George Hacker, director of the Center for Science in the Public Interest's (CSPI) alcohol policies project, the ads for fruit-flavored alcohol drinks are luring millions of teenagers. He says, "Those ads put liquor brand names right in kids' faces (Alcohol Ads Reaching Teens, 2002, p. 3A). An example is alcoholic lemonade; it has the same amount of alcohol as beer, but the alcohol taste is masked by the lemonade. Another product category appealing to young consumers is the "malternative" beverages, ads for which feature loud music and attractive young people laughing or dancing. In a survey taken by a polling firm for CSPI, an estimated 22 million teenagers—3 out of 4 people ages 12 to 18—watch television after 9:00 P.M. on school nights when alcohol ads are typically run; furthermore, 6 in 10 teens could name a specific company or brand that advertises during that time. Another product aimed at young people is "zippers," fruit-flavored gelatin cups containing 12 percent alcohol, roughly the same amount found in a glass of wine. In 2002, "zippers" were sold in at least 20 states, and the Community Anti-Drug Coalition of America spoke out against them. Grocery stores were selling "zippers" without proper labeling, making it easier for underage drinkers to buy them. The packaging looked like the type of dessert packs that thousands of children eat every day, so parents were unaware of what their children were consuming.

*About 30 percent of the American population is under age 21, but certain magazines that run alcohol ads draw a higher percentage of young readers.*

About 30 percent of the American population is under age 21, but certain publications draw a higher percentage of young readers than others. For example, *Spin* magazine draws 48 percent of readers under the legal drinking age of 21, according to data used by ad executives. *Allure* has 44 percent underage readers, and *Rolling Stone* has 35 percent. Each of these magazines has alcohol ads, including products such as V. O. Seagram Co.'s Absolut Vodka (Wells, Burnett & Moriarty, 2000).

Less than socially responsible ads have been removed from circulation, such as those showing people drinking while driving or boating. But in general, liquor ads show well-dressed young adults out as a group in an attractive setting having fun while drinking, so drinking is portrayed as a social activity. In reality, a lot of excessive drinking takes place behind closed doors at home, alone—not an appealing image.

## Smoking and Nicotine Products

*Three out of four smokers cannot quit.*

**Tobacco** refers to the leaves of cultivated plants prepared for smoking, chewing, or using as snuff (Insel & Roth, 2002). **Nicotine** is a poisonous addictive substance found in tobacco that is responsible for many of the effects of tobacco (Insel & Roth, 2002). It is addictive—three out of four smokers want to quit but find they cannot (Insel & Roth, 2002).

Cigarette smoking contains many toxic and carcinogenic (cancer-causing) chemicals that affect both the person smoking and the people breathing in tobacco smoke in the nearby environment. The debate about the use of smoking and nicotine products often circulates around the issue of individual choice versus the rights of others and leads to discussions of how much should be regulated or banned. In various states there are initiatives or laws that limit or ban smoking in restaurants. One state was experimenting with eliminating smoking outside state buildings, requiring employees to smoke at least 50 feet away from state office buildings and specifying that no benches or other seating or shelters would be made available. In the debate, consumers may disagree with one another (smokers versus nonsmokers). Generally consumer groups want more regulations because of the dangers inherent in secondhand smoke inhalation, and the industry (in it for the profit) wants fewer. Other issues include how much to tax smoking and nicotine products, use of age restrictions, health warnings on labels, and advertising. There are related product issues, such as candy cigarettes, which are a bad idea because they encourage children to imitate smoking behaviors. Should tobacco company advertisers be allowed to use cartoonlike characters in ads? How much risk disclosure is necessary on product labels and in advertising?

Many government groups actively set policies, taxation, and regulations on tobacco products. As one example, in 1995 the FDA declared cigarettes to be "drug delivery devices," and restrictions were proposed on marketing and sales to reduce smoking by young people. However, some consumer groups feel there are double messages because tobacco farmers are given crop subsidies (money from the federal government to grow or not grow crops) while at the same time consumption of cigarettes is taxed. They wonder why the government is supporting the industry that has so many devastating effects on the health of the nation—in the United States, more than 400,000 deaths a year are associated with cigarette smoking.

Nicotine products range from gums and chewing tobacco to bottled waters. Some are marketed as a smoking substitute (for example, you can drink when you can't light up on an airplane or in the office, or you can use tobacco as a way to lose weight). Others are marketed as a way to quit or reduce smoking. Nicotine addiction is considered a disease. The FDA has ruled that nicotine water is an unapproved drug under the Federal Food, Drug, and Cosmetic Act and therefore cannot be marketed without going through the approval process. The FDA has warned that nicotine lollipops and lip balm, which had been selling over the Internet without a doctor's prescription, are also illegal. Children were getting hold of the lollipops, lip balm, waters, and gums. Several groups, including the National Center for Tobacco-Free Kids, the AMA, and the American Lung Association, have joined together to ban nicotine water marketed to children.

*Cigarette smoking is declining in the United States.*

The percentage of U.S. adults who smoke cigarettes is dropping. In 2008 the percentage was 20 percent, compared with 28 percent in 1984.

## HEALTHY PEOPLE INITIATIVE

The U.S. government has a national Healthy People Initiative that seeks to prevent unnecessary diseases and disabilities and to achieve a better quality of life for all. It has set two national goals for 2010:

1. Increase quality and number of years of healthy life.
2. Eliminate health disparities among groups in the population.

The second goal is needed because health problems disproportionately affect certain populations such as ethnic minorities, less educated or less wealthy people, and people with disabilities.

The federal government has a vital interest in the health of all citizens because a healthy population is the nation's greatest resource—the foundation of its vitality, creativity, and true wealth. Conversely, poor health is a drain on the nation's resources.

## SUMMARY

As seen in the previous chapter on food and beverages, the Food and Drug Administration (FDA) is the main regulator of health-related products and (as its name implies) of drugs. The emphasis in the chapter was on legal drugs, such as those gained by prescription or sold over the counter. The Harrison Act of 1914 prohibited the use of cocaine, morphine, and opiates for nonmedical purposes.

Besides safety concerns, there are cost maintenance concerns because health care costs are skyrocketing; on average, they are increasing faster than most other areas of consumer expenditures. What consumers seek is the best health care at a reasonable price. Preventive self-help is one way to reduce costs, and another way consumers pay less is by using generic drugs. It is estimated that 44 percent of all prescriptions in the United States are filled with generic drugs. Issues in the twenty-first century include the continued search for cures and the ethical issues surrounding tissue replacement, fertility treatments, and research on gene therapy. The threat of legal action (malpractice lawsuits) has driven up the cost of providing health care, as have labor costs in general. To save money, some American citizens are buying drugs by traveling to other countries or by ordering drugs over the Internet, both of which raise quality-control issues.

About 30 percent of doctors have their own Web sites, and the trend is increasing. More and more medical advice and information are being offered over the Internet, and there is a push to switch to e-records in the entire health industry. With this system, parents could look up their child's vaccination records online, and this type of information would also be beneficial to schools and universities.

Consumers should be aware of quality issues, and guidelines for determining them were given in the chapter. Cosmetics as well as alcohol and tobacco use were covered. There are many health care and cosmetic products that are fraudulent. The chapter presented different reasons for why consumers are so susceptible to this particular area of fraud (mostly false hope winning out over reason), why they may choose not to report fraud problems, and why they may choose to ignore science. Some products are classified as both cosmetics and drugs (for example, dandruff shampoos).

National legislation to stop adult intake of alcohol (most specifically the Eighteenth Amendment to the Constitution passed in 1919 and repealed in 1933, more commonly referred to as Prohibition) has failed. The Federal Trade Commission (FTC) is the main regulator of advertising of alcohol and tobacco/nicotine products. Studies have shown that teenagers are quite aware of the brand names of alcohol products that are advertised on television. In the United States, more than 400,000 deaths a year are related to tobacco use.

## KEY POINTS

1. Consumer health is an umbrella term encompassing the decisions consumers make about their health care and lifestyle.
2. Many health care frauds exist. Be especially wary of suspicious cancer cures and HIV-AIDS cures. The FTC has clamped down on fraudulent treatments. Other government agencies, such as the FDA and the CDC, are dedicated to protecting the public's health.
3. Health is your greatest asset.
4. Health care costs are rising significantly, and about 40 million Americans do not have health insurance.
5. Cigarette smoking is declining in the United States.
6. Congress enacted the Biologics Control Act in 1902, giving the FDA the authority to regulate biological products such as vaccines to ensure their quality.
7. Infectious disease is communicable from person to person; it is caused by invading microorganisms such as viruses and bacteria. One of the great advances of the twentieth century was a decrease in the percentage of deaths due to infectious diseases.
8. The top three causes of death in the United States are heart disease, cancer, and stroke.
9. Botox is a drug that is FDA regulated.
10. When it comes to cosmetics, there are no federal standards or definitions of the term *hypoallergenic*.
11. Some cosmetics and scents are aspirational products, meaning consumers aspire to own them.
12. Debates on limiting cigarette smoking usually revolve around individual rights versus the rights of others.

## KEY TERMS

| | | |
|---|---|---|
| addictions | fetal alcohol syndrome | prescription drugs |
| agent | generic drug | principal |
| alcohol | hedonism | quacks |
| aspirational products | infectious disease | science |
| biologics | junk science | scientific literacy |
| botox | lack of efficacy | tanning |
| chronic disease | malpractice insurance | tobacco |
| consumer health | Medicare | well-being |
| cosmetics | nicotine | wellness |
| cues | over-the-counter (OTC) | |
| drugs |     drugs | |

## DISCUSSION QUESTIONS

1. Why would someone pay $500 an ounce for an antiaging facial cream? Which U.S. government agency regulates cosmetics? How does it define cosmetics?

2. According to Robert Park, author and commentator, how do the media promote fraudulent products?
3. How long does it take before a patent usually runs out on an FDA-approved drug? Are all drugs available in generic form?
4. Why are people hesitant to use generic drugs?
5. How can a product be both a drug and a cosmetic? Give at least three examples of products that are both.
6. Select a Web site in the E-Resources section, and report on what you find on a specific body-related issue such as drugs, biologics, medical devices, or cosmetics.

## E-RESOURCES

*General tip:* If you are looking for someone who works for the government, there is a good chance you can locate that person through a Web page called the U.S. Government Telephone and E-Mail Directories, sponsored by FirstGov; the page is a gateway for contacting elected officials, federal employees, and military personnel. This site links to the National Contact Center where there is information about health issues and Medicare, as well as other topics.

**Medical and Health**

**American Cancer Society**    *www.cancer.org*

**American Dental Association (ADA)**    *www.ada.org*

**American Heart Association**    *www.americanheart.org*

**American Medical Association (AMA)**    *www.amaassn.org*

**American Psychological Association (APA)**    *www.apa.org/psychnet*

**Centers for Disease Control and Prevention (CDC)**    *www.cdc.gov*

**Federal Trade Commission (FTC)**    *www.ftc.gov*

**Healthfinder**    *www.healthfinder.gov*

**Mayo Clinic**    *www.mayoclinic.com*

**Medscape and CBS Healthwatch**    *www.medscape.com*

**National Cancer Institute**    *www.cancer.gov    PersonalPath.com*
Created by doctors and nurses, this Web site covers health, illnesses, treatments, medications, benefits, costs, and ways to find help. It includes direct links to other Web sites, such as the Harvard Health Letter and Care Guides. You can research your symptoms or conditions and learn before your doctor visit about treatment options, tests, free clinical trials, prescriptions, and side effects.

**U.S. Health and Human Services Office on Women's Health**    *www.4women. gov*

**WebMD**    *www.webmd.com*

**Botox and Plastic Surgery**

**American Academy of Dermatology**    *www.aad.org*

**American Society for Aesthetic Plastic Surgery**    *www.asaps.org*

**American Society for Dermatologic Surgery**    *www.aboutskinsurgery.com*

**New England Journal of Medicine**    *www.nejm.org*

If you or someone you know needs guidance or someone to talk to regarding alcohol or drug use, contact your health care provider or a counselor. In addition to services on campus, the following organizations specialize in alcohol and other drug problems:

**Alcohol and Drugs**

**Alateen and Al-Anon (for family members and friends of persons with addictions)**    *www.al-anon-alateen.org*

**Alcoholics Anonymous (AA) (for persons with alcohol problems)**
*www.alcoholics-anonymous.org*

**American Society of Addiction Medicine**    *www.asam.org*

**Narcotics Anonymous (NA) (for persons with other drug problems)**
*www.na.org*

**National Clearinghouse for Alcohol and Drug Information**    *www.health.org*

**National Council on Alcoholism and Drug Dependence**    *www.ncadd.org*

**Smoking and Disease**

**Centers for Disease Control and Prevention (CDC)**    *www.cdc.gov*

**World Health Organization (WHO)**    *www.who.int*

**Smoking, Addiction, and Quitting**

**Centers for Disease Control and Prevention (CDC)**    *www.cdc.gov*

**National Center Institute (NCI)**    *www.nci.nih.gov*

**QuitNet**    *www.quitnet.org*

**U.S. Food and Drug Administration (FDA)**    *www.fda.gov*

**Secondhand Smoke**

**Environmental Protection Agency (EPA)**    *www.epa.gov*

**International Agency for Research on Cancer**    *www.iarc.fr*

## REFERENCES

Alcohol ads reaching teens (July 17, 2002). *Tallahassee Democrat,* p. 3A.

Chase, M., and G. Hitt. (October 21, 2002). Ugly side effects of smallpox vaccine color terror plans. *Wall Street Journal,* p. A1.

Cummings, J. (January 14, 2003). Doctors' activism revives malpractice bill. *Wall Street Journal*, p. A4.

De Graaf, J., D. Wann, and T. Naylor. (2001). *Affluenza: The all-consuming epidemic*. San Franciso, CA: Berrett-Koehler Publishers.

De Lisser, E. (January 14, 2003). The cranky consumer works on its smile. *Wall Street Journal*, p. D1.

Engstrom, P. (September 30, 2002). Medical sleuths. *Wall Street Journal*, p. R6.

Fleck, C. (January 2003). Cancer and snake oil. *AARP Bulletin*, p. 18.

*FTC facts for consumers: Miracle health claims: Add a dose of skepticism* (2003). Washington, DC.

Generics may be "equivalent," cheaper, but consumers resist (July–August 2002). *AARP Bulletin*, p. 13.

Huge profits in drug stocks. (July 2002). *Louis Rukeyser's Wall Street*, pp. 5–6.

Hype in "hypoallergenic," (June 2002). *Consumer Reports*, p. 6.

Insel, P., and W. Roth. (2002). *Core concepts in health*, 9th ed. Boston: McGraw-Hill.

Lewis, C. (July–August 2002). Botox cosmetics: A look at looking good. *FDA Consumer*, pp. 11–13.

Meadows, M. (September–October 2002a). *FDA Consumer*, pp. 12–14.

Meadows, M. (September–October 2002b). *FDA Consumer*, pp. 18–23.

100 years of biologics regulation. (July–August 2002). *FDA Consumer*, 36 (4), pp. 8–10.

Park, R. L. (2000). *Voodoo science: The road from foolishness to fraud*. Oxford: Oxford University Press.

Parker-Pope, T. (October 22, 2002). The ins and outs of getting drugs (the legal kind) from across the border. *Wall Street Journal*, p. D1.

Parker-Pope, T. (January 14, 2003). That veggie wrap you just chowed down is more fattening than a ham sandwich. *Wall Street Journal*, p. D1.

Reagan, B. (October 21, 2002). Handle with care. *Wall Street Journal*, p. R4.

Wells, W., J. Burnett, and S. Moriarty. (2000). *Advertising: Principles & practice*, 5th ed. Upper Saddle River, NJ: Prentice Hall.

Whitney, E., and S. Rolfes. (2002). *Understanding nutrition*, 9th ed. Belmont, CA: Wadsworth.

Yoo, C. J., S. T. Hong, and H. E. Jung. (2006). In-depth study on women's needs for makeup and consumption behavior of cosmetics products. *Journal of Korean Academic Society of Business*, 35 (1), 21–49.

# Ownership, Safety, and Repairs

> There is no right to strike against the public safety by anybody, anywhere, any time.
> —Calvin Coolidge

## Learning Objectives

1. Explain the value of warranties and guarantees.
2. Discuss the fact that many products cause injury and harm.
3. Explain what the U.S. Consumer Product Safety Commission does.
4. Know how to minimize the potential for home improvement and travel frauds.
5. Discuss sources of travel safety alerts and ways to stay safer when traveling.
6. Discuss the postpurchase life of products, including disposition.

---

### Ownership, Safety, and Repairs: Home Remodelers Beware!

*Consumer Reports* editor Daniel DeClerico says, "Whenever possible, get samples of your top choices. Live with them for a few days, seeing how they look under different light conditions (this is especially important with interior paint). And if you have any doubts about performance, don't be afraid to conduct your own tests. 'I tell my clients to cut stone samples, scratch them, spill wine on them, or ink or cooking oil,' says South Carolina kitchen designer Duval Acker.[1]

"As for countertops made from slate or any other stone, slabs do differ from quarry to quarry. 'There are 6,000 varieties of materials, and every one of them is unique,' says Church Muehlbauer, technical director of the Marble Institute of America. That's why it's important for you to work with a reputable distributor who really knows the specific stones it carries."[2]

---

[1]Daniel DiClerico, "Avoid Remodeler's Remorse," Consumer Reports.org, November 7, 2007.
[2]Ibid.

---

## INTRODUCTION

As you can see from the title, this is an eclectic chapter. The previous one focused on health and wellness issues; this one covers a myriad of topics regarding home and vehicle repairs and the safety of consumer products. These are important areas to cover

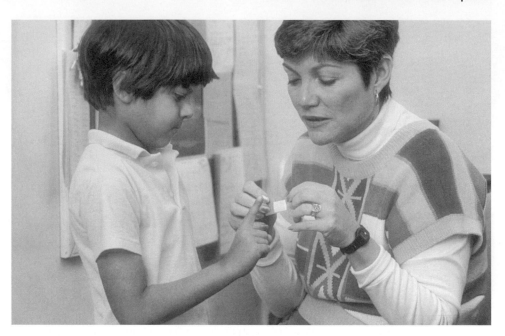

A school nurse places a bandage on a small boy. (Stephen McBrady, PhotoEdit Inc.)

because many consumer complaints arise from faulty repairs and other services that don't live up to expectations. Severe injuries or death can result, so safety concerns go beyond mere inconvenience and questions about restitution. The chapter focuses on how products are used after purchase, how they perform, and how they are disposed of. Public awareness of the hazards of everyday products is also discussed, as are the functions of the main consumer safety agencies that handle complaints.

Can consumers be sure of safety? Federal and state agencies have recalled many products, ranging from lawn motors to toys, because of defects or potential safety hazards. Products for infants and children are covered because child safety is paramount. Manufacturers should pretest toys, and parents should read product labels to determine if their child is old enough for a certain toy. Locking up household chemicals, drugs, and firearms is also an important safety measure. Further, this chapter covers travel fraud and travel safety, including where to find sources of regular alerts about places of particular concern. If planning to travel or work abroad, this section and the E-Resources should not be missed. Keeping yourself and your money safe is part of the general topic of safety.

A recurring theme throughout the chapter is the importance of information gathering. For example, consumers should read and understand warranties. You may recall from Chapter 2 that the right to safety and the right to information are two of the four basic rights in President John F. Kennedy's Consumer Bill of Rights.

## CONSUMER RESEARCH ON PRODUCT USE AND NONUSE

Before we can talk about safety and repairs, we need to explore how goods are used or not used. You read that right. A lot of things that are bought are never used or only partially used. Consumer research typically deals with three processes pertaining to the use of goods and services (Jacoby, Berning & Dietvorst, 1977):

1. Decision making
2. Usage
3. Disposal

We discussed decision making (prepurchase, purchase, and postpurchase) in Chapter 6. This chapter explores the last two on the list, which are the least re-searched. Within these categories is the rather peculiar one of items or services that are bought and never used or rarely used. In an earlier chapter we talked about how foods are bought and never used, but other items include membership in health and fitness clubs, in-home exercise equipment, sports equipment, small kitchen appliances, vitamins and supplements, crafts, sewing machines, high-tech goods, personal care items (such as hair gel, aftershave, and perfume), and clothes. What have you got sitting around your house that you rarely or never use?

**Underutilization** is a condition where consumers use a product, but only to a small fraction of the extent to which they intended to use it (Trocchia & Swinder, 2002). Anger, embarrassment, and guilt may be associated with underutilization, or the buyer may simply have lost interest in the product or service. Interests change frequently regarding foods, books, workout equipment or clubs, and video games. People may throw themselves into a new hobby or life change and buy everything associated with it and then change their minds. For example, an individual may try to grow orchids, put in special growing lights, and in the process spend several thousand dollars and uncountable hours of work; when all the orchids die, he or she decides there must be an easier hobby. There may be concerns about physical injury, or an illness may prevent or lessen use of clubs or equipment. Other life changes include changes in marital status, children, educational or career goals, or geographic location (snow skis aren't much use in Hawaii).

A product may disappoint as well—perhaps it is not as much fun or it does not smell as good or taste as yummy as hoped. The product or service may not trans-form the user into a popular or attractive person, as had been hoped. When it comes to in-home products, there are storage and maintenance issues as well. A waffle iron, for instance, may be too much trouble to haul out and clean after use, so a consumer may decide that a frozen waffle popped in the toaster is nearly as good and a lot less trouble than whipping up waffle mix, cooking, and cleaning up afterward.

To summarize, many products and services are purchased and then rarely or never used. There are various reasons for underutilization or nonuse:

- *Impulsiveness.* One respondent in a survey said, "Even though I knew that the [high-heeled] shoes would hurt my feet, I bought them anyway" (Trocchia & Swinder, 2002, p. 191). As another example, after a cooking demonstration in a store, someone may impulsively think he or she needs a special gadget or ingredient when the one already at home would suffice.
- *Sale purchases.* A sale purchase might be made at a promotion such as three T-shirts for $10 when only one is needed. If the purchase was inexpensive, people may shrug their shoulders and say, "Oh well, it didn't cost much, so if I get only a couple of wearings, that is okay."
- *Function problems.* Purchased items often have maintenance difficulties or disappointing results, and the buyer may have difficulties using the product

(Trocchia & Swinder, 2002). Examples are food preparation devices such as grills, juice machines, lawn mowers, cosmetic/personal care treatments, and clothes that wrinkle easily or are difficult to care for (for example, requiring washing by hand and drying flat).

- *Ill-fitting or malfunctioning products.* After an item is purchased, it either doesn't fit or doesn't work.
- *Self-consciousness.* People are not comfortable using or wearing the product after buying it. The product is not consistent with their self-image or with other people's image of them. An individual may feel like an idiot wearing the item, or a child may say that the style is too young-looking.
- *Concerns about personal injury.* The use of new power tools or recreational equipment may engender safety concerns.
- *Loss of interest or enthusiasm.* Consumers may decide they don't need the product or service; examples include language tapes, humorous items or toys, and exercise equipment.
- *Lifestyle changes.* Soon after an item is bought, the consumer's lifestyle changes and the item is no longer necessary or desired.

It is true that businesses make money from products and services that are bought and never used, but nonuse is not good for repeat business. An unhappy buyer may spread bad word-of-mouth information, which further brings down sales, but money-back guarantees and generous return policies can reduce the number of disgruntled customers. Because of embarrassment or loss of interest, the consumer may not pursue getting a refund or returning a product, representing a waste of resources. Businesses and government agencies that handle complaints and recalls should do all they can to encourage use of products and services, and if the customer is not satisfied, they should do what they can to encourage redress. Presenting realistic views of products and services in the first place would reduce the incidence of nonuse.

Underutilization also points to the fact that consumer behavior is imprecise—mistakes are made. In order to save money and heartache (guilt, anger, or whatever), consumers need to try to lessen nonuse, perhaps by knowing themselves better and by spending more time on the decision end of the consumption process. Another remedy is to take advantage of the warranties and money-back or replacement guarantees (discussed next).

## WARRANTIES AND GUARANTEES: PERCEPTIONS AND REALITIES

In previous chapters, we've covered the importance of price and brand name in consumer decision making, especially in determining quality. National brands are perceived by many as better than generic or store brands. As examples, consumers may think that a Band-Aid from Johnson & Johnson Inc. may be better than a store brand or that a name-brand sweater is better quality than a store-brand sweater. Other indicators of quality are country of manufacture and warranties. A lot of this has to do with perception: Would you think a camera or car from Japan is better than one manufactured in Russia? Do you think Egyptian cotton is better than Malaysian cotton?

Research indicates that the longer and more inclusive the warranty, the better the quality of the product is assumed to be (Boulding & Kirmani, 1993). A product with a five-year warranty is assumed to be better than one with a three-month warranty. But what happens if the company goes out of business? Regardless of length, the warranty may be worthless. Note the word *inclusive* because besides length, consumers need to know what is covered, that is, what types of repairs, replacement parts, and product conditions are included.

In order to sell products, marketers extol the virtues of goods such as an extended warranty. They have found that the more variables or attributes presented, the greater is the perception of reduction of risk, which is referred to as **attribute-based choices**. Warranties and guarantees are very important to risk reduction. One associates them with higher-priced items, but they can apply to less expensive ones. For example, a shampoo can be guaranteed to give satisfaction, or your money is refunded in full. Some clothing stores will allow returns at any time for any reason, and others are more selective, perhaps having a three-month-from-purchase return policy or no returns on sale items.

Besides manufacturers and stores, service businesses such as dry cleaners or home inspection businesses provide warranties or guarantees (a checklist is given in Table 10.1). To complicate things, attributes are not equally weighted. Price may be by far the most important attribute in a product purchase, or it may be quick service or brand name; for example, a person may prefer a certain brand of deodorant and will not buy any other at any price. On the other hand, a product line may be eliminated as too expensive, such as a $2,000 flat-screen television. In a competitive market, one product maker will emphasize price as a dominant evaluative criterion in its advertisement, whereas a competitor will stress other aspects such as safety or warranties. Another example of attributes is features weighting. A person may want not only a safe car with a good warranty but also a car with automatic windows and air conditioning.

In economics, rational choice theory assumes a rational decision maker has well-defined preferences. Each option or alternative in a choice set is assumed to have a value to the consumer that depends on the characteristics of that option, and consumers are assumed to have sufficient skill to determine which options best suit their needs—they will maximize their value, getting the most for their money and needs. As we know from earlier chapters, rationality does not always exist. Consumers are said to have **bounded rationality**, meaning a limited capacity for processing information. What does this have to do with warranties and guaranties? In a word, *everything* because unless they are lawyers, consumers cannot

**Table 10.1**    Product or Service Comparison Checklist*

| Evaluative Criteria | Brand A (Name) | Brand B (Name) |
|---|---|---|
| Price | | |
| Size/dimensions | | |
| Country of origin | | |
| Warranty/guaranty | | |
| Repairs/service/refunds | | |
| Reputation of company | | |

*Suggested rating system: 1 equals very poor and 5 equals very good.

possibly understand every word in a lengthy tiny-print warranty or guaranty, nor are they inclined to take the time to read it. What happens is that most make a **constructive choice**, which is a timely decision based on the situation at hand.

Many businesses now guarantee customer satisfaction with services. This may include free pizza if delivery does not take place in half an hour or a free lunch if not brought to the table in 14 minutes or less. These types of guarantees ensure that service is timely and increases customer satisfaction. Regarding warranties and guarantees, customer service is paramount. Not only does the product have to be fixed, but it also has to be fixed or replaced quickly by courteous employees, whether online, over the telephone, or in person. So customer–employee interaction is important not only at points of sale but also during service encounters. Consumers respond well not only to pleasant people but also to pleasant environments while they wait, which is why car dealerships and repair shops have comfortable waiting rooms with snacks, reading material, and chairs for customers.

The role of competition was covered in previous chapters, and one way firms compete is through guarantees. For example, the United Parcel Service (UPS) competes with FedEx Corp. and the U.S. Postal Service. In a move to erase the service gap between UPS, the world's largest package hauler, and FedEx Corp., UPS rolled out money-back guarantees for U.S. residential shipments in the lower 48 states. About 20 percent of UPS shipments go to homes (Brooks, 2002). Regarding the announcement, "The consumer is the winner," said Satish Jindel, a transportation consultant at SJ Consulting Group Inc., in Pittsburgh. "Now, if they know when to expect it, it tells them when to be ready" (Brooks, 2002, p. D2).

## SERVICE CONTRACTS

True flaws show up quickly, and warranties should take care of most repairs.

When buying a new car, appliance, or computer, you may be offered a **service contract**, which provides repair and/or maintenance for a specific time period (it may also be called an extended warranty). The length of warranty may differ: For a small appliance, the warranty may be for 90 days; for larger, more expensive items, the length of warranty is longer. For example, new cars come with a manufacturer's warranty, which usually offers coverage for 12,000 miles or at least one year, or whichever comes first. A service contract would then extend the warranty and pick up either after 12,000 miles or after that first year. Many consumers buy a service contract for peace of mind, and this is how the contracts are marketed. But are they necessary? Service contracts cost extra and are sold separately; they give extra protection but are rarely worth the cost. For most consumer products, chances are you will never use a service contract, which can run from $20 to $2,000 depending on the length and amount of coverage provided. The problem may be that the service contract covers only certain parts of the product or only specific repairs, or it could also be limited to repairs only at the local dealership (in the case of a car or appliance). Read the contract carefully and ask questions. Labor is probably not included, and there may be deductibles. From a financial standpoint, it may be better to set aside some money for emergencies so that if the rare breakdown occurs, that cash can be used to get things fixed or repaired.

Statistics show that costly consumer products do not break very often within the one- to three-year period covered by service contracts. True flaws show up quickly

The Consumer Sentinel is a secure online database about fraud information that is government operated and useful to law enforcement agencies.

and are covered by regular product warranties that should be included in the purchase price. Service contracts often exclude problems that are most likely to happen, and in many cases the warranties cost more than a repair or replacement would cost. If the car or appliance is sold, the service contract is probably ended because service contracts are rarely transferable to the next owner.

If you have a complaint about a service contract, you should follow the usual procedure of starting with the dealer first. The Federal Trade Commission (FTC) gets many letters from consumers about service contracts. Although the FTC cannot represent you in a dispute, it wants to know if companies are not meeting their obligations. To let the FTC know what is going on, use the complaint form available at www.ftc.gov. The FTC enters fraud-related complaints and also Internet, telemarketing, and identity theft fraud information into Consumer Sentinel, a secure online database available to hundreds of civil and criminal law enforcement agencies in the United States and abroad.

## ARE CONSUMERS COMPLAINING MORE?

Consumers are definitely complaining more—the number of complaints is rising each year, according to statistics keepers such as the FTC and scores of law enforcement and consumer groups. Of course, some of this can be explained by the rise in population, along with a greater public awareness of the problems. There is also a relationship between a downturn in the economy and an upswing in consumer complaints because people are more worried about their money. In addition, in a busier, faster world, consumers expect better and faster service. Fortunately, registering a complaint with a company is getting easier because it can be done over the Internet. One example is that complaints about cleaning products jumped 33 percent in 2001 according to Planet Feedback.com, a company that tracks consumer behavior. Forrester Research, a marketing research company, found in a survey that 84 percent of people wished companies would make it easier to complain (Higgins, 2002). Companies are increasingly viewing consumer complaints not only as a good source of feedback but also as an opportunity to sell more products, which is called **cross-selling**. If the person does not like a certain product, he or she may be given a refund or a coupon to buy another brand that the company sells. For example, if Unilever, which sells everything from Hellmann's mayonnaise to Dove soap, finds out someone doesn't like a taste or a fragrance, it suggests another one of its brands rather than lose a customer (Higgins, 2002).

The cost of beefing up call centers to field complaints poses a dilemma for consumer goods companies that are trying to cut costs. However, one author sees another side:

> But there's also a growing realization that consumers who aren't given a chance to vent can cause damage to a product's reputation by sending mass e-mails, a phenomenon that has become so common, it has a name: the viral effect. In one high-profile case, a businessman became so annoyed at a hotel chain, he designed a scathing PowerPoint slide show that eventually got forwarded from inbox to inbox around the world. (Higgins, 2002, p. D2)

Many old labels were out-of-date, making it difficult for consumers to find company addresses, toll-free complaint numbers, or Internet addresses. It is expensive to redesign a whole line of labels, so companies do it infrequently. A spokeswoman for Shop-Rite pitted olives said that the label for that product had not been redesigned since 1974 and that the company was in the process of redoing it to include an 800 number and a Web address if there was room. Companies have found that many consumers like to talk to a person when they make complaints, so the 800 number is still important (Higgins, 2002).

Companies say they receive not only complaints but also compliments on these lines and through the Internet. "In fact, offering a compliment may be the quickest way to get what you want. John Schachter of Arlington, VA, says he has received everything from free coupons to a transistor radio in the shape of a Tropicana orange, in return for praising products to the manufacturer" (Higgins, 2002, p. D4).

# INJURIES

Each year about a quarter of the population is injured in some way, and about 150,000 Americans die from injuries; disabling injuries (temporary or permanent) are another outcome. Injuries can occur in a variety of places, from cars to homes to leisure to work. Everyone is at risk, but injuries are most common among men, minorities, and people with low incomes due to a variety of factors, including social, environmental, and economic. According to Insel and Roth (2002), in a typical day in the United States the following occur:

- 58 homicides
- 85 suicides
- 265 deaths
- 3,200 suicide attempts
- 20,400 interpersonal assaults
- 100,000 unintentional injury-related emergency room visits

Besides loss of life, unintentional injuries are so common that they account for more **years of potential life lost** (which refers to the difference between an individual's life expectancy and his or her age at death) than any other cause of death (Insel & Roth, 2002). Besides the emotional loss, the economic cost is high. More than $500 billion is spent each year for medical care and rehabilitation of the injured (Insel & Roth, 2002).

**Intentional injuries** are purposely inflicted by oneself or by another person and include homicide, suicide, and assault. **Unintentional injuries** occur when no harm is intended, such as the result of falls, fires, or motor vehicle crashes. The fifth leading cause of death as well as the leading cause of death and disability among children and young adults is unintentional injuries. To lower injuries, engineers help by designing safety belts and safety-related products such as tamper-proof containers for over-the-counter (OTC) and prescription drugs, and law enforcement helps in these same areas by enforcing regulations and laws.

What causes most injuries? The answer is a combination of human and environmental errors. Slick roads, foggy conditions, defective tires, and undertow in the ocean are examples of environmental hazards. Human error involves the following:

- Fatigue, stress, and sleep deprivation
- Risk taking
- Bad judgment

- Distractions (such as children yelling, pets jumping around, cell phones ringing)
- Drugs and alcohol
- Smoking in bed
- Improper or nonuse of safety belts, child safety seats, and air bags (since 1998, all new cars have been equipped with dual air bags for driver and front-seat passenger)
- Nonuse of helmets and other safety equipment when on motorcycles, mopeds, and bicycles
- Inattention (when driving, crossing the street, exercising)

Unintentional injuries occur primarily in three areas:

1. *In the home.* Accidents in the home involve falls, fires, poisoning (carbon monoxide poisoning is the most common type of poisoning by gases), suffocation and choking, and firearm use. Over 100,000 deaths and injuries are caused by firearms each year. To protect yourself in the home from unintentional injuries, remove or fix anything that causes tripping or falling, make sure smoke alarms and fireplaces work properly, use safety equipment, remove electrical cords in pathways, and store firearms appropriately.

2. *During leisure.* Injuries occur during leisure activities such as boating, swimming, and other sports, possibly due to lack of skill or proper equipment. In-line skating accounts for more than 250,000 injuries a year in the emergency room (injuries to head and wrist are most common); scooter injuries account for 27,000 emergency room visits a year.

3. *At work.* Nearly 4 million Americans suffer disabling injuries on the job each year, and many die. Possible causes include falls, exposure to toxic chemicals and radiation, burns, cuts, back sprains, loss of body parts in machinery, and electrical shocks. Back injuries are especially common. Another common injury is **carpal tunnel syndrome**, which is compression of the median nerve in the wrist, often caused by repetitive use of the hands such as in cutting or using a computer; it is characterized by numbness, tingling, and pain in the hands and fingers (webmd.com, June 4, 2008). This can be prevented or lessened by changes both in behavior and in workstations, by the temporary wearing of a splint to stabilize the hand and wrist, and by surgery (in extreme cases). In the workplace, the main federal agency concerned with safety is the Occupational Safety and Health Administration (OSHA), created within the Department of Labor; it was established in 1970 through the Occupational Safety and Health Act.

## Product Safety

Children are often the victims of injuries from consumer products. The government and the public want to lessen the severity and reduce the incidence of accidents, so the question is how to improve product safety. The answers lie in better-designed products, better labeling, removal of hazards and hazardous products, better industry standards, more government regulation (where necessary), and increased consumer awareness. Another question concerns an appropriate number of regulations or warnings. How many accidents happen from lack of common sense and preparedness? In the case of children, how many accidents occur because of parental neglect or ignorance?

Some hazards are known and some are hidden. For example, individuals would not know that a wheel is going to fall off a bicycle or that a pan on a stove would explode. They would also not know that someone's brakes on a car would fail and the car would plow through the front window of a restaurant, injuring customers. On the other hand, known hazards would include driving a faulty car and living in a house with a leaky roof.

Critics of safety regulations often state:

- *People should know better.* Consumers should look out for themselves. It is true that many injuries are the result of misuse of a product, an example being putting plasticware on the stove and cooking in it. These injuries can stem from ignorance, inexperience, and behavioral and environmental errors; examples of behavioral and environmental errors would be riding in a boat or playing golf during a lightning storm and surfing during a hurricane. Product manufacturers would say that behavioral and environmental conditions are beyond their control and that they should not be held responsible. Likewise, a product made for an adult that falls into the hands of a child (such as a prescription drug container left on the sink with the cap off) is primarily the responsibility of the supervising adult.
- *Too much government costs too much money.* Government-mandated safety standards cost manufacturers millions of dollars, and those costs are passed on to consumers.
- *Too much government puts too much power in the hands of a few at the top.* Power can corrupt, so it is better to not let a few make decisions that affect so many consumers.
- *Too many regulations limit freedom.* For example, in some states motorcycle riders have to wear helmets, but in other states it is optional. Motorcycle riders argue that it is their lives that are at stake, so if they don't want to wear helmets, they should not have to. Federal, state, and local governments have passed laws and regulations regarding safety, but how much is too much? All laws and regulations must be considered from several points of view, and the individual's right to freedom is one of them.

## Risks and Factors in Product Safety: Consumer Product Safety Commission

What is an acceptable amount of risk? Everyone has to answer that question for him- or herself. Is one accidental death too many, or do we just assume that a certain percentage of the public will be injured or die every year from consumer products?

To find out how many injuries and deaths occur each year from consumer products, one turns to the National Injury Information Clearinghouse, which disseminates statistics and information relating to the prevention of injuries and deaths associated with consumer products. It is part of the Consumer Product Safety Commission (CPSC). For Web sites, see the E-Resources section at the end of the chapter. Where does the clearinghouse get its statistics and data?

- Hospital emergency rooms
- Health departments (from death certificates when consumer products were involved)
- Victim interviews
- Newspaper accounts
- Reports from medical sources (in addition to hospital emergency rooms)
- Consumer complaints and inquiries sent to the CPSC

Who uses CPSC's injury data?

- Consumer groups
- Manufacturers and industry associations
- Media
- Educators, students, researchers, and attorneys

What can we learn from the clearinghouse statistics? Studying clearinghouse statistics reveals a myriad of problems, including young children getting into problems by using consumer products. Box 10.1 gives a list of categories of consumer product–related statistics categories (and subtopics) used by the CPSC in its Web site.

### Consumer Product Safety: Toys, Baby Equipment, Sports Equipment

As Box 10.1 indicates, a lot of consumer product safety concerns revolve around infants and children. A large category of household consumption is in the area of toys, leisure or recreation or sports equipment, and baby equipment. Americans spend an estimated $22 billion on toys and games each year—and that amount is decreasing (Fetto, 2002). The prime toy market is children between the ages of 2 to 11. American children are more diverse racially and ethnically than the adult population. According to Census 2000, two in five children (39 percent) under the age of 18 are part of a minority group; toy manufacturers are responding by adding Spanish-language Barbie Web sites and making phones and pull toys that use English and Spanish. Video games have expanded "toy" use into the teen years, with teen boys being heavy users, although 44 percent of the video game market is geared for children ages 12 and under (Fetto, 2002). In recent years, according to the London-based market research firm Mintel, sales of toys in the "play sports" category, including foam sports equipment, have grown the fastest, followed by infant/preschool toys, ride-ons like mini-jeeps, activity toys, and dolls. Sales of plush toys have declined.

 **CONSUMER ALERT**

The U.S. Consumer Product Safety Commission and the American Academy of Pediatrics have made recommendations for safe bedding practices for infants under 12 months of age. Among these are specific cautions on the use of soft bedding in cribs. Consult with pediatricians about the latest information.

**BOX 10.1　Consumer Product–Related Statistics**

Children's Products

Toy-Related Injuries and Deaths

Nursery Products

Deaths Associated with Playpens

Asbestos Fibers in Children's Crayons

Sudden Infant Death Syndrome (SIDS) Awareness

Portable Youth Bed Rail Entrapments and Hangings

Hazards Associated with Children Placed in Adult Beds

Child Poisonings

Carbon Monoxide (CO) Poisonings

Electrocutions

Fires

Fires Caused by Children Playing with Lighters

Electric and Gas Clothes Dryers

Halogen Floor Lamps

Hazard Reports for Candle-Related Incidents

Fireworks

Sports and Recreation

Amusement Rides

Children's Playground Equipment

Trampoline-Related Injuries

ATV-Related Injuries and Deaths

Baby Boomer Sports Injuries

Helmets

Go-Cart-Related Injuries and Deaths

Sports-Related Injuries to Persons 65 Years of Age and Older

Other Products

Pool Alarm Reliability

Hazardous Products in Thrift Stores

Shopping Cart Injuries

*Source:* U.S. Consumer Product Safety Commission, http://www.cpsc.gov.

## Toy-Related Injuries to Children

According to the CPSC, in 2006 an estimated 220,500 toy-related injuries were treated in U.S. hospital emergency rooms. There was a rise in estimated toy-related injuries from the previous year due to unpowered scooters. The injury estimates for the years 1999 to 2006 are shown in Table 10.2. Seventy-nine percent (150,800) of the injuries in 2000 were to children under age 15, and 37 percent (70,900) were to children under age 5. Males are more likely to be injured than

**Table 10.2**    Estimated Toy-Related Injuries (1999–2006)

| Year | Estimated Injuries |
|------|--------------------|
| 1999 | 152,600 |
| 2000 | 191,000 |
| 2006 | 220,500 |

*Source:* U.S. Consumer Product Safety Commission, http://www.cpsc.gov.

females. Most of the victims (98 percent) are treated and released from the hospital.

The most likely area of the body to be hurt is the head and face area, followed by the shoulders and fingers. Riding toys (including nonpowered scooters) cause the most injuries.

## Injuries from Nursery Products

According to the CPSC, an estimated 69,500 children under age five were treated in U.S. hospital emergency rooms in 2001 for injuries associated with nursery products. From 1997 to 1999, there were 195 deaths from nursery product–related injuries. The number one cause of injury was infant carriers and car seats (excluding motor vehicle incidents); the number one cause of death was cribs. Table 10.3 shows the injuries and deaths by product.

## Advertising and Children's Products

Advertising plays a vital role in children's safety. Box 10.2 shows messages or images that should not occur in advertising because of potential harm to children.

**Table 10.3**    Nursery Product–Related Injuries and Deaths to Children under Age Five by Product

| Product Category | Estimated Injuries (2001) | Total Deaths (1997–1999) |
|------------------|---------------------------|--------------------------|
| TOTAL | 69,500 | 195 |
| Infant carriers and car seats | 15,370 | 18 |
| Strollers and carriages | 13,070 | 5 |
| Cribs | 11,380 | 80 |
| High chairs | 7,430 | 7 |
| Baby walkers and jumpers | 6,200 | 5 |
| Changing tables | 1,990 | 3 |
| Baby gates and barriers | 1,670 | 2 |
| Playpens and play yards | 1,590 | 23 |
| Baby bath seats | 0 | 18 |
| Other | 10,140 | 34 |

Note: The CPSC used the National Electronic Injury Surveillance System (NEISS) for the 2001 injury estimates and the In-Depth Investigation File, Injury and Potential Injury Incident File, Death Certificate File, and NEISS for 1997 to 1999 for reported deaths.
*Source:* U.S. Consumer Product Safety Commission, http://www.cpsc.gov.

**BOX 10.2    Inappropriate Messages and Images in Advertising for Children**

1. Displaying products children should not use. These products include alcohol, cigarettes, and drugs.
2. Showing adults and children using products in a way they shouldn't, which may be misinterpreted. For example, a "miniaturized" adult could be pictured in a toilet, refrigerator, washing machine, or dishwasher or a child might be seen alone in a swimming pool. Small children may imitate these behaviors.
3. Having young children play with toys and sporting equipment or driving ATVs that are only appropriate for teenagers and adults.
4. Showing children not being accepted by their peers if they do not use or own a product. Messages implying increased popularity are inappropriate. Showing children having fun with a product is okay, but showing mockery, bullying, or loneliness of nonusers or nonowners of a particular brand of toy, shoes, or clothing is not.
5. Picturing children eating less-than-healthy foods. Food advertising directed at children should show foods in the context of a balanced meal. If the food is a snack, it should be clear that it is a snack and not a meal; sugared and fast-food products are especially controversial. Food advertising on Saturday mornings has increased substantially over the last decade.
6. Showing items that do not perform as expected when a child uses them. An example would be an ad showing a boomerang that is thrown by an expert; the same boomerang would not work as well when a seven-year-old throws it.

Note: Advertisements during children's program hours such as Saturday morning and after school are heavily monitored, but increasingly children watch prime-time television (7:30–11:00 P.M.), so this places an additional responsibility on advertisers, marketers, and parents.

As mentioned in previous chapters, the FTC is the main regulator of advertising, and it works for the consumer to prevent fraudulent, deceptive, and unfair business practices in the marketplace and to provide information to help consumers spot, stop, and avoid them.

The regulation of advertising and marketing activities directed at children focuses primarily on the impact messages may have on children's health and safety and also on their values. In other words, physical harm is important, but so is personal and social development. Advertising in a sense is an educator and part of the child's socialization process since children between 2 and 11 years old spend more than 25 hours per week watching television and are exposed to almost 25,000 commercials per year (Weisskoff, 1985). As discussed earlier in the book, television is primarily a one-way process: The viewer sits and watches. Web sites provide the opportunity for two-way interaction, so children are not only being exposed to advertising but also providing information that marketers can use ("Many Kids' Web Sites Continuing to Collect Personal Information," 1999).

## VEHICLE SAFETY AND REPAIR

In an earlier chapter, we covered automobile safety in the discussion of Ralph Nader and his book *Unsafe at Any Speed*, which condemned the auto industry's record on safety and brought about much-needed vehicle safety legislation. Since then, laws have been passed requiring the wearing of seat belts, for example. Earlier in the book we also covered the subject of recalls; an example of a recall was the 1997 and 1998 Yamaha "Warrior" all-terrain vehicles (ATVs) that sold for about $5,000. The problem was that a counting-bracket weld on the rear hub could come loose, resulting in rear brake failure and possible injury to operators. Yamaha received reports from consumers of the weld problems, including the injuries that resulted. Various state departments of consumer services, the CPSC, and Yamaha Motor Corporation, U.S.A., of Cypress, California, announced the voluntary recall of about 14,000 of the vehicles. In a nationwide newspaper announcement, consumers were told to stop using these ATVs immediately and to call their local Yamaha ATV dealer to schedule a free appointment to have their units inspected and repaired if needed.

The Yamaha ATV example illustrates that vehicular safety and repair are often a combination of industry and government cooperation. Recalls are expensive to a company, but not as expensive as bad publicity, loss of sales, lawsuits, and injuries or loss of human life. Likewise, government is charged to protect the welfare and lives of citizens. State governments register auto repair companies and resolve customer complaints. Repair shops have to follow certain rules, so if they are in trouble, they have to get back into compliance and then renew their licenses to operate. There are regulated and nonregulated complaints: Regulated complaints fall under the state's statutory authority to enforce, such as a repair shop's failure to fill out forms or other problems that are specifically listed in statutes; nonregulated complaints may cover car accessories, towing charges, and other things that may not fall under statutes. Across the country, millions of dollars are refunded to consumers each year through consumer divisions in state government. These divisions send in undercover investigators who take in a car that has been prechecked for problems and then see if the repair shops find the correct problem and fix it at a reasonable price. If the shops add on extra charges or even go so far as to damage the car further and ask for more repair money, then they are in trouble.

How can you protect yourself from auto repair fraud? The best way is to go to companies or car dealerships that have existed for a long time and have a reputation for good service and quality work (see Box 10.3). Complaint records can be checked through Better Business Bureaus (BBBs) and motor vehicle divisions in states, most likely under the main consumer protection agency.

One of the worst consumer frauds in the auto repair market is the black market in used auto parts. In this scam, auto parts are switched around, with used ones often being sold to the consumer as new auto parts. A particularly bad practice is the black market on air bags, where used or damaged air bags are sold as new. Law officers in Florida made an arrest when a repair shop was putting cardboard in the slot for the air bag; if there was an accident, cardboard would fly out of the air bag compartment instead of an air bag. Auto safety and repair are not just about paying less or being gypped—they are about saving lives. Fly-by-night repair shops exist; in other words, someone does car repairs and also does other types of repairs, going from one business to another. This is a good example of getting what you pay for—someone without an established business is someone to avoid or at least to check out thoroughly.

The National Institute for Automotive Service Excellence (ASE) located in Herndon, Virginia, is an independent, national nonprofit organization that helps improve the

**BOX 10.3    Vehicle Repairs: Steps to Follow**

1.  Choose a reliable repair shop based on recommendations from family and friends. If you are unsure, check out the repair shop's complaint record with a BBB or local or state consumer protection agency.
2.  Describe the symptoms of the car (what it is doing) when you take it in.
3.  Get more than one estimate in writing if repairs are costly.
4.  Do not allow work to begin until you authorize it and have an estimate.
5.  Don't sign a blank repair order, and understand anything you sign.
6.  Check your warranty—should the repairs be covered?
7.  Pay by credit card if the bill is over $50 because if there is a defect or problem with the repair, payment to the credit card company can be withheld until improvements are made.
8.  Keep copies of all paperwork.
9.  Report complaints to your local or state consumer protection office.

*Source:* These steps have been adapted and modified from *The Consumer Action Handbook,* U.S. General Services Administration, GSA Office of Communications, and Federal Consumer Information Center, 1800 F. Street, NW, Washington, DC 20405.

quality of automotive service and repair through the voluntary testing and certification of automotive repair professionals. Nearly half a million ASE-certified technicians work in car dealerships, automotive repair services, auto parts stores, and service stations. The ASE also publishes consumer publications about auto repair.

## CONSUMER POWER MODEL

### Ultra-Mini Cars and Lamborghini for the Day

Consumers have many choices when it comes to cars today, from serious redesigns to address rising gas prices and environmental concerns to new ways to lease or own cars. Hybrids are one way to go, [and] another is the ultra-mini cars such as the Mercedes-Benz Smart for Two, which is 8.8 feet long and 5 feet wide with a beginning price tag of under $12,000. Making informed choices is the name of the game in difficult economic times.

Since luxury cars are so expensive to repair and most rich people rarely drive them, a company named Gotham offers fractional shares in trophy cars in New York and Miami (minimum package: 20 days for $9,000). Other companies are springing up including San Francisco's Club Sportiva.

"Over the past year, George Johnson, owner of a New Jersey construction company, has spent about $30,000 for a total of 90 days' drive time in a Lamborghini Murcielago and a Bentley Continental GT, among other pricey rides. 'It's not worth it to buy one of these cars when you have to fix them.'"[1]

A target market is companies wishing to reward outstanding managers with an ultra-luxe rental. Gotham's president says the growing number of millionaires is feeding this business. They don't want the hassles of insuring and storing cars on a permanent basis.

[1]David Kiley, "My Lamborghini—Today, Anyway," *Business Week,* January 14, 2008, p. 17.

## VEHICLE WARRANTIES

Standard car warranties are for 3 years or 36,000 miles (whichever happens first) and cover manufacturer defects (labor and parts may be extra). To increase customer satisfaction and to encourage car sales, manufacturers are lengthening warranties and wrapping in new services, such as free car washes with each checkup and free donuts and cappuccinos in the service area waiting room. As may be expected, luxury car dealers offer more services than low-end dealers, including generous free loaner car policies, free wiper blade replacement, and 24-hour roadside service. Warranties that used to be limited to 3 years now go as high as 5 years for a Ford Focus and 10 years for a Hyundai; Daimler-Chrysler introduced 7-year, 70,000-mile power-train warranties. Lengthy contracts are a way to distinguish brands. Whether they are a good idea or not depends on the features (likelihood that they will be needed) and the added price. Most are not transferable to a second buyer, so the original purchaser should decide whether or not to keep the car past 5 or 10 years before buying an extended warranty. From the manufacturer's point of view, extended warranties can be moneymakers or they can be costly.

Consumers are more aware than ever before about the necessity for repairs because of the computer systems on dashboards of vehicles. Sometimes these systems malfunction, and the repair is not needed. This type of warning error wastes the consumer's and the dealer's time. However, usually these systems of blinking lights and warning signals are accurate and let the customer know when repairs are needed, so they are useful safety features. Unquestionably the warning systems have saved lives as well as time and money. Volvos are particularly well known for safety features. The Volvo S60 modules are "fitted with 26 censors that prompt six levels of warning messages, ranging from the mildly unsettling 'FIX NEXT SERVICE' to the more hysterical 'STOP SAFELY ASAP'" (Spencer, 2002, p. D2).

For warranties to remain in effect, it may be in the contract that you must follow all the manufacturer's recommendations for routine maintenance, such as changing the oil and spark plugs and bringing the car in for routine maintenance checks. Keep records and receipts to prove this, although in most cases dealership service offices will keep records of work done on your car as well. There may be clauses in the contracts that say that taking your car to repair shops other than the dealership will not count.

According to a newspaper article, Alan Entin (a clinical psychologist in Richard, Virginia) says, "People who make heavy warranty demands may be seeking parental attention from their mechanics. It's 'Take care of me. You're bigger, you're stronger, you can make all things right in the world if you fix my car,' he says. The warranty represents approval or fixing from their daddy" (Spencer, 2002, p. D2). Entin's interpretation may seem reasonable or extreme depending on your point of view, but nevertheless the trend is toward more lengthy warranties. Box 10.4 explains how to get the most out of any car warranty.

FTC's *Auto Service Contracts* offers the following advice:

When shopping for a used car, look for a Buyer's Guide sticker posted on the car's side window. This sticker is required by the FTC on all used cars sold by dealers. It tells whether a service contract is available. It also indicates whether the vehicle is being sold with a warranty, with implied warranties only, or "as is." If the manufacturer's warranty is still in effect on the used car, you may have to pay a fee to obtain

**BOX 10.4    Vehicle Warranties: How to Get the Most from Them**

First:

- Keep up with the recommended maintenance schedule, especially oil changes.
- Fill out all the necessary paperwork, including service logs; save receipts.

When a repair is needed, follow these recommended steps:

- Find out if other drivers have similar problems. Go to www.autosafety.org for common problems by make of car. Visit www.nhtsa.dot.gov, the National Highway Traffic Safety Administration (NHTSA) site, for posted defect bulletins.
- If the dealer will not fix the problem when it is under warranty (to your satisfaction), appeal to the manufacturer by contacting the manufacturer's regional or national office. Ask for the consumer affairs representative or go to the company Web site for this information.
- If still unsuccessful, consider contacting other organizations (including www.autosafety.org) for legal advice.

After warranties expire:

- Ask the dealer if policy adjustments/extensions are possible. A free fix is possible if the manufacturer has told dealers to authorize repairs.
- If the warranty has recently expired and the service log shows that the repair problem started before the warranty ran out, then there is a possibility of a free or lower-cost repair.

Basic advice: Car dealers want return customers, so most will try to make the needed repairs in a timely fashion.

coverage, making it a service contract. However, if the dealer absorbs the cost of the manufacturer's fee, the coverage is considered a warranty. (2003, p. 3)

Implied warranties are unspoken and unwritten and are based on the principle that the seller stands behind the product. Sold "as is" means there is no warranty—you buy the car and must pay for all repairs even if the car breaks down on the street outside the dealership lot. Some states prohibit "as is" sales; other states have lemon laws under which a consumer can receive a refund or replacement.

*Buying a used car "as is" is risky business.*

## NATIONAL HIGHWAY TRAFFIC SAFETY ADMINISTRATION

The mission of the National Highway Traffic Safety Administration (NHTSA), according to its Web site, is to save lives, prevent injuries, and reduce traffic-related health care and other economic costs by facilitating the development, deployment, and evaluation of safety products and systems. Among other things, this involves research into the science of crash avoidance to enable the development of safety-enhancing products. The agency works with the automobile industry and other technology companies. The goal of the agency is to demonstrate improved capability of collision avoidance systems, to ensure that systems are both effective and usable for consumers, and to provide a basis for understanding the benefits (for example, collisions, injuries, and fatalities that will be avoided).

Air Bag Inflation. An air bag inflates in front of a dummy in the passenger side of a car with a cutaway door during a crash test. (National Highway Traffic Safety Administration.)

NHTSA wants to hear from consumers regarding potential car defects, and it has information on safety recalls, crash tests ratings, child safety seats, bicycles, air bags, and impaired driving prevention. Probably what the public knows best about NHTSA is the results of the crash tests. Have you seen the dummies being tossed around in cars on television announcements or the nightly news? Those demonstrations and tests are part of what NHTSA does.

In 1978 the New Car Assessment Program (NCAP) was initiated with the purpose of providing consumers with a measure of the relative safety potential of vehicles in frontal crashes. NCAP supplies consumers with frontal- and side-crash results to help them in buying decisions. Ultimately NCAP would like the industry to use similar standards and provide better occupant protection in crashes. One thing NCAP would really like to see happen is a significant reduction in the number of rollovers.

If you want to check on the crash test results of a particular vehicle, go to the Web site in the E-Resources and click on one of the icons (a car, truck, van, or SUV). Next, select your vehicle size and year, and keep clicking until you find the exact make, model, and year. The vehicles that are tested are purchased from dealerships so that they are the same vehicles that consumers would buy. The typical models tested are new vehicles that are predicted to have high sales volume or vehicles that either have been redesigned with structural changes or have improved safety equipment for testing. Injury risk curves are obtained from the test dummy in the crash, which demonstrates the probability of injury to a real person in that crash. The lower the injury number is, the less chance an individual will be hurt in a crash.

# FEDERAL AVIATION ADMINISTRATION

How safe are you when you fly? The Federal Aviation Administration (FAA), part of the Department of Transportation (DOT), is in charge of air safety for the general public and the aviation community, and it investigates unsafe aviation practices. According to the FAA home page, the DOT oversees consumer issues such as denied boarding, baggage, overbooking, and ticketing, as well as statistics on on-time performance, while the FAA is in charge of civil aviation safety, including developing safety regulations, certifying pilots, and compiling airport flight delay information. The Transportation Security Administration (TSA) is responsible for all modes of transportation (see www.tsa.dot.gov). On the FAA Web page, there is a list of consumer rights and airline consumer obligations, including guides for traveling smart.

# HOME IMPROVEMENTS

Remodeling can range in price from a $15 can of paint to $100,000 additions. A wide range of minor repairs or upgrades cost under $3,000, and the do-it-yourself market is huge. An estimated 26 million Americans tackle home improvements each year, spending some $180 billion, according to the Remodelers Council of the National Association of Home Builders (Beck, 2002).

With repairs and upgrades also comes the potential for fraud or at least disappointment with the quality of end results. A huge area of consumer complaints is home repair and renovations and related items, such as pool construction and anything else having to do with yards, garages, and outbuildings. Small claims courts are filled with these types of complaints, which pit the consumer against the contractor. Since in-ground swimming pools and kitchen remodeling can cost over $30,000, cases can go to higher courts. Similar to the advice for car repair, one should look for established businesses with good reputations, and the homeowner should be realistic in terms of the amount of time and inconvenience substantial renovations will cause; contractors should be appropriately licensed. See Box 10.5 for more steps to follow in home improvements.

Certain behaviors should draw your attention. Avoid contractors who come door to door, especially those in unmarked vans with out-of-state license plates—busy legitimate contractors wait for you to call them. Very low bids should also be a warning sign, as are exceptionally long guarantees. If you feel any kind of pressure to hurry and pay up front, then that is another warning sign. If you are considering having a home painted, for example, get two or three bids from local services and check references. Not only the price but the availability and quality of materials and workmanship should be compared. According to Beck (2002), to evaluate workmanship, ask previous customers about these four critical measures of the contractor's past work:

- On budget
- On time
- Agreeableness (worked with homeowner)
- Capability of finishing the job to the homeowner's standards

**BOX 10.5   Home Improvements: Steps to Follow**

Choose a reliable contractor or company based on recommendations from family and friends.

Check your BBB or local or state consumer agency for information on contractors' licensing or registration requirements and complaint records (license requirements vary by state).

Get at least three written estimates, and remember that the lowest one may not be the best.

Get references and talk with people who have had work done by the contractor.

Contact your local building inspection department to check for permit and inspection requirements.

Get a complete written contract detailing work to be done, quality of materials, timetables, warranties, subcontractors' names, and total price of the job and payment schedules.

Do not pay completely up front, and try to limit your down payment. Don't make a final payment until you are satisfied.

Remember that you have cancellation rights (usually three business days) in home improvement contracts, meaning you can get out of the contract without penalty.

Pay by credit card because under most laws (in most cases) you have the right to refuse to pay the credit card company until any defects or problems are corrected.

*Source:* These steps have been adapted and modified from *The Consumer Action Handbook,* 2001 edition, U.S. General Services Administration, GSA Office of Communications, Federal Consumer Information Center, 1800 F Street NW, Washington, DC 20405.

## Home Improvement Professionals

Whom do you hire? Home improvement professionals vary by complexity of the project:

- *General contractors.* Those who manage all aspects of a project, including hiring and supervising subcontractors, are called general contractors.
- *Subcontractors or specialty contractors.* A subcontractor would install a particular product, such as staircases, cabinets, or bathroom plumbing fixtures.
- *Architects.* An architect designs homes, buildings, additions, and major renovations, especially those having to do with structural changes. A related specialty area is landscape architecture.
- *Designers.* People who have expertise in design and layout as well as space planning are called designers. For example, they may specialize in kitchens and baths, using contemporary or traditional designs, or they may do it all. Designers may work independently or with a firm, they may charge by the hour or by the project, or they may work for free if you purchase items from the company they work for.
- *Design/builder contractors.* A design/builder contractor oversees projects from start to finish. Some firms have architects on staff; others use certified designers.

Contracts are well advised and can range from a letter of agreement for a modest job to a full-blown contract. In each case, the who, what, where, and when as well as the cost of the project should be spelled out. The agreement should be clear, concise, and complete, including the contractor's or designer's name, address, phone, and license number. Hopefully this information is on the person's letterhead, but if it is not, request it. The kinds of information to be covered include costs, detailed lists of materials, warranties, ways any changes will be handled, estimated start and completion dates, payment schedules for all involved, and cleanup and trash hauling (a "broom clause"); for a major project, you should have a written statement of your right to cancel the contract within three business days, and the contract or letter should be dated. Keep all paperwork in one place, and at the completion of the project, the homeowner and the home improvement professional should do a walk-through, checking that everything was done to expectation and as agreed upon.

## Where to Complain and Where to Find Help

First, try to resolve differences with the home improvement professional; if you are unsuccessful, then follow the other steps listed in the complaint section earlier in the book. Besides the usual sources of help, there are state and local builders' associations and/or remodelers' councils. The Remodelers Council of the National Association of Home Builders can be reached at www.nahb.com. The federal agency having the most to do with housing is the Department of Housing and Urban Development, located in Washington, D.C. It has a home improvement branch, and its Web site is in the E-Resources section at the end of the chapter. The industry self-monitors to some extent. The National Association of Home Builders and any state associations would be the main groups interested in maintaining quality and good relations with the public. The FTC also investigates home improvement scams that are considered to be fraudulent, deceptive, or unfair business practices and would especially check false or misleading advertising in this regard.

If a home has construction defects, there are moves afoot called **right-to-cure laws** (laws stating that homeowners can allow a builder to correct problems before they take legal action) that have passed in California, Washington, Arizona, and Nevada and that are being considered in other states. Since this is a rapidly changing area, check the laws in your state before buying a home or hiring a builder for major home improvements. "The laws generally set up a procedure for homeowners to give builders a chance to repair their homes before they can file a lawsuit. But while the requirement sounds logical, some consumer advocates fear builders will gain an advantage over unsophisticated home buyers, who may sign away their rights to sue later if the problem isn't fixed properly. Tom Miller, a Newport Beach, Calif., lawyer who has built a national specialty in suing home builders, says that "'right to cure' laws benefit builders more than consumers" (Perez, 2003, p. D2). The National Association of Home Builders, a Washington, D.C., residential builders' lobby group, supports right-to-cure laws. The whole issue is similar to malpractice insurance for doctors: The lawsuits are affecting the insurance industry, so some builders cannot get insurance or are limited in the types of policies available—and their premiums keep going up and up. "The construction-defect problem is considered one of the most serious problems in the insurance market today," says Bob Harwig, chief economist for the Insurance Information Institute of New York (Perez, 2003, p. D2). Consumer advocates and plaintiff attorneys complain that builders are largely to blame for the increasing amounts of defects mainly because they are relying more and more on cheap unskilled labor; the builders counter by saying that it is getting more and more difficult to find reliable skilled labor. To give perspective to the whole issue of right-to-cure laws, building complaints are far down the list compared with complaints about car dealerships, for example. Nevertheless, the fact remains that building defects are moving up the list, indicating that potential and current homeowners should be especially cautious about the quality of construction and the reputation of builders.

## Home Improvements as Investments

Are home improvements good investments? It depends on several factors. If you rent out a house, then the monthly check from the renter can be considered a dividend. If you live in the house yourself, then it can be considered "imputed rent," which means you get to live in the house rent-free. A capital gain from housing on a national average is modest. According to Freddie Mac (a federal government mortgage program), over the past 27 years home prices have appreciated at 5.8 percent a year, which is 1.2 percentage points a year faster than inflation (Clements, 2002). This does not include regular costs of home maintenance (painting, fixing, replacing), and these usually come to 1 percent or 2 percent of the home's value each year. When owning a home, most people do not stop at simple maintenance and begin to add rooms, pools, air-conditioning systems, and so forth. The bottom line is that usually home prices do not outpace inflation once maintenance and remodeling costs are figured in, unless a person lives in a high-growth area. Another way people make money on houses is to buy the worst house on the block and bring it up to comparable houses on the same street. A mistake (from a financial point of view) would be to upgrade the house so much that it is far grander than all its neighbors because usually this type of investment will not be regained at resale.

Historically, kitchen and bathroom remodeling provide the greatest return at resale time.

Another way to look at the value of home improvements from a consumer point of view is that the consumer will save money by adding on to a cheaper house rather than moving up to a much more expensive and bigger house. Staying in an existing neighborhood (if it is a good one) is usually cheaper than incurring the costs involved in buying and selling houses. Home improvements should not be made with an eye solely on resale unless the house is going on the market within a year because home improvements age (just like any other consumer product or service) and become worth less as time goes on. *Remodeling* magazine says that the most likely recoup on money spent on home improvements is 70 percent to 80 percent, assuming the house is sold within one year of making improvements. Kitchen and bath remodeling historically provide the best return at resell; for example, according to *Remodeling* magazine, you can get back 80 percent to 87 percent of what you spend on a kitchen upgrade. Perhaps how quickly remodeling ages is discouraging, but the biggest return on home ownership is the dividend discussed earlier, whether collected in rent or in the ability to live rent-free. Fixing a place up gives a person the chance to express him- or herself, a more pleasant place to live, and personal comfort, all of which also have value. Further, there are other paybacks, including immediate cost savings in home energy. For example, it is estimated that upgrading kitchen appliances will result in a significant energy savings: If the refrigerator, dishwasher, and range are updated, about $50 to $130 will be saved in energy a year; in the laundry, an energy-smart washer alone can save as much as $110 a year on utility bills, depending on local rates and specific appliances.

Unless a homeowner is planning to sell soon, any remodeling should start with his or her needs first. A budget or spending plan may be set up to take care of short- and long-term goals. If you are doing it yourself, work safe and smart. Use safety goggles, and protect yourself from splashes, spills, falls, scrapes, dropped tools, and flying debris. Wear sturdy shoes (not sandals or slippers); add a dust mask (if sanding), work gloves, long-sleeved shirts, and so forth—in short, do what the professionals do.

## TRAVEL: WAYS TO SAVE MONEY, AVOID FRAUD, AND STAY SAFE

Numerous travel magazines and Web sites exist both to help cost-conscious consumers compare services and prices and to sell products and services. Travel agencies can individualize consumers' wants and experiences and can provide advice tailor-made for each individual. Increasingly, consumers are booking airline tickets directly at sites like www.delta.com and www.southwest.com, making reservations by themselves for the hotel or cruise line; they also use shopping bots or Internet travel Web sites. Examples of comprehensive sites include www.bestfares.com, www.expedia.com, www.fodors.com, www.frommers.com, www.orbitz.com, www.sidestep.com, and www.travelocity.com. The advantages of these sites are 24/7 service and the ability to rapidly compare prices.

Many hotels offer a variety of prices based on days of the week, occupancy rates, and discounts to government employees, students or faculty members, senior citizens or members of the American Association of Retired Persons (AARP), and members of the American Automobile Association (AAA). People should seek the best discounts by inquiring about who qualifies for discounts, and there may also be point systems (such as Marriott Rewards) or frequent-flyer points that may serve as incentives or that offer upgrades, discounts, or services. Most hotels are interested in increasing occupancy rates and would rather rent a room out for 70 percent of the "rack" rate than let it sit vacant. Whether the hotel is full or empty, it still has to pay maids, front desk workers, managers, wait staff, cooks, and so on.

Travel bargaining may be confusing to many U.S. travelers who are mostly used to a **one-price system**, meaning there is one price for one product or service; for example, a shopper goes into a grocery store or a Wal-Mart and pays whatever is on the price sticker. If the advertised rate for a hotel room is $100 a night, consumers may assume they will pay $100 because bargaining is less common in the United States than in many other countries in the world. Curiously, in the United States we are used to a system where high-priced items such as homes and new cars can be bargained for but low-priced items such as toothpaste or fresh fruit have a set price. Some consumers enjoy bargaining and others find it distasteful. According to Meg Whitman, founder of eBay, over 150,000 people make their living, either full-time or part-time, by buying and selling on eBay, the online auction house with new and used items, so obviously a sizable portion of the population is reaping the benefits of people who enjoy bargaining. As this online auction house has risen in popularity, so has the public's understanding of the pleasures of bargaining, which should impact a number of industries and product sales.

Another pricing issue is whether airlines should charge an obese person more because he or she requires more space on the plane. Some airlines currently have a policy of charging for an extra seat, but some would argue that this is unfair. It could be reasoned that obesity is a health issue and that given the customs in our pricing system, oversized people should not have to pay extra for larger seats any more than they do for larger clothes (Stark, 2002). But what about the comfort and the rights of the person sitting next to the obese person? As with any issue, there are several perspectives to consider (the airline, the obese person, the other passengers) as well as related considerations such as individual rights, safety, and personal dignity.

Another issue in the travel industry is the extensive amount of fraud or deception that exists—each year travel moves up higher on the list of consumer complaints. The steps to follow to avoid being ripped off are similar to those for auto repairs and home improvements. When going out of the country especially, start with reputable, established travel agencies or tour companies. Make sure that you understand the terms of the contract, and remember that brochures are mostly marketing hype. Be wary of very low fares, sweepstakes wins, and off-season bargains (they may not be bargains if you have to endure hurricanes and closed museums). For example, one woman booked an August museum tour of Paris; on arrival, she found out that nearly every August the museum workers go on strike and the museums are closed. Watch out for paying in advance; if the trip is a long time away, you may want travel insurance. In some states, some travel agencies and tour operators have to be registered and insured, but in others there is less regulation. Contact the attorney general in your state or the one where the company is located to see if any complaints have been lodged. Foreign travel is especially susceptible to fraud and problems; again, the main protection is to deal with reputable companies. The American Society of Travel Agents helps resolve disputes with member agents, airlines have their own toll-free complaint lines, and state and local consumer protection agencies can help as well (see E-Resources).

Regarding travel safety, Australia, Japan, Denmark, Canada, Great Britain, and the United States regularly issue travel warnings. These are handy because they provide information pertaining to traveler safety, but they can wreak havoc on a country's tourism industry. One of the outcomes of the information provided is that whole countries are often shut down due to travel warnings when just a small area

## CONSUMER ALERT

College students are especially susceptible to travel fraud. Beware of ads in student newspapers and flyers posted on campus for extremely inexpensive trips at spring break and holiday times such as ski trips. Students have been stranded in Mexico and the Caribbean without hotels to stay in or have been sent to extremely low-quality hotels. In Europe, students are approached at railway stations and sometimes led to shoddy hotels or, worse, mugged. Pickpocketing is much more common in Europe and other parts of the world than in the United States and Canada; there are fraudulent on-the-street ticket sales to Broadway and London plays. Group travel is usually safer than singles traveling alone, and groups can usually negotiate better prices. A tour guide or faculty member with a student trip can provide additional guidance and protection.

be really thorough, other nations' Web sites should be checked as well. Given that they have different forms of intelligence gathering, nations don't always agree on where the risky places are and why. For example, in October 2002, Denmark and Great Britain reported on Web sites that they had received information that terrorists might target resorts in Phuket, Thailand, so tourists were told to "exercise extreme caution."

At the same time the U.S. government sources did not report the need for extreme caution but did issue a broad warning about Southeast Asia; fortunately, nothing of a terrorist nature happened in Thailand in the fall of 2002. However, tragedy did strike in Bali in October 2002 when more than 190 people (many of them foreign tourists) were killed in the deadly bombing of the Sari Club in Kuta Beach, Bali. This was not predicted or preannounced by the major Web sites; however, it is still recommended to gather advice from several governments (see E-Resources section) before traveling abroad. Several companies specialize in providing security advice, including medical aid and evacuation services, but they charge a price. If you work for a business that involves traveling to foreign countries or working abroad, the company may have in-house advice as to security and the safe conduct of business. As an added measure, many international businesses, resorts, and hotels are stepping up security measures. Travelers are encouraged to use common sense by avoiding standing out or appearing lost, and they should be aware of surroundings, keep up with the news and changing events, and have an exit plan.

## UNORDERED MERCHANDISE

The FTC has ruled on merchandise sent through the mail directly to the consumer who did not order the merchandise. Only two kinds of merchandise may be sent legally in this way (without the consumer's consent):

1. Free samples that are clearly marked as such (besides arriving in the mail, these may also be attached to newspapers)
2. Merchandise (such as address labels) from charitable organizations

If you receive anything that does not fit these two categories, be wary—especially of opening unexpected packages, unlabeled packages, and packages with no return address or an unknown return address—but you have the right to keep whatever is in the package if it is clearly addressed to you, the occupant, and you should not pay anything. You can also simply return the package to the post office.

## DISPOSITION

Some products are entirely consumed (for example, an ice cream cone); others are disposed of after use (for example, chewing gum). **Disposition** (disposal) of a product can occur before, during, or after its use. How can it occur before? It has been estimated that as much as 30 percent of the food brought into the home is disposed of before use. Examples of product waste include fruits and vegetables that spoil or milk and bread that go bad before use. Millions of pounds of packaging are disposed of each year—think about the cardboard packaging in cereal boxes and the foil on snack packages. Disposition is about not only the product but also the packaging around it. Manufacturers are concerned about disposition. The absence of a package or minimal packaging can be used as an attempt to attract environmentally oriented consumers.

Besides the obvious reason of spoilage, why do people get rid of things? Other reasons may be that the product no longer functions in a manner that the consumer desires, wear and tear are visible, or a newer model or style may be better. There is a market for used products that still function or have value, as the success of eBay as well as millions of garage sales attest. Dissatisfaction is caused by a failure of performance—the product does not live up to expectations or has worn out its welcome.

## SUMMARY

Good buying and ownership tactics were covered in this chapter. Even following all the tips and rules, consumers sometimes make mistakes and seek remedies or solutions. Sometimes bad purchases are buried in the back of closets or in the corner of basements or garages, only to be found during moving. Disposition (disposal) of a product can occur at any time, even before use. Warranties are included in the price of the product, while service contracts cost extra and are sold separately. Care should be taken before signing a service contract; often consumers pay for more protection than they need.

Home improvement scams are rampant. Investigating the credentials and past work of designers, architects, contractors and subcontractors, and other home improvement professionals can go a long way in reducing potential problems. Letters of agreement or contracts up front are imperative.

The travel market responds to terrorist attacks and epidemics. There are many ways to reduce risks, the foremost including being informed before traveling, keeping aware of news and world events while traveling, changing itineraries when necessary, and using common sense.

Consumer safety is a serious issue. Most infant equipment injuries are caused by infant carriers and car seats, and most infant deaths result from cribs. Riding toys, including unpowered scooters, are associated with more injuries than any other toy category for older children. An estimated 220,500 children a year end up in the hospital emergency room from consumer product–related injuries, with boys more likely to be injured than girls. The most typical injury is to the head or face. The Consumer Product Safety Commission actively monitors injury statistics and tries to reduce the number of consumer product injuries through regulations, recalls, and education.

Americans are used to a one-price system for most things, meaning the sticker price is what they expect to pay at a grocery or discount store. However, bargaining and sliding price systems (price variation) are on the rise, and savvy shoppers seek to find out if they qualify for discounts on hotel rooms, airplane tickets, and so forth. Careful shoppers also look for warranties, read labels, pay cash when feasible to save credit card fees, keep records and receipts, and file complaints or send letters or online complaints when necessary. The steps in the buying process are to find out all you can before buying, make sure the product or service is truly needed, and then find the best supplier at the best price.

## KEY POINTS

1. Consumers underutilize products for a variety of reasons, from impulse buying to changes in lifestyle and interests. The use of products influences the need for safety and repairs.
2. Warranties are useful, but in most cases service contracts are unnecessary. The Federal Trade Commission keeps a database of fraud-related complaints and enters them into the Consumer Sentinel, a secure online database available to law enforcement agencies.
3. The Consumer Product Safety Commission assembles consumer product–related statistics not only for child-related products but also for other products such as fireworks, helmets, and candles.
4. The Federal Trade Commission regulates advertising and especially monitors advertising aimed at children.
5. Travel prices are increasingly negotiable. More than one price exists for the same flight or the same hotel, and discount and frequent user programs are increasing.
6. Travel fraud, especially at holiday time and during spring break, is aimed at college students.
7. Before traveling abroad, Web sites of several countries should be checked to find out if there are particular concerns or warnings.
8. Home improvement fraud is rampant. Right-to-cure laws set up a procedure for homeowners to give builders a chance to repair their homes before they file a lawsuit. Builder associations support these laws, but plaintiff attorneys and consumer advocates are skeptical.

## KEY TERMS

| | | |
|---|---|---|
| attribute-based choices | disposition | service contract |
| bounded rationality | intentional injuries | underutilization |
| carpal tunnel syndrome | one-price system | unintentional injuries |
| constructive choice | right-to-cure laws | years of potential life lost |
| cross-selling | | |

## DISCUSSION QUESTIONS

1. Why would someone buy a product and never use it? What is an example of a product that you have bought and rarely or never used? Describe the reasons why you underutilized the product.
2. Have you or a family member ever had a problem with car repairs? What happened as a result? What was the process, from problem to the final fix-up?
3. Why is it said that information is the smart traveler's secret weapon? For safety purposes, what are some information sources that a traveler could use before and during travel?
4. What is the Consumer Sentinel, and why is it useful?
5. Select a Web site from the E-Resources list and report on what you find.

## E-RESOURCES

### Travel Information

**American Society of Travel Agents**   *www.astanet.com*
Travel clearinghouse, tips, education

**Consumer Product Safety Commission (CPSC)**   *www.cpsc.gov*
*clearinghouse@cpsc.gov*
National Injury Information Clearinghouse

**Department of Housing and Urban Development, Home Improvement Branch**   *www.hud.gov/homeimpr.html*
Information on home improvements

**Federal Aviation Administration (FAA)**   *www.faa.gov*
Information on regulations and on certification for pilots

**Federal Trade Commission (FTC)**   *www.ftc.gov*
Complaint filing, free information on consumer issues (including advertising)

**National Center for Injury Prevention and Control**   *www.cdc.gov/ncipc*
Information on prevention of unintentional injuries and violence

**National Highway Traffic Safety Administration (NHTSA)**   *www.nhtsa.dot.gov*
Education and safety regulations, crash test results, statistics on economic losses from crashes

**National Institute for Automotive Service Excellence (ASE)**   *www/asecert.org*
Training, certification, publications

**National Safety Council (NSC)**   *www.nsc.org*
Information on prevention of unintentional injuries

**World Health Organization (WHO)**   *www.who.int/violence_injury_prevention*
Information and statistics on consequences of intentional and unintentional injuries worldwide

### Travel Warnings and Advisories

**Australian Department of Foreign Affairs and Trade**   *www.dfat.gov.au*
Travel information

**Bureau of Consular Affairs (U.S. Department of State)**
*www.travel.stat.gov/travel_warnings.html*
Foreign travel, adoptions, passports, career information

**Canada's Consular Affairs Bureau**   *www.voyage.gc.ca*
Travel information

**Great Britain's Foreign & Commonwealth Office**   *www.fco.gov.uk/travel*
Travel information

**Internet Public Library**   *www.ipl.org/reading/news*
International news when traveling (also use BBC, CNN, local papers for news)

# REFERENCES

Beck, E. (2002). Get with the remodeling boom. *Home Improvement: A Great Investment.* Lowes.com/investment.

Boulding, W., and A. Kirmani. (June 1993). A consumer-side experimental examination of signaling theory. *Journal of Consumer Research,* 11–23.

Brooks, R. (August 1, 2002). UPS guarantees home deliveries on time, following FedEx's lead. *Wall Street Journal,* p. D2.

Clements, J. (August 28, 2002). Skip the imported granite countertops: Home remodeling is a lousy investment. *Wall Street Journal,* p. D1.

Fetto, J. (October 2002). Babes in toyland. *American Demographics,* 14.

*FTC Facts: Auto Service Contracts,* (2003). Washington, DC.

Higgins, M. (August 28, 2002). "My cookies are crumbled": The art of consumer griping. *Wall Street Journal,* pp. D1 and D4.

Insel, P., and W. Roth. (2002). *Core concepts in health,* 9th ed. Boston: McGraw-Hill.

Jacoby, J., C. K. Berning, and T. G. Dietvorst. (1977). What about disposition? *Journal of Marketing, 41,* 22–28.

Many kids' Web sites continuing to collect personal information. (July 19, 1999) Center for Media Education.

Neuman, S. (2002). Travel warnings pose threat to tourism in Asian countries. *Wall Street Journal,* p. D3.

Perez, E. (January 23, 2003). Builders push "right-to-cure" laws. *Wall Street Journal,* p. D2.

Spencer, J. (November 12, 2002). The best care deal around: Never paying for repairs. *Wall Street Journal,* p. D1.

Stark, A. (2002). Saving up for the lean times ahead. *Wall Street Journal,* p. D8.

Stark, E. (November 1996). Which charities merit your money. *Money,* 100–02.

Trocchia, P., and J. Swinder. (2002). An investigation of product purchase and subsequent non-consumption. *Journal of Consumer Marketing, 19* (3), 188–204.

Weisskoff, R. (March 1985). Current trends in children's advertising. *Journal of Advertising Research,* 12–14.

# The Internet and Issues of Identity Theft and Fraud

> True security lies not in the things one has, but in the things
> one can do without.
> —Og Mandino

## Learning Objectives

1. Discuss the role of the Internet in consumption patterns.
2. Explain the environmental impact of the Internet.
3. Define identity theft, biometrics, and privacy protection.
4. Describe how to do self-background checks.
5. Discuss the federal agencies involved in resolving identity theft.
6. List some deceptions occurring over the Internet in regard to charitable giving.

---

### E-Images: Employers and Advertisers Pay Attention

Whatever you put on the Internet is public, with few exceptions. Employers and advertisers know and are using what is there. In the case of employers, many are searching the Internet to see if they can find out more about the students they are interviewing or as a way to find out more about recent hires. Compromising photographs or stories put on the Web by the students themselves or their friends can cause difficulty in the job market. Here are examples:

"A chemical engineering student at a university in the Northeast was eliminated from consideration for a job opening after a company recruiter Googled the student's name, discovering, among other things, that he liked to blow things up."[1]

"A recent graduate of a small Upper Midwest university was only a few weeks into her postgraduation job when the boss called her into his office. He had discovered the young woman's personal blog, where she had been writing in detail about how miserable she was in her new position. She soon became a former employee."[2]

Jill Wesley, a former Purdue career counselor and now Director of Career Services, Distance Education, at Indiana Business College, and former Purdue colleague Kimberly Shea created a checklist of how to inspect your online presence. It starts with Googling yourself, assessing social network sites such as Facebook and MySpace, and then conducting a content inventory of personal Web sites or blogs. Is there anything that might turn off future employers?

Facebook.com is a social network where people make friends and exchange likes and dislikes as well as news about their activities. Facebook has begun selling ads that

---

display people's profiles along with what they buy or that register an opinion about people's brand preference or movie choice. So far people have been asked if this is okay, but once they say okay, that preference or movie can be sent to friends along with an ad.

The Federal Trade Commission has stepped in regarding the advertising and expressed concern about privacy. Hearings are being held. The fundamental question is how much information about people's online activities should be made public, including their purchasing behavior. What do you think?

_____

[1]www.youngmoney.com/careers/monstertrak/career, November 1, 2007.
[2]Ibid.
*Reference:* Louise Story, "Facebook Is Marketing Your Brand Preferences," *New York Times,* November 7, 2007, p. C5.

# INTRODUCTION

The last chapter dealt with safety issues. This chapter continues along that same theme of safety and protection but emphasizes the growing consumer and privacy problems associated with the broad scope of the Internet. It also explores the new ways of handling security, such as verifying identities through biometrics. **Biometrics** refers to using people's unique physical traits (such as fingerprints) to verify identity. As one example, many laptops come equipped with fingerprint readers so passwords aren't needed. In the future, biometrics will be used more for identification purposes.

This chapter also builds on the consumer-in-control movement, which means consumers want more say about products and services. Relevant to this chapter is that consumers want more input about what is available on the Internet and want to be assured of safety. They are using the Internet more and more to perform information searches as well as to actually buy and to put their own messages out to the public. One student told the author, "I go online before I shop to read what other people are buying and to see what is out there. Then I go to the mall."

Consumers want to be more directly involved and to be heard; they also want to control more of what they see and how they react. Part of this stems from the interactivity that the Internet (as a pull medium) provides, compared with the push medium of television and radio. Television is more passive, requiring little of the viewer but to watch and listen—think of local car salesmen screaming at you in television commercials. The Internet requires action. Knowing this, several television shows have Internet sites so that after a show is over, the viewer is directed to more information and conversation at the site. Thus, the shows are keeping the viewer more involved for a longer period of time and providing interactivity, such as the ability to vote on issues or download recipes.

As we all know, the Internet has opened up consumer choice and worldwide communication. These are great developments. Few among us can live without e-mail, text messaging, or information searches via search engines such as Google, Yahoo!, AOL, or MSN. According to Harris Interactive, about 80 percent of Internet traffic begins with a search engine (Klaassen, 2006). Increasingly, students are using Wikipedia and GoogleScholar (www.Scholar.google.com) for information searches.

Although there are many positives, the darker side of the marketplace looms in the ease with which identity theft can take place and the deceptive practices and sales pitches aimed at children and adults. It is more difficult than ever to be a careful consumer and to maintain privacy. Many online problems stem from auction fraud, general merchandise fraud, and a wide range of e-mail scams. The growth of the Internet has resulted in a need for new laws and governmental scrutiny. Another issue is the **digital divide**, which refers to how the Internet is not accessible equally by all; not everyone has the benefit of this new technology. It is another case of the haves and the have-nots.

**Identity theft** refers to someone using your name or personal information, such as your Social Security number, driver's license number, student identification number, credit card number or other account number, telephone number, or e-mail or street address, without your permission. Identity theft involves more than a loss of immediate cash—it can destroy a person's credit score or financial or personal reputation, which may take months or years to reestablish. Steps to follow to prevent identity theft will be covered in this chapter, along with suggestions about what to do if it happens to you.

The U.S. Federal Trade Commission reports that for the last four years identity theft is at the top of consumer complaints.

Media reports of stolen veterans' records, bank account numbers, college student records, and employee records are rampant. All these may be stolen from computers by hackers. A hacker is a person who breaks into a computer—in-person or remotely. Break ins can happen to computers in your home, workplace, or businesses you patronize. Besides stealing files, hackers can corrupt files through the use of computer viruses and can use password detection software to steal people's identities. Hackers generally steal passwords first and then break into computers to obtain personal information. So identity theft can happen to individual consumers or to hundreds of thousands of consumers through mistakes, mishaps, and fraudulent behavior.

Before addressing the safety issues, first we will look at how consumers are using the Internet: Who buys what, when, and where online? We'll also discuss

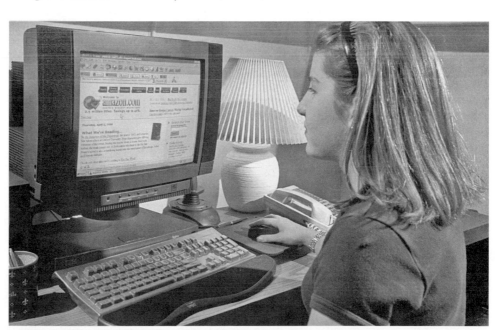

Online shopping is the fastest-growing category of consumer buying. (Frank LaBua, Pearson Education/PH College.)

trust issues related to buying online and the use of online personal shoppers or shopbots. Then we will delve into the subject of biometrics as it relates to security. Some areas involving trust issues are charitable giving and political campaign support. How do you separate legitimate charities from the quasi-legitimate or fraudulent charities? Although giving to charities can be done in person, over the phone, or through the mail, more and more charities are using the Internet as their primary form of solicitation, so charities are included at the end of this chapter. Online donating was heavily used in the 2008 presidential campaigns as well.

## THE INTERNET: CONSUMPTION PATTERNS AND CONSUMER ISSUES

E-commerce is a major driving force in the worldwide economy. From the consumer point of view, buying online offers convenience and selection: Web sites are open 24/7, products and prices can be easily compared, and an immediate purchase can be made.

There are several complaints about online shopping:

- Product return policies
- Quality of merchandise
- Slow or poor customer service
- Refund and billing pursuits
- Privacy, security, and trust issues
- Complex or difficult-to-navigate Web sites

Consumers process a lot of information from a variety of sources such as media, families and friends, work colleagues, coupons and promotions, in-store presentations, personal experiences, and other influences. Consumers cite past experience as the number one influencer when buying, so a proven brand name, store name, or Web site is a powerful factor in repeat buying behavior. Examples of Web sites that sell only brand names are Tee-zone, Shopbop, and Bluefly. Having brand names on Web sites was found to be an important influence on purchase decisions for consumers (Kim & Shim, 2002).

Access to the Internet as well as actual use varies significantly by country (the digital divide referred to in the Introduction), and the gap is changing so rapidly that in a book such as this reporting too many statistics would be foolhardy since the numbers will be outdated immediately. This chapter will offer an overview and research results that indicate not only what is but what is predicted to come. The focus, therefore, is not so much on the numbers, percentages, or specific equipment but on trends of usage and the consumer issues involved.

Research indicates that use of the Internet is based on several factors:

- Household income
- Age
- Gender
- Country
- Education level

Regarding Internet users, one general trend is that the higher their income and the higher their education level are, the more they use the Internet. Many early

**CONSUMER ALERT**

Be especially wary of a phone call, letter, unsolicited fax, e-mail, or postcard telling you that you have won a free or incredibly inexpensive trip. It is probably a trap. When you respond, the salesperson will want your credit card number as a way of confirming, but he or she could use this to build up charges for something you do not want. A typical scam is when your first night is free but subsequent nights are overpriced. Some offers do not include hotel taxes or service fees, transportation, or even basics like air conditioning and working televisions. One family with young children found themselves in Nassau in a very seedy, bug-ridden hotel; they had to pay to get a decent room in another hotel, and their "free" trip was ruined. Their return flight didn't leave for several days, so they were stuck. They had been had and they knew it. Protect yourself by being wary of great deals, do not be pressured into buying, ask detailed questions, get all information in writing before buying, don't buy part of the package, don't give credit card numbers over the phone, and don't send money by messenger or overnight mail. The best protection is to make travel plans on your own. Beware of all unsolicited offers.

To round out your perspective, visit several nations' Web sites where their travel warnings are posted.

of the country is experiencing unrest. As a potential traveler to a certain country, it is difficult to tell from the news on television and in newspapers just how unsettled the country or region is or how much an infectious disease has spread, so travel warnings issued by governments are useful. Usually, there is a lag time between the expiration of a threat, the reevaluation of the warning, and the return of tourists. During this lag time, adventuresome tourists find bargain prices, but as with most purchases, consumers are also taking a risk. They should weigh the risk factors and search for more information before making a decision about proceeding with travel plans.

A useful Web site in this regard is that of the U.S. State Department, which gives information on travel.state.gov for citizens traveling abroad. Box 10.6 gives a description of the types of information available on the site. This site is extremely popular for tourists, business travelers, job seekers with the federal government, and those interested in world conditions—it receives 95 million hits a year (Neuman, 2002). To

**BOX 10.6    U.S. State Department Travel Information (travel.state.gov)**

The Web site travel.state.gov contains the following sections:

- *Travel warnings.*  The warnings include reports of dangerous conditions in certain countries.
- *Public announcements.*  The public announcements list warnings of significant risks to the security of travelers because of terrorist threats as well as short-term unsafe conditions.
- *Consular information sheets.*  The consular information sheets give the locations of U.S. embassies and consulates in individual countries; information on health conditions, entry regulations, crime, security, and drug policies; and immigration policies.
- *Additional information.*  This site also provides information on ways to apply for jobs with the state department and foreign service, on international adoptions, and on visas and passports, and it offers travel publications.

studies showed that men were heavier users of the Internet than women, but more recent studies show that both men and women are heavy users, although they may be accessing different Web sites and using the Internet slightly differently in communicating with friends, shopping, and so forth. In regard to shopping, both men and women shop online, but they may shop for different product categories and for different reasons. Internet shoppers tend to be younger than conventional in-store shoppers or mail-order catalog shoppers. Take, for example, the Saks Fifth Avenue store chain. Shoppers on the Saks Web site are "on the average about seven years younger than the typical Saks customer and spend more per transaction" (O'Connell, 2007, p. B2). According to a Television Bureau of Advertising–sponsored media study on where adults are most likely to learn about products or brands, it found that those younger than 55 are heavier users of the Internet than older persons. Young people are heavy browsers. Because browsing activity often does not result in an immediate purchase but does result in a future purchase, companies try to encourage consumers to stay online or to come back for another visit. Interestingly, when it comes to actual purchasing, older Internet-savvy shoppers were more likely to purchase online than younger shoppers (Sorce, Perotti & Widrick, 2005). Perception of product price is especially important to older shoppers (Loke & Chan, 2007).

To reach all consumers, many print magazines have online versions to attract younger audiences who do not want subscriptions. Most magazines (such as *Consumer Reports*) and newspapers have online versions as well as print versions.

The Internet is just one player in the information world but is a growing one. Besides magazines and newspapers, other sources of brand and product information are television and radio as well as word of mouth. Depending on the particular study, sometimes newspapers come before magazines in terms of consumers learning about products or brands. But the main message is that the younger the group (such as ages 18 to 34) is, the more likely they will be to choose the Internet over other types of media.

In a study of the 25- to 34-year-old age group with Internet access, 78 percent shopped online in the past month (*How America Shops & Spends,* 2006). Comparing the 1990s to today's shopping patterns, there is a gradual decrease of shopping in malls and a rise in shopping in neighborhood stores and shopping online. To combat this trend, malls are encouraging cinemas, entertainment, activities such as fashion shows, extended hours, and restaurants or food courts to give more reasons for consumers to come to the mall. The popularity of malls varies by time of year, climate, location, and available alternatives. The Internet, of course, is a convenient alternative.

In the *How America Shops & Spends* study, here are the ways consumers used the Internet (from highest to lowest):

Doing shopping-related activities

Researching goods and services

Buying something on the Internet

Buying something locally after checking it out on the Internet

Buying an item after checking local stores for that product

The research for this age group showed that the main category they searched was electronics, such as types of cameras; other categories of interest included computers, home and garden equipment, sports and outdoor equipment, and clothing and accessories. The growing trend is the role of the Internet in influencing consumer decision making and purchasing.

## Shopbots: Intelligent Agents

When you go online to buy a wedding gift, the bridal registry or department store may supply a list of gifts for $50 and under or for $50 to $100. You have encountered a personal shopper or shopbot (also called a shopping agent or shopping bot, with bot being short for robot). **Shopbots** (or browser-based shopping assistants) are intelligent agent programs that scan the Internet and compile the information they are asked to locate in a format convenient for users. In other words, they aggregate information from various databases and recommend or list choices. Sometimes what appears at the top of the lists are the most commonly chosen or most authoritative sources, but other times they are paid placements, which are text ads targeted to keyword search results, or paid inclusion, which involves a fee structure (paid by the store or company) commonly used in shopping comparison sites. So what is at the top of the list may or may not be the wisest choice in terms of accurate information and the best price.

As mentioned earlier, most readers are probably familiar with Google and Yahoo! as general types of search engines that find and organize Web information. Shopbots, however, are specialized search engines that locate desired products and present a side-by-side comparison of online offerings, including the prices charged by each online merchant. Many of these services exist, one of the better known being MySimon; other examples are IBuy, Shopper, and Pricewatch as well as the various travel sites that compare prices and deals such as Expedia.com. and Travelocity. Since this is an evolving phenomenon, many competitors will come and go.

Shopbots are essentially personal online shoppers that enable quick comparison shopping. As an example, the way the bots work is that shoppers type in a brand name such as Nike and a specific model of athletic shoe along with a maximum price they are willing to pay. Another example would be to omit the brand name and enter a more general subject such as a man's oxford cloth blue dress shirt at less than $40. In both examples, the shopbot would search and reveal sellers' names, prices, and further details, including links to sellers such as Lands' End or Kohl's. To be useful, search functions have to be adaptive (responsive and able to make appropriate connections between buyers and sellers), organized (logical), and communicative (understandable). With the link to the merchants, searchers can go directly to the companies to find out more about the product and to buy from them.

A study by Goldsmith and Goldsmith (2003) revealed that users were more experienced and more innovative with regard to using the Internet for shopping than were nonusers. Users rated their experience with shopbots as generally positive (easy, convenient, fast, enjoyable). Higher income and higher socioeconomic status were associated with higher ratings of the convenience, speed, and enjoyment of using bots.

Since a list of sellers and prices is given for a selected product such as shoes or a shirt, will the customer most likely select the first merchant on the list, or will they go through the whole list and consider other details such as warranty and return terms, delivery date and conditions, prices, name or brand recognition, and availability? An ethical question is whether retailers should pay (paid placement or paid inclusion) to have their products listed first on the shopbot's page, and if so, should the buyer be made aware of this fact?

Following is one author's description of shopbots:

> Today's newer bots are more intelligent and more efficient. They store information on a site's thousands of products in a local cache (storage) and refresh them daily. They gather data about a merchant responsibly, search during off hours, and give merchants the option to release product prices rather than spidering their way through the sites with each request. They also compare customer service, delivery options, warranties, and the like. (Awad, 2007, p. 293)

This last sentence is so important. Customer satisfaction rests heavily on service quality: Was the online buying experience pleasant? Was product delivery on time?

## Online Auctions

Looking for a signed baseball glove or a wooden sled from 1930? An Internet auction may be the place for you. Since it appeared in 1995, this has been a fast-growing phenomenon in the Internet marketplace. The most famous is eBay. "The key to eBay's success is trust among buyers, sellers, and the company that facilitates the auctions" (Awad, 2007, p. 378).

The global flea market has items going from dollars to millions of dollars, from kitchen gadgets to yachts. Prohibited auction items include counterfeit goods, illegal drugs, guns, and government IDs such as passports. Usually individual sellers offer one item at a time, although companies unload large amounts of unsold merchandise. Typically the seller sells items at the price of the highest successful bid. The seller may set a minimum acceptable price. The bidding closes at a scheduled time, and the highest bidder wins. Afterward, the seller and the buyer communicate to arrange payment and delivery. This describes person-to-person sales, but there can also be business-to-person sales.

Buyers may pay by credit card, debit card, personal check, cashier's check, money order, cash on delivery, and escrow services. Credit cards offer buyers the most consumer protection, and typically this is the form of payment that business-to-person sales want, but person-to-person auctions often do not. The main choices for paying for online purchases are:

Paypal

Credit cards

Money orders

Cashier's checks

Some sellers use an escrow fee arrangement in which the buyer pays 5 percent of the cost of the item. The escrow service accepts payment from the buyer by check, credit card, or money order; then the service releases the money to the seller after the buyer receives and accepts the merchandise. This offers more protection to the buyer but slows up the transaction process. Another option is for the seller to agree to send purchases COD (collect on delivery) and the buyer to pay when the item is received.

## CONSUMER ALERT

Beware of shill bids that are put there either by the sellers themselves (using made-up names) or by friends or relatives of the seller. Many people have been caught doing this. It is a technique used in live auctions as well as online auctions where a seller's friend bids against potential buyers, driving up the price, and then the friend backs out at the last minute. There are also shill testimonials available online and in print. These made-up testimonials usually relate to product performance.

The Federal Trade Commission (FTC) receives complaints about auction fraud, and most complaints center on sellers:

- They do not deliver the goods as advertised.
- They deliver something far less valuable.
- They do not deliver on time.
- They fail to disclose relevant information (cracks, missing pieces, etc.).

Buyers can protect themselves by identifying the seller, checking the seller's feedback rating, and reviewing comments supplied by previous buyers. They should also know products and prices and should establish a top price and stick with it, avoiding getting caught up in bidding fever. Find out about payment options, payment of shipping and delivery fees, and return policies before bidding. Know all you can about the site itself. What protections does it offer buyers?

Sellers can protect themselves by providing accurate information, dealing with a reputable site, responding quickly to potential buyers' questions, contacting the highest bidder immediately, and shipping the merchandise as soon as possible. They cannot sell illegal goods or place shill bids or false testimonials. Sellers increase sales by offering photos of items.

## Security and Trust

In order to buy online in the **marketspace** (the Internet realm in which buying and selling take place), a consumer must be able to have **trust** in (reliance on) the process. The issue of trust is described this way:

> Trust is the psychological status of involved parties who are willing to pursue further interactions to achieve a planned goal. A trading party makes itself vulnerable to the other party's behavior; in other words, both parties assume risk. In the marketspace, sellers and buyers do not meet face to face. The buyer can see a picture of the product but not the product itself. (Turban et al., 2000, p. 86)

## CONSUMER ALERT

Be aware of damaged goods, and watch for words such as "refurbished," "flood sale," "close-out," "discontinued," and "off-brand." Take special caution when buying electrical or mechanical goods.

The buyer must trust not only the seller but also the e-commerce infrastructure and environment. Can someone look in on the transaction and take information away from it? Security mechanisms can help solidify the trust between buyer and seller in the marketspace.

Trust is also a basic expectation of brands—customers are more likely to buy brand names than unknown products online. According to an article in *Advertising Age,* "When we ask consumers to tell us about those they believe are the 'best brands,' the No. 1 attribute mentioned is 'it's a brand I trust.' Trust is the foundation for building relationships and for sustaining loyalty. Trust is critical when you introduce new ideas, products and benefits" (Keller, 2003, p. 28). According to this same article, trust was severely eroded with all the corporate scandals, including bloated chief executive officer (CEO) compensation, in 2002 and the continuing downturn of the economy in 2003. Not only did these factors affect stock valuations, but they also eroded people's confidence in business. In a survey, 6 in 10 people believed that the scandals resulted in a loss of trust that would take a long time to restore (Keller, 2003). Regulation is part of the solution, but businesses, through sound practices, must make a conscious effort to build trust.

In Chapter 2 on consumer movement history, we discussed the rise of antitrust legislation. The Internet has made the application of these laws even more important. One case in point is the worldwide practice of downloading or pirating copyrighted music without paying fees. A study found that many students felt downloading music was an acceptable act and that the majority of people were doing it (Siegfried, 2006). The legalities surrounding downloading are complex and involve competition laws and intellectual property laws in addition to antitrust and antimonopoly laws.

Since 2000, companies have faced serious penalties for not being careful with consumer information. Privacy-related regulations include the following:

Sarbanes-Oxley Act

Gramm-Leach-Bliley Act

Fair Credit Reporting Act

Health Insurance Portability and Accountability Act (HIPAA)

Customer service and legal compliance are critical to the success of an online business. According to Charles Hofacker, author of *Internet Marketing* (2000), trust is essential in facilitating exchange, and consumers need three kinds of trust before buying:

1. Trust in the mechanics of the selling process
2. Trust in the fairness and integrity of the specific people involved
3. Trust in the firm or institution and its ability to fulfill its delivery promise

The benefits of shopping online are that the Internet is always open—7 days a week, 24 hours a day—and comparison shopping is easier. Good deals, convenience, and selection abound, but how do you make sure your online shopping experience is safe? Here are some rules to follow when buying online:

- *Use secure connections and websites.* Computers come with browsers installed, and you can program them to filter secure and insecure sites.
- *Shop for known brands with known companies.* You should also determine companies' refund and mailing policies.

**CONSUMER POWER MODEL**

**Virtual Office Hours**

The Internet has opened up new ways for faculty and students to interact. "The days when students had to trek across campus to get professors' help during office hours may be slipping away. Harvard University computer science professor David Malan has launched 'virtual office hours,' allowing students to chat via text or microphone in live, online help sessions. 'It's especially convenient if they're in their dorm, at Starbucks or on vacation. They can get help without physically making their way to the office,' he says. 'And it allows instructors to pop in at 11 p.m. or 1 a.m. . . . It's not feasible for us to be on campus at that time.'"[1]

[1] Angela Haupt, "Professors Help Students Virtually." *USA Today*, January 8, 2008, p. 7D.

- *Keep passwords private.* The most secure passwords use a combination of numbers, letters, and symbols that have nothing to do with other parts of your life; in other words, avoid mailing addresses, phone numbers, and birthdays.
- *Pay by credit card.* When you pay by credit card, your transaction is protected by the Fair Credit Billing Act. In fact, this is usually the only way you can pay online, so it should be automatic. More and more sites are allowing payment with checks and bank accounts. These transactions are covered by the Electronic Funds Transfer Act.
- *Update virus program.* Run an updated virus scanner and legitimate spyware scanner weekly.
- *Keep a record.* You should maintain a personal record of purchases by printing a copy of any transaction.
- *Read the company's online privacy policy.* The policy should disclose what information is being collected about you and how the company may use the information. As mentioned before, opt out of having your information passed on to others whenever possible.

## Children as Online Consumers

The Computer Decency Act (CDA) has added some safeguards to Internet access, but content on the Internet is still difficult to control. As a counterpoint, there are issues of free speech. But most everyone agrees that children need to be protected from pornography and other inappropriate images and messages. Before delving into Internet issues regarding children, let us first discuss children as consumers in general.

Children are consumers of breakfast cereals, toys, games, entertainment, clothes, snack foods, technology, and sports equipment and exert a great deal of influence on family purchases such as vacations and cars. More than half of U.S. children are playing video games by the time they are five years old, and many are doing so as young as ages two and three. You may or may not agree with the following sentiment: "Childhood in recent decades has been defined . . . by parents who see their job as building self-esteem, by soccer coaches who give every player a trophy, by schools that used to name one 'student of the month' and these days name 40" (Zaslow, 2007, p. W1).

Parents and children are often seen as partners in consumerism. "Moms want the best for their children and that includes teaching them to realize that they have the power to make their own choices and decisions—and these decisions count!" (Coffey, Siegel & Livingston, 2006, p. x). Children are exposed to brands on the Internet, on television, and in a variety of other ways. Brands that are used in childhood are often preferred in adulthood, and this knowledge makes children a target for marketers. For example, Home Depot has workshops for parents and children to build birdhouses or other small items, and during the workshops the children wear orange Home Depot aprons. This is both cute and purposeful—the brand and the store are being mentally imprinted.

One study found that children were influenced by brand names and what the brands represented, so massive marketing campaigns by clothing and athletic shoe companies such as Tommy Hilfiger, Nike, and Adidas are undertaken (Zollo, 1999). In this study, two-thirds of teens interviewed associated "cool" brands with quality; they assumed that a marketing campaign message of "cool" meant that the brands were of high quality, that the two characteristics go together. At any age, the meaning of quality is not easy to define, but characteristics of quality may include durability.

Children as young as 4 years may have made their first independent purchase, although 8 is a more likely age (McNeal & Yeh, 1993). Consumers 8 to 18 years old spend over $30 billion a year mainly in these categories (Janof, 1999):

- Food and beverages
- Toys
- Clothing, entertainment, and personal care

It is during the preadolescent years, ages 8 to 12, that buying really takes off and purchasing behaviors are established. Countless media messages about consumption bombard children, parents, and teachers.

The Federal Communications Commission (FCC) regulates children's TV programming to make sure that children are not deceived by advertising, but this is not so easy to do because children watch television more times than on Saturday mornings. Generally, the TV ads aimed at children are for toys, food, games, and clothing. The Internet is largely unregulated, so if children are online, it is likely they are exposed to messages and images that parents would consider inappropriate. There are millions of personal blogs (daily accounts of people's lives) that are unregulated, which raises ethical issues about censorship in the home as well as in the greater society. **Censorship** is an attempt to control or the act, process, or policy of control. In the case of children, what might need to be censored are inappropriate materials (such as pornographic, offensive, hate, and other potentially dangerous materials) plus the solicitation of children for information about their parents, their families, or themselves. Possible approaches include training children how to be careful, getting parents involved, installing blocking software, and having government and Internet providers take steps to protect children.

The Children's Online Privacy Protection Act (COPPA), enforced by the FTC, requires commercial Web site operators to get parental consent before collecting personal information from children under the age of 13; this act also allows teachers to act on behalf of a parent during online school activities but does not require them to do so. Many school districts have adopted acceptable use policies to educate parents and children about both Internet use and issues of online safety, privacy, and parental consent, cautioning about the use of children's full names, addresses, and telephone numbers. Teachers are encouraged to notice the Web sites students are using and to steer them away from ones asking for personal information. Violators of COPPA should be reported to the FTC at www.ftc.gov/kidzprivacy.

**Strong encryption** means the ability to achieve unbreakable confidentiality. Parents can put filters on messages coming into the home on their home computers, thus limiting what content can be viewed by their children. Monitoring software will allow parents to view their child's activity on the computer. Some employers may use filters to screen what employees can see and do on work computers. Following are some tips for parents from www.secureflorida.org:

1. Create rules for Internet use in the home.
2. Know what your kids are doing online.
3. Use the Internet with your kids.
4. Don't allow solitary surfing.
5. If you agree to let your child meet an online buddy in person, go with them.
6. Don't rely solely on technology as a substitute for you.

## Environmental Impact of the Internet

There is no doubt that the Internet has an impact on the environment, but no one has measured the full impact mainly because it is changing so rapidly and is so profuse. The best that we can do is to provide estimates. The obvious sorts of impact have been in the areas of reduced use of paper, problems involved with equipment disposal, and decreased use of electricity. As one example, consider the movement of money. Payment systems in the paper world involve cash, checks, vouchers, coupons, and stamped and mailed credit card statements and bills. All this paper is saved in the digital world of e-commerce, which has the same look and feel and should be at least as secure as paper transactions. Electronic financial transactions should be properly encrypted, meaning security is embedded in the transactions.

Discussing the environmental impact of the Internet is important because issues about the natural environment such as global warming and the destruction of the rain forests have grown massively in the public's awareness. Environmental impact is of worldwide concern. The United States is particularly of interest because it leads the world in energy consumption, representing 24 percent of the world's primary energy consumption (Caruso, 2003).

"Moving businesses online and marketing by pixels instead of packages, e-commerce can reduce the need for such wasteful products as printed catalogues, telephone books, newspapers, and magazines" (Sui & Rejeski, 2002). Other areas of environmental impact include shipping, warehouse space, and employee productivity. Electronic purchasing and inventory have made the recording of the buying, selling, and storing of goods and services much more efficient, but it is difficult to say how much energy is saved. For example, in some cases more fuel is used because half-filled delivery trucks are sent so that a company can back up its promise of rapid delivery. Less warehouse space may be needed, or all the warehousing may be done in one central place rather than in scattered storage facilities. More people working at home would seem to indicate a reduction both in travel (meaning less fuel) and in the need for outside office space (meaning less energy), so one would assume that more teleworkers would indicate less stress on the environment.

Using less paper would indicate less stress on most resources; for example, less wood would be needed for paper products and less energy would be used in processing the wood into paper. E-commerce has also affected the packaging and display of products. If products are sold online, that reduces the need for packaging and displaying products and for driving to the store to see the products. Internet billing and direct depositing use less paper and envelopes. To conclude, the full extent of the environmental impact from use of the Internet (versus other forms of getting information, conducting business, and buying and selling products) is yet to be determined.

If every U.S. household switched to online billing and statements, it would save 16.5 million trees, 13 billion gallons of water, and 1.6 billion pounds of solid waste.

## Biometrics

As covered in the Introduction section, biometrics refers to the use of one's unique physical traits to verify identity. "One day soon, it may not matter that you lost the house key or can't find all five documents required to renew your driver's license, Instead, you'll need just your fingerprints for identification. That's the future painted by a number of companies that are touting fingerprints as the preferred way to use biometrics" (Keeton, 2007, p. B4).

In Japan, the use of biometrics is common on cell phones, at bank automated teller machines (ATMs), and for point-of-purchase credit card purchases. Home Depot stores in Canada and the United States are selling keyless door entries, and so are car manufacturers around the world. Fingerprint sensors have been used for many years at universities for dormitory or cafeteria entrance by students and at companies where security is important for entrance by employees. One manufacturer of biometric devices has a sensor that reads below the fingerprint to living tissue, which is harder to fake with a piece of tape or some other substitute.

Airports, laboratories, and border patrol stations are experimenting with biometrics. Law enforcement already uses them. One of the problems is the vast amount of data. Imagine managing a fingerprint database of over 300 million Americans; then imagine doing this for the worldwide population of over 6 billion.

Are there privacy issues? Yes, there are. Barry Steinhart of the American Civil Liberties Union (ACLU) says that "the use of biometric identification raises legal privacy issues, particularly if a big database were used for national drivers' license or ID-card program. In the worse case, the government could use personal information to keep tabs on innocent citizens" (Keeton, 2007, p. B4). Surveys of Americans show that most are comfortable with biometric identification and that they like the convenience of not carrying keys or cards or remembering passwords.

In addition to fingerprint scanners, there are eye readers (referred to as retinal scanners), which have people look at a sensor that causes a garage door to open or makes something else happen. Other biometrics include facial analysis, speech analysis, body odor analysis, and signature analysis, but currently fingerprint analysis leads the way for identification. "The reason is the one in a billion chance that two people will have the same fingerprint" (Awad, 2007, p. 441). The main goal of using biometrics would be to make identification hacking or spoofing more difficult, which makes biometrics a safe and secure identity tool. Biometric methods should be used in combination with other security methods. For example, to enter a secure area an individual would need to supply a password, enter a code, and provide a fingerprint.

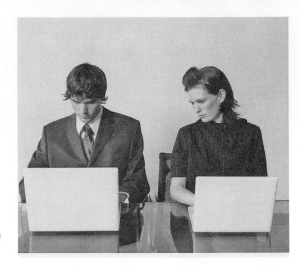

How do you keep laptop information private? (Getty Images—Stockbyte.)

## IDENTITY THEFT AND PRIVACY PROTECTION

**E-consumerism** is defined as actions of consumers or their agents to protect and promote consumer interest and to seek empowerment in the context of the electronic marketplace (Rha, Widdows & Montalto, 2003). In order to participate in the marketplace, consumers have to provide codes or personal information as a way of identifying themselves to vendors. This is part of the transaction between consumers and producers.

E-commerce is still evolving. A leading car manufacturer conducted a study of car-buying habits and predicted that consumers might buy used cars via the Internet but would still want to touch and drive the cars before purchasing them (Drucker, 2002). It is true that most consumers still want to test-drive a new car before buying it, but increasingly they are turning to the Internet for the final purchase. Dealers may soon serve as only deliverers of cars or as showrooms rather than places of purchase, which has incredible implications for one of America's leading and most profitable industries. For years General Motors was the leading Fortune 500 company in the nation but is now surpassed by Wal-Mart in terms of revenue (sales).

Another aspect of e-commerce is that new distribution channels change who the customers are. "They change not only how customers buy but also what they buy. They change consumer behavior, savings patterns, industry structure—in short, the entire economy. This is what is now happening, and not only in the United States but increasingly in the rest of the developed world, and in a good many emerging countries, including mainland China" (Drucker, 2002, pp. 15–16).

Models of decision making that are based on economic considerations of utility, value maximization, and scarcity predict that consumers would evaluate the utility provided by each offering and choose the option that provides the maximum utility. Choice is narrowed by these considerations. Consumers want the best product at the lowest price with the maximum return or benefit; they also want ease of use, which leads to the increased use of credit cards and the Internet as modes of purchase (as opposed to in-person cash transactions where identity theft is not a

Identity theft is a federal crime.

problem). No one is identified, the cash is exchanged, and that is the end—there is no paper trail. This is the starting point in our discussion. Times have changed, and the frauds have kept pace.

As defined in the Introduction section to this chapter, identity theft refers to someone using your name or personal information, such as your Social Security number, driver's license number, credit card number or other account number, telephone number, or street address, without your permission. Essentially the identity thief is stealing your identity for personal gain, such as using the information to open up credit accounts or bank accounts, take out loans, place long-distance calls, or make major purchases. Identity theft can result in the loss of money and the loss of reputation. An example of the latter would be the loss of a good credit rating.

**Privacy** is a state of an individual or group which keeps information about their lives and activities from public consumption. It means to not be bothered by unwanted intrusions such as unsolicited sales calls. The right to privacy is recognized by federal and state laws in the United States and by the laws of many other countries. Box 11.1 gives a list of some federal privacy legislation. The question is how much government regulation is necessary. Some degree of regulation and authority is necessary, but not at the expense of individual freedoms and civil liberties. In the long run, the best defense against unwanted scams and other intrusions is through using self-regulation and discretion and by being aware, making wise choices, being careful about participation, learning about security, knowing legal rights, and seeking redress.

According to Mason et al. (1995), ethical issues can be categorized in several ways:

- *Privacy*. The collection, storage, and dissemination of information about individuals all impact privacy. A question in this category would be: What information about oneself should one have to reveal in order to get a product or service?
- *Accuracy*. Accuracy involves the authenticity and fidelity of information collected and processed. A question in this category would be: Who is to be held accountable for errors in information?
- *Property*. The ownership and value both of information and of intellectual property are property issues. A question in this category would be: Who owns the information?
- *Accessibility*. The term *accessibility* refers to the right to access information and the payment of fees to access it. Questions in this category would be: Who is allowed access to information? Should I be afraid to give information that may be sold, used, or revealed in an inappropriate manner? Research reveals that this issue comes up again and again and is one of the main reasons people refuse to buy over the Internet.

## It's the Law: Federal and State Legislation

The Identity Theft and Assumption Deterrence Act of 1998 makes it a federal crime if someone "knowingly transfers or uses, without lawful authority, a means of identification of another person with the intent to commit, or to aid or abet, any unlawful activity that constitutes a violation of federal law, or that constitutes a felony under any applicable state or local law." A Social Security number is considered a means of

**BOX 11.1    Main Federal Privacy Legislation**

Privacy rights are built into many state and federal laws. Here is a list of representative federal privacy legislation acts:

*Privacy Act of 1974.* This act prohibits the government from collecting information secretly, or if it is collected, it must be for a specific purpose.

*Privacy Protection Act of 1980.* This act provides protection of privacy in computerized and related documents.

*Electronic Communications Privacy Act of 1986.* This act prohibits citizens from intercepting data communications without authority.

*Computer Matching and Privacy Act of 1988.* This act regulates the matching of computer files by state and federal agencies.

*Video Privacy Protection Act of 1988.* This act protects privacy in picture transmissions.

*Fair Health Information Practices Act of 1997.* This act sets a code of fair information practices.

*Consumer Internet Privacy Protection Act of 1997.* This act requires prior written consent before a computer service can disclose information about subscribers.

*Federal Internet Privacy Protection Act of 1997.* This act prohibits federal agencies from disclosing personal records from the Internet.

*Communications Privacy and Consumer Empowerment Act of 1997.* This act protects online commerce in terms of privacy rights.

*Data Privacy Act of 1997.* This act limits the use of personal information and regulates spamming.

*Children's Online Privacy Act of 1998.* This act, an amendment to the Internet Tax Freedom Act, requires companies to verify a person's age before showing online material that could be harmful to minors. This can be done through credit cards or access numbers.

*Internet School Filtering Act of 1998.* This act attempts to limit access to inappropriate material by controlling federal funds and grants to school and libraries. Schools provide blocking software.

*USA PATRIOT Act of 2001.* This act attempts to unite and strengthen the United States by providing appropriate tools required to intercept and observe terrorism; see www.epic.org/privacy/terrorism/usapatriot. It also expands government law enforcement powers, especially with regard to the Internet.

identification, as are credit card numbers. The penalties are stiff: A conviction of identity theft carries fines and prison sentences of up to 15 years, and states have passed laws related to identity theft, as well. To find out rules in your state, contact the state attorney general's office (www.naag.org) or local consumer protection agencies.

Many federal government agencies are involved in educating the public about identity theft and hunting down criminals. The E-Resources section lists many of the places consumers can turn to for information and help. The following agencies are particularly important in the fight to protect personal information:

- *Federal Trade Commission (FTC).* The FTC provides education and publications, and it has an electronic database called the Identity Theft Clearinghouse, which is a system of records covered under the Privacy Act of 1974. The Privacy Act prohibits unauthorized use of these records, but the information may be shared with FTC attorneys and investigators or certain private entities such as credit bureaus if the FTC deems it necessary to resolve problems (see E-Resources section).

- *U.S. Department of Justice.* The Justice Department and its U.S. attorneys prosecute federal identity theft cases.
- *Federal Bureau of Investigation (FBI).* The FBI investigates cases connected with bank fraud, mail fraud, wire fraud, bankruptcy fraud, insurance fraud, fraud against the government, and terrorism. Field offices are listed in a telephone directory's Blue Pages.
- *Secret Service.* The Secret Service investigates financial crimes involving identity theft, usually cases involving substantial dollar loss. Field offices are listed in a telephone directory's Blue Pages.
- *U.S. Department of the Treasury.* The Treasury Department has a financial crimes division that specializes in identity theft problems.

## Identity Theft: Methods and Protections

Skilled identity thieves have a number of methods to gain access to personal information (see Box 11.2). Box 11.3 shows how the thieves use the personal information they obtain. No one can prevent identity theft entirely, but you can minimize the risk by doing the following:

- Watch credit card statements, and order a copy of credit reports from each of the three major credit bureaus (Equifax, Experian, and TransUnion).

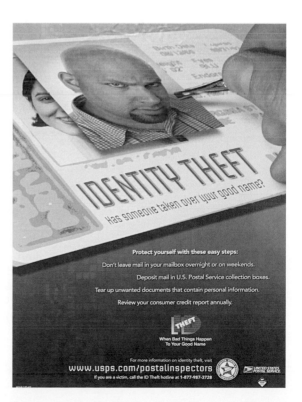

Poster from a nationwide push to educate the public about identity theft. (AP Wide World Photos.)

**BOX 11.2    Methods of Identity Thieves**

Here are nine methods that identity thieves use to get personal information:

1. They steal wallets and purses containing your identification as well as credit and bank cards.
2. They steal your mail, including your bank and credit card statements, preapproved credit offers, new checks, and tax information.
3. They complete a "change of address form" to divert your mail to another location.
4. They rummage through your trash or the trash of businesses for personal data in a practice known as "dumpster diving."
5. They fraudulently obtain your credit by posing as a landlord, employer, or someone else who may have a legitimate need for and a legal right to the information.
6. They find personal information in your home.
7. They use personal information you share on the Internet.
8. They scam you, often through e-mail or telephone, by posing as a legitimate organization.
9. They get your information from the workplace in a practice known as "business record theft" by stealing files out of offices where you're a customer, employee, patient, or student; by bribing an employee who has access to your files; or by hacking into electronic files.

*Source: ID Theft: When Bad Things Happen to Your Good Name.* Washington, DC: Federal Trade Commission, September 2002, p. 3.

- Be careful with the following items: checkbooks, pay stubs, receipts with credit card numbers, credit cards, ATM cards, Palm pilots, business cards, driver's licenses, and health insurance cards (especially those with Social Security numbers). If you think you are safe because you have never lost any of these or put them in the wrong hands, think again. Anyone processing your

**BOX 11.3    How Identity Theft Information Is Used**

Following are eight ways that identity thieves may use personal information:

1. They call your credit card issuer while pretending to be you and ask to change the mailing address on your credit card account. The imposter then runs up charges on your account. Because your bills are being sent to the new address, it may take some time before you realize there's a problem.
2. They open a new credit card account using your name, date of birth, and Social Security number. When they use the credit card and don't pay the bills, the delinquent account is reported on your credit report.
3. They establish phone or wireless service in your name.
4. They open a bank account in your name and write bad checks on that account.
5. They file for bankruptcy under your name to avoid paying debts they've incurred under your name or to avoid eviction.
6. They counterfeit checks or debit cards and drain your bank account.
7. They buy cars by taking out auto loans in your name.
8. They give your name to the police during an arrest. If they're released from police custody but don't show up for their court date, an arrest warrant is issued in your name.

*Source: ID Theft: When Bad Things Happen to Your Good Name.* Washington, DC: Federal Trade Commission, September 2002, p. 4.

credit card or taking information about you (for example, in a video rental store) can turn around and sell that information to a fraud ring. Be especially cautious when traveling.

- Use hard-to-figure-out passwords or passphrases on credit card, bank, and phone accounts. An example of a strong password from www.secureflorida.org is A&Bh3cnJ,P,&E.

  Ann and Bob have three children named Jason, Paul, and Elizabeth. Ann, who made up the password, can remember it because it is based on her family.
- Secure personal information at home if there are roommates. At work, be watchful of people who are in and out doing remodeling or repairs.
- Secure personal information at work.
- Update virus protection software regularly on computers.
- Never click on hyperlinks sent from strangers or download unknown files.
- Take special care with laptops, and log off when finished.
- Take mail with checks and personal information to the post office instead of putting it in unsecured mailboxes.
- Delete personal information using a "wipe" utility program to overwrite the entire hard drive when disposing of a computer. For more information about how to do this, go to www.hq.nasa.gov/office/oig/hq/harddrive.pdf from NASA or go to www.ftc.gov.

## Self-Background Checks

There is an upsurge of interest in background checks, both personal background checks and those by outside parties such as employers, who hire a corporate background-screening agency such as ChoicePoint (employers can do this once consent is provided on the application form). ChoicePoint has information from government public records and some courts and can do employment and education verification, such as finding out if someone really graduated from Harvard or Stanford. A free annual report can be gathered from www.choicetrust.com, but pre-employment self-checks may cost a fee. LexisNexis also provides a free copy of information contained in background-screening reports; call 877-913-6245 or e-mail compliance@wxpscreening.lexisnexis.com. LexisNexis may charge a fee for a more thorough report. It should be noted that contact information and fee structures are subject to change, but you should be able to find out a great deal about yourself for free. Unfortunately, as has been mentioned in this part of the chapter, fraudsters can find out about you, too.

What is the first step in a self-background check? Googling yourself is a beginning, but it is not enough—you should order your credit report. This can be obtained by going to www.annualcreditreport.com, by calling 877-322-8228, or by contacting credit-reporting agencies such as Experian, TransUnion, or Equifax. Under a 2004 federal law, consumers have access to these reports, those by ChoicePoint, and others. The credit-reporting agencies keep records on your credit history as well as personal information such as previous addresses. A free annual credit report is available from them and is required by federal law at the phone number given or the Web site www.annualcreditreport .com. Another place to check is www.ssa.gov. Through this Web site, you can check your Social Security earnings and find out if anyone has been using your

**CONSUMER ALERT**

When it comes to identity theft, the most victimized age group is 18–29. This is due to:

- Transient nature
- Prevalence on the Internet
- Simple naivety

number. For example, someone else could be working under your Social Security number.

One of the hardest things to fix is a damaging online set of postings. ReputationDefender.com scours the Web for unflattering material on you and can work to remove it, but they charge a fee for this service.

Another option is to hire a private investigator or professional screening service, but these are quite costly and are more likely to be used for executive-level screenings. Background-screening check services require proof of identity before releasing information. There are other groups as well, such as the trade association called the National Association of Professional Background Screeners (www.napbs.com). Identity theft insurance is another option available to consumers.

When filling out information cards in person or over the computer, choose the opt-out option as a way to reduce the number of people and organizations that receive personal information about you. Use work phone numbers and addresses rather than home phone numbers and addresses whenever possible. You can notify the three major credit bureaus that you do not want personal information about you shared for selling or promotional purposes.

## Recourse for Victims of Identity Theft

Here are four steps to follow if you are a victim of identity theft:

1. Contact the fraud department of the three credit bureaus. Following an investigation, there may be a dispute; if there is, use the sample dispute letter in Box 11.4 as a guide.
2. Close the accounts that you think may have been tampered with or opened fraudulently. In most cases, the Truth in Lending Act limits your liability for unauthorized credit card charges to $50 per card. The Fair Credit Billing Act establishes procedures for resolving billing errors, including fraudulent charges on accounts.
3. File a police report with your local police department; also get a copy of the report and send it to Experian, Equifax, and TransUnion.
4. File a complaint with the FTC. This can be done online at www.consumer. gov/idtheft. The FTC does not bring criminal cases but can help victims by providing information to assist them in resolving the financial and other problems that can result from this crime, and reporting this information can help law enforcement officials track down identity thieves and stop them.

## CONSUMER ALERT

The elderly are particularly at risk for identity theft when they are in nursing homes or assisted living centers. Seniors are also vulnerable because they tend to have good credit, they are less likely to use their cards often, and they are unlikely to request their credit reports from credit bureaus. Their lack of use makes them easy targets. The cardholder's name can be used to open bank accounts, to forge checks, and even to take out bank loans for cars. Seniors' relatives can look out for them by lowering their credit card limit to $300 or $500; relatives should also be familiar with the security policies at any residential facility. Besides relatives, sheriff department detectives can look out for the elderly and give talks on what to notice. Nursing homes and assisted living centers should do background checks on potential employees before hiring them.

**BOX 11.4    Sample Dispute Letter for Credit Bureau**

Date

Your Name
Your Address
Your City, State, Zip Code

Complaint Department
Name of Credit Bureau
Address
City, State, Zip Code

Dear Sir or Madam:
I am writing to dispute the following information in my file. The items I dispute also are circled on the attached copy of the report I received. (Identify item[s] disputed by name of source, such as creditors or tax court, and identify type of item, such as credit account, judgment, etc.)

The item is (inaccurate or incomplete) because (describe what is inaccurate or incomplete and why). I am requesting that the item be deleted (or request another specific change) to correct the information.

Enclosed are copies of (use this sentence if applicable and describe any enclosed documentation, such as payment records or court documents) supporting my position. Please investigate this (these) matter(s) and (delete or correct) the disputed item(s) as soon as possible.

Sincerely,

Your Name

Enclosures: (List what you are enclosing)

*Source: ID Theft: When Bad Things Happen to Your Good Name.* Washington, DC: Federal Trade Commission, September 2002.

## CHARITIES: WHEN GIVING HELPS AND WHEN IT HURTS

As noted in the introductory part of this chapter, many charities are moving toward the Internet as their main way of advertising what they do and of soliciting donations. Charities can be legitimate, quasi-legitimate, or outrightly fraudulent. Americans donate billions of dollars a year to the 400 largest charities in the United States. Curiously, low-income people are often more generous donors than wealthier people; some speculate this is because they can more easily relate to those in need. For many years, the Salvation Army has received the largest donations, but following the September 11, 2001, disaster, donations to the American Red Cross skyrocketed. These are both legitimate charities and not to be confused with ones that are not. An estimated $2 billion a year falls into the hands of fraudulent solicitors.

The problem is there are so many charities that it is difficult to sort the good ones from the bad ones. There are hundreds of thousands of charities vying for your contribution, and new ones join their ranks every year. How do you make good choices? Your first thought should center on the causes or charities you believe in because your donations should be a reflection of your values and principles. This will narrow the field. The next guide should be how the charity ranks on the basis of how efficiently its dollars are spent. For example, the American Red Cross ranks consistently high in the percentage of its income that goes directly to programs to help those in need. *Money* magazine regularly reports the rankings of charities; other magazines, Better Business Bureaus (BBBs), newspapers, state government consumer protection agencies, and consumer watchdog organizations also offer lists and rankings (see the E-Resources for a list of charity watchdog Web sites). Go online and investigate the charity itself; all large charities have Web sites with information.

The surest way to avoid fraud is to know about the charity and its activities, so ask questions about how money is used (make sure most of it gets to those who are in need), and be sure the money will be spent where you want it spent. Do you want it to go to terrorist causes that blow up buildings? Do you want your hard-earned money to go to fake religious leaders for building their mansions or for adding to their fleet of luxury cars? Sometimes the surface organization seems okay, but the money is funneled to other organizations, people, and causes that you would not normally support. Box 11.5 provides a charity checklist to ensure that your donation dollars benefit the people and organizations that you want. Be especially wary of charities or persons you do not know who ask for donations over the Internet.

Special care should be taken when giving large donations, especially those made through trusts and wills. Donations of this sort should not be made without legal and tax advice from professionals.

**CONSUMER ALERT**

Look out for fraudulent middlemen representing real charities. For example, they may say "buy this raffle ticket and the proceeds will go to the Red Cross," but the person pockets all or some of the cash.

**BOX 11.5    Charity Checklist**

1. Ask for written information. Do not go by what is said on the telephone or in e-mail. Be especially wary of unsolicited e-mails with sad stories from foreign countries.
2. Ask for identification. If the solicitor refuses, call the local authorities.
3. Call the charity back to find out if the caller was legitimate.
4. Watch for similar-sounding names. The fraudulent name may differ by only one word from a legitimate charity's name.
5. Be skeptical about being pressured to pledge money. Be wary if anyone says that you or someone in your family has already pledged money.
6. Ask how the donation will be spent.
7. Find out how much of the donation is tax-exempt or tax-deductible if there are special events or tickets. If tax deductibility is important to you, ask for a receipt showing the amount of your contribution and stating that it is tax-deductible. For security reasons, pay by check. Beware of any solicitor insisting on cash.
8. Discourage employers from pushing employees or schools from pushing schoolchildren to donate to charities. Donations should be by individual choice, not by force.
9. Be wary of any gifts or sweepstakes offers connected with a contribution. To be eligible to win, a donation is not necessary (depending on state regulations).
10. Be wary of people who gather money at street corners or at traffic intersections; they may or may not be legitimate.
11. Be wary of fraudsters operating immediately after a crisis. They prey on your sympathy.
12. Let the attorney general, your local consumer protection office, and the FTC know of any organization that is making misleading solicitations.

 **CONSUMER ALERT**

For years, common consumer fraud relied on the victim's desire to help organizations and individuals. The way it works is that you are first led to feel sorry for the charity or source; then it evolves into not only charity fraud but also mail and investment fraud. A particularly enduring and costly one is a proposal that asks individuals to assist government officials in transferring "tied-up" funds by establishing accounts in their country. The offer claims you can earn millions as a percentage of the money you help transfer into new accounts. For example, you provide a bank account where they can deposit millions of dollars that the Nigerian government has "tied up" in bureaucracy. Initially, the proposal states that you need not invest any money up front. However, as time passes, you begin receiving letters or faxes stating that the Nigerian government has snagged the transaction of depositing money into the account you set up; then they ask you to provide your own money to complete the transaction, stating that afterward "millions" will be deposited into your account. Victims have been known to pump thousands of dollars into this scam. U.S. postal officials believe that this type of mail fraud has cost victims more than $100 million a year.

*Reference:* Florida Department of Consumer Services Web site, January 22, 2003.

## SUMMARY

Online buying offers convenience and selection, with the main negatives being security and potential for fraud. The Internet has revolutionized the shopping experience and information searches. From the sellers' point of view, hard-to-reach populations are no longer difficult to reach.

Consumer information processing is fundamental to the study of consumer economics. Greater access to information should lead to greater confidence in decision making and more choices for consumers. The downside to greater access is greater exposure to identity theft. In short, technology brings with it new opportunities and challenges for regulators, consumers, and marketers.

In terms of demographics, Internet customers tend to be younger than the usual in-store customers, but older online shoppers are often more likely to actually purchase. The Internet is a pull medium, meaning there is interactivity between the consumer and the Internet. The Internet requires action; it is less passive than watching television or listening to radio.

The Identity Theft and Deterrence Act of 1998 made it a federal crime for someone to steal your identity. The Internet creates numerous problems in the area of privacy, identity protection, sales, and children's issues. The risk to privacy can be minimized if the buyer trusts the mechanics of the selling process, the fairness and integrity of the people involved, and the firm or the institution and its ability to deliver as promised. This chapter showed how to conduct a self-background check to find out what information is out there about you. The USA PATRIOT Act of 2001 confers extra powers on the executive branch of government, especially in regard to the Internet. This act unites and strengthens America by providing appropriate tools required to intercept and obstruct terriorism.

## KEY POINTS

1. More consumers are using the Internet for prepurchase and purchase activities.
2. Biometrics such as fingerprints and retinal scans is being used more frequently for identity purposes.
3. Shopbots, a type of search engine, are used by consumers to locate and compare products.
4. Identity theft has challenged the trust among consumers and between consumers and markets and can lead to a loss of money, reputation, and time. It is a worldwide problem, and in the United States it is a federal crime.
5. Children are at risk on the Internet due to predators and fraudsters who take advantage of them.
6. The spread of the Internet has an environmental impact, and the extent of this impact is being studied.
7. Under a 2004 federal law, consumers can perform self-background checks, which begin with ordering free credit reports.

## KEY TERMS

| | | |
|---|---|---|
| biometrics | identity theft | shopbots |
| censorship | marketspace | strong encryption |
| digital divide | privacy | trust |
| e-consumerism | | |

## DISCUSSION QUESTIONS

1. How is the subject of the consumer-in-control movement related to the Internet?
2. Why are children particularly vulnerable when it comes to the Internet? What steps can be taken to lessen the risk?
3. Since e-commerce is evolving, it is not clear how many different kinds of goods and services will eventually be offered for sale online. Some, like dry cleaning, are unsuitable, but books and cars have been sold successfully online. Can you think of another category of goods or services that would sell well online? Explain your answer.
4. What federal agencies are involved in monitoring the Internet?

## E-RESOURCES

### U.S. Government Sites

*Note:* You have the option to submit information about identity theft or any other fraud problem anonymously. However, if you do this, law enforcement and other entities cannot contact you for further information to assist in identity theft investigations and prosecutions.

**Department of Justice (DOJ)**   *www.usdoj.gov*

**Federal Bureau of Investigation (FBI)**   *www.fbi.gov*

**Federal Trade Commission (FTC)**   *www.ftc.gov*
Library of consumer publications registering complaints

**Secret Service**   *www.treas.gov/usss*

### Banking Fraud

**Federal Deposit Insurance Corporation (FDIC)**   *www.fdic.gov*

**Federal Reserve System**   *www.federalreserve.gov*

**National Credit Union Administration (NCUA)**   *www.ncua.gov*

**Office of the Comptroller of the Currency**   *www.occ.treas.gov*

**Office of Thrift Supervision**   *www.ots.treas.gov*

**Bankruptcy Fraud**

**U.S. Trustee**   *www.usdoj.gov/ust*

**Investment Fraud**

**Securities and Exchange Commission (SEC)**   *www.sec.gov*

**Mail Theft**

**U.S. Postal Inspection Service**   *www.usps.gov*

**Passport Fraud**

**U.S. Department of State**   *www.travel.state.gov/passport_services.html*

**Phone Fraud**

*Note:* First contact your local phone service before going to a higher-level agency.

**Federal Communications Commission (FCC)**   *www.fcc.gov*

**Social Security Number Theft and Misuse**

**Social Security Administration (SSA)**   *www.ssa.gov*

**Tax fraud**

**Internal Revenue Service (IRS)**   *www.treas.gov/irs/ci*

**Online Buying Information and Privacy Protection**

**American Express Company**   *www.americanexpress.com*
Full description of Web site security, ways to decline e-mail offers

**Call for Action, Inc.**   *www.callforaction.org*
International nonprofit, ABC's of privacy

**Consumer Information Center**   *www.pueblo.gsa.gov*
Publications from federal agencies

**Direct Marketing**   *www.the-dma.org*
Trade association, intermediary association between consumers and companies

**Charitable Giving**

**Charity Watchdogs**
Charity scams reported

**Council of Better Business Bureaus**   *www.bbb.org*
Overall guide to consumer complaint filings

**Internet Nonprofit Center**   *www.nonprofits.org*
IRS database of 1.2 million nonprofits, information on whether a charity is registered

**Money magazine**   *www.money.mag.com*
Rankings of nation's largest charities

**National Charities Information Bureau**   *www.give.org*
Monitoring of charities receiving $500,000 or more annually

# REFERENCES

Awad, E. M. (2007). *Electronic commerce from vision to fulfillment,* 3rd ed. Upper Saddle River, NJ: Pearson Prentice Hall.

Caruso, G. (2003). *United States: Environmental issues.* Retrieved March 29, 2007, from Energy Information Administration, www.eia.doe.gov/emeu/cabs/usenv.html.

Coffey, T., D. Siegel, and G. Livingston. (2006). *Marketing to the new super consumer mom & kid.* Ithaca, NY: Paramount Market Publishing.

Drucker, P. (2002). *Managing in the next society.* New York: St. Martin's Press.

Goldsmith, R., and E. Goldsmith. (2003). The use of shopping bots by online buyers. Proceedings of Marketing Theory and Practice Annual Meeting. Hilton Head, SC.

Hofacker, C. (2000). *Internet marketing,* 3rd ed. New York: John Wiley.

*How America Shops & Spends.* (2006). Newspaper Association of America.

Keeton, A. (April 12, 2007). Fingerprints give a hand to security. *Wall Street Journal,* p. B4.

Keller, E. (February 24, 2003). To regain trust, faking won't do. *Advertising Age,* p. 28.

Kim, Y., and K. Shim. (2002). The influence of Internet shopping mall characteristics and user traits on purchase intent. *Irish Marketing, 15* (2), 25–34.

Klaassen, A. (2006). *Search Marketing Fact Pack 2006.* New York: Crain Communications.

Loke, Y. J., and W. Y. Chan. (2007). Seasoned and potential Internet shoppers. A multinomial logit analysis. *Applied Economics Letters, 14,* 43–47.

Mason, R. O., et al. (1995). *Ethics of information management.* Thousand Oaks, CA: Sage Publishers.

McNeal, J., and C. Yeh. (June 1993). Born to shop. *American Demographics,* 34–39.

O'Connell, V. (April 20, 2007). Park Avenue classic or Soho trendy? *Wall Street Journal,* pp. B1–B2.

Rha, J. R., N. H. Widdows, and C. Montalto. (2003). E-consumerism as a tool for empowerment. *Journal of Consumer Education, 19* (20), 61–69.

Secure Florida. Best Practices for Parents and Online Safety, www.secureflorida.org, accessed May 15, 2008.

Siegfried, R. (2006). Student attitudes on software piracy and related issues of computer ethics. *Ethics and Information Technology, 6,* 215–22.

Sorce, P., V. Perotti, and S. Widrick. (2005). Attitude and age differences in online buying. *International Journal of Retail & Distribution Management, 33* (2/3), 122–33.

Sui, D., and D. Rejeski. (2002). Environmental impacts of the emerging digital economy: the e-for-environment e-commerce. *Environmental Management, 29* (2), 155–63.

Turban, E., J. Lee, D. King, and H. M. Chung. (2000). *Electronic commerce: A managerial perspective.* Upper Saddle River, NJ: Prentice Hall.

Zaslow, J. (April 20, 2007). The most-praised generation goes to work. *Wall Street Journal,* p. W1.

Zollo, P. (1999). *Wise up to teens: Insights into marketing and advertising to teenagers.* Ithaca: NY: New Strategist Publications.

# Being a Better Consumer of Housing and Vehicles

> A comfortable house is a great source of happiness. It ranks immediately
> after health and a good conscience.
> —Sydney Smith

## Learning Objectives

1. Define consumer unit, and describe a typical unit's expenditures.
2. Explain the pros and cons of owning versus renting housing.
3. Explain the different types of home mortgages.
4. Discuss change points in people's lives and their effect on consumption.
5. Discuss the cost of utilities.
6. Explain the pros and cons of leasing versus owning vehicles.
7. Discuss how to buy new or used vehicles and what deceptive practices to avoid.

"This summer Mary Mooney and her husband were soaking up the sun in Florida when they saw a Buick Enclave, a big, seven-passenger vehicle, and decided they just had to have one. But when the couple called two dealers back in Michigan, where they live most of the year, the model they wanted was sold out at both. So instead of flying home, the Mooneys bought an Enclave in Florida and drove it 1,300 miles back to Michigan. Sitting in her opal-colored Enclave on Saturday, Mrs. Mooney said, 'We fell in love with it.'"[1]

The tight supply of Enclaves and other cars is an example of supply and demand, and sometimes amount of demand is a surprise to automakers and sometimes it is done on purpose. Cars in short supply and in high demand drive up sales and market mavenism, good word of mouth. "'We want to keep [the Enclave] hot,' says GM Vice Chairman Robert Lutz. 'Nothing destroys the value of a new product faster than over producing.'"[2]

High gas prices affect the sale of new vehicles, especially gas-guzzlers. Many consumers are attracted to crossovers, which are cars which look like SUVs but are lighter, give a smoother ride, and get better gas mileage. The Enclave is considered a crossover with a large cargo space behind the third row of seats. This is not to say this is the car for everyone; many young single consumers are drawn to smaller cars.

Future years can bring changes in consumer demand, but Paul Ballew, a GM sales analyst, says, "Of course we don't want to have too little supply on dealer lots, but the situation we're looking at now is definitely a good problem to have."[3] What is considered a healthy supply? About 65 days or less is considered healthy.

---

[1]John D. Stoll, "How GM Handles a Hit: Build Fewer," *Wall Street Journal*, October 31, 2007, p. B1.
[2]Ibid.
[3]Ibid.

## INTRODUCTION

Wise consumer practices are needed to survive the ups and downs of the real estate market. Because homes and cars are the most visible high-ticket items that most consumers have, this chapter is devoted to how to become better consumers of both. In the typical family's budget, housing represents 32.8 percent and transportation 19.1 percent. Thus, homes are the most expensive single purchase that most consumers make. The pie chart in Figure 12.1 shows a typical family budget. Since Chapter 10 covered repairs (such as vehicular repairs and home improvements), the emphasis in this chapter is on the prebuying and purchasing part of these investments, starting with the decision of whether to buy or rent housing. To provide context and historical perspective, it should be noted that "no century began with as much promise for change as the twentieth. The automobile and airplane, motion pictures and radio, the electric light and appliances, bottled soft drinks and canned soups, all so prosaic and common at the end of the century, were the new wonders of 1900" (Cross, 2000, p. 17). Can the same be said for the twenty-first century? What developments bode well for our future? One trend discussed in this chapter is the growth in home technology, in particular home monitoring systems. Is owning a home still the American dream? The numbers reveal that it is. About 67 percent of households own their homes, and home equity accounts for 23.5 percent of household net worth. These percentages and many others in the chapter, including those in the pie chart, come from the Consumer Expenditure Survey reported by the Bureau of Labor Statistics.

According to the bureau, the terms *household* and *consumer unit* are used interchangeably for convenience. The definition of a **consumer unit** is members of a household related by blood, marriage, adoption, or other legal arrangement; a single person living alone or sharing a household with others but who is financially independent; or two persons living together who share responsibilities for at least two out of three major types of expenses (food, housing, and other expenses). In the United States, the average number of persons in a consumer unit is 2.5, with 1.3 earners, and they have two vehicles and spend 13.1 percent of their budget on food.

With ownership come responsibility and the need to make lasting choices. Before buying, nearly everyone rents, so the chapter begins with a discussion of renting and leasing. In the second half of the chapter, we'll discuss the pros and cons of leasing and buying vehicles and the traps to avoid.

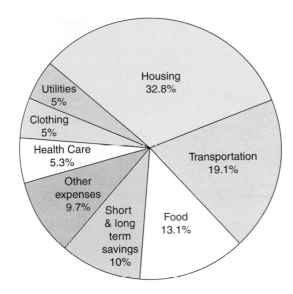

**Figure 12.1**  Typical Household or Consumer Unit Budget.

## LEASING AND RENTING HOUSING

### Advantages of Leasing vs. Renting

Millions of students sign their first leases while in college. Leases may be difficult to get out of, so caution is advised. There are month-to-month leases, school year leases, and yearly leases. Landlords give financial incentives or make improvements to keep the same renters year in and year out. **Rent** is payment for the use of property. Most students will continue to pay rent for the first few years out of college with the intention of eventually buying housing. A great advantage of renting is that it is a temporary arrangement; you pay month to month, so money is not tied up. Even with this advantage, increasingly people are buying homes at a younger and younger age because low mortgage rates make buying more affordable than or just as affordable as renting. As one 24-year-old said, "Why pay $700 a month for a small apartment when I can own a town house for the same price and then have something to sell when I move on?" But one has to make these decisions while weighing other parts of one's financial life. For example, a 33-year-old Atlanta hospital administrative assistant bought a $50,000 condominium whose $473 monthly mortgage and carrying charges she could easily meet, but trouble came after moving in. The problem was she already had about $12,000 in credit card debt and student loans and then spent another $5,000 for bedroom and dining room furniture ("Making Your House Pay Off," 2002). She ended up in credit counseling to get things straightened out (a subject that is discussed in the next chapter).

Renting usually involves a **security deposit**, which is a payment required by the landlord in advance to cover wear and tear of the unit and (as the name implies) to secure a unit for the renter. Most typically this is one month's rent, on top of writing a check for the first month's rent, so a renter would probably pay $1,800 to move in if the rent was $900 a month plus the security deposit. There may also

## CONSUMER ALERT

Before signing a lease, do the following:

- Review its contents in order to know what you are signing.
- Look for features such as time and conditions. Is it a one-year lease or a month-to-month lease? Are you liable for damages and what kind?
- Look over the property. How well maintained are the grounds and the interiors? Are there newer appliances?
- Find out about subleasing. Is there a fee for the privilege of subleasing?
- Remember that landlords are not bound to anything they promise orally. If landlords make an oral promise, ask that it be written into the lease.
- Final advice: Write everything down.

be a refundable or nonrefundable pet fee or deposit to take care of cleaning carpets and so forth when the renter moves out. Many landlord–tenant disputes are over the return of the security deposit at the end of the renting period.

Another part of renting is the signing of a **lease**, a legal document between the renter and the landlord describing the rights and responsibilities of both. Part of the lease is a clause about **subleasing**, which means the property can be leased by the original tenant to another person or persons; this clause describes what is allowed or what is not allowed and under what circumstances.

## Landlord–Tenant Disputes

Disputes between landlords and tenants are common, especially in college towns. Before moving in, renters should take photos showing the condition of the rental unit, especially focusing on any damaged or substandard areas that may come into dispute later. If the landlord promises repairs such as retiling a bathroom or recarpeting, get that promise in writing. Upon leaving the unit, if it has been kept clean and undamaged, the tenants have the right to expect a prompt return of the security deposit. Tenants should give ample notice of vacating (usually at least a month) in order for the landlord to inspect the unit and line up another tenant. If there is a dispute about the return of the security deposit or the conditions of subleasing, the tenant should try first to work something out with the landlord or leasing agent. If

## CONSUMER ALERT

A common problem is bait and switch regarding the quality of the apartment rented. For example, two students may look at a model apartment in a large complex in the spring and sign a lease to rent an apartment similar to that apartment in the fall. When they arrive in the fall, their apartment is not of the same quality as the model apartment they were shown. Perhaps the carpet is not new, or the apartment has not been repainted; if it is furnished, the furniture may be broken and so forth. As mentioned in the text, the students' first step is to try to resolve the issue with the landlord. Are there other apartments? Will the landlord agree in writing to fix the problems immediately?

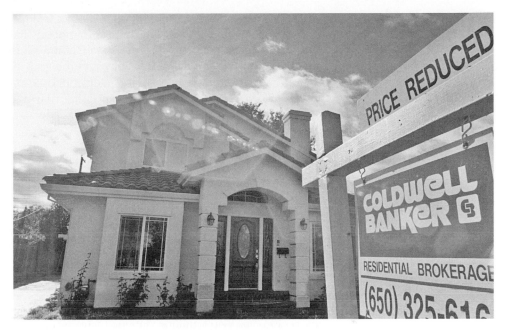

Home ownership is up, but supply exceeded demand in 2008 as home prices leveled or fell. (Paul Sakuma, AP Wide World Photos.)

this does not work, most campuses offer free legal services to students to try to resolve issues such as landlord–tenant disputes, and you can locate this service through university student services. Another alternative is small claims court.

## HOME OWNERSHIP

"Minorities, immigrants, and single people are buying homes in record numbers."

As mentioned in the Introduction section, owning a home is often referred to as the American dream. We have sentimental songs like Stephen Foster's "Home Sweet Home" that extol the virtues of home. Can you picture this as "Apartment Sweet Apartment"? According to the U.S. Census Bureau, record home ownership rates are taking place. Half of all Americans live in the suburbs, and nearly three-quarters (73 percent) of homes are owner occupied. Between 1990 and 2000, the number of owner-occupied units rose 18 percent while renter-occupied units edged up only 8 percent.

"The typical buyer of a new house lays out $9,000 for furnishings and improvements in the first year."

When buying a home, what do most people want? Usually the answer for a middle-income family is a single-family detached house with three or four bedrooms, multiple bathrooms, central heating and air conditioning, an up-to-date kitchen, a two-car garage, and a yard. With higher income comes the desire for a three-car garage for the extra car or for the storage space. One of the biggest changes in homes has been the increasing size of kitchens. According to the Census Bureau, from 1950 to 2004 the average size of the kitchen increased 216 percent while the home itself only increased 72 percent in size. Consumers not only want spacious kitchens but also may specify granite or solid-surface countertops and stainless steel appliances.

A starter home may be a town house, half of a duplex, a condominium, a small home in a new development, or a house that needs fixing up. Some people, especially dual-income couples, skip the starter home phase and head straight for the three-bedroom, two-bath house in the suburbs or a deluxe city or beach condominium. "Minorities, immigrants and single people are buying homes in record numbers. They have transformed the housing market over the past 10 years and will likely be leading the charge in the decade to come" ("The New 'Starter' Home," 2002, p. 53).

Larger homes usually mean the purchase of more furniture as well as higher utility bills and property taxes, so size and location of the home have financial implications beyond the home's price. "Credit counselors say that new homeowners often get into financial trouble by spending too much after they move in. The typical buyer of a new house lays out $9,000 for furnishings and improvements in the first year, according to Harvard's Joint Center for Housing Studies" ("Making Your House Pay Off," 2002, p. 15).

Another development is adding more technology, including "green" technology, to homes. This ranges from compact fluorescent light bulbs to high-tech laundry equipment to home monitoring systems using cameras, cell phones, and computers. "The market for home-monitoring systems is expected to grow from $91 million in 2007 to $400 million in 2012, according to Parks Associates, a Dallas research firm" (Goodloe & Jurgensen, 2007, p. P6). Real estate agents can use the monitors to check who is looking at a house. Homeowners use the monitors to turn on air conditioning so that the house is cool when they return after work or to see if their children got home safely from school; they can also watch renovations from afar. Costs can range from a monthly fee to a start-up package of over $15,000, sold by big box stores or individual installers who customize home monitoring or security devices. The technology is being promoted by telephone, electronics, contractors, security, and computer companies—the more indispensable the devices, the better. It is easy to see how consumers get hooked on technology so they can be anywhere and see what is going on at home. You no longer have to worry whether you left a door unlocked or not; you can see if you did. On the joys of home monitoring systems, here is one example: "For some, it's pure escapist. Zach Glenwright spends most of his day editing video for a local news station. But every 30 minutes or so, he takes a break on this work computer to check on a camera of his own, monitoring the squirrels and birds in the backyard of his home in York, Pa. 'It's kind of like watching a TV show,' says the 25-year-old" (Goodloe & Jurgensen, 2007, p. P6).

## LIFE CHANGE POINTS AND CONSUMPTION

The discussion of people going from renting to owning a home is a good example of a visible change point in people's lives. It is a signal of settling down and putting down roots. Other change points in people's lives include going to college, getting married, having children, getting a first professional job, moving, and retiring. These all usually involve increased expenses.

Marriage or having a first or second child or even getting a dog often signals the need for owning rather than renting. Families, friends, and work colleagues may help celebrate transitions with moving-in parties, baby showers, wedding showers, housewarming parties, and retirement parties, which involve presents for the changing family and/or household needs. Since life changes involve the spending of money, media and business are well aware of this and try to capitalize on it by sponsoring bridal shows or giving free sample gift packs at marriage license bureaus and at maternity wards in hospitals. The thinking is that free magazines; free Tide, Secret, or Pampers samples; or discount coupons given at the right moment can set the mood for future sales. Condé Nast, publisher of *Bride's* and *Modern Bride,* estimates that U.S. newlyweds spend $70 billion in the first year after marriage on their households. Consumers buy more in their first six months of marriage than a settled household does in five years (Ellison & Tejada, 2003). Consider the following:

*Newlyweds are the ultimate consumers.*

> Corporate marketers say certain points in life make consumers especially vulnerable to sales pitches, with the soon-to-be married often being the most susceptible. It's a time when they aren't just choosing a marriage partner but also are making brand decisions about toothpaste, detergent and appliances that could last even longer. Unless a couple has been living together for years, wedding represents a moment when two sets of habits and brand preferences meet and usually only one survives. "Newlyweds," says James Stengel, global marketing officer at Procter & Gamble Co. in Cincinnati, "are in some ways the ultimate consumer." (Ellison & Tejada, 2003, p. B1)

Change points surge at certain times of the year. For example, graduations and weddings peak in June. Also, one-fifth of wedding proposals occur in December, causing a huge spike in advertising in January bridal magazines; these ads are not just for wedding gowns and bridesmaid dresses but for vacation destinations, household goods, shampoos, cosmetics, fragrances, and cars. American List Counsel, a marketing firm, gathers names of newlyweds from county clerk's offices and photographers and sells the names to marketers, including realtors. "Newlywed names 'are like gold,' says Pete Hunsinger, president of Condé Nast's bridal group" (Ellison & Tejada, p. B3). House sales peak in the summer because people with children want to be settled before the new school year begins, so movers can charge more in the summer than they can during the rest of the year.

## HOMES AS INVESTMENTS

Technically speaking, housing is considered a consumer good, not a pure investment; however, most people think of their homes as an investment. It is a consumer good because the house is typically used by the owners—90 percent of all single-family homes are owner occupied. Homeowners typically stay in their homes for eight years, which is longer than most people hold shares of stock. Even with all that said, real estate investments are compared to investing in stocks. This is important to do to gain perspective, even though they are not truly equivalent. As former Federal Reserve Board Chairman Alan Greenspan said, "The transaction costs of homes are very high. You can't readily sell a home without a very large cost, and perhaps more importantly, you have to move. The type of underlying conditions that creates bubbles is very difficult to create in the housing market" (*The Freddie Mac Reporter Fact Book,* 2002–2003, p. 17).

Home values in recent years have had their ups and downs. Location, as always, matters greatly.

Home values fell nationally during the depression of the 1930s but held up well for much of the rest of the twentieth century and into the twenty-first century with a slowdown in 2008. Home values tend to hold up even during recessions. Over the last 50 years, home values have gone up on average 4 percent per year compared to stocks at 7 percent per year, so some would say stocks are better investments.

When the economy dipped from 1999 to 2003, real estate held its value because of low mortgage rates and actually increased considerably in value in places such as Greenwich, Connecticut; Washington, D.C.; and Southern California. In fact, the housing market was so good that an article in the *Wall Street Journal* said, "Forget watching the stock market. The best—maybe the only—game in town these days is the remarkably resilient real-estate market. Last year alone, amid all the bad news, home prices still rose by 7% nationally—and some economists believe things will be almost as strong this year" (Fletcher, 2003, p. W1). What followed this article was a slowing down of the real estate market, and in most areas of the United States in 2006 and 2007, there were more sellers than buyers and many homes were sitting on the market for six months or more. Real estate values declined, leveled off, or kept pace with inflation. At the same time, property insurance and taxes skyrocketed in many parts of the country, making real estate investing less attractive. The practice of flipping houses to make quick profits slowed; extravagant remodeling jobs were also reconsidered in terms of their added value at resale time. So land and/or a home may or may not be a good investment, depending on the time, the location, taxes, and interest rates. Realtors and wise buyers study the national economy as well as the local market when comparing house values. The "takeaway" from this is that the real estate market cycles and that a boom will be followed by a downswing or a more stable period when values do not rise sharply.

## RENTING VS. BUYING HOMES: TIME FACTOR

If living in an area for less than three years, it may be wiser to rent than to buy.

"The longer you stay in a house, the more you will benefit from the ability to live rent-free and the less you need to worry about short-term price dips. 'Over seven or eight years, you can be pretty sure that buying a house will financially dominate renting,' according to Chris Mayer, a real estate professor at the University of Pennsylvania's Wharton School" (Clements, 2003, p. D1). But if your time horizon is shorter than that, what should you do? The shorter the time horizon, the more risk there is, so more care should be taken in choosing the type of housing and the location. As a general rule, condominiums and high-end houses should be avoided because during market downturns these are hit harder than middle-income single-family homes. The cutoff point is three years, so if you are going to be in an area less than three years, renting may be a better option from a financial standpoint. The reasons are the high expense that is involved in buying and selling the house (including closing and financing costs) and the possibility that the home will not rise significantly in value in a short amount of time. Of course, an area where housing prices are soaring would be an exception to this.

**CONSUMER ALERT**

As stocks declined in the early 2000s and real estate rose in value, scam artists shifted their attention to the real estate market. Newlyweds can be a target since they are new to the housing market. State and federal regulators reported a decided increase in complaints regarding time-shares and other types of real estate investments, including land in places like Texas. One scam was the promise of oil on land in Texas, the basic pitch being that because of unrest in the world, Texas oil was going to be worth more. As readers of this book know, geopolitical situations and the economy change, and fraudsters take advantage of whatever they can to prey on fear and uncertainty. Whether for personal use or as a way to build wealth, real estate investments should be carefully scrutinized. Ask yourself if the seller is legitimate (established) and if the price is reasonable. In general, investigate before you invest. The best way to protect yourself is to remember, as always, "If it sounds too good to be true, it probably isn't." Does the offer pass the sniff test?

Homes can be an **illiquid asset**, meaning they are difficult to sell readily to get the cash. It is not unusual for homes to take more than a year to sell; if they are vacant during that time, the homeowners are paying the mortgage, property taxes, and upkeep expenses while at the same time paying rent or mortgage payments in the new location.

## DECISION POINTS

### Readiness to Buy

After years of renting, individuals want to own. The main reason first time home buyers give for looking for a home is that they are tired of paying rent, according to the National Association of Realtors, so the first determinant of readiness to buy is the feeling that it is time to buy. When asking people why they want to buy, the second most-cited reason is tax advantages and the third is a desire for a larger place. Box 12.1 gives other reasons why someone may prefer buying over renting. Owning a home has several advantages, including the most basic—supplying the need for shelter. A home is an investment as well, offering an opportunity to build equity; when someone buys, he or she hopes the house will go up in value. Emotional reasons include the need to lay down roots, pride, an opportunity for self-expression, security, and a sense of ownership.

Financially, how does someone determine how much house he or she can afford? Several formulas exist to determine readiness to buy: The simplest is the 2½ times rule, which gives a person a general idea of the maximum amount he or she could spend. To calculate this, multiply the annual household income by two and one-half; for example, a person earning $40,000 a year could afford a $100,000 house. A typical down payment is 10 to 20 percent of the purchase price, so for the $100,000 house, a person should save up $10,000 to $20,000

**BOX 12.1    Pros and Cons of Renting and Buying Housing**

|  | Renting | Buying |
|---|---|---|
| Pros | Extras like swimming pools | Pride of ownership |
| | Few responsibilities | Tax deductions |
| | No yard work, no repairs | Equity building |
| | Feeling of not being tied down | Feeling of community |
| | Close neighbors offering security | Ability to borrow against equity |
| | Problems handled by manager | Improved credit rating |
| | Utilities possibly included | Garage and/or yard possibly included |
| Cons | No tax deductions | Feeling of being tied down |
| | Transient neighbors | Down payment |
| | Inability to make many changes | Closing costs |
| | No pets policy | Repair bills |
| | Not much storage | Yard work |
| | Rent increase with little notice | Property taxes |
| | Inability to build equity | Homeowners' association dues |
| | | Money tied up |

before seriously looking to buy. Ads for new developments will often say no money down; in that case, the person would not need a down payment, although it is usually a good idea because there are more choices and a higher down payment will diminish how much is owed. **Mortgages**, loans to purchase real estate in which the real estate serves as collateral, are what remains after the down payment is subtracted from the purchase price. Lenders such as banks can help a person determine how much house he or she can afford. Lenders estimate mortgages based on the down payment and the buyer's ability to handle monthly payments of **PITI**, which stands for principal, interest, taxes, insurance. Another method for determining whether one is ready to buy or not is the 28/36 qualifying rule: Monthly gross income is multiplied by 0.28 (28 percent) or 0.36 (36 percent) to show the range that lenders would consider appropriate.

For example, if someone had a $4,000 monthly income, the person could afford a mortgage of between $1,120 and $1,440 per month, assuming the person does not have large amounts owed on cars or on credit cards. The lender will look at the person's total **net worth** (assets minus liabilities) to determine how much he or she can afford. **Assets** are what is owned; **liabilities** are what is owed. The 2½ times rule and the 28/36 qualifying rule are starting points. An online tutorial that helps consumers determine if they are ready for home ownership and that provides descriptions of the mortgage process and options is available at www.freddiemac.com/homebuyers. Through a congressional charter in 1970, **Freddie Mac** became a stockholder-owned corporation designed to increase the supply of money that lenders can make available to home buyers and multifamily investors. Because of Freddie Mac, more people have access to better home financing and lower monthly mortgage payments, the goal being to make housing more accessible and affordable to a wide range of Americans.

Table 12.1

|                | 28 Qualifying Rule | 36 Qualifying Rule |
|----------------|--------------------|--------------------|
| Monthly income | $4,000             | $4,000             |
|                | × 0.28             | × 0.36             |
|                | $1,120             | $1,440             |

## Housing Types

The two main housing types are unattached single-family dwellings and multiunit dwellings such as duplexes, town houses, condominiums, and cooperatives. **Condominiums** and town houses are homes attached to one another: You own a unit, but you and your neighbors share common areas such as swimming pools and lobbies. Condominiums can be found anywhere but are most often associated with beaches, ski areas, golf courses, theme parks, and other types of resort, retirement, or recreational areas. The monthly maintenance or repair fees for common areas collected from owners of town houses or from condominium owners are called **homeowner's fees**. **Cooperative apartments** are similar, except you own shares in the building as a whole, with the right to lease a certain unit. Cooperative apartments are found mostly in big cities such as Boston and New York City. **Manufactured housing** includes units that are fully or partially assembled in a factory and moved to the living site.

## Housing Quality

Regardless of housing type, care should be taken in assessing housing quality—availability of services, zoning laws, school zones, and covenants. Potential buyers should inquire about **home warranties**, which provide additional protection for the buyer, and **home inspections**, which assess the condition of the home. States vary in how much is disclosed to the potential buyer before or at **closing**, the meeting in which real estate is transferred from seller to buyer. States also vary in how much is paid by the seller and how much is paid by the buyer at closing in terms of fees and add-ons; many of these can be negotiated before going into the closing. An anxious seller is more likely to pick up extra costs and fees than a seller with many potential buyers. **Defect-disclosure forms** that describe the condition of the home are required in some states, and termite inspections are required in others. Before purchasing, find out what the rules are in your area. Realtors should be up front about a home's or a neighborhood's defects, but they are usually paid commission by the seller and therefore are more likely to be working in the seller's interest. Many realtors, however, take the long-term view and realize it is equally important to have satisfied buyers who either may hire them again to buy or sell a house or may give good word-of-mouth publicity to other potential buyers and sellers. About 90 percent of homes are sold by realtors, although this percentage may be declining slightly for a number of reasons, including the use of the Internet. More homeowners are using the Internet to sell their house, and more buyers are searching online on their own, at least initially.

One would assume a new home bought directly from the builder would not require a home inspection, but today hiring inspectors for new housing is becoming more and more common. The potential buyer hires the home inspector and pays the fee. Investing in real estate is very much about the old adage that "you get what you pay for"—using highly recommended realtors and inspectors and buying well-built houses pay off in the long run.

## Mortgages

This section provides a quick overview of the main types of mortgages. Following are three hints when shopping for a mortgage:

1. Educate yourself. Current interest rates are reported in the newspaper and over the Internet, and mortgages are available locally and over the Internet.
2. Know your lending institution.
3. Visit Web sites providing home buying information (see the E-Resources section for examples).

Most people get a fixed-rate, fixed-term, fixed-payment loan, which is usually carried for 15 or 30 years and is called a **fixed-rate conventional mortgage**. When mortgage rates are low, this is a good choice because the housing costs are known, budgeting is easier, and the mortgage rate is set. If mortgage rates increase sharply, more people consider **adjustable-rate mortgages (ARMs)**, which allow the interest rates to fluctuate within a range which is based on changes in the economy. Usually with ARMs, less is paid initially, as much as 2 percent less (a teaser rate) than with fixed-rate conventional mortgages, so ARMs may be a good option for people starting out as new hires or as newlyweds, assuming their incomes will build. At preset intervals, the ARM would be revisited and go up or down within a range (for example, between 5 and 10 percent).

Mortgage seekers can get mortgages either online or at mortgage companies, banks, or credit unions. A home buyer can negotiate with the lender (online or in person) rather than assuming a published rate is final. If a person has a good credit rating, the amount may be reduced. See the E-Resources section for Web sites with mortgage quotes.

Sometimes, the seller offers help with financing. Potential buyers should weigh all the financial options and the state of the economy at the time of purchase.

If mortgage rates drop considerably (at least two percentage points) after the house is bought, then the homeowner can look into refinancing. For example, if the mortgage was 9 percent and the current fixed-rate conventional mortgage is at 5 percent, it would be worthwhile to look into refinancing. The problem is this change involves paperwork, time, and fees, so the homeowner will have to weigh the costs and the benefits of changing to a different mortgage. Usually refinancing makes the most sense if the homeowner is planning to stay several more years in the same home.

**Predatory Home Mortgage Abuses.**  Most people get their homes financed through legitimate mortgage companies or banks, but as with anything involving money (and in this case, large sums of money), the potential for fraud is enormous. May the borrower beware! **Predatory lending** lures people into loans they really can't afford, usually by borrowing against the equity in their homes or a relative's home. The predatory practice could involve a new mortgage or a home equity loan on a home already owned. Consumers' rights in this regard are partially protected by the Home Ownership and Equity Protection Act of 1994, and consumer advocates would like to strengthen this act to provide further protection, which would include wider regulation of the high-interest subprime lending market where predatory practices are common. Here are five warning signs of predatory lenders:

1. Advertising "We give credit to anyone" or "Poor credit, no problem"
2. Rushing the person to sign immediately
3. Asking for a large fee up front to see if the potential homeowner qualifies for a loan
4. Offering an unusually low mortgage rate compared to the general market
5. Offering small monthly payments with a large balloon payment at the end

Older people and low-income people are prime targets for predatory home mortgage sellers. Many people do not understand that they could lose their homes if they do not keep up payments. Loan origination fees are part of the problem; these may run as high as 10 to 25 percent of the total loan amount (versus a more typical lender fee of around 2 percent). Advocacy groups such as the American Association of Retired Persons (AARP) have successfully represented homeowners in suits against mortgage lenders in New York, West Virginia, and Washington, D.C. For copies of settlements, go to the Federal Trade Commission (FTC) Web site. Freddie Mac's information on predatory lending is available at www.freddiemac. com/singlefamily/predlend.html. For examples of beneficial lending practices and their predatory potential, see Table 12.2.

**Mortgage Pitfalls and Fraud Potential.**   Once individuals own a home and start building equity, they may take out a second mortgage, a home equity line of credit, cash-out refinancing, or a reverse mortgage (the latter is discussed in a later section). Each financial instrument has pitfalls, the main one being that all forms of home equity borrowing leech value from the home. Here are the main types:

- In a second mortgage, a person pays a fixed rate of interest (usually around 6 or 7 percent) for a set amount of money repaid over 5 to 10 years to finance a single project such as renovations.

**Table 12.2**   Beneficial Lending Practices and Their Predatory Potential

| **Lending Practice** | **Benefit** | **Predatory Potential** |
|---|---|---|
| Higher-than-market interest rates | Enables relatively risky borrowers to obtain credit | Can financially ruin borrowers who lack financial capacity to repay the loan with its excessive interest rate |
| Ability to refinance | Enables borrowers to take advantage of lower interest rates | Can invite loan flipping, resulting in high loan fees and unnecessary credit costs |
| Prepayment penalties | Provides borrowers with lower rates | Can prevent borrowers from refinancing or can unnecessarily drive up loan balance (as penalties are financed as part of a new loan) |

*Source:* Adapted from *The Freddie Mac Reporter Fact Book 2007*, McLean, VA, p. 25.

- The **home equity line of credit** carries a variable interest rate (usually around 4 percent, but it varies, so investigate current rates) and allows the homeowner to borrow up to a set amount. This can work well to finance home improvement projects.
- Cash-out refinancing allows the homeowner to replace the first mortgage with another, perhaps larger, loan and repocket the difference. The drawback here is that a person may be starting over with a new 30-year loan.

These are the basic types, but there are new combinations being offered, including a combination of a first mortgage with a home equity line of credit. One of the features is that the credit line automatically increases as the borrower pays down the mortgage and the home's value grows.

The main advantages of home-based loans are that they offer low interest rates and that the interest paid is usually deductible from income tax. Rates are usually tied to the prime rate and move up when the prime rate increases.

Here is an example:

> Chris Englin, an executive recruiter who lives near Seattle, took out a home equity line from Wells Fargo when she refinanced her $200,000 mortgage in December. Ms. Englin says her loan officer suggested the credit line when she mentioned she needed cash to buy a half-interest in a 24-foot fishing boat. Taking out the home-equity line "was really easy," she says. "We did the whole thing by e-mail." (Simon, 2003, p. D1)

The main drawback of home-based loans is that the home is at risk if the person does not keep up with the monthly loan payments. Before taking out a home equity loan, the homeowner should ask some questions:

1. Do I really need the money?
2. Is there a minimum or maximum monthly payment?
3. What is the annual percentage rate? Is it set or adjustable? (If rates are low, a set rate is usually a better choice.)
4. Are there any annual fees or transaction fees?
5. How long is the loan for?

See the Consumer Alert at the top of the next page for further advice.

Fraud, through advertisements on television, high-pressure telephone sales calls, and door-to-door salespeople, abounds. The elderly are often targeted because they have built up so much equity in their homes yet may be cash poor. The best way to go about this is to apply for an equity loan through a local credit union or bank or at least to talk with a loan officer, which provides a sense of baseline amounts and terms. Do not sign anything unless it is completely understood. Home equity lines of credit, refinancing arrangements, and second mortgages may carry closing costs, fees, points, and taxes that may total up to 10 percent of the loan, so a $40,000 loan could end up costing an additional $4,000—and this is with a legitimate business.

**Reverse mortgages** pay the homeowner, usually an elderly person, in monthly advances or through a line of credit. Reverse mortgages convert home equity into cash with no repayment required for as long as the borrowers live in their homes. The main drawback is that the homeowners are taking value away from their home, so when they move elsewhere or die, the home equity for them or their heirs is reduced. It is prudent to consult an attorney, an accountant, or another financial

**CONSUMER ALERT**

Banks are aggressively marketing home equity lines, but they are not for everyone:

- They make the most sense for short-term loans (two or three years) for things such as home improvements.
- If money is needed for a longer period of time, the borrower should seek fixed-rate loans.
- Pay attention to the interest rate, and compare rates. One source is Bankrate.com, a consumer finance Web site. The best home equity line may be from the same lender as the mortgage lender because usually banks look favorably on someone they already know and have a relationship with.

advisor before taking out a reverse mortgage. For further information, homeowners should gather data from their state office of consumer protection or the other sources listed in the E-Resources section.

As mentioned in an earlier chapter, in 1969 the Truth in Lending Act became a federal law as part of the Consumer Protection Act. It requires disclosure of a truth-in-lending statement on consumer loans, including mortgages. The consumer has to know the total cost of credit, such as the annual percentage rate and other specifics of the loan. The law was updated in 1980 as part of the Depository Institutions Deregulation and Monetary Control Act.

**Discrimination and Redlining.**   **Discrimination** is an act based on prejudice or bias. In housing, it means that someone may not be treated fairly in terms of renting, buying, or financing. **Redlining**, prohibited by law, refers to the practice of drawing a red line or any other color around an area and marking that area as not receiving the same treatment as other areas regarding financing (redlining can also exist for insurance and credit). Typically state laws protect consumers from being discriminated against regarding housing and financing; however, there are exceptions, such as private clubs and religious organizations. There have been many lawsuits about discriminatory practices, including retirement living developments that have tried to keep out

**CONSUMER ALERT**

If you or someone you know has been discriminated against, complain to the lender; then check your state consumer affairs department or attorney general's office to see if the creditor has violated state laws. Many states have their own equal credit opportunity laws. If a mortgage application is denied, the lender must provide the name and address of the appropriate government agency to contact. Another option is suing the lender in federal district court—you can sue as an individual or join others to file a class-action suit. Another source for advice is the National Fair Housing Alliance (go to www.incacorp.com/nfha). You can file a complaint with the U.S. Department of Housing and Urban Development (HUD) in Washington, D.C., and HUD will investigate the complaint and determine if there is reasonable cause to believe the Fair Housing Act has been violated.

younger occupants. The Home Mortgage Disclosure Act requires the lenders to report where they make loans. No loans may be available in certain locations, usually low-income or crime-ridden areas; if loans are available, they may be significantly over-priced. Box 12.2 lists the protections against discrimination that the Equal Credit Opportunity Act (ECOA) and the Fair Housing Act (FHA) offer. These acts cover purchasing and refinancing homes as well as making home improvements.

Lenders cannot discourage an individual from applying for a mortgage or reject an application due to race, national origin, religion, sex, marital status, age, or support from public assistance, but it is legal for lenders to factor in a person's income, expenses, debts, and credit history. Stable employment is also an important factor in how a lender will evaluate an application. When a mortgage is denied, the lender has to give specific reasons. Before applying for mortgages, potential home buyers should check their credit report, and any errors should be corrected; credit bureaus are required to investigate any errors in dispute.

### BOX 12.2    Mortgage Discrimination

The Equal Credit Opportunity Act (ECOA) and the Fair Housing Act (FHA) protect against discrimination when an individual applies for a mortgage to purchase or refinance a home or to make home improvements.

Under ECOA, discrimination is prohibited in any aspect of an applicant's credit transaction based on the following:

Race or color

Religion

National origin

Sex

Marital status

Age (provided the applicant has the capacity to contract)

Applicant's income derived from any public assistance program

Applicant's exercise, in good faith, of any right under the Consumer Credit Protection Act (the umbrella statute that includes ECOA)

Under FHA, discrimination is prohibited in all aspects of residential real estate-related transactions:

Loans to buy, build, repair, or improve a dwelling

Sale, brokering, or appraisal of residential real estate

Sale or renting of a dwelling

Borrower's race or color

Borrower's national origin

Borrower's sex

Borrower's familial status (defined as children under age 18 living with a parent or legal guardian, pregnant women, and people with custody of children under age 18)

Borrower's handicap

*Source:* Adapted from FTC Facts for Consumers, Mortgage Discrimination, at www.ftc.gov.

## UTILITIES: COSTS AND ENVIRONMENTAL IMPACT

Since the first edition of this book, there has been a tremendous energy-saving pro-environment push, with earth-friendly products and ideas showing up everywhere. Specially designed products and programs can cut energy bills and decrease greenhouse gas emissions by up to 30 percent. When it comes to going green, a lot of people are jumping on board.

In the typical household, the utilities, including electricity, natural gas, and water, take about 5 percent of the budget (see Figure 12.1). Sometimes telephone services are included in a list of utilities, but because of the variety of new phone systems, most of them are not tied to home use (telephone services are addressed in Chapter 15). Consumers have choices of energy suppliers (including natural gas suppliers) in most states, and these choices include a local private or public utility company or a cooperative. Water comes from local water agencies; the main government protection in this area comes from the Environmental Protection Agency (EPA). Costs as well as services should be compared.

When looking at national averages, the highest utility cost is for residential space heating at 33 percent, followed by water heating at 15 percent; next comes space cooling at 10 percent. Of course, in warm climates the space cooling can run higher on a yearly basis than heating bills. Small appliances, such as small motors, electric knives, DVD players, and sewing machines, use very little energy and won't affect utility bills much one way or the other. Appliances, devices, and lights that are large and left on for long periods of time use more energy than appliances that are turned off and on and only used for a few minutes (for example, a blender uses far less energy than a refrigerator).

To address the new ways people cook and the reduced spaces in which they live, appliance manufacturers are developing refrigerators that are multifunctional, including a single appliance that looks like an oven but also has a refrigeration feature. For example, with this appliance the homeowner could put meatloaf in the unit in the morning and it would stay cold; then at 4:00 P.M. the oven would go on and cook the meatloaf. If the homeowner should get home later than expected, the unit would have gone back into the refrigeration mode (after a certain amount of warming/holding time) and would have cooled the meatloaf. Combination washer/dryers, which are rare in the United States, are common in Europe, and other multipurpose appliances are in development.

ENERGY SMART is a government program that requires appliance manufacturers to label the energy use of new appliances so the consumer will know how much energy the appliance uses in a typical year. A growing number of appliances and systems in the home are said to be getting smarter by communicating with each other, ascertaining workloads, and so on. Microprocessors and computer networking have made these connections possible; for example, new washing machines can measure how heavy a wash load is and how soiled the clothing is and then react accordingly. Over the next 10 years, the majority of new appliances will have some type of electronics that makes them smarter—appliances can be put on timers that will have them run during off-peak energy times for energy savings and potential money savings. As another way to reduce utility bills, most utility companies or government energy offices have inspectors or auditors who will provide free home energy audits so that homeowners can learn how to save energy costs in their specific house.

In the long run, though, "There isn't a silver bullet," says David Garman, the U.S. Energy Department's assistant secretary for energy-efficiency programs. "There isn't a single 'gee whiz' technology that changes everything. You usually have to try to do a lot of little things to achieve energy savings" (Moore, 2001). That said, builders and architects are working on this concept to the point that energy savings with fluorescent lighting and tankless water heaters can be as much as 75 percent compared with those in conventional homes. Saving on utilities while saving on the environment is a good example of the crossover between consumerism and environmentalism (discussed in Chapter 2). Environmentally friendly building practices, spurred by home buyers' values, the cost savings derived from greater energy efficiency, and pressure from environmentalists, have become increasingly popular in the custom building industry.

## VEHICLES

The rest of the chapter turns to a discussion of vehicles. Daniel Gilbert (2006) says that cars might seem like good purchases because of their lasting value, but actually cars experience depreciation (a loss of value quickly, especially right after purchase) and slowly deteriorate. This is in comparison to homes, which generally see **appreciation** (an increase in value). That said, most of us need cars, so questions revolve around which ones to buy, how to maintain them, how long to keep them, and whether to lease them or not. Do you want a hybrid or not? How do

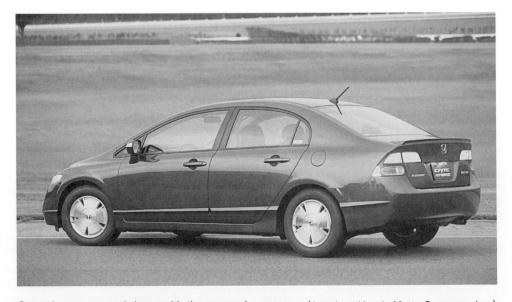

Car sales go up and down with the general economy. (American Honda Motor Company, Inc.)

you feel about fuel efficiency and the environment? How important are added safety features? Will a less expensive car bring as much satisfaction as a more expensive car?

There is no question that a vehicle that runs well is useful and enjoyable and that vehicles are needed to get you where you want to go. Some consumers also get great satisfaction from owning, collecting, showing, and restoring cars. This discussion goes back to the beginning of the first chapter, which explored the connection between happiness and consumption. If ever there was a purchase category where this is true (or not), it is vehicle ownership. Have you had good or bad experiences when purchasing cars? The following section begins with an exploration of leasing as an option.

## LEASING VEHICLES

### Pros and Cons

**Leasing** is a contractual arrangement with terms concerning the monthly payment, security deposit, and condition of the vehicle on return. It is estimated that about 30 percent of new cars are leased, with some consumers leasing a new car every three years. There are several advantages to leasing:

- Less money is needed up front. A down payment is not needed; the car can be leased with a security deposit (similar to renting an apartment). During promotions and in competitive markets, the security deposit may be waived.
- Monthly payments may be less than the payments when a car is bought.
- The lease may be paid by an employer or may be a tax deduction if the owner owns a business that uses the car.
- There are no worries about getting a trade-in or having to personally sell the car.
- People in businesses such as real estate where having a fairly new and presentable car is an asset may find that leasing is a good option.

Following are the disadvantages of leasing:

- The vehicle isn't owned, so it is not an investment with a return.
- Extra charges may be added when the vehicle is turned in; for example, if more than the recommended mileage has accrued or repairs are needed beyond average wear, the lease agreement may not cover those expenses.

Before leasing, read the contract thoroughly; focus on the number of miles recommended, and determine if that number meets your needs. Contracts are usually written for 12,000–15,000 miles per year, which was figured as reasonable given that the average car is driven 15,100 miles; however, with commutes getting longer, it is expected that the average mileage will increase. To figure total cost, a leaser should find out what the additional per-mile charge is for going over the minimum—typically this runs 20 to 25 cents a mile.

When reading the contract, be alert to other charges such as conveyance, disposition, and preparation fees. If there was a trade-in allowance, make sure the contract includes it.

## CONSUMER ALERT

A lease covering 12,000–15,000 miles is typical, but big names in the luxury car business are pushing low-payment leases to spur consumer traffic. Many of these deals allow motorists just 10,000 miles of driving a year before severe penalties occur. Here were two options for a BMW 325i three-year lease:

| Lease Miles | Monthly Payment |
|---|---|
| 10,000 | $299 |
| 15,000 | $321 |

If mileage was exceeded by 5,000 miles/year, the charge was $3,000. If the cost was added at the time of the lease (up front), the 5,000 extra miles/year would be $792 (White, 2003). To win at this game, the driver should be realistic about the average number of miles that will be driven and pick the best option.

## Types of Leases

Not all leases are created equal. There are three main types:

1. *Closed-end or "walk-away" lease.* In a closed-end lease, the leaser returns the vehicle at the end of the lease period (usually three years) and pays only for additional miles or repairs.
2. *Open-end or finance lease.* The leaser pays the difference between the expected value of the leased vehicle and the amount for which the leasing company sells it in an open-end lease. There may also be an end-of-lease payment.
3. *Single-payment lease.* A single-payment lease allows the consumer to obtain a discount on the vehicle rental agreement if certain standards are met.

Consumer rights and responsibilities regarding leasing vehicles are given in Box 12.3.

## CONSUMER ALERT

When leases first became available, some consumers did not understand that they were renting a vehicle rather than owning it outright, so when it came time to get a new model, they did not understand that they could not sell it or get any money back—in fact, they most likely owed money. Others have been less than happy at the extra add-on charges when they brought the vehicle in for a new one. Still other consumers felt pressured to buy from the same dealership and found there were financial penalties involved in switching manufacturers, making them feel locked in to the same make for years—the only choices being a new color and updated features. On the other hand, some consumers have found a type of car they want and get it over and over again, and the leasing process makes this process easy.

BOX 12.3    Know Your Rights and Responsibilities When Leasing Vehicles

The federal Consumer Leasing Act gives you the right to information that helps you understand and negotiate your lease. When you lease a vehicle, you have these rights:

1. To use it for an agreed-on number of months and miles
2. To turn it in at lease end, pay any end-of-lease fees and charges, and "walk away"
3. To buy the vehicle (if you have a purchase option)
4. To take advantage of any warranties, recalls, or other services that apply to the vehicle

Your responsibilities include the following:

1. To pay excess mileage charges when you return the vehicle
2. To pay excess wear charges when you return the vehicle
3. To make substantial payments if you end the lease early

*Source:* Adapted from *Keys to Vehicle Leasing: A Consumer Guide* from the Board of Governors of the Federal Reserve System, Washington, D.C.

## VEHICLE PRELEASING AND PREBUYING: INFORMATION SEARCH

Before leasing or buying a car, many consumers take a spin around the Internet. A search reveals makes, models, features such as color choices, upgrade packages, and dealer locations. Some individual dealers have put their whole inventory online, so in addition to information from the manufacturer, you can get specific information from the lot down the street. Before leasing or purchasing, most consumers want to test-drive a few cars to get a sense of how they feel and fit, but as a first step, it is hard to beat an online search. Of course, Web sites vary: Some provide much-needed information, and others are more heavily into marketing and sales without the necessary concrete information. The best ones give energy-use figures and 360-degree photo tours of the interiors, including zoom-in features so that the dashboard and engine can be examined (see the E-Resources section for a list of sites).

## BUYING VEHICLES

### Pros and Cons

The main advantage of buying is that you own the vehicle—it is an asset. Up-front costs include the cash price or a down payment, taxes, registration and other fees, and other charges. A drawback is that the monthly loan payments are usually higher than monthly lease payments because the total cost includes interest and other charges, and if you end the loan early, there may be fees. Future value will be determined by the condition of the vehicle and the vehicle's market value at time of sale or trade. Another drawback is that a lot of money can be tied up in car payments that could be spent or invested elsewhere. Advantages to owning versus leasing include no limits on the number of miles driven and no charges for excessive wear. Once the car is paid for in full or at the end of the loan term (typically

**GLOBAL CONSUMER**

**The World's Cheapest Car**

How to build a car for $2,500 or less was the question posed to the engineers at TaTa Motors of India. Their answer was this was possible. The prototype is dubbed "the People's Car." Some of the changes included one windshield wiper rather than two and a small engine with a horsepower of 30 to 35. Compare this to the Honda Fit, one of the smallest cars sold in the U.S., with 109 horsepower. TaTa's primary market is the hundreds of millions of Indians and others in the developing world because the car is not ready for U.S. highways, considering safety and emissions.

What does it look like? Sort of a hatchback shaped like a jellybean with four doors and five seats. There are no power windows, air conditioning or a radio. We're talking basic transportation here. What do you think? Who might buy a car like this in your country? Even if it does not meet Western nation standards, there is talk that the car will influence global car makers. One such spin-off may be tinier trunks.

*Reference:* Anand Giridharadas, "How to Build a $2,500 Car." *New York Times,* January 8, 2008, p. C1.

four to six years), there are no further loan payments. Being debt free is a positive feeling, a goal many people hope to attain.

## New Cars

**Information Gathering.**   Besides researching cars online, another option is to read *Consumer Reports, Popular Mechanics,* and *Motor Trend* for car ratings, service, and safety. Information gathering of this sort can be pleasurable and

A salesman shakes hands with a couple while handing them the keys to their new car at a car dealership. (Michael Newman, PhotoEdit Inc.)

useful since a new car is a major purchase, second only to a house in terms of expense. Once the make and model have been selected, here are some other suggestions:

- Do comparison shopping at area dealerships or through online services or buying services such as the American Automobile Association (AAA). Examples of sources of online price quotes are autoweb.com, autovantage.com, carpoint.com, and autobytel.com. Buy only from reputable dealers or services. Complaint records are available from state and local consumer protection agencies and Better Business Bureaus (BBBs).
- Shop in advance for the best financing option. Local or online credit unions and banks often offer better interest rates than dealerships.
- Test-drive cars to get a sense of how they handle and whether they fit your size, shape, and driving behavior. Get price quotes from several dealers. If buying from a dealer, test-drive the specific car you are going to buy, do not allow a substitute car or one that is coming in next week. If you order a car from a dealership, test-drive it before buying it.
- Read the "Buyer's Guide" sticker required to be displayed in the window of the car.
- Don't buy on impulse or when you are pressured by salespeople.
- Negotiate the price. Dealer profit margin is usually between 10 and 20 percent. The difference may be between the manufacturer's suggested retail price and the invoice price. The **invoice price** is the manufacturer's initial charge to the dealer (in other words, what the car cost the dealer). The **sticker price** or **suggested retail price** is the price of the car, including options, transportation charges, and any "market adjustments." Look at the total price, not just the monthly payment.
- Find out if the manufacturer is offering rebates.
- Remember that buying off the lot may bring the lowest price because that is in-stock inventory that has to move, but ordering a car from a dealer or service will get the desired features and will omit the ones not cared about. Volume, especially the cars sitting on a dealer's lots, tends to drive down prices.

**Sales Techniques.**    A common sales technique is to polish up cars and put them under flattering lights in showrooms. A second one is to encourage the buyer of a new car to become a loyal repeat customer, and there are several ways of doing this, including offering good dealer repair services (with free donuts in the waiting room). Another sales technique is for the salesperson to build a relationship with the buyer. As a first step, the salesperson calls recent buyers to find out if they are satisfied with their car. But some salespeople go further than that. Joe Girard, known as the "world's greatest car salesman" (how is that for puffery), says the secret of his success was getting customers to like him. He did this by sending every one of his more than 13,000 customers holiday greeting cards every month (Happy New Year, Happy Thanksgiving, etc.), and each card had the same printed message: "I like you." Joe explained, "There's nothing else on the card, nothin' but my name. I'm just telling 'em that I like 'em" (Cialdini, 2001, p. 152). Joe had learned that flattery worked. We tend to believe praise, and we like the people who give it (Cialdini, 2001).

Another sales technique involves pressure. This can work selling cars (new and used) and houses. If the salesperson can convince potential buyers that this is the one and only car or house for them, that is a very hard pitch for buyers to resist. Making the buyer feel special (smart, unique, forward-thinking) is a strong sales ploy.

## Used Cars

As a potential buyer of a used car, the first step is to figure out how much you can afford, and the next step is to narrow the choices by going online, researching the frequency of repair and maintenance costs on the models, knowing sellers, and checking the U.S. Department of Transportation's Auto Safety Hotline (1-800-424-9393) to find out about recalls. Average prices can be located in *Edmund's Used Car Prices* and the *Kelley Blue Book* (see the E-Resources section) as well as other guides and Web sites. For paying, there are two options: pay in full or finance over time. Financing will be more costly than paying cash because of the interest and other loan costs. Annual percentage rates (APRs) are usually higher and loan periods shorter on used cars than on new ones.

Where do you find used cars? Choices include new car dealers selling trade-ins, used-car dealers specializing locally in used cars, and dealers such as CarMax with huge national inventories. One option to consider is buying a certified pre-owned car backed by a warranty from a dealership. Find out how many years or miles the warranty protection covers (some go as high as six years or 100,000 miles). Previously leased cars were usually well maintained. There are also rental car companies, friends, relatives, coworkers, and strangers selling cars on the side of the road or out of driveways. The FTC Used Car Rule requires dealers to post a Buyer's Guide in every used car they sell. Note this rule applies only to dealers, specifically to dealers that sell six or more cars a year. There are fewer protections (if any) when buying from friends or on the side of the road. Be especially careful of private sellers since generally they are not covered by the Used Car Rule; they sell cars "as is." Box 12.4 shows the parts of the Buyer's Guide.

States vary on whether dealers can offer "as is—no warranty." State divisions of consumer services will know the laws in your state and can also tell you about

**BOX 12.4   Buyer's Guide for Used Cars**

If a car is bought from a dealer, the Buyer's Guide must tell you whether the vehicle is being sold "as is" or with a warranty as well as what percentage of the repair costs a dealer will pay under the warranty. Remember to do the following:

- Get all promises in writing (spoken promises are difficult to enforce).
- Keep the buyer's guide for reference after the sale.
- Check out the mechanical and electrical systems on the car as well as any other major problem areas.
- Ask to have the car inspected by an independent mechanic before you buy.

*Source:* Adapted from *Buying a Used Car: A Consumer Guide from the Federal Trade Commission.* Bureau of Consumer Protection, March 2002, p. 3.

state requirements regarding implied warranties, warranty of merchantability, and warranty of fitness for a particular purpose (for example, whether a dealer is liable if he or she says a car can haul a trailer and it turns out that it can't). You need to find out whether the used car has a full or limited warranty and what the warranty covers. Before buying, the purchaser has the right to see a copy of the dealer's warranty. According to the FTC, warranties are included in the price of a product, but service contracts cost extra and are sold separately. As discussed in Chapter 10, service contracts provide extra protection at a price, and it is questionable whether a service contract is needed. Many used-car service contracts only last 90 days, so the time limit should be noted as well as what it covers.

What is truly necessary is to have a used car inspected by an independent mechanic, particularly if the used car is being purchased from a private seller, the main concern being safety. Inspections may run $100 or less and are worth the expense. The inspection will indicate the mechanical condition of the vehicle and any needed repairs, and the mechanic should provide a written report. Mechanics can be found by going to "Automotive Diagnostic Service" in the Yellow Pages or by asking friends or relatives for referrals. The Automotive Service Excellence (ASE) seal is a certification to look for when choosing mechanics. Auto repair or diagnostic centers should be licensed or registered with the state.

To summarize, take these steps before buying a used car:

1. Examine the car yourself in daylight. Research the make and model, and know prices and the seller.
2. Test-drive the car over varied road conditions.
3. Inspect the car's maintenance record. Check with the dealership or the previous owner if the current owner's record is incomplete.
4. Hire a mechanic to inspect the car. Safety is the main concern.

After the purchase, any problem should be worked out first with the dealer; the next step would be to contact the manufacturer if the warranty is backed by a car manufacturer. Then a consumer would go to the next level, dispute resolution (as suggested in Chapter 4); the last step would be small claims court (if the amount falls within the dollar limit in a particular state). Suspected fraud should be reported to the state or the FTC. To file a complaint or to get information on consumer issues, go to www.ftc.gov.

## Lemon Laws

Some states have **lemon laws**, which allow owners of new vehicles that repeatedly break down to get their money back or get the car replaced. Rules vary by state regarding how many miles the car was driven, how long the person has had the car, and the amount of repair problems that exist. A common rule of thumb is whether the car has been out of service for 30 days within the first 12,000 miles/12 months; another is whether the car has been in the repair shop four or more times during the first year of ownership. The procedure to get the money back or to replace the car is called **revocation of acceptance**, which must be in writing and is usually handled between the buyer and the seller. Customers suspecting they have a lemon should follow a number of steps, including contacting their state or local consumer protection office, giving the dealer a list of symptoms, keeping repair order copies, and contacting the manufacturer as well as the dealer. Most

**CONSUMER ALERT**

A common fraud involves moving water-damaged cars (from floods) to another state, drying them out, and selling the cars to unsuspecting consumers. A mechanic inspecting the engine will find this out. Stolen cars are another potential problem when purchasing from private sellers. There is also the problem of dealers posing as private individuals. To avoid this problem, look at the title and the registration to determine whether the seller is the registered owner of the vehicle. Remember that private sellers have less responsibility than dealers to disclose defects.

states require dealers of used cars to label cars that have been returned as lemons so that future buyers know the car has had problems.

## Unfair Vehicle Pricing

When buying a car, one of two unfair price-setting practices may be used:

1. *High-balling.* The term **high-balling** means that a high amount is offered for a trade-in, but the extra amount is made up in an increased new car price. It is possible that car owners would be better off selling their old car themselves rather than going through the dealer.
2. *Low-balling.* The term **low-balling** refers to a very low price being quoted, but there are add-on costs at the end that drive the final price up.

On a more minor level, some dealers add on extra frills at the end that buyers don't want, such as vinyl racing stripes or floor mats. This may have nothing to do with whether there is a trade-in, so this practice is not necessarily high-balling. Buyers should mention that they do not want these extras; by doing so, they can either save hundreds of dollars when they are removed or use them as part of the negotiation. The best advice is to know the fair market price for new vehicles and for trade-ins—a little knowledge goes a long way in the car business. Because many people dislike the haggling part of car buying, they use auto brokers or car-buying services or they go through dealers such as Saturn that offer a no-haggling car-selling method.

**CONSUMER ALERT**

When it comes to cars, all sorts of financial frauds can occur. In a real case in an unnamed state, the attorney general sued a dealership for damages and penalties under the state's Deceptive and Unfair Trade Practices Act, according to courthouse records. The lawsuit alleges that a car dealership sent promotional mailings to residents promising (among other things) it would pay off their trade-ins; instead, customers were obliged to pay off their former vehicles themselves, were enticed into unfavorable financing agreements, and were denied the promised discounts. Customers filed complaints with the attorney general's office. This is an example of a classic bait-and-switch scheme in which customers are lured in (the bait being the paying off of the trade-in), and once they are there, the switch takes place.

## SUMMARY

The Bureau of Labor Statistics, through its Consumer Expenditure Survey, provides a picture of American consumption habits, noting that there are two cars per household or consumer unit and that housing makes up the major part of the typical budget. Renting was suggested as a preferred alternative to owning if a person is staying less than three years in an area; the exception to this would be if home prices are rising rapidly, making owning a more viable option. A benefit to buying is that homeowners receive tax deductions for interest on mortgage and property taxes. The American dream is still to own a house, with 67 percent of American households owning their own house. Housing represents 32.8 percent, transportation 19.1 percent, food 13.1 percent, and utilities 5 percent of a typical household budget. Environmentally friendly building practices reduce the cost of utilities and are examples of the crossover between consumerism and environmentalism. There is a growth in home monitoring systems; one of their benefits is that what is happening in and around a house (such as renovations) can be watched from afar. A significant change has been in the average size of the kitchen: It increased 216 percent from 1950 to 2004 while the home itself increased in size only 72 percent.

People's lives go through change points that accelerate consumption, including the desire to own a home and buy new furnishings and appliances. Buying a house is the single most expensive purchase most people make, and a house is their most visible asset. There are a number of ways to determine how much house a person can afford, two of the most common being the 2½ times rule and the 28/36 qualifying rule.

To pay for improvements or to get cash, four financial instruments based on home ownership include the second mortgage, the home equity line of credit, cash-out refinancing, and the reversible mortgage. Fraud potential and other problems, such as losing one's house or paying too much in fees, are rampant. The Truth in Lending Act, a federal law enacted in 1968, provides some protection. The lender must disclose in a truth-in-lending statement the total cost of a consumer loan, including a mortgage loan. Redlining is illegal.

The discussion of the pros and cons of leasing cars and buying new and used cars included a number of steps to follow to avoid being fleeced. The Federal Trade Commission works to prevent fraudulent, deceptive, and unfair business practices involved in leasing and buying vehicles. Some states have lemon laws to cover new cars with repeated repair problems in the first year of ownership or the first 12,000 miles. Vehicle sales techniques include the use of flattery and praise because repeat business is sought.

## KEY POINTS

1. A lease is a legal document.
2. Appreciation means the increase in a home's value.
3. Mortgages are loans to purchase real estate. Rates can be compared online, and mortgages can be negotiated online.

4. Net worth is calculated as assets minus liabilities. Lenders will look at net worth before loaning money for a house because they are trying to determine a person's ability to pay the mortgage.

5. Car leases are typically for 12,000–15,000 miles per year, and if the driver goes over that amount, there are financial penalties. Some luxury car dealers are offering teaser rates for 10,000 miles to attract customers, but the average car is driven 15,100 miles per year. A down payment may be required.

6. Buyers of used cars should hire their own independent mechanic to inspect the car they are interested in buying.

7. When shopping for used vehicles, consumers should consider buying a certified pre-owned vehicle backed by warranties.

8. Car buyers should be aware of unfair pricing practices such as high-balling and low-balling.

9. Dealer profit margins on new cars are usually between 10 and 20 percent.

## KEY TERMS

| | | |
|---|---|---|
| adjustable-rate mortgages (ARMs) | home equity lines of credit | net worth |
| appreciation | home inspections | PITI |
| assets | homeowner's fees | predatory lending |
| closing | home warranties | redlining |
| condominiums | illiquid asset | rent |
| consumer unit | invoice price | reverse mortgages |
| cooperative apartments | lease | revocation of |
| defect-disclosure forms | leasing | acceptance |
| discrimination | lemon laws | security deposit |
| fixed-rate conventional mortgage | liabilities | sticker price |
| Freddie Mac | low-balling | subleasing |
| high-balling | manufactured housing | suggested retail price |
| | mortgages | |

## DISCUSSION QUESTIONS

1. Why have corporate executives called newlyweds the ultimate consumers? And why are their names like gold? How do companies get lists of newlyweds' names?

2. What are the pros of renting versus owning? What are the reasons people give for buying a home?

3. What are the pros and cons of leasing vehicles? What is the typical financial arrangement for a lease?

4. Go to the E-Resources list, select one from the housing or vehicle sites, and report on what it offers.

## E-RESOURCES

### U.S. Government Sites

**Bureau of Labor Statistics (BLS)**   *www.bls.gov*
Household or consumer unit expenses reported in the Consumer Expenditure Survey

**Department of Housing and Urban Development (HUD)**
*www.hud.gov/places.html*
Fraud hotline (1-800-347-3735)

**Environmental Protection Agency (EPA) Safe Drinking Water**
*www.epa.gov/safewater*

**Federal Trade Commission (FTC)**   *www.ftc.gov*
Predatory lending settlements, publications about buying cars, leasing, and warranties

*Note:* You can send a letter to FTC Consumer Response Center, Rm. 130, 600 Pennsylvania Ave., NW, Washington, DC 20580.

**Federal Citizen Information Center**   *www.pueblo.gsa.gov*
Gateway to home buying publications

### Housing Sites

**Bankrate.com**   *www.bankrate.com*
Comparisons of mortgage and home equity loan rates

**Freddie Mac**   *www.freddiemac.com*
Statistics on housing, mortgages, and online fact book updates

**Homes Advisor**   *www.homesadvisor.com*

**HomePath**   *www.homepath.com*

**Homes.com**   *www.homes.com*

**National Association of Realtors**   *www.realtor.org*
Gateway to housing and money advice

**National Consumer Law Center (NCLU)**   *www.consumerlaw.org*
Representation for low-income consumers, research, advocacy

### Mortgage Rate Sites

*Note:* Each of these four sites offers mortgage rates; there are dozens more sites.

**ditech**   *www.ditech.com*

**Yahoo! Finance**   *www.finance.yahoo.com/loans*
National rate averages, articles about ways to finance

**Quicken Loans**   *www.quickenloans.com*

**LendingTree**   *www.lendingtree.com*

### Vehicle Sites

**autobytel.com**   *www.autobytel.com*
Side-by-side comparison chart of several vehicles, relations with thousands of dealers

**CarPoint**   *www.carpoint.msn.com*
Model car data, tours, "surround video"

**ConsumerGuide**   *www.consumerguide.com*
Specs, prices, shopping tips, best buys

**ConsumerReports.org**   *www.consumerreports.org*
Tips on narrowing choices and negotiating prices, tips on saving money on leases

**Buyer's Guides**

*Note:* Check out motor vehicle magazine Web sites such as roadandtrack.com and motortrend.com.

**Edmund's Automobile**   *www.edmunds.com*
Vehicle information, consumer chat rooms, used-car and new car prices

**Kelley Blue Book**   *www.kbb.com*
Used-car prices, trade-in values

## REFERENCES

Cialdini, R. (2001). *Influence: Science and practice,* 4th ed. Boston: Allyn and Bacon.

Clements, J. (February 5, 2003). Bubble? What bubble? Housing isn't that pricey, so go ahead and buy. *Wall Street Journal,* p. D1.

Cross, G. (2000). *An all consuming century.* New York: Columbia University Press.

Ellison, S. and C. Tejada. (January 30, 2003). *Wall Street Journal,* pp. B1, B3.

Fletcher, J. (January 31, 2003). How's your town doing? *Wall Street Journal,* p. W1.

Gilbert, D. (2006). *Stumbling on happiness.* New York: Alfred A. Knopf.

Goodloe, K., and J. Jurgensen (April 21–22, 2007). Remote control. *Wall Street Journal,* p. P7.

Making your house pay off. (November 2002). *Consumer Reports,* 12–18.

Moore, B. (September 17, 2001). Inventive answers. *Wall Street Journal.*

Simon, R. (January 29, 2003). Getting a two-fer on a home loan. *Wall Street Journal,* pp. D1–D2.

*The Freddie Mac Reporter Fact Book 2002–2003.* McLean, VA: Freddie Mac Corporate Communications.

The New "Starter" home. (October 2002). *American Demographics,* 53.

White, J. (February 10, 2003). Low lease price on luxury cars may cost you. *Wall Street Journal,* p. B1.

# Saving, Banking, Debt, and Credit Issues

> If one wants to harvest quickly, one must plant carrots and salads; if one has the ambition to plant oaks, one must have the sense to tell oneself: my grandchildren will owe me this shade.
>
> —Leon Walras

## Learning Objectives

1. Identify the three steps in the financial management process.
2. Explain budgets, net worth statements, and the role of taxes.
3. Describe banking and savings strategies, scams, and advances.
4. Discuss financial planner credentials and fees.
5. Explain credit, common pitfalls, and consumer rights.
6. Explain bankruptcy and how to avoid it.

---

### Saying No to Unexpected Sales Calls

"In June Rosemary McDougall got an unsolicited phone call at dinnertime from a telemarketer selling automotive warranties. 'I find it more than coincidental,' says her son Graham, 'that she had taken her car to the dealer for repairs the day before. But they deny providing her car or contact information to the caller.' The phone solicitor had specific details about her 2002 Dodge Durango...and persuaded her to buy a 'protection' policy for $295. 'It sounded like a good deal,' says the 82-year-old-widow, a cancer survivor who lives in Metairie, La."[1]

She gave her credit card number to the salesperson and immediately regretted it and tried to get out of the policy. She called to cancel and Graham, a gerontologist at the University of Texas School of Nursing, Austin, called and left messages to cancel but to no avail. Then two weeks later a bill showed up demanding $2,700. The bill stated that it was the balance due on the $295 policy, which had been charged to Rosemary's credit card. Graham says there was no doubt in his mind that they were trying to scam her. He complained to the Better Business Bureau, AARP, and the Federal Trade Commission. Finally, the policy was cancelled and the $295 returned. Moral of the story: do not give credit card information out over the phone to anyone you did not call first.

To make matters worse, Rosemary was on the "do not call list," yet this salesperson got through. The FTC manages the list, but calls manage to leak through. The FTC gets 3 million complaints a year from registrants. They recommend that consumers re-register after five years. To sign up for the first time or to re-register, call 1-800-382-1222 toll free or visit www.donotcall.gov. Another source of help is the National Fraud Information Center at www.fraud.org; click on Telemarketing Fraud.

[1]Sid Kirchheimer, "When Trouble Calls." *AARP Bulletin*, November 2007, p. 22.

## INTRODUCTION

In capitalism, economic decisions are made by individuals, households, and families, mainly in their roles as consumers and owners of privately held goods and services such as houses, cars, and retirement plans. It takes money to have these things, and this section of the book explores how consumers can make the most of the money they have through wise planning.

We've also discussed the connection between happiness and consumption in preceding chapters. Someone living in poverty will get a boost from more money, but studies show that once you go further up the income scale, the connection between income and happiness is less clear. One reason may be **nexting**, meaning that when people buy or attain something, their minds are already thinking of the next purchase or goal. Those with considerable financial wealth do score slightly higher on the happiness scale, but what appears to make most happy is not the actual amount of money but what they do with it or plan to do with it. Daniel Gilbert, author of *Stumbling on Happiness,* says, "Our brains are made for nexting and that's just what they'll do. When we take a stroll on the beach, our brains predict how stable the sand will be when our foot hits it and adjust the tension in our knee accordingly" (2006, p. 8). Saving is all about nexting. You save in order to have more money to spend or invest or give away.

In this chapter, we will also go over steps to financial success as well as common pitfalls and frauds related to finances. Throughout the life cycle, we spend, save, borrow, and lend. As one ages, the goal is to become more of a saver and a lender in order to build financial wealth and maintain stability. This chapter introduces the topic of personal finance and shows how it fits into life plans. **Personal finance** is an umbrella term that covers the spending, saving, investing, and protecting of financial resources. Financial planning is a lifelong process, and no matter how much or how little money a person has, the principles of financial planning are useful.

According to former Federal Reserve Chairman Alan Greenspan, "Making informed decisions about what to do with your money will help build a more stable financial future for you and your family" (Ip, 2003, p. D3). Consumers are besieged by investment schemes and quasi-legitimate financial schemes on television and over the Internet. To counteract these negative information sources, the Federal Reserve has stepped in with public service announcements and a Web site (www.federalreserveeducation.org) with links to dependable financial information sources.

The goal of this chapter is to make readers more aware of how money can be more successfully managed (including where to go for help) and in so doing increase life satisfaction. Most consumption requires money—to get in the consumer game, one needs money or something worth trading. An individual's or family's standard of living and future financial stability hinge on the ability to accumulate, save, invest, protect, and spend money wisely. Personal finance also takes place within the ups and downs of the general economy, and as covered earlier in the book, the ways consumers spend, save, and invest affect the way the economy cycles, so there is both cause and effect when talking about consumers and their financial behavior.

## FINANCIAL MANAGEMENT PROCESS

Money management should be a no-brainer—you work, you earn money, you save, and you build an independent financial life. Over a million personal bankruptcies are filed each year, indicating that this set of tasks is not so easy to accomplish; as further evidence, credit card debt is at an all-time high, and a smaller percentage of consumers are keeping up with their monthly bills. The numbers of loan defaults and home foreclosures are up. In short, more and more people are having trouble making ends meet. As college students, you are in a uniquely positive position to begin a habit of good money management. The bottom line is being responsible, being a wise consumer, and handling income and expenditures in a prudent manner by avoiding debt and putting your hard-earned money where you want it go, where it will do the most good. It is not simply about helping yourself but also helping others. Personal finance is a process involving three steps (as shown in Table 13.1), and each of the steps is described next.

### Step 1: Setting and Prioritizing Financial Goals and Creating Plans

The first question financial planners ask clients is "What are your financial goals?" In other words, "What are you saving for—a primary residence, a comfortable life, a vacation home, a secure retirement, or the college education of children? What are you striving for?" Your answers may involve short-range goals such as paying bills each month. As mentioned in Chapter 1, goals are end results, things worth striving for, things to be achieved. Goals are based on **values** (principles that guide behavior), **attitudes** (likes and dislikes), and **resources** (source of wealth) and are affected by **decision making** (process of making a choice between two or more alternatives). Idealism is a value, and a sample behavior associated with idealism is the choice that more students are making to be active in their communities—many students have a tradition of volunteering to help others. According to U.S. Census Bureau data, the number of people ages 16 to 24 engaged in volunteer work is rising significantly. "For a lot of my friends from college and high school, the buzz word is finding your passion," says Sean Smith, age 24, a University of Notre Dame graduate and Peace Corps volunteer (Shellenbarger, 2006, p. D1). Table 13.2 provides a space for you to fill in your own financial goals based on time—short-term, intermediate, and long-range goals—along with estimated prices and a

**Table 13.1**    Three Steps in the Personal Finance Process

1. Setting Financial Goals and Creating Plans
2. Activating Plans
3. Evaluating and Revising Plans: Going Forward

**Table 13.2**    Setting of Financial Goals

| Time | Example of a Goal | Estimated Cost | Priority* |
|------|-------------------|----------------|-----------|
| Short-term (less than 2 months) | 1 _____  2 _____ | $ _____  $ _____ | _____  _____ |
| Intermediate (2 months to 1 year) | 1 _____  2 _____ | $ _____  $ _____ | _____  _____ |
| Long-range (1 year or more) | 1 _____  2 _____ | $ _____  $ _____ | _____  _____ |

*In each category, select a or b (a = 1st priority, b = 2nd priority).

place to rank their priority. People in their forties may have the following long-range goals: (1) to provide a college education for two children, (2) to move to a more expensive house, (3) to buy a vacation home, and (4) to retire at age 62. Not all of these goals will be held as equally important, which is where prioritizing comes in. Financial planners (to be discussed later in this chapter) help people make informed decisions about their financial future.

So the first step in the financial process is setting and prioritizing goals and (on the basis of those goals) creating plans. To be successful, goals should be flexible, action oriented, specific, and realistic. Financial goals are affected by risk, the possibility of experiencing loss or harm. Examples of risk are income risk (loss of income), investment risk, personal risk (health and safety), status risk, time risk, liquidity risk, interest rate risk, and inflation risk. Several of these were discussed in previous chapters, but as a recap inflation is a rise in prices and liquidity refers to how readily something can be turned into cash. Everyone varies in the amount of risk they can handle, which is referred to as risk tolerance. In regard to time, the longer one has until money is needed (the time horizon), the more chances or risks can be taken. Plans involve setting a course of action and then making decisions about what to do, such as continuing at the same pace, expanding (earning more, spending more, investing more), cutting back (saving more), or choosing an entirely new course of action.

## Step 2: Activating Plans

In this step, plans are actually carried out. Individuals make calls, go on appointments, open up a savings or brokerage account, or put a down payment on a house. Flexibility at this stage is important because plans may need to change due to circumstances. For example, 20 houses may need to be looked at before the right one is found, and then the desired one may be more expensive, requiring a reworking of the budget. At this step, there will be gains and losses, and learning takes place that will affect future decisions.

## Step 3: Evaluating and Revising Plans

This step involves looking back at how the plans went. Did they succeed or fail? Was the success total or partial? Evaluation is probably the least attractive of the steps but in many ways is the most important: People learn what works and what doesn't. Personal comfort level with risk is reassessed. Every day some level of assessment takes place, but a more formal once-a-year evaluation of financial plans is recommended. This usually takes place when people are filing taxes and have W-2 forms and other records of earnings and expenditures in hand. At the end of the evaluation, they reset their course by going back to step one and asking themselves, For next year, what do I want to accomplish, what goals do I want to achieve, and what plans do I need to make?

A deeper life evaluation may take place at the change points (discussed in the last chapter) such as graduations, weddings, and births of children. Another evaluation point may occur around a significant birthday such as age 30, 40, 50, or 60. The evaluation may not take place right on the birthday but in the surrounding years. For example turning 30 years old can involve an evaluation anywhere from age 29 to age 32. People do look back on the last decade of their lives and evaluate how it went. Career exploration is common between the ages of 20 and 29, and it is not until the ages of 45 to 54 that median income peaks. Self-evaluation involves an assessment of career, education, and personal and family progress. See Appendix A for job information that may be of assistance when beginning a career or when redirecting career goals.

## BUDGETS AND NET WORTH STATEMENTS

If you don't know your net worth or where your money is going, you need to find out.

A budget is a financial plan based on income and expenditures in a month. To develop a budget, one needs financial records that show consumption (for example, bank and credit card statements) and organized paperwork. Budgets show how much money is flowing in (earnings, dividends, gifts) and how much is flowing out (rent, expenses). Budgets have **fixed expenses** such as rent and **variable expenses** such as food and entertainment. In the last chapter, net worth was defined as assets minus liabilities; net worth statements are useful because they give an overall picture of financial worth, and lenders and creditors use them to determine whether to extend credit. Box 13.1 gives a budget. Box 13.2 gives an example of a net worth statement. You can do budgets and net worth statements yourself or with the help of a financial advisor. A negative net worth is not unusual for college students, but your goal should be to get on the plus side (having more assets than debts).

## SAVINGS

We all need cash for small immediate needs and savings for longer-range needs. Savings provide a safety net and are also helpful for putting together money for future needs such as a down payment on a house. Savings provide a sense of comfort and security, so they are useful from an emotional as well as a fiscal point of view. Traditionally, an **emergency fund** of three to six months of salary set aside as savings is recommended as a financial goal; these funds should be kept in a liquid interest-bearing account such as a money market fund, short-term certificates of deposit (CDs), or a savings account. During recessionary times with higher-than-usual unemployment, six or more months' salary is recommended for extra cushioning in case of job loss or other major setbacks or expenses, such as unexpected auto or home repairs or medical bills. Americans save zero percent on average of disposable income per year, a rate much lower than is found in most other industrialized countries. Yes,

**BOX 13.1    Budget: Tracing the Flow of Income and Expenses**

A budget is made up of cash inflows and cash outflows, usually figured on a monthly basis.

**Cash Inflows**

| | |
|---|---|
| Net salary | $ |
| Interest or dividends from savings accounts or investments | $ |
| Financial aid checks, scholarships | $ |
| Gifts | $ |
| Other sources of income* | $ |
| **Total of Cash Inflows** | $ |

**Cash Outflows**

| | |
|---|---|
| Housing (rent or mortgage payment) | $ |
| Utilities (electric, water, cable TV) | $ |
| Educational expenses, tuition and books | $ |
| Telephone | $ |
| Auto payments | $ |
| Gasoline, auto repairs | $ |
| Gifts | $ |
| Food (including restaurant expenses) | $ |
| Clothing | $ |
| Credit card payments | $ |
| Entertainment | $ |
| Medical/dental/prescriptions | $ |
| Personal care | $ |
| Pet care | $ |
| Savings | $ |
| Other expenses | $ |
| **Total of cash outflows** | $ |

Subtract outflow total from inflow total to determine what is left          $
over at the end of a typical month.

*Example: Josh, a college junior, gets $1,000 a month to live on from his mom while he is in college. His biggest expense is a combination of rent and utilities (he shares an apartment with a friend), followed by food. She pays for his tuition and books, and he drives an old used car that is paid for. He noticed friends coming over and eating all his food, so he put an end to that. When he eats out, he goes for the cheap all-you-can-eat places. Josh eats at his mom's house when he can. In exchange, he mows the yard and takes care of the pets when his mom travels. He had jobs in high school but is currently not working.

you read that last sentence correctly: The American savings rate has dropped from 4–5 percent to 3 percent to 2 percent and now is at 0 percent. Some would say the savings rate is in the negative zone, meaning more money is being spent than is brought into the household; for example, someone owes more for his or her mortgage and credit cards each month than he or she brings home in income.

**BOX 13.2   Net Worth Statement**

Net Worth: Assets − Liabilities = Net Worth

Assets are what a person owns, and liabilities are debts (what is owed).

Step 1: Figure out Total Assets.

**Current Assets**

| | |
|---|---|
| Checking accounts | $ |
| Money market or savings accounts | $ |
| Cash value of life insurance | $ |

**Investments**

| | |
|---|---|
| Stocks, bonds, mutual funds (estimated worth) | $ |
| Individual retirement accounts | $ |
| Employer retirement accounts | $ |

**Other Assets**

| | |
|---|---|
| Worth of house, other real estate | $ |
| Value of car, appliances, computers | $ |
| Jewelry | $ |
| Other belongings such as furniture | $ |

Add together each asset category to get Total Assets.                      $

Step 2: Figure out Total Liabilities.

**Current Liabilities**

| | |
|---|---|
| Credit card bills | $ |
| Medical/dental bills | $ |
| Car payments | $ |
| Other | $ |

**Long-Term Liabilities**

| | |
|---|---|
| Mortgage | $ |
| Student loans | $ |
| Other | $ |

Add together each liability category to get Total Liabilities.             $

Step 3: Subtract Total Liabilities from Total Assets to determine Net Worth.   $

Savings accounts in banks and credit unions earn interest that is compounded continuously. The **Truth in Savings Act** requires financial institutions to reveal the annual percentage yield (the amount of interest earned on a yearly basis expressed as a percentage), fees charged, and information about rules regarding maintaining a minimum balance.

One of the best ways to build savings is to automate savings through payroll deduction or transfers from a checking account to a savings account. Young adults in their twenties and thirties should be developing an overall savings and investment

**GLOBAL CONSUMER**

### What Do the Richest Men in the World Invest In?

The three richest men in the world are Bill Gates (founder of Microsoft), Carlos Slim Helu (Mexican businessman), and Warren Buffett of investment fame. Stockpickr tracks their portfolios to see what stocks they invest in, from which we can all learn. Do they have much in common? Surprisingly, the answer is no. Slim and Buffett own shares of Kraft Foods (symbol KFT), the worldwide food conglomerate with everything from cookies to cheese. This is not a recommendation to buy this stock or any other, but what do you think of the idea of tracking what billionaires invest in as a strategy?

*Reference:* James Altucher, "The World's Richest Men Own These Stocks." The Street.com, January 7, 2008.

plan and putting together an emergency fund. By the ages of 40 to 50, a goal should be to increase savings by holding on to money and making it grow. Middle-age adults should be saving for retirement based on estimates of how much they will need per year, and older adults are interested in trying to make their savings last and, in some cases, leaving a legacy.

## BANKS AND FINANCIAL PRODUCTS

The new financial marketplace has several features, including electronic banking, 24/7 access to accounts, automatic teller machines (ATMs), electronic transfer of funds, stockbrokerages offering checking and savings accounts (including money market funds), banks offering investment services, and deregulation. Overall, in recent years there has been a crossover of services that has benefited consumers. One of the few exceptions to this is that the wide variety of services has created some confusion as to safety and security. For example, today neighborhood banks offer mutual funds and other types of investments that are not protected by the **Federal Deposit Insurance Corporation (FDIC)**, which is government insurance of bank or savings and loan (S&L) accounts (up to $100,000 per account). Offerings that are not FDIC-protected are subject to risk, which confuses some elderly consumers who assume that everything offered by a bank is insured. Credit unions are insured by the National Credit Union Administration.

### Taxes

Since there are so many kinds of financial professionals, Table 13.3 gives a list of providers as well as products and services. Notice on this list the category of tax preparers. **Taxes** are payments of money to federal, state, and local governments. Each level of government has various methods of taxation. For example, sales taxes on items such as autos, clothing, and furniture are set by state and local governments. Another example of a tax is an **excise tax**, which is collected from the manufacturer of a product. You pay an excise tax every time you purchase a gallon

**Table 13.3**    Financial Services Providers and Their Products and Services

| Financial Services Providers | Typical Products and Services |
|---|---|
| Accountants | Budgets, advice, preparation of tax returns and audits, financial planning |
| Attorneys | Lawsuits, estate plans, trusts, legal matters regarding adoption or divorce, bankruptcy, wills, mediation, dispute resolution |
| Banks, credit unions, savings and loans (S&Ls) | Checking accounts, share and savings accounts, money market accounts, CDs, loans, safety deposit boxes, ATMs, debit and credit cards, trusts |
| Brokerage firms (financial counselors) | Online or in-person stock purchases or sales, bonds, mutual funds, money market and asset management accounts (including checking accounts), mortgages, IRAs, financial planning |
| Credit counselors | Debt management, credit consolidation, budgets, 24-hour hotlines (sometimes free, sometimes sliding-scale fees), bankruptcy issues |
| Financial planners | Fee- and commission-based financial planning services (budgets, investments, life insurance, mutual funds) |
| Insurance companies | Annuities, retirement plans, sales of insurance |
| Real estate companies | Housing and land sales, investments, rentals |
| Tax preparation services | Income tax returns, tax advice |

of gasoline; these taxes are considered regressive taxes, meaning they take a smaller share of people's income as their income grows. The majority of state and local taxes are regressive—they tend to hit low- and middle-income earners harder than higher-income individuals.

The federal income tax is progressive: The more you make, the more you pay. Income taxes are taxes on income, which includes salaries, wages, interest from savings accounts and other investments, commissions, and tips. Both individuals and businesses pay taxes. For individuals, the most-used forms are Form 1040 and Form 1040A. Throughout the year, it is important to keep good records of expenditures, including charitable contributions, because you may be able to itemize **deductions**, which are expenses subtracted from income before figuring out the amount of taxes owed. A simpler form is Form 1040EZ, often used by college students because it is most appropriate if someone is single or married but without dependents or a lot of money. All forms are available online from the Internal Revenue Service (IRS). The greatest percentage of federal income dollars is spent on human resources.

For a citizen to not pay taxes is cause for fines or various penalties, including jail sentences. **Tax avoidance** is a legal money management strategy to reduce one's taxes through such investments as tax-deferred individual retirement accounts (IRAs) or charitable donations, which are allowed under the tax code and should be properly documented. Before making or selling an investment such as a house or a stock or bond, the tax consequences should be considered. A well-trained financial planner, realtor, banker, or stock broker should be able to assist in these

BOX 13.3    **Nonprofit Organizations with Information on Wise Money
and Debt Management**

> *Consumer Action.* This national consumer advocacy organization directs consumers to complaint-handling agencies and offers educational materials. Go to www.consumer-action.org.
>
> *Consumer Counseling Centers of America, Inc.* These centers offer free and low-fee counseling and services to help people manage their debts. Go to www.consumercounseling.org.
>
> *Consumer Federation of America.* This is a pro-consumer advocacy and educational organization. Go to www.consumerfed.org.
>
> *Debtors Anonymous.* This national 12-step organization is dedicated to helping people overcome debt problems. Go to www.debtorsanonymous.org.
>
> *National Foundation for Credit Counseling.* This network of 150 member agencies at 1,300 locations offers educational programs on money management, budgeting, credit, and debt counseling, including help with arranging debt-repayment plans. Go to www.nfcc.org.
>
> *National Institute for Consumer Education.* This professional development, training, and research institute promotes personal finance education in workplaces, communities, and schools. Go to www.nice.emich.edu.

matters. Most people want to pay what they owe and not a penny more. **Tax evasion** is illegal because of the methods involved, such as not paying taxes or not reporting all income. Box 13.3 gives a list of nonprofit organizations that can help with money management, including how to manage debt.

## Bank Products and Issues

Banks and brokerage firms offer CDs with a maturity of at least seven days, with penalties on early withdrawals. CDs, a type of **time deposit**, are usually safe ways to store money from seven days to several years. The longer the money is deposited and the larger the amount is, the higher the interest rate offered. After the CD reaches maturity (the designated period of time has passed), the CD can be cashed in or rolled over to a new CD, hopefully at a higher rate. Banks compete

     **CONSUMER ALERT**

Although banks usually exercise good judgment, there are exceptions. Is your bank selling your secrets? In 1999 the U.S. Bancorp allegedly sold information on 930,000 account holders to a telemarketing firm called MemberWorks, which then pitched these customers "trial memberships" for a variety of services such as phones and discount travel. Even though some people said no to these offers, their accounts were charged anyway (the bank received a commission). Allowing these kinds of withdrawals without the customers' permission is illegal and resulted in lawsuits totaling $6.5 million. Selling information is legal, so to stop it customers must tell banks to keep their dealings confidential. Consumer groups are lobbying for tougher laws; for more information, go to www.privacyrightsnow.com (Stirland, 2001).

for CD business, and rates are compared in newspapers or can be found by going online or making phone calls.

Money market accounts are a type of account that offers a higher rate of interest than most checking or savings accounts. Many require a minimum balance to be maintained.

Checking accounts are offered by banks, and share accounts are offered by credit unions. "Americans write about 42 billion checks each year, and each one must be shipped from a bank to a central operations center to an intermediary (such as the Federal Reserve, a correspondent bank or a clearinghouse) before finally reaching the bank on which it's drawn. By the time a typical check lands back in your mailbox, it's been handled more than 15 times" ("The Check Is in the Air," 2003, p. 46). Since processing costs $1.25 to $5 a check, legislation is under way to streamline this process, which typically takes five days per check. Fraud runs rampant. The current cost to banks and credit unions is about $700 million a year in processing and fraud investigations. Congress is considering legislation that would involve banks sending images of each check electronically rather than by couriers coming to bank branches every afternoon for the paper checks. The savings in transportation alone would be $250 million, and it would slash fraud by 80 percent. The reason is that the more float time involved and the more people who handle a check, the greater the chances are for fraud. Once the legislation passes, banks will need check-imaging technology, and while big banks have already done this, smaller community banks will have to come up to speed.

Banks or credit card companies offer **debit cards**, which are issued to allow customers access to their funds electronically in places like grocery stores, and **smart cards** (also called **chip cards** or **stored value cards**), which may be worth $20 or $50 and can be used for placing phone calls or buying sodas or snacks from vending machines. Most retailers sell stored value cards in place of paper gift certificates. Some cards can be "reloaded" with additional value at a cash machine; other cards are disposable—when their value is gone, you throw them away. Debit cards can be used to withdraw money from ATMs and have no float like credit cards because debit card funds are withdrawn immediately. Cards may have combinations of these so that the owner does not have to carry three separate cards.

Credit card usage is expected to rise due to convenience of use. (Getty Images—Stockbyte.)

## CONSUMER ALERT

Under the Electronic Fund Transfer Act (EFTA), if there is a mistake or unauthorized withdrawal from a bank account through the use of a debit card or other electronic fund transfers, the person must notify the financial institution of the problem or error not later than 60 days after the statement containing the problem or error was sent. If someone uses your debit card without your permission, you can lose from $50 to $500 or more, depending on when you report the loss or theft. If you report the loss within 2 business days after the discovery of the problem, you will not be responsible for more than $50 of unauthorized use. The longer you wait to report the loss, the higher the amount you could lose. If you do not report an unauthorized transfer or withdrawal within 60 days after your statement is mailed to you, you risk unlimited loss.

## CONSUMER ALERT

Be careful in selecting a **personal identification number (PIN)** for use in ATMs and other forms of cash management. Usually you are better off using the one assigned to you by the bank, but if you select one yourself, don't make it too easy. A number like 1111 and one too easily traced to you (like your street address number, telephone number, or birth date) would be examples. Never keep the PIN with your card—memorize it. When using an ATM, be careful of your surroundings and take your receipt. If the ATM card is lost or stolen, report it immediately to the financial institution. Watch out for ATM charges, especially if you use your bank card in another bank's machine. On the plus side, ATMs have made it possible to get cash anytime and nearly anywhere, including abroad, reducing the need to carry traveler's checks and large sums of cash.

## CONSUMER ALERT

ATM thieves target customers in a variety of ways according to the Florida Division of Consumer Services Web site. A new scheme works like this. The ATM customer attempts to make an ATM withdrawal, and there is a malfunction, resulting in the card being held by the machine. An official-looking sign posted on the machine reads, "If for any reason your card gets stuck, punch in your PIN." The customer does as instructed, but the card is not returned. Later the customer learns money has been withdrawn from his or her account. Police investigators believe that the suspect inserts some type of plastic sleeve into the card slot and then waits for a customer to use the machine. When a customer arrives, he or she inserts the ATM card and keys in the PIN. Investigators believe the suspect may be using binoculars to watch the victim enter the PIN; then after the customer leaves, the suspect retrieves the card and starts making withdrawals. The advice to consumers is that if an ATM malfunctions, report it immediately to bank officials. In addition, ignore all signs, no matter how official looking, and report all suspicious-looking persons or vehicles in the ATM vicinity to the bank and the local police department immediately.

## Deregulation of Banking

With deregulation, there are different rules and more players in the financial market. For consumers, the good news is that the Depository Institutions Deregulation and Monetary Control Act of 1980 opened up competition: New forms of banking emerged, including banks without main offices or branches, which became even more popular with the advent of the Internet in the 1990s; new services opened up as well, and mergers took place more readily. So to recap regarding money and savings, with deregulation consumers have benefited by having more choices of financial institutions, including commercial banks, S&Ls, credit unions, and brokerage firms. Consumers should take advantage of this by comparing interest rates, features, risk, and convenience.

## Online Banking and E-Payments

*Online banking outpaces online auctions and stock trading.*

The Pew Internet and American Life Project survey revealed that online banking is the fastest-growing Internet application, outpacing online auctions and stock trading. In 2003 there were more than 37 million online bank users in the United States (versus 14 million in 2000). The best way to start banking online is with your current bank. Check its Web site to see what online banking services it offers and what the costs and fees are; these could be free or cost up to $10 a month. Also, investigate what your bank offers in terms of automatic bill paying. If you don't like what it offers, check out other local banks or consider using services like Yahoo! Finance (finance.yahoo.com) and MSN Money (billpay.msn.com), which allow you to have all your online activities from banking, e-mail, and stocks in one place.

The goal is to make handling finances, shopping, and bill paying simpler. Cards of any kind or the use of the Internet stimulates consumption, so financial institutions and retailers are motivated to provide cards for consumers in as many shapes and forms as they can. Most consumers use credit or debit cards to pay for online purchases, but other payment methods, such as "e-wallets" and automatic bill paying systems, are coming into vogue. The Federal Trade Commission (FTC) wants these payments and transactions to be as safe as possible and encourages the use of secure browsers and care in using PINs. **E-wallets** are Internet-based payment systems that allow value to be transmitted through computers. You can use e-wallets to make "micropayments"—very small online or offline payments for things like books or fast food. It works this way: When you buy something using your e-wallet, the balance on your online account decreases by that amount. E-wallets may be connected to your credit or debit card account, and e-payments include authorizing your financial institution to pay recurring bills in regular amounts, such as mortgages or rent, and irregular amounts, such as utility bills or credit cards, which is an especially useful service if a person is traveling or moving. If a biller does not accept e-payments, your bank can send a check instead. As explained earlier, check first with your bank to see what its policies are. New services are springing up daily; for example, a company called Paytrust (**www.paytrust.com**) will process any bill you instruct to have sent there for a monthly fee.

## Money Laundering and Terrorist Financing

Since this chapter is about global as well as personal financial issues, it would be remiss not to address the global problems regarding money laundering and

**CONSUMER ALERT**

Several steps can be taken for safety when you do online banking:

- Make sure that your bank uses Secure Socket Layer (SSL) encryption technology or another such system.
- Look for a liability guarantee against late payments and fraudulent activity.
- Make sure you have the ability to regularly log on to your account and see what is happening.
- Secure your system with antivirus software and a firewall program.
- Pick a hard-to-trace PIN code.

terrorist financing. In the United States, the Bank Secrecy Act (BSA) requires all national banks to file a Suspicious Activity Report (SAR) when they detect certain known or suspected violations of federal law or suspicious transactions related to a money-laundering activity or a violation of the BSA. There are a number of systems, controls, and rules too lengthy to go into here in regard to BSA and SARs, but generally speaking, movements of money in amounts over $5,000 are likely to be noted. Bank employees are trained to coordinate and maintain compliance. Under section 326 of the USA PATRIOT Act, every bank adopted a customer identification program. To learn more, go online to the Comptroller of the Currency Administrator of National Banks in the U.S. Department of Treasury. Other countries have similar money movement detection policies through their departments of the treasury or a related department.

## FINANCIAL PLANNER CREDENTIALS AND SCAMS

A **financial planner** looks at a person's or a family's total financial picture, helps that person or family define and prioritize goals, and then works out a plan to achieve those goals. Once the plan is in place, the financial planner may help implement or manage the plan, prepare tax returns, discuss investments, and obtain insurance coverage. A financial planner is really an asset manager, which is different from a financial counselor who tries to reduce a client's debts.

### Regulations and Credentials

Financial planning requires involvement and commitment from everyone in the family or household in order to succeed. Individuals availing themselves of financial planning help are trying to gain control over their money and move in a better financial direction. Over 500,000 people in the United States call themselves financial planners. This is an industry that is largely unregulated; hence the phrase "may the buyer beware" applies. The amount of regulation varies and is carried out by states, by credentialing associations, and by the Securities and Exchange Commission (SEC). It is not possible for the SEC to send investigators and auditors to visit every person claiming to be a financial planner, and better ways to regulate the industry are under discussion. That said, there are many financial planners who are legitimate and well trained. The most recognized credential is **Certified Financial Planner (CFP)** because of the rigorous examinations, the required three years of practical experience, and the code of ethics. New planners receive experience from established CFPs; nationally, there are more than 40,000 CFPs (Hoffman, 2003). Other credentials are Chartered Financial Consultant (ChFC) and the Personal Financial Specialist (PFS). To search for a planner where you live, see the E-Resources section.

Often certified public accountants (CPAs) have taken the exams and are also CFPs—this is a strong set of credentials. After individuals check for these types of credentials, then they would interview two or three potential financial planners before final selection. The more that is known about the planner, the better. Recommendations from several people whom you trust and a careful questioning of the financial planner's way of working should help screen out the fraudulent ones. The next Consumer Alert below gives other clues.

How much do financial planners charge? Most charge an hourly fee, but an initial consultation may be free. For example, Andy Claybrook, a CFP in Franklin, Tennessee, is a fee-only planner who charges $135 an hour (Hoffman, 2003). Others charge a flat fee, such as $300, to do a net worth statement and write an initial plan; still others charge commissions on products they sell such as mutual funds and life insurance. Some charge a combination fee and commission. Charles Schwab and other brokerage houses may offer financial planning online or in person for free or at a reduced cost (such as $99) if a person has an account with them—especially a sizable account.

If going with a CFP, generally it is accepted that the fee-only advisor brings the least-biased advice (Clements, 2003). The CFP may charge a yearly fee of 1 percent to maintain your records and update your investments once they are set up. With this setup, the advisor has an incentive to manage money wisely because as the portfolio grows, the advisor will make more money. As might be expected, the more work CFPs do, the more they will charge. Through commissions, the advisors make their money by selling life insurance, mutual funds, or other investments that will pay them a commission. A lot of planners like the flexibility and the income derived from the combination fee and commission method. What it boils down to is matching the client's needs with what is being offered, whether it be help with a particular problem that needs immediate attention (such as an impending divorce or sudden job loss) or more long-term planning. Some planners specialize in a certain type of client (widow, doctor, entertainer, executive, small-business owner) and may not want to work with other types of clients.

See E-Resources to find a list of financial planning services and calculators on the Internet. Other resources offering free financial advice include bankers, credit union managers, and employer-based human resources departments.

## Divorce Planners: New Breed of Financial Planner

A **certified divorce planner** is a specialist who is trained to focus on who gets the assets in divorces and who works alongside attorneys who handle legal documents and child custody issues. Divorce planners help couples divvy up retirement accounts and stock options, divide up businesses, calculate alimony payments, and decide who keeps the primary house and vacation home. "Nearly 70% of them have a financial title such as CPA or certified financial planner. About

**CONSUMER ALERT**

Rapport, setting, Web sites, and materials give an indication of how a financial planner operates. Do the materials look professional or amateurish? Is the office nice but not over the top? Are calls returned promptly? Does the financial planner really listen? Remember that the courts are filled with horror stories about judges, bankers, relatives, and personal friends who acted as financial advisors and robbed others of everything they have. Be wary, be cautious, start small, and keep your eyes open. No matter which financial planner is selected, make sure to obtain a written estimate of what services are to be expected and at what price; then check records of purchases.

1,000 divorce planners have been certified since 1993, with about 500 more in training right now. They generally charge between $100 and $200 and client work usually lasts about 12 hours" (Silverman, 2003, p. D1). Most of the clients have been married at least 10 years and have over $250,000 in assets, and they are usually women who want help with dividing up the finances. The certifying bodies are the Institute for Certified Divorce Planners in Michigan and the College for Divorce Specialists in Boulder, Colorado (see the E-Resources for Web sites).

## FREE FINANCIAL SEMINARS AND BEST-SELLING "GET RICH" BOOKS

A popular mode of communication about financial matters involves free seminars at hotels, schools, churches, and libraries that are given by financial planners, stockbrokers, insurance agents, and motivational speakers. The worth of these has to do with who is sponsoring the talk or seminar and who is the speaker. Be wary of direct mailings or advertisements in newspapers offering free financial talks—in some cases, the quality of information is suspect, and in others the "free" seminar is really a sales presentation. There is nothing wrong with a sales pitch as long as it is clear from the beginning that is what the seminar is about. Scams occur when seminars are given in public places that are followed up by high-pressure in-home one-on-one sales talks for a product or service.

A more dependable source of financial information is available from employers who offer it as a perk. For example, companies such as Honeywell, Dell, Pitney Bowes, and Procter & Gamble pay for reliable financial services specialists both to help executives prepare their taxes and set up estate plans and to help lower-ranking employees with college savings plans and retirement planning, including offering 800 numbers they can call for advice. The basic financial planning help may be one-on-one meetings or full-day seminars. The reasons employers are doing this is because of the growing role that workers assume in managing their personal finances and the knowledge that financial worries take employees' attention away from their work. As the 401(k) and 403(b) savings accounts for retirement and benefit plans become more employee controlled, workers are forced to make investment decisions that were normally made by higher management. About 28 percent of workers receive financial planning advice through their employer, and the percentage is climbing (Higgins & Simon, 2003).

Regardless of source or sponsor, realize that no one speaker or author has the key to financial success; if that person did, he or she would be on a yacht enjoying it and not sharing financial secrets with the public. A speaker or author who supports diversification (a variety of investments) and is not selling any one way to get rich, such as buying options or investing in foreign real estate, is on the right track. Television programs on money management as well as in-person talks can be enjoyed as long as one realizes that a personal viewpoint is being given and that this perspective is one among many. The best advice is tailored to individuals based on their circumstances and goals as well as changes in the economy and the financial marketplace, which is why the one-on-one consultations or 800 numbers are beneficial. Because there are so many changes in tax rules and in investments (including real estate), books and advice quickly become outdated. Few things are more worthless than a five-year-old "how to get rich" book.

## CREDIT, LOANS, AND DEBT WARNING SIGNS

People borrow money through the use of credit and loans. The "buy now, pay later" philosophy is ingrained in American society. Credit can be used for luxury items or for longer-term investments such as educational expenses:

> The difference between using credit to purchase luxury products and using it to finance an education is that the former usage is more consumption-oriented, while the latter is more investment-oriented. The commonality is that both incur long-term financial obligation, or consumer debt. Although the growth of consumer credit has contributed to the expansion of the U.S. economy and raised the quality of life for millions of American consumers, it also has brought about extensive consumer debt. (Lee & Lee, 2001/2002, pp. 25–26)

A study by Eun-Ju Lee and Jinkook Lee (2001/2002) found that consumers who approved of using credit for luxury purchases had more credit cards and greater credit card debt than consumers who disapproved of using credit for such purchases but found this was not the case for using consumer debt to finance education. So they concluded that "learn now and pay later" is a reasonable credit choice for most consumers but that people should beware of "buy luxury now and pay later" since this strategy tends to lead to more serious financial burdens on households. Another reason that using credit to finance education is a sounder choice is because higher education significantly enhances future earning potential, so borrowing money for educational purposes can be viewed as an investment.

The cost of using money is called **interest**. The rate of interest is determined by supply (amount of money lenders are willing to lend) and demand (amount of money borrowers are willing to pay). Interest rates are expressed as percentages (for example, 4 percent per year). You are a receiver of interest when you have a savings account that pays interest, and you are a payer of interest if you use a credit card or take out a student loan. Interest rates do not exist in a vacuum; they respond to changes in other parts of the financial market or the economy, so they may change daily or weekly. Naturally, when people borrow, they seek the lowest interest rate with the best terms.

Convenience is the main benefit of credit. **Credit cards**, which came into being in 1973, are used to purchase something or to get cash now with the promise of

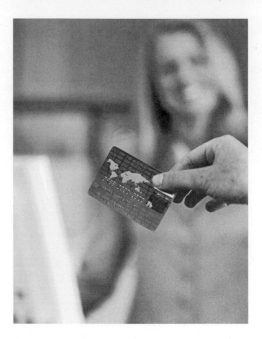

Global use of credit cards is spreading, making international travel and transactions easier. (Getty Images—Stockbyte.)

Credit cards began in 1973.

future payment. The typical cardholder carries 8 to 10 cards and owes over $4,000. Credit cards are also useful for identification purposes, rebates, emergencies, and purchases of big-ticket items.

A number of laws, most notably the Consumer Credit Protection Act of 1968, have been passed to reduce the problems with and confusion about consumer credit. The laws make several stipulations:

- You cannot be denied a credit card because you are a single woman.
- You can limit your risk if a credit card is lost or stolen.
- You can resolve errors in your monthly bill without damage to your credit rating.
- You cannot have credit shut off just because you've reached age 62.

The main drawback is overextension—people overuse credit and go into debt. Other problems include loss of cards, loss of privacy, and loss of financial freedom as money becomes more and more tied up in past purchases and interest payments.

 **CONSUMER ALERT**

Use caution when signing for a loan or acting as a cosigner. As a cosigner, if the borrower defaults, you will have to repay the loan. Not only would you lose money, but also failure to pay promptly will affect your credit rating.

**Loans** are sums of money lent at interest. A person considering taking out a loan should consider the source, the interest rate, and the terms, including the repayment schedule and any fees or penalties. Loans can be divided up into two types: by the reason for the loan (education, furniture, cash) and by the repayment schedule (monthly or yearly). Loans come from universities, stores, car dealerships, brokerage firms, banks, S&Ls, credit unions, consumer finance companies, sales finance companies, and life insurance companies. With the Internet, applying for a loan has never been easier, but that also causes problems because although applying is easy, paying up is another matter. A **cosigner** agrees to repay the loan if the borrower does not (defaults). Property such as a car, recreational vehicle, or boat used to secure a loan is called **collateral**. **Liens** are legal rights to take and hold property if the person with the loan does not pay up. When the loan is paid off, the liens are removed. When someone buys a house, a title search will reveal if there is a lien on the property, and the buyer will not purchase the house until the liens are cleaned up. A mortgage is a lien against a house.

Different types of loans such as mortgages, home equity loans, and car loans have been covered in previous chapters. The main thing to focus on is the annual percentage rate (APR), known as the interest rate; for example, the APR could be 8 percent a year or 12 percent a year—obviously the lower, the better. Most students are familiar with car or student loans. Regarding education loans, upon graduation students should schedule an exit counseling session with their lender or university financial aid office to determine their rights and responsibilities and to set up a repayment schedule. Choices are going to include stretching out payments over 10 years or having higher payments and getting them paid off faster; there will also be choices about how soon the repayment begins. Some people never pay off their student loans, and lenders are getting more aggressive about getting their money back (sooner or later). In some cases, lenders can get their money back when a person starts getting Social Security—they go through a process to remove a part of the Social Security payment each month until the student loan is paid off. Recent graduates should review loan statements, and if they could have trouble making payments, then the lender should be contacted and a new repayment schedule developed.

## Credit and Consumer Rights

A good credit rating (paying off student loans promptly is part of this) is important for a number of reasons, including the fact that potential employers may check your credit history before hiring you and landlords may check it to see if they

**CONSUMER ALERT**

Is it possible to be turned down for a new credit card because you have no balance on another card because it is paid off each month? Yes. Lenders like people who borrow wisely and pay their bills; however, too much financial discipline can be a negative from their point of view, which is to make money off you in finance charges. Is this fair for consumers? No. If you still want a card, one option is to spend a moderate amount on the current card each month and make smaller repayments. After six months, reapply, and you should get a new card, which you can then pay off each month. Or you can forget this credit card company and try another.

would be wise to give you a lease. Sometimes things happen in the system that can cause credit problems, so credit records should be checked. The FTC enforces credit laws and protects your rights to obtain, use, and maintain credit; it cannot guarantee that everyone will get credit but can require businesses to be fair and equal in their treatment of customers and their resolution of disputes.

**Consumer reporting agencies (CRAs)**, more commonly known as **credit bureaus**, have files that contain information about your income, debt, and credit payment history as well as information on whether you have been sued or arrested or have filed for bankruptcy. A **credit score** is given that includes all this information plus assets, length of employment, and length of living in one place. Negative events such as bankruptcies or failure to pay bills impact heavily on the credit score. There are two types of credit scores:

1. The **FICO score** was developed by the San Rafael, California–based firm named Fair, Isaac & Co. (the three credit reporting centers listed below all provide a FICO score to lenders). FICO is the score most widely used by lenders and also the one you have to pay to see. FICO scores range from 300 to 850, and a score below 500 is considered subprime lending, which means it may be hard to get loans or very high interest may be charged because a subprime borrower is considered more of a risk than someone with a high FICO score. The median score is 623, so someone with a score above that is preferred by lenders such as mortgage lenders; a score over 750 is considered a very high score and anything above 800 is unusual. FICO scores are often checked by employers before they hire someone, so it is a good idea to get your financial house in order before job hunting. How consistent and reliable individuals are at paying their bills and loans is a major factor in the score. FICO scores tend to go up and down slowly because they reflect many years of consumption, payments, and financial patterns. Students who have dealt strictly in cash or whose parents paid all the bills may not have a FICO score, but employers will not hold that against them if they realize that is the case.

2. Other scores available for free use factors that are similar to (but not the same as) those used by FICO. These scores are available online from such companies as FreeCreditReport.com and eLoan.com. However, in exchange for the free score, you may get e-mails from e-loan companies or other financial services.

Below are the three main credit reporting centers:

Equifax Information Service Center
PO Box 10596
Atlanta, GA 30348-5496

www.econsumer.equifax.com

Experian Consumer Assistance Center
PO Box 2104
Allen, TX 75013

www.experian.com

Trans Union LLC Consumer Disclosure Center
PO Box 1000
Chester, PA 19022

www.transunion.com

## ⚠ CONSUMER ALERT

Each credit bureau keeps a separate file on each person with information supplied to it by creditors. It is possible one of the reports has serious inaccuracies that could damage credit while the other two would not have the error in the file. So if there are problems, some experts would suggest getting copies from all three bureaus. If everything is going okay, then a check may not be necessary, or it may be prudent to receive a copy of your credit report each year from one bureau to check for errors and to make sure you have not been a victim of identity theft. If there is a mistake, contact the credit bureau in writing or online and explain the situation. The way to raise a FICO score is by paying down your current account balances and by paying bills on time.

Your credit rights are protected under the Fair Credit Reporting Act (FCRA), which is designed to ensure that CRAs furnish correct and complete information to business when evaluating your application. According to the FTC, under FCRA your rights are as follows:

- You have the right to receive a copy of your credit report.
- You have the right to know the name of anyone who received your credit report in the last year for most purposes and in the last year for employment purposes.
- Companies that deny your application must supply the name and address of the CRA.
- You have the right to a free copy of your credit report when your application has been denied.
- If you disagree with the accuracy of information, you can file a dispute with the CRA and the company that furnished the information. Afterward, you should receive a summary explanation of the settling of the dispute.

Your credit rights are also protected under the Equal Credit Opportunity Act (ECOA), which prohibits credit discrimination. According to the FTC, under ECOA your rights are as follows:

- You cannot be denied credit based on your race, sex, marital status, religion, age, national origin, or receipt of public assistance.
- You have the right to reliable public assistance that is considered in the same manner as other income.
- If you are denied credit, you have a legal right to know why.

According to the FTC, your credit rights under the Fair Credit Billing Act (FCBA) and the EFTA establish procedures for resolving mistakes on credit billing and electronic fund transfer statements, including the following areas:

- Charges or electronic fund transfers that you—or anyone you have authorized to use your account—have not made
- Charges or electronic fund transfers that are incorrectly identified or that show the wrong amount or date
- Computation or similar errors that have been made

- Failure to reflect payments, credits, or electronic fund transfers properly
- Failure to mail or deliver credit billing statements to your current address (as long as that address was received by the creditor in writing at least 20 days before the billing period ended)
- Charges or electronic fund transfers for which you request an explanation or documentation, due to a possible error

Most credit laws apply to open-ended credit (up to a maximum such as $5,000 or $10,000), revolving charge accounts such as department store accounts, and overdraft checking accounts. The EFTA applies to ATMs, debit transactions, and other electronic banking transactions.

To take advantage of consumer protection laws regarding incorrect charges, the person falsely charged must first write to creditors to straighten things out. The letter should be sent by certified mail, return receipt requested, so the person has proof that the creditor has received the letter; copies of sales slips and other documents should be included. The sender should keep a copy of the dispute letter. A sample dispute letter is given in Box 13.4.

## Students and Credit Cards

Credit card companies target students before their freshman year in college and hit them again before graduation. "When Laura Caccavone set off for her first semester

**BOX 13.4    Sample Dispute Letter to Credit Card Issuers**

---

Date

Your Name
Your Address
Your City, State, Zip Code
Your Account Number

Name of Creditor
Billing Inquiries
Address
City, State, Zip Code

Dear Sir or Madam:

I am writing to dispute a billing error in the amount of $ _____ on my account. The amount is inaccurate because (describe the problem). I am requesting that the error be corrected, that any finance and other charges related to the disputed amount be credited as well, and that I receive an accurate statement.

   Enclosed are copies of (use this sentence to describe any enclosed information, such as sales slips, payment records) supporting my position. Please investigate this matter and correct the billing error as soon as possible.

Sincerely,

Your Name

Enclosures: (List what you are enclosing.)

*Source: ID Theft: When Bad Things Happen to Your Good Name.* Federal Trade Commission publication, February 2000, Washington, DC.

**CONSUMER ALERT**

A person's liability for lost or stolen credit cards is limited to $50. If this happens, notify card issuers promptly upon discovery of loss. Most companies have toll-free numbers and 24/7 service. Companies will instruct on the next steps to be taken (if any).

of college last month, she brought along her favorite stuffed animals, hot pink sheets—and a Capital One Visa with a $300 credit limit. 'I know I have it if I need it,' says the 18-year-old freshman at Drew University in Madison, N.J., who also uses the card to buy gas and the occasional must-have accessory" (Simon & Whelan, 2002, p. D1). The $300 limit won't get her into too much trouble, but overuse of credit can lead to substantial debt loads that affect students the rest of their lives. Percentages of students who have major credit cards in their own name are as follows: freshmen, 36 percent; sophomores, 55 percent; juniors, 51 percent; and seniors 64 percent (Simon & Whelan, 2002). The trend is upward. Students should shop carefully because rates and introductory credit limits vary widely. When this book went to press, examples of cards targeted to students included Discover Card (issuer Discover) with a minimum interest rate of 17.99 and a $1,000 credit limit and Blue for Students (issuer American Express) at an 8.90 minimum interest rate and $500 introductory credit limit. The Senate Banking Committee has held hearings on the marketing of credit cards to college students because concerns have been raised about credit abuse.

Debit cards, ATM cards, and stored value cards are other options that students can use. A growing number of colleges now give students identification cards that can be used to buy everything from books to pizza, with the school getting a share of the revenue. Alumni cards are also being used by schools as a source of revenue.

## Debt Collectors and Creditor Rights

**Debts** are what is owed. Examples of debts are bonds, notes, mortgages, and other forms of paper evidencing amounts owed and payable on specified dates or on demand. A debtor is a person who owes money. If a debtor does not keep up with debts (such as not keeping up with car payments) or if there has been an error in the record or account, a debt collector may call. A debt collector is any person other than the creditor who collects debts. Lawyers can be debt collectors. The Fair Debt Collection Practices Act (FDCPA) prohibits debt collectors from using unfair, deceptive, or abusive practices while collecting debts. According to the FTC, these are your rights under the FDCPA:

- Debt collectors may contact you only between 8:00 A.M. and 9:00 P.M.
- Debt collectors may not contact you at work if they know your employer disapproves.
- Debt collectors may not harass, oppress, or abuse you.
- Debt collectors may not lie when collecting debts, such as falsely implying that you have committed a crime.
- Debt collectors must identify themselves to you on the phone.
- Debt collectors must stop contacting you if you ask them to in writing.

**BOX 13.5   How to Avoid Credit Card Scams**

- Beware of television or radio ads for "easy credit."
- Beware of the phrase "Anyone can qualify for a major credit card, even bankrupts!"
- Look out for calls to a "900" number for a credit card. This call may not be toll-free and may not result in a credit card. The FTC has found that calls can run from $2 to $50 or more.
- Watch out for credit repair companies or clinics. There are no tricks or shortcuts—only time and consistently paid bills will repair damaged credit. If someone advertises help consolidating debts into one check instead of several, find out how much has to be paid and for how long.

## Solutions to Credit Problems

Your credit record or report influences your purchasing, getting a job, renting or buying a house, and buying insurance. Negative information can stay on a report for 7 years and bankruptcy for 10. Any problems paying bills should be reported at once to creditors and a modified payment plan worked out. In other words, be up front about problems and take care of them before creditors turn to debt collectors. Creditors want the money even if it takes a long time; it costs them to hire debt collectors, an expense they want to avoid. People who have been turned down for credit may get desperate and fall for credit card scams. See Box 13.5 for advice on how to avoid scams.

## CREDIT COUNSELING SERVICES

After a person tries everything to straighten out credit problems, an alternative is to turn to credit counseling services such as the National Foundation for Credit Counseling or the Consolidated Credit Counseling Service. They have offices throughout the United States and offer Web sites and toll-free 24-hour hotlines. For services in your area, check the Yellow Pages of the phone book under credit counseling, or refer to the E-Resources section at the end of the chapter. Services may be free or low cost. How can they afford to operate for free or with low fees? The answer is that they are supported by local businesses and banks that want to help consumers be fiscally responsible and by foundations and groups such as the United Way.

 **CONSUMER ALERT**

Women have often had trouble establishing a good credit history—a record of how bills were paid—because they have made name changes and because creditors report accounts shared by married couples in the husband's name only. Women should make sure all relevant information in the credit bureau's file is in their name. The credit bureaus should be informed of any changes in names and in marital status, including getting married, separated, divorced, or widowed.

Also universities, military bases, credit unions, employers (through employee assistance programs [EAPs]), and housing or community authorities may offer free or low-cost money management or credit counseling services. Counselors look at the bills and try to arrange repayment plans that are acceptable to the people with credit problems and to their creditors. This may mean debt consolidation or the formation of a debt repayment plan. The Federal Consumer Information Center (1-888-878-3256) offers publications on credit counselors and debt management as well as checklists of questions to ask when choosing a counseling agency.

Who has financial or credit problems? Nearly everyone has experienced a bounced check or problems with electric or telephone bills, but credit counseling services are primarily for people who really have gotten in over their heads. The average customer at the National Foundation for Credit Counseling is a woman, is 35.4 years old, is married (or has never married) with children, has low to middle income, and owes several thousand dollars to over 10 creditors. How do you know when things are getting out of hand? This typical profile provides a few indicators, such as having dependents and several creditors. There are other signs:

- Is routinely fighting about money with a spouse or partner
- Is being continually anxious about money, never feeling there is enough, or is worried about spending what is available
- Is not able to save, feels that spending is out of control, seeks instant gratification through shopping, or rationalizes purchases (such as the tenth pair of running shoes)
- Has no idea where money goes and is not balancing a checkbook or looking at statements
- Lives paycheck to paycheck, usually running out of money before the next paycheck
- Is being turned down for credit cards
- Bounces checks regularly and is having problems with bank accounts
- Has trouble paying the rent and car payment
- Has to regularly borrow money from family members and friends
- Pays the minimum each month on credit cards and never pays them off completely
- Does not want to hear about money problems and uses avoidance
- Has a history of falling into debt, getting out of debt, and falling back into it
- Is attracted to people who have money problems as kindred souls
- Has to have the best of everything (such as the most expensive set of golf clubs or a showy car) even if it is not affordable

## DEBT AND RELATIONSHIPS/SELF-WORTH

Debt affects relationships. In a magazine article, a 31-year-old registered nurse revealed that she owed $57,000 and was afraid to tell her fiancé. When she told him, it turned out he had $27,000 in debt, so they postponed the wedding. Later, they disagreed about money; for example, he bought a new car instead of paying his bills. Eventually they broke up. Since then she has been paying off her debts each month and so far has reduced it by $5,000. Her goal is to be debt free in three years (Orman, 2001). In the same article, another woman, age 34, who was in debt set a financial goal to save for a down payment for a house and eventually wanted to start a family. She gained control of her finances by paying off three credit cards, which changed the dynamic between her husband and her for the better, and she reported they don't argue as much about money anymore.

**Self-worth** is a system of thoughts and feelings concerning or focused on self. Research indicates that self-worth is a driving force in people's perceptions of their financial situation and spending behavior. In an article on self-worth and finances, the relationship was explained this way:

> Some people spend because they have low self-worth. This spending helps them feel better about themselves, at least momentarily. On the other hand, some people engage in excessive spending behavior and feel guilty, thereby diminishing their self-worth. The positive and significant relationship between self-worth and financial satisfaction is an important finding that has significant implications for educators and financial advisors. (Hira & Mugenda, 1999, p. 220)

# BANKRUPTCY

## Causes

Credit counseling is encouraged and bankruptcy is discouraged by credit counseling services. A person should try everything possible before resorting to **bankruptcy**, which is a form of legal recourse open to insolvent debtors. A debtor would petition a federal court for protection from creditors and arrange for the liquidation of assets. The bankruptcy rate is about 1.4 million Americans a year, and the number is rising. Some of it is caused by credit overextension; other times it is caused by health crises, business failures, job losses, divorces, accidents, and natural disasters. Usually the debtors are under stress and unable to think clearly about the ramifications of bankruptcy, which remains on credit reports for up to 10 years. The person may get out from under debt but will be unable to buy a car, rent an apartment, or buy a house and may not be able to get a job or do other things most people take for granted. Over 25 percent of employers look into credit backgrounds before hiring, especially for jobs involving money and accounting such as retail, bank, and management positions (on an employment application, the potential employee authorizes the employer to do background checks, including credit records).

## Options

Most bankrupt individuals want to choose Chapter 7 of the federal bankruptcy code, but because of changes, most bankrupt individuals are steered to Chapter 13. **Chapter 7 bankruptcy** is known as "Straight Liquidation Chapter" because in return for eliminating debts, the debtor agrees to turn over nonexempt assets and pay as much as possible to creditors. However, the way it usually goes is that there are no nonexempt assets to sell, so creditors receive nothing. Exempt items differ by state but usually include houses, tools of trade, cars, and farm animals. Chapter 7 bankruptcy is popular because if it is granted, the court erases all dischargeable debt. In this situation, assets are turned over to an appointed trustee who will sell the assets to pay debts, making partial payments to creditors. Usually the first one to be paid is the attorney who handles the bankruptcy, and it is suggested that people hire an attorney for these cases. Costs include attorney fees, a filing fee, and trustee fees.

Another choice is **Chapter 13 bankruptcy**, which allows debtors to repay some of the debt they owe, and in return they get to keep most of their property; usually this type of debtor is a person with regular income. Through a court-approved plan, the debtor pays back some of the debt, and this looks better on the person's future credit report. Under Chapter 13 bankruptcy, the debtor retains some assets, and debts have to be paid within five to seven years. States differ about what assets the debtor may keep. People may hide such assets as jewelry, cars, or boats at relatives' and friends' houses, but the courts are quite shrewd and try to determine whether the debtor has given an honest accounting of assets and liabilities before final decisions are made.

Bankruptcy, then, represents an issue with several sides to it. Sometimes the debtor may have been fiscally irresponsible and may be bilking creditors and lenders; in other cases, the debtor has been through an unfortunate set of circumstances, such as ill health or an injury, and the laws are there to protect him or her from being harassed or unfairly treated. In recent years, Congress has considered bankruptcy legislation that would make declaring bankruptcy more difficult and might also include education requirements (similar to traffic school for drivers with traffic tickets). Repeated or serial bankruptcies are not uncommon, and stopping the cycle for the debtors' sake and their families' sake, as well as for the sake of the economy and of creditors, is a goal. Ultimately, the cost of bankruptcy is passed down to the people who pay their bills and are responsible through higher interest rates, more credit charges, and higher taxes. Somewhere along the line, someone has to pay for other people's misfortunes and mistakes.

## Steps to Follow

When people declare bankruptcy, they file petitions and schedules with the clerk's office of the federal bankruptcy court. In the petition, there will be a list of assets, income sources, liabilities (including lists of creditors and amounts owed), and living expenses (including number and ages of dependents). Proof will be needed in the form of deeds, mortgages, tax returns, credit card bills, medical bills, savings records, and loan papers. The process will take from four to six months to complete. One of the positive aspects is that debt collectors stop calling until things are settled, giving people breathing space. Attorneys also provide a buffer zone because debtors can refer creditors to them. Lenders may show up during the court case and will talk to the debtors and their attorneys immediately after the case ends, trying to get their money first. Attorneys do the following:

- Advise the person of rights and options in bankruptcy.
- Complete the forms (or have someone in their office complete the forms) and file them.
- Attend the "First Meeting of Creditors" with the debtor (this is also called the 341 meeting).
- Represent the debtor in the courtroom.

A trustee is appointed by a U.S. trustee, who works for the Department of Justice, and administers the case but cannot give legal advice. The trustee's job is to ensure that the debtor and creditors (people, banks, institutions, and stores to which the debtor owes money) are treated in accordance with the rules and procedures established in the U.S. Bankruptcy Code. Even though people go bankrupt, they still have to pay taxes, alimony, child support, property settlements, and student loans. A judge decides disputes, and usually debtors only see a judge if someone objects to their case.

## GOVERNMENT'S ROLE IN CONSUMER FINANCES

Throughout this chapter, the government's role as defender of consumers' rights, regulator, law setter, holder of hearings, and mediator has been emphasized. The government also has a role in providing financial education; examples of this were mentioned earlier and include public service announcements and the Web site of the Federal Reserve. Since the 1970s, financial and credit rights have been at the forefront of the consumer movement. As this chapter has shown, there are many agencies and laws regulating the use of credit. The leading agency is the FTC, which works for the consumer to prevent fraudulent, deceptive, and unfair business practices in the marketplace and to provide information to help consumers spot, stop, and avoid scams. Complaints against all kinds of creditors can be filed with the Department of Justice, Civil Rights Division, Washington, DC 20530.

An example in the chapter of government legislation aiding consumers and the banking business is the legislation being considered by Congress as this book went to press that would give electronic check images the same legal weight as paper checks. Instead of couriers arriving at bank branches to pick up checks to be processed, the checks would be sent electronically—this makes so much more sense in terms of time efficiency, cost-effectiveness, and gasoline savings. Technology in e-finance is one of the fastest-growing areas of e-commerce.

Besides federal agencies and Congress, state agencies and legislators also work to protect consumers. Each state has usury laws that limit how high an interest rate pawnbrokers and other lenders can charge. State attorney generals can prosecute creditors who have violated state equal credit opportunity laws, and in state governments, the office of the attorney general has the muscle to stop anticonsumer practices.

### CONSUMER ALERT

People file for bankruptcy with the idea of being free from debt, but as noted in the chapter some debts (such as student loans) are not dischargeable—they keep going. Also, a Chapter 7 bankruptcy only eliminates past debt, debt owed before the filing, so debtors are not absolved from future debt. They have to keep paying rent, telephone, electricity, and water bills or face losing services or being evicted even while they are in the process of filing for bankruptcy.

## SUMMARY

It is never too soon or too late to work on improving finances. Financial planning is a lifelong process, and sound money management is a means (although not the sole means) to personal power, success, stability, esteem, and general well-being. Research indicates that self-worth, financial beliefs, behavior, and satisfaction are linked. Reaching financial goals requires setting realistic targets and creating a plan to reach them; the best strategy is to set short-, medium-, and long-term goals and to build savings. The sum that Americans save, as a percentage of their disposable income, has fallen sharply in recent years. Most of our federal tax dollars go to human resources. When it comes to taxes, money management, and investments, seeking financial advice will help, but the quality of financial advice varies. With the deregulation of financial institutions in 1980, the market opened up, mergers happened, and more choices were available to consumers. Americans write about 42 billion checks each year, and the antiquated processing system is being overhauled. Banks are offering products such as mutual funds that are not backed by the FDIC, and this is confusing to some investors who thought all bank products and services were secure and backed by the federal government.

Online banking, a fast-growing use of the Internet for bill paying and account checking, is more popular than online auctions or stock trading. The chapter covered a number of ways to make sure that your online banking is conducted in a safe way and that your liability is limited. Streamlining bill paying saves time and reduces clutter.

There are few controls or regulations for financial planners. The Certified Financial Planner (CFP) is the most recognized certification. Many different situations, such as significant changes in lifestyle or marital status, can trigger the need for professional help. Certified divorce planners are financial planners who specialize in dividing assets in divorce cases.

The three main consumer reporting agencies (CRAs), which are also known as credit bureaus, keep credit scores and records. Credit is used by many consumers to finance educations, buy houses, remodel homes, and buy cars. A number of acts ensure that consumers are given equal access to credit and are treated fairly. The list of uses for credit scores is growing and includes auto and homeowner insurance companies; every lender looks at credit scores to gauge the likelihood of customers' future claims and then sets their premiums accordingly. More employers are using credit scores to screen job applicants, and landlords use them before renting. A credit score may be the earliest indication of an identity theft problem. Credit counseling is recommended for people with credit or bill-paying problems. If the problems cannot be solved, an alternative is filing for bankruptcy, which is a form of legal recourse open to insolvent debtors; the two main types of personal bankruptcy are Chapter 7 and Chapter 13.

## KEY POINTS

1. Financial management is a three-step process.
2. In recent years, Americans and Canadians have been saving 0 percent of disposable income on average each year, but there are indications this is changing for the better.

3. An emergency fund is recommended as a fallback in case of job loss or other major setbacks.
4. With deregulation, money markets opened up, and consumers had more choices because of increased competition.
5. Four main kinds of financial institutions are commercial banks, credit unions, brokerage firms, and savings and loan associations.
6. Under the old check-processing system, paper checks took five days to go through the system and were handled more than 15 times. In the proposed electronic system, processing time and the chance for fraud will be reduced. Banks will know much faster whether a check is good, and consumers will have increased security.
7. Online banking and online tax forms for the Internal Revenue Service offer convenience.
8. Progressive taxes (for example, income taxes) and regressive taxes (for example, taxes on gasoline) have different impacts on the population. Tax avoidance is legal, but tax evasion is illegal.
9. There are over 500,000 financial planners in the United States; 40,000 have the CFP credential, which requires having three years of practical experience, passing exams, and adhering to a code of ethics.
10. Consumer credit can be used for a variety of reasons, including financing education and buying luxury items. Financing education is an investment in human capital.
11. A credit score is a key factor in determining access to credit as well as the interest rate a person may be charged. The FICO score is the credit industry standard. FICO scores, which range from 300 to 850, allow lenders to rank loan applicants according to the likelihood they will repay on time.
12. Federal law sets procedures for correcting inaccurate information on credit reports.

## KEY TERMS

attitudes
bankruptcy
certified divorce planner
Certified Financial Planner (CFP)
Chapter 7 bankruptcy
Chapter 13 bankruptcy
chip cards
collateral
consumer reporting agencies (CRAs)
cosigner
credit bureaus
credit score
debit cards

debts
decision making
deductions
emergency fund
e-wallets
excise tax
Federal Deposit Insurance Corporation (FDIC)
FICO score
financial planner
fixed expenses
interest
liens
loans

nexting
personal finance
personal identification number (PIN)
resources
self-worth
smart cards
stored value cards
tax avoidance
taxes
tax evasion
time deposit
Truth in Savings Act
values
variable expenses

## DISCUSSION QUESTIONS

1. Are you pleased or disappointed with your financial situation? What steps are you taking to get on sounder footing? What are your short-, medium-, and long-range goals? Why does financial planning require flexibility?
2. Why is it true that it is never too soon or too late to start working on improving a financial situation?
3. What is your potential liability if your debit card is lost or stolen? What is your potential liability if your credit card is lost or stolen? In either case, what should you do first?
4. Look at the E-Resources list and select one Web site to investigate. Report what you find.

## E-RESOURCES

### Banking and Savings Bonds Sites

**American Bankers Association (ABA)**   *www.aba.com*
General information on banking and loans

**Bank Online**   *www.bankonline.com*
Links to banks throughout the United States

**Federal Deposit Insurance Corporation (FDIC)**   *www.fdic.gov*
Insurer of bank accounts

**Federal Reserve**   *www.federalreserveeducation.org*
Government-based source of financial information on how the Federal Reserve operates, links to topics on banking and more

**Gomez Advisors**   *www.gomez.com*
Ranking of bank Web sites

**Treasury Department's Bureau of Public Debt**   *www.savings-bonds.gov*
Source for U.S. savings bond information and purchase

### Financial Plans and Financial Planners

*Note:* There are over 1,000 Web sites with financial calculators, and all of them produce different results, depending on how they are set up and the depth of information that the person seeking advice gives. So these are useful for a beginning estimate of net worth and financial well-being, but they are not the last word. Examples of some leading sources follow.

**American Bankruptcy Institute (ABI)**   *www.abiworld.com*
Provides information on bankruptcy

**American Bar Association (ABA)**   *www.abanet.org*
Provides legal information and lists of attorneys

**American Express**   *www.americanexpress.com/advisors*
Provides ways to calculate net worth, cash flow, etc.

**CFP Board of Standards**   *www.cfpp-board.org* (click on "Consumers")
Provides "10 Questions to Ask When Choosing a Financial Planner" and other consumer brochures

**Citibank**   *www.finance.com*
Offers financial advice and plans

**College for Divorce Specialists**   *www.cdscollege.com*
Has search engine for divorce planners by keyword and geography

**Consolidated Credit Counseling Services (CCCS)**   *www.cccs.org*
Offers credit counseling help

**Federal Trade Commission (Credit/Bankruptcy)**   *www.ftc.gov*
Provides information on credit, rights, frauds, scams

**Financial Planning Association**   *www.fplanet.org*
Aids in locating planners (fee and commission based), will work with modest sums

**Garrett Planning Network**   *www.garrettplanningnetwork.com*
Aids in locating planners who charge by the hour, will work with modest sums

**Institute for Certified Divorce Planners**   *www.institutecdp.com*
Has search engine for divorce planners by zip code, state, or last name

**John Hancock Mutual Life Insurance Company**   *www.jhancock.com*
Offers computer-generated financial plan

**Jump$tart Coalition for Personal Financial Literacy**   *www.jumpstart.org*
Educates K–12 students about financial matters

**National Association of Insurance Commissioners (NAIC)**   *www.naic.org*
Maintains links to all state insurance regulators whose credit scores are used in predicting future claims under auto and homeowner policies

**National Association of Personal Financial Advisors (fee-only)**
*www.napfa.org*
Aids in locating planners, will work with modest sums

**National Foundation for Credit Counseling (NFCC)**   *www.nfcc.org*
Provides information on credit and credit reporting centers, tells where nonprofit credit counselors can be found by area of the country, offers tips on how to get credit reports and how to budget

**West's Legal Dictionary**   *www.wld.com*
Provides legal terminology and definitions

## REFERENCES

Clements, J. (February 19, 2003). Finding a financial adviser who won't sneer at your little nest egg. *Wall Street Journal,* p. D1.

Gilbert, D. (2006). *Stumbling on happiness.* New York: Alfred A. Knopf.

Higgins, M., and R. Simon. (February 12, 2003). Getting stock picks from your boss. *Wall Street Journal*, p. D1.

Hira, T., and O. Mugenda. (1999). The relationships between self-worth and financial beliefs, behavior, and satisfaction. *Journal of Family and Consumer Sciences, 91* (4), 214–20.

Hoffman, E. (February 2003). Want some outside advice? *AARP Bulletin*, p. 26.

Ip, G. (May 20, 2003). New role for Greenspan: Pitching financial advice. *Wall Street Journal*, p. D3.

Lee, E., and J. Lee. (2001/2002). Credit choices: An examination of consumer approval for the financing of luxury items and education. *Journal of Consumer Education*, pp. 25–34.

Orman, S. (September 2001). Your net worth? Priceless. *O Magazine*, pp. 66–70.

Shellenbarger, S. (June 26, 2006). Doing well vs. doing good: Parents struggle with their grad's idealism. *Wall Street Journal*, p. D1.

Silverman, R. (February 12, 2003). How to plan the perfect divorce. *Wall Street Journal*, p. D1.

Simon, R., and C. Whelan. (September 3, 2002). The credo on campus: "Just Charge It." *Wall Street Journal*, p. D1.

Stirland, S. (October 2001). Is your bank selling the world your secrets? *Good Housekeeping*, pp. 229–30.

The Check is in the air. (April 2003). *SmartMoney*, p. 46.

# Insurance and Investment Issues

> You can fool some of the people all of the time, and all of the people some of the time, but you cannot fool all of the people all of the time.
> —Abraham Lincoln

## Learning Objectives

1. Explain the purpose and types of insurance.
2. Describe the different parts of insurance contracts.
3. Explain the purpose and types of investments.
4. Describe frauds and scams involved in insurance and investments.
5. Discuss state and federal government agencies that look out for insurance and investment frauds.

---

### Pay Attention to What People Do

How much to invest and how much to put into insurance are questions all of us face. Many financial decisions are affected by consumer confidence in the present and estimated future economy. A potential slowdown "was a hot topic at the meeting of the American Society of Plastic Surgeons in Baltimore this fall. One breast-implant maker sees hints of a slowdown in demand. The number of vision-correction surgeries appears to be falling as well. 'This whole mortgage credit crisis is making people think twice,' said J. Peter Rubin, a Pittsburgh plastic surgeon. 'It's something I've noticed and some colleagues have noticed as well.' Consumers spend more on housing, health care, education, travel, restaurants and other services—$4.6 trillion last year—than they do on food, gasoline, clothing, electronics, cars and other goods—$3.6 trillion. . . . Breast jobs and tummy tucks aren't covered by insurance, so patients need a chunk of cash—or a healthy credit line."[1] Dave Harmon, President of Market Scope LLC, estimates that 80% of the change in volume in such surgeries can be explained by changes in consumer confidence. Dean Croushore, a University of Richmond economist, adds, "Pay attention to what people do, not what people say. As long as people's incomes are doing fine and they have money to spend, they'll spend it."[2]

---

[1] Rhonda L. Rundle and Kelly Evans, "Evidence Grows That Consumers Are Pulling Back." *Wall Street Journal*, December 8–9, 2007, pp. A1, A12.
[2] Ibid.

# INTRODUCTION

Insurance and investments are little-understood yet important parts of our financial lives and are multifaceted. As evidence of their role in the economy, consider the following two facts:

1. Over one-half of Americans own stocks through mutual funds and their retirement plans.
2. In the United States, $1 out of every $12 is connected to the insurance industry.

This chapter explains the basic forms of insurance and investments as well as the most common fraud problems. Since this is an ever-evolving area, readers need to keep abreast of changes in the general economy and the legislation that affects products and services.

As in all areas, the Internet brings with it increasing choices along with increasing opportunities for fraud. Since large sums of money are involved in insurance and investments, the attraction to swindlers is easily seen—swindlers go where the money is. But let's say you are a cautious person and unlikely to fall victim to obvious fraud. Why should you care? Insurance fraud alone can inflate your premiums as much as 30 percent, according to the National Insurance Crime Bureau. Whether you fall victim directly or not, you pay for the insurance fraud that involves others because the cost is passed on to all consumers.

The chapter begins with a brief overview of the purpose of and types of insurance because this type of fraud cannot be explained until the reader understands the way insurance works. Specifics on the different types of insurance will be given, leading to a discussion of consumer rights and responsibilities. After the insurance section, the chapter turns to a description of different types of investments and the connected frauds. The purpose of this end section of the chapter is to give a thumbnail sketch of the main types of investments.

Is there one surefire way to get rich? The answer to this is no. A basic principle in economics is that the greater the expected return on investment, the greater the risks associated with it. Before putting money into either insurance or investments, read this chapter and then investigate further.

# INSURANCE

## Purpose

Insurance, a financial arrangement between consumers and insurers, is for protection.

**Insurance** is a financial arrangement between individuals and insurance companies to protect against loss or injury, and it provides peace of mind. The primary purpose of insurance is protection. This protection can be for a house, a business, or an automobile and also protection from possible liability claims. Another purpose is that some types of insurance, such as whole life insurance, can be used as a form of investment. By buying insurance, individuals are trying to protect themselves, their families, and their assets such as homes and cars.

College courses in insurance usually fall under the category of risk management and is taught in the business school. Individuals take out policies (contracts) and make premiums (payments) to insurers. The policies include agreements, **exclusions** (items not covered), conditions, deductibles, and endorsements (amendments or additions to the basic policy). An example of an exclusion would be exempting claims stemming from nuclear explosions or radioactive fallout. State Farm, the nation's largest auto and residential insurer, changed its car insurance policies to exclude such claims in the wake of heightened awareness of terrorism and the realization that there was no specific language in its existing contracts regarding nuclear-related claims. Letters were sent to 40 million auto policy holders saying that nuclear blasts and radioactive damage are not normal road hazards, whether the incidents are accidental or intentional, and in so doing, the company clarified that cars damaged by nuclear incidents are not covered. **Deductibles** are amounts policy holders pay toward a loss before insurance coverage begins. If there is a loss or injury, the insurer pays up.

Insurance is sold through agents in person, over the telephone, or online. Auto insurance is one type of insurance that is increasingly being sold online. **Exposures** such as driving are sources of risks; **perils** are events such as car accidents that cause financial loss.

The buying of insurance can be thought of as a process beginning with awareness of need, moving through analysis and action (including purchase), and ending with evaluation. Insurance policies should be revisited at least once a year—and more often when there are significant lifestyle changes. One kind of thing that could change, for example, is peril exposure, such as when a consumer takes up skydiving or starts traveling extensively.

An insurer can turn down an applicant. If this happens, the applicant can ask the insurer why he or she was denied coverage and request a copy of personal medical information. The individual denied insurance can try other companies as well as check with the state department of insurance to find out about rights and responsibilities.

## Automobile Insurance

Many states (but not all) require auto insurance, and most require liability coverage. Liability insurance is described by three numbers; as an example, 25/50/25 means that the policy would pay a maximum of $25,000 for bodily injury to one person, a maximum of $50,000 to more than one person, and $25,000 maximum for property damage in one accident. To find out coverage in your state, go to your department of insurance Web site or to the Insurance Information Institute Web site at http://www.iii.org.

Since not all states require auto insurance, it is possible to get in an accident with an uninsured motorist, so what you may want to have is **uninsured motorist coverage**, which pays for bodily injury caused by an uninsured motorist or by a hit-and-run driver or a negligent driver with an insolvent insurer. A driver may be underinsured as well. In the case of an accident, whether or not a claim is paid depends on the insurance of the two drivers who were legally liable, agreements between the people involved, the amount of damage, and the amount of maximum limit on the policies.

In the last chapter, it was stated that banks and other institutions are crossing lines by adding more and more types of financial products. Similarly, there is a new twist in car insurance: In order to control cost, insurers (such as Progressive Corporation, the nation's third largest auto insurer) have opened their own chain of one-stop auto claims centers. Customers make an appointment and bring in their

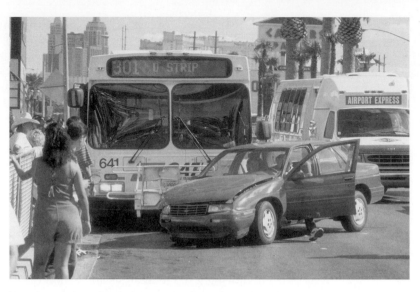

People watch curiously from a sidewalk after witnessing an automobile accident in Las Vegas, Nevada. (Jeff Greenberger, PhotoEdit, Inc.)

cars, and the company takes it from there. At the centers, Progressive will inspect crashed vehicles, hand customers keys to rental cars, take crashed cars to a body shop for repairs, and inspect them afterward before giving them back to customers. This hands-on approach is different from the usual procedure of owners of damaged cars finding their own repair shops and sending the paperwork to the company. From a convenience standpoint, this new service by Progressive is attractive, but critics are worried that the quality of repairs may suffer as insurers scrimp on costs. To save money, generic auto parts may be used instead of brand-name auto parts, a practice that may be okay or may cause problems. In the past, the use of generic parts that were deemed inferior has led to lawsuits. A pro argument for using the insurance company–repair shop combinations is that Farmers Home Insurance estimates that 40 percent of repair jobs found on the general market

 **CONSUMER ALERT**

Protect yourself when buying insurance online by doing research. Determine which insurance coverage best fits your needs; then shop around for companies, premiums, and coverage. In order to sell insurance in your state, the company and the agent must be licensed. You can link to your state insurance department's Web site by going to www.naic.org, clicking on "State Insurance Regulators Web Sites," and then clicking on your state. Remember that security is important—protect your personal information, taking extra precautions when paying with credit cards. Keep detailed records, get all rate quotes, and print out forms and information. You should receive a copy (not a photocopy) of new policies within 30 to 60 days of purchase. If you do not, contact the company immediately.

involve some type of fraud. According to one author, "The next time you need to take your vehicle to the body shop, don't assume all the repairs were necessary or that the parts of work you were charged for were even used or completed" (Oster, 2003b, p. D1). Since this combination of repair shop and insurance company is limited in availability, it is too soon to tell if this service will dominate the market-place; however, the trend is under way because other insurance companies such as Allstate and Farmers Home are experimenting with similar services.

Regarding the differences between states in auto insurance coverage required, in Louisiana you must have liability coverage, which pays for property damages or personal injury for which the driver is legally responsible. No-fault insurance (after an auto accident, each party collects from his or her insurer) is available in only a few states; no-fault insurance policies are rife with fraud, and motorists are paying too much for limited coverage. There are several other types of insurance:

- *Bodily injury liability.* Coverage of bodily injury liability pays for serious and permanent injury or death to others when you cause an accident involving your automobile.
- *Collision.* Collision coverage pays for repair or replacement of your vehicle if it collides with another vehicle or flips over or crashes into an object, regardless of who causes the accident. People often drop collision coverage after a car is more than 10 years old because the car is not worth much, so the cost of insurance does not make financial sense.
- *Comprehensive.* Comprehensive coverage pays for losses from incidents other than a collision, such as fire, theft, windstorm, vandalism, or flood.
- *Uninsured or underinsured motorist.* Coverage for uninsured or underinsured drivers pays for bodily injuries to you, your family members, and any other person occupying your covered vehicle if the injuries are caused by the negligence of others.
- *Medical payments.* Another type of coverage pays for medical expenses for accidental injury up to the limit of your policy.
- *Towing.* Coverage can be added to basic auto insurance for towing and road service.

Actually there are additional kinds of auto insurance, but they tend to be for unique situations. The point is that auto insurance is something that individuals buy on their own (not through an employer) and that the states vary in what they require. Following are some factors that affect premiums:

- *Driving history.* A driving history includes past accidents and traffic violations.
- *Type of vehicle.* Premiums are impacted by the vehicle's model, year, and value.
- *Gender and age.* Insurance companies typically charge higher premiums for males under the age of 25.
- *Territory.* Where you drive and where you keep your car influence premiums. Urban drivers typically pay more than rural drivers; for example, insurance is higher in New York than it is in Wyoming or North Dakota.

Ways to reduce premiums include having a good driving record, being a non-drinker and nonsmoker, driving low-profile automobiles, getting older, raising your deductible, getting good grades, having restraint systems, dropping collision on older cars, and installing antitheft devices. The price of insurance (the average premium for full coverage) varies greatly by type of vehicle. *Consumer Reports* found

**BOX 14.1   Types of Fraud Schemes and Scams Related to Auto Insurance**

*Agent sliding.* The term *agent sliding* refers to an agent selling a consumer optional coverage or services without his or her full consent.

*Deceptive claim.* When an accident victim files a claim for lost wages and medical bills following an accident and investigators find out that the injury was preexisting and had nothing to do with the accident, that would be a deceptive claim.

*Fictional theft.* When a policy holder files a phony claim for a stolen luxury car when the car is actually hidden in storage or at a friend's house, that is fictional theft.

*Repair shop rip-off.* An example of a repair shop rip-off is when an owner of a repair shop offers to inflate the damage estimate as a favor, and the dishonest owner of the vehicle submits the inflated claim.

*Understatement of risk.* A dishonest applicant lying about the number of miles frequently driven per year in order to get a lower premium is an understatement of risk.

*Note:* Some of these scams and schemes are caused by the insurer and some by the consumer.

that small sedans are usually the least expensive and that midsize high-end sedans are the highest. Surprisingly SUVs were in the middle ("What a Difference the Car Makes," 2002). Insurers base their rates on their claims experience. Box 14.1 lists the typical types of insurance frauds related to autos.

## Credit Insurance

Credit insurance is one of the lesser known forms of insurance. It protects a loan or mortgage on the chance that a person cannot make the payments. Usually it is optional, meaning the lender will not demand it. The Federal Trade Commission (FTC) says it is against the law for a lender to deceptively include credit insurance in your loan without your knowledge or permission. There are four types of credit insurance:

1. *Credit disability insurance.* A credit disability insurance policy pays off all or some of your loan if you become ill or injured and can't work.
2. *Credit life insurance.* A credit type of life insurance pays off all or some of your loan if you die.
3. *Credit property insurance.* Credit property insurance protects personal property used to secure a loan.
4. *Involuntary unemployment insurance.* Insurance coverage for involuntary unemployment makes loan payments if you lose your job through no fault of your own, such as a layoff.

Several of these credit insurance types are covered by other kinds of insurance an individual may already have, such as health or auto insurance, so before buying credit insurance, he or she should check this first. Alternatives, such as life insurance instead of credit life insurance, may make more sense. Before buying credit insurance, find out about these issues and the length of loan, as well as the usual issues about insurance such as coverage, cost of premiums, and ratings of companies.

## CONSUMER ALERT

When applying for auto insurance policies, individuals must disclose past tickets or accidents; otherwise, individuals risk policies being cancelled, leaving them without coverage. Applicants must also be truthful about the number of drivers in their family. An insurance company can cancel the policy if the driver has been in three or more accidents in a three-year period; failure to make premiums can also result in cancellation. As with any other major purchase, individuals should shop around. To see how companies are rated, go to the E-Resources section. If you receive phone calls after an accident, it could be someone trying to involve you in a fraud scheme. Always carry auto and health insurance cards with you, and protect insurance identification numbers as you would credit card numbers.

## Homeowners' (Property and Liability) Insurance

Homeowners' insurance helps pay to repair or rebuild your home and to replace personal possessions lost to theft, fire, storm, or other disasters. Most states do not require the purchase of homeowners' insurance but may require it for specific purposes (for example, liability insurance if you have a swimming pool). **Property insurance** pays for losses to homes and personal property due to theft, fire, vandalism, natural disaster, or another cause such as trees falling on houses. **Liability insurance** pays for losses from negligence resulting in bodily injury or property damage to others for which the policy holder is responsible; all homeowners' policies provide liability coverage. From a consumer point of view, the main thing is to have replacement-cost coverage. If the home or apartment is destroyed by fire, a person wants to replace the contents, and if the dwelling was owned, replacing the structure should be covered as well. There are a variety of forms. The most popular of all policies for homeowners that cover the basics is HO-3, HO-4 is for renters. Policy seekers look for a match between what they need and what the policy covers while keeping costs to a minimum. If a person owns only a beat-up bicycle, a three-year-old computer, and clothes, renters' insurance is probably not necessary. The more valuable the possessions are, the more insurance is needed. To save money, homeowners and renters should raise the deductible, use security systems and smoke detectors, not smoke, and take advantage of available discounts such as those offered to groups.

Liability may be related to homes, autos, situations involving bodily injury, libel (a written, printed, or pictorial statement that damages a person by damaging his or her character or reputation), or other damages caused by the insured.

There are three red flags that may prevent an insurer from covering a home:

1. Water claims
2. Wind/hail damage
3. Burglaries

The insurance industry has been cracking down on houses with a past. The message from the insurer is "It is not you—it is your house."

Policies usually cover the basics, but for extras such as jewelry, furs, and expensive computers, a person may need additional coverage that can be obtained

**CONSUMER POWER MODEL**

**Will You Have to Buy Flood Insurance?**

Basic homeowners' insurance does not cover water that enters from the outside so if the levee breaks or the hurricane comes, you might be out of luck. More and more homeowners are looking into buying flood insurance policies. If you live in a flood-prone area, you may be required to buy flood insurance. The Federal Emergency Management Agency (FEMA) has maps showing flood-prone areas in states such as Texas, Louisiana, Ohio, and Florida. If you get FEMA flood coverage, the most it typically covers is $100,000 for household contents and up to $250,000 for the house. Not everything is covered like finished basements. If you live in high-risk areas like a coastline, premiums might double.

Before buying a house, find out about insurance coverage and if the house is in a high-risk area for flooding. Flood damage is much more common than most people realize. Do you have a house in a flood zone or do your parents? Do you know if you or they have flood insurance?

*Reference:* Anne Field, "Why You Could Soon Be in a Flood Zone." *Business Week,* January 14, 2008, p. 65.

as an **endorsement**, an addition to an insurance policy. "The truth is that homeowners insurance can be very limited in protecting valuable possessions. It's common to encounter special clauses that exclude fine art and antiques, or that cap payments on losses. . . . Standard policies also rarely protect against common causes of loss to fine art, like water damage and breakage" (Whitehouse, 2003, p. D2). Decisions about insurance should hinge on how losses are reimbursed. Some insurers use a method that gives replacement value minus depreciation. Usually sentimental value is not included, so the policy holder has to decide how much coverage is appropriate. Cost is going to vary by part of the country; for example, in coastal areas of Florida, endorsement or additions for breakables like china are going to be higher than in Utah. Box 14.2 gives a list of typical insurance frauds related to homeowners' policies. An **adjuster** is a person who determines the amount of claim, loss, or damage payable under a contract and should be properly licensed. If there is a loss, insurers require that you notify them immediately.

**CONSUMER ALERT**

If a housing unit is vacant for 30 days in a row, it may be considered abandoned, and insurance coverage may halt. If you are going to be gone for longer than 30 days, check your policy. A housesitter or someone checking your property regularly, including police, may take care of this problem. Also some policies do not cover floods or other disasters, so if you live in a flood-prone area, you may need extra insurance or you can take your chances.

**BOX 14.2    Types of Insurance Fraud Related to Homeowners' Policies**

*Arson for profit.* Financially strapped homeowners who intentionally set fires to destroy property in hopes of collecting insurance claims are committing arson for profit.

*Duplicate policies for profit.* When consumers buy multiple policies on the same house or property (such as a piece of jewelry), hoping to collect from more than one company when the item is destroyed or lost, that is use of duplicate policies for profit.

*Fictional theft.* A fictional theft includes exaggerating the value of missing items.

*Unlicensed public adjuster.* It is illegal to use a public adjuster who lacks a license and who solicits distraught homeowners during claims settlement after a disaster. The trick would include the homeowner paying more than 10 percent of the settlement and paying the money up front.

*Note:* Some of these insurance frauds are caused by insurers and some by consumers.

## Health Insurance

Of all the types of insurance, health insurance is the most costly and the most vital. Understanding who health care consumers are and how they are changing is a primary concern of health insurance companies, hospitals, nurses, doctors, pharmaceutical companies, government policy makers, and the media. Health care is one of the nation's largest industries, and insurance is a big part of it. Some of the issues related to health insurance include the rapid rise of health care spending, the diversity of health care consumers, the Internet's growing importance to health care, the growing use of alternative medicine, the aging of the population, the de institutionalization of medical care, the growth of outpatient care, and the change in attitudes toward disability, mental health, psychiatry, and even death.

Health care costs are rising
steeply.

Health care costs are rising steeply, which is affecting the cost of insurance. On a yearly basis, health care costs are increasing 20 percent faster than the general inflation rate, and the cost of prescription drugs is rising more than 20 percent per year. People can have no insurance, private health insurance, or government-linked or managed care insurance through employers. Increasingly, employers are cutting health care benefits or raising deductibles so that employees pay more before health insurance kicks in. The annual percent increase in health care costs to U.S. employers was 12 percent in 2000, 13 percent in 2001, 14 percent in 2002, and 16 percent in 2003 and is currently over 20 percent. This upward progression shows the burden that employers are under. Private health insurance (meaning that not obtained through an employer) is very expensive, and consumer difficulties generally fall into the categories of cost-related issues, communications-based problems of convenience, and serious medical concerns. As noted in Chapter 12, health care costs make up 5.3 percent of the typical household budget, and this percentage is rising.

An average doctor visit lasts 7
to 10 minutes.

The number one problem people report having with their health care plan is payment or billing for services (Paul, 2002). Another major problem is that "more than half of all Americans are not satisfied with the availability of their doctors and the amount of information they receive in an office visit, which now averages seven to ten minutes. . . . Fifty-two million adults now use the Internet as their primary source of health-care information" (Zuboff & Maxmin, 2002, p. 6).

## CONSUMER ALERT

Consumers with insurance from employers may think they are fully covered, but they may not be. Increasing copayments and deductibles are often not apparent until someone gets sick or disabled. According to the Commonwealth Fund's survey of people ages 19 to 64, 13 percent of insured consumers did not fill a prescription in the previous year due to cost, and 17 percent were unable to pay medical bills ("The Unraveling of Health Insurance," 2002). The shift is away from employers to employees, making them more responsible for their health care, including more financially responsible. As the survey results show, people are cutting corners by not filling prescriptions or are having trouble paying bills.

Two criticisms of health care plans are that they do not cover a particular treatment or kind of care that is needed and that there is difficulty getting someone from the plan on the phone to answer questions. Also, a company has the right to refuse to sell coverage if a person is in ill health or if a person provides false information on the application. The bottom line is that Americans want to feel in control of their health care services, and this includes having more types of self-care such as at-home diagnostics and self-monitoring of benefits (Paul, 2002). During every presidential election, health care costs and programs are issues for debate, with each candidate offering remedies.

*People like their own health care plans but are less happy with "the system."*

The majority of Americans are at least partially insured under governmental or managed care plans. An example of managed care is a health maintenance organization (HMO). Employers with at least 25 employees have to offer an HMO choice. In the past, a lot of people were dissatisfied with managed care, but recent polls show the public is discontented with "the system" but not with their own health care plans. So despite a general atmosphere of frustration with the health care industry and with hassles with insurance companies, a Harris Interactive survey found that two-thirds of Americans gave their plan a grade of A or B, three-fourths said they would recommend their plan to someone who is healthy, and 68 percent would recommend it to friends or family with a serious or chronic disease.

About one in five Americans has either Medicare or Medicaid; more Medicaid than Medicare beneficiaries gave their plans low marks (Paul, 2002). **Medicaid** is the federal health care program for low-income people who qualify, and **Medicare** is the federal health insurance program for people age 65 or older and for many people with disabilities. You may have heard of **Medicare Part D**, a newer option that reduces the cost of some generic and brand-name prescription drugs for those who qualify. From a consumer point of view, of course it is good to get a reduction in the cost of necessary drugs, but the guidelines are complicated and difficult to follow. The American Association of Retired Persons (AARP) and other consumer advocacy groups say that rather than the guidelines getting easier, they appear to be getting more difficult (Barry, 2007). In basic Medicare, the two main parts are hospital insurance and medical insurance. Medicare and Medicaid are government programs, so they are not forms of insurance that people buy in the for-profit market. Because Medicare is mostly for elderly people, a lot of fraud and misconceptions are involved—padded bills are not unusual. Box 14.3 lists common red flags. The U.S. Administration on Aging and Social Security offices look out for

**BOX 14.3    Common Red Flags Regarding Medicare Fraud**

Look out for people who say the following:

* I represent Medicare.
* I have free service or equipment.
* I need your Medicare number or Social Security number.
* I want to tell you how you can get more out of Medicare.
* I offer free tests, exams, or consultations.

Also beware of people who pressure you to buy Medigap insurance or who use scare tactics as well as those who show up at your front door or call you over the phone.
  Doing any of the following is illegal:

* Billing for services not rendered or equipment not received
* Billing twice for the same services
* Misrepresenting a diagnosis or the place of diagnosis to get a higher payment
* Falsifying documents
* Soliciting, offering, or receiving kickbacks, bribes, or illegal rebates
* Seeking to defraud Medicare or the government in any way other than those previously mentioned

Medicare fraud. For example, there has been a crackdown on people who purposely make themselves poor so the government will pay for their nursing home care. "For years, thousands of middle class and even affluent retirees—terrified that long-term health care costs could wipe out their savings—have transferred their assets to relatives in order to qualify for Medicaid, the government health plan for the poor. Their goal is to make themselves poor by Medicaid's definition, generally meaning they have no more than $2,000 in assets, excluding their house and their car" (Higgins, 2003, p. D1). A whole industry has sprung up helping seniors to qualify, and often it is aided by children who are doing asset transfers for sick parents. This is a form of defrauding the government if the elderly person is not actually poor. Therefore, guidelines are being looked into so this is not so easy to do. It is also unfortunate that people feel they have to do this to take care of sick parents—better solutions need to be found.

## Disability Income Insurance

**Disability income insurance** pays benefits to policy holders when they are incapable of working; it can be for temporary or long-term disability and typically pays 60 to 80 percent of their paycheck. Most people get this coverage through employers, but someone can buy it as an individual (for example, if a person is self-employed or owns a small business). The policies have an elimination period, meaning a period of time that must elapse before insurance begins. Obviously, it is linked to employment, so this type of insurance does not make sense for retirees or other nonworkers. Social Security also has disability insurance. In **workers' compensation**, money is paid if a disability is due to illness or injury received on the job. If someone becomes disabled, there are a variety of options: Benefits usually go to the injured or ill person, but there are situations in which the benefits go to the spouse or underage children if the person dies.

Employers and unions sometimes offer disability income insurance, and if it is offered at a low cost or for free, it should be considered, especially if one travels to high-risk parts of the world or if one performs high-risk work. Even desk work can bring injuries such as carpal tunnel syndrome, so a case could be made for every worker to have disability income insurance and/or workers' compensation. To keep premiums low, an employee should reduce coverage time, pay a high deductible, lower the monthly benefit, and lengthen the elimination period.

## Life Insurance

In the United States, 70 percent of adults have life insurance policies.

About 70 percent of U.S. adults have life insurance policies. **Life insurance** is a contract between a policy holder and an insurer that says what sum will be paid to beneficiaries on the insured's death. These can be bought on your own or through employers; some employers offer, for example, a free $100,000 policy as a perk. Most new policies are bought by people between the ages of 25 and 44, often when they have children, because life insurance is a protection for survivors. Other reasons people have life insurance are to protect or make a more secure life for a surviving spouse or an aging or disabled relative, to protect a business and business partners, and to leave money to a charity or a cause. College students without dependents generally don't need it, but if an employer provides it at a low cost or for free, this is a benefit to consider.

How much is needed depends on life circumstances such as age, income, and number and ages of children. One rule of thumb is the five to seven times rule; for example, a person earning $30,000 a year should have life insurance in the range of $150,000 to $210,000. Someone with several young children who is the main support of the family needs more than someone whose children are grown.

The two main types of life insurance are term (for a fixed time such as 5 years, 10 years) and whole (with a savings feature). With term, protection expires when the contract expires, so an individual with 5-year term insurance would have to renew it to keep it going. Term is considered pure protection; in other words, it only offers insurance and does not have a savings feature. It costs less than whole life insurance and is therefore recommended by most personal financial experts.

---

### CONSUMER ALERT

**Churning** is an illegal practice of encouraging insureds (consumers) to switch policies in order to generate commissions. Insurance agents make commissions when consumers purchase a policy, especially a whole life policy. When switching policies is not in the best interest of the client and is done solely to generate more commissions, this is considered churning, a practice disdained by the legitimate insurance industry. Multimillion-dollar class-action suits about churning have been brought by bilked policy holders.

If an agent offers to replace your old life insurance policy, which has a high cash value, with a new and "better" one, carefully review the premium schedule, benefits, and restrictions on benefits, such as preexisting conditions. Also, if a life insurance pitch comes at a time when there is no apparent need to change insurance coverage, such as a marriage, a new child, or a similar life change, be cautious. Do not buy insurance from a door-to-door salesperson or sign blank insurance claims forms.

Whole life insurance offers savings but at a very low rate of interest; most investors could make better money elsewhere. Policies should be reviewed every few years and changed if there are major life changes such as a marriage, a divorce, the birth or adoption of children, a new house, a different employer, a promotion, retirement, or an empty nest.

## Long-Term Care Insurance

"Advances in medical research and technology have exploded the numbers of people who will live longer lives than at any other time in human history. New treatments are also responsible for prolonging the lives of people with chronic illness, no matter what their age" (Zuboff & Maxmin, 2002, p. 200). **Long-term care (LTC) insurance** provides benefits for nursing home, assisted living, or in-home care not covered by Medicare insurance as well as for other types of long-term care. For example, a severe auto accident at age 40 could lay a person up for several months, and LTC insurance could help with the bills. About 40 percent of the people receiving long-term care today are younger than age 65 (Greene, 2003). However, most people buy LTC insurance with the intention of using it in old age, and most policies have the same basic features such as covering Alzheimer's disease. There may also be coverage if you can no longer perform two of the following activities of daily living:

Bathing

Being continent

Dressing

Eating

Transferring from one location to another

Using the toilet

The policies pay for a certain amount of care. The most important feature is the dollars paid per day that the policy will cover toward eventual care, but the problem is that these costs keep going up, and no one knows if and when they will need assisted living or other help. Currently, the cost of care averages over $200 per day for an individual in a U.S. nursing home; the cost varies widely by city and state as well as by the care needs of the patient. People buy LTC insurance because the high cost of care could wipe out any savings they have accumulated. Some of the policies cost from $1,000 to $10,000 a year, depending on the age of the person and the coverage offered. The older you are, the more expensive LTC insurance becomes because it is more likely that you will actually access it.

A fundamental problem occurs when your personal finances decrease and you cannot keep up with premiums—you could lose the policy, or you may get a check for some of the residual value, depending on the state where you live and what the policy says. Policies may have riders (add-ons) as well, one of the most important being a compound-inflation option; this is a desirable feature because costs keep going up as the years pass.

Who sells LTC insurance? Many insurance agents sell it, but they vary in their skills and credentials. A person seeking a policy should look for an agent who specializes in LTC insurance. The letters after an agent's name refer to training programs, time, and testing; for example, the credential CLTC stands for certified in

## CONSUMER ALERT

LTC is a fairly new form of insurance, and regulations between states vary widely. Low-income people can rarely afford it and may be better off putting money into current health care or other investments. Web sites of rating services where the financial strength of companies can be checked are given in the E-Resources section. This is important to know because especially in the case of LTC insurance the company will have to last a long time. If the insurer goes bankrupt, you could be left with little or no coverage.

long-term care, which is awarded by the Corporation on Long-Term Care and requires two classroom days or four to six weeks of correspondence courses.

Most people buy LTC insurance in their fifties or older as a protection in old age, although some buy it when they are in their thirties. The decision to buy it or not rests on whether it is affordable and whether someone thinks it will be needed because of either personal health problems or the lack of another caregiver (for example, there may be no children who could provide care when a parent ages), as well as a number of other factors. No one knows if they will absolutely need it, although statistics indicate that 60 percent of the U.S. population will need it. Besides providing money for care, it may be sought to preserve assets for a spouse, children, or grandchildren. The point is that it can be used for more than nursing home care: It could be used for assisted living, hospice, or in-home care; because most seniors want to stay in their own homes as long as possible, LTC can help with that.

The younger you are when you purchase it, the lower the premiums will be. Medicare or private health insurance does not cover all aspects of long-term care. Medicaid covers long-term care, but an elderly person has to "spend down" assets to at or near the federal poverty level in order to qualify. Another problem is that Medicaid-approved facilities have to be used, which narrows the choices, some of which may be far from families and friends. Women are especially vulnerable because they outlive men by an average of seven years and are more likely to need LTC insurance or other arrangements.

## OVERPRICED AND UNNEEDED INSURANCE

The previous sections listed some of the major kinds of insurance that consumers buy. There are rarer kinds that for the most part are not needed:

- *Private mortgage or mortgage life insurance.* It would be better to pick other forms of investing or add on to existing life insurance policies rather than taking out a new mortgage or life insurance policy.
- *Service contracts and extended warranties.* These are usually both unnecessary and too expensive (they were described in previous chapters).
- *Separate policies versus riders.* When a rider is added to an existing policy, it usually costs less than buying a whole new policy; a new boat or motorcycle, for example, could be added to an existing policy.

- *Flight insurance.* Statistics show an individual can fly on an airline every day for 26,000 years before that person would be involved in a plane crash, and even then the odds are in that person's favor that he or she would survive.
- *Credit insurance.* Lenders cannot make you buy credit insurance (this was also covered in a previous chapter).
- *Short-term (cash value) life insurance.* If a policy holder does not keep cash value (whole life) insurance for a long time, the policy is a waste of money.
- *Life insurance for children.* Children do not have debts or dependents, so they do not need life insurance.
- *Cancer or other disease-specific insurance.* Unless the specific disease runs in your family, you don't need insurance coverage for it. Conventional health insurance will cover most illnesses and diseases.
- *Add-ons to homeowners' insurance.* Insurance for such things as "family protection" is unnecessary for most individuals. This type of insurance covers victims of home invasion, child abductions, and stalking threats, and it pays medical bills, consulting, and other expenses (but not ransom payments). A wealthy high-profile person may need this, but for most people this is unneeded insurance.
- *Short-term medical coverage.* Under the federal COBRA law, an employee's old insurance policy can follow him or her (if his or her employer has 20 or more employees) for about 18 months after the end of employment, but there is a catch—the person has to pay the whole premium, so the cost of coverage is high. A single healthy person may pass on short-term medical coverage after a job that has insurance coverage ends, but someone with a family may go ahead and get it. The idea is that buying employer-based insurance should be less expensive than having the former employee buy it in the open market as a private individual. This may or may not be the case, so a former employee should comparison-shop.

What to buy and what to pass on both refer back to the beginning of the chapter and the discussion of matching insurance to a person's needs and not paying for protection that is unnecessary. In terms of overpriced insurance, studies show that the poor pay more for goods and services, mostly due to a lack of creditworthiness indicated by low credit scores (Lee, 2002). That puts the poor in a disadvantaged position in the financial market, including the area of insurance. Policy makers and regulators continue to evaluate how the poor are affected in the financial market and are on the lookout for discrimination, includeing procedures such as redlining (not providing services in certain areas) addressed in the previous chapter.

## CONSUMER RIGHTS AND RESPONSIBILITIES

### Rights

Consumers have these rights:

    To choose insurance companies and agents

    To obtain fair quotes for coverage

    To receive policies in a timely manner

To receive proper and timely investigations of claims

To receive payments for repairs or whatever is necessary

To buy policies free of unfair discrimination due to age, gender, occupation, marital status, national origin, or physical handicap (for example, a handicap that does not impair someone's ability to drive)

To file complaints

To receive copies of all forms and applications signed by the applicant and insurer

### Responsibilities

Consumers are responsible for doing the following:

- Evaluating their needs and choosing the policy or contract that meets those needs
- Shopping around and comparing costs and services
- Watching for exclusions and limitations
- Investigating insurance salespeople's credentials, and finding out about licensure
- Reading policies or contracts and understanding what is covered
- Keeping insurance policies and records at home, and keeping copies in safe-deposit boxes or with a trusted friend or attorney
- Telling beneficiaries about the kinds and amounts of health and life insurance owned and where policies are kept
- Reviewing coverage periodically to make sure it is still meeting needs
- Being truthful when applying, and disclosing pertinent information
- Contacting the insurance company or agent immediately after auto accidents
- Keeping up with premiums, and reviewing all bills

## SCAMS AND FRAUDS

Remember the line "Oh, what a tangled web we weave, when first we practice to deceive"? The insurance industry is rampant with scams and frauds. Insurance scams are more subtle than the snake oil salesmen of old and thus more difficult to root out. The frauds in the financial area feed on greed and fear rather than the need for a quick cure sought from patent medicines and weight-reduction pills. In financial fraud, victims are susceptible to things they do not understand and fall prey to promises of large returns on their money. The area of insurance is particularly vulnerable because it is a subject few like to think about or discuss. The chance that something bad will happen—illness, disability, theft, destruction, death—makes it all the easier to perpetuate fraud. The sources for much of the following information are the state departments of insurance and the Coalition against Insurance Fraud Report. The next section covers scams by companies, and the section after that discusses how customers defraud companies.

### Company Scams

Most agents are reputable professionals who have been trained in their area of expertise; they take classes and pass tests to be licensed. But there are **rogue agents** who are not associated with established companies and who are engaging in illegal activities. They will sell insurance and pocket the premiums, and when people try to file a claim, they find out they have been had—there is no policy and there is no money. Naturally the industry wants to root out rogue agents and drive them from business because they give the whole industry a bad name.

One trick is for an agent to drain the cash value of one policy to buy a new policy with the same insurer. Another fraud is called failure to forward premiums: An insurance agent convinces a consumer to pay each premium by a check written directly to the agent or to pay in cash; the agent then pockets these payments, leaving the consumer without coverage.

Understatement of risk or "cleansheeting" is another type of fraud. In this case the agent omits pertinent health information from a consumer's application to make a sale that might not otherwise meet the insurance company's risk management requirements.

Overselling refers to selling too much insurance to one individual. For example, in a testimony at a National Association of Insurance Commissioners (NAIC) meeting in Atlanta in March 2003, an Alabama attorney said that an elderly woman with a house worth $19,000 had 17 homeowners' insurance policies on it—far too much coverage for the modest house. He said that she would sign anything that was put before her and that unscrupulous agents took advantage.

## Consumer Frauds

One survey reports the following:

> Nearly one in four Americans says it is acceptable to defraud an insurance company, according to a survey by consulting firm Accenture Ltd. The results appear to confirm the worst suspicions of insurance companies, which say fraudulent claims are costing them—and honest policyholders—billions of dollars a year. The Insurance Services Office Inc., the main provider of claims data to the industry, estimates the annual cost of fraud to insurers at $24 billion. (Oster, 2003a, p. D2)

According to the survey (Oster, 2003b), there are at least three kinds of fraud that consumers engage in:

1. Overstating the value of a claim to an insurance agency
2. Submitting claims for items that aren't actually lost or damaged
3. Submitting claims for personal injuries that did not occur

Why do people do it? Nearly half of the survey respondents said it was because people could get away with it; others said that people needed the money or that they paid too much to insurance companies and thought it was their due. The study subjects said it was important that insurers track down deceptive claims. Another study found that "four out of ten Americans have tried to pad an insurance bill to cover the deductible" (Solomon, 2003, p. 234).

Another type of fraud is applicant fraud. In this case, the applicant provides false information to a life insurance company to obtain a lower premium or to prevent the application from being rejected.

Another fraud called deceptive claims happens when a financially strapped consumer files false claims on credit disability and health insurance policies after staging an accident and exaggerating a preexisting injury—in other words, they are faking it. Insurance companies have investigators who can prove fraud by filming claimants with bad backs hauling lumber out of trucks or working out in gyms. One of the reasons that states got rid of or altered no-fault auto insurance is because people would fake their own accidents (purposely run into a tree, have a friend's car nudge their car) and claim huge repairs, emotional damage, or medical expenses. Along these same lines, people have faked accidents such as slipping and falling in a theme park or at a hotel and tried to sue the park or hotel. The use of more security cameras should diminish these types of cases.

## ROLE OF STATE DEPARTMENTS OF INSURANCE

Insurance is largely regulated by states. The objectives of state regulators are to protect consumers and to help maintain the financial stability of the insurance industry. Regarding health insurance:

> Most states impose only minimal regulation on benefits and premiums. Individual policies are also underwritten, meaning that premiums vary according to an applicant's health status, age, and gender. . . . Paying more doesn't always buy more. . . . To buy your own health-insurance policy, begin by investigating those sold by at least four or five carriers in your area, interview agents, and find one who offers policies from several different companies. ("Shopping for Your Own Policy," 2002)

Consumers should find out how their company is rated. Consumers residing in states that set minimum standards for coverage and limit how high premiums can go tend to have better protection. If a person is turned down for health insurance, he or she can investigate state requirements for obtaining a policy of last resort, and anyone with low income should find out if he or she qualifies for Medicaid.

For over 50 years, the NAIC and the states have enacted disclosure rules defining what insurers may and may not say to consumers about a variety of things, including pricing and product features. Over the course of time, policies have become more complex, and consumer advocates are calling for more fairness and transparency in information provided by insurers to consumers.

## INVESTING

### Purpose

The chapter switches gears now away from insurance to the subject of investment. Most simply stated, **investment** is the commitment of funds (capital) to long-term growth, and the purpose of investing is to build and maintain wealth. People invest to feel more secure or comfortable in retirement or in midlife and to acquire funds for vacations, for children's educations, and for homes. Investing should be based on goals; it is an important means for getting ahead, keeping ahead of inflation, and becoming independent and self-supporting.

## Guiding Principles

Concerted attempts at investing start after people have stabilized their lives, meaning they have a job, they can meet basic life needs, and their debt is under control. Retirement plans through an employer or individually through individual retirement accounts (IRAs) are forms of investing. A guiding principle is that the sooner you start, the greater the return (money needs time to grow) and that even a modest start (like $10 a week in a savings account) is better than no start at all. In investing, one assesses risk and return. As stated in the Introduction to this chapter, the higher the risk (uncertainty) is, the greater the chance for a greater return. Taking financial risks in your youth makes more sense than taking risks in old age when you have fewer years to recover from loss; when you are young, your income keeps growing and you can replace lost income from poorly performing investments. How you feel about risk is called risk tolerance. "Your risk tolerance is your ability or willingness to endure declines in the value of your investments while you wait for them to return a profit that will help you meet your investment goal" ("Your Risk Tolerance," 2001). Following is a widely used risk assessment question from the Federal Reserve Board Survey of Consumer Finances (SCF):

Which of the following statements comes closest to the amount of financial risk that you are willing to take when you save or make investments?

1. Substantial financial risks expecting to earn substantial returns
2. Above-average financial risks expecting to earn above-average returns
3. Average financial risks expecting to earn average returns
4. No financial risks

There are no completely risk-free investments. For example, government bonds and savings accounts may guarantee principal but may fall behind in keeping up with inflation. Because principal is guaranteed, these are considered safer investments compared with investments such as stocks when much or all of the principal can be lost. Utah State University Professor Jean Lown, in an article in the *Journal of Consumer Education,* suggested that educators can help investors adopt a more realistic view of risk tolerance and investment selection based on a time horizon (for example, the number of years until retirement) for financial goals. Further, she says that **volatility** (the ups and downs of a security or a commodity or of the stock market itself) should be of little concern to the long-term investor. A person needs to do the following to be a successful investor:

- Keep perspective, staying in through the ups and downs
- Keep investing, even with small amounts
- Believe in the growth of business (stocks and corporate bonds) or the strength of government (bonds)

Some investments provide interest or **dividends**, which are distributions of money from companies or government to investors. Most typically, dividends are paid twice a year and can come from stocks or bonds. Sometimes stocks and bonds can be bought in such a way (usually directly, such as bonds from the federal government) that there are no fees for transactions; other times there are fees that vary greatly. Charges for transactions should be weighed against services rendered and probable returns. A consideration in investing is the tax implications of

**CONSUMER ALERT**

Every investment has advantages and disadvantages—there are no "magic" investments that fit all of the people, all of the time. There is little hope of more than average returns without extraordinary luck or knowledge and, of course, risk. A realistic approach works best, basing investments on goals, acceptable levels of risk, personality, and a time horizon (how many years until the money will be needed). Knowledge is power, so find out everything you can about a potential investment from reliable sources.

certain types of investing, such as tax-deferred retirement savings plans and municipal bonds or municipal bond funds.

Another guiding principle is that investors should use **diversification**, meaning the spreading of money over several categories of investments such as bonds, blue-chip stocks, small and large companies, foreign shares, real estate, and real estate investment trusts. In this way, an investor will have a balanced **portfolio**, a combined set of holdings to increase diversification and to reduce risk. At any given time, some of the holdings will be in favor and some will be out of favor, but in the long run this strategy, rather than putting all one's money into a single investment, should work. To summarize, the least risk is involved in cash, government savings bonds, money market funds, and CDs; the most risk is associated with speculative investments such as options, commodities, and junk bonds. The Securities and Exchange Commission (SEC) is a good source for information about investing wisely and avoiding fraud. In the next sections, the most widely used types of investing, along with potential frauds and scams, are discussed.

## TYPES OF INVESTMENTS AND INCOME

### Stocks

As noted in the Introduction, more than half of Americans own stock. **Stocks** represent ownership in a company. For example, if you own one share of Microsoft stock, you own part of Microsoft. Is the stock market rational (meaning reasonable, predictable)? The answer is no—it rises and falls, and it is very difficult to predict how well an individual stock will do. It is useful to know a company's financial history and future prospects as a guide in choosing well. The best advice is to buy and hold, ride out the ups and downs, invest in quality companies, and keep transaction (buying and selling) costs low. Over the last 50 years, stocks have far exceeded inflation, but in the short run investing can be risky.

Most stocks are called **common stock**, which refers to shares or units of ownership in a public corporation such as Apple or Coca-Cola. You can buy stock online or in person through brokerage firms such as Charles Schwab, Ameritrade, or Merrill Lynch, or you can buy stock directly from the company. One of the values of having a broker is that you have someone with whom to discuss your investment choices and to create a financial plan. To invest directly in a company (called a **direct investment plan**), go to the company Web site and look for investor

## CONSUMER ALERT

Millions of dollars worth of consumer lawsuits, for everything from faulty cell phones to stock fraud, are filed each year, but consumers are not always aware that money is owed to them. More than half the people who are eligible for compensation never follow up (Kalis, 2003). Fraud happens when companies charge substantial finder's fees (money to find out if you should be getting a consumer lawsuit settlement) when in reality you can check yourself for free. One place to look for the latest settlements is www.bigclassaction.com. Go to the "class action settlements" link. A site that charges for claim information is www.classactionamerica.com. Announcements of settlements are often given in newspapers, or information can be obtained from law enforcement agencies in your state. An example of a Web site that focuses on shareholder suits is Securities.stanford.edu. Be forewarned that the gains may be small; for example, one settlement going back to 1984 had a maximum award of $80 for anyone who had leased a phone from AT&T.

relations. You could then purchase a certain number of shares of stock for a set amount of money or set up a payroll deduction so that $50 a month goes into buying shares of that particular company's stock. Over 1,000 companies (including most of the larger ones such as McDonald's) offer direct investment plans. Another choice is a **dividend reinvestment plan (DRIP)**, which also eliminates the need for a broker (who will charge a fee called a commission to buy or sell a stock). DRIPs allow dividends to be automatically reinvested in additional shares purchased directly from the company.

Investors may engage in **socially responsible investing**, meaning they invest in stocks that directly express their values. For example, they will not invest in companies that are involved in practices they do not believe in, such as making alcohol or tobacco products, or that have unfair labor practices, such as using child labor. "They seek to influence corporate decision-making by including social and ethical criteria in their investment choices. According to the Social Investment Forum, a nonprofit organization that promotes social investing, the total level of socially and environmentally responsible investing in the United States grew by 8 percent, from $2.16 trillion in 1999 to $2.34 trillion in 2001, despite a significant stock market decline during that period" (Zuboff & Maxmin, 2002, p. 110).

## Bonds

**Bonds** are investments involving the lending of money. If you have a bond for a corporation, you have lent money to that corporation (to build a new factory, for example). Bonds can be for corporations or for state, local, or federal government (as in U.S. savings bonds). When the stock market took a downturn in the late 1990s and early 2000s, many investors switched to bonds for these reasons:

- They are considered safer than stocks.
- In many cases, the rate of return is guaranteed.
- There may be the added benefit of biannual dividends paid to the bondholder, so the bonds serve as a source of income.

Government bonds are more secure than corporate bonds. Bonds from corporations are rated, and these ratings should be used as a guide. The two types of U.S. savings bonds are Series EE and Series I. For information about these, go to www.savingsbonds.gov. By going to this Web site, you can buy bonds online directly from the government, or you can buy savings bonds at local banks or through your employer.

## Mutual Funds

American investors are increasingly turning to mutual funds to save for retirement and other financial goals. **Mutual funds** are groups of investments. Over 100 million Americans own mutual funds, mostly in their retirement accounts through their employers and in their IRAs. There are over 7,000 mutual funds of stocks and bonds from which to choose. If you buy one share of a mutual fund such as Capital Growth Fund, you are buying a small amount of several different holdings and spreading your risk, which is a positive feature of mutual funds. Funds come in different types such as growth, international, and value. Growth funds are the largest category and focus on stocks that have the potential for large capital gains. The name of the fund implies the type of fund that it is; for example, the Capital Growth Fund would be a growth mutual fund. In 2001, rulings were passed calling for more alignment of fund names with fund holdings and requiring funds to include after-tax return data. Since each fund has to have a unique name, the names can get creative: the Rydex Velocity 100 Fund, the Columbia Thermostat Fund, the Amidex Cancer Innovations, and Health-care Mutual Fund. Investors purchase fund shares from the fund itself or through a broker for the fund.

There are several advantages:

- *Affordability*. Some funds set relatively low dollar amounts for initial purchases and subsequent monthly purchases, or both.
- *Diversification*. Spreading investments across a wide range of companies and industry sectors is advantageous to the investor.
- *Liquidity*. Funds can be redeemed for cash, although there may be fees and charges at redemption time.
- *Professional management*. Money managers research, select, and monitor funds.

Disadvantages include the following:

- Front-end or management fees
- Taxes
- Lack of control (managers choose what stocks are in funds, not investors)

Mutual funds are also not guaranteed or insured by the Federal Deposit Insurance Corporation (FDIC) or any other government agency—even if bought at a bank. A person can lose money investing in mutual funds, and past performance is not a totally reliable indicator of future performance; however, past performance is one factor to consider because it shows a pattern over time. The SEC offers a Mutual Fund Cost Calculator to compare the costs of owning different funds before an individual makes a purchase (see E-Resources). Another source for mutual fund information is Morningstar.com.

## CONSUMER ALERT

Investment con artists thrive during times of uncertainty. Low-interest rates and poor investment returns in conventional markets drive risk-taking consumers to look for something other than traditional investments. They are looking for excitement and want to be part of the action, which includes investing in defense industries. Do not play this game. Protect yourself:

1. Hang up on aggressive cold callers promoting investments in mutual funds; foreign currencies; precious metals such as gold, platinum, and silver; or oil and gas schemes.
2. Ignore tips about tiny companies with great growth potential, especially those involved in war industries or bioterrorism.
3. Contact state securities regulators or check with the National Association of Securities Dealers (1-800-288-9999) when you suspect fraud.
4. Request written information about investments. Promotions with the word *safe*, *secure*, or *guaranteed* are usually rip-offs.

When it comes to investing, being rash and feeling pressured are warning signs—don't do anything in a hurry. Use common sense, and do not succumb to confusion and fear. An example is that after the anthrax-laced mail tragedy in 2001, con artists began selling fake anthrax detectors, security-enhancing technologies, and stock in phony technology companies. Hucksters are surprisingly quick and resourceful at dreaming up schemes overnight.

## Real Estate

**Real estate** refers to a piece of land and everything related to it, including houses, landscaping, and fencing, plus the right to the airspace above and the earth below (with limits, of course). In Chapter 12, we covered how to be a better consumer of housing and included advice on buying homes. This chapter discusses real estate more from an investment angle. About 67 percent of American households own their own homes, which is a type of **direct investment**; other examples include owning apartment buildings, raw land, and other houses. One of the main disadvantages of real estate over other types of investments is illiquidity, meaning it is difficult to turn it quickly into cash. **Indirect investments** refer to investing with a group of investors to own **real estate investment trusts (REITs)**, apartment buildings, or

## CONSUMER ALERT

Do not buy time-shares or vacation homes without investigating all the costs, rules, fees, taxes, and resale terms. Many people have had trouble selling time-shares and wish they had rented instead of tying up their money. Consumers are more satisfied if they purchase time-shares in companies with cooperative arrangements across the country because this opens up more choices of places to visit and the types of available units. Remember that all buildings age—the brand-new model time-share unit will not look so good after a few years of wear and tear.

**CONSUMER ALERT**

REITs fluctuate with the ups and downs of the market and with the quality of the investment. While some parts of the country are having marvelous success with new office buildings and shopping malls, others are overbuilt, so care should be taken in selecting REITs. There are about 300 REITs that are traded publicly on the New York Stock Exchange.

office buildings. REITs are traded on the major stock exchanges, so you can buy a share in them the same way that you can buy a share in a stock or mutual fund.

REITs are sold through stock brokerage firms or over the counter and are listed in the *Wall Street Journal* and other financial news sources. One of the main advantages is the pooling of money with others to buy a bigger investment than one normally could alone. Another advantage is the professional management aspect, meaning one could invest in apartments without having landlord worries. With any investment, however, there is both a risk of loss and tax consequences.

Owning a primary residence has tax advantages, but the tax advantages of second homes and vacation homes are less attractive. **Time-shares** are apartments, units, or homes with several owners that are normally used for vacation purposes.

## Franchises

Another form of investing is franchises. A **franchise** is a right to operate a business and sell the franchisor's products or services in a given area. This may or may not be an exclusive right; in other words, you could be the only franchisee at a certain intersection or the only one in a whole city. Arrangements are formalized in a franchisee agreement, a contract between the franchisee and the franchisor. Television infomercials and advertisements in newspapers suggest there is easy money to be had in franchises, playing on people's dreams of being entrepreneurs, of being their own boss. Although franchises can be legitimate (such as a franchise for a McDonald's or a Subway restaurant), many are investments with little or no guarantee of success. If you have never heard of the franchise before, this is a warning sign to slow down.

**Benefits.**   The benefit to this type of arrangement is that investment risk is reduced by being associated with an established company. Also the franchisor will often grant the right to use the company name for a limited amount of time and provide assistance, initial training, marketing, and so on. There will probably be ongoing technical support and training.

**Loss Potential.**   The downside of being associated with an established company is that the franchisee has to conform to its standards and is essentially giving up a lot of individual control. In exchange for the name and the services, the franchisee will have to pay both fees, such as an initial franchise fee, and other expenses, for rent, building and equipment, signs, insurance, and licenses (this can run from thousands of dollars to several hundred thousand dollars). Over time, the franchisee will pay royalty payments to continue to use the name. The start-up costs are very high, and since most businesses fail in the first two years, many people lose money.

**Responsibilities.**   Before investing, potential franchisees should consider their goals, abilities, and experience and determine how much this investment is going to cost as well as the current strength and potential growth of the parent company. Is the product or service in demand? What is the competition like? For example, a common type of franchise is a janitorial service franchise. Before investing, find out how businesses, schools, and government agencies in your area hire janitorial services. If you had a franchise, would there be a demand for it? How much are locals willing to pay? Often figures given by franchisors are national and may be far higher than what you could charge locally.

Before attending a franchise exposition, investors should know how much they have to invest and what type of business is the best for them. Before investing, the franchisee should get a copy of the franchisor's disclosure document. Under the Federal Trade Commission (FTC) Franchise Rule, a potential franchisee must receive the document at least 10 business days before being asked to sign any contract or paying any money to the franchisor. Things to look out for include business background, litigation history, bankruptcy, costs, restrictions, terminations, training, advertising, current and former franchisees' experiences, earnings potential, and financial history. Besides doing research, potential franchisees should talk with attorneys with franchise experience, accountants, banks, the local Better Business Bureau (BBB), government departments that regulate the particular business (provide licenses), and the FTC before investing. A bank or other financial institution can give an unbiased view of a franchise opportunity and can obtain a Dun & Bradstreet report on a franchisor. If ever there was an area where the phrase "investigate before you invest" is true, it is in the franchise industry.

## All That Glitters: Precious Gems, Metals, and Collectibles

Diamonds are the most regulated gems and the ones most likely to hold their value; they mostly come from Botswana and Russia, but Canada is moving up the ranks. Canada has three diamond mines and hopes to have 12 percent of the world's rough gem–quality diamonds by the end of the decade. One of the questions is whether consumers care where their diamonds come from. Some engaged couples have driven to Canada to purchase certified Canadian diamonds. Canada's diamond mines have strict environmental guidelines and pay miners well, which makes them more politically correct. Some jewelers say people won't care about origin, but Oren Sofer, a New York wholesaler, says, "If you can put water in a bottle and sell it under a brand name, then trust me, you can brand a diamond. It just takes time" (Baglole, 2003, p. B1). Consider as examples Swiss watches, Idaho potatoes, and French wines—we associate certain products with places, but with other products, location is unimportant. How do you know the diamond is from Canada? Each diamond comes with a certificate of where it was mined, cut, and polished, and the certificate has a serial number engraved by laser on the diamond. A microscopically laser-engraved polar bear is sometimes put on larger Canadian diamonds.

Over a third of Americans collect something.

Rubies are mined in Burma; sapphires come from Tanzania, Madagascar, and Sri Lanka. The gems are flown into Thailand, where they are sorted and treated before export.

The most precious metal available to consumers is platinum, followed by gold and silver. Gold is produced primarily in Russia and South Africa and can be purchased as

One of the costly items a young
couple might buy is a diamond ring.
(Mika, Corbis Zefa Collection.)

gold coins, gold certificates, gold mutual funds, bullion accounts, and stock
shares in existing companies. People have lost and gained fortunes from investing in diamond and gold mines—it is not for amateurs. The price of precious
metals usually rises when inflation rises and falls when inflation falls, but international events can disturb this. International incidents tend to drive up the price of
gold, but it fluctuates widely. Before investing in precious metals, an investor
should know the current price per ounce and the market's ups and downs during
the last several years.

Over a third of Americans collect something. Collectibles include everything
from books to stamps, coins, athletic shoes, lunch boxes with cartoon characters
on them, and priceless antiques. In collectibles, knowledge is crucial, and this includes trusting one's source or dealer. There is no substitute for education and
knowledge of prices and quality. Special care should be taken when buying valu-
ables at auctions or over the Internet (see the next section). Generally speaking,
gems, metals, and collectibles should be purchased primarily because the owner
likes them or could use them and secondly as an investment.

## Online Investing

The Internet has opened up a whole new world of investment opportunities—
some legitimate and some not. Many of the schemes are the same as have been
played out for centuries, only in a glossy new format. Beware of promoters who
make their companies look like venerable old established Wall Street firms, and
look out for the usual promise of high profits in short amounts of time. On the Internet, you may find a Web site asking you to submit personal financial information
such as income level, bank accounts, Social Security numbers, and other personal
information. Read the site's privacy policy and consider the source, but never give
PIN numbers, account information, or Social Security numbers. Do not invest in
tax-free investments. Before putting money in offshore investments, get a second

**CONSUMER ALERT**

Gemstone scandals include using heat treatments and additives to turn lesser sapphires and rubies into copies of better gems. In Chanthaburi, Thailand, the market was suddenly flooded with padparadschas—a rare orange-pink sapphire. Gem collectors swarmed in, some paying as high as $4,000 a carat (more than 10 times the going rate). After a gem alert, the prices started falling. U.S. scientists charged that the gems had been altered with coloring agents, a technique which breaks no law but which violates the ethics of the trade. "The degree to which gems are treated has spun out of control," says Stuart Robertson, research director of Gemworld, a U.S. company. He says, "Unless treatments are reined in . . . and disclosure taken seriously, the market will drop. . . . All color traits [that buyers] are led to believe occur in nature are being produced in ovens. All of the romance is taken out of the stone" (Mazurkewich, 2003, p. B1).

opinion and learn about the tax implications. For information about Internet investment sources, see the E-Resources section.

## Retirement and Social Security

For most Americans, retirement support comes from several sources such as Social Security; private, employer-sponsored, or government pensions or retirement plans; and personal savings and investments. Social Security (from the U.S. government) is the primary source of retirement income for 20 percent of beneficiaries, and one in four U.S. households has someone getting monthly income from Social Security, but not everyone who receives Social Security is retired. According to Reno (2005), here is a breakdown of beneficiaries:

- 30 million retired workers
- 5 million widows
- 6 million disabled workers
- 3 million young children
- 750,000 adults disabled since childhood

The benefits are financed by workers and employers. Traditionally Americans started receiving partial benefits at age 62 (if they chose to do so) and full Social Security at age 65, but in recent years the eligible age for full benefits has been sliding up from 65 to 67, depending on date of birth. One issue is whether to raise the age of eligibility higher or to lower benefits. According to the Social Security Administration, increases in the number of projected beneficiaries per 100 workers will rise from 26 in 2010 to 32 in 2020 and 39 in 2030.

## Annuities

A common myth is that once one saves for retirement, the need for financial planning is over—nothing could be further from the truth. While people are retired, investments have to keep growing to keep up with inflation. Often when nearing retirement, people consider **annuities**, which are contracts in which the insurer promises the insured a series of periodic payments and are a type of investment that provides investors with tax-deferred growth. Annuities do not limit how much can be contributed each year and can be purchased directly from insurance companies or indirectly from stock brokers. They come in several forms, including fixed annuities, which guarantee fixed payments for life or a specific number of years, and variable annuities, which provide returns based on the performance of the assets in the annuities; there are different payout options, from lump sums to more periodic sums. Fixed annuities are invested in financial securities that pay a fixed interest rate, such as certificates of deposit, bonds, and treasury securities (safe investments), but money in variable annuities is more likely to be put into stocks and mutual funds. An investor could put money into both fixed and variable annuities and thus spread the risk and return.

Fixed annuities are being sold in record numbers as baby boomers retire and can be an especially good hedge in a volatile market; still confusion, fraud, and deception are rampant. Consumers should use caution before buying annuities, making sure they understand what they are getting, what the amount of risk is, and how much it is going to cost. Annual expense fees vary by product. The major disadvantage of annuities is illiquidity, meaning money is locked in for a long time.

## INVESTMENT SWINDLES

Investment swindles abound because people are drawn to high and quick returns on their money. They fall victim to various schemes and scams that can be nationally or internationally based.

Certain catchy phrases should be warning signs:

"This is a once-in-a-lifetime opportunity."

"Learn the secret of the wealthy."

"Quickly invest now in this low-risk short-term offer."

"Only a few will be invited to participate."

"Get in on the ground floor."

"You are assured of list of products such as display racks for greeting cards or vending machines for candy."

"This is approved by a celebrity or a doctor or the IRS and is IRA approved."

"The market is moving, so don't be left behind."

You will notice from this list that many financial scams sound a lot like the come-on phrases used in weight-loss scams. Swindlers (also called con artists and fraudsters) prey on the same emotions of fear, greed, and excitement, and even though they cheat people out of their money, they often advertise in legitimate sources such as *USA Today* and campus newspapers.

### Multilevel Marketing Plans

**Pyramids.    Multilevel marketing plans** are ways of selling goods and services through distributors. The plans promise that if someone signs up as a distributor, he or she will receive commissions both from his or her own sales and from those of people who are recruited to become distributors. The FTC cannot tell anyone which plans are legal and which are illegal—you must decide for yourself—but it

## CONSUMER ALERT

Be wary of the sales pitches and products sold on infomercials, which are a half hour or longer, as well as radio and television commercials for gold, real estate, and other forms of investing. If it sounds too good to be true, it probably is. Common techniques are endorsements by actors and actresses (many of whom later regret getting involved), by motivational speakers, and by "satisfied" past investors. Often they are selling sets of 12 tapes or videos and books or asking $1,000 per person for an in-person investment seminar "coming to your area soon!" Is someone really going to watch 12 videos about an investment technique? And once past the first video, how much can one say that is new and original?

does say that if a plan offers to pay commissions for recruiting new distributors, consumers should watch out. Most states outlaw this practice, which is called **pyramiding**. It is legal to pay commissions for retail sales of goods or services but not for recruiting of new distributors. Why are states so cautious about pyramiding? In the past, plans such as these invariably collapsed when new distributors could not be recruited—the people who began the scam (at the top of the pyramid) often benefited, but the late recruits lost their money. An example of a pyramid scheme was one in which an "investor" gave $100 to become a member, and the money was passed on to the president of the scheme; then the investor had to sign up 2 more people and collect $100 from each of them. After 10 people were recruited, the investor would become a president and form a new pyramid. The problem was finding new recruits to keep the money flow going. Unfortunately, pyramid schemes exist worldwide. Box 14.4 gives a list of sales pitches to avoid.

### BOX 14.4    FTC Web Site: Seven Tips

Consider these tips before investing in multilevel marketing plans:

1. Avoid any plan that includes commissions for recruiting additional distributors. It may be an illegal pyramid.
2. Beware of plans that ask new distributors to purchase expensive inventory. These plans can collapse quickly—and also may be thinly disguised pyramids.
3. Be cautious of plans that claim you will make money through continued growth of your "downline"—the commissions on sales made by new distributors you recruit—rather than through sales of products you make yourself.
4. Beware of plans that claim to sell miracle products or promise enormous earnings. Just because a promoter of a plan makes a claim doesn't mean it's true! Ask the promoter of the plan to substantiate claims with hard evidence.
5. Beware of shills—"decoy" references paid by a plan's promoter to describe fictional success in earning money through the plan.
6. Don't pay or sign any contracts in an "opportunity meeting" or any other high-pressure situation. Insist on taking your time to think over a decision to join. Talk it over with your spouse, a knowledgeable friend, an accountant, or a lawyer.
7. Do your homework! Check with your local Better Business Bureau and state attorney general about any plan you're considering—especially when the claims about the product or your potential earnings seem too good to be true.

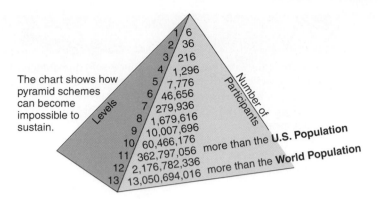

**Figure 14.1**    Ponzi Scheme. (Courtesy of the U.S. Securities and Exchange Commission.)

**Ponzi Schemes.**    **Ponzi schemes** are a kind of pyramid scheme with enticing come-ons that promise to make huge profits from a small investment in a very short time (Figure 14.1). They are named after Charles A. Ponzi, a dapper five-foot two-inch Italian immigrant who in 1920 raked in an estimated $15 million in eight months by persuading tens of thousands of Bostonians that he had unlocked the secret to easy wealth (Darby, 1998). Ponzi claimed to have found a way to profit by speculating in international postal-reply coupons, a form of prepaid return postage used in foreign correspondence. The first round of investors made money, and at the height of his success, Ponzi had offices from Maine to New Jersey, but later recruits lost everything, and half a dozen banks crashed. The problem was that there was no actual investing going on, just a shuffling of money from new investors to old ones. Ponzi was offering 50 percent interest in 90 days (later he shortened the investment period to 45 days), so it's no wonder people joined up, but these kinds of returns should raise any thinking person's suspicions.

Some modern-day Ponzi swindlers explain losses by telling people that investments went sour; other times the swindlers just disappear. Ponzi schemes involve the idea that something is for sale, whether it is coupons, foreign real estate, or racehorses. Legitimate multilevel plans involve the selling of actual products, such as clothing, home furnishings, cookware, and cosmetics, that one can see and examine in person. These plans involve in-home or at-workplace sales that do not differ too much from conventional store sales, other than the fact that sellers are given incentives of free products or deep discounts on products and that any money they make is based on commissions rather than salaries (for the most part). Examples of legitimate multilevel plans are Avon and Amway; as a customer, you can purchase the merchandise, as opposed to pyramid or Ponzi schemes where you walk away with nothing and you have to endure the hassle of trying to recruit new members.

## Ways to Avoid Swindles

The main ways to avoid swindles are to use common sense and to ask questions—research is by far the best protection. Find the investment that meets your needs

**BOX 14.5    Investment-Related Frauds to Avoid**

Coupon scams

Get-rich-quick and self-employment schemes

Gifting clubs

Hoaxes aimed at the elderly or minority groups

International lottery scams

Investment schemes involving rare coins or stamps

Chain letters*

At-home medical billing scams

Online investment opportunities

Invention patent scams

Publishing of your own book (for a price)

Work-at-home schemes

Learn-at-home schemes

*Note:* Check out the source and the company's background, and talk with previous owners or investors (in addition to the ones the company recommends).

*These are violations of the mail fraud statute and can carry fines and prison sentences. Report any chain letter (especially those involving money schemes or threats) to the U.S. Postal Service if the letter was received in the mail because the government will go after the starters of the letters— not the recipients. See www.usps.gov for details.

and goals; then shop around for companies and choices, double-checking the source and the seller. It is important to keep detailed records. Avoid high-pressure tactics, and seek advice from attorneys, accountants, and banks as well as government agencies and consumer watchdog organizations. Do not be taken in by television infomercial hype or late-night commercials when your sales resistance may be low. The FTC is a leader in alerting the public to investment fraud. Box 14.5 gives a list of some types of fraud to avoid.

## SUMMARY

Hopefully, this chapter has provided a start toward understanding insurance and investments as well as the possible deceptions. Those who wish to stay ahead of inflation (rising prices) need to invest, but they also need to protect what they have. Insurance buys protection for loved ones and for assets such as homes and cars; it is a financial arrangement wherein individuals are concerned about potential hazards, so they pay premiums (payments) to insurers who reimburse them in the case of loss or injury. Policies have different components, including exclusions. An example of an exclusion is exempting car insurance claims stemming from nuclear explosions or radioactive fallout.

Nearly all insurance is sold through agents, but the trend is to buy insurance over the Internet. Group plans usually cost less than plans sold to individuals. Health insurance is the most expensive and the most vital, yet with growing costs many individuals and their families do not have health insurance. Employers are the main source of health insurance. Most Americans have either a government plan such as Medicaid or Medicare or a managed plan. Medicare Part D reduces the cost of generic and prescription drugs for those who qualify.

To protect valuable possessions such as an engagement ring, art, or antiques, a homeowner may want to add an endorsement or rider to a basic homeowners' insurance policy. Life insurance is a contract between the policy holder and the insured. Some types of automobiles are less expensive to insure than others; most states require liability coverage for vehicles, and seven states have no-fault auto insurance. In general, the poor are in a disadvantaged position in the insurance marketplace.

Today more and more employees are being asked to make investment decisions, and consumers are actively looking for ways to invest so that their money grows and lasts for their lifetime. Investments are used to build or maintain wealth; they involve risks and returns, and they should be based on goals. A guiding principle is that the greater the risk is, the higher the potential return. Diversification refers to reducing the risk by spreading investments around to different categories such as bonds, blue-chip stocks, small and large companies, mutual funds, real estate, and real estate investment trusts. Stocks represent ownership in a company; bonds are loans to the government or to companies. Mutual funds, owned by 93 million Americans, are groups of stocks or bonds.

Other forms of investing such as real estate, real estate investment trusts, franchises, gems, precious metals, collectibles, and annuities were also discussed in the chapter. Diamonds mainly come from Botswana, Canada, and Russia. Gem scandals exist when rubies and sapphires are colored or treated in some way to imitate more expensive stones. Gold is mined mostly in Russia and South Africa. When the world becomes less stable, investors often rush to buy precious gems and metals (especially gold), but careful investors have an accurate knowledge of current and past prices and ride out the ups and the downs. Although there are legitimate investment opportunities for precious metals, this area tends to be risky and is inappropriate for beginning investors.

Investors should be suspect of unknown companies that pop up overnight with new cures or security devices. Web-based technologies hold great potential for providing investment information.

Multilevel marketing plans are a way of selling goods or services through distributors—some are legal and some are illegal. Pyramiding, a type of multilevel marketing wherein most people lose money except for the people who started the plan, is prohibited. Better Business Bureaus are a useful source for checking into the complaint record of local businesses and of franchise opportunities because they can report on whether any consumers have complained about a company's products, services, or personnel.

The Federal Trade Commission and the Securities and Exchange Commission are sources of information on investments and ways to avoid frauds. The FTC works for the consumer to prevent fraudulent, deceptive, and unfair business practices in the marketplace; the SEC works specifically to prevent investment fraud.

## KEY POINTS

1. The primary purpose of insurance is protection. Most health insurance comes from employers or government programs such as Medicare and Medicaid.
2. Not everyone needs life insurance, but those who do usually have dependents.
3. Term insurance is less expensive than whole life insurance.
4. Life insurance needs increase in midlife and decrease in old age.
5. Life insurance policies cannot be cancelled because of an insured's poor health.
6. Credit insurance protects a loan or mortgage if a person cannot make payments.
7. Homeowners' insurance pays to repair or rebuild a home and to replace personal possessions.
8. Long-term care insurance provides for nursing homes, assisted living, hospice, and in-home care.
9. The purpose of investing is to build and maintain wealth, and successful investors are in it for the long term.
10. More than half of all Americans own stock. Historically, stocks have gained in value more rapidly than bonds and most other forms of investing.
11. There is no one miracle or foolproof investment that fits everyone all of the time.
12. Con artists take advantage of times of confusion and fear by promoting bogus investment scams. Investors are vulnerable when traditional investment returns have dipped. Low interest rates and poor investment returns drive potential investors into uncertain markets—they take chances that they otherwise would not take.
13. Socially responsible investing is based on the investor's values and beliefs of supporting or not supporting certain types of industries or business practices.
14. Franchises should be thoroughly investigated before investing in them.
15. Pyramid investment schemes, a type of speculation, are illegal; Ponzi schemes are a type of pyramid scheme.

## KEY TERMS

| | | |
|---|---|---|
| adjuster | dividends | Medicare |
| annuities | endorsement | Medicare Part D |
| bonds | exclusions | multilevel marketing plans |
| churning | exposures | mutual funds |
| common stock | franchise | perils |
| deductibles | indirect investments | Ponzi schemes |
| direct investment | insurance | portfolio |
| direct investment plan | investment | property insurance |
| disability income | liability insurance | pyramiding |
| insurance | life insurance | real estate |
| diversification | long-term care (LTC) | real estate investment |
| dividend reinvestment | insurance | trusts (REITs) |
| plan (DRIP) | Medicaid | rogue agents |

|                          |                          |                          |
|--------------------------|--------------------------|--------------------------|
| socially responsible     | time-shares              | volatility               |
| investing                | uninsured motorist       | workers' compensation    |
| stocks                   | coverage                 |                          |

## DISCUSSION QUESTIONS

1. If current age and employment rates continue, there will be fewer working Americans to support the nonworking older adult population in the year 2020. What can be done to make the Social Security system more viable?
2. According to a survey, one in four Americans says it is acceptable to defraud an insurance company. Why would people say that? What is your opinion about falsely taking money from an insurance company?
3. Why do you think survey polls show that Americans are satisfied with their own health care plans but are critical of managed care in general?
4. The famous philosopher George Santayana (1863–1952) said, "Nonsense is so good only because common sense is so limited." Considering this saying, why do you think so many people fall prey to scams and frauds? List five financial phrases or scams that attract investors.
5. Why do people have collections? Do you or any of your friends collect anything? If so, what is it, and how did the collection start? How can someone tell if a collectible is correctly priced?

## E-RESOURCES

**Insurance Sites**

**Ecoverage**  *www.ecoverage.com*
Instant quotes for most types of insurance policies

**Insurance Information Institute (III)**  *www.iii.org*
Tips how to cut insurance costs

**Insurance Regulatory Information Network (IRIN)**  *www.irin.org*
General information on the industry as well as links to state departments of insurance

**InsWeb.com**  *www.insweb.com*
Instant quotes for car insurance

**National Association of Insurance Commissioners (NAIC)**  *www.naic.org*
Consumer information on insurance

*Note:* NAIC is a voluntary organization of the chief insurance regulatory officials of the 50 states, Washington, D.C., and 4 U.S. territories. An example of its publications is "A Shopper's Guide to Long Term Care Insurance."

**Quotesmith**  *www.quotesmith.com*
Instant quotes for all kinds of insurance

### Rating Systems of Insurance Companies' Financial Strength

**A.M. Best Co.**   *www.ambest.com*

**Fitch Investors Services Inc.**   *www.fitchibca.com*

**Moody's Investor Service Inc.**   *www.moodys.com*

**Standard & Poor's Insurance Rating Service**   *www.standardandpoors.com*

**Weiss Ratings Inc.**   *www.weissratings.com*

### Investment Information (Including Internet Investments)

**Alliance for Investor Education**   *www.investoreducation.org*

**American Savings Education Council (ASEC)**   *www.asec.org*

**Commodity Futures Trading Commission (CFTC)**   *www.cftc.gov*

**Employee Benefit Research Institute (EBRI)**   *www.ebri.org*

**Federal Trade Commission (FTC)**   *www.ftc.gov*
Information on investment frauds and scams

**InvestorGuide**   *www.investorguide.com*

**InvestorWords**   *www.investorwords.com*

**Morningstar**   *www.morningstar.com*
Information on mutual funds

**National Association of Investors Corporation**   *www.better-investing.org*

**National Association of Securities Dealers (NASD)**   *www.nasd.com*

**National Fraud Information Center**   *www.fraud.org*

**North American Securities Administrators Association (NASAA)**
*www.nasaa. org*

**Securities and Exchange Commission (SEC)**   *www.sec.gov*
Information about investing wisely and avoiding fraud (go to Investor Information section of Web site)

**Small Business Administration (SBA)**   *www.sba.gov*

**The Motley Fool**   *www.fool.com*
General investing advice

**The Online Investor**   *www.theonlineinvestor.com*

## REFERENCES

Baglole, J. (April 17, 2003). Political correctness by the carat. *Wall Street Journal,* pp. B1, B3.
Barry, P. (December 2007). The going gets tougher. *AARP Bulletin.*
Darby, M. (December 1998). In Ponzi we trust. *Smithsonian.*

Greene, K. (March 24, 2003). Buying a security blanket. *Wall Street Journal Reports,* pp. R1, R3.

Higgins, M. (February 25, 2003). Getting poor on purpose. *Wall Street Journal,* p. D1.

Kalis, L. (February 18, 2003). Tracking consumer suits. *Wall Street Journal,* p. D1.

Lee, J. (2002). The poor in the financial market: Changes in the use of financial products, institutions, and services from 1995 to 1998. *Journal of Consumer Policy, 25,* 203–31.

Lown, J. (2001/2002). Educating consumers about investment risk. *Journal of Consumer Education, 19* (20), 1–8.

Mazurkewich, K. (April 17, 2003). Gemstone scandals. *Wall Street Journal,* pp. B1, B3.

Oster, C. (February 12, 2003a). Insurance-fraud survey confirms industry worries. *Wall Street Journal,* p. D2.

Oster, C. (April 8, 2003b). Car insurers get into the repair business. *Wall Street Journal,* p. D1.

Paul, P. (July/August 2002). Managed care. *American Demographics,* p. 24.

Reno, V. (Spring 2005). How social security works. *Generations: Journal of the American Society of Aging.*

Shopping for your own policy. (September 2002). *Consumer Reports,* pp. 38–41.

Solomon, M. (2003). *Conquering consumerspace.* New York: AMACOM.

The unraveling of health insurance. (July 2002). *Consumer Reports,* pp. 48–49.

What a difference the car makes. (October 2002). *Consumer Reports,* p. 22.

Whitehouse, K. (March 6, 2003). Is that Picasso covered by your home insurance? *Wall Street Journal,* p. D1.

Your risk tolerance. (2001). http://personal.vanguard.com/educ/inveduc.html. Select: Course 4: The basics of asset allocation: Your risk tolerance.

Zuboff, S., and J. Maxmin. (2002). *The support economy.* New York: Viking.

# PART 5

# Emerging Consumer Issues and the Global Perspective

## CHAPTER 15
### Consumer Issues, Ethics, and Globalization

# CHAPTER 15

# Consumer Issues, Ethics, and Globalization

> We keep on waiting; waiting on the world to change.
> —John Mayer

## Learning Objectives

1. Describe the four drives impacting consumer behavior.
2. Explain globalization and the need for a global perspective.
3. Explain what it means to be a pro-environment sustainability consumer.
4. Discuss the need for consumer and financial literacy.

---

### International Taste Exploration

More and more our consumption patterns are influenced by international travel, study abroad programs, and global products and ideas. For example, Americans "are taught from an early age that there are four basic tastes—sweet, salty, sour and bitter. But what describes the taste of chicken soup? To an increasing number of chefs and food-industry insiders, the answer is 'umami,' dubbed 'the fifth taste.' First identified by a Japanese scientist a century ago, umami has long been an obscure culinary concept. Hard to describe, it is usually defined as a meaty, savory, satisfying taste. . . . While umami is a relatively new concept in this country, it has been well known in parts of Asia for nearly 100 years. It was identified in the early 20th century by Kidunae Ikeda, a Japanese scientist who coined the name umami (pronounced 'oo-Ma-mee') using the Japanese term for deliciousness. . . . In mid-July, Frito-Lay, a unit of PepsiCo, hired its executive chef, Stephen Kalil. Mr. Kalil says he is experimenting with umami ingredients from Latin and Asian cultures—like cheese powder, anchovy powder, fermented soybean products and mushroom powder—to create new flavors for brands including Lay's and Flat Earth vegetable and fruit crisps."[1] Do any of these sound yummy to you?

[1] Katy McLaughlin, "A New Taste Sensation." *Wall Street Journal*, December 8–9, 2007, pp. W1, W8.

---

## INTRODUCTION

There is no question that our concept of consumerism is rapidly changing. The products and the foods we crave are considerably different than our tastes 20 years ago when there were no flat-screen TVs or lime and pepper potato chips. As this

451

book has continually pointed out, consumer economics as a field of study has had to advance and move with the times; also, controversy and concerns about the planet have always been part of consumer economics, and there is every indication that the future holds more of the same. E-commerce has had the effect of eliminating geography or distance from the consumer–market exchange. Making decisions and choices after careful consideration of every possible course of action is not possible, so how do consumers narrow their selection and in the process avoid as much fraud as possible? Unfortunately protecting themselves in the marketplace has become more difficult. The saving grace is that "our brains have a unique structure that allows us to mentally transport ourselves into future circumstances and then ask ourselves how it feels to be there" (Gilbert, 2006, p. 262). In addition, "with a little detective work, a pencil, and a good eraser, we can usually estimate—at least roughly—the probability that a choice will give us what we desire" (Gilbert, 2006, p. 260).

Ethics was introduced earlier in the book, and it underlies consumer decisions about courses of action. Ethics is the study of the general nature of morals and of specific moral choices made by individuals within the context of the larger society.

The essence of modern consumer economics is its eclectic approach. This chapter begins with a description of four drives that affect consumer behavior and then uses these drives as an organizing principle for the rest of the chapter. One of the drives, the drive to bond, is linked with gifting behavior; the subject of gift cards (a growing phenomenon) is covered. Another drive, the one to learn and make sense of the world and ourselves, is tested when it comes to selecting a phone service and the add-on equipment and services, so the practical application of this drive, that of trying to make sense of a purchase plan, is included in this chapter. Next, the chapter moves on to discussions of global and environmental perspectives, which are so blended together that often they are difficult to differentiate. An example is the use of pesticides, which is of worldwide concern. In the United States, we ban the use of certain pesticides that are acceptable in other parts of the world, and vice versa, so because food is imported and exported globally, there are real differences among nations about what is acceptable and safe.

The chapter wraps up with a retrospective on the book and the consumer movement in general. What have we learned? Where are we going? Even though consumer fraud has been with us since the beginning of trade and exchange, there are always new wrinkles, new swindlers, and new issues. By this time in the course and the book, you should be far less gullible. The money and heartache you will save—and the increased peace of mind you will gain—are beyond price, and in the process your knowledge of consumer economics should have increased tremendously.

## FOUR DRIVES IMPACTING CONSUMER BEHAVIOR

We talked earlier in the book about consumer behavior, and following is some additional information on the subject. Paul Lawrence and Nitin Nohria, two Harvard-based researchers, conclude that the way we act is a result of the conscious choices we make, often based on our ethics. These choices are fueled by an internal battle among four drives (Lawrence & Nohria, 2002, p. 5):

> The drive to acquire objects and experiences that improve our status relative to others
>
> The drive to bond with others in long-term relationships of mutual care and commitment
>
> The drive to learn and make sense of the world and of ourselves
>
> The drive to defend ourselves, our loved ones, our beliefs, and our resources from harm

## Drive to Acquire

The drive to acquire is crucial to the understanding of consumerism and was addressed in the Chapter 1 in the discussion of needs versus wants. Here is further evidence of this drive:

> When subjects are given the choice of living in two worlds, in which prices are the same, but in one they earn $90,000 and their neighbors earn $100,000 versus another in which they earn $110,000 but their neighbors earn $200,000, they are more likely to choose the former situation. Such behavior is at odds with standard utility-maximizing models of human behavior—in absolute terms subjects would be better off earning $110,000 instead of $90,000. (Lawrence & Nohria, 2002, p. 66)

What this experiment suggests is that humans compare themselves to others and care about relative status. It sheds light on such concepts as competition, ambition, envy, and status.

In an earlier chapter, we discussed prospect theory, developed by Daniel Kahneman and Amos Tversky in 1979 as an alternative to expected utility theory. What they found was that people frame outcomes or transactions in their minds, affecting how they behave and what they expect to receive. Prospect theory has been used to explain various gambling and betting behaviors; for example, even though the odds are very poor, consumers go ahead and bet or gamble anyway. In short, consumers aren't always rational, they engage in risky behaviors, they have a drive to acquire even if the odds are not in their favor, and their behavior is not always consistent. For example, someone could be conservative in stock market investments but regularly play the lottery.

Connected with the drive to acquire is the desire to use something we have paid for. This reluctance to waste a purchase is called the **sunk-cost fallacy**, a decision-making bias. An example given in Michael Solomon's book *Conquering Consumerspace* is that if there is a sudden snowstorm that makes it dangerous to go to a big football game, the person who paid for the ticket will more likely brave the storm and go than the person who was given a free ticket. The person who paid—in other words, who sunk money into the ticket—is more determined to go.

As consumers, we are always weighing wins and losses, taking chances, and comparing costs and benefits. This example also illustrates the theory of mental accounting in which decisions are influenced by the way a problem is framed, meaning how it is posed, so purchases should not be looked at solely in terms of price but also in terms of circumstances or conditions. For example, someone may not balk at paying $60 for a haircut in a fancy salon but might object to that price at a Cost Cutters or Wal-Mart Supercenter.

As an example of the drive to acquire, employees may be perfectly happy with 5 percent raises until they find out that their colleagues received 7 percent raises;

then they will want to know why the difference exists, but probably no explanation will appease them because they have a bad taste in their mouth. This reaction illustrates that drives are not always positive—they can lead to personal unhappiness, unsettling comparisons, and unproductive consequences. Reward systems cannot always live up to expectations. But it should be pointed out that the drive to acquire is counterbalanced with other drives such as the need for more time. Most people would rather spend time relaxing at home than fighting for a parking space at the mall. Many report being more pressed for time than ever before, and they are actively seeking solutions to be less pressured, resulting in growth in the interest in prepared foods and in yoga and other relaxing or stretching forms of exercise. About a third of Americans report always feeling rushed, and the average American sleeps 7 hours a night, 90 minutes less than people did a century ago (Solomon, 2003).

*One-third of Americans report always feeling rushed. The average American sleeps seven hours a night.*

## Drive to Bond

**Relational Issues.**   Human relationships contain a mix of both competitive and cooperative elements (Lawrence & Nohria, 2002). Self-interest is not the only motivator—caring about others (extended family, friends, communities, the world) and a sense of fairness serve as counterbalances. Acts of selfless generosity or altruism, such as giving to charities, returning found wallets, helping strangers with flat tires, and doing volunteer work, abound in human affairs. The drive to bond also refers to the drive to seek experiences. The experience of studying and working in another society and culture transforms individuals and has a multiplier effect that extends to their communities and their own countries on their return. The needs both to acquire and to bond cannot be underestimated, and the benefits in terms of improving global understanding are enormous.

The drive to bond is part of what it means to be a consumer because we, as consumers, wonder how other consumers are faring, and we care about their rights as well as our own. How does what we do on a daily basis affect others? What skills do we need in an ever-changing society to preserve and enhance not only our own lives but the lives of others? Furthermore, on the subject of the drive to bond, customer loyalty, which is the bonding of customers to companies, is fundamental to such firms as Ben & Jerry's, whose Waterbury, Vermont, factory pumps out 190,000 pints of ice cream each day. "Their consumer affairs staff matches up the pint with the 225 calls and e-mails received each week, checking to see if there were any complaints, and if so, which supplier's milk, eggs, or cherries didn't meet the [company's] near-obsession with quality" (Schlosser, 2003, p. 114). Although Ben & Jerry's cultivates a "down home" image, it is a multimillion-dollar company that ships to 50,000 grocery stores in the United States and multiple other countries. Attention to detail, in particular to consumer complaints, has been one of the reasons for its success, along with consistent quality, unusual flavors, and colorful names.

*Each American buys on average six birthday gifts a year.*

**Gifting and Gift Cards.**   An example of the drive to bond is the experience of giving and receiving gifts. **Gifting** is a symbolic act of voluntarily bestowing and occurs in nearly every culture as a means of celebration. "Each American on average buys about six birthday gifts a year—about one billion gifts in total. Business gifts are used strategically to define and nurture professional relationships, to the tune of more than $1.5 billion per year" (Solomon, 2003, p. 204). Other gifting occasions include Hanukkah, Christmas, anniversaries, Easter, weddings, Mother's

Day, Father's Day, and graduations. If you are a reader from another country, supply your own list of typical gifting occasions and behaviors; for U.S. readers who have traveled extensively, you may supply your own memories of gifting and celebrating in other countries. One U.S. visitor to Italy celebrated her birthday in Venice and the usual cake and singing happened, as are typical in the United States, but the difference was that the restaurant turned the lights off so the candles would show and that everyone in the restaurant joined in the singing—it was quite the occasion.

Gift cards are enormously popular with people because of the choices they provide and have largely replaced paper gift certificates from stores and restaurants. What sometimes happens is that customers leave a little money on the gift cards and the stores keep the money. As a piece of advice, if you buy an $18.99 item from a $20.00 gift card and the store clerk offers you the change, take it because the likelihood is that you couldn't find another item for a dollar or less or that you would forget about it and the card would expire or get mislaid. A significant problem is that people lose the cards, so as a form of proof, companies should make a copy at the time of sale of the card.

Fights have broken out as retailers and consumers tussle over who should get the unspent money on cards and whether the cards should carry expiration dates. It sounds like small change, but the sale of cards totals over $50 million a year and is a significant source of revenue for retail companies. Besides making 5 percent to 10 percent of value stored on gift cards that are never spent, stores also profit because a customer with a card often spends over the amount, paying more. For example, with a $25 gift card, someone might spend $30 and pay the extra $5.

"Laws in most states require retailers to turn over unused gift-card value as lost property, so that state officials can try to return it to consumers. . . . But enforcement is spotty at best. Most merchants don't keep thorough records of gift-card sales, making returns difficult" (McCarthy, 2003, pp. A1, A12). Some states are trying to pass a ban on expiration dates. The New York Attorney General's office and Home Depot reached an agreement on lost and stolen cards under which the chain will cancel them and reissue new cards to individuals who can prove they bought a card. The reason this came to a head in New York was over a complaint filed by Ann Becchina of Stony Brook, New York, who was trying to get a refund of a $1,879 balance on a $2,500 Home Depot card she had lost. She said, "I spent a frantic two days taking apart my home, cars, retracing my steps, checking lost-and-founds" (McCarthy, 2003, p. A12). She had bought the card herself and had a receipt for it, but her local store refused to replace it. The company has since revised its computer software to build in a way to repatriate the money to the holder. Before that, the company explained that losing the card was like losing cash: Once you lost the card, you were out of luck. Until this issue is completely sorted out across all stores, consumers would be wise to treat the card as they would cash, but if the card is lost or stolen, they should contact the store immediately and then follow steps like Ms. Becchina did.

### Drive to Learn and to Make Sense of the World and Ourselves

The drive to learn is inherent in consumer education, and a section on that can be found near the end of this chapter. The second part of that drive, the need to make sense of the world and of ourselves, is covered in the section on obtaining a global perspective.

### Drive to Defend

The last drive, the drive to defend, has a lot to do with insurance, identity theft, and privacy protection, which were discussed earlier in the book. The drive to defend is innate—we want to defend ourselves, our loved ones, and our resources from unwanted intrusions.

## TELEPHONE SERVICES

### Pricing Issues

The drive to make sense comes into play when comparing prices of telephone services. If ever there was an industry that ranks high on the list of student complaints, this is it. Advances in cell phone technology and deregulation brought more consumer choice but also more consumer confusion. Advertising about how bills will be figured and how much calls will actually cost can be misleading. A case in point is Sarah Kalliney, a time-starved Manhattan executive, who bills out at roughly $200 an hour for her business services. She ended up spending nearly 10 hours battling her cell phone company over $9 in late fees. Is such a battle worth her time? No, not in purely economic terms, but she said it was worth it for the satisfaction. She finally won the battle, but only after she tracked down the phone number for the president of the company (Spencer, 2003). The company says it has taken steps to improve customer service, including making it easier to reach operators.

### Prepaid Phone Cards

Telephone time paid for in advance can be put on prepaid phone cards. For example, a person pays $10 or $20 up front for the use of the card; the amount of time bought depends on the rate-per-minute charge. For most people, these cards are a convenience and are used in travel. The cards are sold at post offices, travel agencies, retail stores, grocery and convenience stores, and book shops. Some of the prepaid cards can be recharged by billing the additional cost to credit cards. Some all-purpose credit cards have a prepaid phone feature; the way they work is that most cards display a toll-free access telephone number and require a personal identification number (PIN), and the companies have computers that use the PIN to keep track of card usage. Here are the key players:

- Carriers have the telephone lines that carry calls.
- Distributors get the cards to retailers so they can be sold.
- Issuers set the rates and the services.
- Resellers buy telephone minutes from carriers.
- Retailers sell the cards.

When things go wrong, here are some typical problems:

- PINs or access numbers do not work.
- Issuers go out of business or did not set up the cards right in the first place.
- Customer service numbers are overloaded, so consumers' needs are not met.

- Rates are higher than advertised (there may be hidden fees such as connection charges, taxes, and surcharges).
- The connections or services are of poor quality.

Consumers can protect themselves in several ways. First, they should know their issuer and retailer. Are they reliable? Second, consumers should understand how the card works; if it does not function, they should know what their avenue of recourse is. Customers should also note any extra fees that may be charged as well as card expiration dates. If the card does not work and the customer service number is not responsive, further steps, including writing or calling state offices of consumer services, the Better Business Bureau (BBB), and the Federal Trade Commission (FTC), should be taken.

## Cramming and Slamming

**Cramming** means unexplained charges on phone bills for services never ordered, authorized, received, or used. Most cramming schemes occur through the use of an 800 or other toll-free number, and some are initiated by sweepstakes and contests; all are deceptive and to be avoided. Crooks can get your phone number and cram charges on your bill in any of these areas:

- *900 number calls.* Your phone number is captured and billed, and your number can be sold to others such as date lines, psychics, and adult entertainment. Be aware that 900 numbers cost money.
- *Contests and sweepstakes.* You may receive calls about sweepstakes and contests from filling out entry forms and sweepstakes promotions—be careful that the source is legitimate.
- *Dating services.* A dating service call may be made to meet someone locally for free, but it may turn out that the call has been routed out of town and long-distance charges show up on the bill.
- *Free-minute deals.* Some free-minute offers have a come-on of free initial minutes, but the service puts you on hold until the charges start.
- *International calls.* A phone number is said to be local access but uses an unfamiliar area code, which may mean the call is international and costly. Usually these are linked to entertainment scams.

The main way to protect yourself or your family from cramming is to check the phone bill every month and look into unfamiliar charges. Sometimes there is an error on the bill; other times someone in the family has become entangled in a scam (teenagers are particularly vulnerable). If there is an error on the bill, follow the instructions on the statement and try to resolve the problem by contacting the telephone company, information provider, or billing agent. A call should be followed up by a letter. If not satisfied, a consumer should follow the usual steps of making a complaint to the state office of consumer service and upward. The FTC has information about cramming at www.ftc.gov.

If a consumer's long-distance telephone company switches to another company without his or her permission, it is called **slamming**. Victims' legal rights regarding this are covered by rulings by the Federal Communications Commission (FCC). Basically, a person has 30 days to rectify the situation without paying long-distance charges and to switch back to the original carrier. This has been one of the most frustrating areas of consumer complaints, and the best defense is to check phone bills carefully and to take the steps necessary for remedy.

## DEVELOPMENT OF A GLOBAL PERSPECTIVE

Technological and distribution advances are shrinking the distances in the world, with the Internet and communications technology making it possible for global businesses to operate at far less cost in time and money than ever before. Consumers are responding not only at home but also at work; many consumers no longer visit the mall but instead shop online for gifts, shoes, and clothing.

New global markets have led to more affluence and more competition worldwide. The major competitors in the global market come from Australia, Europe, Asia, and North America, and the largest economies in the world are found in the United States, Japan, and Germany. **Globalization** refers to the distribution of goods and services worldwide, with consumer goods eventually becoming universally accepted and homogeneous (Du Plessis & Rousseau, 1999). It is a centrist international marketing approach with business at the center, and it also implies a materialistic view of consumers.

This is different from the term **global perspective**, which is a philosophy, a way of thinking, a type of ethics—it delves into moral choices we all make. According to one source: "A global perspective entails the challenging of materialism and commercialism and an examination of one's role as citizen. It further includes global ethics" (Erasmus, Kok & Retief, 2001, p. 116). The global perspective en-

The world is going more urban with large metropolitan areas spreading throughout the globe. (Ambient Images, Creative Eye/MIRA.com.)

courages and appreciates local small businesses, including home-based businesses, as well as the balance, creativity, and job opportunities they bring to the world economy. Even the bigger companies are increasingly expected to put money and support back into the communities that purchase from them or where their headquarters are located. People are feeling that those who generate profits have more of an obligation, a **social responsibility**, to do something worthwhile with at least some of those profits. To be truly socially responsible or to engage in social marketing, companies must address the needs of the masses as well as the needs of the few and balance individual quality with societal and environmental quality. For example, it does not work to give money to charities while at the same time polluting the streams and rivers that run past the homes of the recipients of those charities—a more complete view of corporate responsibility is needed.

To go back to the concept of globalization, a large-scale economy is beyond the purview of one person or one company, although James Bond and Austin Powers movies would lead us to believe that there are wealthy, power-hungry individuals out there who would like to rule the world. One of the leading management experts in the world, Peter Drucker, says, "When we talk about the global economy, I hope nobody believes it can be managed. It can't. There is no information on it. But if you are in the hospital field, you can know hospitals. If you were to parachute into some strange place and make your way to the lights in the valley, you would be able to identify the correct building as the hospital" (2002, p. 49).

No one can completely manage the global economy, but a single person, an expert, can know how a specific industry or area of business operates. This is not to say that there are not some extremely powerful individuals and pervasive businesses. The retail giant Wal-Mart founded by Sam Walton is the biggest single employer in many states in the United States and the largest grocer in the United States, and its expansion in the United States and abroad is continuing. Carrefour, a company started in France in 1959 by two families, is the biggest retailer in Europe and the second largest worldwide, with stores in over 30 countries including some in Asia and South America. Its three leading formats are hypermarket, supermarket, and hard discount. The largest foundation in the world is the Bill & Melinda Gates Foundation. According to its Web site, simple values are at the center of the foundation's work:

- All lives—no matter where they are being led—have equal value.
- To whom much is given, much is expected.

The Bill & Melinda Gates Foundation is an example of developing a global perspective, a world attitude that shifts away from self-interest to consideration of both behavior and assets within a greater context. One of the foundation's principles is to invest resources responsibly, for example, to help reduce inequities in neglected areas.

Along these same lines, the United Nations and the International Labour Organization came up with a list of universally felt human needs (Harman, 1998, pp. 176–177):

- Basic human needs ("enough" food, shelter, health care, education, employment, and security of the person)
- Sense of the dignity of being human
- Sense of becoming (a chance to achieve a better life)
- Sense of justice or equity
- Sense of achievement, of being involved with something worth achieving
- Sense of solidarity—of belonging to a worthy group and of participating in decisions that affect the group's and one's own destiny

**GLOBAL CONSUMER**

### Hm, Cocoa!

Most cultures around the world like chocolate. *Consumer Reports* rated the best hot chocolates for taste from the Swiss-based company Nestlé to 10 others. The worst were a thin reddish concoction, which tasted weak and oily. The best had more chocolate flavor. Their recommendation is you can't go wrong with Ghirardelli or Cacao Reserve. Two less expensive yet still good hot chocolates made with milk were Hershey's Cocoa and Swiss Miss Dark Chocolate Sensation. The sensory panelists said milk not only added flavor but covered up some of the defects. Milk adds calories and fat. Are you a cocoa drinker? Do you consult *Consumer Reports* before making purchases?

*Reference:* "Which Cocoa's a Go?" ConsumerReports.org, January 7, 2008.

Besides all these needs, one of the greatest challenges that consumers face is knowing what outside information to access in order to make sound decisions. Who to believe? What to buy or not buy? The global economy has opened up the world to limitless possibilities. Customers are changing and distribution systems are changing, and the effects on technology and competition are immeasurable. Drucker says, "Under e-commerce, delivery will become the one area in which a business can truly distinguish itself. It will become the critical 'core competence.' Its speed, quality, and responsiveness may well become the decisive competitive factor even where brands seem to be entrenched. And no existing multination and altogether very few businesses are organized for it" (2002, pp. 57–58). An example of a fast-growing area of e-commerce is new cars being bought through such businesses as CarsDirect.com, Autobytel.com, and CarPoint.com. Since there is no reason an e-seller must limit itself to one brand or make of car, for example, it opens up new possibilities in competitive pricing, styling, and options beyond the traditional ways of selling cars. In this new economy, sales aren't necessarily linked to production, which is a significant paradigm shift. Lest this section and chapter appear too positive about the benefits of e-commerce, it should be noted that certain goods and services cannot be sold online. There are limitations; for example, haircuts, manicures, and massages still require the personal touch, and most brides would like to try on a wedding dress (or several of them) before making a purchase.

## CONSUMER TERRORISM

**Consumer terrorism** refers to a variety of activities conducted by individuals or groups whose purpose is to disrupt the marketplace. It includes making threats and deliberately spreading misinformation and fear, as well as actually tampering with products. Product tampering is a form of bioterrorism that can cause great harm to individuals (such as those made ill by tampered-with foods or drugs) and can ruin or temporarily cripple companies. The wise company immediately addresses any problems with its products by alerting the public and by handling recalls and rebates efficiently. The increased use of surveillance cameras in stores and in factories should reduce product tampering.

Another form of consumer terrorism is tampering with Web sites, company data, and personal computers through computer viruses. Sophisticated hackers can wreck company records, invade individual and government accounts, and steal identities. This is such a new concept that it is difficult to envision all the ways consumer terrorism may take place, but suffice it to say that disruptions of financial, food, electronic, health, and water supply networks are disconcerting, as well as potentially fatal. The main concern is the vastness of the problem, in other words, the huge number of people who could be hurt given the new modes (specifically the Internet) of consumer terrorism.

## STEALTH MARKETING

Global marketing strategies come and go, but one with lasting power is called **stealth marketing**, the provision of a unique service or product in a way that is not too public. Rather than being overt in offering a new product or service, in stealth marketing the company's intent is to "come in under the radar" by introducing something new without it being too obvious to competitors. Once a marketing plan is established, the company may keep new offerings or changes under wraps until it is time to launch. Stealth is used as a tool to gain competitive advantage. This term is mentioned at this point in this chapter to show that both companies and consumers (including consumer terrorists) can engage in less-than-obvious behaviors or have less-than-obvious motivations. Attention may be drawn, for example, to a side product or event as a means of keeping the main event under the radar. In stealth marketing, a program or strategy may be targeted to a select group of customers or prospects (such as millionaires, yacht owners, urban teenagers) based on targeting criteria that are not obvious.

In the public's mind, mainstream marketing is often thought of as being obvious, pushy, slick, and pressured and as being highly publicized in magazines and newspapers (for example, celebrity-filled product launches for fashions, perfumes, or restaurant chains). Stealth marketing is the opposite of this. Stealth marketing is not illegal, nor is it fully developed, but it is a consumer issue involving protection and awareness.

## PRO-ENVIRONMENT CONSUMERISM

One of the biggest shifts in consumer behavior in recent years has been toward green consumerism. In 2007, 58 percent of Americans said that they wanted to receive gifts that were green and that the green items they were most interested in were clothes made from organic cotton (Puente, 2007).

### Relationship between Environment and Economics

The relationships between environment and economics can be looked at from a variety of perspectives. The specialization in economics that focuses on these

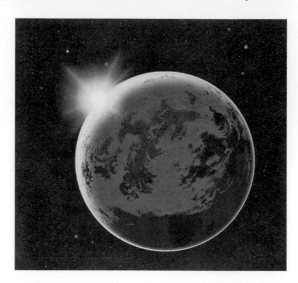

Environmental concerns such as global warming are spurring "green" consumerism. (David Gifford, Photo Resarchrs, Inc.)

relationships is called **ecological economics**, with a particular emphasis in changes in **natural capital**, which consists of natural resources and ecological systems. "Natural capital is defined as the whole endowment of land and resources available to us, including air, water, fertile soil, forests, fisheries, mineral resources, and the ecological life-support systems that make economic activity, and indeed life itself, possible" (Harris, 2002). In ecological economics, changes in these realms are viewed as important as changes in human-made capital. The gross national product (GNP) measures human production, not the state of the environment; the quality of our lives is a combination as well as the state of social issues of family, well-being, health, education, and harmony. "The economic indicators, such as the GNP, which measure how well the society is doing, are essentially measures of how rapidly resources are being used up—converted to economic product. The more economic the product, the 'healthier' the economy and, by implication, the society. Is that good, you ask, on a finite planet to place a premium on the maximum rate of using up resources?" (Harman, 1998, p. 123).

One way to determine if ecosystems are being strained is by noting the increased prevalence of large-scale or global environmental problems such as global climate change, ozone layer destruction, ocean pollution, soil degradation, and species loss (Harris, 2002). **Sustainable development** would mean not using up natural resources or endangering ecosystems. One author states that sustainable development is "economic development that provides for human needs without undermining global ecosystems and depleting essential resources" (Harris, 2002, p. 28). Although it may seem like a contradiction in terms, abundance and affluence bring new forms of scarcity—"scarcity of natural resources, of fresh air and water, of arable land, of the waste-absorbing capacities of the natural environment, of resilience of the planet's life-support systems, of spirit-renewing wilderness. . . . The 'new scarcities' are of course also related to population growth, which in turn is a consequence of improved sanitation and public health measures" (Harman, 1998, p. 125).

The industrialized world places a high value on economic and financial signals, yet because of the pollution problems caused by Eastern Europe in the

1980s and the pervasive smog worldwide, the public today is more aware of the effects of production, transportation, and consumption on the environment. As mentioned earlier, many consumers feel that business has a social responsibility to look out for the quality of the environment as part of the consumer–market exchange. Wal-Mart even has sustainability experts on its headquarters staff. Green advocate Amanda Freeman, a founder of VitalJuiceDaily.com, says that "social responsibility is hot this year as well, so everyone is trying to be less consumption-oriented and more cause-oriented" (Puente, 2007, p. 2D). Consumers have a responsibility to consume in environmentally friendly ways and to engage in recycling behaviors.

According to South African authors Alet C. Erasmus, Martha Kok, and Arda Retief, "Consumer behavior of the Western world can generally be described as materialistic. . . . Driven by economic principles, the retail environment encourages and even promotes a materialistic value system. Although many consumers will deny being materialistic, every day consumer related behavior in the Western world unfortunately bears testimony of the opposite" (2001, p. 116).

They also say that a global perspective results in an appreciation for voluntary simplicity and conservation and a respect for past and future generations. **Voluntary simplicity** refers to a conscious effort to live more modestly, with fewer possessions and at lower consumption levels. Erasmus, Kok, and Retief (2001) call for decisions to be based on these types of considerations, of the effect on interactive environments rather than with a passion for consumption. Does anyone really need a 17-bedroom, 20-bathroom house? Many are calling for a "mind shift" away from indiscriminate consumption to a socially conscious and environmentally responsible consumer behavior where the consumer is regarded as a citizen (McGregor, 1998a, 1998b, 1999). "Voluntary simplifiers range from senior citizens who downsize their homes to young, mobile professionals who don't want to be tied down to their possessions . . . clearly, most mainstream consumers are not about to give up their Prada bags any time soon. However, many of us are overwhelmed by the profusion of stuff out there" (Solomon, 2003, p. 248). Voluntary simplifiers believe that once their basic needs are met, there is no reason to keep consuming on top of that—they do not believe that more is better.

The word *environment* can refer to so many things, from energy alternatives to air quality to use of fuels to water quality. There is also the consumer right to a healthy environment. As mentioned in Chapter 2 on the history of consumerism, President John F. Kennedy, inspired by Rachel Carson's book *Silent Spring,* was an early advocate for better environmental protection. The Consumer Federation of America (CFA)—one of the most active consumer organizations advocating for a cleaner environment—believes that we must all reduce, reuse, and recycle more. The main government agency regarding environmental control is the Environmental Protection Agency (EPA).

**ENERGY STAR** is a cooperative effort between the EPA and the Department of Energy. It is estimated that if a typical household normally spends $1,900 a year on energy, it can save more than $600 when using ENERGY STAR products and practices. In essence, this government program offers energy-efficient solutions. A new house can earn an ENERGY STAR rating, as can individual products such as appliances, heating and cooling systems, insulation, roofing, home electronics, office equipment, lighting (for example, compact fluorescent light bulbs [CFLs]), and ceiling fans; new products such as CFLs have the ENERGY STAR designated on the package. One goal of the program is the reduction of air pollution, which can be done by following these five steps:

1. Change five lights.
2. Include more ENERGY STAR products.
3. Heat and cool more efficiently, and use a programmable thermostat.
4. Seal your home or apartment to prevent air leaks.
5. Tell family and friends about ways to reduce air pollution and buy fuel-efficient cars.

The CFA often says that the EPA is not doing enough and that more regulation and enforcement are needed, especially in regard to water quality and air pollution. It is a constant battle within the United States, within other countries, and cross-nationally because polluted air and water do not stop at state or national boundaries. How does this relate to consumerism (besides the obvious fact that we breathe air and drink water)? Perhaps it would be useful to focus on one aspect of consumption such as packaging. The manufacture of packaging involves raw materials such as wood, energy, and water. First, when making packaging materials, there can be an awareness of the negative effect of certain manufacturing procedures on the environment and a consideration of redesign and acceptable alternatives. A next step could be eliminating unnecessary packaging, such as double and triple layers of packaging. Have you ever noticed how much packaging you throw out? Biodegradable and recyclable packaging could be alternatives. **Biodegradability** means that packaging material will decompose naturally through biological processes; in homes, packaging could be recycled for another use.

Another way to look at the environment–consumption interchange is to consider the environmental costs of producing goods from cradle to grave (from inception to disposal). How much electricity, raw materials, water, and gasoline (for transportation) are used? New methods and materials are needed, as is support for consumers when they are offered more environmentally friendly goods. Consumers have to be informed about the larger part they play, and education is one of the keys to making informed decisions (more on this in a later section).

The discussion of caring about the environment harkens back to the beginning of the book when values (individual or collective beliefs that are considered desirable), standard of living, and quality or quantity of goods and services were introduced. Values and standards of living impact economic life in the home. This approach is part of a far greater concept: life satisfaction (including the concept of buying wisely). This is in direct contrast to the concept that consumption just happens. On the contrary, consumption is far more complex and involves a set of behaviors, presumptions, and perspectives, including a global, environmental, or citizen-oriented approach.

All of us are at some degree of risk in terms of consumption. For example, we can select a sandwich with bean sprouts, spinach, or peanut butter that has been infected. It is estimated that a third or more of the American population get sick each year from poorly prepared or handled food. From a global perspective, one of the growing concerns is how much food is imported from countries such as China and India that do not have the sanitation and pesticide rules regarding farming that are common in other nations. As mentioned earlier, this is a two-way street—infected food has been produced, exported, and circulated in more developed nations as well.

### Consumer and Financial Literacy on the Agenda

By reading this book, you have experienced consumer education and improved your financial acumen. This is important because "the ability of consumers to make sound financial decisions has never been more challenged. . . . Educators, community leaders and policy makers face the challenge of bringing financial literacy and consumer education effectively to their constituencies" (Toussaint-Comeau & Rhine, 2001–2002, p. 9). Changes in technology—most notably the Internet—have affected both the type and the delivery of consumer goods and services, making the exchange process more complex and in some ways easier (speedier transporation, for example). The goal of consumer education is to provide a broad range of people the information, technology, and confidence needed to give them a sense of control over their decisions. Formal **consumer education** (knowledge about today's marketplace) in grades K–12 varies by state but is usually part of several courses in high schools, colleges vary in what they offer as well.

"Consumer education is concerned with the skills, attitudes, knowledge and understanding that individuals need to cope in an increasingly complex marketplace. Adding to the complexity is a growing recognition of accommodating the needs of multicultural and multilingual learners" (Allison & Rehm, 2007, p. 8). "Consumer education aims to protect consumers, inform them, promote an understanding between buyer and seller, and contribute to society as a whole, including providing a sense of economic well-being and fair play. The consumer experience relies on trust and dependability" (Goldsmith & McGregor, 2000, p. 126). Consumer education curricula require a three-prong attack:

1. *Consumer decision making.* External and internal factors affect consumer decisions as well as the stages of the decision-making process.
2. *Resource management.* Goal setting, personal finance, buying skills, technological developments, and conservation are all part of resource management.
3. *Citizen and government participation.* Both individual citizens and their government as a whole need to have an awareness of economic conditions and to make legislative changes.

In modern consumer economics, there is an intense relationship among economic, social, and geopolitical forces that focuses on how market forces operate and how individuals and families make choices in a complex society and a diverse economy. Consumer education has its challenges in terms of getting students at all levels to identify needs, allocate resources, and recognize the harsh reality of scarcity. Some needs are going to go unmet; in the process of determining who gets what and who is left out of the loop, there are issues of equity, justice, and fairness. These all fall under the subject of economic education as well as the more general category of character education. Discussions such as these are not for the faint of heart or the perfectionist, but these issues should be debated with many sides represented. Legislators and governors constantly struggle with how to disburse tax dollars in a fair and effective way. Should budget money go to border control, space programs, or consumer protection? No matter which way they turn, some program will have to do with less than in the past in order that other programs or new programs can thrive—growth requires hard choices. Consumer education straddles family and consumer sciences and other subjects within the social sciences such as economics, so it sometimes falls through the cracks when money is being disbursed and programs set up.

The majority of high school seniors taking financial literacy tests fail to comprehend basic subjects such as banking products, credit cards, taxes, savings, and investments (Mandell, 1998). Further, the National Council on Economic Education has said that most high school students and adults score failing grades on their understanding of basic economics. A multiprong approach is suggested. The Jump$tart Coalition for Personal Financial Literacy is an example of an effective program aimed at high school students.

Besides teaching these types of courses in school settings, it is clear that adult outreach programs are needed in consumer economics, including e-consumerism. Extension programs and Internet resources are available to those outside school environments. Consumer educators see their role as encompassing both the formal and informal learning environments. As more and more people become lifelong learners and because consumerism is a lifelong process, it makes sense that this topic transcends age and income groups. The Internet will increasingly play a bigger role in our consumption experiences and certainly in the search for information; other delivery modes include information seminars, pamphlets and booklets, newspapers, magazines, radio, television, and videos. Scam alerts are part of the information exchange.

## CONSUMER ECONOMICS RETROSPECTIVE

A modern boutique hotel has a saying. When you call down to the front desk, the first thing the receptionist says is, "How can I inspire you today?" The goal of this book, especially as we look to the future, is to address that very question. As we have traced the unfolding of consumer economic thought, we concentrated on economic thinking while keeping the welfare of the individual and the family in mind. In assessing economic ideas, it is important to remember that what we are seeing today has a history.

> In an advanced industrial society, consumption is a necessity, not a luxury. It is what people must do to survive. It is the way that individuals take care of themselves and their families, much as hunting and gathering or growing crops were for people of earlier societies. For today's women and men, consumption decisions encompass everything from education to health care, insurance, transportation, and communication, as well as food, shelter, clothing and luxuries. (Zuboff & Maxmin, 2002, p. 7)

We also consume experiences as well through such activities as travel and work.

Theories guide us on the right road. It is difficult to fully appreciate the development of economic thought as applied to consumerism without an examination of a variety of ideas and viewpoints. The Consumer Power Model of consumer economics (introduced in Chapter 3) shows the interaction among various components such as the media, consumers, businesses, the government, and consumer organizations. We also learned about the less noble aspects of consumerism, namely, frauds and scams, which both have a history and tend to repeat themselves in new and "improved" forms; where money is concerned, fraud and deception are never far behind. As counterpoints, the concepts of citizenship and regulatory action were introduced.

"The search for better answers needs to go on at all levels—societal, organizational, family, local community, and individual—as people struggle with the difficult choices in their lives. . . . We have many reasons to be grateful that we, as members of the human species, come well equipped for these challenges. We are truly marvelous, adaptable creatures" (Lawrence & Nohria, 2002, pp. 283–284). This book provides the armor to protect yourself and those you care about from the unscrupulous and directs you toward the better part of the marketplace, a place we all need. "No one can escape the centrality of consumption. There is no distinct class of consumers. Everyone is a consumer, no matter what their status or income level" (Zuboff & Maxmin, 2002, p. 7).

## SUMMARY

Researchers have conceptualized human drives as being the drive to acquire, the drive to bond, the drive to learn, and the drive to defend. Thinking and caring about others relates to the drive to bond as well as the drive to learn and make sense of the world and of ourselves, and the example of the Bill & Melinda Gates Foundation was used. A global perspective is a way of thinking, a philosophy, in which local small businesses are appreciated and seen as part of the worldwide economy. Ethics and citizenship are important considerations in the interchange between environmentalism and consumer behavior, and choosing wisely with an eye to future generations takes present consumption into a higher realm, that of thinking of others besides oneself. This requires a shift from individual consumer rights to an awareness of collective human responsibilities. The underlying principles of a global perspective require a mind shift to the greater good, to an awareness of a greater role.

## KEY POINTS

1. Globalization refers to international marketing and exchange, the distribution of goods and services worldwide.
2. The global perspective includes global ethics and consideration of others.
3. Establishing trust is fundamental to the consumer–market exchange. Governments need to agree on food production, sanitation rules, and other areas in which cross-border trade takes place.
4. Consumer terrorism refers to activities whose purpose is to disrupt the marketplace.
5. Stealth marketing, engaged in to gain competitive advantage, refers to targeting an audience or market without being too obvious about it.
6. No one person or company manages the worldwide economy.
7. ENERGY STAR is a U.S. government program that reduces energy bills and protects the environment.

8. Educating consumers about the long-term effects of consumption, including environmental impact and sustainable development, is part of building a global perspective.
9. Work, internships, and study abroad or exchange programs, along with volunteering, are ways to get involved in international consumer and environmental issues.

## KEY TERMS

| | | |
|---|---|---|
| biodegradability | gifting | stealth marketing |
| consumer education | globalization | sunk-cost fallacy |
| consumer terrorism | global perspective | sustainable development |
| cramming | natural capital | voluntary simplicity |
| ecological economics | slamming | |
| ENERGY STAR | social responsibility | |

## DISCUSSION QUESTIONS

1. Have you or a friend or family member ever pursued getting money back from a telephone company or had trouble getting a bill corrected? If so, what was the result, and was it worth the effort?
2. How important is gifting to you? Do you think there is too much or too little emphasis in our society on gifting and celebrating holidays? For your holiday gift, how would you feel about someone donating a goat to a family in an African village? Explain your answers.
3. Look at consumer economics from the global perspective, and list five issues or areas of concern that require international cooperation.

## E-RESOURCES

**International Consumer Information, Statistics, and Data**

**Bill & Melinda Gates Foundation**   *www.gatesfoundation.org*

**United Nations**   *www.un.org*

**Consumer Current Events (U.S.-Based Consumer News Media Sources)**

**abc News**   *abcnews.go.com*

**FOX News**   *www.foxnews.com*

**CBS News**   *www.cbsnews.com*

**msnbc**   *www.msnbc.msn.com*

**PBS**   *www.pbs.org/news*

Consumer Current Events (Canadian-Based Consumer News Media Sources)

**CBC**    *www.cbc.ca*

**CTV**    *www.ctv.ca*

**Consumer Current Events (United Kingdom–Based Consumer News Media Sources)**

*www.bbc.co.uk*

**U.S. Telephone Services**

Note: First contact local services and state regulators before going to the federal level.

**Federal Communications Commission (FCC)**    *www.fcc.gov*

**Free and Low-Cost Consumer Publications**

**Consumer Information Center**    *www.pueblo.gsa.gov*

**ENERGY STAR program**    *www.energystar.gov*

**Study Abroad and Exchange Programs**

**Institute of International Education (IIE)**    *www.iie.org*

## REFERENCES

Allison, B., and M. Rehm. (2007). Teaching strategies for diverse learners in FCS classrooms. *Journal of Family & Consumer Sciences, 99* (2), 8–10.

Drucker, P. (2002). *Managing in the next society.* New York: St. Martin's Press.

Du Plessis, R., and G. Rousseau. (1999). *Buyer behavior: A multicultural approach,* 2nd ed. Johannesburg, South Africa: Thomson.

Erasmus, A., M. Kok, and A. Retief. (2001). Adopting a global perspective in the discipline consumer science. *Journal of Family Ecology and Consumer Sciences, 29,* 116–23.

Gilbert, D. (2006). *Stumbling on happiness.* New York: Alfred A. Knopf.

Goldsmith, E., and S. McGregor. (2000). E-commerce: Consumer protection issues and implications for research and education. *Journal of Consumer Studies and Home Economics, 24* (2), 124–27.

Harman, W. (1998). *Global mind change: The promise of the 21st century.* San Francisco, CA: Berrett-Koehler Publishers.

Harris, J. (2002). *Environmental and natural resource economics.* Boston: Houghton Mifflin.

Lawrence, P., and N. Nohria. (2002). *Driven: How human nature shapes our choices.* Cambridge, MA: Harvard Business School.

Mandell, L. (1998). *Our vulnerable youth: The financial literacy of American 12th graders.* Jump$tart Coalition for Personal Financial Literacy.

McCarthy, M. (February 26, 2003). Why merchants are so happy you lost that gift card. *Wall Street Journal,* pp. A1, A12.

McGregor, S. (1998a). Reinterpreting economic theory in a global reality. *Journal of Family and Consumer Sciences, 90* (3), 35–40.

McGregor, S. (1998b). Towards adopting a global perspective in the field of consumer studies. *Journal of Consumer Studies and Home Economics, 22* (2), 111–19.

McGregor, S. (September 1999). Globalizing consumer education: Shifting from individual consumer rights to collective human responsibilities. Proceedings of the 19th International Consumer Studies and Home Economics Research Conference, pp. 43–52.

Puente, M. (December 11, 2007). Oh, you shouldn't have—really! *USA Today*, p. 1D.

Schlosser, J. (March 17, 2003). Looking for intelligence in ice cream. *Fortune*, pp. 114–20.

Solomon, M. (2003). *Conquering consumerspace.* New York: AMACOM.

Spencer, S. (February 26, 2003). How much is your time worth? *Wall Street Journal*, pp. D1, D2.

Toussaint-Comeau, M., and S. Rhine. (2001/2002). Delivery of financial literacy programs. *Journal of Consumer Education,* 9–17.

Zuboff, S., and J. Maxmin. (2002). *The support economy.* New York: Viking.

# Consumer Careers and Graduate School

## OVERVIEW

If you have enjoyed this class and perhaps are majoring in consumer economics, financial planning, merchandising, nutrition, or a related field, you may be thinking about pursuing a consumer career or going on to graduate school. Consumer careers are many and varied; most exist in government, business, media, organizations, law enforcement, community development, and education.

A popular Web site for college graduates seeking employment is monster.com, where over 5,000 jobs are listed with the word *consumer* in the title. Most require a bachelor's degree, although a few require advanced degrees and/or two or three years of work experience. Once you are at monster.com, click on "Search Jobs." The employers listed include Pfizer, Pepsi, eBay, Bank of America, Disneyland Resort, Sprint, Johnson & Johnson, Goody, Ashley Furniture Industries, Bank One, The Clorox Company, Wachovia, Toys 'R' Us, the Federal Reserve System, and Bonne Bell. Job titles include consumer affairs manager, consumer promotions/marketing positions, consumer lending manager, consumer product sales positions, consumer fabrics manager, consumer insights manager, consumer researcher, and consumer services representative. For each job opening, click on it and find out more about the position and the employer. This Web site also lists jobs abroad. The term *consumer affairs* usually refers to careers that advocate for the consumer and that involve activities in the public interest, specifically fairness in the marketplace and improvement of consumer well-being.

## JOB PROSPECTS

When reading job advertisements, be forewarned that not all jobs with the word *consumer* in the title require college degrees or even a course or two in the subject, and in many existing consumer positions, one will find employees with all sorts of work experience and coursework backgrounds. Often employees start out in human resources or accounting and then find that they have skills in consumer affairs and are drawn to the subject, or they are promoted to be head of a division. As another example, anyone can say he or she is a financial planner, but to be a certified financial planner requires rigorous exams and training/apprenticeships. Another job category that may be of interest is that of stockbroker. Do all stockbrokers have college degrees? The answer is no, but they must pass the Series 7 licensing examination, and sometimes a Series 63 exam, too. The successful completion of the exams allows the broker to provide advice, solicit business, and execute transactions for clients.

Perhaps this knowledge of the level of credentials necessary for some jobs in financial and consumer fields is disheartening, but what it means to you as a job candidate is that it is a wide-open field and that your credentials will be stronger than most. As mentioned previously, each day monster.com lists over 5,000 openings with the word *consumer* in the title—this is a tremendously large job bank. Then add all the related possibilities, not to mention what may be found on other search engines as well as all the jobs that are never listed (only by word of mouth), and the number of potential jobs is astronomical. Because of the number of different jobs, it also means that it is not unusual for consumer specialists to work for one industry such as the airlines and then switch to a food company and then work for a government regulatory agency. There are few fields as versatile as those in consumerism.

## JOBS IN BUSINESS

Consumer positions in business may involve communicating with consumers; evaluating consumer applications for loans, mortgages, or insurance; writing publications or press releases; representing a service or industry; designing exhibits or working at conventions; serving customers or clients; being a salesperson; or reporting consumer trends or consumer information gained from toll-free lines, consumer surveys, and other forms of research and communications to higher management. Consumer affairs departments may be called consumer care centers or consumer service; the consumer-related functions may be part of public relations, sales, management, or marketing. Monster.com suggests using related search terms such as banker, relationship banker, financial services officer, and private banking officer. When searching, do not limit yourself to the word *consumer.* You can also put in the area of the country or the type of industry (consumer products, banking, and so on) that you are interested in. Promotions can lead to jobs such as vice president of consumer affairs or another type of corporate officer.

At a consumer conference on the issue of how to protect children in cyberspace, representatives from Microsoft Corporation, Visa USA, and AOL spoke, and they were joined by representatives from the Federal Trade Commission (FTC) and consumer organizations, so being a spokesperson is a career option in a variety of settings. It is not unusual for consumer advocates from a number of employers to join together on a common theme or concern.

In a small company, the consumer services specialist may be a jack-of-all-trades, performing a myriad of functions from testing products to proofreading advertisements and brochures to conducting survey research to responding to customer complaints; in a larger company, a consumer affairs professional (CAP) may specialize in one function. Another way the function may be specialized is that someone with coursework or a major in consumer economics may become a stockbroker, a mortgage lender, a real estate developer, a product designer, an owner of a consumer services company, or a mutual fund manager. Forming a partnership is another way to go, and more and more students like the idea of owning their own company or business (either initially or in the long run).

Many companies belong to the Society of Consumer Affairs Professionals (SOCAP), and its Web site (www.socap.org) could be used as a way to find potential employers. SOCAP has members from more than 1,500 companies, including multinational firms. The organization's goal is to improve the marketplace for consumers by addressing their concerns within corporate structures. One member company is Mobil, and Exxon Mobil Customer Relations in Exton, Pennsylvania, can be reached at www.exxonmobil.com. Other sources of company names, addresses, and information include *Standard & Poor's Register of Corporations, Directors, and Executives; Trade Names Directory; Standard Directory of Advertisers;* and *Dun & Bradstreet Directory.* The *Thomas Register of American Manufacturers* lists the makers of thousands of products.

Trade associations offer other options where you would represent an entire industry or a group of industries. Examples would be the Soap and Detergent Association located in Washington, D.C.; the Toy Industry Association located in New York; and the Certified Financial Planner Board of Standards in Denver. Lobbying (for businesses, trade associations, or nonprofit organizations) would be another possibility.

## JOBS IN GOVERNMENT

In government, the consumer specialist role has many options: designing educational programs, Web sites, and brochures; evaluating and setting policy; sculpting model laws; testing products; collecting and analyzing data; doing public speaking; writing reports; testifying; interviewing and giving interviews; and engaging in arbitration or mediation. Your goal would be to advance pro-consumer views on a variety of issues. A person with consumer economics coursework could become a leader in energy policy, tourism, or environmental protection or an expert on a state's lemon laws (for cars). Thus, the Environmental Protection Agency (EPA), as well as many other agencies or branches of the state and federal government (such as the Departments of Commerce) would be appropriate job categories. The E-Resources section at the end of each chapter can serve as a guide for finding government careers as well as other types of jobs. Anything involving money, credit, or finances or the public welfare would have positions requiring consumer expertise. Military bases have positions in community and family services, including financial counseling; also included would be the U.S. Military Family Centers (http://mfrc.calib.com) for the Navy, Air Force, Marine Corps, Coast Guard, and Army as well as the Commissary and Exchange Offices.

America's Jobline, an audio version of the federal government's America's Job Bank, is available at no cost by telephone: Dial 1-800-414-5748 and follow the voice prompts. The Jobline also has information about employment services for the state you are calling from. Jobs are available in the state attorney general's offices and other offices listed earlier in the book; in addition, county and city governments have openings.

Places to look for jobs include offices of consumer affairs, housing authorities or neighborhood community watches, departments of human resources, departments of aging or community affairs, licensing agencies, social services offices, energy administrations or public utility commissions, insurance commissions or financial offices, legislative or congressional offices, and departments of commerce, finance, or motor vehicles. The Consumer Price Index and the Consumer Expenditure Survey are compiled by the Bureau of Labor Statistics (BLS) (go to www.bls.gov), and the BLS regularly has openings for consumer analysts and economic assistants.

The Federal Trade Commission (FTC), the Consumer Product Safety Commission (CPSC), the Food and Drug Administration (FDA), and any other agency mentioned in this book have positions and internships, and often the main way into state or federal jobs is through internships. A government job search may take six months or more. If you type in the word *consumer* when you do government searches, you will find hundreds of matches or leads, but do not limit yourself to this word because (as the list suggests) consumer functions may fall under many different bureaus and agencies.

Another specific example is the U.S. General Services Administration (GSA) in Washington, D.C., which has many positions related to consumer economics, such as program manager for the Federal Citizen Information Center (FCIC); a degree (a bachelor of arts or science or a master's) in consumer sciences, marketing, or a related field is required, and the person should be someone who is interested in educating citizens through a coordinated program of print publications, electronic information, and a national contact center. The FCIC is known for promoting and delivering consumer information from Pueblo, Colorado, and also publishes the annual *Consumer Action Handbook,* a 150-page compendium of the best consumer purchasing and complaint advice. To receive a free copy of the current *Consumer Action Handbook,* order it through the FCIC Web site (www.pueblo.gov); the handbook can also be viewed there. For information that is updated weekly, visit www.consumeraction.gov, a useful guide to all kinds of government, trade association, media, community/education, and corporate jobs; it lists names, addresses, and contact information.

Following is a list of other federal agencies with enforcement and/or complaint-handling duties for products and services used by the general public not previously mentioned in this section:

Architectural and Transportation Barriers Compliance Board

Centers for Disease Control and Prevention

Commodity Futures Trading Commission

Department of Agriculture

Department of Defense

Department of Education

Department of Energy

Department of Health and Human Services

Department of Homeland Security

Department of Housing and Urban Development

Department of Justice

Department of Labor

Department of State

Department of the Interior

Department of the Treasury

Department of Transportation

Department of Veterans Affairs (Consumer Affairs Service)

Equal Employment Opportunity Commission

Federal Communications Commission (Consumer and Governmental Affairs Bureau)

Federal Deposit Insurance Corporation (Consumer Affairs Section)

Federal Emergency Management Agency

Federal Maritime Commission

Federal Reserve System (Division of Consumer and Community Affairs)

Government Printing Office

Immigration and Naturalization Service

National Archives and Records Administration

National Council on Disability

National Credit Union Administration

National Labor Relations Board

Nuclear Regulatory Commission (Office of Consumer Affairs)

Pension Benefit Guaranty Corporation (Customer Service Division)

Postal Rate Commission (Office of the Consumer Advocate)

Railroad Retirement Board

Securities and Exchange Commission

Small Business Administration

Social Security Administration

Surface Transportation Board

U.S. Postal Inspection Service

U.S. Postal Service (Office of Consumer Advocate)

## JOBS IN MEDIA

In media, the role may be that of a consumer reporter on television or radio (common in bigger cities), a writer for newspapers or magazines such as *Consumer Reports,* or an Internet supervisor or designer of consumer Web sites. Newspapers such as the *Washington Post* and the *St. Petersburg Times* have consumer reporters; smaller newspapers often have consumer news in their business sections. Magazines such as *Southern Living, Woman's Day, Family Circle, Ladies' Home Journal,* and *Better Homes and Gardens* are written for consumers. In the case of *Consumer Reports* (published by Consumer Union located in Yonkers, New York), there are positions in product testing, lobbying, management, and public relations, as well as writing and editing jobs.

Whole cable networks are devoted to consumer news. How-to networks such as HGTV (Home and Garden Television Network) and individual news shows such as the *Today Show* have segments on consumer-related matters—finances, homes, gardens, nutrition, and health. NBC at 30 Rockefeller Plaza in New York has a consumer division; go to its Web site, or call 212-664-2333.

The Internet opens up vast new frontiers. Financial information is one of the main areas on the Web, and someone has to design Web sites, oversee and update the sites, provide site content, and respond to consumers' questions.

## JOBS IN NONPROFIT ORGANIZATIONS

Potential employers include all the organizations already listed in the book such as the Consumer Federation of America (CFA), Center for Auto Safety, American Association of Retired Persons (AARP), Better Business Bureaus (BBBs), U.S. Public Interest Research Group, Legal Services, Public Citizen, and Common Cause. An example of an area within the CFA is its Food Policy Institute. Consider nonprofit and community action groups, legal services organizations, and policy think tanks. For example, the Consumer Protection Division of AARP, located in Washington, D.C., is charged with both examining those consumer problems and issues that impact the financial security of people 50 years of age and older and helping its members protect themselves from marketplace fraud and deception (www. aarp.org). Another example is Public Citizen, which has a division called Congress Watch in Washington, D.C., that works for consumer-related legislation, regulation, and policies in such areas as health, safety, and campaign financing (www. citizen.org). Other examples of organizations involved in consumer affairs are the Urban Institute, the Heritage Foundation, Trial Lawyers for Public Justice, the American Council for an Energy-Efficient Economy, and the Center for Policy Integrity.

BBBs are nonprofit organizations supported primarily by the business community to promote ethical marketplaces; to find locations in the United States and Canada, go to www.bbb.org. Vehicle disputes are settled by several nonprofit groups, including an arm of BBBs, the Center for Auto Safety, and the RV consumer group.

## JOBS IN COMMUNITY DEVELOPMENT AND EDUCATION

This is a crossover category since many consumer jobs in government or business involve community development or education. A prime example is the Cooperative Extension Service, a government agency under the U.S. Department of Agriculture, found in every county in the nation that serves rural and urban consumers (children and adults) through programs and information. Most jobs in K–12 require teaching certificates, and most college instructors have master's or PhDs.

Community development jobs can also be found in nonprofit organizations (such as those previously mentioned) and in neighborhood revitalization programs, Habitat for Humanity, government-sponsored programs such as Vista and Peace Corps, and church-sponsored programs. Nearly all consumer-oriented positions in government, the media, nonprofit organizations, and businesses involve some form of education or outreach.

## ADVANCED DEGREES

Consumer economics often serves as a launch pad for graduate school specialization in family and consumer sciences (or human sciences or human ecology), law, and public education or business school administration, among others. To find out more about graduate school in any of these fields, go to the Web site of the specific school you are interested in or go to general search Web sites such as www.abanet.org (law school information from the American Bar Association). Books found in career planning areas of bookstores can also be useful resources for locating schools and programs. Many employers allow employees to take one or two classes during office hours or grant a leave of absence to enroll full-time. Some pay tuition or have agreements with universities so that courses are free; others set up on-premises courses or encourage employees to enroll in night and weekend classes, with the reward of a salary hike or promotion when a degree or certificate is completed.

# B Journals

## ACADEMIC JOURNALS WITH "CONSUMER" IN TITLE*

*Advances in Consumer Research*

*Family and Consumer Sciences Research Journal*

*International Journal of Consumer Studies*

*International Review of Retail, Distribution and Consumer Research*

*Journal of Consumer Affairs*

*Journal of Consumer Behaviour*

*Journal of Consumer Education*

*Journal of Consumer Marketing*

*Journal of Consumer Policy*

*Journal of Consumer Psychology*

*Journal of Consumer Research*

*Journal of Consumer Satisfaction, Dissatisfaction and Complaining Behavior*

*Journal of Family and Consumer Sciences*

*Journal of International Consumer Marketing*

*Journal of Retailing and Consumer Services*

*The Forum for Family and Consumer Issues* (electronic journal)

## GENERAL JOURNALS

*Academy of Marketing Science Review*

*American Journal of Psychology*

*American Sociological Review*

---

*This is a partial list. New journals appear, and some on the list may be discontinued or re-named. In addition, there is a growing number of electronic journals. A few are listed and noted as such.

*Asian Journal of Marketing*

*Asia Pacific Journal of Marketing and Logistics*

*Australasian Marketing Journals*

*British Food Journal*

*Cambridge Journal of Economics*

*Canadian Home Economics Journal*

*Child Development*

*Clothing and Textile Research Journal*

*Consumption, Markets and Culture*

*Corporate Reputation Review*

*Der Markt* (in German)

*Developmental Psychology*

*Economic Journal*

*Educational and Psychological Measurement*

*European Journal of Marketing*

*Family Relations*

*Human Relations*

*Industrial Marketing Management*

*Interactive Marketing* (electronic journal)

*Marketing Science*

*Marketing Theory*

*Marketing* (*Zeitschrift fur Forschung und Praxis* in German)

*Perceptual and Motor Skills*

*Personality and Social Psychology Bulletin*

*Psychological Bulletin*

*Psychological Reports*

*Psychology & Marketing*

*Public Opinion Quarterly*

*Qualitative Market Research*

*Quarterly Journal of Electronic Commerce*

*Recherche et Applications en Marketing* (in French)

*Review of Marketing Science* (electronic journal)

*Social Behavior*

*The Gerontologist*

*The New England Journal of Medicine*

*The Service Industries Journal*

*Utrecht Business Review*

## JOURNALS STARTING WITH *INTERNATIONAL* IN TITLE[*]

*International Journal of Advertising*
*International Journal of Bank Marketing*
*International Journal of Electronic Commerce*
*International Journal of Market Research*
*International Journal of Research in Marketing*
*International Journal of Retail and Distribution Management*
*International Journal of Retailing*
*International Journal of Wine Marketing*
*International Marketing Review*

## JOURNALS STARTING WITH *JOURNAL* IN TITLE[†]

*Journal of Advertising*
*Journal of Advertising Research*
*Journal of Applied Psychology*
*Journal of Applied Social Psychology*
*Journal of Brand Management*
*Journal of Business Research*
*Journal of Current Issues and Research in Advertising*
*Journal of Database Marketing*
*Journal of Economic Issues*
*Journal of Environmental Systems*
*Journal of Euromarketing*
*Journal of Experimental Social Psychology*
*Journal of Family and Economic Issues*
*Journal of Fashion Marketing and Management*
*Journal of Financial Planning and Counseling*
*Journal of Financial Services Marketing*
*Journal of Food Distribution Research*
*Journal of Global Marketing*
*Journal of Hospitality and Leisure Marketing*
*Journal of Insurance Regulation*

---

[*]This list includes journals starting with the word *International* that have not been previously listed.

[†]This list includes journals starting with the word *Journal* that have not been previously listed.

*Journal of International Marketing*

*Journal of Marketing*

*Journal of Marketing Channels*

*Journal of Marketing Communications*

*Journal of Marketing Education*

*Journal of Marketing History*

*Journal of Marketing Management*

*Journal of Marketing Research*

*Journal of Marketing Theory and Practice*

*Journal of Marriage and Family*

*Journal of Nonprofit and Voluntary Sector Marketing*

*Journal of Personality and Social Psychology*

*Journal of Personal Selling & Sales Management*

*Journal of Product and Brand Management*

*Journal of Promotion Management*

*Journal of Public Policy & Marketing*

*Journal of Relationship Marketing*

*Journal of Retailing*

*Journal of Service Research*

*Journal of Social Behavior and Personality*

*Journal of Social Issues*

*Journal of Social Psychology*

*Journal of Socio-Economics*

*Journal of Strategic Marketing*

*Journal of the Academy of Marketing Science*

*Journal of Travel and Tourism Marketing*

*Journal of Vacation Marketing*

# U.S. Presidents and Their Terms in Office

| | | | |
|---|---|---|---|
| Washington | 1789–1797 | B. Harrison | 1889–1893 |
| J. Adams | 1797–1801 | Cleveland | 1893–1897 |
| Jefferson | 1801–1808 | McKinley | 1897–1901 |
| Madison | 1809–1817 | T. Roosevelt | 1901–1909 |
| Monroe | 1817–1825 | Taft | 1909–1913 |
| J. Q. Adams | 1825–1829 | Wilson | 1913–1921 |
| Jackson | 1829–1837 | Harding | 1921–1923 |
| Van Buren | 1837–1841 | Coolidge | 1923–1929 |
| W. H. Harrison | 1841–1841 | Hoover | 1929–1933 |
| Tyler | 1841–1845 | F. D. Roosevelt | 1933–1945 |
| Polk | 1845–1849 | Truman | 1945–1953 |
| Taylor | 1849–1850 | Eisenhower | 1953–1961 |
| Fillmore | 1850–1853 | Kennedy | 1961–1963 |
| Pierce | 1853–1857 | L. B. Johnson | 1963–1969 |
| Buchanan | 1857–1861 | Nixon | 1969–1974 |
| Lincoln | 1861–1865 | Ford | 1974–1977 |
| A. Johnson | 1865–1869 | Carter | 1977–1981 |
| Grant | 1869–1877 | Reagan | 1981–1989 |
| Hayes | 1877–1881 | G. H. Bush | 1989–1993 |
| Garfield | 1881 | Clinton | 1993–2001 |
| Arthur | 1881–1885 | G. W. Bush | 2001–2008 |
| Cleveland | 1885–1889 | | |

# Glossary

**ability to trade** The trading of one good for another.

**acquisitive** A trait meaning a strong desire for things, ideas, and information.

**actively acquired information** Any information sought after for its own sake.

**addictions** Psychological and/or physiological dependencies on habit-forming substances or practices (e.g., gambling).

**additives** Substances added to food either intentionally or accidentally.

**adjustable-rate mortgages (ARMs)** Mortgages with fluctuating interest rates within a specific range, based on changes in the economy.

**adjuster** A person who determines the amount of claim, loss, or damage payable under a contract.

**advertising** A paid communication of a product, service, or idea by a company/sponsor to a select group of people or the general public.

**agent** The provider of health care.

**alcohol** An intoxicating liquor containing various levels of alcohol.

**annuities** Contracts in which the insurer promises the insured a series of periodic payments.

**antitrust laws** Regulations to prevent business monopolies.

**appreciation** An increase in value (usually referring to a home).

**arbitration** The process by which the parties in a dispute submit their differences to the judgment of an impartial person or group appointed by mutual consent.

**aspirational products** Commodities that appeal to consumers' desires to own a brand-name product or service.

**assets** Tangible things that are owned.

**association** The method advertisers use when linking their products with something fun or pleasant to help sell their products.

**attitudes** Likes and dislikes.

**attribute-based choices** Selections that are made based on several variables or attributes, thus reducing the perception of risk.

**authenticity** An attribute of an original, innovative, or distinctive product or service.

**bankruptcy** A form of legal recourse open to insolvent debtors.

**banner ad** Any promotional information found at the top of a Web site.

**behavioral economics** A specialization within economics that emphasizes the impact of psychological or behavioral factors.

**behavioral finance** A specialization within economics that emphasizes saving and investing behaviors (accumulation of wealth) related to personal finance.

**biodegradable** A characteristic of material that decomposes naturally through biological processes.

**biologics** A broad product category including vaccines, blood and blood derivatives, allergenic patch tests and extracts, tests to detect HIV and hepatitis, gene therapy products, cells and tissues for transplantation, and treatments for cancers and arthritis.

**biometrics** The use of unique physical traits to determine a person's identity.

**biotechnology** The use of biological systems or organisms to create or modify products.

**bonds** Investments involving lending money to governments or corporations.

485

**Botox** A shortened name for botulinum toxin type A; a product used for a number of treatments including lessening of facial lines by injection.

**bounded rationality** The limited capacity consumers have for processing information.

**boycott** The act of refraining from or refusing to purchase certain items in protest to achieve a certain objective.

**brand** A distinctive name identifying a product or a manufacturer (usually talked about in terms of a popular brand of a product).

**brand extension** The addition of a new product to an already existing brand to satisfy a consumer need.

**brand image** The set of perceptions that consumers have formed about a brand.

**brand perception** The way consumers rate or consider a brand.

**bricks and clicks** A store or business (e.g., a bank) that has a physical as well as an online presence.

**budget constraints** Relationships between the money available to spend and the products or services on which to spend it.

**bunko** A swindle in which an unsuspecting person or group of people is cheated.

**business cycle** The normal cyclical expansion and contraction in the economy.

**calories** Units by which energy is measured.

**capitalism** An economic system characterized by open competition in a free market.

**carpel tunnel syndrome** The compression of the median nerve in the wrist, resulting in numbness, tingling, and pain in hands and fingers, that is caused by repetitive use of the hands (e.g., during computer use).

**caveat emptor** A Latin phrase translated "may the buyer beware."

**cease-and-desist order** An administrative or judicial order to a business to stop its unfair or deceptive acts or practices.

**censorship** An attempt to control; the act, process, or policy of control.

**certified divorce planner** A specialist trained to focus on who gets the assets in divorces.

**Certified Financial Planner (CFP)** A person with the most recognized financial planning credential (based on rigorous examinations, three years of practical experience, and adherence to a code of ethics).

**Chapter 7 Bankruptcy** A type of bankruptcy in which the court is asked to erase all dischargeable debt, with few exceptions (those vary by state).

**Chapter 13 Bankruptcy** A type of bankruptcy that allows debtors to repay some of the debt they owe and in return they get to keep most of their property.

**chip cards** *See* smart cards.

**chronic disease** A sickness that develops and continues over a long period of time, usually caused by a variety of factors (including lifestyle).

**churning** An illegal practice of encouraging insured consumers to switch policies, often in order to generate commissions.

**civil cases** Court cases involving the settling of private conflicts between people or between businesses.

**claim rates** Percentages of consumers who mail in rebate coupons.

**closing** The meeting in which real estate is transferred from seller to buyer.

**cognitive dissonance** The tendency to accentuate the benefits and downplay the deficits.

**collateral** Any property used to secure a loan.

**command or centrally controlled economy** An economy in which most decisions about what, how, and for whom to produce are made by those who control the government.

**common law** An unwritten system of rights of buyers and competitors that is the foundation of both the U.S. and English legal systems.

**common stock** A share or unit of ownership in a public corporation.

**communism** A social or economic system in which nearly all capital is collectively owned.

**conciliation** A type of dispute-resolution program.

**condominiums** Types of dwellings that are attached to each another and that share common areas such as swimming pools and lobbies; also called town houses.

**confidence man** A person who swindles and defrauds victims after winning their trust; also called con man.

**conglomerate merger** A combining of different companies in widely divergent fields into a single entity.

**con man** *See* confidence man.

**consent decree** A notice from the Federal Trade Commission to an advertiser whose ads are deceptive asking the advertiser to sign a consent decree saying it will stop the deceptive ads.

**conspicuous consumption** The act of people who pay an extremely high price for a product because of its prestige value, leading to a much higher demand for the product.

**constitutional law** The fundamental regulations of the U.S. federal system of government based on the U.S. Constitution.

**constructive choice** A timely decision based on the situation at hand.

**consumer behavior** The buying choices of customers (individuals, families, and households) who buy goods and services for personal consumption

**consumer confidence** A measure of customer well-being by the Conference Board and the University of Michigan's Survey Research Center.

**consumer cost** The total cost involved in owning or using a product; also called the nonprice cost.

**consumer durables** Products bought by consumers that are expected to last three years or more, including automobiles, appliances, and furniture.

**consumer economics** A specialization within economics that studies how people deal with scarcity, fulfill needs, and select among alternative goods, services, and actions.

**consumer education** The teaching of skills, attitudes, knowledge, and understanding that individuals need to cope in an increasingly complex marketplace.

**Consumer Expenditure Survey** The published result of data collected by Bureau of Labor Statistics that provides detailed information on spending habits.

**consumer health** An umbrella term encompassing the decisions people make about their health care, including products and services that they buy or that their insurance covers, and the decisions they make about their lifestyle, including those that affect health care needs.

**consumer-in-control movement** A movement that refers to consumers wanting more say not only in designing ads and promotions but also in creating the products and services, which can happen when companies ask consumers to vote on ads or products.

**consumerism** The belief that goods give meaning to individuals and their roles in society.

**consumer–market conflict** A situation where one side, either the customer or the seller, is not satisfied with the exchange.

**consumer-mediated environment (CME)** The process of buying and selling over the Internet.

**consumer movement** A movement that refers to policies aimed at regulating products, services, methods, and standards of manufacturing, selling, and advertising that are in the interests of the buyer.

**consumer payoff** A positive result experienced by the consumer after searching and making the best choice.

**Consumer Power Model** A model incorporating many economic theories that is designed to show the constant motion of the activities and exchanges of the parties involved in marketplaces.

**Consumer Price Index (CPI)** An index that measures monthly prices of a fixed basket of 400 goods and services (durables and nondurables) bought by a typical consumer.

**consumer reporting agencies (CRAs)** Centers that have files containing information about consumers' incomes, debts, credit payment histories, lawsuits, arrests, and bankruptcies; also called credit bureaus.

**consumers** Individuals or groups such as families who obtain, use, maintain, and dispose of products and services to increase life satisfaction and fulfill needs.

**consumer satisfaction** The pleasant result when a consumer's product or service expectations are met.

**consumer sovereignty** The assumption that the customer is king by deciding which goods will survive because producers cannot dictate consumer tastes.

**consumer style** The totality of a consumer's economics, history, culture, personality, biology or environment, technology, and politics or political climate.

**consumer terrorism** Any activity conducted by individuals or groups whose purpose is to disrupt the marketplace.

**consumer unit** The consumption of each household that is reported in the Consumer Expenditure Survey conducted by the Bureau of Labor Statistics.

**consumption** The use of goods by consumers.

**contracts** Agreements or promises that are legally enforceable.

**cooperative apartments** Types of housing units (most commonly located in large cities) in which homeowners own shares in the building as a whole and have the right to lease their units; also called co-ops.

**corrective advertising** The type of advertisement pursuant to an Federal Trade Commission order disclaiming previously false advertising claims that is run by a firm to cause consumers to "unlearn" inaccurate information from prior advertisements; also called counteradvertising.

**cosigner** A person who agrees to repay the loan if the borrower does not (defaults).

**cosmetics** Any substance applied to the body that is used to improve or alter the appearance.

**counteradvertising** *See* corrective advertising.

**cramming** Any unexplained charges on phone bills for services never ordered, authorized, received, or used.

**credence goods** Commodities such as drugs for which the consumer can never get relevant information.

**credit bureaus** *See* consumer reporting agencies (CRAs).

**credit cards** Cards used to purchase something or to get cash now with the promise of future payment.

**credit score** A rating based on an individual's financial, workplace, and lifestyle information, including assets, debts, length of employment, and length of living in one place, that is negatively affected by any bankruptcy or failure to pay bills on time.

**criminal cases** Legal charges brought by the government against people or entities for violations or injustices deemed to have been committed by them.

**cross-selling** The process that occurs when a company offers another one of its brands (using coupons or samples) so that a customer remains loyal to the company.

**cues** Reminders or hints such as ads, signs, packaging, and other stimuli that prompt a consumer to buy.

**customer satisfaction** A customer's pleasure derived both from the value and use of a product and from the prebuying, buying, and postbuying experience.

**customization** The process of individually tailoring a product because consumers want uniqueness.

**debit cards** Cards that allow customers access to their funds electronically.

**debts** Amounts that are owed.

**decision making** The process of choosing between two or more alternatives.

**deductibles** Amounts that policy holders pay toward a loss before insurance coverage begins.

**deductions** Expenses subtracted from income before calculation of the amount of taxes owed.

**defect-disclosure forms** Forms that describe the condition of the home (required in some states).

**defendant** The party against which a legal action is brought.

**deflation** A general decline in prices.

**Delaney clause** A clause stating that no substance known to cause cancer in animals or human beings at any dose level shall be added to foods.

**demographics** The information and data used to describe populations or subgroups.

**demography** The study of human populations, including characteristics such as size, growth, density, distribution, movement, and other vital statistics.

**depreciation** The loss of value of an item over time.

**depression** A drastic and long-lasting decline in the economy characterized by high unemployment, falling prices, and decreasing business activity.

**deregulation** The reduction or removal of government intervention.

**digital divide** A term referring to the fact that the Internet is not equally accessible to everyone.

**diminishing marginal utility** The decrease in satisfaction that a buyer experiences from each successive unit consumed in a given period of time.

**direct investment** Any consumer purchase of a home, apartment building, raw land, or other structures.

**direct investment plan** The option of personally making an investment in a company rather than using a broker.

**disability income insurance** A type of insurance that pays benefits to policy holders when they are incapable of working.

**discrimination** An act based on prejudice or bias.

**disposition** The process of getting rid of a product that can occur before, during, or after its use.

**distribution** A marketing concept wherein products are available in places near target customers.

**diversification** The use of money to buy several categories of investments, such as bonds, blue-chip stocks, small and large companies, foreign shares, real estate, and real estate investment trusts, thereby diminishing risk.

**dividend reinvestment plan (DRIP)** A procedure that takes dividends and automatically uses them to purchase additional shares directly from the company.

**dividends** Distributions of money from companies or the government to investors.

**drugs** Chemicals (not including food) that can affect the function of the body.

**ecological economics** A specialization within economics that focuses on the relationships between the environment and economics.

**e-commerce** Any exchange transaction that takes place on the Internet.

**economics** The study or science of production, distribution, and consumption.

**e-consumerism** The act of protecting, empowering, and informing consumers on the Internet.

**emergency fund** An amount of money equal to three to six months of salary set aside as savings in case of an unforeseen situation such as loss of job.

**end-of-aisle displays** Groups of featured products placed at the end of store aisles that sometime cost more than similar products of another brand placed midaisle.

**endorsement** An addition to an insurance policy that covers extra things such as jewelry or collectibles.

**endowment effect** The theory that if people are given something (e.g., a present, a sample), they will think it is worth more than someone who has not received the item because people put a value on what they own.

**ENERGY STAR** A government program offering energy-efficient solutions.

**entrepreneurs** Unique industry-changing leaders who relentlessly pursue new business opportunities (e.g., executives, inventors, small-business owners).

**environmentalism** A concern for the environment.

**equilibrium price** The price that is reached when supply and demand for a product or service are equal.

**e-wallets** Internet-based payment systems that allow value to be transmitted through computers.

**exchange process** The procedure people (as individuals or groups) go through when they negotiate with a goal of reaching an agreement.

**excise tax** A type of tax collected from the manufacturer of a product.

**exclusions** Items not covered under insurance.

**expansion** A period of prosperity marked by growth, higher output, low unemployment, increased retail sales, and increased housing sales that is the preferred stage in the business cycle.

**experience goods** The relevant information that the consumer gets after purchasing commodities such as food and entertainment.

**expiration date** The last day the consumer should use the product.

**exposures** Sources of risks (e.g., driving).

**external search** The process that occurs when a consumer looks at advertisements, reads articles, goes on the Internet, or asks others what they think about a product or service.

**extortion** The illegal use of position, power, or knowledge to obtain money, goods, funds, or favors.

**family** A unit that consists of two or more persons related by birth, marriage, or adoption and residing together in a household (U.S. Census definition); more broadly, a group that includes other couples and groups who share resources.

**family brand** The same brand name given to several products.

**Federal Deposit Insurance Corporation (FDIC)** The government-backed insurance of bank and savings and loan accounts up to $100,000 per account.

**fetal alcohol syndrome** The long-term effects that babies suffer because of their mothers' alcohol abuse.

**FICO score** The score most widely used by lenders to determine who gets a loan and how much the loan is, developed by California-based Fair, Isaac & Co.

**financial planner** A professional who looks at a person's or a family's total financial picture, helps that person or family define and prioritize goals, and then works out a plan to achieve those goals.

**fixed expenses** Expenses that do not vary from month to month (e.g., rent, car payments).

**fixed-rate conventional mortgage** A fixed-payment loan that is usually carried for 15, 20, or 30 years.

**food allergy** A reaction of the body's immune system to a food or food ingredient (usually a protein).

**food irradiation** The process of treating food with gamma rays, X rays, or high-voltage electronics to kill potentially harmful pathogens that cause food-borne illnesses; also a process used to reduce spoilage and extend shelf life of food products.

**foods** Products from plants or animals that can be taken into the body for energy and nutrients to sustain life and growth.

**forecast** A prediction by marketers of sales of existing or new products or services.

**franchise** The privilege to operate a business that sells the franchisor's products or services in a given area.

**fraud** An intentional deception perpetrated to deprive another person of assets.

**Freddie Mac** A stockholder-owned corporation designed to increase the supply of money that lenders can make available to home buyers and multifamily investors.

**generic drug** A copy of a brand-name drug that is the same in dosage, safety, strength, method of ingestion, quality, performance, and intended use.

**genetic engineering** The modification of genetic materials to produce new substances or perform new functions through the use of biotechnology.

**gifting** A symbolic act of voluntarily bestowing.

**globalization** The distribution of goods and services worldwide so that they are more consistent and universally accepted.

**global perspective** The view that challenges materialism and commercialism and that asks citizens to examine their role in consumption and how it affects the world.

**goals** End results; also things people strive for.

**GRAS** An acronym for "generally recognized as safe" that refers to food additives that have long been in use and that are believed to be safe.

**grifter** A person who uses position to derive profit or advantage by unscrupulous means.

**hedonism** The view that people want certain products (e.g., chocolate) because the products taste, look, feel, or smell good and that people engage in certain behaviors (e.g., tanning) because the behaviors provide sensory benefits.

**high-balling** The act of offering a large amount of money up front for a commodity (e.g., a trade-in) but making up that extra amount in an increased price (e.g., a higher-priced new car).

**home equity lines of credit** Loans often used to finance home improvements that carry a variable interest rate and that allow homeowners to borrow up to a certain amount based on their home's value.

**home inspections** Assessments of the condition of a home, usually done by a home inspector hired by the prospective buyer before purchasing the home.

**homeowner's fees** Monthly maintenance or repair costs for common areas collected from single-family homeowners or from condominium owners.

**home warranties** Types of insurance that provide additional protection for home buyers.

**horizontal merger** A combining of direct competitors in the same product lines or markets into a single entity.

**household** A group of related family members and all the unrelated persons who share a housing unit.

**hucksterism** An act of extreme promotion.

**Human Development Index (HDI)** A measurement that quantifies quality of life and compares the progress of nations by combining several measures of well-being.

**identity marketing** The act of a consumer who wears or displays product logos.

**identity theft** The act of someone using your name or personal information (e.g., Social Security number, driver's license number, credit card number or other account number, telephone number, street address) without your permission, often to illegally make a profit.

**illiquid asset** A personal possession that is difficult to readily turn into cash.

**image** An impression or attitude.

**implied warranties** Guarantees that are not written but are inherently understood in a transaction.

**implied warranty of fitness** A guarantee that holds for the correct use of the product.

**implied warranty of merchantability** A guarantee that implies the product should work and should be salable and fit for the market.

**impulse buying** The act of someone who purchases an item without taking time to think about the ramifications (e.g., costs, benefits, values, needs).

**indirect investments** Actions of a group of investors to form a partnership, to own real estate investment trusts (REITs), or to invest in apartment, commercial, or office buildings.

**infectious disease** A communicable disease spread from person to person by invading microorganisms (e.g., viruses, bacteria).

**inflation** A steady increase in prices.

**infomercials** Program-long advertisements running an hour or more for products or services (e.g., cooking products, cosmetics, tools, exercise equipment, diet programs or supplements).

**information economy** An economy where those who produce, have access to, and influence the spread of information have power in the global society.

**information search rule** A rule stating that a consumer will search as long as the cost of the search is less than or equal to the expected savings from the search.

**injurious consumption** A decision to consume that has negative consequences or that misuses products in such a way as to cause injury to the consumer or to others.

**innovation** A newly introduced product or method.

**innovators** People or a group of people who created a newly introduced product or method.

**insurance** A financial arrangement between individuals and insurance companies that protects against loss or injury.

**intentional injuries** Bodily hurts that are purposely inflicted either personally or by other people (e.g., assaults, homicides, suicides).

**interest** The cost of using money (the rate of interest) that is determined by supply.

**internal search** The act that occurs when a consumer analyzes what is known about a product based on past searches or personal experience.

**investment** The commitment of funds (capital) to long-term growth as an important means to getting ahead, keeping ahead of inflation, and becoming independent and self-supporting.

**invoice price** The manufacturer's initial charge to or cost paid by the dealer.

**jingles** Music memory devices used by advertisers.

**junk science** A term referring to an area or field where there is little or no evidence or proof to support a claim.

**lack of efficacy** The failure of a pill or treatment to produce the desired effect or outcome.

**law of demand** A rule stating that as the price of a good or service rises, the quantity demanded of that good or service falls.

**law of supply** A rule stating that as the supply of a good or service goes up, the price comes down.

**lease** A legal document between the renter and the landlord describing the rights and responsibilities of both.

**leasing** A contractual arrangement outlining the terms of a car lease, including monthly payments, security deposit, condition of the returned vehicle, and number of miles driven.

**lemon laws** Regulations that allow owners of new vehicles that repeatedly break down to get their money back or get the cars replaced.

**level of living** The way consumers are actually living.

**liabilities** Sum totals of people's or entities' debts.

**liability insurance** A type of insurance that pays for losses from negligence resulting in bodily injury or property damage to others for which the policy holder is responsible (all homeowner's policies provide liability coverage).

**liens** Legal rights to take and hold property if the person with the loan does not repay the loan.

**life insurance** A type of insurance that is a contract between a policy holder and an insurer saying what sum will be paid to beneficiaries on the insured's death.

**lifestyle** The sum of a person's life choices, including pattern of time use, type of living space, values and issues considered important, and ways of spending money.

**litigants** Consumers who are claiming damages or resolving disputes.

**loans** Sums of money lent with interest.

**lobbyists** People who represent special-interest groups.

**locking power** The property of an advertisement that plays on two forms of memory, recognition (seeing) and recall (more complex associations); also called memorability.

**long-term care (LTC) insurance** A type of insurance that provides benefits for nursing home, assisted living, or in-home care not covered by Medicare insurance as well as for other types of long-term care.

**loss aversion** The avoidance of risk; also the fear of loss.

**loss leader** A very low-priced advertised special to bring in shoppers.

**low-balling** The act of initially quoting a very low price but then adding on costs that drive the final price up.

**Magnuson-Moss Warranty–FTC Improvement Act of 1975** An act that empowers the Federal Trade Commission to obtain consumer redress when a person or firm engages in deceptive practices (e.g., false or misleading advertising).

**malpractice insurance** A type of insurance that doctors and clinics have in case they are sued by patients.

**manufactured housing** A unit that is partially or fully assembled in a factory and moved to the living site.

**market economy** An economy where exchanges are controlled by marketplace forces of demand and supply rather than by outside forces (e.g., government control).

**market extension merger** A combining of firms selling the same products in different markets.

**marketing communications** Any advertising, public relations, coupons, labels, packaging, billboards, in-store displays, and other signals or messages that a company provides about itself and its products.

**marketing mix** The use of communications and information along with price, distribution, and service to sell a product.

**marketing strategy** A plan or operation created to give customer value to the target market.

**market mavens** Consumers who are very involved in the marketplace by spreading the word about a product or service.

**market segment** A portion of a larger market whose needs differ somewhat from those of the larger market.

**marketspace** A situation where a seller and a buyer do not meet face to face (e.g., a buyer may see a picture of a product but not examine the product itself).

**mass consumption** The action of millions of consumers making similar choices that has a tremendous impact on the general economy.

**media** Means of mass communications (e.g., newspapers, magazines, radio, television, the Internet).

**media mix** The combination of media and marketing communications used to reach a target audience.

**mediation** The process of negotiating to resolve differences; also an attempt to bring about a peaceful settlement or compromise between the consumer and the business through the intervention of a third party.

**Medicaid** The federal health care program for low-income people who qualify.

**Medicare** The federal health insurance program for people who are age 65 or older and for people who have disabilities.

**Medicare Part D** The federal health insurance option that reduces the cost of brand-name and prescription drugs for those who qualify.

**mental accounting** The context in which people do their buying and selling.

**merger** A combining of two or more companies into a single entity.

**message framing** The choice of positive or negative communications (e.g., in advertisements).

**models** Representations, schematics, or illustrations of relationships.

**monopoly** The situation where there is only one producer of a product or service and there is no substitute for the product or service.

**mortgages** Loans used to purchase real estate in which the real estate serves as collateral and the loan amount equals the down payment subtracted from the purchase price.

**muckraker** A person (e.g., writer, politician, journalist, public speaker) who searches out and exposes political or commercial corruption.

**multilevel marketing plans** Strategies for selling goods and services through distributors.

**mutual funds** Groups of investments that are usually stocks and/or bonds.

**natural capital** The whole endowment of landed resources that are available; also the natural environment that makes our lives possible.

**needs** Things that are deemed necessary.

**need set** The term used to reflect the fact that most products satisfy more than one need.

**net worth** A sum arrived at by subtracting liabilities from assets that determines how much a person can borrow or spend.

**neuroeconomics** A specialization within economics that takes into account how personal choices, attitudes, and emotions affect consumers' selection of products and services.

**nexting** The term that refers to a consumer anticipating what will happen next.

**nicotine** The chief active ingredient in tobacco that is found in cigarettes, cigars, and chewing tobacco.

**nonfamily households** Groups of people who live together who are not related to each other; also a single person living alone would compose a nonfamily household.

**nutrition** The science of foods and nutrients and their actions within the body.

**ombudsperson** A person who works with the court system to accelerate the bureaucratic process.

**one-price system** An arrangement where a consumer pays the price for a product that is stated on its price tag, without bargaining.

**ongoing search** A search conducted to acquire information for possible later use.

**open dating** A system of placing a date on a perishable product that indicates when the product should be sold or consumed.

**opportunity** A favorable outlook; also a chance for progress, advancement, and action.

**opportunity costs** Expenses incurred or attached when one alternative is selected over other choices.

**organically grown foods** Crops grown and processed according to USDA regulations.

**over-the-counter (OTC) drugs** Nonprescription medications.

**pack date** The date that a product is packaged or manufactured.

**Pareto principle** A rule stating that 20 percent of the time expended produces 80 percent of the results and 80 percent of the time expended results in only 20 percent of the outcomes; also called the 80-20 rule.

**Parkinson's law** A principle stating that a job expands to fill the time available to accomplish the task (e.g., finding and purchasing a product).

**passive information** The type of information encountered when someone is doing something else.

**perils** Events that cause financial loss (e.g., car accidents).

**personal finance** An umbrella term that covers the spending, saving, investing, and protecting of financial resources.

**personal identification number (PIN)** The number used for ATMs and other forms of cash management.

**pirating** The act of stealing an original idea or product and selling it.

**PITI** An acronym for "principal, interest, taxes, insurance" that refers to how lenders estimate mortgages based on the down payment and the buyer's ability to handle monthly payments of principal, interest, taxes, and insurance.

**plaintiff** The party bringing legal charges or a suit against the defendant.

**pollution** Any undesirable change in biological, chemical, or physical characteristics of air, land, or water that harms activities, health, or survival of living organisms.

**Ponzi schemes** Pyramid scams using enticing come-ons that promise to make huge profits from a small investment in a very short time.

**portfolio** A group of investments that an individual owns.

**predatory lending** A type of lending that lures people into loans that they really can't afford, usually by borrowing against the equity in their homes or a relative's home.

**prepurchasing** A consumer's thoughts and behaviors before the person actually purchases a product or service.

**prescription drugs** Medications obtained by written instructions from a physician for their preparation and use.

**preservatives** Substances added to food to maintain a desired quality.

**price** The amount of money a person pays to buy or use a product.

**price discrimination** The variation in prices charged, a process that can be illegal if individuals or groups are treated unfairly (e.g., if people are charged a different price based on their ethnicity).

**price variation** The act of a single seller charging different consumers different prices at different times for the same item.

**principal** The consumer of health care services.

**privacy** The state of an individual or group that keeps information about their lives and activities from public consumption.

**privatization** The allocation of some functions of government to business.

**product** Anything a consumer acquires or perceives to need.

**product extension merger** A combining of firms selling different but related products in the same market into a single entity.

**product positioning** The projecting of a specific image of a brand to consumers within a target market.

**property insurance** A type of insurance that pays for losses to homes and personal property due to theft, fire, vandalism, natural disaster, or other causes (e.g., a tree falling on a house).

**property rights** Legal rights over the use, sale, and proceeds from a good or resource.

**prospect theory** A system of ideas that states people feel more pain from loss than pleasure from profit, a fact that affects their decisions to make a change in their condition.

**public policy** A plan or decision by government to act in a certain way or go in a particular direction.

**public service announcements (PSAs)** Messages sent out to the public, usually arranged by the Ad Council in conjunction with government agencies or nonprofit organizations.

**puffery** Any advertising that exaggerates the characteristics of a product or service.

**pull date** The day by which a product should be sold.

**pyramiding** An illegal practice that involves offers to pay commission for recruiting new distributors.

**quacks** Unscrupulous individuals specializing in medical or health swindles.

**quality assurance date** The latest day when a product is at its peak quality.

**quality of life** A consumer's perception of and satisfaction with life.

**radio frequency identification (RFID)** A computer chip embedded in a product that allows it to be tracked.

**rational** The characteristic of having the ability to reason.

**rational self-interest** A mind-set that selects choices giving the greatest amount of satisfaction at a particular time based on known information.

**reactance** A reaction by a consumer of wanting a product or service even more after hearing a warning or negative message about it.

**real estate** A piece of land and everything related to it, including houses, landscaping, and fencing, plus right to the airspace above and the earth below (within specified limits).

**real estate investment trusts (REITs)** Investments in property bought in shares and traded on the major stock exchanges.

**real gross domestic product (real GDP)** A measure of the value of all the goods and services newly produced in a country during some period of time, usually a year or a quarter, adjusted for inflation.

**reasonable person** A person who is rational, attentive, knowledgeable, and capable of making judgments in his or her best interest.

**recession** A temporary and moderate decline or downturn in the economy.

**recovery** A period in the business cycle when economic activity picks up, leading to expansion.

**redlining** The illegal practice of drawing a red (or any other color) line around an area so that area does not receive the same treatment as other areas regarding financing, insurance, or credit.

**reference groups** Collections of people who influence other people's decisions and behaviors.

**regional subcultures** Groups that have characteristic differences in environment, resource use, history, and traditions based on location.

**regulation** An attempt by government to control the workings of the marketplace; also called rule.

**regulatory laws** Rules or regulations enacted by agencies of the federal or state government to protect consumers.

**rent** The payment for the use of property.

**rent-to-own (RTO)** Dealers who rent to individuals a variety of goods, from furniture to electronics to appliances, with an option to buy.

**resources** Assets that are available for personal use.

**reversible mortgages** Conversions of home equity into cash paid to (often elderly) homeowners either in monthly advances or through a line of credit, with no repayment required for as long as the borrowers live in their homes.

**revocation of acceptance** A procedure to get either a monetary refund or a replacement for a defective car.

**right-to-cure laws** Regulations that allow homeowners to give builders a chance to repair defects in their homes before filing a lawsuit.

**right to redress** The right of consumers to seek and obtain satisfaction for damages incurred through the use of a product or service.

**risk** The possibility or perception of harm, suffering, danger, or loss.

**rogue agents** Agents who are not associated with established companies and who are engaging in illegal activities (usually involving insurance).

**rule** *See* regulation.

**rule of reciprocation** The principle that people try to repay what someone has given to them.

**rules of thumb** Principles that guide purchases (e.g., only buying certain brands, only shopping in certain stores, only buying certain styles).

**sandwich generation** The group of people who are supporting or taking care of children as well as aging parents.

**scarcity** A condition where there is an insufficient amount or a shortage in supply of a product or service.

**science** The observation, identification, description, experimental investigation, and theoretical explanation of phenomena.

**scientific literacy** The promotion of science education in schools and in communities.

**second mortgages** Loans based on their homes' value taken out by homeowners to get money in a lump sum for home improvements or other expenses.

**security deposit** A payment required by the landlord in advance to secure a unit for the renter and to cover wear and tear of the unit.

**self-worth** A system of thoughts and feelings concerning or focused on self.

**service** Any activity that is performed to enhance and sustain the primary product or service.

**service contract** The type of contract that provides repairs and/or maintenance of a product for a specific time period.

**shopbots** Browser-based shopping assistants that aggregate Internet information and list choices.

**slamming** A term referring to a situation where a consumer's long-distance phone company switches to another company without permission.

**slogans** Memory devices consisting of short phrases used by advertisers.

**small claims court** A civil court that allows litigants claiming damages or resolving disputes that involve modest amounts of money; also called conciliation or magistrates court.

**smart cards** Cards embedded with computer chips for a prepaid amount of money, often used for making phone calls or buying snacks from vending machines; also called chip cards and stored value cards.

**socialism** An economic system in which the government centrally plans, owns, and controls most of the capital and makes decisions about prices and quantities.

**socialization** The process of learning to interact with others, forming cooperative relationships, participating in society, and learning the ways of daily life.

**socially responsible investing** A type of investing that is consistent with the investor's values and attitudes.

**social marketing** A type of marketing strategy designed to create or alter behavior so that it has a positive rather than negative effect on or outcome for individuals, society, and the environment.

**social responsibility** A broad term meaning that companies should address the needs of the masses as well as the needs of the few and must balance individual quality with societal and environmental quality.

**Society of Consumer Affairs Professionals (SOCAP)** An international professional organization that offers training, conferences, and publications to encourage and maintain the integrity of businesses in their transactions with consumers and in communications with government regulatory groups and agencies.

**socioeconomic index (SEI)** A measure based on people's education level and occupation.

**special-interest groups** Units of two or more persons who have a common interest and seek to influence government policy and enforcement.

**standard of living** The quality of life at which consumers aspire to live.

**statutory laws** Regulations enacted by the legislative branch of government.

**stealth marketing** A type of marketing strategy that targets a unique service or product that is not too public, that is "under the radar."

**sticker price** The cost of the car, including options, transportation charges, and any market adjustments; also called suggested retail price.

**stocks** Shares representing ownership in a company.

**store bands** Products sold under the store name, usually for a lower price than nationally advertised brands.

**stored value cards** *See* smart cards.

**strong encryption** The ability to achieve unbreakable confidentiality online.

**structure–function claims** Health claims that can be made without FDA approval.

**style** The individuality expressed by a person's actions and tastes.

**subleasing** The process that allows property to be leased by the original tenant to another person or persons.

**subliminal advertising** A message about a product or service that is delivered in such a way that the person is not consciously aware of receiving it.

**subpoena** A written statement requiring a person's appearance in court to give testimony.

**suggested retail price** *See* sticker price.

**summons** A notice requiring a person to appear in court.

**sunk-cost fallacy** The desire to use something that has been paid for.

**sustainable development** A type of economic development that provides for human needs while not depleting global ecosystems and natural resources.

**taglines** End messages used as memory devices by advertisers to sell a product or service.

**tanning** The body's response to skin exposed to ultraviolet (UV) radiation from the sun.

**targeted advertising** A type of advertising geared to a specific group based on its environment or culture.

**target market** The largest and most likely group to purchase a product or service.

**tax avoidance** A money management strategy to reduce taxes owed through tax-deferred investments and charitable donations.

**taxes** Payments of money to local, state, and federal governments.

**tax evasion** An illegal strategy of not paying taxes or not reporting all taxable income.

**technological obsolescence** The process that occurs when a product becomes outdated soon after it was purchased or before it is worn out.

**technology** The application of scientific knowledge to useful purposes.

**theory** An organized system of ideas or beliefs that can be measured.

**theory of mental accounting** A system of ideas that examines the framework of people's saving and spending behaviors.

**theory of reasoned action** A system of ideas that posits that actions are based on a combination of attitudes and beliefs and that motivations are linked to attitudes and beliefs.

**third-party complaint-handling sources** People or organizations used when consumers need help regarding complaints about products or services that they couldn't resolve by themselves.

**tie-ins** A term referring to the technique of placing complementary products side by side, one being the loss leader and one having its price jacked up to compensate for the loss leader.

**time deposit** A safe way to store money from seven days to several years (e.g., certificates of deposit).

**time-shares** Apartments, units, or homes, usually for vacation purposes, that have several owners who use them for specific time periods.

**tobacco** A plant native to America whose leaves are processed for use in cigarettes, cigars, etc.

**tort** A civil wrong (either intentional or negligent) that causes emotional or physical injury, or both.

**trademark** A legal term referring to words, symbols, and marks that are legally registered for use by a company.

**trade-offs** Anything that is sacrificed (or traded) in order to obtain something else.

**transaction** A transfer that leads to completion of the exchange process.

**trans fats** Substances produced when hydrogen is added to vegetable oil in a process known as hydrogenation.

**trust** The psychological status of involved parties who are willing to pursue further interactions to achieve a planned goal.

**Truth in Savings Act** An act requiring financial institutions to reveal the annual percentage yield (amount of interest earned on a yearly basis expressed as a percentage), fees charged, and rules regarding a minimum balance.

**underutilization** A condition where a consumer does not use a product to the full extent to which it is intended to be used.

**Uniform Commercial Code (UCC)** A set standard by which merchants operating in more than one state can more easily comply with that state's laws.

**uninsured motorist coverage** A type of insurance that pays for bodily injury caused by an uninsured motorist, a hit-and-run driver, or a negligent driver with an insolvent insurer.

**unintentional injuries** Bodily hurts that occur accidentally when no harm was intended (e.g., results of falls, fires, or motor vehicle crashes).

**uniqueness theory** A system of ideas proposing that individuals vary in the extent to which they wish to be different.

**unit pricing** The presentation on store shelves of price information on a common basis (e.g., per ounce).

**utility** The usefulness of a product, service, or idea.

**values** Principles that guide behavior.

**variable expenses** Costs that vary from month to month (e.g., food, entertainment).

**vertical merger** A combining of supplier and company or customer and company into a single entity.

**volatility** The movement up and down of a security, a commodity, or the stock market.

**voluntary simplicity** A conscious effort by consumers to live more modestly, with fewer possessions and at lower consumption levels.

**wants** Things wished for or desired.

**well-being** The state of being healthy, happy, and/or prosperous, of having both mental and physical health as well as the finances to keep healthy, comfortable, and contented.

**wellness** The condition of good physical and mental health, maintained by good diet and exercise.

**workers' compensation** The money paid to a person whose disability is due to illness or injury received on the job.

**written warranties** Promises in writing that the character and quality of the product are as the manufacturer represents them.

**years of potential life lost** A term referring to the difference between an individual's life expectancy and age at death.

# Index